How To Use This Book

This book starts at the beginning, taking people who know n
2 and stepping them through 21 lessons and on to program

Within this book, you'll find hands-on tutorials, timely tips, and easy-to-understand technical information to help you get your footing with Visual C++ 2. You begin by writing simple programs and progress to complex, useful programs that you can apply to your day-to-day situations.

Specific features that you'll see throughout the book are:

DO DON'T **Do/Don't boxes:** These give you specific guidance on what to do and what to avoid doing when programming in C.

Notes: These provide essential background information so that you not only do things with C, but have a good understanding of what you're doing and why.

Warnings: A warning alerts you to a hazard regarding the topic currently being discussed.

Who Should Read This Book

Teach Yourself Visual C++ 2 in 21 Days has you, the beginner, in mind when explaining concepts and techniques within programming. No prior programming experience is required; however, knowing how to program in other languages, such as BASIC or Pascal, certainly helps. This book is not for the faint-hearted, because learning to program in C++ and to write 32-bit programmed applications in C++ are two non-trivial tasks!

Conventions

This book uses various typefaces to help you differentiate between Visual C++ code and regular English, and also to help you identify important concepts. Actual Visual C++ code is typeset in a special `monospace` font. Placeholders—terms used to represent what you actually type within the code—are typeset in an *`italic monospace`* font. New or important terms are typeset in *italic*. In addition, when new terms are introduced in the text, a New Term icon appears to the left of the text to indicate that a term is being defined.

Teach Yourself Visual C++™ 2 in 21 Days

Third Edition

Teach Yourself Visual C++™ 2 in 21 Days

Third Edition

Namir Clement Shammas

SAMS PUBLISHING

201 West 103rd Street, Indianapolis, Indiana 46290

THIRD EDITION

International Standard Book Number: 0-672-30534-8

Library of Congress Catalog Number: 94-66271

97 96 95 94 4 3 2 1

Interpretation of the printing code: the rightmost double-digit number is the year of the book's printing; the rightmost single digit, the number of the book's printing. For example, a printing code of 94-1 shows that the first printing of the book occurred in 1994.

Composed in AGaramond and MCPdigital by Macmillan Computer Publishing

Printed in the United States of America

Trademarks

Publisher
Richard K. Swadley

Acquisitions Manager
Stacy Hiquet

Acquisitions Editor
Rosemarie Graham

Development Editor
Angelique Brittingham

Managing Editor
Cindy Morrow

Production Editor
Anne Owen

Editorial Coordinator
Bill Whitmer

Editorial Assistants
Carol Ackerman
Sharon Cox
Lynette Quinn

Technical Reviewer
Robert Zigon

Marketing Manager
Gregg Bushyeager

Cover Designer
Dan Armstrong

Book Designer
Michele Laseau

Director of Production and Manufacturing
Jeff Valler

Imprint Manager
Juli Cook

Production Analysts
Dennis Clay Hager
Mary Beth Wakefield

Proofreading Coordinator
Joelynn Gifford

Indexing Coordinator
Johnna VanHoose

Graphics Image Specialists
Jason Hand
Clint Lahnen
Shawn MacDonald
Dennis Sheehan

Team Leader
Katy Bodenmiller

Production
Georgiana Briggs
Michael Brumitt
Elaine Brush
Cheryl Cameron
Mary Ann Crosby
Rob Falco
Donna Harbin
Chad Poore
Casey Price
Brian-Kent Proffitt
Marc Shecter
Kim Scott
Susan Springer
Scott Tullis
Dennis V. Wesner

Indexer
Bront Davis

Overview

Contents

Acknowledgments

I would like to thank the many people at Sams Publishing for encouraging me and working with me on this project. I would like to thank publisher Richard Swadley and associate publisher Jordan Gold for their vital support. Many thanks go to Stacy Hiquet for sharing the vision for this book project. Special thanks to development editors Dean Miller and Angelique Brittingham. My appreciation to technical reviewer Bob Zigon for his valuable comments. Thanks to Cindy Morrow, managing editor, and Anne Owen, production editor, who both ensured that this is a quality book. Finally, I want to thank all those who participated in producing this book.

About the Author

Namir Clement Shammas is a software engineer and an expert in object-oriented programming. He has written many articles for leading computer magazines and is responsible for many books on computer programming, including *Windows Programmer's Guide to Object Windows Library, Teach Yourself QBasic in 21 Days,* and *Teach Yourself Mac C++ Programming in 21 Days.*

WEEK 1

AT A GLANCE

1

2

3

4

5

6

7

The first week of your journey into learning to write Windows applications starts with an introduction to the Visual C++ environment—the Workbench. The remaining days in this week present the basics of the C++ language itself. You learn about predefined data types; naming constants, variables, and functions; C++ operators and expressions; managing basic input and output; making decisions; writing loops; and declaring and using arrays. Thus, this week covers the basic components of the C++ language.

1

Getting Started

WEEK 1

Welcome to the world of C++ and Windows programming! Your journey into this exciting venture begins today. Most of the information in today's lesson familiarizes you with the Visual C++ Workbench. You learn about the following topics:

- The basics and history of C++ programs
- Loading and using the Visual C++ Workbench
- The Console applications
- Typing and running your first C++ program

The Basics of C++ Programs

You don't need any previous experience in programming to learn Visual C++ with this book, but if you've programmed before, things will be easier. As with other languages, C++ is made up of declarations and statements that specify exact instructions to be executed when the program runs.

C++ was developed by Bjarn Stroustrup at Bell Labs. The language is meant to succeed and build on the popular C language, mainly by adding object-oriented language extensions.

NEW TERM An *object-oriented language* represents the attributes and operations of objects.

In addition, C++ offers a number of enhancements to C that are not object-oriented. Thus, learning C++ gives you the bonus of becoming very familiar with C. Unlike C, which has been standardized, C++ is still undergoing the standardization process.

Programming in C++ requires that you become aware of the supporting libraries which perform various tasks such as input, output, text manipulation, math operations, file I/O (input/output), and so on. In languages such as BASIC, support for such operations is transparent to programs, because it is automatically available to these programs. As a result, many programs come across as single components that are independent of any other programming components. By contrast, programming in C++ makes you more aware of the dependency on various libraries. The advantage of this language feature is that you are able to select between similar libraries, including ones that you develop. Thus, C++ programs are modular. C++ compilers, including Visual C++, use project files and program files. The Visual C++ Workbench uses project files to manage the creation and update of a program.

NEW TERM *Project files* specify the library. *Program files* create an application.

Loading the Visual C++ Workbench

The Visual C++ Workbench is the visual interface for the C++ compiler, linker, debugger, and other tools used to create, manage, and maintain C++ programs. You can load the Workbench by simply clicking on the Visual C++ icon or by double-clicking the MSVC20.EXE program from the File Manager. (The file MSVC20.EXE is located in the directory \MSVC20\BIN.)

The Visual C++ Workbench does not use command-line switches to fine-tune how it loads and operates. Instead, it uses one of its menu options (more about this later in today's lesson).

An Overview of the Visual C++ Workbench

The Visual C++ Workbench is the environment, shown in Figure 1.1, used to develop C and C++ applications. The Workbench is a versatile tool which facilitates developing both MS-DOS and Windows applications as well as libraries. Throughout this book, you use the Workbench to learn about programming in C++ and writing Windows applications.

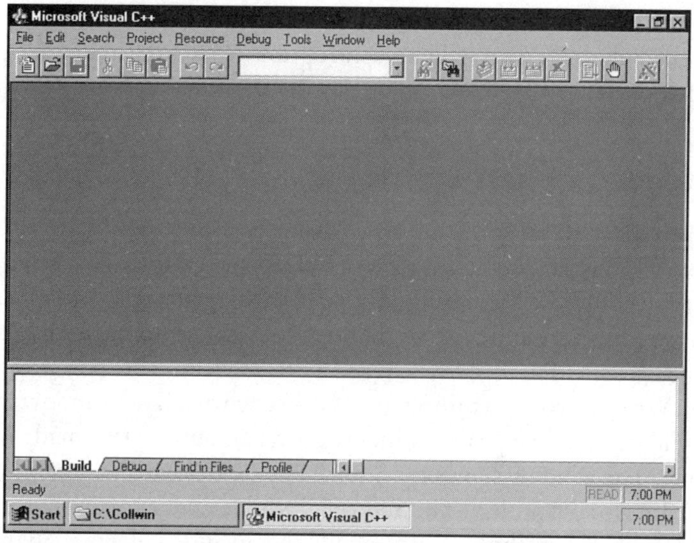

Figure 1.1. *The Visual Workbench.*

The Visual C++ Workbench has menu options, a tool bar, a status bar, and a display area. The built-in editor uses this area to display and edit files in MDI (Multi-Document Interface) windows.

One of the valuable features of the Workbench is the extensive on-line help. Using the Help option, you can inquire about every aspect of the Workbench, the C++ language, and other aspects of developing programs.

The Visual C++ Workbench contains a menu with nine main options. You don't need to understand what all these options mean exactly. This is just an overview. Each option contains a family of selections which performs a task or sets an option. The next sections introduce you to the menu options of the Visual C++ Workbench.

The File Option

The File option essentially manages loading and saving files, printing, and exiting the Workbench. This option includes the selections in the next subsections.

The New Selection

The **N**ew selection brings up the New dialog box, shown in Figure 1.2. This dialog box allows you to create a new source code window, project, resource script, binary file, bitmap file, icon file, or cursor file. The first option creates a new source code window with the default title TEXT1. The second option invokes the integrated project manager. The other options in the New dialog box invoke the integrated App Studio utility.

The Open Selection

The **O**pen selection brings up the Open dialog box shown in Figure 1.3. This dialog box permits you to open source code files (with the extensions .C, .CPP, .CXX, and .H), .MAK project files, or .RC resource files. The dialog box allows you to select a file from any existing directory and drive. In addition, the dialog box has a wildcard filenames text box which permits you to choose the set of files to view before selecting an individual file to open. When you open a project, the Workbench displays a window that resembles the one in Figure 1.4. The project window shows an outline tree made up of folders and filenames. The window shows the Source Files folder which contains the .CPP, .DEF, and .RC files for the project. The Source Files folder also contains the nested Dependencies folder, which lists the header files and other included files used in the project. Figure 1.5 shows a sample source code window. By default, the Workbench editor colors the source code to highlight reserved words, comments, and strings.

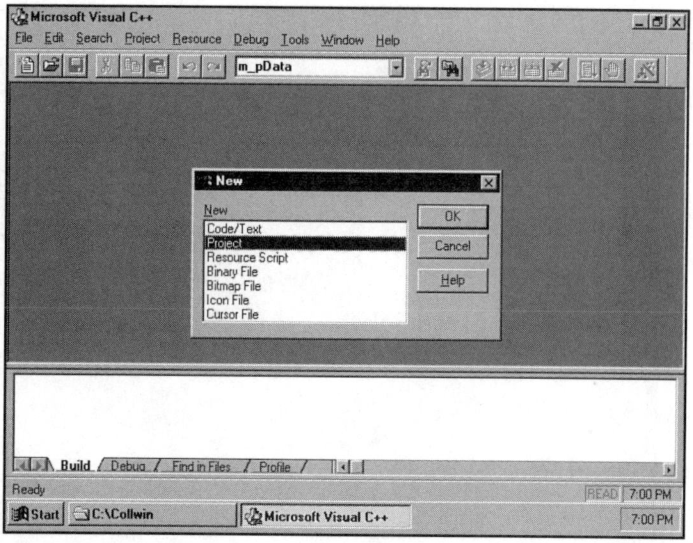

Figure 1.2. *The New dialog box.*

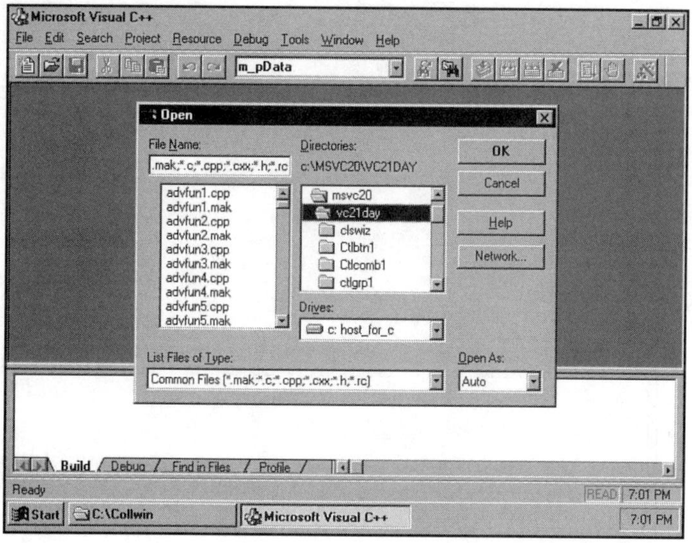

Figure 1.3. *The Open dialog box.*

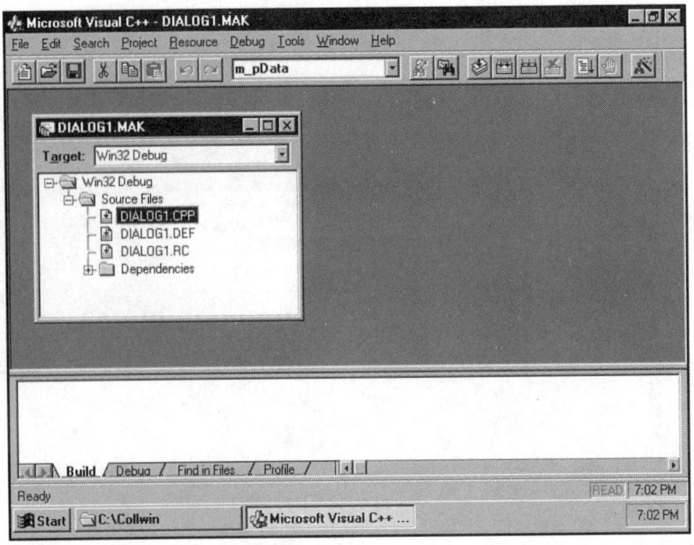

Figure 1.4. *A sample project window.*

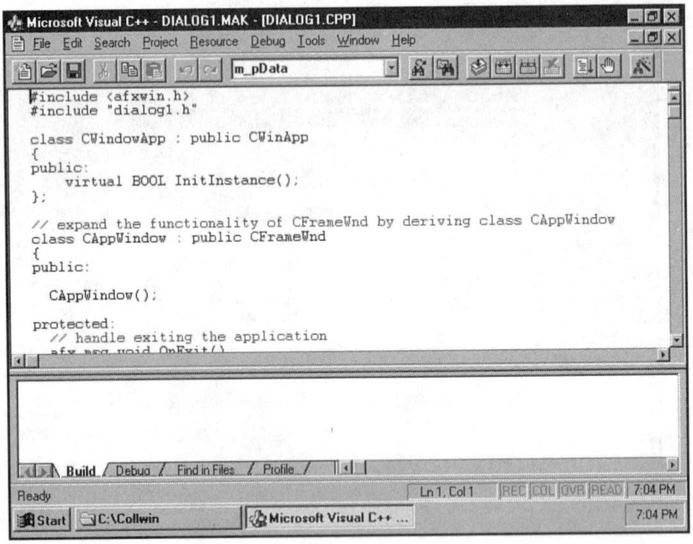

Figure 1.5. *A sample source code window.*

The Close Selection

The **C**lose selection closes the currently edited window. If the contents of that window (which may contain source code or a resource) have not been saved or updated, the **C**lose selection displays a message dialog box. This dialog box asks you if you want to save the contents of the window before closing.

The Save Selection

The **S**ave selection updates the file which is associated with the currently edited window (which may contain source code or a resource). If you invoke this selection with a new window, the Workbench invokes the Save As dialog box.

The Save As Selection

The Save **A**s selection allows you to save a new window or write the contents of the currently edited window to a different file. The selection invokes the Save As dialog box to allow you to specify the filename as well as the target directory and drive (see Figure 1.6).

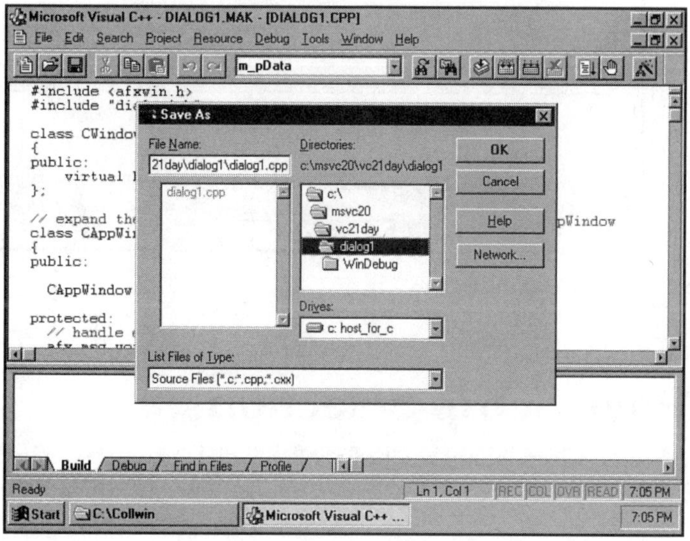

Figure 1.6. *The Save As dialog box.*

The Save All Selection

The Save All selection quickly saves all the windows in the Workbench. The selection invokes the Save As dialog box to save new windows.

The Print Selection

The **Print** selection allows you to print part or all of the currently edited window. The selection invokes the Print dialog box, shown in Figure 1.7, which allows you to select the printer, to select printing all or part of the edited text, and to invoke the printer setup. The Print dialog box invokes other dialog boxes for the printer setup.

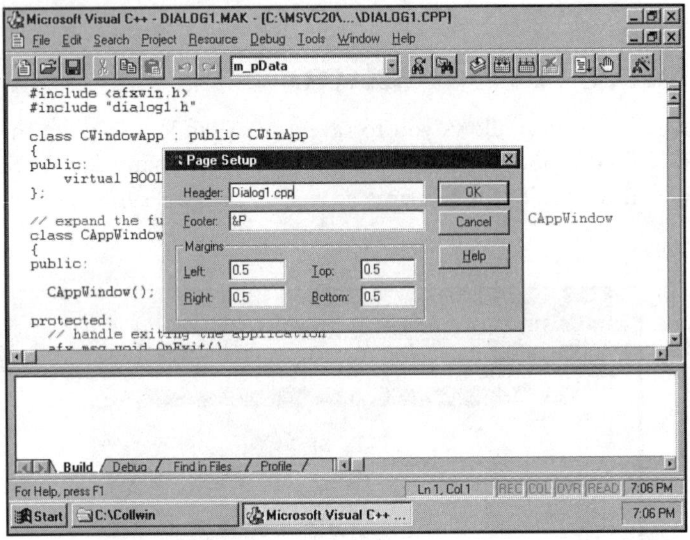

Figure 1.7. *The Print dialog box.*

The Page Setup Selection

The Page Setup selection invokes the Page Setup dialog box, shown in Figure 1.8, which permits you to specify the header, footer, and the four document margins.

The Exit Selection

The Exit selection allows you to exit the Visual C++ Workbench. If there are edited windows that are not saved, the Workbench gives you the opportunity to save these windows before exiting.

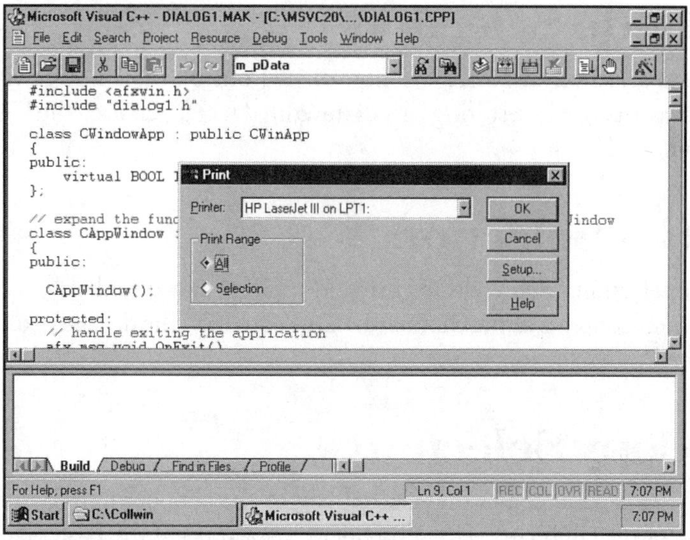

Figure 1.8. *The Print Setup dialog box.*

The Most Recent Files Selections

The Visual C++ Workbench remembers the most recent files and project files that you have worked with. The Workbench displays the names of these files in the **F**ile option above the E**x**it selection.

The Edit Option

The **E**dit option has selections that perform four kinds of operations: undoing changes, cut-and-paste operations, find/replace operations, and toggling read-only mode.

The Undo Selection

The **U**ndo selection allows you to undo previous editing tasks. The number of editing tasks which you can undo depends on the size of the Undo buffer (a memory location used to track and store changes in the text). The default size of the buffer is 4K and can be set anywhere from 0 to 64K. The **E**ditor selection in the **O**ptions option allows you to alter the size of the Undo buffer.

The Redo Selection

The **R**edo selection undoes the action carried out by the **U**ndo selection. The **R**edo selection assists you in restoring part of the edited text if you used the **U**ndo selection too many times.

The Cut Selection

The Cu**t** selection deletes selected text and copies that text to the clipboard (overwriting the previous contents of the clipboard). Consequently, the deleted text can be reinserted using the **P**aste selection.

The Copy Selection

The **C**opy selection copies the selected text to the clipboard, overwriting the previous contents of the clipboard. The subsequent invocation of the **P**aste selection inserts the copied text.

The Paste Selection

The **P**aste selection inserts the text in the clipboard at the current cursor location. You can move text from one location to another with the Cu**t** and **P**aste selections. You can duplicate text in one or more windows with the **C**opy and **P**aste selections.

The Delete Selection

The **D**elete selection deletes the selected text or the character at the cursor (if there is no selected text). The deleted text or character is not copied into the clipboard.

The Select All Selection

The **S**elect All selection enables you to quickly select all of the text in the active window.

The ClassWizard Selection

The Class**W**izard selection invokes the ClassWizard utility, which allows you to fine-tune the source code generated by the AppWizard utility. The first two bonus chapters discuss the AppWizard and ClassWizard utilities.

The Properties Selection

The Pr**o**perties selection brings up the dialog box which shows the properties associated with the item in the active window. Figure 1.9 shows the Text File Properties dialog box which shows the properties associated with a text file.

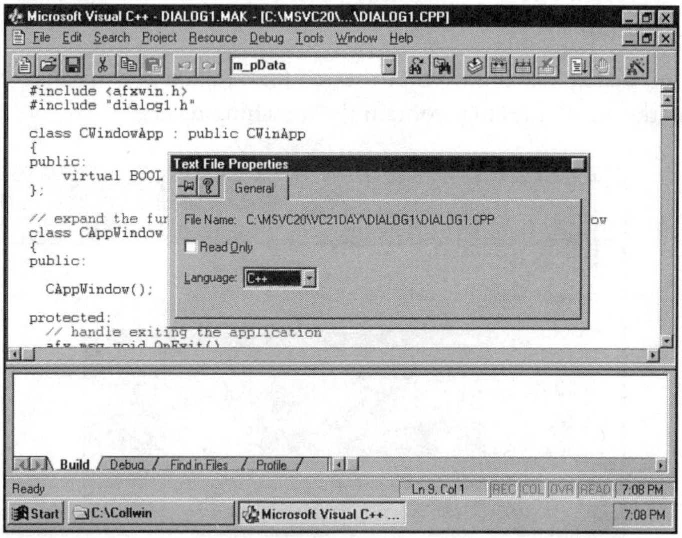

Figure 1.9. *The Text File Properties dialog box.*

The Search Option

The **S**earch option contains selections which allow you to search for various kinds of information, such as text, function definitions, and error messages.

The Find Selection

The **F**ind selection allows you to search for text in the currently edited window. The selection invokes the Find dialog box, shown in Figure 1.10. This dialog box allows you to specify the following search options:

- The search text (the dialog box uses a combo box control which allows you to specify previous search text)
- The search for a whole word (the dialog box offers a check box to toggle the search for a whole word)

- The case-sensitive search (the dialog box offers a check box to toggle the case-sensitive search)
- The use of regular expressions to search for text using more advanced text patterns
- The search direction (the dialog box offers radio buttons to specify the search direction)

The Find dialog box allows you to search for a match one instance at a time, or to set bookmarks on all lines that contain the matching text.

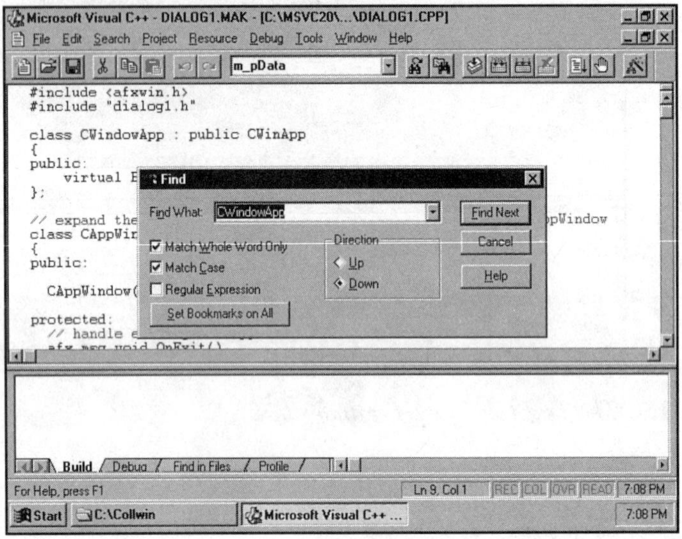

Figure 1.10. *The Find dialog box.*

The Replace Selection

The Replace selection replaces text in the currently edited window. The selection invokes the Replace dialog box, shown in Figure 1.11. This dialog box allows you to specify the following search options:

- The search text (the dialog box uses a combo box control which allows you to specify previous search text)
- The replacement text (the dialog box uses a combo box control which allows you to specify previous replacement text)

- The search for a whole word (the dialog box offers a check box to toggle the search for a whole word)
- The case-sensitive search (the dialog box offers a check box to toggle the case-sensitive search)
- The use of regular expressions to search for text using more advanced text patterns
- The scope of replacement which can be in the entire file or only in the selected text

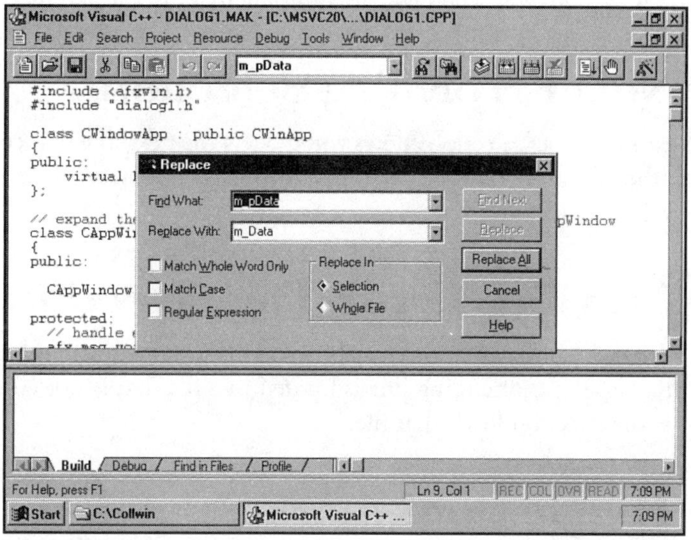

Figure 1.11. *The Replace dialog box.*

The Replace dialog box replaces some or all the occurrences of the search text with the replacement text. The dialog box also contains a **F**ind Next command button, which allows you to search for text.

The Find In Files Selection

The Find in Files selection invokes the Find In Files dialog box which enables you to find text in other files that are not opened by the Workbench.

The Match Brace Selection

The **M**atch Brace selection empowers you to find matching curly braces—{ and }. C++ uses the braces to define a block of statements. When you write complex programs which contain nested blocks, this selection ensures that the blocks are properly closed.

The Go To Selection

The **Go** To selection invokes a dialog box which prompts you for the line number to view. This selection allows you to make accurate jumps to specific lines. The benefit of this selection is even greater when you are jumping to a distant line in a very large file.

The Next Error/Tag Selection

The **N**ext Error/Tag selection allows you to view the next line that contains an error or a tag. If the offending line is located in a file that is not currently in an MDI window, the selection loads that file.

The Previous Error/Tag Selection

The **P**revious Error/Tag selection enables you to view the previous line that contains an error or a tag. If the offending line is located in a file that is not currently in an MDI window, the selection loads that file.

The Toggle Bookmark Selection

The **T**oggle Bookmark selection toggles the highlight of the line that contains the cursor. When this selection highlights a line, it sets a bookmark at that line. When the selection clears the highlight of a line, that line is no longer marked.

The Next Bookmark Selection

The Ne**x**t Bookmark selection visits the next line with a bookmark. You can create such lines by using the **T**oggle Bookmark selection or by using the **F**ind selection in the Edit option.

The Previous Bookmark Selection

The Pre**v**ious Bookmark selection visits the previous line that has a bookmark.

The Clear All Bookmarks Selection

The **C**lear All Bookmarks selection removes all the bookmarks. Use this selection before you employ the **F**ind selection in the **E**dit option to mark lines that match a specific text.

The Go to Definition Selection

The Go to **D**efinition selection jumps to the first location where a name is defined. The selection loads the file that contains the definition if the definition is not located in any window in the workspace.

The Go to Reference Selection

The Go to **R**eference selection jumps to the first location where a name is referenced. The selection loads the file that contains the reference if the reference is not located in any window in the workspace.

The Next Definition Selection

The **N**ext Definition selection jumps to the next definition or reference of a name. The action of this selection depends on which of the last two selections was most recently invoked.

The Previous Definition Selection

The **P**revious Definition selection jumps to the previous definition or reference of a name. The action of this selection depends on which selection was most recently invoked—Go to Definition or Go to Reference.

The Pop Context Selection

The Pop **C**ontext selection jumps to the name that you used before the last invocation of the Go to Definition selection or the Go to Reference selection.

The Browse Selection

The **B**rowse selection opens the Browse dialog box, shown in Figure 1.12, which allows you to browse through the various components of a program. This advanced-level selection serves you later when you create modular programs.

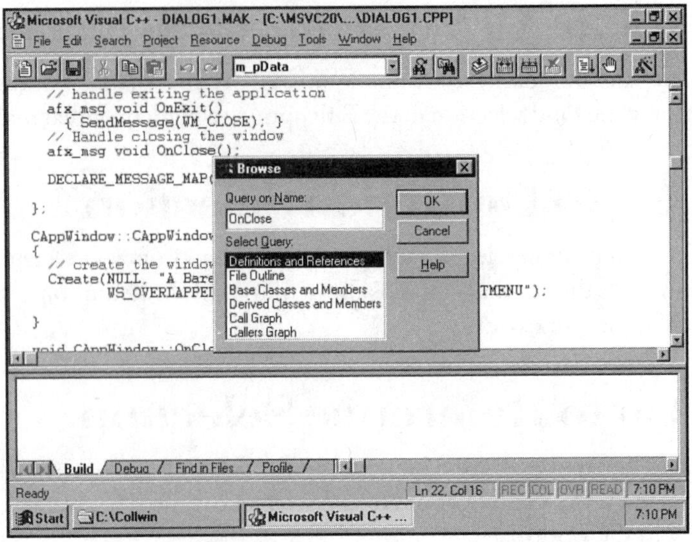

Figure 1.12. *The Browse dialog box.*

The Project Option

The **P**roject option allows you to manage the creation and update of an application. You use various selections in the **P**roject option to compile and run C++ programs.

The Files Selection

The **F**iles selection brings up the Project Files dialog box, shown in Figure 1.13. This dialog box allows you to load any needed files. Use this selection to complete and update files in existing projects.

The New Group Selection

The New **G**roup selection brings up the New Group dialog box which allows you to create a logical set of files from the collection of files in the current project.

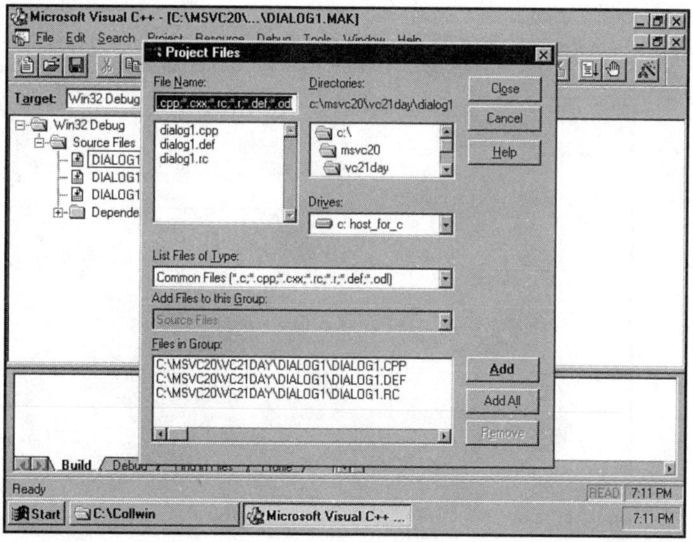

Figure 1.13. *The Project Files dialog box.*

The Settings Selection

The **S**ettings selection brings up the Project Settings dialog box, shown in Figure 1.14. This dialog box enables you to fine-tune the operations of the C/C++ compiler, the debugger, the linker, and the resource compiler. The default settings are adequate for the programs in this book.

The Targets Selection

The **T**argets selection brings up the Targets dialog box, shown in Figure 1.15. This dialog box allows you to select the targeted code. You can choose, for example, between the release version or the debug version of a program. The debug version contains additional information which allows the debugger to trace and examine the program flow. The price for this advantage is that the .EXE files generated are large. By contrast, the release version of a program is smaller.

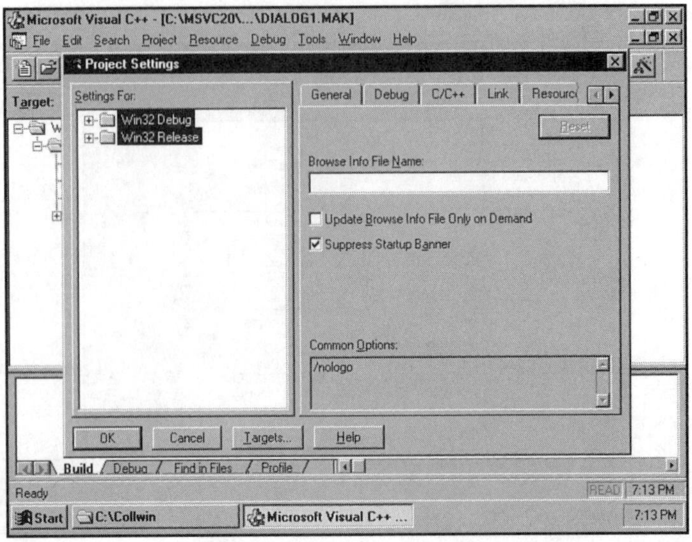

Figure 1.14. *The Project Settings dialog box.*

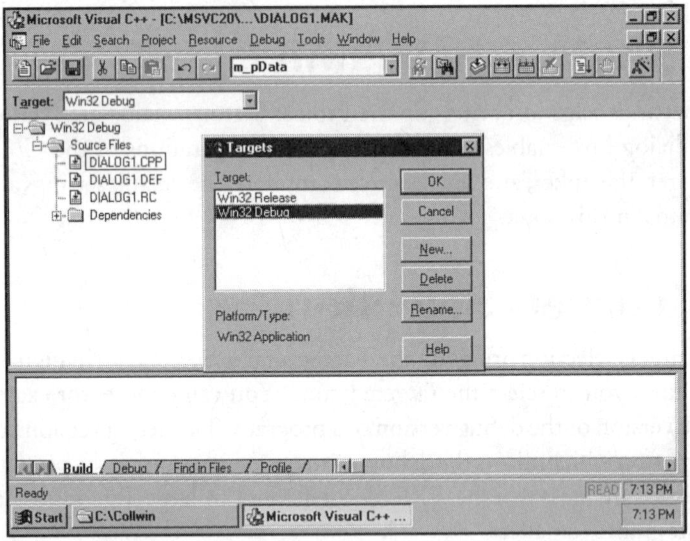

Figure 1.15. *The Targets dialog box.*

The Compile Selection

The Com**p**ile selection compiles the statements in the active window. The option saves the contents of that window if necessary. The Workbench displays an output window which displays the status of the compilation and any errors generated by the compiler.

NEW TERM C++ allows you to create a program using several components. Each component is stored in a *source file*. The compiler generates .OBJ object files from each source file. The linker creates the .EXE program file by combining the various .OBJ files with run-time library files.

The Build Selection

The **B**uild selection creates the .EXE program file by compiling (or recompiling) the source files. The selection works on only those files that either

- Have not yet been compiled
- Have been compiled earlier, but their corresponding source codes were changed

The project file stores information which specifies the dependencies of files on other files. This information allows the **B**uild selection to determine the hierarchical level of dependencies between files.

The Rebuild All Selection

The **R**ebuild All selection creates the .EXE program file by systematically recompiling all its components.

The Batch Build Selection

The Batch B**u**ild selection brings up the Batch Build dialog box, shown in Figure 1.16. This dialog box permits you to specify multiple targets. The Workbench stores the compiled files of each target in a different subdirectory to prevent similarly named files from being overwritten.

The Stop Build Selection

The S**t**op Build selection halts the creation of the application as soon as possible. This selection empowers you to halt building a project if you realize that you still have some code changes to make.

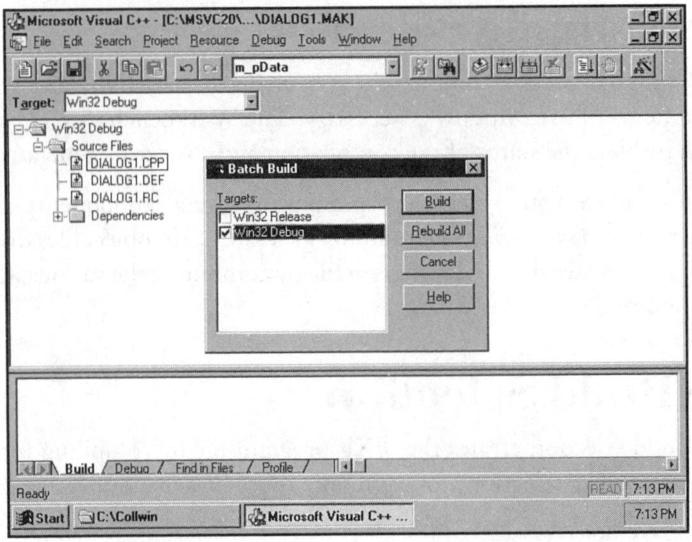

Figure 1.16. *The Batch Build dialog box.*

The Execute Selection

The Execute selection runs the program in the project. This selection recompiles and links the components source file if needed. You use this option to run the programs in this book.

The Update Dependencies Selection

The Update Dependencies selection updates the list of dependent files for the currently edited file.

The Update All Dependencies Selection

The Update All Dependencies selection updates the list of dependent files for the entire project.

The Build Browse Info File Selection

The Build Browse Info File selection creates the browse information file.

The Close Browse Info File Selection

The Close Browse Info File selection closes the browse information file.

The Resource Option

The **R**esource option contains selections that permit you to create, update, view, test, and manage various kinds of resources. These resources include menus, icons, bitmaps, and cursors. The selections in the **R**esource option invoke the integrated App Studio utility which uses visual programming methods to create and update resources.

The Debug Option

The **D**ebug option contains selections that permit you to monitor program execution in order to catch run-time errors. Debugging techniques assign breakpoints to specific statements. The **D**ebug option has selections that enable you to single-step through a program and watch the values of variables.

NEW TERM *Breakpoints* cause the program to temporarily stop, allowing you to inspect various components.

The Tools Option

The **T**ools option is a flexible menu that you can customize. Its selections are utilities that are invoked from within the Workbench.

The Toolbars Selection

The **T**oolbars selection brings up the Toolbars dialog box, shown in Figure 1.17. This dialog box allows you select the toolbars to display. The dialog box offers the options of the Standard, Edit, Resource, Debug, and Browse toolbars.

The Customize Selection

The **C**ustomize selection brings up the Customize dialog box, shown in Figure 1.18. This paged (or tabbed) dialog box allows you to customize the toolbars, the tools, and the keyboard.

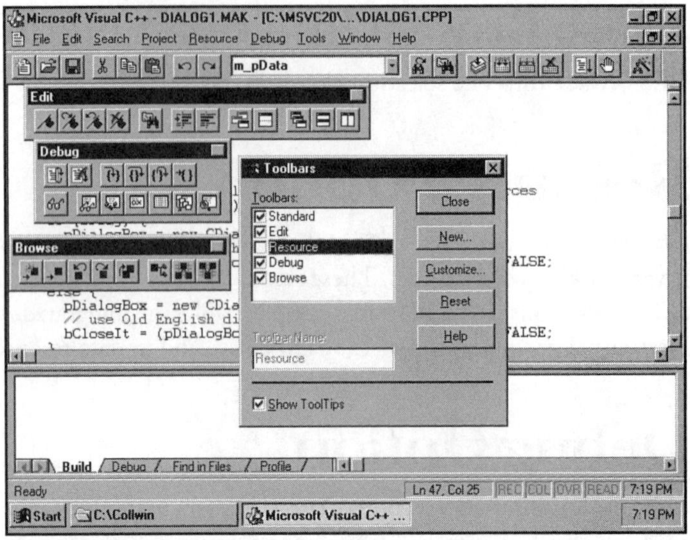

Figure 1.17. *The Toolbars dialog box.*

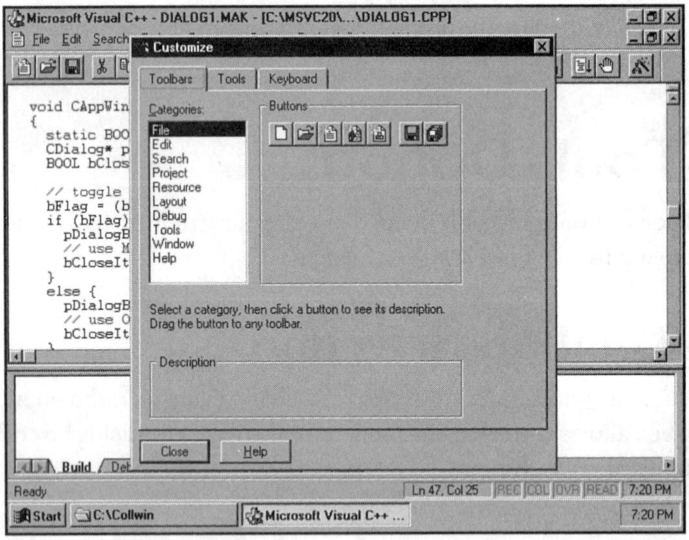

Figure 1.18. *The Customize dialog box.*

The Options Selection

The **O**ptions selection invokes the Options dialog box, shown in Figure 1.19. This dialog box sets the options for the editor, colors, fonts, debugger, directories, workspace, and the on-line help.

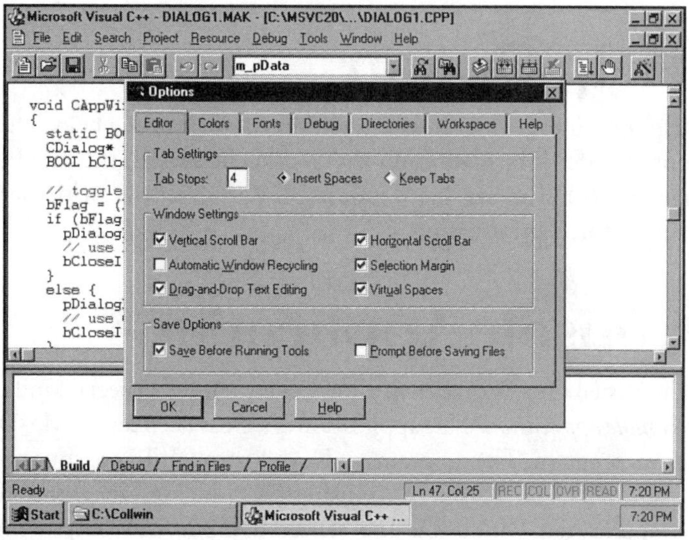

Figure 1.19. *The Options dialog box.*

The Record Keystrokes Selection

The **R**ecord Keystrokes selection allows you to record keystrokes in the current editor window. These keystrokes enable you to quickly and efficiently repeat tasks.

The Playback Recording Selection

The **P**layback Recording selection allows you to play back the keystroke sequences that you recorded using the **R**ecord Keystrokes selection.

The Profile Selection

The Pro**f**ile selection opens the Profile dialog box, which permits you to view and analyze the performance of your program.

The Window Option

The **W**indow option has a group of selections that allow you to tile, cascade, close, and duplicate windows in the workspace. In addition, the Window option allows you to display special windows that view program variables and the CPU registers.

The Help Option

The **H**elp option provides versatile and time-saving on-line help. The selections of the **H**elp option offer information on the Workbench itself, the build tools, the C/C++ languages, the MFC library, the Windows SDK (Software Development Kit), and where to obtain technical information.

The Console Applications

NEW TERM The Visual C++ Workbench allows you to build a special kind of program called a *console application.* This application is a cross between an MS-DOS program and a Windows program. The programs in Days 1 through 12 are console applications that allow you to focus on learning C++ using DOS-like interface and input/output. The console application window is the standard input and output for C++ programs (compiled as console applications). The console application window has a simple menu with few options and a few selections.

To create a console application, perform the following steps:

1. Load the Visual C++ Workbench.
2. Choose the **N**ew selection in the **F**ile option.
3. Select the Code/Text option and click the OK button.
4. The Visual Workbench creates a new source code window.
5. Type in the C++ program in the new window.
6. Choose the Save **A**s selection in the **F**ile option. Save the C++ programs with a .CPP extension. The Save As dialog box allows you to select the drive and/or directory to store the new program.
7. Close the currently edited window using the **C**lose selection in the **F**ile option.
8. Choose the **N**ew selection in the **F**ile option. Select the **P**roject option and then click the OK button.

9. The Visual Workbench displays the New Project dialog box. Select the Console Application option from the Project Type list box.
10. Enter the name of the project (use the same name as the .CPP file). If necessary, select a new directory to be the host directory. Click on the Create button when you are finished.
11. The Workbench displays the Project Files dialog box which allows you to select the file or files that make up a project. The dialog box includes controls for selecting another drive and/or another directory. Use these controls to locate the program you just entered. To add a file to the list of project files, either double-click on that file or select it and then click on the Add button. To remove a file from the list of project files, select that file and click on the Delete button. When you have finished selecting files, click on the Close button.
12. Invoke the **B**uild selection in the **P**roject option. This step compiles and links your program.
13. Choose the E**x**ecute selection in the **P**roject option to run the program. The output appears in a console application window that has the title of the project name.

Note: The programs in this book are located in the directory \MSVC20\VC21DAY. Please create the subdirectory VC21DAY and attach it to directory \MSVC20.

Your First C++ Program

The first C++ program that I present displays a one-line greeting message. This simple program enables you to see the very basic components of a C++ program.

Listing 1.1 contains the source code for program HELLO.CPP with numbered lines. Do not enter the line numbers when you type in the program. These line numbers serve as reference only. The trivial program displays the string `"Hello Programmer!"`. Carry out the following steps to create and run your first C++ program:

1. Load the Visual C++ Workbench.
2. Choose the **N**ew selection in the **F**ile option.
3. Select the Code/Text option and click the OK button.

4. The Visual Workbench creates a new source code window.
5. Enter in the new window the program found in Listing 1.1.
6. Choose the Save **A**s selection in the **F**ile option. Save the C++ program as HELLO.CPP in directory \MSVC20\VC21DAY.
7. Close the currently edited window using the **C**lose selection in the File option.
8. Choose the **N**ew selection in the File option. Select the **P**roject option and then click the OK button.
9. The Visual Workbench displays the New Project dialog box. Select the Console Application option from the Project Type list box.
10. Enter `hello` of the project and then click the Create button.
11. The Workbench displays the Project Files dialog box which allows you to select the HELLO.CPP file. Add this file to the list of project files by selecting it and then clicking on the Add button. Click on the Close button.
12. Invoke the **B**uild selection in the **P**roject option. This step compiles and links your HELLO.CPP program.
13. Choose the Execute selection in the **P**roject option to run the program HELLO.EXE. The output appears in a console application window.

Type

Listing 1.1. Source code for the program HELLO.CPP.

```
1: // a trivial C++ program that says hello
2:
3: #include <iostream.h>
4:
5: main()
6: {
7:   cout << "Hello Programmer!";
8:   return 0;
9: }
```

The program displays the greeting message in a console application window.

Examine the short code of the C++ program and notice the following characteristics:

- C++ uses the `//` characters for comments that run to the end of the line. C++ also supports the C-style comments that begin with the `/*` characters and end with the `*/` characters. Line number 1 contains a comment that briefly describes the program.

NEW TERM *Comments* are remarks that you put in the program to explain or clarify certain parts of the program. The compiler ignores comments.

- The C++ program has no reserved keywords that declare the end of a program. In fact, C++ uses a rather simple scheme for organizing a program. This scheme supports two levels of code: global and single-level functions. In addition, the function `main`, which starts in line 5, plays a very special role because run-time execution begins with this function. Therefore, there can be only a single function `main` in a C++ program. You can place the function `main` anywhere in the code.
- The C++ strings and characters are enclosed in double and single quotes, respectively. Thus, `'A'` is a single character, whereas `"A"` is a single-character string. Mixing C++ single-character strings and characters is not allowed.

> **Note:** Strings can have any number of characters, including no characters—the empty string.

- C++ defines blocks using the `{` and `}` characters (see examples in lines 6 and 9, respectively).
- Every statement in a C++ program must end with a semicolon (;).
- C++ contains the `#include` compiler directive. An example of this is in line 3, instructing the Visual C++ compiler to include the IOSTREAM.H header file. C++ extends the notion of streams, which already exists in C. IOSTREAM.H provides the operations that support basic stream input and output. The C++ language does not include built-in I/O routines. Instead, the language relies on libraries specializing in various types of I/O.

NEW TERM A *compiler directive* is a special instruction for the compiler. A *header file* contains the declarations of constants, data types, variables, and forward (early) declarations of functions. A *stream* is a sequence of data flowing from part of a computer to another.

- The C++ program outputs the string `"Hello Programmer!"` to the standard output stream `cout`, which is the Console Application window. In addition, the program uses the extractor operator, <<, to send the emitted string to the output stream.
- The function `main` must return a value that reflects the error status of the C++ program. Returning the value `0` signals to the operating system that the program terminated normally.

Exiting the Workbench

To exit the Workbench, close the current project (using the **C**lose selections in the **P**roject option) and choose the **Ex**it selection in the **F**ile option.

Summary

Today's lesson introduces you to the Visual C++ Workbench and presents you with the first C++ program. You learn these basics:

- C++ programs are modular and rely on standard and/or custom libraries.
- The two ways to load the Visual C++ Workbench are by clicking on the Visual C++ icon or double-clicking on the MSVC.EXE file when using the File Manager (or any similar utility).
- The Visual C++ Workbench is a versatile environment for developing, maintaining, and debugging C and C++ programs and libraries for MS-DOS and Windows applications.
- The **F**ile option allows you to manage files, print text, and exit the Workbench.
- The **E**dit option permits you to undo text changes, manage text (cut, paste, copy, and delete), search for text, and replace text.
- The **V**iew option allows you to view compiler errors, manage bookmarks, toggle the status bar, and toggle the toolbar.
- The **P**roject option enables you to manage programs by compiling source files, building projects, running programs, managing workspaces, and managing the dependencies of files.
- The **B**rowse option permits you to locate the definition and references of a name.
- The **D**ebug option offers choices that allow you to manage breakpoints in source files, single-step program execution, and watch variables.
- The **T**ools option invokes utilities that assist in developing, managing, and maintaining programs.
- The **O**ptions option fine-tunes projects, directories, the editor, syntax color, fonts, tools, the workspaces, and the debugger.

- The **Window** option allows you to manage windows and open special windows.
- The **Help** option provides versatile on-line help on a variety of topics, such as the Workbench, the C/C++ language, and the MFC library.
- The console applications are Windows applications providing special windows that act as standard input and output devices. Console applications allow you to write DOS-like programs.
- The first C++ program is a simple greeting program that illustrates the basic components of a C++ program. These components include comments, the `#include` directive, and the `main` function.
- You exit the Workbench through the E**x**it selection in the **F**ile option.

Q&A

Q Does C++ use line numbers?

A No. I am using line numbers in the listings only for the sake of reference.

Q Does the Workshop's editor monitor what I type?

A Yes it does. In fact, when you type in a C++ keyword, the Workbench quickly colors that keyword.

Q What happens if I forget to type the second double quote in the first program?

A The compiler tells you that there is an error in the program. You need to add the second double quote and build the project.

Q How do I delete text in the currently edited window?

A Use the **R**eplace selection in the **E**dit option and specify nothing for the replacement string.

Workshop

The Workshop provides quiz questions to help you solidify your understanding of the material covered and exercises to provide you with experience in using what you've learned. Try to understand the quiz and exercise answers before continuing on to the next day's lesson. Answers are provided in Appendix B, "Answers."

Quiz

1. What is the output of the following program?

```
// quiz program #1

#include <iostream.h>

main()
{
  cout << "C++ in 21 Days?";
  return 0;
}
```

2. What is the output of the following program?

```
// quiz program #2

#include <iostream.h>

main()
{
  // cout << "C++ in 21 Days?";
  return 0;
}
```

3. What is wrong with the following program?

```
// quiz program #3

#include <iostream.h>

main()
{
  cout << "C++ in 21 Days?"
  return 0;
}
```

Exercise

Write a program that displays the message `I am a C++ Programmer.`

2

C++ Program Components

Day 1 presents the Visual C++ Workbench and a simple C++ program. Today we focus on the basic components of C++ programs, including data types, variables, constants, and functions. You learn about the following topics:

- The predefined data types in Visual C++
- Naming items in Visual C++
- The `#include` directive
- Declaring variables
- Declaring constants
- Declaring and prototyping functions
- Local variables in functions
- Static variables in functions
- Inline functions
- Exiting functions
- Default arguments
- Function overloading

Predefined Data Types in Visual C++

Visual C++ offers the `int`, `char`, `float`, `double`, and `void` data types to represent integers, characters, single-precision floating-point numbers, double-precision floating point numbers, and valueless data, respectively. C++ uses the `void` type with a function's returned values to indicate that the function acts as a procedure.

C++ adds more flexibility to data types by supporting data type modifiers. The type modifiers are: `signed`, `unsigned`, `short`, and `long`. Table 2.1 shows the predefined data types in C++ (and includes the type modifiers) along with their sizes and ranges. Notice that the `int` and `unsigned int` are system-dependent. The table shows the 16-bit values for these data types.

NEW TERM *Data type modifiers* alter the precision and the range of values.

Table 2.1. Predefined data types in C++.

Data Type	Byte Size	Range	Examples
`char`	1	-128 to 127	`'A','!'`
`signed char`	1	-128 to 127	`23`
`unsigned char`	1	0 to 255	`200,0x1a`
`int`	2	Depends on system -32768 to 32767 for 16-bit	`3000`
`unsigned int`	2	Depends on system 0 to 65535 for 16-bit	`0xffff, 65535`
`short int`	2	-32768 to 32767	`100`
`unsigned short int`	2	0 to 65535	`0xff, 40000`
`long int`	4	-2147483648 to 2147483647	`0xfffff -123456,`
`unsigned long int`	4	0 to 4294967295	`123456`
`float`	4	3.4E-38 to 3.4E+38 and -3.4E-38 to -3.4E+38	`2.35, -52.354, 1.3e+10`
`double`	8	1.7E-308 to 1.7E+308 and -1.7E-308 to -1.7E+308	`12.354 -2.5e+100 -78.32544`
`long double`	10	1.2E-4932 to 1.2E+4932 and -1.2E-4932 to -1.2E+4932	`8.5e-3000`

NEW TERM C++ supports *hexadecimal numbers*. Such numbers begin with the characters `0x` followed by the hexadecimal value. For example, the number `0xff` is the hexadecimal equivalent of the decimal number `255`.

Naming Items in Visual C++

Visual C++ requires you to observe the following rules with identifiers:

1. The first character must be a letter or an underscore (_).
2. Subsequent characters can be letters, digits, or underscores.
3. The maximum length of an identifier is 247 characters.
4. Identifiers are case-sensitive in C++. Thus, the names `rate`, `RATE`, and `Rate` refer to three different identifiers.
5. Identifiers cannot be reserved words such as `int`, `double`, or `static` (to name just a few).

Here are examples of valid identifiers:

```
X
x
aString
DAYS_IN_WEEK
BinNumber0
bin_number_0
bin0Number2
_length
```

DO | **DON'T**

DO use descriptive names that have a reasonable length.

DON'T use identifier names that are too short or too long. Short names yield poor readability and long names are prone to typos.

The *#include* Directive

Recall that a directive is a special instruction for C and C++ compilers. A directive begins with the # character and is followed by the directive name. Directives are usually placed in the first column of a line. They can be preceded only by spaces or tab characters. The C++ program in Day 1 contains the `#include` directive. This directive tells the compiler to include the text of a file as if you have typed that text yourself. Thus, the `#include` directive is a better alternative than cutting text from one file and pasting in another file. Recall from Day 1 that programs use the `#include` directive to include header files.

Syntax

The *#include* Directive

The general syntax for the `#include` directive is

```
#include <filename>
#include "filename"
```

Example:

```
#include <iostream.h>
#include "string.h"
```

The filename represents the name of the included file. The two forms differ in how the `#include` directive searches for the included file. The first form searches for the file in the special directory for included files. The second form extends the search to involve the current directory.

Declaring Variables

Declaring variables requires you to state the data type of the variable and the name of the variable. The word *variable* indicates that you can alter the data of these data containers.

NEW TERM *Variables* are identifiers used to store and recall information. You can regard a variable as a labeled data container.

Syntax

Declaring Variables

The general syntax for declaring variables is

```
type variableName;
type variableName = initialValue;
type var1 [= initVal1], var2 [= initVal2], ...;
```

Example:

```
int j;
double z = 32.314;
long fileSize, diskSize, totalFileSize = 0;
```

C++ allows you to declare a list of variables (that have the same types) in a declarative statement. For example:

```
int j, i = 2, k = 3;
double x = 3.12;
double y = 2 * x, z = 4.5, a = 45.7;
```

The initializing values may contain other variables defined earlier.

DO	DON'T

DO resist using global variables.

DON'T declare variables, within the same program unit, with names that are different in character case (such as `rate` and `Rate`).

Let's look at a simple example which uses variables. Listing 2.1 shows the source code for the program VAR1.CPP. The program declares four variables, two of which are initialized during their declarations. The program then assigns values to the uninitialized variables and displays the contents of all four variables. Create the project VAR1 and include the VAR1.CPP file. Build and run the VAR1.MAK project.

Type

Listing 2.1. Source code for the program VAR1.CPP.

```
1: // C++ program that illustrates simple variables
2:
3: #include <iostream.h>
4:
5: main()
6: {
7:   int i, j = 2;
8:   double x, y = 355.0 / 113;
9:
10:    i = 3 * j;
11:    cout << "i = " << i << "\n"
12:         << "j = " << j << "\n";
13:
14:    x = 2 * y;
15:    x = x * x;
16:    cout << "y = " << y << "\n"
17:         << "x = " << x << "\n";
18:    return 0;
19:
20: }
```

Here is a sample session with the program in Listing 2.1:

Output

```
i = 6
j = 2
y = 3.14159
x = 39.4784
```

Analysis

The program uses the `#include` directive in line 3 to include the stream I/O header file IOSTREAM.H. The function `main` appears in line 5. The function contains the declarations of the `int`-typed variables `i`, `j` in line 7, and the `double`-typed variables x and y in line 8. The declarations initialize the variable j and y. The statement in line 10 multiplies the value in variable j (which is 2) by 3 and stores the result in variable x. The stream output statement in lines 11 and 12 displays the values of variables i and j. The statement includes strings that label the output.

The statement in line 14 doubles the value in variable y and stores it in variable x. The statement in line 15 squares the value in variable x and assigns the result back to variable x. This statement uses the variable x on both sides of the equal sign. The stream output statement in lines 16 and 17 displays the values in variable x and y. The statement in line 18 returns 0 as the result of function main.

Declaring Constants

Many languages such as BASIC (the more recent implementations), Modula-2, Ada, C, Pascal, and C++ support constants. No one can deny that constants enhance the readability of a program by replacing numeric constants with identifiers that are more descriptive. Moreover, using constants enables you to change the value of a program parameter by merely changing the value of that parameter in one location. This capability is certainly easier and less prone to generate errors that may occur when you employ your text editor to replace certain numbers with other numbers.

NEW TERM *Constants* are identifiers that are associated with fixed values. C++ offers constants in two flavors: *macro-based* and *formal*. The macro-based constants are inherited from C and use the #define compiler directive.

Syntax

The *#define* Directive

The general syntax for the #define directive is

```
#define constantName constantValue
```

The #define directive causes the compiler to invoke the preprocessor and perform text substitution to replace the macro-based constants with their values. This text replacement step occurs before the compiler processes the statements in the source file. Consequently, the compiler never sees the macro-based constants themselves—only what they expand to.

Examples:

```
#define ASCII_A 65
#define DAYS_IN_WEEK 7
```

The second type of constant in C++ is the *formal constant.*

Syntax

The Formal Constant

The general syntax for the formal constant is

```
const dataType constantName = constantValue;
```

The `dataType` item is an optional item that specifies the data type of the constant values. If you omit the data type, the C++ compiler assumes the `int` type.

Examples:

```
const unsigned char ASCII_A = 65;
const DAYS_IN_WEEK = 7;
const char FIRST_DISK_DRIVE = 'A';
```

DO	DON'T

DO use uppercase names for constants. This naming style enables you to quickly determine if an identifier is a constant.

DON'T assume that other people who read your code will know what embedded numbers mean. Use declared constants to enhance the readability of your programs.

Using Macro-Based Constants

Let's look at an example that uses macro-based constants. Listing 2.2 shows the source code for program CONST1.CPP. The program prompts you to enter the number of hours, minutes, and seconds since midnight. The program then calculates and displays the total number of seconds since midnight. Create the project CONST1 and include the CONST1.CPP file. Build and run the CONST1.MAK project.

Type

Listing 2.2. Source code for the program CONST1.CPP.

```
// C++ program that illustrates constants

#include <iostream.h>

#define SEC_IN_MIN 60
#define MIN_IN_HOUR 60

main()
```

```
9: {
10:    long hours, minutes, seconds;
11:    long totalSec;
12:
13:    cout << "Enter hours: ";
14:    cin >> hours;
15:    cout << "Enter minutes: ";
16:    cin >> minutes;
17:    cout << "Enter seconds: ";
18:    cin >> seconds;
19:
20:    totalSec = ((hours * MIN_IN_HOUR + minutes) *
21:                SEC_IN_MIN) + seconds;
22:
23:    cout <<"\n\n" << totalSec << " seconds since midnight";
24:    return 0;
25: }
```

Here is a sample session with the program in Listing 2.2:

Output

```
Enter hours: 10
Enter minutes: 0
Enter seconds: 0


36000 seconds since midnight
```

Analysis The program uses the `#include` directive in line 3 to include the header file IOSTREAM.H. Lines 5 and 6 contain the `#define` directive that declares the macro-based constants `SEC_IN_MIN` and `MIN_IN_HOUR`. Both constants have the value 60, but each value has a different meaning. The function `main` which starts at line 8 declares four long-typed variables: `hours`, `minutes`, `seconds`, and `totalSec`.

The function uses pairs of statements to output the prompting messages and receive input. Line 13 contains the stream output statement which prompts you for the number of hours. Line 14 contains the stream input statement. The identifier `cin` is the name of the standard input stream and uses the insertion operator >> to read data from the keyboard and to store it in the variable hours. The input and output statements in lines 15 through 18 perform a similar task of prompting for input and obtaining keyboard input.

Line 20 contains a statement which calculates the total number of seconds since midnight and stores the result in variable `totalSec`. The statement uses the macro-based constants `MIN_IN_HOUR` and `SEC_IN_MIN`. As you can see, using these constants enhances the readability of the statement compared to using the number 60 in place of both constants. Line 23 contains a stream output statement which displays the total number of seconds since midnight (stored in variable `totalSec`), followed by qualifying text to clarify the output.

Using Formal Constants

Now let's look at a new version of the program, one which uses the formal C++ constants. Listing 2.3 shows the source code for program CONST2.CPP. This program works like the CONST1.CPP program. Create the project CONST2 and include the CONST2.CPP file. Build and run the CONST2.MAK project.

> **Note:** At this point, I assume that you are familiar with the process of creating the .CPP source file and the .MAK project file. From now on, I will not mention creating these files unless there is a special set of source files in a project.

Type

Listing 2.3. Source code for the program CONST2.CPP.

```
// C++ program that illustrates constants

#include <iostream.h>

const SEC_IN_MIN = 60; // global constant

main()
{
  const MIN_IN_HOUR = 60; // local constant

  long hours, minutes, seconds;
  long totalSec;

  cout << "Enter hours: ";
  cin >> hours;
  cout << "Enter minutes: ";
  cin >> minutes;
  cout << "Enter seconds: ";
  cin >> seconds;

  totalSec = ((hours * MIN_IN_HOUR + minutes) *
               SEC_IN_MIN) + seconds;

  cout <<"\n\n" << totalSec << " seconds since midnight";
  return 0;
}
```

Here is a sample session with the program in Listing 2.3:

Output

```
Enter hours: 1
Enter minutes: 10
Enter seconds: 20

4220 seconds since midnight
```

Analysis

The programs in Listings 2.2 and 2.3 are similar. The difference between them is in how they declare their constants. In Listing 2.3, I use the formal C++ constant syntax to declare the constants. In addition, I declare constant `SEC_IN_MIN` in line 5, outside the function `main`. This kind of declaration makes the constant global. That is, if there were another function in the program, it would be able to use the constant `SEC_IN_MIN`. By contrast, I declare the constant `MIN_IN_SEC` inside the function `main`. Thus, the constant `MIN_IN_SEC` is local to the function `main`.

Declaring and Prototyping Functions

Most programming languages use functions and procedures. C++ does not support formal procedures. Instead, all C++ routines are functions!

NEW TERM *Functions* are the primary building blocks that conceptually extend the C++ language to fit your custom programs.

Syntax

Declaring Functions

The general form for the ANSI C style of declaring functions (which is maintained by C++) is

```
returnType functionName(typedParameterList)
```

Examples:

```
double sqr(double y)
{ return y * y; }

char prevChar(char c)
{ return c - 1; }
```

Remember the following rules when declaring C++ functions:

1. The return type of the C++ function appears before the function's name.
2. If the parameter list is empty, you still use empty parentheses. C++ also allows you the option of using the `void` keyword to explicitly state that the parameter list is void.

3. The typed parameter list consists of a list of typed parameters that use the following general format:

   ```
   [const] type1 parameter1, [const] type2 parameter2, ...
   ```

   This format shows that the individual parameter is declared like a variable—you state the type first and then the parameter's identifier. The list of parameters in C++ is comma-delimited. In addition, you cannot group a sequence of parameters that have the exact same data type. You must declare each parameter explicitly. If a parameter has the `const` clause, the compiler makes sure that the function does not alter the arguments of that parameter.

4. The body of a C++ function is enclosed in braces (`{}`). There is no semicolon after the closing brace.

5. C++ supports passing arguments either by value or by reference. By default, parameters pass their arguments by value. Consequently, the functions work with a copy of the data, preserving the original data. To declare a reference parameter, insert the `&` character after the data type of the parameter. A reference parameter becomes an alias to its arguments. Any changes made to the reference parameter also affect the argument. The general form for reference parameters is

   ```
   [const] type1& parameter1, [const] type2& parameter2, ...
   ```

   If a parameter has the `const` clause, the compiler makes sure that the function does not alter the arguments of that parameter.

6. C++ supports local constants, data types, and variables. Although these data items can appear in nested block statements, C++ does not support nested functions.

7. The return keyword returns the function's value.

8. If the function's return type is `void`, you do not have to use the return keyword, unless you need to provide an exit route in the middle of the function.

NEW TERM C++ dictates that you either declare or define a function before you use it. Declaring a function, which is commonly called *prototyping*, lists the function name, return type, and the number and type of its parameters. Including the name of the parameter is optional. You also need to place a semicolon after the close parenthesis. C++ requires that you declare a function if you call it before you define it.

The following is a simple example of prototyping:

```
// prototype the function square
double sqr(double);

main()
{
  cout << "5^2 = " << sqr(5) << "\n";
  return 0;
}

double sqr(double z)
{ return z * z; }
```

Notice that the declaration of function `sqr` only contains the type of its single parameter.

Typically, the declaration of a function is global. You may still prototype a function within its client function. This technique conceals the prototype from other functions.

Calling a function requires that you supply its parameter with arguments. The arguments are mapped onto the parameter by the sequence in which the parameters are declared. The arguments must be data types that match or are compatible with those of the parameters. For example, you may have a function `volume` which is defined as follows:

```
double volume(double length, double width, double height)
{
  return length * width * height;
}
```

To call the function `volume` you need to supply double-typed arguments or arguments with compatible types (which in this case are all of numeric data types). Here are a number of sample calls to function `volume`:

```
double len = 34, width = 55, ht = 100;
int i = 3;
long j = 44;
unsigned k = 33;

cout << volume(len, width, ht) << "\n";
cout << volume(1, 2, 3) << "\n";
cout << volume(i, j, k) << "\n";
cout << volume(len, j, 22.3) << "\n";
```

Note: C++ allows you to discard the result of a function. This kind of function call is used when the focus is on what the function does rather than its return value.

Local Variables in Functions

Sound structured programming techniques foster the notion that functions should be as independent and as reusable as possible. Consequently, functions can have their own data types, constants, and variables to give them this independence.

NEW TERM The *local variable* in a function exists only when the host function is called. Once the function terminates, the run-time system removes the local variables. Consequently, local variables lose their data between function calls. In addition, the run-time system applies any initialization to local variables every time the host function is called.

DO	DON'T

DO use local variables to store and alter the values of parameters that are declared with the `const` clause.

DON'T declare a local variable to have the same name of a global variable which you need to access in the function.

Let's look at an example. Listing 2.4 displays the value of the following mathematical function:

```
f(X) = X2 - 5 X + 10
```

and its slope at the argument 3.5. The program calculates the slope using the following approximation:

```
f'(X) = (f(X + h) - f(X - h)) / 2h
```

where `h` is a small increment.

Type

Listing 2.4. Source code for the program VAR2.CPP.

```
// C++ program that illustrates local variables in a function

#include <iostream.h>

double f(double x)
{
  return x * x - 5 * x + 10;
}

double slope(double x)
{
  double f1, f2, incrim = 0.01 * x;
```

```
13:    f1 = f(x + incrim);
14:    f2 = f(x - incrim);
15:    return (f1 - f2) / 2 / incrim;
16: }
17:
18: main()
19: {
20:   double x = 3.5;
21:
22:    cout << "f("  << x << ") = " << f(x) << "\n"
23:         << "f'(" << x << ") = " << slope(x) << "\n";
24:
25:    return 0;
26: }
```

Here is a sample session with the program in Listing 2.4:

```
f(3.5) = 4.75
f'(3.5) = 2
```

The program in Listing 2.4 declares three functions, namely `f` (in line 5), `slope` (in line 10), and `main` (in line 18). The function `f` is simple and returns the value of the mathematical function. The function `f` is void of local variables. By contrast, the function slope declares the local variables `f1`, `f2`, and `incrim`. This function also initializes the latter variable. Line 13 assigns the value of `f(x + incrim)` to the local variable `f1`. Line 14 assigns the value of `f(x - incrim)` to the local variable `f2`. Line 15 returns the value for function `slope` using the local variables `f1`, `f2`, and `incrim`. The function `main` simply displays the values of the mathematical function and its slope when `x = 3.5`.

Static Variables in Functions

In Listing 2.4, the local variables in function `slope` lose their values once the function terminates. C++ allows you to declare a local variable as static by simply placing the static keyword to the left of its data type. Static variables are usually initialized. This initialization is performed once, when the host function is called the first time.

NEW TERM There are a number of programming techniques that require maintaining the values of local variables between function calls. These special local variables are called *static variables.*

When the host function terminates, the static variables maintain their values. The compiler supports this language feature by storing static variables in a separate memory location that is maintained while the program is running. You can use the same names for static variables in different functions. This duplication does not confuse the compiler because it keeps track of which function owns which static variables.

Let's look at a simple program. Listing 2.5 uses a function with static variables to maintain a moving average. The program supplies its own data and calls that function several times to obtain and display the current value of the moving average.

Type

Listing 2.5. Source code for the program STATIC1.CPP.

```
1: // C++ program that illustrates static local variables
2:
3: #include <iostream.h>
4:
5: double mean(double x)
6: {
7:   static double sum = 0;
8:   static double sumx = 0;
9:
10:   sum = sum + 1;
11:   sumx = sumx + x;
12:   return sumx / sum;
13: }
14:
15: main()
16: {
17:   cout << "mean = " << mean(1) << "\n";
18:   cout << "mean = " << mean(2) << "\n";
19:   cout << "mean = " << mean(4) << "\n";
20:   cout << "mean = " << mean(10) << "\n";
21:   cout << "mean = " << mean(11) << "\n";
22:   return 0;
23: }
```

Here is a sample session with the program in Listing 2.5:

Output

```
mean = 1
mean = 1.5
mean = 2.33333
mean = 4.25
mean = 5.6
```

Analysis

The program in Listing 2.5 declares the function `mean` which contains static local variables. Lines 7 and 8 declare the static variables `sum` and `sumx`, respectively. The function initializes both static variables with 0. The statement in line 10 increments the variable `sum` by 1. The statement in line 11 increments the variable `sumx` by the value of parameter `x`. Line 12 returns the updated moving average, obtained by dividing `sumx` by `sum`.

The function main issues a series of calls to function mean. The stream output statements in lines 17 through 21 display the updated moving average. These results are possible thanks to the static local variables sum and sumx in function mean. If static variables are not supported by C++, you must resort to using global variables—a highly questioned programming choice!

Inline Functions

Using functions requires the overhead of calling them, passing their arguments, and returning their results. C++ allows you to use inline functions that expand into their statements. Thus, inline functions offer faster execution speed—especially where speed is critical—at the cost of expanding the code.

Syntax

The inline Function

The general syntax for the inline function is

```
inline returnType functionName(typedParameterList)
```

Examples:

```
inline double cube(double x)
{ return x * x * x; }

inline char nextChar(char c)
{ return c + 1; }
```

The alternative to using inline functions is the use of the #define directive to create macro-based pseudofunctions. Many C++ programmers (including me) strongly recommend abandoning this method in favor of inline functions. The justification for this inclination is that inline functions provide type checking. Macros created with the #define directive do not.

DO	DON'T

DO start by declaring inline functions as ordinary functions when you develop your programs. Non-inline functions are easier to debug. Once your program is working, insert the inline keyword where needed.

DON'T declare inline functions with too many statements. The increase in .EXE program size may not be acceptable.

Here is a simple example of a program that uses inline functions. Listing 2.6 contains the source code for program INLINE1.CPP. The program prompts you for a number. Then the program calculates and displays the square and cube values for your input.

Listing 2.6. Source code for the program INLINE1.CPP.

```
// C++ program that illustrates inline functions

#include <iostream.h>

inline double sqr(double x)
{
  return x * x;
}

inline double cube(double x)
{
  return x * x * x;
}

main()
{
  double x;

  cout << "Enter a number: ";
  cin >> x;

  cout << "square of "  << x << " = " << sqr(x) << "\n"
       << "cube of " << x << " = " << cube(x) << "\n";

  return 0;
}
```

Here is a sample session with the program in Listing 2.6:

```
Enter a number: 2.5
square of 2.5 = 6.25
cube of 2.5 = 15.625
```

The program in Listing 2.6 declares the inline functions `sqr` and `cube`. Each function heading starts with the keyword inline. The other aspects of the inline functions resemble short normal functions. The function `main` calls the function `sqr` and `cube` to display the square and cube values, respectively.

Exiting Functions

Usually you make an early exit from a function because particular conditions do not allow you to proceed with executing the statements in that function. C++ provides the return statement to exit from a function. If the function has the void type, then you employ the statement return and include no expression after the return. By contrast, if you exit a non-void function, the return statement should produce a value that indicates the purpose for exiting the function.

Default Arguments

Default arguments are a language feature that is quite simple and yet very powerful. When you omit the argument of a parameter that has a default argument, that argument is automatically used.

NEW TERM C++ permits you to assign *default arguments* to the parameters of a function.

Using default arguments requires that you follow these rules:

1. Once you assign a default argument to a parameter, you must do so for all subsequent parameters in the same parameter list. You cannot randomly assign default arguments to parameters. This rule means that the parameter list can be divided into two sublists: the leading parameters which do not have default arguments, and the trailing parameters which do.
2. You must provide an argument for every parameter that has no default argument.
3. You may omit the argument for a parameter that has a default argument.
4. Once you omit the argument for a parameter with a default argument, the arguments for all subsequent parameters must also be omitted.

Note: The best way to list the parameters with default arguments is to locate them according to the likelihood of using their default arguments. Place the least likely used arguments first and the most likely used arguments last.

Let's look at a simple example that uses a function with default arguments. Listing 2.7 shows the source code for program DEFARGS1.CPP. The program prompts you to enter the X and Y coordinates of two points. Then the program calculates and displays the distance between the two points and between each point and the origin (0, 0).

Listing 2.7. Source code for the program DEFARGS1.CPP.

```
1: // C++ program that illustrates default arguments
2:
3: #include <iostream.h>
4: #include <math.h>
5:
6: inline double sqr(double x)
7: { return x * x; }
8:
9: double distance(double x2, double y2,
10:                  double x1 = 0, double y1 = 0)
11: {
12:   return sqrt(sqr(x2 - x1) + sqr(y2 - y1));
13: }
14:
15: main()
16: {
17:   double x1, y1, x2, y2;
18:
19:   cout << "Enter x coordinate for point 1: ";
20:   cin >> x1;
21:   cout << "Enter y coordinate for point 1: ";
22:   cin >> y1;
23:   cout << "Enter x coordinate for point 2: ";
24:   cin >> x2;
25:   cout << "Enter y coordinate for point 2: ";
26:   cin >> y2;
27:
28:   cout << "distance between points = "
29:        << distance(x1, y1, x2, y2) << "\n";
30:   cout << "distance between point 1 and (0,0) = "
31:        << distance(x1, y1, 0) << "\n";
32:   cout << "distance between point 2 and (0,0) = "
33:        << distance(x2, y2) << "\n";
34:
35:   return 0;
36: }
```

Here is a sample session with the program in Listing 2.7:

```
Enter x coordinate for point 1: 1
Enter y coordinate for point 1: 1
Enter x coordinate for point 2: -1
Enter y coordinate for point 2: 1
distance between points = 2
distance between point 1 and (0,0) = 1.41421
distance between point 2 and (0,0) = 1.41421
```

The program in Listing 2.7 includes not one but two header files. Line 4 uses the `#include` directive to include the MATH.H header file which declares the square root math function, `sqrt`. The program declares the inline `sqr` function in line 6.

This function returns the square value of the arguments for parameter `x`. The program also declares the function `distance` with four double-typed parameters. The parameters `x2` and `y2` represent the X and Y coordinates, respectively, for the second point, whereas the parameters `x1` and `y1` represent the X and Y coordinates, respectively, for the first point. Both parameters `x1` and `y1` have the default argument of 0. The function returns the distance between the two points. If you omit the arguments for `x1` and `y1`, the function returns the distance between the point (x2, y2) and the origin (0, 0). If you omit only the argument for the last parameter, the function yields the distance between the points (x2, y2) and (x1, 0).

The function `main` prompts you to enter the X and Y coordinates for two points, using the statements in lines 19 through 26. The output statement in lines 28 and 29 calls the function `distance`, providing it with four arguments, namely, `x1`, `y1`, `x2`, and `y2`. Therefore, this call to function `distance` uses no default arguments. By contrast, the statement in lines 30 and 31 calls function `distance`, supplying it with only three arguments. This call to function `distance` uses the default argument for the last parameter. The statement in lines 32 and 33 calls function `distance`, providing it with only two arguments. This call to function `distance` uses the two default arguments for the third and fourth parameters. I can omit the third argument in the second call to function `distance` and still compile and run the program.

Function Overloading

Function overloading is a language feature in C++ that has no parallel in either C, Pascal, or BASIC. This new feature enables you to declare multiple functions that have the same name but different parameter lists. The function's return type is not part of the function signature because C++ allows you to discard the result type. Consequently, the compiler is not able to distinguish between two functions with the same parameters and different return type when these return types are omitted.

NEW TERM A parameter list is also called the *function signature.*

> **Warning:** Using default arguments with overloaded functions may duplicate the signature for some of the functions (when the default arguments are used). The C++ compiler is able to detect this ambiguity and generate a compile-time error.

DO / DON'T

DO use default arguments to reduce the number of overloaded functions.

DON'T use overloaded functions to implement different operations.

Let's look at a simple program that uses overloaded functions. Listing 2.8 contains the source code for program OVERLOAD.CPP. The program performs the following tasks:

- Declares variables that have the `char`, `int`, and `double` types, and initializes them with values
- Displays the initial values
- Invokes overloaded functions that increment the variables
- Displays the updated values stored in the variables

Type

Listing 2.8. Source code for the program OVERLOAD.CPP.

```
// C++ program that illustrates function overloading

#include <iostream.h>

// inc version for int types
void inc(int& i)
{
  i = i + 1;
}

// inc version for double types
void inc(double& x)
{
  x = x + 1;
}

// inc version for char types
void inc(char& c)
{
  c = c + 1;
}

main()
{
  char c = 'A';
  int i = 10;
  double x = 10.2;

  // display initial values
```

```
30:   cout << "c = " << c << "\n"
31:        << "i = " << i << "\n"
32:        << "x = " << x << "\n";
33:   // invoke the inc functions
34:   inc(c);
35:   inc(i);
36:   inc(x);
37:   // display updated values
38:   cout << "After using the overloaded inc function\n";
39:   cout << "c = " << c << "\n"
40:        << "i = " << i << "\n"
41:        << "x = " << x << "\n";
42:
43:   return 0;
44: }
```

Here is a sample session with the program in Listing 2.8:

Output

```
c = A
i = 10
x = 10.2
After using the overloaded inc function
c = B
i = 11
x = 11.2
```

Analysis

The program in Listing 2.8 declares three versions of the overloaded void function `inc`. The first version of function `inc` has an `int`-typed reference parameter, `i`. The function increments the parameter `i` by 1. Because the parameter `i` is a reference to its arguments, the action of function `inc(int&)` affects the argument outside the scope of the function. The second version of function `inc` has a `double`-typed reference parameter, `x`. The function increments the parameter `x` by 1. Because the parameter `x` is a reference to its arguments, the action of function `inc(double&)` affects the argument beyond the scope of the function. The second version of function `inc` has a `char`-typed reference parameter, `c`. The function increments the parameter `c` by 1. The reference parameter affects its arguments outside the scope of the function.

The function `main` declares the variables `c`, `i`, and `x` to have the `char`, `int`, and `double` types, respectively. The function also initializes the variables `c`, `i`, and `x` using the values `'A'`, `10`, and `10.2`, respectively. The statement in lines 30 through 32 displays the initial values in variables `c`, `i`, and `x`. The function `main` invokes the overloaded function `inc` in lines 34 through 36. The call to function `inc` in line 34 ends up calling the function `inc(char&)` because the argument used is a `char`-typed variable. The call to function `inc` in line 35 results in calling the function `inc(int&)` because the argument used is an `int`-typed variable. The call to function `inc` in line 36 invokes the function `inc(double&)` because the argument used is a `double`-typed variable. The output statement in lines 39 through 41 displays the updated values in variable `c`, `i`, and `x`.

Summary

Today's lesson presents the basic components of C++ programs. These components include data types, variables, constants, and functions. You learned these basics:

- The predefined data types in Visual C++ include the `int`, `char`, `float`, `double`, and `void` data types. C++ adds more flexibility to data types by supporting data type modifiers. These modifiers alter the precision and the range of values. The type modifiers are: `signed`, `unsigned`, `short`, and `long`.

- Visual C++ identifiers can be up to 247 characters long and must begin with a letter or an underscore. The subsequent characters of an identifier may be a letter, digit, or underscore. C++ identifiers are case-sensitive.

- The `#include` directive is a special instruction to the compiler. The directive tells the compiler to include the contents of the specified file as though you typed it in the currently scanned source file.

- Declaring variables requires you to state the data type of the variable and the name of the variable. C++ allows you to initialize a variable when you declare it. You can declare multiple variables in a single declarative statement.

- Declaring constants involves using the `#define` directive to declare macro-based constants, or using the `const` keyword to declare formal constants. The formal constants require that you specify the constant's type (the default is `int`, when omitted), the name of the constants, and the associated value.

- The general form for defining functions is

  ```
  returnType functionName(parameterList)
  {
  <declarations of data items>

  <function body>
  return returnValue;
  ```

  You need to prototype a function if it is used by a client function before the prototyped function is defined. The general form for prototyping functions is

  ```
  returnType functionName(parameterList);
  ```

  You can omit the name of the parameters from the parameter list.

- Local variables in a function support the implementation of highly independent functions. Declaring local variables is similar to declaring global variables.

- Static variables in functions are declared by placing the keyword `static` before the data type of the variables. Static variables retain their values between function calls. In most cases, you need to initialize static variables. These initial values are assigned to the static variables the first time the program calls the host function.
- Inline functions allow you to expand their statements in place, like macro-based pseudofunctions. However, unlike these pseudofunctions, inline functions perform type checking.
- You exit functions with the return statement. Void functions do not need to include an expression after the return keyword.
- Default arguments allow you to assign default values to the parameters of a function. When you omit the argument of a parameter that has a default argument, that argument is automatically used.
- Function overloading enables you to declare multiple functions that have the same name but different parameter lists (also called the function signature). The function's return type is not part of the function signature because C++ allows you to discard the result type.

Q&A

Q Is there a specific style for naming identifiers?

A There are a few styles that have become popular in recent years. The one I use has the identifier begin with a lowercase character. If the identifier contains multiple words, such as `numberOfElements`, make the first character of each subsequent word an uppercase letter.

Q Can C++ functions declare nested functions?

A No. Nested functions actually add a lot of overhead at run time.

Q When can I use static global variables?

A Never! Global variables need not be declared static because they exist for the entire program's lifetime.

Workshop

The Workshop provides quiz questions to help you solidify your understanding of the material covered and exercises to provide you with experience in using what you've learned. Try to understand the quiz and exercise answers before continuing on to the next day's lesson. Answers are provided in Appendix B, "Answers."

Quiz

1. Which of the following variables is valid and which is not (and why)?

```
numFiles
n0Distance_02_Line
0Weight
Bin Number
static
Static
```

2. What is the output of the following program? What can you say about the function swap?

```
#include <iostream.h>

void swap(int i, int j)
{
  int temp = I;
  i = j;
  j = temp;
}

main()
{
  int a = 10, b = 3;
  swap(a, b);
  cout << "a = " << a << " and b = " << b;
  return 0;
}
```

3. What is the output of the following program? What can you say about the function swap?

```
#include <iostream.h>

void swap(int& i, int& j)
{
  int temp = I;
  i = j;
  j = temp;
}

main()
{
```

```
  int a = 10, b = 3;
  swap(a, b);
  cout << "a = " << a << " and b = " << b;
  return 0;
}
```

4. What is the problem with the following overloaded functions?

```
void inc(int& I)
{
  i = i + 1;
}

void inc(int& i, int diff = 1)
{
  i = i + diff;
}
```

5. Where is the error in the following function?

```
double volume(double length, double width = 1, double
height)
{
  return length * width * height
}
```

6. Where is the error in the following function?

```
void inc(int& i, int diff = 1)
{
  i = i + diff;
}
```

7. What is the error in the following program, and how can you correct it?

```
#include <iostream.h>

main()
{
  double x = 5.2;

  cout << x << "^2 = " << sqr(x);
  return 0;
}

double sqr(double x)
{ return x * x ; }
```

Exercise

Create the program OVERLOD2.CPP by adding a second parameter with default arguments to the overloaded `inc` functions in program OVERLOAD.CPP. The new parameter should represent the increment value, with a default argument of 1.

3

Operators and Expressions

WEEK 1

The manipulation of data involves expressions that are made up of operands and operators. C++ supports several kinds of operators and expressions.

Operators are special symbols that take the values of operands and produce a new value.

Each category of operators manipulates data in a specific way. Today you learn about the following topics:

- Arithmetic operators and expressions
- Increment operators
- Arithmetic assignment operators
- Typecasting and data conversion
- Relational operators and conditional expressions
- Bit-manipulating operators
- The comma operator

Arithmetic Operators

Table 3.1 shows the C++ arithmetic operators. The compiler carries out floating-point or integer division depending on the operands. If both operands are integer expressions, the compiler yields the code for an integer division. If either or both operands are floating-point expressions, the compiler generates code for floating-point division.

Table 3.1. C++ arithmetic operators.

C++ Operator	Purpose	Data Type	Example
`+`	Unary plus	Numeric	`x = +y + 3;`
`-`	Unary minus	Numeric	`x = -y;`
`+`	Add	Numeric	`z = y + x;`
`-`	Subtract	Numeric	`z = y - x;`
`*`	Multiply	Numeric	`z = y * x;`
`/`	Divide	Numeric	`z = y / x;`
`%`	Modulus	Integers	`z = y % x;`

Let's look at an example that uses the mathematical operators with integers and floating-point numbers. Listing 3.1 shows the source code for program OPER1.CPP. The program performs the following tasks:

- Prompts you to enter two integers (one integer per prompt)
- Applies the `+`, `-`, `*`, `/`, and `%` operators to the two integers, storing the results in separate variables
- Displays the result of the integer operations
- Prompts you to enter two floating-point numbers (one number per prompt)
- Applies the `+`, `-`, `*`, and `/` operators to the two numbers, storing the results in separate variables
- Displays the result of the floating-point operations

Type

Listing 3.1. Source code for the program OPER1.CPP.

```
// simple C++ program to illustrate simple math operations

#include <iostream.h>

main()
{

    int int1, int2;
    long long1, long2, long3, long4, long5;
    float x, y, real1, real2, real3, real4;

    cout << "\nType first  integer : ";
    cin >> int1;
    cout << "Type second integer : ";
    cin >> int2;
    cout << "\n";
    long1 = int1 + int2;
    long2 = int1 - int2;
    long3 = int1 * int2;
    long4 = int1 / int2;
    long5 = int1 % int2;
    cout << int1 << " + " << int2 << " = " << long1 << '\n';
    cout << int1 << " - " << int2 << " = " << long2 << '\n';
    cout << int1 << " * " << int2 << " = " << long3 << '\n';
    cout << int1 << " / " << int2 << " = " << long4 << '\n';
    cout << int1 << " mod " << int2 << " = " << long5 << '\n';
    cout << "\n\n";
    cout << "Type first  real number : ";
    cin >> x;
    cout << "Type second real number : ";
    cin >> y;
```

continues

Listing 3.1. continued

```
32:     cout << "\n";
33:     real1 = x + y;
34:     real2 = x - y;
35:     real3 = x * y;
36:     real4 = x / y;
37:     cout << x << " + " << y << " = " << real1 << '\n';
38:     cout << x << " - " << y << " = " << real2 << '\n';
39:     cout << x << " * " << y << " = " << real3 << '\n';
40:     cout << x << " / " << y << " = " << real4 << '\n';
41:     cout << "\n\n";
42:     return 0;
43: }
```

Here is a sample session with the program in Listing 3.1:

Output

```
Type first  integer : 10
Type second integer : 5

10 + 5 = 15
10 - 5 = 5
10 * 5 = 50
10 / 5 = 2
10 mod 5 = 0


Type first  real number : 1.25
Type second real number : 2.58

1.25 + 2.58 = 3.83
1.25 - 2.58 = -1.33
1.25 * 2.58 = 3.225
1.25 / 2.58 = 0.484496
```

Analysis The program in Listing 3.1 declares a set of `int`-typed, `long`-typed, and `float`-typed variables in the function `main`. Some of these variables store your input and others store the results of the mathematical operations. The output statement in line 12 prompts you to enter the first integer. The input statement in line 13 obtains your input and stores it in the variable `int1`. Lines 14 and 15 perform a similar operation to prompt you for the second integer and store it in variable `int2`.

The program performs the integer math operation in lines 17 through 21 and stores the results of these operations in variables `long1` through `long5`. I declared these variables as `long`-typed to guard against possible numeric overflow. The output statements in lines 22 through 26 display the integer operands, the operators used, and the results.

The output statement in line 28 prompts you to enter the first floating-point number. The input statement in line 29 obtains your input and stores it in the variable `x`. Lines

30 and 31 perform a similar operation to prompt you for the second floating-point number and to store it in variable y.

NEW TERM A floating-point number is also known as a *real number*.

The program performs the floating-point math operation in lines 33 through 36 and stores the results of these operations in variables real1 through real4. The output statements in lines 37 through 40 display the operands, the operators used, and the results.

Arithmetic Expressions

The simplest kinds of expressions are the ones that contain literals, such as

```
-12
34.45
'A'
"Hello"
```

NEW TERM In general terms, an *arithmetic expression* is part of a program statement which contains a value.

The literal constants -12 and 35.45 are the simplest arithmetic expressions. The next level of arithmetic expressions includes single variables or constants, such as

```
DAYS_IN_WEEK // a constant
i
x
```

The next level of arithmetic expressions contains a single operator with numbers, constants, and variables as operands. Here are a few examples:

```
355 / 113
4 * i
45.67 + x
```

More advanced arithmetic expressions contain multiple operators, parentheses, and even functions, such as

```
(355 / 113) * square(radius)
PIE * square(radius)
(((2 * x - 3) * x + 2) * x - 5
(1 + x) / (3 - x)
```

I discuss the order of executing the operators at the end of today's lesson, after introducing the other types of operators.

Increment Operators

C++ supports the special increment and decrement operators.

NEW TERM *Increment* (++) and *decrement* (- -) operators allow you to increment and decrement, respectively, by one the value stored in a variable.

Syntax

Increment Operators

The general syntax for the increment operators is

```
variable++  // post-increment
++variable  // pre-increment
```

Example:

```
lineNumber++;
++index;
```

Syntax

Decrement Operators

The general syntax for the decrement operators is

```
variable-- // post-decrement
--variable  // pre-decrement
```

Example:

```
lineNumber--;
--index
```

This general syntax demonstrates that there are two ways to apply the ++ and - - operators. Placing these operators to the left of their operand changes the value of the operand before the operand contributes its value in an expression. Likewise, placing these operators to the right of their operands alters the value of the operand after the operand contributes its value in an expression. If the ++ or - - operators are the only operators in a statement, there is no practical distinction between using the pre- or post- forms.

Here are a few simple examples:

```
int n, m, t = 5;

t++; // t is now 6, same effect as ++t
--t; // t is now 5, same effect as t--
t = 5;
n = 4 * t++; // t is now 6 and n is 20
m = 5;
m = 4 * ++m; // m is now 6 and n is 24
```

The first statement uses the post-increment ++ operator to increment the value of variable t. If you write ++t instead, you get the same result once the statement finishes executing. The second statement uses the pre-decrement -- operator. Again, if I write t-- instead, I get the same result. The next two statements assign 5 to variable t and then use the post-increment ++ operator in a simple math expression. This statement multiplies 4 by the current value of t (that is, 5), assigns the result of 20 to the variable n, and then increments the values in variable t to 6. The last two statements show a different outcome. The statement first increments the value in variable m (the value in variable m becomes 6), then performs the multiplication, and finally assigns the result of 24 to the variable m.

Let's look at a simple program that illustrates the feature of the increment operator. Listing 3.2 shows the source code for program OPER2.CPP. The program requires no input from you. It simply displays two integers whose values were obtained using the increment operator.

Type

Listing 3.2. Source code for the program OPER2.CPP.

```
/*
   C++ program to illustrate the feature of the increment operator.
   The ++ or -- may be included in an expression.  The value
   of the associated variable is altered after the expression
   is evaluated if the var++ (or var--) is used, or before
   when ++var (or --var) is used.
*/

#include <iostream.h>

main()
{
    int i, k = 5;

    // use post-incrementing
    i = 10 * (k++); // k contributes 5 to the expression
    cout << "i = " << i << "\n\n"; // displays 50 (= 10 * 5)

    k--; // restores the value of k to 5

    // use pre-incrementing
    i = 10 * (++k); // k contributes 6 to the expression
    cout << "i = " << i << "\n\n"; // displays 60 (= 10 * 6)
    return 0;
}
```

Here is a sample session with the program in Listing 3.2:

Output

```
i = 50

i = 60
```

Analysis The program in Listing 3.2 has the function `main`, which declares two `int`-typed variables, `i` and `k`. The function initializes the variable `k` by assigning it the value 5. Line 16 contains a statement which applies the post-increment operator to the variable `k`. Consequently, the statement multiplies 10 by the initial value in `k`, 5, and assigns the product, 50, to variable `i`. After assigning the result to variable `i`, the program increments the value in variable `k`. The output statement in line 17 displays the value in variable `i`. The statement in line 19 decrements the value in variable `k` back to 5. The statement in line 22 applies the pre-increment operator to the variable `k`. Therefore, the program first increments the value in variable `k` (from 5 to 6) and then multiplies 10 by the updated value in `k`. The program assigns the result of the multiplication, 60, to the variable `i`. The output statement in line 23 displays the current value of variable `i`.

Assignment Operators

As a programmer, you often come across statements that look like this:

```
IndexOfFirstElement = IndexOfFirstElement + 4;
GraphicsScaleRatio = GraphicsScaleRatio * 3;
CurrentRateOfReturn = CurrentRateOfReturn / 4;
DOSfileListSize = DOSfileListSize - 10;
```

The variable that receives the result of an expression is also the first operand. (Of course, the addition and multiplication are communicative operations. Therefore, the assigned variable can be either operand with these operations.) Notice that I chose relatively long names to remind you of your need to shorten the expression without making the names of the variables shorter.

NEW TERM C++ offers *assignment operators* that merge with simple math operators.

You can write the following statements:

```
IndexOfFirstElement += 4;
GraphicsScaleRatio *= 3;
CurrentRateOfReturn /= 4;
DOSfileListSize -= 10;
```

Notice that the name of the variable appears only once. In addition, notice that the statements use the operators `+=`, `*=`, `/=`, and `-=`. Table 3.2 shows the arithmetic assignment operators. C++ supports other types of assignment operators.

Table 3.2. Arithmetic assignment operators.

Assignment Operator	Long Form	Example
`x += y`	`x = x + y`	`x += 12;`
`x -= y`	`x = x - y`	`x -= 34 + y;`
`x *= y`	`x = x * y`	`scale *= 10;`
`x /= y`	`x = x / y`	`z /= 34 * y;`
`x %= y`	`x = x % y`	`z %= 2;`

Let's look at a program that applies the assignment operators to integers and floating-point numbers. Listing 3.3 shows the source code for program OPER3.CPP. The program performs the following tasks:

- Prompts you to enter two integers (one integer per prompt)
- Applies a set of assignment and increment operators to the two integers
- Displays the new values of the integers
- Prompts you to enter two floating-point numbers (one number per prompt)
- Applies a set of assignment and increment operators to the two numbers
- Displays the new values of the floating-point numbers

Listing 3.3. Source code for the program OPER3.CPP.

```
// C++ program to illustrate math assignment operators

#include <iostream.h>

main()
{
    int i, j;
    double x, y;

     cout << "Type first  integer : ";
     cin >> i;
     cout << "Type second integer : ";
     cin >> j;
     i += j;
     j -= 6;
     i *= 4;
     j /= 3;
     i++;
```

continues

Listing 3.3. continued

```
19:     j--;
20:     cout << "i = " << i << "\n";
21:     cout << "j = " << j << "\n";
22:
23:     cout << "Type first  real number : ";
24:     cin >> x;
25:     cout << "Type second real number : ";
26:     cin >> y;
27:     // abbreviated assignments also work with doubles in C++
28:     x += y;
29:     y -= 4.0;
30:     x *= 4.0;
31:     y /=  3.0;
32:     x++;
33:     y—;
34:     cout << "x = " << x << "\n";
35:     cout << "y = " << y << "\n";
36:     return 0;
37: }
```

Here is a sample session with the program in Listing 3.3:

Output

```
Type first  integer : 55
Type second integer : 66
i = 485
j = 19
Type first  real number : 2.5
Type second real number : 4.58
x = 29.32
y = -0.806667
```

Analysis

The program in Listing 3.3 contains the function `main`, which declares two `int`-typed variables (`i` and `j`) and two `double`-typed variables (`x` and `y`) in lines 7 and 8, respectively. The output statement in line 10 prompts you to enter the first integer. The input statement in line 11 receives your input and stores it in the variable `i`. Lines 12 and 13 are similar to lines 10 and 11—they prompt you for the second integer and store it in variable `j`.

The program manipulates the values in variable `i` and `j` using the statements in lines 14 through 19. In line 14, the program uses the `+=` operator to increment the value in variable `i` by the value in variable `j`. Line 15 uses the `-=` operator to decrement the value in variable `j` by 6. Line 16 applies the `*=` operator to multiply the value in variable `i` by 4 and to assign the result back to variable `i`. Line 17 utilizes the `/=` operator to divide the value in variable `j` by 3 and to store the result in `j`. Lines 18 and 19 apply the increment and decrement operators to variables `i` and `j`, respectively. The output statements in lines 20 and 21 display the contents of variables `i` and `j`, respectively.

The output statement in line 23 prompts you to enter the first floating-point number. The input statement in line 24 receives your input and saves it in the variable `x`. Lines 25 and 26 are similar to lines 23 and 24—they prompt you for the second floating-point number and store it in variable `y`.

The program manipulates the values in variables `x` and `y` using the statements in lines 28 through 33. In line 28, the program uses the `+=` operator to increment the value in variable `x` by the value in variable `y`. Line 29 uses the `-=` operator to decrement the value in variable `y` by 4. Line 30 applies the `*=` operator to multiply the value in variable `x` by 4 and to save the result back to `x`. Line 31 utilizes the `/=` operator to divide the value in variable `y` by 3 and to store the result in `y`. Lines 32 and 33 apply the increment and decrement operators to variables `x` and `y`, respectively. The output statements in lines 34 and 35 display the contents of variables `x` and `y`, respectively.

3

The *sizeof* Operator

Frequently your programs need to know the byte size of a data type or of a variable. C++ provides the `sizeof` operator, which takes for an argument either a data type or the name of a variable (`scalar`, `array`, `record`, and so on).

Syntax

The *sizeof* Operator

The general syntax for the sizeof operator is

```
sizeof({variable_name ¦ data_type})
sizeof {variable_name ¦ data_type}
```

Example:

```
int sizeDifference = sizeof(double) - sizeof(float);
int intSize = sizeof int;
```

DO	DON'T

DO use `sizeof` with the name of the variable instead of its data type. This approach is the safest because if you alter the data type of the variable, the `sizeof` operator still returns the correct answer. By contrast, if you use the `sizeof` operator with the data type of the variable and later alter the variable's type, you create a bug if you do not update the argument of the sizeof operator.

DON'T use numbers to represent the size of a variable. This approach often causes errors.

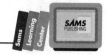

Let's look at an example that uses the `sizeof` operator with variables and data types. Listing 3.4 contains the source code for program SIZEOF1.CPP. The program displays two similar tables that indicate the sizes of the short `int`, `int`, `long int`, `char`, and `float` data types. The program displays the first table by applying the `sizeof` operators to variables of the above types. The program displays the second table by directly applying the `sizeof` operator to the data types.

Type

Listing 3.4. Source code for the program SIZEOF1.CPP.

```
/*
  simple program that returns the data sizes using the sizeof()
  operator with variables and data types.
*/

#include <iostream.h>

main()

{
     short int aShort;
     int anInt;
     long aLong;
     char aChar;
     float aReal;

     cout << "Table 1. Data sizes using sizeof(variable)\n\n";
     cout << "    Data type          Memory used\n";
     cout << "                         (bytes)\n";
     cout << "------------------    -----------";
     cout << "\n     short int              " << sizeof(aShort);
     cout << "\n      integer               " << sizeof(anInt);
     cout << "\n    long integer            " << sizeof(aLong);
     cout << "\n     character              " << sizeof(aChar);
     cout << "\n      float                 " << sizeof(aReal);
     cout << "\n\n\n\n";

     cout << "Table 2. Data sizes using sizeof(dataType)\n\n";
     cout << "    Data type          Memory used\n";
     cout << "                         (bytes)\n";
     cout << "-------------------   -----------";
     cout << "\n     short int              " <<  sizeof(short int);
     cout << "\n      integer               " <<  sizeof(int);
     cout << "\n    long integer            " <<  sizeof(long);
     cout << "\n     character              " <<  sizeof(char);
     cout << "\n        float               " <<  sizeof(float);
     cout << "\n\n\n\n";

     return 0;
}
```

Here is a sample session with the program in Listing 3.4:

```
Table 1. Data sizes using sizeof(variable)

Data type              Memory used
(bytes)
------------------     -----------
short int                  2
integer                   42
long integer               4
character                  1
float                      4


Table 2. Data sizes using sizeof(dataType)

Data type              Memory used
(bytes)
------------------     -----------
short int                  2
integer                   42
long integer               4
character                  1
float                      4
```

The program in Listing 3.4 declares five variables in function `main`. Each variable has a different data type and derives its name from its data type. For example, the variable `anInt` is an `int`-typed variable, the variable `aLong` is a `long`-typed variable, and so on.

The statements in lines 17 through 25 display the table of data sizes. The output statements in lines 21 through 25 use the `sizeof` operator with the variables.

The statements in lines 28 through 36 also display the table of data sizes. The output statements in lines 32 through 36 use the `sizeof` operator with the data type identifiers.

Typecasting

Automatic data conversion of a value from one data type to another compatible data type is one of the duties of a compiler. This data conversion simplifies expressions and eases the frustration of both novice and veteran programmers. With behind-the-scene data conversion, you do not need to examine every expression that mixes compatible data types in your program. For example, the compiler handles most expressions that mix various types of integers or that mix integers and floating-point types. You get a compile-time error if you attempt to do something illegal!

NEW TERM *Typecasting* is a language feature that allows you to specify explicitly how to convert a value from its original data type into a compatible data type. Thus, typecasting instructs the compiler to perform the conversion you want and not the one the compiler thinks is needed!

Syntax

Typecasting

C++ supports the following forms of typecasting:

type_cast(expression)

and

(type_cast) expression

Examples:

```
int i = 2;
float a, b;
a = float(i);
b = (float) i;
```

Let's look at an example that illustrates implicit data conversion and typecasting. Listing 3.5 shows the source code for program TYPCAST1.CPP. The program declares variables that have the character, integer, and floating-point data types. Then the program performs two sets of similar mathematical operations. The first set relies on the automatic conversions of data types, performed by the compiler. The second set of operations uses typecasting to explicitly instruct the compiler on how to convert the data types. The program requires no input—it provides its own data—and displays the output values for both sets of operations. The program illustrates that the compiler succeeds in generating the same output for both sets of operations.

Type **Listing 3.5. Source code for the program TYPCAST1.CPP.**

```
// simple C++ program that demonstrates typecasting

#include <iostream.h>

main()
{
    short shortInt1, shortInt2;
    unsigned short aByte;
    int anInt;
    long aLong;
    char aChar;
    float aReal;

    // assign values
```

```
    shortInt1 = 10;
    shortInt2 = 6;
    // perform operations without typecasting
    aByte = shortInt1 + shortInt2;
    anInt = shortInt1 - shortInt2;
    aLong = shortInt1 * shortInt2;
    aChar = aLong + 5; // conversion is automatic to character
    aReal = shortInt1 * shortInt2 + 0.5;

    cout << "shortInt1 = " << shortInt1 << '\n'
         << "shortInt2 = " << shortInt2 << '\n'
         << "aByte = " << aByte << '\n'
         << "anInt = " << anInt << '\n'
         << "aLong = " << aLong << '\n'
         << "aChar is " << aChar << '\n'
         << "aReal = " << aReal << "\n\n\n";

    // perform operations with typecasting
    aByte = (unsigned short) (shortInt1 + shortInt2);
    anInt = (int) (shortInt1 - shortInt2);
    aLong = (long) (shortInt1 * shortInt2);
    aChar = (unsigned char) (aLong + 5);
    aReal = (float) (shortInt1 * shortInt2 + 0.5);

    cout << "shortInt1 = " << shortInt1 << '\n'
         << "shortInt2 = " << shortInt2 << '\n'
         << "aByte = " << aByte << '\n'
         << "anInt = " << anInt << '\n'
         << "aLong = " << aLong << '\n'
         << "aChar is " << aChar << '\n'
         << "aReal = " << aReal << "\n\n\n";
    return 0;
}
```

Here is a sample session with the program in Listing 3.5:

Output

```
shortInt1 = 10
shortInt2 = 6
aByte = 16
anInt = 4
aLong = 60
aChar is A
aReal = 60.5


shortInt1 = 10
shortInt2 = 6
aByte = 16
anInt = 4
aLong = 60
aChar is A
aReal = 60.5
```

Analysis

The program in Listing 3.5 declares the following variables in the function `main`:

- The `short`-typed variables `shortInt1` and `shortInt2`
- The unsigned `short`-typed variable `aByte`
- The `int`-typed variable `anInt`
- The `long`-typed variable `aLong`
- The `char`-typed variable `aChar`
- The `float`-typed variable `aReal`

Lines 15 and 16 assign the integers 10 and 6 to variable `shortInt1` and `shortIn2`, respectively. Lines 18 through 22 perform various mathematical operations and assign the results to variables `aByte`, `anInt`, `aLong`, `aChar`, and `aReal`.

Note: C and C++ treat the `char` type as a special integer. Each `char`-typed literal (such as `'A'`), constant, or variable has an integer value that is equal to its ASCII representation. This language feature enables you to store an integer in a `char`-typed variable and treat a `char`-type data item as an integer. The statement in line 21 adds the integer 5 to the value of the variable `aLong` and assigns the result, an integer, to variable `aChar`. The value of the assigned integer, 65, represents the ASCII code for the letter A.

The output statement in lines 24 through 30 displays the values stored in the variables. Notice that the output for variable `aChar` is the letter `A`. If I write the output term for variable `aChar` as `<< (int) aChar`, I get `65`, the ASCII code of the character stored in `aChar`.

The statements in lines 32 through 37 perform similar operations to the statements in lines 18 through 22. The main difference is that the statements in lines 32 through 37 use typecasting to explicitly instruct the compiler on how to convert the result. The output statement in lines 39 through 45 displays the contents of the variables.

Relational and Logical Operators

Table 3.3 shows the C++ relational and logical operators. Notice that C++ does not spell out the operators `AND`, `OR`, and `NOT`. Rather, it utilizes single- and dual-character symbols. Also notice that C++ does not support the relational `XOR` operator. You can use the following `#define` macro directives to define the `AND`, `OR`, and `NOT` identifiers as macros:

NEW TERM The *relational operators* (less than, greater than, and equal to) and logical operators (AND, OR, and NOT) are the basic building blocks of decision-making constructs in any programming language.

```
#define AND &&
#define OR ||
#define NOT !
```

Table 3.3. C++ relational and logical operators.

C++ Operator	Meaning	Example
`&&`	Logical AND	`if (i > 1 && i < 10)`
`||`	Logical OR	`if (c==0 || c==9)`
`!`	Logical NOT	`if (!(c>1 && c<9))`
`<`	Less than	`if (i < 0)`
`<=`	Less than or equal to	`if (i <= 0)`
`>`	Greater than	`if (j > 10)`
`>=`	Greater than or equal to	`if (x >= 8.2)`
`==`	Equal to	`if (c == '\0')`
`!=`	Not equal to	`if (c != '\n')`
`? :`	Conditional assignment	`k = (i<1) ? 1 : i;`

Although these macros are permissible in C++, you might get a negative reaction from veteran C++ programmers who read your code. Who said that programming is always objective?

Warning: Do not use the = operator as the equality relational operator. This common error is a source of logical bugs in a C++ program. You may be accustomed to using the = operator in other languages to test the equality of two data items. In C++, you must use the == operator. What happens if you employ the = operator in C++? Do you get a compiler error? The answer is that you may get a compiler warning. Other than that, your C++ program should run. When the program reaches the expression that is supposed to test for equality, it actually attempts to assign the operand on the right of the = sign to the operand on the left of the = sign. Of course, a session with such a program most likely leads to weird program behavior, or even a system hang!

Note: C++ does not support predefined Boolean identifiers. Instead, the language regards 0 as false and a nonzero value as true. To add clarity to your programs I suggest that you declare global constants `TRUE` and `FALSE` and assign them 1 and 0, respectively.

Notice that the last operator in Table 3.3 is the `?:`. This special operator supports what is known as the conditional expression.

NEW TERM The *conditional expression* is shorthand for a dual-alternative simple `if-else` statement (see Day 5 for more information about the `if` statement).

For example, the following is an `if-else` statement:

```
if (condition)
  variable = expression1;
else
  variable = expression2;
```

The equivalent conditional expression is

```
variable = (condition) ? expression1 : expression2;
```

The conditional expression tests the condition. If that condition is true, it assigns `expression1` to the target variable. Otherwise, it assigns `expression2` to the target variable.

Boolean Expressions

Often, you need to use a collection of relational and logical operators to formulate a nontrivial condition. Here are examples of such conditions:

```
x < 0 || x > 11
(i != 0 || i > 100) && (j != i || j > 0)
x != 0 && x != 10 && x != 100
```

NEW TERM *Boolean* (also called *logical*) *expressions* are expressions that involve logical operators and/or relational operators.

DO	DON'T

DO double-check to avoid Boolean expressions that are either always true or always false. For example, the expression `(x < 0 && x > 10)` is always false, because no value of `x` can be negative and greater than 10 at the same time.

DON'T use the = operator to test for equality.

Let's look at an example that uses relational and logical operators and expressions. Listing 3.6 shows the source code for program RELOP1.CPP. The program prompts you to enter three integers, and then proceeds to perform a battery of tests. The program displays the relational and logical operations, their operands, and their results.

Type

Listing 3.6. Source code for the program RELOP1.CPP.

```
/*
   simple C++ program that uses logical expressions
   this program uses the conditional expression to display
   TRUE or FALSE messages, since C++ does not support the
   BOOLEAN data type.
*/

#include <iostream.h>

const MIN_NUM = 30;
const MAX_NUM = 199;
const int TRUE = 1;
const int FALSE = 0;

main()
{
    int i, j, k;
    int flag1, flag2, in_range,
        same_int, xor_flag;

    cout << "Type first  integer : "; cin >> i;
    cout << "Type second integer : "; cin >> j;
    cout << "Type third  integer : "; cin >> k;

    // test for range [MIN_NUM..MAX_NUM]
    flag1 = i >= MIN_NUM;
    flag2 = i <= MAX_NUM;
    in_range = flag1 && flag2;
    cout << "\n" << i << " is in the range "
         << MIN_NUM << " to " << MAX_NUM << " : "
         << ((in_range) ? "TRUE" : "FALSE");

    // test if two or more entered numbers are equal
```

continues

Listing 3.6. continued

```
    same_int = i == j || i == k || j == k;
    cout << "\nat least two integers you typed are equal : "
         << ((same_int) ? "TRUE" : "FALSE");

    // miscellaneous tests
    cout << "\n" << i << " != " << j << " : "
         << ((i != j) ? "TRUE" : "FALSE");
    cout << "\nNOT (" << i << " < " << j << ") : "
         << ((!(i < j)) ? "TRUE" : "FALSE");
    cout << "\n" << i << " <= " << j << " : "
         << ((i <= j) ? "TRUE" : "FALSE");
    cout << "\n" << k << " > " << j << " : "
         << ((k > j) ? "TRUE" : "FALSE");
    cout << "\n(" << k << " = " << i << ") AND ("
         << j << " != " << k << ") : "
         << ((k == i && j != k) ? "TRUE" : "FALSE");

    // NOTE: C++ does NOT support the logical XOR operator for
    // boolean expressions.
    // add numeric results of logical tests.  Value is in 0..2
    xor_flag = (k <= i) + (j >= k);
    // if xor_flag is either 0 or 2 (i.e. not = 1), it is
    // FALSE therefore interpret 0 or 2 as false.
    xor_flag = (xor_flag == 1) ? TRUE : FALSE;
    cout << "\n(" << k << " <= " << i << ") XOR ("
         << j << " >= " << k << ") : "
         << ((xor_flag) ? "TRUE" : "FALSE");
    cout << "\n(" << k << " > " << i << ") AND("
         << j << " <= " << k << ") : "
         << ((k > i && j <= k) ? "TRUE" : "FALSE");
    cout << "\n\n";
    return 0;
}
```

Here is a sample session with the program in Listing 3.6:

Output

```
Type first  integer : 55
Type second integer : 64
Type third  integer : 87

55 is in the range 30 to 199 : TRUE
at least two integers you typed are equal : FALSE
55 != 64 : TRUE
NOT (55 < 64) : FALSE
55 <= 64 : TRUE
87 > 64 : TRUE
(87 = 55) AND (64 != 87) : FALSE
(87 <= 55) XOR (64 >= 87) : FALSE
(87 > 55) AND(64 <= 87) : TRUE
```

Analysis

The program in Listing 3.6 declares four global constants. The constants `MIN_NUM` and `MAX_NUM` define a range of numbers used in the logical tests. The constants `TRUE` and `FALSE` represent the Boolean values. The function `main` declares a number of `int` variables which are used for input and various testing. The statements in lines 21 through 23 prompt you for three integers and store them in the variables `i`, `j`, and `k`, respectively.

The statements in lines 26 through 31 deal with testing whether the value in variable `i` lies in the range of `MIN_NUM` and `MAX_NUM`. The statement in line 26 tests if the value in `i` is greater than or equal to the constant `MIN_NUM`. The program assigns the Boolean result to the variable `flag1`. The statement in line 27 tests whether the value in `i` is less than or equal to the constant `MAX_NUM`. The program assigns the Boolean result to the variable `flag2`. The statement in line 28 applies the `&&` operator to the variable `flag1` and `flag2`, and assigns the Boolean result to the variable `in_range`. The output statement in lines 29 through 31 states what the test is and displays `TRUE` or `FALSE` depending on the value in variable `in_range`. The statement uses the conditional operator `?:` to display the string `TRUE` if `in_range` has a nonzero value, and to display the string `FALSE` if otherwise.

The statements in lines 34 through 36 determine whether at least two of the three integers you entered are equal. The statement in line 34 uses a Boolean expression that applies the `==` relational operators and the `||` logical operators. The statement assigns the Boolean result to the variable `same_int`. The output statement in lines 35 and 36 states the test and displays the `TRUE`/`FALSE` outcome. The output statement uses the conditional operator to display the string `TRUE` or `FALSE` depending on the value in variable `same_int`.

The statements in lines 39 through 49 perform miscellaneous tests that involve the input values, and display both the test and the results. Please feel free to alter these statements to conduct different tests.

Note: The statements in lines 54 through 60 perform an `XOR` test and display the outcome. The program uses a simple programming trick to implement the `XOR` operator. The statement in line 54 adds the Boolean value of the subexpressions `(k <= i)` and `(j >= k)`. The result is 0 if both subexpressions are false, 1 if only one of the subexpressions is true, and 2 if both subexpressions are true. Since the `XOR` operator is true only if either subexpression is true, the statement in line 57 assigns `TRUE` to the variable `xor_flag` if the previous value is 1. Otherwise, the statement assigns `FALSE` to `xor_flag`. The statements in lines 61 through 63 perform another miscellaneous test.

Bit-Manipulation Operators

C++ is a programming language that is suitable for system development. System development requires bit-manipulating operators.

NEW TERM *Bit-manipulating operators* toggle, set, query, and shift the bits of a byte or a word.

Table 3.4 shows the bit-manipulating operators. Notice that C++ uses the symbols `&` and `|` to represent the bitwise `AND` and `OR`, respectively. Recall that the `&&` and `||` characters represent the logical `AND` and `OR` operators, respectively. In addition to the bit-manipulating operators, C++ supports the bit-manipulating assignment operators, shown in Table 3.5. (Using bit-manipulating operators is part of advanced programming, which involves fiddling with single bits. As a novice C++ programmer, you will most likely not use these operators in the near future.)

Table 3.4. C++ bit-manipulating operators.

C++ Operator	Meaning	Example
`&`	Bitwise `AND`	`i & 128`
`|`	Bitwise `OR`	`j	64`
`^`	Bitwise `XOR`	`j ^ 12`
`~`	Bitwise `NOT`	`~j`
`<<`	Bitwise shift left	`i << 2`
`>>`	Bitwise shift right	`j >> 3`

Table 3.5. C++ bit-manipulating assignment operators.

C++ Operator	Long Form	Example
`x &= y`	`x = x & y`	`i &= 128`
`x |= y`	`x = x	y`	`j |= 64`
`x ^= y`	`x = x ^ y`	`k ^= 15`
`x <<= y`	`x = x << y`	`j <<= 2`
`x >>= y`	`x = x >> y`	`k >>= 3`

Let me present a C++ program that performs simple bit manipulation. Listing 3.7 contains the source code for program BITS1.CPP. The program requires no input because it uses internal data. The program applies the `|`, `&`, `^`, `>>`, and `<<` bitwise operators and displays the results of the bitwise manipulation.

Listing 3.7. Source code for the program BITS1.CPP.

```
1: // C++ program to perform bit manipulations
2:
3: #include <iostream.h>
4:
5: main()
6: {
7:
8:      int i, j, k;
9:
10:      // assign values to i and j
11:      i = 0xF0;
12:      j = 0x1A;
13:
14:      k = j & i;
15:      cout << j << " AND " << i << " = " << k << "\n";
16:
17:      k = j | i;
18:      cout << j << " OR " << i << " = " << k << "\n";
19:
20:      k = j ^ 0x1C;
21:      cout << j << " XOR " << 0x1C << " = " << k << "\n";
22:
23:      k = i << 2;
24:      cout << i << " shifted left by 2 bits = " << k << "\n";
25:
26:      k = i >> 2;
27:      cout << i << " shifted right by 2 bits = " << k << "\n";
28:      return 0;
29: }
```

Here is a sample session with the program in Listing 3.7:

```
26 AND 240 = 16
26 OR 240 = 250
26 XOR 28 = 6
240 shifted left by 2 bits = 960
240 shifted right by 2 bits = 60
```

The program in Listing 3.7 declares three `int`-typed variables, `i`, `j`, and `k`. The statements in lines 11 and 12 assign hexadecimal numbers to the variables `i` and `j`, respectively. The statement in line 14 applies the bitwise `AND` operator to the variables `i` and `j`, and stores the result in variable `k`. The output statement in line 15 displays the operands, the bitwise operator, and the results. The statement in line 17 applies the bitwise `OR` operator to the variable `i` and `j`, and saves the result to variable `k`. The output statement in line 18 displays the operands, the bitwise operator, and the results. The statement in line 20 applies the bitwise `XOR` operator using the variable `j` and the hexadecimal integer 0x1C. The output statement in line 21 displays the operands, the bitwise operator, and the results.

The statements in lines 23 through 27 apply the shift left and shift right operators to variable `i`. These operators shift the bits of variable `i` by 2 bits and assign the result to variable `k`. The effect of the left shift operator is the same as multiplying the value in variable `i` by 4. Similarly, the effect of the right shift operator is the same as dividing the value in variable `i` by 4.

The Comma Operator

The comma operator requires that the program completely evaluates the first expression before evaluating the second expression. Both expressions are located in the same C++ statement! What does *located in the same C++ statement* mean exactly? Why utilize this rather unusual operator in the first place? Because the comma operator with its peculiar role does serve a specific and very important purpose in the `for` loop.

NEW TERM *Loops* are powerful language constructs that enable computers to excel in achieving repetitive tasks. The *comma operator* enables you to create multiple expressions that initialize multiple loop-related variables.

Syntax

The Comma Operator

The general syntax for the comma operator is

```
expression1, expression2
```

Example:

```
for (i = 0, j = 0; i < 10; i++, j++)
```

You learn more about the for loop in Day 6. For now, this example shows you how to apply the comma operator.

Operator Precedence and Evaluation Direction

Now that you are familiar with most of the C++ operators (there are a few more operators that deal with pointers and addresses), there are two related aspects you need to know:

first, the precedence of the C++ operators; second, the direction (or sequence) of evaluation. Table 3.6 shows the C++ precedence of the C++ operators that I have covered so far and also indicates the evaluation direction.

Table 3.6. C++ operators and their precedence.

Category	Name	Symbol	Evaluation Direction	Precedence
Monadic				
	Post-increment	`++`	Left to right	2
	Post-decrement	`-`	Left to right	2
	Address	`&`	Right to left	2
	Bitwise `NOT`	`~`	Right to left	2
	Typecast	`(type)`	Right to left	2
	Logical `NOT`	`!`	Right to left	2
	Negation	`-`	Right to left	2
	Plus sign	`+`	Right to left	2
	Pre-increment	`++`	Right to left	2
	Pre-decrement	`-`	Right to left	2
	Size of data	`sizeof`	Right to left	2
Multiplicative				
	Modulus	`%`	Left to right	3
	Multiply	`*`	Left to right	3
	Divide	`/`	Left to right	3
Additive				
	Add	`+`	Left to right	4
	Subtract	`-`	Left to right	4

continues

Table 3.6. continued

Category	Name	Symbol	Evaluation Direction	Precedence
Bitwise Shift				
	Shift left	<<	Left to right	5
	Shift right	>>	Left to right	5
Relational				
	Less than	<	Left to right	6
	Less or equal	<=	Left to right	6
	Greater than	>	Left to right	6
	Greater or equal	>=	Left to right	6
	Equal	==	Left to right	7
	Not equal	!=	Left to right	7
Bitwise				
	AND	&	Left to right	8
	XOR	^	Left to right	9
	OR	|	Left to right	10
Logical				
	AND	&&	Left to right	11
	OR	||	Left to right	12
Ternary				
	Cond. express.	?:	Right to left	13
Assignment				
	Arithmetic	=	Right to left	14
		+=	Right to left	14
		-=	Right to left	14
		*=	Right to left	14

Category	Name	Symbol	Evaluation Direction	Precedence
		`/=`	Right to left	14
		`%=`	Right to left	14
	Shift	`>>=`	Right to left	14
		`<<=`	Right to left	14
	Bitwise	`&=`	Right to left	14
		`¦=`	Right to left	14
		`^=`	Right to left	14
	Comma	`,`	Left to right	15

Summary

Today's lesson presents the various C++ operators and discusses how to use these operators to manipulate data. You learn the following:

- The arithmetic operators include `+`, `-`, `*`, `/`, and `%` (modulus).
- The arithmetic expressions vary in complexity. The simplest expression contains a single data item (literal, constant, or variable). Complex expressions include multiple operators, functions, literals, constants, and variables.
- The increment and decrement operators come in the pre- and post- forms. C++ allows you to apply these operators to variables that store characters, integers, and even floating-point numbers.
- The arithmetic assignment operators allow you to write shorter arithmetic expressions in which the primary operand is also the variable receiving the result of the expression.
- The `sizeof` operator returns the byte size of either a data type or a variable.
- Typecasting allows you to force the type conversion of an expression.
- Relational and logical operators permit you to build logical expressions. C++ does not support a predefined Boolean type and instead considers 0 as false and any nonzero value as true.

- Boolean expressions combine relational and logical operators to formulate nontrivial conditions. These expressions allow a program to make sophisticated decisions.
- The conditional expression offers you a short form for the simple dual-alternative `if-else` statement.
- The bit-manipulation operators perform bitwise `AND`, `OR`, `XOR`, and `NOT` operations. In addition, C++ supports the << and >> bitwise shift operators.
- The bit-manipulation assignment operators offer short forms for simple bit-manipulation statements.

Q&A

Q How does the compiler react when you declare a variable but never assign a value to it?

A The compiler issues a warning that the variable is unreferenced.

Q What is the Boolean expression to check that the value of a variable, call it `i`, is in the range of values (for example, defined by variables `loVal` and `hiVal`)?

A The expression that determines whether the value in variable `i` is located in a range is

```
(i >= lowVal && i <= hiVal)
```

Workshop

The Workshop provides quiz questions to help you solidify your understanding of the material covered and exercises to provide you with experience in using what you've learned. Try to understand the quiz and exercise answers before continuing on to the next day's lesson. Answers are provided in Appendix B, "Answers."

Quiz

1. What is the output of the following program?

```
#include <iostream.h>

main()
{
```

```
  int i = 3;
  int j = 5;
  double x = 33.5;
  double y = 10.0;

  cout << 10 + j % i << "\n";
  cout << i * i - 2 * i + 5 << "\n";
  cout << (19 + i + j) / (2 * j + 2) << "\n";
  cout << x / y + y / x << "\n";
  cout << i * x + j * y << "\n";
  return 0;
}
```

2. What is the output of the following program?

```
#include <iostream.h>

main()
{
  int i = 3;
  int j = 5;

  cout << 10 + j % i++ << "\n";
  cout << -i * i - 2 * i + 5 << "\n";
  cout << (19 + ++i + ++j) / (2 * j + 2) << "\n";
  return 0;
}
```

3. What is the output of the following program?

```
#include <iostream.h>

main()
{
  int i = 3;
  int j = 5;

  i += j;
  j *= 2;
  cout << 10 + j % i << "\n";
  i -= 2;
  j /= 3;
  cout << i * i - 2 * i + j << "\n";
  return 0;
}
```

4. What is the output of the following program?

```
include <iostream.h>

main()
{
  int i = 5;
  int j = 10;
```

```
    cout << ((i > j) ? "TRUE" : "FALSE") << "\n";
    cout << ((i > 0 && j < 100) ? "TRUE" : "FALSE") << "\n";
    cout << ((i > 0 && i < 10) ? "TRUE" : "FALSE") << "\n";
    cout << ((i == 5 && i == j) ? "TRUE" : "FALSE") << "\n";
    return 0;
}
```

Exercises

1. Use the conditional operator to write the function `max`, which returns the greater of two integers.
2. Use the conditional operator to write the function `min`, which returns the smaller of two integers.
3. Use the conditional operator to write the function `abs`, which returns the absolute value of an integer.
4. Use the conditional operator to write the function `isOdd`, which returns 0 if its integer argument is an odd number and yields 1 if otherwise.

4

Managing I/O

WEEK
1

C++, like its parent language C, does not define I/O operations that are part of the core language. Instead, C++ and C rely on I/O libraries to provide the needed I/O support. Such libraries are mainly aimed at non-GUI (Graphics User Interface) environments such as MS-DOS. These libraries usually work with console applications, which is why they are of interest in this book. However, because my primary goal is to teach you how to write Windows programs, I keep the discussion of these I/O libraries to a minimum. Today's short lesson looks at a small selection of input and output operations and functions that are supported by the STDIO.H and IOSTREAM.H header files. You learn about the following topics:

- Formatted stream output
- Stream input
- The `printf` function

Formatted Stream Output

C++ brought with it a family of extendable I/O libraries. The language designers recognized that the I/O functions in STDIO.H, inherited from C, have their limitations when dealing with classes (more about classes in Day 11). Consequently, C++ extends the notion of streams. Recall that streams, which already exist in C, are a sequence of data flowing from part of a computer to another. In the programs that I have presented so far, you have seen the extractor operator << working with the standard output stream, `cout`. You also saw the inserter operator >> and the standard input stream, `cin`. In this section I introduce you to the stream functions width and precision which help in formatting the output. The C++ stream libraries have many more functions to further fine-tune the output. However, as I stated earlier, because these functions work for non-GUI interfaces, I don't want to overwhelm you with information that is relevant to Windows programming. The `width` function specifies the width of the output. The general form for using this function with the `cout` stream is

```
cout.width(widthOfOutput);
```

The `precision` function specifies the number of digits for floating-point numbers. The general form for using this function with the `cout` stream is

```
cout.precision(numberOfDigits);
```

Let's look at an example. Listing 4.1 contains the source code for program OUT1.CPP. The program, which requires no input, displays formatted integers, floating-point numbers, and characters using the `width` and `precision` stream functions.

Type

Listing 4.1. Source code for the program OUT1.CPP.

```
1: // Program that illustrates C++ formatted stream output
2: // using the width and precision functions
3:
4: #include <iostream.h>
5:
6: main()
7: {
8:   short    aShort     = 4;
9:   int      anInt      = 67;
10:   unsigned char aByte = 128;
11:   char     aChar      = '@';
12:   float    aSingle    = 355.0;
13:   double   aDouble    = 1.130e+002;
14:   // display sample expressions
15:   cout.width(3); cout << int(aByte) << " + ";
16:   cout.width(2); cout << anInt << " = ";
17:   cout.width(3); cout << (aByte + anInt) << '\n';
18:
19:   cout.precision(4); cout << aSingle << " / ";
20:   cout.precision(4); cout << aDouble << " = ";
21:   cout.precision(5); cout << (aSingle / aDouble) << '\n';
22:
23:   cout << "The character in variable aChar is "
24:        << aChar << '\n';
25:   return 0;
26: }
```

Here is a sample session with the program in Listing 4.1:

Output

```
128 + 67 = 195
355 / 113 = 3.1416
The character in variable aChar is @
```

Analysis

The program in Listing 4.1 declares a set of variables which have different data types. The statements in lines 15 through 17 use the stream function `width` to specify the output width for the next item displayed by a `cout` statement. Notice that it takes six statements to display three integers. In addition, notice that in line 15 the program uses the expression `int(aByte)` to typecast the `unsigned char` type into an `int`. Without this type conversion, the contents of variable `aByte` appear as a character instead of a number. If I use the stream output to display integers that have default widths, I can indeed replace the six stream output statements with a single one.

Lines 19 through 21 contain the second set of stream output statements for the floating-point numbers. The statements in these lines contain the stream function precision to specify the total number of digits to display. Again, it takes six C++ statements to output three floating-point numbers. Once more, if I use the stream output to display numbers that have default widths, I can replace the six stream output statements with a single one.

Stream Input

Like the standard output stream, C++ offers the standard input stream, `cin`. This input stream is able to read predefined data types, such as `int`, `unsigned`, `long`, and `char`. Typically, you use the inserter operator >> to obtain input for the predefined data types. The programs that I have presented so far use the >> operator to enter a single item. C++ streams allow you to chain the >> operator to enter multiple items. In the case of multiple items, you need to observe the following rules:

1. Enter a space between two consecutive numbers to separate them.
2. Entering a space between two consecutive `char`s is optional.
3. Entering a space between a `char` and a number (and vice versa) is necessary only if the `char` is a digit.
4. The input stream ignores spaces.
5. You can enter multiple items on different lines. The stream input statements are not fully executed until they obtain all the specified input.

> **Note:** I postpone discussing the input of character strings for now. Day 9 covers strings and includes the input of strings.

Let's look at a program which illustrates both the input of multiple items and different combinations of data types. Listing 4.2 shows the source code for program IN1.CPP. The program performs the following tasks:

- ☐ Prompts you to enter three numbers
- ☐ Calculates the sum of the three numbers
- ☐ Displays the sum and the average of the three numbers you entered
- ☐ Prompts you to type in three characters
- ☐ Displays your input
- ☐ Prompts you to enter a number, a character, and a number
- ☐ Displays your input
- ☐ Prompts you to enter a character, a number, and a character
- ☐ Displays your input

Listing 4.2. Source code for the program IN1.CPP.

```
1: // Program that illustrates standard stream input
2:
3: #include <iostream.h>
4:
5: main()
6: {
7:   double x, y, z, sum;
8:   char c1, c2, c3;
9:
10:   cout << "Enter three numbers separated by a space : ";
11:   cin >> x >> y >> z;
12:   sum = x + y + z;
13:   cout << "Sum of numbers = " << sum
14:        << "\nAverage of numbers = " << sum / 3 << "\n";
15:   cout << "Enter three characters : ";
16:   cin >> c1 >> c2 >> c3;
17:   cout << "You entered characters '" << c1
18:        << "', '" << c2 << "', and '"
19:        << c3 << "'\n";
20:   cout << "Enter a number, a character, and a number : ";
21:   cin >> x >> c1 >> y;
22:   cout << "You entered " << x << " " << c1 << " " << y << "\n";
23:   cout << "Enter a character, a number, and a character : ";
24:   cin >> c1 >> x >> c2;
25:   cout << "You entered " << c1 << " " << x << " " << c2 << "\n";
26:
27:   return 0;
28: }
```

Here is a sample session with the program in Listing 4.2:

```
Enter three numbers separated by a space : 1 2 3
Sum of numbers = 6
Average of numbers = 2
Enter three characters : ABC
You entered characters 'A', 'B', and 'C'
Enter a number, a character, and a number : 12A34.4
You entered 12 A 34.4
Enter a character, a number, and a character : A3.14Z
You entered A 3.14 Z
```

The program in Listing 4.2 declares four `double`-typed variables and three `char`-typed variables. The output statement in line 10 prompts you to enter three numbers. The input statement in line 11 obtains your input and stores the numbers in variables `x`, `y`, and `z`. You need to enter a space character between any two numbers. You can also enter each number on a separate line. The statement stores the first number you enter in variable `x`, the second number in variable `y`, and the third one in variable `z`. This sequence is determined by the sequence in which these variables appear in line 11. The statement in line 12 calculates the sum of the values in variables `x`, `y`, and `z`. The output statement in lines 13 and 14 displays the sum and average of the numbers that you entered.

The output statement in line 15 prompts you to enter three characters. The input statement in line 16 obtains your input and sequentially stores the characters in variables `c1`, `c2`, and `c3`. Your input need not separate the characters with a space. Thus, you can type in characters such as `1A2`, `Bob`, and `1 D d`. The output statement in lines 17 through 19 displays the characters you type in, separated by spaces.

The output statement in line 20 prompts you to enter a number, a character, and a number. The input statement in line 21 sequentially stores your input in variables `x`, `c1`, and `y`. You need to type in a space between the character and either number only if the character can be interpreted as part of either number. For example, if you want to enter the number 12, the dot character, and the number 55, type in `12 . 55`. The spaces around the dot ensure that the input stream does not consider it as a decimal part of either floating-point number. The output statement in line 22 displays the values you entered, separated by spaces.

The output statement in line 23 prompts you to enter a character, a number, and a character. The input statement in line 24 sequentially stores your input in variables `c1`, `x`, and `c2`. You need to enter a space between the characters and the number only if the characters can be interpreted as part of the number. For example, if you want to enter the character `-`, the number `12`, and the digit `0`, type in `- 12 0`. The output statement in line 25 displays the values you entered, separated by spaces.

The *printf* Function

As a novice C++ programmer you have a wealth of I/O functions to choose from. In this section I discuss the formatting features of function `printf` which is part of the standard I/O of C. The function is prototyped in the header file STDIO.H.

The `printf` function offers much power and presents formatted controls. The general syntax for the individual formatting instruction is

```
% [flags] [width] [.precision] [F ¦ N ¦ h ¦ l] <type character>
```

The `flags` options indicate the output justification, numeric signs, decimal points, and trailing zeros. In addition, these flags also specify the octal and hexadecimal prefixes. Table 4.1 shows the options for the `flags` in the format string of the `printf` function.

The `width` option indicates the minimum number of displayed characters. The `printf` function uses zeros and blanks to pad the output if needed. When the `width` number begins with a 0, the `printf` function uses leading zeros, instead of spaces, for padding. When the `*` character appears instead of a `width` number, the `printf` function obtains the actual width number from the function's argument list. The argument that specifies the required width must come before the argument actually being formatted. The following is an example which displays the integer 3 using 2 characters, as specified by the third argument of `printf`:

```
printf("%*d", 3, 2);
```

The `precision` option specifies the maximum number of displayed characters. If you include an integer, the `precision` option defines the minimum number of displayed digits. When the `*` character is used in place of a precision number, the `printf` function obtains the actual precision from the argument list. The argument that specifies the required precision must come before the argument that is actually being formatted. The following is an example which displays the floating-point number 3.3244 using 10 characters, as specified by the third argument of `printf`:

```
printf("%7.*f", 3.3244, 10);
```

The `F`, `N`, `h`, and `l` options are sized options used to overrule the argument's default size. The `F` and `N` options are used in conjunction with far and near pointers, respectively. The `h` and `l` options are used to indicate short `int` or `long`, respectively.

Table 4.1. The escape sequence.

Sequence	Decimal Value	Hex Value	Task
`\a`	7	0x07	Bell
`\b`	8	0x08	Backspace
`\f`	12	0x0C	Formfeed
`\n`	10	0x0A	New line
`\r`	13	0x0D	Carriage return
`\t`	9	0x09	Horizontal tab
`\v`	11	0x0B	Vertical tab
`\\`	92	0x5C	Backslash
`\'`	44	0x2C	Single quote

continues

Table 4.1. continued

Sequence	Decimal Value	Hex Value	Task
`\"`	34	0x22	Double quote
`\?`	63	0x3F	Question mark
`\000`			1 to 3 digits for octal value
`\Xhhh` and `\xhhh`		0xhhh	Hexadecimal value

The `printf` function requires that you specify a data type character with each `%` format code. Table 4.2 shows the options for the flags in the format string of `printf`. Table 4.3 shows the data type characters used in the format string of `printf`.

Table 4.2. Options for the flags in the format string of the `printf` function.

Format Option	Outcome
-	Justifies to the left within the specified field
+	Displays the plus or minus sign of a value
blank	Displays a leading blank if the value is positive; displays a minus sign if the value is negative
#	No effect on decimal integers; displays a leading 0X or 0x for hexadecimal integers; displays a leading zero for octal integers; displays the decimal point for reals

Table 4.3. Data type characters utilized in the format string of `printf`.

Category	Type Character	Outcome
Character	`c`	Single character
	`d`	Signed decimal int
	`i`	Signed decimal int

Category	Type Character	Outcome
	`o`	Unsigned octal int
	`u`	Unsigned decimal int
	`x`	Unsigned hexadecimal int (the set of numeric characters used is 0123456789abcdef)
	`X`	Unsigned hexadecimal int (the set of numeric characters used is 0123456789abcdef)
Pointer	`p`	Displays only the offset for near pointers as OOOO; displays far pointers as SSSS:OOOO
Pointer to int	`n`	
real	`f`	Displays signed value in the format [-]dddd.dddd
	`e`	Displays signed scientific value in the format [-]d.dddde[+|-]ddd
	`E`	Displays signed scientific value in the format [-]d.ddddE[+|-]ddd
	`g`	Displays signed value using either the `f` or `e` formats, depending on the value and the specified precision
	`G`	Displays signed value using either the `f` or `E` formats, depending on the value and the specified precision
String pointer	`s`	Displays characters until the null terminator of the string is reached

Note: Although the function `printf` plays no role in the output of Windows applications, its sister function, `sprintf`, does. The latter function creates a string of characters which contains the formatted image of the output. I discuss the `sprintf` function in Day 9, and use that function in the latter lessons of this book to create a dialog box that contains messages that include numbers.

Let's look at a simple example. Listing 4.3 shows the source code for program OUT2.CPP. I created this program by editing the OUT1.CPP in Listing 4.1. The new version displays formatted output using the `printf` function. The program displays the same floating-point numbers using three different sets of format code.

Type

Listing 4.3. Source code for the program OUT2.CPP.

```
// C++ program that uses the printf function for formatted output

#include <stdio.h>

main()
{
  short    aShort    = 4;
  int      anInt     = 67;
  unsigned char aByte = 128;
  char     aChar     = '@';
  float    aSingle   = 355.0;
  double   aDouble   = 1.130e+002;
  // display sample expressions
  printf("%3d %c %2d = %3d\n",
          aByte, '+', anInt, aByte + anInt);

  printf("Output uses the %%lf format\n");
  printf("%6.4f / %6.4lf = %7.5lf\n", aSingle, aDouble,
                                aSingle / aDouble);
  printf("Output uses the %%le format\n");
  printf("%6.4e / %6.4le = %7.5le\n", aSingle, aDouble,
                                aSingle / aDouble);
  printf("Output uses the %%lg format\n");
  printf("%6.4g / %6.4lg = %7.5lg\n", aSingle, aDouble,
                                aSingle / aDouble);

  printf("The character in variable aChar is %c\n", aChar);
  printf("The ASCII code of %c is %d\n", aChar, aChar);
  return 0;
}
```

Here is a sample session with the program in Listing 4.3:

Output

```
128 + 67 = 195
Output uses the %lf format
355.0000 / 113.0000 = 3.14159
Output uses the %le format
3.5500e+002 / 1.1300e+002 = 3.14159e+000
Output uses the %lg format
355 / 113 = 3.1416
The character in variable aChar is @
The ASCII code of @ is 64
```

Analysis The program in Listing 4.3 declares a collection of variables with different data types. The output statement in lines 14 and 15 displays integers and characters using the `%d` and `%c` format controls. Table 4.4 shows the effect of the various format controls in the `printf` statement at line 14. Notice that the `printf` function converts the first item in the output from an unsigned `char` to an `int`.

Table 4.4. Effects of the various format controls in the `printf` statement at line 16.

Format Control	Item	Data Type	Output
`%3d`	`aByte`	`unsigned char`	Integer
`%c`	'+'	`char`	Character
`%2d`	`anInt`	`int`	Integer
`%3d`	`aByte + anInt`	`int`	Integer

The output statement in line 18 displays the variable `aSingle`, the variable `aDouble`, and the expression `aSingle / aDouble` using the format controls `%6.4f`, `%6.4lf`, and `%7.5lf`. These controls specify precision values of 4, 4, and 5 digits, respectively, and minimum widths of 6, 6, and 7 characters, respectively. The last two format controls indicate that they display a `double`-typed value.

The output statement in line 21 is similar to that in line 18. The main difference is that the `printf` in line 21 uses the `e` format instead of the `f` format. Consequently, the three items in the `printf` statement appear in scientific notations.

The output statement in line 24 is similar to that in line 18. The main difference is that the `printf` in line 24 uses the `g` format instead of the `f` format. Consequently, the first two items in the `printf` statement appear with no decimal places, because they are whole numbers.

The output statement in line 27 displays the contents in variable `aChar` using the `%c` format control. The output statement in line 28 displays the contents of variable `aChar` twice: once as a character and once as an integer (the ASCII code of a character, to be more exact). The `printf` function in line 28 performs this task by using the `%c` and `%d` format controls, respectively.

Summary

Today's lesson examines the basic input and output operations and functions that are supported by the IOSTREAM.H and STDIO.H header files. You learn the following:

- Formatted stream output uses the precision and width functions to provide some basic formatting output.
- Standard stream input supports the insert operator >> to obtain input for the predefined data types in C++.
- The format codes involved in the format string of the `printf` function empower the `printf` function to control the appearance of the output and even perform type conversion.

Q&A

Q How can I chain >> or << operators?

A Each of these operators returns a special stream data type which can be the input for another similar stream operator.

Q Why can't I use the stream I/O operators in Windows applications?

A Windows applications have a fundamentally different way of interacting with you. When a console application (which emulates a non-GUI MS-DOS application) executes an input statement, it goes into a special mode where it monitors the keyboard input. By contrast, Windows programs (which are GUI applications) are always monitoring the mouse (its movements and its button clicks) and the keyboard and reporting the current status to the part of Windows which monitors events. The vast difference between GUI and non-GUI applications renders non-GUI input functions useless in GUI applications.

Workshop

The Workshop provides quiz questions to help you solidify your understanding of the material covered and exercises to provide you with experience in using what you've learned. Try to understand the quiz and exercise answers before continuing on to the next day's lesson. Answers are provided in Appendix B, "Answers."

Quiz

1. What is wrong with the following statement?

```
count << "Enter a number " >> x;
```

2. What happens in the following statement?

```
cout << "Enter three numbers : ";
cin >> x >> y >> x;
```

Exercises

1. Write the program OUT3.CPP, which displays a table of square roots for whole numbers in the range of 2 to 10. Use the MATH.H header file to import the `sqrt` function, which calculates the square root of a `double`-typed argument. Because I have not discussed C++ loops, use repetitive statements to display the various values. Employ the format controls `%3.0lf` and `%3.4lf` to display the number and its square root, respectively.

2. Write the program OUT4.CPP, which prompts you for an integer and displays the hexadecimal and octal equivalent forms. Use the `printf` format controls to perform the conversion between decimal, hexadecimal, and octal numbers.

5

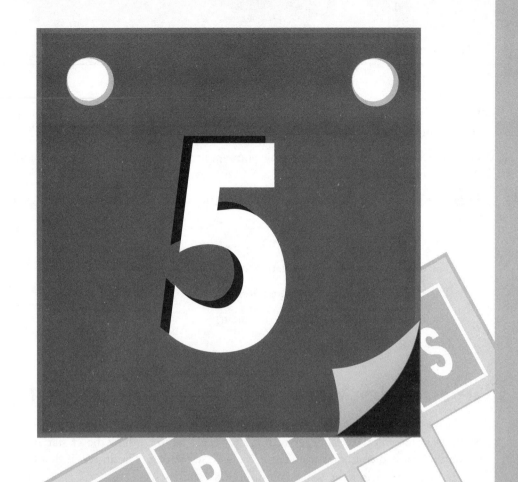

The Decision-Making Constructs

WEEK 1

The support of different programming languages varies depending on their decision-making constructs.

NEW TERM Decision-making constructs enable your applications to examine conditions and designate courses of action.

Today's lesson looks at the decision-making constructs in C++ and covers the following topics:

- The single-alternative `if` statement
- The dual-alternative `if-else` statement
- The multiple-alternative `if-else` statement
- The multiple-alternative `switch` statement
- Nested decision-making constructs

The Single-Alternative *if* Statement

Unlike many programming languages, C++ does not have the keyword `then` in any form of the `if` statement. This language feature may lead you to ask how the `if` statement separates the tested condition from the executable statements. The answer is that C++ dictates that you enclose the tested condition in parentheses.

NEW TERM An `if` statement is a *single-alternative* statement.

Syntax

The Single-Alternative *if* Statement

The general syntax for the single-alternative `if` statement is

```
if (condition)
statement;
```

for a single executable statement, and

```
if (tested_condition) {
<sequence of statements>
}
```

for a sequence of executable statements.

Examples:

```
if (numberOfLines < 0)
  numberOfLines = 0;
```

```
if ((height - 54) < 3) {
  area = length * width;
  volume = area * height;
}
```

C++ uses the open and close braces ({})to define a block of statements. Figure 5.1 shows the flow in a single-alternative `if` statement.

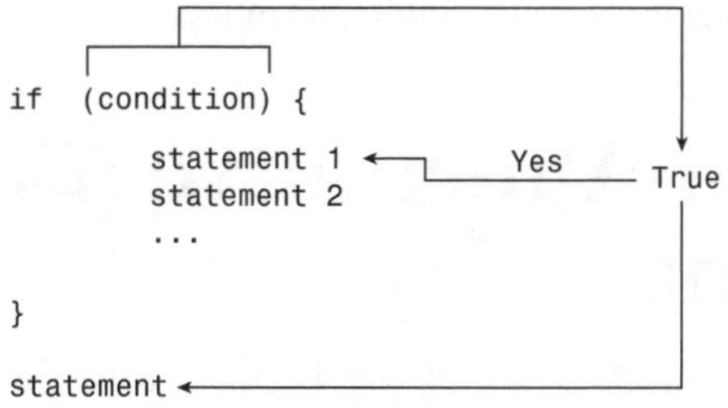
if (condition) {
statement 1
statement 2
...
}
statement
Yes
True

Figure 5.1. *The program flow in the single-alternative* `if` *statement.*

Let's look at an example. Listing 5.1 shows a program with a single-alternative `if` statement. The program prompts you to enter a non-zero number and stores the input in the variable `x`. If the value in `x` is not zero, the program displays the reciprocal of `x`.

Type

Listing 5.1. Source code for the program IF1.CPP.

```
// Program that demonstrates the single-alternative if statement

#include <iostream.h>

main()
{
  double x;
  cout << "Enter a non-zero number : ";
  cin >> x;
   if (x != 0)
     cout << "The reciprocal of " << x
          << " is " << (1/x) << "\n";
   return 0;
}
```

Here is a sample session with the program in Listing 5.1:

Output

```
Enter a non-zero number : 25
The reciprocal of 25 is 0.04
```

Analysis The program in Listing 5.1 declares the double-typed variable `x` in function `main`. The output statement in line 8 prompts you to enter a non-zero number. The input statement in line 9 stores your input in variable `x`. The `if` statement in line 10 determines whether `x` does not equal zero. If this condition is true, the program executes the output statement in lines 11 and 12. This statement displays the value of `x` and its reciprocal, `1/x`. If the tested condition is false, the program skips the statement in lines 11 and 12 and resumes at the statement in line 13.

The Dual-Alternative *if-else* Statement

In the dual-alternative form of the `if` statement, the `else` keyword separates the statements used to execute each alternative.

NEW TERM The *dual-alternative* `if-else` statement provides you with two alternate courses of action based on the Boolean value of the tested condition.

Syntax

The Dual-Alternative *if-else* Statement

The general syntax for the dual-alternative `if-else` statement is

```
if (condition)
statement1;
else
statement2;
```

for a single executable statement in each clause, and

```
if (tested_condition) {
  <sequence #1 of statements>
}
else {
  <sequence #2 of statements>
}
```

for a sequence of executable statements in both clauses.

Example:

```
if (moneyInAccount > withdraw) {
  moneyInAccount -= withdraw;
  cout << "You withdrew $" << withdraw << "\n";
  cout << "Balance is $" << moneyInAccount << "\n";
}
else {
  cout << "Cannot withdraw $" << withdraw << "\n";
  cout << "Account has $" << moneyInAccount << "\n";
}
```

Figure 5.2. shows the program flow in the dual-alternative `if-else` statement.

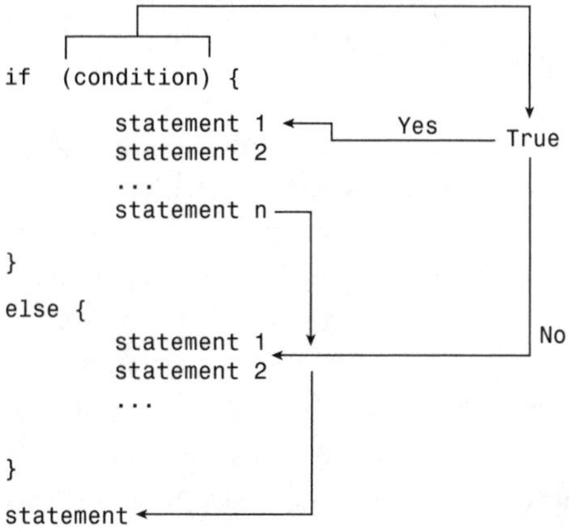
if (condition) {
statement 1
statement 2
...
statement n
}
else {
statement 1
statement 2
...
}
statement
Yes
True
No

Figure 5.2. *The program flow in the dual-alternative* `if-else` *statement.*

Let's look at an example that uses the dual-alternative `if-else` statement. Listing 5.2 contains the source code for the program IF2.CPP. The program prompts you to enter a character and then determines whether or not you entered a letter. The program output classifies your input as either a letter or a nonletter character.

Type

Listing 5.2. Source code for the program IF2.CPP.

```
// Program that demonstrates the dual-alternative if statement

#include <iostream.h>
#include <ctype.h>

main()
{
  char c;
  cout << "Enter a letter : ";
   cin >> c;
   // convert to uppercase
   c = toupper(c);
   if (c >= 'A' && c <= 'Z')
     cout << "You entered a letter\n";
   else
     cout << "Your input was not a letter\n";
   return 0;
}
```

Here is a sample session with the program in Listing 5.2:

Output

```
Enter a character : g
You entered a letter
```

Analysis

The program in Listing 5.2 declares the `char`-typed variable `c` in line 8. The output statement in line 9 prompts you to enter a letter. The input statement in line 10 obtains your input and stores it in variable `c`. The statement in line 12 converts the value in the variable to uppercase by calling the function `toupper` (prototyped in the CTYPE.H header file). This character case conversion simplifies the tested condition in the `if-else` statement at line 13. The `if-else` statement determines if the variable `c` contains a character in the range of A to Z. If this condition is true, the program executes the output statement in line 14. This statement displays a message stating that you have entered a letter. By contrast, if the tested condition is false, the program executes the `else` clause statement in line 16. This statement displays a message stating that your input was not a letter.

Potential Problems with the *if* Statement

There is a potential problem with the dual-alternative `if` statement. This problem occurs when the `if` clause includes another single-alternative `if` statement. In this case, the compiler considers that the `else` clause pertains to the nested `if` statement. (A nested `if` statement is one that contains another `if` statement in the `if` and/or `else` clauses—more about nesting in the next section.) Here is an example:

```
if (i > 0)
  if (i == 10)
    cout << "You guessed the magic number";
else
  cout << "Number is out of range";
```

In this code fragment, when variable `i` is a positive number other than 10, the code displays the message `Number is out of range`. The compiler treats these statements as though the code fragment meant

```
if (i > 0)
  if (i == 10)
    cout << "You guessed the magic number";
  else
    cout << "Number is out of range";
```

To correct this problem, enclose the nested `if` statement in a statement block:

```
if (i > 0) {
  if (i == 10)
  cout << "You guessed the magic number";
}
else
  cout << "Number is out of range";
```

The Multiple-Alternative *if-else* Statement

C++ allows you to nest `if-else` statements to create a multiple-alternative form. This alternative gives a lot of power and flexibility to your applications.

NEW TERM The *multiple-alternative* `if-else` statement contains nested `if-else` statements.

Syntax

The Multiple-Alternative *if-else* Statement

The general syntax for the multiple-alternative `if-else` statement is

```
if (tested_condition1)
  statement1; ¦ { <sequence #1 of statement> }
else if (tested_condition2)
  statement2; ¦ { <sequence #2 of statement> }
...
else if (tested_conditionN)
  statementN; ¦ { <sequence #N of statement> }
 [else
  statementN+1; ¦ { <sequence #N+1 of statement> }]
```

Example:

```
char op;

int opOk = 1;
double x, y, z;
cout << "Enter operand1 operator operand2: ";
cin >> x >> op >> y;
if (op == '+')
  z = x + y;
else if (op == '-')
  z = x - y;
else if (op == '*')
  z = x * y;
else if (op == '/' && y != 0)
  z = x / y;
else
  opOk = 0;
```

The multiple-alternative `if-else` statement performs a series of cascaded tests until one of the following occurs:

1. One of the conditions in the `if` clause or in the `else if` clauses is true. In this case, the accompanying statements are executed.
2. None of the tested conditions is true. The program executes the statements in the catch-all else clause (if there is an `else` clause).

Figure 5.3 shows the program flow in the multiple-alternative `if-else` statement.

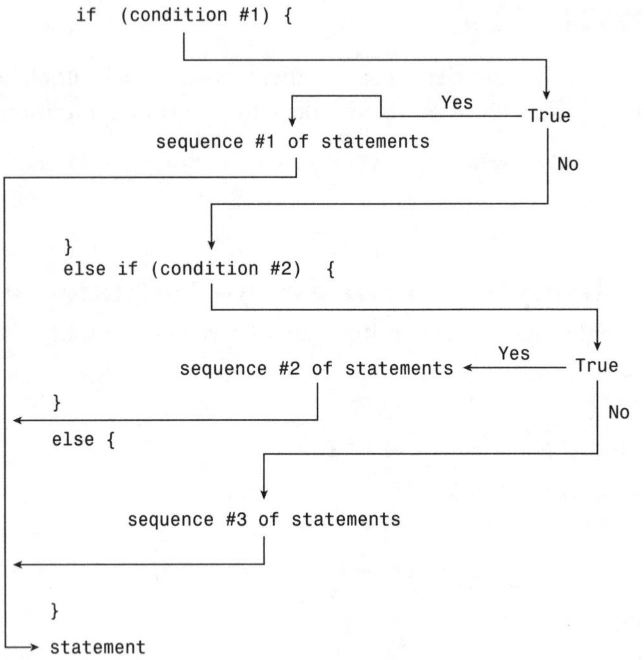

Figure 5.3. *The program flow in the multiple-alternative* `if-else` *statement.*

Let's look at an example. Listing 5.3 shows the source code for program IF3.CPP. The program prompts you to enter a character and uses the multiple-alternative `if-else` statement to determine whether your input is one of the following:

- An uppercase letter
- A lowercase letter
- A digit
- A non-alphanumeric character

Type

Listing 5.3. Source code for the IF3.CPP program.

```
// Program that demonstrates the multiple-alternative if statement

#include <iostream.h>

main()
{
```

```
7:    char c;
8:    cout << "Enter a character : ";
9:    cin >> c;
10:    if (c >= 'A' && c <= 'Z')
11:      cout << "You entered an uppercase letter\n";
12:    else if (c >= 'a' && c <= 'z')
13:      cout << "You entered a lowercase letter\n";
14:    else if (c >= '0' && c <= '9')
15:      cout << "You entered a digit\n";
16:    else
17:      cout << "You entered a non-alphanumeric character\n";
18:    return 0;
19: }
```

Here is a sample session with the program in Listing 5.3:

Output

```
Enter a character : !
You entered a non-alphanumeric character
```

Analysis

The program in Listing 5.3 declares the `char`-typed variable `c` in line 7. The output statement in line 8 prompts you to enter a letter. The input statement in line 9 obtains your input and stores it in variable `c`. The multi-alternative `if-else` statement tests the following conditions:

1. In line 10, the `if` statement determines if the variable `c` contains a letter in the range of A to Z. If this condition is true, the program executes the output statement in line 11. This statement confirms that you entered an uppercase letter. The program then resumes at line 18.
2. If the condition in line 10 is false, the program jumps to the first `else if` clause in line 12. There the program determines whether the variable `c` contains a letter in the range of A to Z. If this condition is true, the program executes the output statement in line 13. This statement confirms that you entered a lowercase letter. The program then resumes at line 18.
3. If the condition in line 12 is false, the program jumps to the second `else if` clause in line 14. There the program determines whether the variable `c` contains a digit. If this condition is true, the program executes the output statement in line 15. This statement confirms that you entered a digit. The program then resumes at line 18.
4. If the condition in line 14 is false, the program jumps to the catch-all `else` clause in line 16 and executes the output statement in line 17. This statement displays a message telling you that your input was neither a letter nor a digit.

The *switch* Statement

The switch statement offers a special form of multiple-alternative decision-making. It enables you to examine the various values of an integer-compatible expression and choose the appropriate course of action.

Syntax

The *switch* Statement

The general syntax for the switch statement is

```
switch (expression) {
  case constant1_1:
    [    case constant1_2: ...]
    <one or more statements>
    break;
  case constant2_1:
    [    case constant2_2: ...]
    <one or more statements>
    break;
...
  case constantN_1:
    [    case constantN_2: ...]
    <one or more statements>
    break;
 default:
    <one or more statements>
}
```

Example:

```
OK = 1;
switch (op) {
  case '+':
    z = x + y;
    break;
  case '-':
    z = x - y;
    break;
  case '*':
    z = x * y;
    break;
  case '/':
    if (y != 0)
      z = x / y;
    else
    OK = 0;
    break;
  default:
    Ok = 0;
}
```

The rules for using a `switch` statement are

1. The `switch` statement requires an integer-compatible value. This value may be a constant, variable, function call, or expression. The `switch` statement does not work with floating-point data types.
2. The value after each `case` label must be a constant.
3. C++ does not support `case` labels with ranges of values. Instead, each value must appear in a separate `case` label.
4. You need to use a `break` statement after each set of executable statements. The `break` statement causes program execution to resume after the end of the current `switch` statement. If you do not use the `break` statement, the program execution resumes at the subsequent `case` labels.
5. The `default` clause is a catch-all clause.
6. The set of statements in each `case` label or grouped `case` labels need not be enclosed in open and close braces.

> **Note:** The lack of single `case` labels with ranges of values makes it more appealing to use a multiple-alternative `if-else` statement if you have a large contiguous range of values.

Figure 5.4 shows the program flow in the multiple-alternative `switch` statement.

Let's look at an example that uses the `switch` statement. Listing 5.4 contains the source code for program SWITCH1.CPP that I obtained by editing Listing 5.3. The new program performs the same task of classifying your character input, this time using a `switch` statement.

Type

Listing 5.4. Source code for the SWITCH1.CPP program.

```
// Program that demonstrates the multiple-alternative switch
  statement

#include <iostream.h>

main()
{
  char c;
  cout << "Enter a character : ";
  cin >> c;
```

continues

Listing 5.4. continued

```
10:   switch (c) {
11:     case 'A':
12:     case 'B':
13:     case 'C':
14:     case 'D':
15:     // other case labels
16:       cout << "You entered an uppercase letter\n";
17:       break;
18:     case 'a':
19:     case 'b':
20:     case 'c':
21:     case 'd':
22:     // other case labels
23:       cout << "You entered a lowercase letter\n";
24:       break;
25:     case '0':
26:     case '1':
27:     case '2':
28:     case '3':
29:     // other case labels
30:       cout << "You entered a digit\n";
31:       break;
32:     default:
33:       cout << "You entered a non-alphanumeric character\n";
34:   }
35:   return 0;
36: }
```

Here is a sample session with the program in Listing 5.4:

Output

```
Enter a character : 2
You entered a digit
```

Analysis

The program in Listing 5.4 declares the `char`-typed variable `c`. The output statement in line 8 prompts you to enter a character. The statement in line 9 stores your input in variable `c`. The `switch` statement starts at line 10. Lines 11 through 14 contain the `case` labels for the letters A to D. I omitted the `case` labels for the rest of the uppercase letters to keep the program short. If the character in variable `c` matches any value in lines 11 through 14, the program executes the output statement in line 16. This statement confirms that you entered an uppercase letter. (Because I reduced the number of `case` labels, the program executes the statement in line 16 only if you enter the letters A to D.) The break statement in line 17 causes the program flow to jump to line 35, past the end of the `switch` statement.

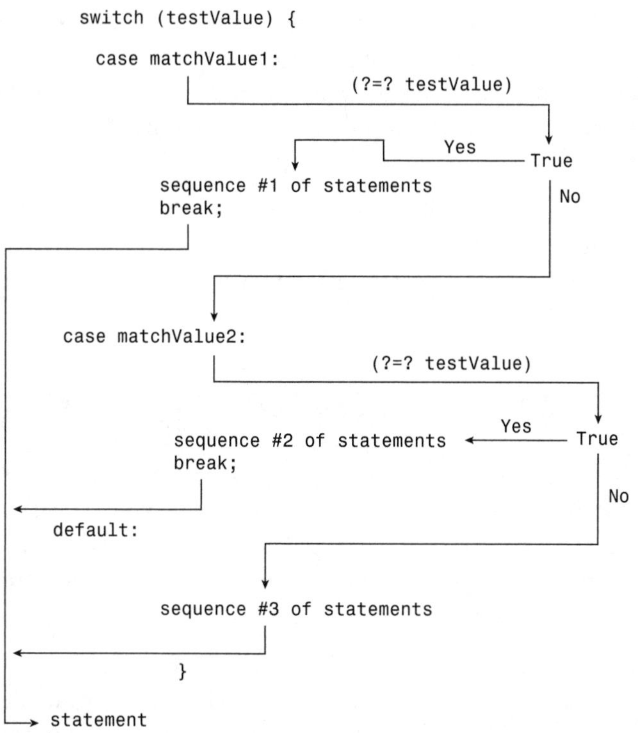
switch (testValue) {
case matchValue1:
(?=? testValue)
Yes
True
sequence #1 of statements
break;
No
case matchValue2:
(?=? testValue)
Yes
sequence #2 of statements
True
break;
No
default:
sequence #3 of statements
}
statement

Figure 5.4. *The program flow in the multiple-alternative* `switch` *statement.*

If the character in variable c does not match any of the `case` labels in lines 11 through 14, the program resumes at line 18, where it encounters another set of `case` labels. These labels are supposed to represent lowercase characters. As you can see, I reduced the number of labels to shorten the program. If the character in variable c matches any value in lines 18 through 21, the program executes the output statement in line 23. This statement confirms that you entered a lowercase letter. (Because I reduced the number of `case` labels, the program executes the statement in line 23 only if you enter the letters a to d.) The `break` statement in line 24 causes the program flow to jump to line 35, past the end of the `switch` statement.

If the character in variable c does match any of the `case` labels in lines 18 through 21, the program resumes at line 25, where it encounters another set of `case` labels. These labels are supposed to represent digits. Again, you can see that I reduced the number of labels to shorten the program. If the character in variable c matches any value in lines 25 through 28, the program executes the output statement in line 30. This statement confirms that you entered a digit. (Because I reduced the number of `case` labels, the program executes the statement in line 30 only if you enter the digits 0 to 3.) The `break` statement in line 31 causes the program flow to jump to line 35, past the end of the `switch` statement.

If the character in variable `c` does not match any `case` label in lines 25 through 28, the program jumps to the catch-all clause in line 32. The program executes the output statement in line 33. This statement tells you that you entered a non-alphanumeric character.

Nested Decision-Making Constructs

Often you need to use nested decision-making constructs to manage nontrivial conditions. Nesting decision-making constructs enables you to deal with complicated conditions using a divide-and-conquer approach. The outer-level constructs help you to test preliminary or more general conditions. The inner-level constructs help you deal with more specific conditions.

Let's look at an example. Listing 5.5 shows the source code for program IF4.CPP. The program prompts you to enter a character. Then the program determines if your input is an uppercase letter, a lowercase letter, or a character that is not a letter. The program displays a message that classifies your input.

Type

Listing 5.5. Source code for the program IF4.CPP.

```
// Program that demonstrates the nested if statements

#include <iostream.h>

main()
{
  char c;
  cout << "Enter a character : ";
  cin >> c;
   if ((c >= 'A' && c <= 'Z') || (c >= 'a' && c <= 'z'))
     if (c >= 'A' && c <= 'Z')
       cout << "You entered an uppercase letter\n";
     else
       cout << "You entered a lowercase letter\n";
   else
     cout << "You entered a non-letter character\n";
   return 0;
}
```

Here is a sample session with the program in Listing 5.5:

Output

```
Enter a character : a
You entered a lowercase letter
```

Analysis

The program in Listing 5.5 declares the `char`-typed variable `c`. The output statement in line 8 prompts you to enter a character. The statement in line 9 stores your input in variable `c`. The program uses nested `if-else` statements that begin at lines 10 and 11. The outer `if-else` statement determines whether or not the variable `c` contains a letter. If the tested condition is true, the program executes the inner `if-else` statement in line 11. Otherwise, the program resumes at the `else` clause of the outer `if-else` statement and executes the output statement in line 16. This statement tells you that your input was not a letter.

The program uses the inner `if-else` statement to further examine the condition of the outer `if-else` statement. The `if-else` statement in line 11 determines whether or not the variable `c` contains an uppercase letter. If this condition is true, the program executes the output statement in line 12. Otherwise, the program executes the `else` clause statement in line 14. These output statements tell you whether you entered an uppercase or a lowercase letter. After executing the inner `if-else` statement, the program jumps to line 17, past the end of the outer `if-else` statement.

Summary

Today's lesson presents the various decision-making constructs in C++, including the following:

- The single-alternative `if` statement, such as

```
if (tested_condition)
  statement; ¦ {  <sequence of statements> }
```

- The dual-alternative `if-else` statement, such as

```
if (tested_condition)
  statement1; { <sequence #1 of statements> }
else
  statement1; { <sequence #1 of statements> }
```

- The multiple-alternative `if-else` statement, such as

```
if (tested_condition1)
  statement1; ¦ { <sequence #1 of statement> }
```

```
else if (tested_condition2)
  statement2; ¦ { <sequence #2 of statement> }
...
else if (tested_conditionN)
   statementN; ¦ { <sequence #N of statement> }
[else
  statementN+1; ¦ { <sequence #N+1 of statement> }]
```

- The multiple-alternative `switch` statement, such as

```
switch (caseVar) {
  case constant1_1:
  case constant1_2:
    <other case labels>
    <one or more statements>
    break;
  case constant2_1:
  case constant2_2:
    <other case labels>
    <one or more statements>
    break;
...
  case constantN_1:
  case constantN_2:
    <other case labels>
    <one or more statements>
    break;

  default:
    <one or more statements>
    break;
}
```

You also learn about the following topics:

- The `if` statements require you to observe two rules:

  The tested condition must be enclosed in parentheses.

  Blocks of statements are enclosed in pairs of open and close braces.

- Nested decision-making constructs empower you to deal with complex conditions using a divide-and-conquer approach. The outer-level constructs help you in testing preliminary or more general conditions. The inner-level constructs assist in handling more specific conditions.

Q&A

Q Does C++ impose any rules for indenting statements in the clauses of an `if` statement?

A No. The indentation is purely up to you. Typical indentations range from 2 to 4 spaces. Using indentations makes your listings much more readable. Here is the case of an `if` statement with unindented clause statements:

```
if (i > 0)
  j = i * i;
else
  j = 10 - i;
```

Compare the readability of that listing with this indented version:

```
if (i > 0)
  j = i * i;
else
  j = 10 - i;
```

The indented version is much easier to read.

Q What are the rules for writing the condition of an `if-else` statement?

A There are two schools of thought. The first one recommends that you write the condition so that it is more often true than not. The second school recommends avoiding negative expressions (those that use the relational operator `!=` and the Boolean operator `!`). Programmers in this camp translate this `if` statement:

```
if (i != 0)
  j = 100 / i;
else
  j = 1;
```

into the following equivalent form:

```
if (i == 0)
  j = 1;
```

```
else
  j = 100 \ i;
```

even though the likelihood of variable `i` storing 0 might be very low.

Q How do I handle a condition such as the following that divides by a variable that can possibly be zero?

```
if (i != 0 && 1/i > 1)
  j = i * i;
```

A C++ does not always evaluate the entire tested condition. This partial evaluation occurs when a term in the Boolean expression renders the entire expression false or true, regardless of the values of the other terms. In this case, if variable `i` is 0, the run-time system does not evaluate the term `1/i` > 1. This is because the term `i != 0` is false and would render the entire expression false, regardless of what the second term yields.

Q Is it really necessary to include an `else` or default clause in multi-alternative `if-else` and `switch` statements?

A Programmers highly recommend the inclusion of these catch-all clauses to ensure that the multiple-alternative statements handle all conditions.

Workshop

The Workshop provides quiz questions to help you solidify your understanding of the material covered, and exercises to provide you with experience in using what you've learned. Try to understand the quiz and exercise answers before continuing on to the next day's lesson. Answers are provided in Appendix B, "Answers."

Quiz

1. Simplify the following nested `if` statements by replacing them with a single `if` statement:

```
if (i > 0)
  if (i < 10)
    cout << "i = " << i << "\n";
```

2. Simplify the following `if` statements by replacing them with a single `if` statement:

```
if (i > 0) {
  j = i * i;
  cout << "j = " << j << "\n";
}
if (i < 0) {
  j = 4 * i;
  cout << "j = " << j << "\n";
}
if (i == 0) {
  j = 10 + i;
  cout << "j = " << j << "\n";
}
```

3. True or false? The following `if` statements perform the same tasks as the `if-else` statement:

```
if (i < 0) {
  i = 10 + i;
  j = i * i;
  cout << "i = " << i << "\n";
  cout << "j = " << j << "\n";
}
if (i >= 0) {
  k = 4 * i + 1;
  cout << "k = " << k << "\n";

}

if (i < 0) {
  i = 10 - i;
  j = i * i;
  cout << "i = " << i << "\n";
  cout << "j = " << j << "\n";
}
else {
  k = 4 * i + 1;
  cout << "k = " << k << "\n";
}
```

4. Simplify the following `if-else` statement:

```
if (i > 0 && i < 100)
  j = i * i;
else if (i > 10 && i < 50)
  j = 10 + i;
else if (i >= 100)
  j = i;
else
  j = 1;
```

5. What is wrong with the following `if` statement?

```
if (i > (1 + i * i)) {
  j = i * I
  cout << "i = " << i << " and j = " << j << "\n";
}
```

Exercises

1. Write the program IF5.CPP to solve for the roots of a quadratic equation. The quadratic equation is

   $AX^2 + B^X + C = 0$

   The roots of the quadratic equation are

   ```
   root1 = √(-B + (B2 - 4AC)) / (2A)
   root2 = √(-B - (B2 - 4AC)) / (2A)
   ```

   If the term in the square root is negative, the roots are complex. If the term in the square root term is zero, the two roots are the same and are equal to `-B/(2A)`.

2. Write the program SWITCH2.CPP, which implements a simple four-function calculator. The program should prompt you for the operand and the operator and display both the input and the result. Include error checking for bad operators and the attempt to divide by zero.

6

Loops

WEEK
1

Recall from Day 3 that loops are powerful language constructs that enable computers to excel in achieving repetitive tasks. Computers are able to repeat tasks quickly, accurately, and tirelessly—an area where computers seem to do a better job than humans. Today's lesson presents the following loops in C++:

- The `for` loop statement
- The `do-while` loop statement
- The `while` loop statement
- Skipping iterations
- Exiting loops
- Nested loops

The *for* Loop

The `for` loop in C++ is a versatile loop because it offers both fixed and conditional iterations. The latter feature of the `for` loop deviates from the typical use of the `for` loop in other programming languages, such as Pascal and Basic.

Syntax

The *for* Loop

The general syntax for the `for` loop statement is

```
for (<initialization of loop control variables>;
     <loop continuation test>;
     <increment/decrement of loop control variables>)
```

Example:

```
for (i = 0; i < 10; i++)
  cout << "The cube of " << i << " = " << i * i * i << "\n";
```

The `for` loop statement has three components, all of which are optional. The first component initializes the loop control variables. (C++ permits you to use more than one loop control variable.) The second part of the loop is the condition that determines whether or not the loop makes another iteration. The last part of the `for` loop is the clause that increments and/or decrements the loop control variables.

Note: The C++ `for` loop allows you to declare the loop control variables. Such variables exist in the scope of the loop.

Let's look at an example. Listing 6.1 contains the source code for program FOR1.CPP. The program prompts you to define a range of integers by specifying its lower and upper bounds. Then the program calculates the sum of integers in the range you specify, as well as the average value.

Type

Listing 6.1. Source code for the program FOR1.CPP.

```
 1: // Program that calculates a sum and average of a range of
 2: // integers using a for loop
 3:
 4: #include <iostream.h>
 5:
 6: main()
 7: {
 8:     double sum = 0;
 9:     double sumx = 0.0;
10:     int first, last, temp;
11:
12:     cout << "Enter the first integer : ";
13:     cin >> first;
14:     cout << "Enter the last integer : ";
15:     cin >> last;
16:     if (first > last) {
17:       temp= first;
18:       first = last;
19:       last = temp;
20:     }
21:     for (int i = first; i <= last; i++) {
22:       sum++;
23:       sumx += (double)i;
24:     }
25:     cout << "Sum of integers from "
26:          << first << " to " << last << " = "
27:          << sumx << "\n";
28:     cout << "Average value = " << sumx / sum;
29:     return 0;
30: }
```

Here is a sample session with the program in Listing 6.1:

Output

```
Enter the first integer : 1
Enter the last integer : 100
Sum of integers from 1 to 100 = 5050
Average value = 50.5
```

Analysis

The program in Listing 6.1 declares a collection of `int`-typed and `double`-typed variables in function `main`. The function initializes the summation variables, `sum` and `sumx`, to 0. The input and output statements in lines 12 through 15 prompt you to enter the integers that define a range of values. The program stores these integers in the variables first and last. The `if` statement in line 16 determines whether or not the value in variable `first` is greater than the value in variable `last`. If this condition is true, the program executes the block of statements in lines 17 through 19. These statements swap the values in variables `first` and `last`, using the variable `temp` as a swap buffer. Thus, the `if` statement ensures that the integer in variable `first` is less than or equal to the integer in variable `last`.

The program carries out the summation using the `for` loop in line 21. The loop declares its own control variable, `i`, and initializes it with the value in variable `first`. The loop continuation condition is `i <= last`. This condition indicates that the loop iterates as long as `i` is less than or equal to the value in variable `last`. The loop increment component is `i++`, which increments the loop control variable by 1 for every iteration. The loop contains two statements. The first statement increments the value in variable `sum`. The second statement adds the value of `i` (after typecasting it to `double`) to the variable `sumx`.

Note: I can rewrite the `for` loop to move the first loop statement to the loop increment component:

```
for (int i = first; i <= last; i++, sum++)
  sumx += (double)i;
```

The output statement in lines 25 through 27 displays the sum and average of integers in the range you specified.

To illustrate the flexibility of the `for` loop, I created the program FOR2.CPP, shown in Listing 6.2, by editing program FOR1.CPP. The two programs perform the same tasks and interact identically with you. The changes I made are in lines 10 and 21 through 25. Line 10 declares the loop control variable. In line 21, I initialize the variable `i` using the value in variable `first`. The `for` loop is located at line 22. The loop has no initialization part because I took care of that in line 21. In addition, I removed the loop increment component and compensated for it by applying the post-increment operator to variable `i` in line 24.

Type

Listing 6.2. Source code for the program FOR2.CPP.

```
1: // Program that calculates a sum and average of a range of
2: // integers using a for loop
3:
```

```
#include <iostream.h>

main()
{
    double sum = 0;
    double sumx = 0.0;
    int first, last, temp, i;

    cout << "Enter the first integer : ";
    cin >> first;
    cout << "Enter the last integer : ";
    cin >> last;
    if (first > last) {
      temp= first;
      first = last;
      last = temp;
    }
    i = first;
    for (; i <= last; ) {
      sum++;
      sumx += (double)i++;
    }
    cout << "Sum of integers from "
         << first << " to " << last << " = "
         << sumx << "\n";
    cout << "Average value = " << sumx / sum;
    return 0;
}
```

Here is a sample session with the program in Listing 6.2:

Output

```
Enter the first integer : 10
Enter the last integer : 100
Sum of integers from 10 to 100 = 5005
Average value = 55
```


Open Loops Using the *for* Loops

When I introduced you to the C++ `for` loop, I stated that the three components of the `for` loop are optional. In fact, C++ permits you to leave these three components empty!

NEW TERM When you leave the three components of a loop empty, the result is an *open loop*.

It is worthwhile pointing out that other languages, such as Ada and Modula-2, do support formal open loops and provide mechanisms to exit these loops. C++ permits you to exit from a loop in one of the following two ways:

1. The `break` statement causes the program execution to resume after the end of the current loop. Use the `break` statement when you wish to exit a `for` loop and resume with the remaining parts of the program.
2. The `exit` function (declared in the STDLIB.H header file) allows you to exit the program. Use the `exit` function if you want to stop iterating and also exit the program.

Let's look at an example. Listing 6.3 contains the source code for program FOR3.CPP. The program uses an open loop to repeatedly prompt you for a number. The program takes your input and displays it along with its reciprocal value. Then the program asks you whether or not you wish to calculate the reciprocal of another number. If you type in the letter `Y` or `y`, the program performs another iteration. Otherwise, the program ends. If you keep typing `Y` or `y` for the latter prompt, the program keeps running—at least until the computer breaks down!

Type

Listing 6.3. Source code for the program FOR3.CPP.

```
// Program that demonstrates using the
// for loop to emulate an infinite loop.

#include <iostream.h>
#include <ctype.h>

main()
{
   char ch;
    double x, y;

    // for loop with empty parts
    for (;;) {
       cout << "\nEnter a number : ";
       cin >> x;
       // process number if non-zero
       if (x != 0) {
         y = 1/ x;
         cout << "1/(" << x << ") = " << y << "\n";
         cout << "More calculations? (Y/N) ";
         cin >> ch;
         ch = toupper(ch);
         if (ch != 'Y')
            break;
       }
       else
         // display error message
         cout << "Error: cannot accept 0\n";
    }
    return 0;
}
```

Here is a sample session with the program in Listing 6.3:

Output

```
Enter a number : 5
1/(5) = 0.2
More calculations? (Y/N) y

Enter a number : 12
1/(12) = 0.0833333
More calculations? (Y/N) y

Enter a number : 16
1/(16) = 0.0625
More calculations? (Y/N) n
```

Analysis

The program in Listing 6.3 declares the `char`-typed variable c and two `double`-typed variables, x and y. The function `main` uses the `for` loop, in line 13, as an open loop by eliminating all three loop components. The output statement in line 14 prompts you to enter a number. The input statement in line 15 obtains your input and stores it in variable `x`. The `if-else` statement in line 17 determines if the value in variable x is not zero. If this condition is true, the program executes the block of statements in lines 18 through 24. Otherwise, the program executes the `else` clause statement in line 28. This statement displays an error message.

The statement in line 18 assigns the reciprocal of the value in variable `x` to variable `y`. The output statement in line 19 displays the values in variables `x` and `y`. The output statement in line 20 prompts you for more calculations, and requires a Y/N (in either uppercase or lowercase) type of answer. The input statement in line 21 stores your single-character input in variable `c`. The statement in line 22 converts your input into uppercase, using the function `toupper` (this function is prototyped in the CTYPE.H header file). The `if` statement in line 23 determines whether or not the character in variable `c` is not the letter Y. If this condition is true, the program executes the `break` statement in line 24. This statement causes the program execution to exit the open loop and to resume at line 30.

6

The *do-while* Loop

The `do-while` loop in C++ is a conditional loop. Therefore, the `do-while` loop iterates at least once.

NEW TERM A *conditional loop* iterates as long as a condition is true. This condition is tested at the end of the loop.

Syntax

The *do-while* Loop

The general syntax for the `do-while` loop is

```
do {
  sequence of statements
} while (condition);
```

Example:

The following loop displays the squares of 2 to 10:

```
int i = 2;
do {
  cout << i << "^2 = " << i * i << "\n";
} while (++i < 11);
```

Let's look at an example. Listing 6.4 shows the source code for program DOWHILE1.CPP, which essentially calculates square root values. The program performs the following tasks:

- Prompts you to enter a number (if you enter a negative number, the program reprompts you for a number)
- Calculates and displays the square root of the number you keyed in
- Asks you if you wish to enter another number (if you enter the letter Y or y, the program resumes at step number 1; otherwise, the program ends)

Type

Listing 6.4. Source code for the program DOWHILE1.CPP.

```
// Program that demonstrates the do-while loop

#include <iostream.h>

const double TOLERANCE = 1.0e-7;

double abs(double x)
{
  return (x >= 0) ? x : -x;
}

double sqroot(double x)
{
  double guess = x / 2;
  do {
    guess = (guess + x / guess) / 2;
  } while (abs(guess * guess - x) > TOLERANCE);
  return guess;
}

double getNumber()
```

```
22: {
23:   double x;
24:   do {
25:     cout << "Enter a number: ";
26:     cin >> x;
27:   } while (x < 0);
28:   return x;
29: }
30:
31: main()
32: {
33:    char c;
34:    double x, y;
35:
36:    do {
37:       x = getNumber();
38:       y = sqroot(x);
39:       cout << "Sqrt(" << x << ") = " << y << "\n"
40:            << "Enter another number? (Y/N) ";
41:       cin >> c;
42:       cout << "\n";
43:    } while (c == 'Y' || c == 'y');
44:    return 0;
45: }
```

Here is a sample session with the program in Listing 6.4:

Output

```
Enter a number: 25
Sqrt(25) = 5
Enter another number? (Y/N) y

Enter a number: 144
Sqrt(144) = 12
Enter another number? (Y/N) n
```

Analysis

The program in Listing 6.4 declares the global constant TOLERANCE and the functions `abs`, `sqroot`, `getNumber`, and `main`. The function `abs`, located in line 7, returns the absolute value of `double`-typed arguments.

The function `sqroot`, located in line 12, returns the square root of the parameter `x`. The function sets the initial guess for the square root to `x / 2` in line 14. Then the function uses a `do-while` loop to refine iteratively the guess for the square root. The condition in the `while` clause determines if the absolute difference between the square of the current guess and the parameter `x` is greater than the allowable error (represented by the constant `TOLERANCE`). The loop iterates as long as this condition is true. The function returns the guess for the square root in line 18. The function `sqroot` implements Newton's method for iteratively obtaining the square root of a number.

The function `getNumber`, located in line 21, prompts you for a number and stores your input in the local variable `x`. The function uses a `do-while` loop to ensure that you enter a non-negative number. The `while` clause in line 27 determines if the value in variable `x` is negative. As long as this condition is true, the `do-while` loop iterates. In line 28 the return statement yields the value of `x`.

The function `main`, located in line 31, uses a `do-while` loop to perform the following tasks:

- Prompts you for a number by calling function `getNumber` (the statement in line 37 contains the function `call` and assigns the result to the local variable `x`)
- Calculates the square root of `x` by calling function `sqroot`, and assigns the result to variable `y` (the statement which contains this function `call` is in line 38)
- Displays the values in variables `x` and `y`
- Asks you if you want to enter another number (the input statement in line 41 takes your single-character Y/N input and stores it in variable `c`)

The `while` clause, located in line 43, determines if the variable `c` contains either the letter Y or y. The `do-while` loop iterates as long as this condition is true.

The program in Listing 6.4 illustrates the following uses for the `do-while` loop:

1. *Iterative calculations.* The loop in function `sqroot` shows this aspect.
2. *Data validation.* The loop in function `getNumber` illustrates this aspect.
3. *Program continuation.* The loop in function `main` shows this aspect.

The *while* Loop

The `while` loop in C++ is another conditional loop that iterates as long as a condition is true. Thus, the `while` loop may not iterate if the tested condition is initially false.

Syntax

The *while* Loop

The general syntax of the `while` loop is

```
while (condition)
  statement; | { sequence of statements }
```

Example:

```
function power(double x, int n)
{
  double pwr = 1;
```

```
  while (n-- > 0)
    pwr *= x;
  return pwr;
}
```

Let's look at an example. Listing 6.5 shows the source code for program WHILE1.CPP. This program performs the same operations as program FOR1.CPP, in Listing 6.1. The two programs interact in the same way and yield the same results.

Type

Listing 6.5. Source code for the program WHILE1.CPP.

```
// Program that demonstrates the do-while loop

#include <iostream.h>

main()
{
    double sum = 0;
    double sumx = 0.0;
    int first, last, temp, i;

     cout << "Enter the first integer : ";
     cin >> first;
     cout << "Enter the last integer : ";
     cin >> last;
     if (first > last) {
       temp= first;
       first = last;
       last = temp;
     }
     i = first;
     while (i <= last) {
       sum++;
       sumx += (double)i++;
     }
     cout << "Sum of integers from "
          << first << " to " << last << " = "
          << sumx << "\n";
     cout << "Average value = " << sumx / sum;
     return 0;
}
```

Here is a sample session with the program in Listing 6.5:

Output

```
Enter the first integer : 1
Enter the last integer : 100
Sum of integers from 1 to 100 = 5050
Average value = 50.5
```

Analysis Because the programs in Listings 6.5 and 6.1 are similar, I focus on lines 20 through 24 where the main difference between the two programs lies. The statement in line 20 assigns the value of variable first to variable `i`. The `while` loop starts at line 21. The loop iterates as long as the value in variable `i` is less than or equal to the value in variable `last`. The variable `i` plays the role of the loop control variable. The statement in line 22 increments the value in variable `sum`. The statement in line 23 adds the value in variable `i` to the variable `sumx` and also increments the variable `i`. The statement performs the latter task by applying the post-increment operator to the variable `i`.

Skipping Loop Iterations

C++ enables you to jump to the end of a loop and resume the next iteration using the `continue` statement. This programming feature permits your loop to skip iteration for special values, which may cause run-time errors.

Syntax

The *continue* Statement

The general form for using the *continue* statement is

```
<loop-start clause> {
  // sequence #1 of statements
  if (skipCondition)
    continue;
  // sequence #2 of statements
} <loop-end clause>
```

Example (in a `for` loop):

```
double x, y;
for (int i = -10; i < 11; i++) {
  x = i;
  if (i == 1)
    continue;
  y = 1/sqrt(x * x - 1);
  cout << "1/sqrt(" << (x*x-1) << ") = " << y << "\n";
}
```

This form shows that the evaluation of the first sequence of statements in the `for` loop gives rise to a condition tested in the `if` statement. If that condition is true, the `if` statement invokes the `continue` statement to skip the second sequence of statements in the `for` loop.

Let's look at an example. Listing 6.6 shows the source code for program FOR4.CPP. The program displays the table of values for the function $f(X) = \sqrt{(X^2 - 9)}$ at integer values between -10 and 10. Because the integers between -2 and 2 yield complex results, which the program avoids, the table does not display the complex values for f(X) between -2 and 2.

Type

Listing 6.6. Source code for the program FOR4.CPP.

```
// Program that demonstrates using the continue statement
// to skip iterations.

#include <iostream.h>
#include <math.h>


double f(double x)
{
   return sqrt(x * x - 9);
}

main()
{
    double x, y;

    cout << "        X";
    cout << "          f(X)\n";
    cout << "_________________________________\n\n";
    // for loop with empty parts
    for (int i = -10; i <= 10; i++) {
      if (i > -3 && i < 3)
        continue;
      x = (double)i;
      y = f(x);
      cout << "      ";
      cout.width(3);
      cout << x << "        ";
      cout.width(7);
      cout << y << "\n";
    }
    return 0;
}
```

Here is a sample session with the program in Listing 6.6:

Output

```
X          f(X)
_________________________________

-10        9.53939
-9         8.48528
-8         7.4162
-7         6.32456
```

```
-6          5.19615
-5                4
-4          2.64575
-3                0
3                 0
4           2.64575
5                 4
6           5.19615
7           6.32456
8            7.4162
9           8.48528
10          9.53939
```

Analysis The program in Listing 6.6 declares the function `f` to represent the mathematical function `f(X)`. The function `main` declares the `double`-typed variables `x` and `y` in line 15. The output statements in lines 17 through 19 display the table's heading. The `for` loop in line 21 declares its own control variable and iterates between -10 to 10, in increments of 1. The first statement inside the loop is the `if` statement located at line 22. This statement determines if the value in variable `i` is greater than -3 and less than 3. If this condition is true, the program executes the `continue` statement in line 23. Thus, the `if` statement enables the `for` loop to skip error-generating iterations and resume with the next iteration. The statement in line 24 assigns the value in variable `i` to variable `x`. The statement in line 25 calls the function `f` and supplies it with the argument `x`. The statement then assigns the result to variable `y`. The output statements in lines 25 through 30 display the values of variable `x` and `y`. The statements use the function `width` for simple formatting.

Exiting Loops

C++ supports the `break` statement to exit a loop. The `break` statement makes the program resume after the end of the current loop.

Syntax

The *break* Statement

The general form for using the `break` statement in a loop is

```
<start-loop clause> {
  // sequence #1 of statements
  if (exitLoopCondition)
    break;
  // sequence #2 of statements
} <end-loop clause>
// sequence #3 of statements
```

Example:

```
// calculate the factorial of n
factorial = 1;
for (int i = 1; ; i++) {
  if (i > n)
    break;
  factorial *= (double)i;
}
```

This form shows that the evaluation of the first sequence of statements in the `for` loop gives rise to a condition tested in the `if` statement. If that condition is true, the `if` statement invokes the `break` statement to exit the loop altogether. The program execution resumes at the third sequence of statements.

For a good example that uses the `break` statement, I recommend that you reexamine the FOR3.CPP program in Listing 6.3.

Nested Loops

Nested loops enable you to contain repetitive tasks as part of other repetitive tasks. C++ allows you to nest any kind of loops to just about any level needed. Nested loops are frequently used to process arrays (covered in Day 7).

An example that uses nested loops, Listing 6.7 shows the source code for program NESTFOR1.CPP. The program displays a table for square roots for whole numbers in the range of 1 to 10. The program uses an outer loop to iterate over the above range of numbers, and employs an inner loop to iteratively calculate the square root.

Type

Listing 6.7. Source code for the program NESTFOR1.CPP.

```
// Program that demonstrates nested loops

#include <stdio.h>

const double TOLERANCE = 1.0e-7;
const int MIN_NUM = 1;
const int MAX_NUM = 10;

double abs(double x)
{
  return (x >= 0) ? x : -x;
}

main()
{
   double x, sqrt;

```

continues

Listing 6.7. continued

```
18:     printf("  X        Sqrt(X)\n");
19:     printf("______________________\n\n");
20:     // outer loop
21:     for (int i = MIN_NUM; i <= MAX_NUM; i++) {
22:       x = (double)i;
23:       sqrt = x /2;
24:       // inner loop
25:       do {
26:         sqrt = (sqrt + x / sqrt) / 2;
27:       } while (abs(sqrt * sqrt - x) > TOLERANCE);
28:       printf("%4.1f     %8.6lf\n", x, sqrt);
29:     }
30:     return 0;
31: }
```

Here is a sample session with the program in Listing 6.7:

Output

```
X       Sqrt(X)
______________________

1.0     1.000000
2.0     1.414214
3.0     1.732051
4.0     2.000000
5.0     2.236068
6.0     2.449490
7.0     2.645751
8.0     2.828427
9.0     3.000000
10.0    3.162278
```

Analysis

The program in Listing 6.7 includes the header file STDIO.H in order to use the `printf` output function with its powerful formatting capabilities. The lines 5 through 7 define the constants, `TOLERANCE`, `MIN_NUM`, and `MAX_NUM`, to represent the tolerance in square root values, the first number in the output table, and the last number in the output table. The program defines the function `abs` to return the absolute number of a `double`-typed number.

The function `main` declares the `double`-typed variables `x` and `sqrt`. The output statements in lines 18 and 19 display the table's heading. Line 21 contains the outer loop, a `for` loop. This loop declares its control variable, `i`, and iterates from `MIN_NUM` to `MAX_NUM`, in increments of 1. Line 22 stores the typecast value of `i` in variable `x`. The statement in line 23 obtains the initial guess for the square root and stores it in variable `sqrt`. Line 25 contains the inner loop, a `do-while` loop that iterates to refine the guess for the square root. The statement in line 26 refines the guess for the square root. The `while` clause in line 27 determines whether or not the refined guess is adequate. The output statement in line 28 displays the formatted values for the variables `x` and `sqrt`.

Summary

Today's lesson covers the C++ loops and topics related to loops. You learn about the following:

- The `for` loop in C++ has the following general syntax:

  ```
  for (<initialization of loop control variables>;
       <loop continuation test>;
       <increment/decrement of loop control variables>)
  ```

  The `for` loop contains three components: the loop initialization, the loop continuation condition, and the increment/decrement of the loop variables.

- The conditional loop `do-while` has the following general syntax:

  ```
  do {
    sequence of statements
  } while (condition);
  ```

  The `do-while` loop iterates at least once.

- The conditional `while` loop has the following general syntax:

  ```
  while (condition)
  statement; ¦ { sequence of statements }
  ```

  The `while` loop may not iterate if its tested condition is initially false.

- The `continue` statement enables you to jump to the end of the loop and resume with the next iteration. The advantage of the continue statement is that it uses no labels to direct the jump.

- Open loops are for loops with empty components. The `break` statement enables you to exit the current loop and resume program execution at the first statement that comes after the loop. The `exit` function (declared in STDLIB.H) enables you to make a critical loop exit by halting the C++ program altogether.

- Nested loops empower you to contain repetitive tasks as part of other repetitive tasks. C++ allows you to nest any kind of loop to just about any level needed.

Q&A

Q How can a `while` loop simulate a `for` loop?

A Here is a simple example:

```
                                       int i = 1;
for (int i = 1; i <= 10; i +=2) {      while (i <= 10) {
  cout << i << "\n";                     cout << i << "\n";
                                         i += 2;
}                                      }
```

The `while` loop needs a leading statement that initializes the loop control variable. Also notice that the `while` loop uses a statement inside it to alter the value of the loop control variable.

Q How can a `while` loop simulate a `do-while` loop?

A Here is a simple example:

```
i = 1;                        i = 1;
do {                          while (i <= 10) {
  cout << i << "\n";            cout << i << "\n";
  i += 2;                       i += 2;
} while (i <= 10);            }
```

The two loops have the same condition in their `while` clauses.

Q How can the open `for` loop emulate the `while` and `do-while` loops?

A The open `for` loop is able to emulate the other C++ loops by placing the loop-escape `if` statement near the beginning or end of the loop. Here is how the open `for` loop emulates a sample `while` loop:

```
i = 1;                        i = 1;
while (i <= 10) {             for (;;) {
  if (i > 10) break;
  cout << i << "\n"             cout << i << "\n"
  i += 2;                       i += 2;
}                             }
```

Notice that the open `for` loop uses a loop-escape `if` statement as the first statement inside the loop. The condition tested by the `if` statement is the logical reverse of the `while` loop condition. Here is a simple example showing the emulation of the `do-while` loop:

```
i = 1;                          i = 1;
do {                            for (;;) {
  cout << i << "\n"               cout << i << "\n"
  i += 2;                         i += 2;
  if (i > 10) break;
} while (i <= 10);              }
```

The open `for` loop uses a loop-escape `if` statement right before the end of the loop. The `if` statement tests the reverse condition as the `do-while` loop.

Q In nested `for` loops, can I use the loop control variable of the outer loops as part of the range of values for the inner loops?

A Yes. C++ does not object to such use. Here is a simple example:

```
for (int i = 1; i <= 100; i += 5)
for (int j = i; j <= 100; j++)
cout << i * j << "\n";
```

Q Does C++ restrict nesting of the various types of loops?

A No, you can nest any combination of loops in a C++ program.

Workshop

The Workshop provides quiz questions to help you solidify your understanding of the material covered and exercises to provide you with experience in using what you've learned. Try to understand the quiz and exercise answers before continuing on to the next day's lesson. Answers are provided in Appendix B, "Answers."

Quiz

1. What is wrong with the following loop?

```
i = 1;
while (i < 10) {
  j = i * i - 1;
  k = 2 * j - I;
  cout << "i = " << i << "\n";
  cout << "j = "  <<  j << "\n";
  cout << "k = " << k << "\n";
}
```

2. What is the output of the following for loop?

```
for (int i = 5; i < 10; i + 2)
  cout << i - 2 << "\n";
```

3. What is the output of the following for loop?

```
for (int i = 5; i < 10; )
  cout << i - 2 << "\n";
```

4. What is wrong with the following code?

```
for (int i = 1; i <= 10; I++)
  for (i = 8; i <= 12; I++)
    cout << i << "\n";
```

5. Where is the error in the following nested loops?

```
for (int i = 1; i <= 10; I++)
  cout << i * i << "\n";
for (int i = 1; i <= 10; I++)
  cout << i * i * i << "\n";
```

6. Where is the error in the following loop?

```
i = 1;
while (1 > 0) {
  cout << i << "\n";
  i++;
}
```

7. The factorial of a number is the product of the sequence of integers from 1 to that number. The following general equation defines the factorial (which uses the symbol !):

```
n! = 1 * 2 * 3 * ... * n
```

Here is a C++ program that calculates the factorial of a number. The problem is that for whatever positive value you enter, the program displays 0 value for the factorial. Where is the error in the program?

```
int n;
double factorial;
cout << "Enter positive integer : ";
cin >> n;
```

```
for (int i = 1; i <= n; i++)
  factorial *= i;
cout << n << "!= " << factorial;
```

Exercises

1. Write the program for FOR5.CPP which uses a `for` loop to obtain and display the sum of odd integers in the range of 11 to 121.
2. Write the program WHILE2.CPP which uses a `while` loop to obtain and display the sum of the squared odd integers in the range of 11 to 121.
3. Write the program DOWHILE2.CPP which uses a `do-while` loop to obtain and display the sum of the squared odd integers in the range of 11 to 121.

```
[illegible]
[illegible]
[illegible]
```

Exercises

1. Write the program [illegible]FOR[illegible], which uses a for loop to [illegible] and display the [illegible] in the range of [illegible].

2. Write the program [illegible], which uses a while loop to [illegible] and display the [illegible] in the range of [illegible].

3. Write the program DOWHILE[illegible], which uses a do-while loop to [illegible] and display [illegible] in the range of [illegible].

7

Arrays

WEEK 1

Arrays are among the most popular data structures. They allow programs to store data for processing later on. Most popular programming languages support static arrays. Many languages also support dynamic arrays.

NEW TERM An *array* is a group of variables.

Today, you learn about the following topics related to static arrays:

- Declaring single-dimensional arrays
- Using single-dimensional arrays
- Initializing single-dimensional arrays
- Declaring single-dimensional arrays as function parameters
- Sorting arrays
- Searching arrays
- Declaring multidimensional arrays
- Using multidimensional arrays
- Initializing multidimensional arrays
- Declaring multidimensional arrays as function parameters

Declaring Single-Dimensional Arrays

The single-dimensional array is the simplest kind of array. In a single-dimensional array, each variable is individually accessed using a single index.

NEW TERM A *single-dimensional array* is a group of variables that share the same name (which is the name of the array).

Syntax

A Single-Dimensional Array

The general syntax for declaring a single-dimensional array is

```
type arrayName[numberOfElements];
```

C++ requires you to observe the following rules in declaring single-dimensional arrays:

1. The lower bound of a C++ array is set at 0. C++ does not allow you to override or alter this lower bound.
2. Declaring a C++ array entails specifying the number of members. Keep in mind that the number of members is equal to the upper bound plus one.

The valid range of indices for this general form extends between `0` and *`numberOfElements - 1`*.

Examples:

```
int intArray[10];
char name[31];
double x[100];
```

Using Single-Dimensional Arrays

Using a single-dimensional array involves stating both its name and the valid index to access one of its members. Depending on where the reference to an array element occurs, it can either store or recall a value. The simple rules to remember are

1. Assign a value to an array element before accessing that element to recall data. Otherwise, you get garbage data.
2. Use a valid index.

DO	DON'T

DO make reasonable checks for the indices that access the arrays.

DON'T assume that indices are always valid.

Let's look at an example. Listing 7.1 shows the source code for the program ARRAY1.CPP. The program uses a 30-element numeric array to calculate the average for the data in a numeric array. The program performs the following tasks:

- Prompts you to enter the number of actual data points (this value must lie in the range of valid numbers indicated by the prompting message)
- Prompts you to enter the data for the array elements
- Calculates the average of the data in the array
- Displays the average value

Type

Listing 7.1. Source code for the program ARRAY1.CPP.

```
/*
  C++ program that demonstrates the use of one-dimension
  arrays. The average value of the array is calculated.
*/

#include <iostream.h>

const int MAX = 30;

main()
{

    double x[MAX];
    double sum, sumx = 0.0, mean;
    int i, n;

    do { // obtain number of data points
        cout << "Enter number of data points [2 to "
             << MAX << "] : ";
        cin >> n;
        cout << "\n";
    } while (n < 2 || n > MAX);

    // prompt user for data
    for (i = 0; i < n; i++) {
        cout << "X[" << i << "] : ";
        cin >> x[i];
    }

    // initialize summations
    sum = n;

    // calculate sum of observations
    for (i = 0; i < n; i++)
        sumx += x[i];

    mean = sumx / sum; // calculate the mean value
    cout << "\nMean = " << mean << "\n\n";
    return 0;
}
```

Here is a sample session with the program in Listing 7.1:

Output

```
Enter number of data points [2 to 30] : 5

X[0] : 12.5
X[1] : 45.7
X[2] : 25.6
X[3] : 14.1
X[4] : 68.4

Mean = 33.26
```

The program in Listing 7.1 declares the global constant `MAX` as the size of the array used in the program. The function `main` declares the `double`-typed array `x`, in line 13, to have `MAX` elements. The function also declares other nonarray variables in lines 14 and 15.

The `do-while` loop, which is located in lines 17 through 22, obtains the number of data points you want to store in the array `x`. The output statement in lines 18 and 19 prompts you to enter the number of data points. The output indicates the range of valid numbers, which is `2` to `MAX`. The statement in line 20 obtains your input and stores it in variable `n`. The `while` clause validates your input. The clause determines if the value in variable `n` is less than 2, or is greater than `MAX`. If this condition is true, the `do-while` loop iterates again to obtain a correct input value.

The `for` loop statement, in lines 25 through 28, prompts you to enter the data. The loop uses the control variable `i` and iterates from 0 to n-1, in increments of 1. The output statement in line 26 prompts you to enter the value for the indicated array element. The input statement in line 27 obtains your input and stores it in the element `x[i]`.

The statement in line 31 assigns the integer in variable `n` to the double-typed variable `sum`. The `for` loop in lines 34 and 35 adds the values in array `x` to the variable `sumx`. The loop uses the control variable `i` and iterates from 0 to n-1, in increments of 1. The statement in line 35 uses the increment assignment operator to add the value in element `x[i]` to the variable `sumx`.

The statement in line 37 calculates the mean value and stores it in variable `mean`. The output statement in line 38 displays the mean value.

Note: The program in Listing 7.1 shows how to use a `for` loop to process the elements of an array. The loop continuation test uses the < operator and the value beyond the last valid index. You can use the <= operator followed by the last index. For example, I can write the data input loop as

```
24:        // prompt user for data
25:        for (i = 0; i <= (n - 1); i++) {
26:            cout << "X[" << i << "] : ";
27:            cin >> x[i];
28:        }
```

However, this form is not popular, because it requires an additional operator, whereas the condition `i < n` does not.

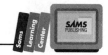

DO | **DON'T**

DO write the loop continuation expression so that it uses the minimum number of operators. This approach reduces the code size and speeds up loop execution.

DON'T use the <= operator in the loop continuation condition, unless using the operator helps you write an expression that minimizes the number of operations.

Initializing Single-Dimensional Arrays

C++ enables you to initialize arrays and is flexible about the initialization. You need to enclose the list of initializing values in a pair of open and close braces ({}). The list is comma-delimited and may continue on multiple lines. If there are fewer items in the initializing list than there are array elements, the compiler assigns 0 to balance the array elements. By contrast, if the list of initializing values has more items than the number of array elements, the compiler flags a compile-time error.

The next program, Listing 7.2, modifies the last program to supply data internally. Consequently, I eliminate the steps that prompt you for the number of data and the data itself. The program simply displays the array elements (obtained from the initialization list) and the average value for the data. Although this program does not interact with the user, it offers a version that stores data in the source code. You can edit the program periodically to add, edit, and delete data before recalculating a new average value.

Type **Listing 7.2. Source code for the program ARRAY2.CPP.**

```
/*
  C++ program that demonstrates the use of single-dimensional
  arrays.  The average value of the array is calculated.
  The array has its values preassigned internally.
*/

#include <iostream.h>

const int MAX = 10;

main()
{

```

```
14:     double x[MAX] = { 12.2, 45.4, 67.2, 12.2, 34.6, 87.4,
15:                       83.6, 12.3, 14.8, 55.5 };
16:     double sum = MAX, sumx = 0.0, mean;
17:     int n = MAX;
18:
19:     // calculate sum of observations
20:     cout << "Array is:\n";
21:     for (int i = 0; i < n; i++) {
22:         sumx += x[i];
23:         cout << "x[" << i << "] = " << x[i] << "\n";
24:     }
25:
26:     mean = sumx / sum; // calculate the mean value
27:     cout << "\nMean = " << mean << "\n\n";
28:     return 0;
29: }
```

Here is a sample session with the program in Listing 7.2:

Output

```
Array is:
x[0] = 12.2
x[1] = 45.4
x[2] = 67.2
x[3] = 12.2
x[4] = 34.6
x[5] = 87.4
x[6] = 83.6
x[7] = 12.3
x[8] = 14.8
x[9] = 55.5

Mean = 42.52
```

Analysis

Let me focus on the initialization of the array `x` in Listing 7.2. Line 14 contains the declaration of array `x` and its initialization. The initializing list, which runs to line 15, is enclosed in a pair of braces and has comma-delimited values. The statement in line 16 declares the variables `sum` and `sumx` and initializes these variables to `MAX` and `0`, respectively. The statement in line 17 declares the `int`-typed variable `n` and initializes it with the value `MAX`. The rest of the program resembles parts of the program in Listing 7.1.

If you are somewhat dismayed by the fact that you have to count the exact number of initializing values, then I have some good news for you: C++ allows you to size an array automatically using the number of items in the corresponding initializing list. Consequently, you don't need to place a number in the square brackets of the array, and you can let the compiler do the work for you.

DO | **DON'T**

DO include dummy values in the initializing list if the initialized array needs to expand later.

DON'T rely on counting the number of items in the initializing list to provide the data for the number of array elements.

Listing 7.3 shows the source code for the program ARRAY3.CPP. This new version uses the feature of automatic array sizing.

Type

Listing 7.3. Source code for the program ARRAY3.CPP.

```
/*
  C++ program that demonstrates the use of single-dimensional
  arrays.  The average value of the array is calculated.
  The array has its values preassigned internally.
*/

#include <iostream.h>

main()
{

     double x[] = { 12.2, 45.4, 67.2, 12.2, 34.6, 87.4,
                    83.6, 12.3, 14.8, 55.5 };
     double sum,  sumx = 0.0, mean;
     int n;

     n = sizeof(x) / sizeof(x[0]);
     sum = n;

     // calculate sum of observations
     cout << "Array is:\n";
     for (int i = 0; i < n; i++) {
         sumx += x[i];
         cout << "x[" << i << "] = " << x[i] << "\n";
     }

     mean = sumx / sum; // calculate the mean value
     cout << "\nNumber of data points = " << n << "\n"
          << "Mean = " << mean << "\n";
     return 0;
}
```

Here is a sample session with the program in Listing 7.3:

Output

```
Array is:
x[0] = 12.2
x[1] = 45.4
x[2] = 67.2
x[3] = 12.2
x[4] = 34.6
x[5] = 87.4
x[6] = 83.6
x[7] = 12.3
x[8] = 14.8
x[9] = 55.5

Number of data points = 10
Mean = 42.52
```

Analysis

Notice that the program in Listing 7.3 does not declare the constant `MAX` which appears in the previous version, shown in Listing 7.2. How does the program determine the number of array elements? Line 17 shows that the program calculates the number of elements in array `x` by dividing the size of the array `x` (obtained by using `sizeof(x)`) by the size of the first element (obtained by using `sizeof(x[0])`). You can use this method to obtain the size of any array of any data type.

Array Parameters in Functions

C++ allows you to declare function parameters that are arrays. In fact, C++ permits you to either be specific or general about the size of the array parameter. If you want an array parameter to accept arrays of a fixed size, you can specify the size of the array in the parameter declaration. By contrast, if you want the array parameter to accept arrays with the same basic type but different sizes, use empty brackets with the array parameter.

Syntax

A Fixed-Array Parameter

The general syntax for declaring a fixed-array parameter is

```
type parameterName[arraySize]
```

Examples:

```
int minArray(int arr[100], int n);
void sort(unsigned dayNum[7]);
```

An Open-Array Parameter

The general syntax for declaring an open-array parameter is

```
type parameterName[]
```

Examples:

```
int minArray(int arr[], int n);
void sort(unsigned dayNum[]);
```

DO	DON'T

DO use open-array parameters in functions.

DON'T forget to check the upper bounds of an open-array parameter in general-purpose functions.

Let's look at a simple example. Listing 7.4 shows the source code for program ARRAY4.CPP. The program performs the following tasks:

- Prompts you to enter the number of data points, which ranges from 2 to 10
- Prompts you to enter the integer values for the arrays
- Displays the smallest value in the array
- Displays the largest value in the array

Listing 7.4. Source code for the program ARRAY4.CPP.

```
// C++ program that passes arrays as arguments of functions

#include <iostream.h>

const int MAX = 10;

main()
{
  int arr[MAX];
  int n;

  // declare prototypes of functions
  int getMin(int a[MAX], int size);
  int getMax(int a[], int size);

  do { // obtain number of data points
    cout << "Enter number of data points [2 to "
         << MAX << "] : ";
```

```
    cin >> n;
    cout << "\n";
  } while (n < 2 || n > MAX);

  // prompt user for data
  for (int i = 0; i < n; i++) {
    cout << "arr[" << i << "] : ";
    cin >> arr[i];
  }

  cout << "Smallest value in array is "
       << getMin(arr, n) << "\n"
       << "Biggest value in array is "
       << getMax(arr, n) << "\n";
  return 0;
}


int getMin(int a[MAX], int size)
{
  int small = a[0];
  // search for the smallest value in the
  // remaining array elements
  for (int i = 1; i < size; i++)
    if (small > a[i])
      small = a[i];
  return small;
}

int getMax(int a[], int size)
{
  int big = a[0];
  // search for the biggest value in the
  // remaining array elements
  for (int i = 1; i < size; i++)
    if (big < a[i])
      big = a[i];
  return big;
}
```

Here is a sample session with the program in Listing 7.4:

```
Enter number of data points [2 to 10] : 5

arr[0] : 55
arr[1] : 69
arr[2] : 47
arr[3] : 85
arr[4] : 14
Smallest value in array is 14
Biggest value in array is 85
```

Analysis

The program in Listing 7.4 declares the global constant `MAX`, in line 5, to size up the array of data. The function `main` declares the `int`-typed array `arr` in line 9. Line 10 contains the declaration of the `int`-typed variable `n`. Lines 13 and 14 declare the prototypes for the functions `getMin` and `getMax`, which return the smallest and biggest values in an `int`-typed array, respectively. The prototype of function `getMin` indicates that it uses a fixed-array parameter. By contrast, the prototype of function `getMax` indicates that it uses an open-array parameter. I use both kinds of array parameters for the sake of demonstration.

The `do-while` loop, located in lines 16 through 21, obtains the number of data points you want to store in the array `arr`. The output statement in lines 17 and 18 prompts you to enter the number of data points. The output indicates the range of valid numbers, which runs between 2 and `MAX`. The statement in line 19 obtains your input and stores it in variable `n`. The `while` clause validates your input. The clause determines if the value in `variable n` is less than 2 or is greater than `MAX`. If this condition is true, the `do-while` loop iterates again to obtain a correct input value.

The `for` loop statement in lines 24 through 27 prompts you to enter the data. The loop uses the control variable `i` and iterates from 0 to n-1, in increments of 1. The output statement in line 25 prompts you to enter the value for the indicated array element. The statement in line 26 obtains your input and stores it in the element `arr[i]`.

The output statement in lines 29 through 32 displays the smallest and biggest integers in array `arr`. The statement invokes the functions `getMin` and `getMax`, supplying each one of them with the arguments `arr` and `n`.

The program defines function `getMin` in lines 37 through 46. The function has two parameters: the `int`-typed, fixed-array parameter `a`, and the `int`-typed parameter size. The function declares the local variable `small` and initializes it with `a[0]`, the first element of parameter `a`. The function searches for the smallest value in parameter `a` using the `for` loop in line 42. This loop declares the control variable `i`, and iterates from 1 to size-1, in increments of 1. The loop contains an `if` statement that assigns the value in element `a[i]` to variable `small`, if the latter is greater than element `a[i]`. The function returns the value in variable `small`. The function `getMin` only accepts `int`-typed arrays that have `MAX` elements.

The program defines function `getMax` in lines 48 through 57. This function, which is similar to function `getMin`, has two parameters: the `int`-typed, open-array parameter `a`, and the `int`-typed parameter size. The function declares the local `variable big` and initializes it with `a[0]`, the first element of parameter `a`. The function searches for the smallest value in parameter `a` using the `for` loop in line 53. This loop declares the control variable `i`, and iterates from 1 to size-1, in increments of 1. The loop contains an `if` statement that assigns the value in element a[i] to variable big, if the latter is less than element a[i]. The function returns the value in variable big. The function getMax accepts int-typed arrays of any size.

Sorting Arrays

Sorting and searching arrays are the most common nonnumerical operations for arrays. Sorting an array arranges its elements in typically ascending order. The process uses parts or all of the value in each element to determine the precedence of the elements in the array. Searching for data in sorted arrays is much easier than in unordered arrays.

Computer scientists have spent much time and effort studying and creating methods for sorting arrays. Discussing and comparing these methods is beyond the scope of this book. I only mention that my favorite array-sorting methods include the QuickSort, Shell-Metzner sort, heap sort, and the new Comb sort. The QuickSort method is the fastest method, in general, but requires some operational overhead. The Shell-Metzner and Comb sort methods do not require similar overhead. The example in this section uses the new Comb sort method, which is more efficient than the Shell-Metzner method.

The Comb sort method uses the following steps, given an array A with N elements:

1. Initializes the Offset value, used in comparing elements, to N
2. Sets the Offset value to either 8*Offset/11 or 1, whichever is bigger
3. Sets the InOrder flag to true
4. Loops for values 0 to N-Offset, using the loop control variable i:

   Assigns I + Offset to J

   If A[I] is greater than A[J], swaps A[I] with A[J] and sets the InOrder flag to false
5. Resumes at step 2 if Offset is not 1 and InOrder is false

Let's look at a program that sorts an array of integers. Listing 7.5 shows the source code for program ARRAY5.CPP. The program performs the following tasks:

- Prompts you to enter the number of data points
- Prompts you to enter the integer values for the array
- Displays the elements of the unordered array
- Displays the elements of the sorted array

Listing 7.5. Source code for the program ARRAY5.CPP.

```
// C++ program that sorts arrays using the Comb sort method

#include <iostream.h>

const int MAX = 10;
const int TRUE = 1;
const int FALSE = 0;

int obtainNumData()
{
  int m;
  do { // obtain number of data points
    cout << "Enter number of data points [2 to "
         << MAX << "] : ";
    cin >> m;
    cout << "\n";
  } while (m < 2 || m > MAX);
  return m;
}

void inputArray(int intArr[], int n)
{
  // prompt user for data
  for (int i = 0; i < n; i++) {
    cout << "arr[" << i << "] : ";
    cin >> intArr[i];
  }
}

void showArray(int intArr[], int n)
{
  for (int i = 0; i < n; i++) {
    cout.width(5);
    cout << intArr[i] << " ";
  }
  cout << "\n";
}

void sortArray(int intArr[], int n)
{
  int offset, temp, inOrder;

  offset = n;
  do {
    offset = (8 * offset) / 11;
    offset = (offset == 0) ? 1 : offset;
    inOrder = TRUE;
    for (int i = 0, j = offset; i < (n - offset); i++, j++) {
      if (intArr[i] > intArr[j]) {
        inOrder = FALSE;
        temp = intArr[i];
        intArr[i] = intArr[j];
        intArr[j] = temp;
```

```
54:        }
55:      }
56:    } while (!(offset == 1 && inOrder == TRUE));
57: }
58:
59: main()
60: {
61:    int arr[MAX];
62:    int n;
63:
64:    n = obtainNumData();
65:    inputArray(arr, n);
66:    cout << "Unordered array is:\n";
67:    showArray(arr, n);
68:    sortArray(arr, n);
69:    cout << "\nSorted array is:\n";
70:    showArray(arr, n);
71:    return 0;
72: }
```

Here is a sample session with the program in Listing 7.5:

```
Enter number of data points [2 to 10] : 10
arr[0] : 55
arr[1] : 68
arr[2] : 74
arr[3] : 15
arr[4] : 28
arr[5] : 23
arr[6] : 69
arr[7] : 95
arr[8] : 22
arr[9] : 33
Unordered array is:
55     68     74     15     28     23     69     95     22     33

Sorted array is:
15     22     23     28     33     55     68     69     74     95
```

The program in Listing 7.5 declares the constants `MAX`, `TRUE`, and `FALSE` in lines 5 through 7. The constant `MAX` defines the size of the array used in the program. The constants `TRUE` and `FALSE` define the Boolean values. The program also defines the functions `obtainNumData`, `inputArray`, `showArray`, `sortArray`, and `main`.

The parameterless function `obtainNumData`, which is defined in lines 9 through 19, prompts you to enter the number of values. The output statement in lines 13 and 14 also specifies the valid range for your input. The statement in line 15 stores your input in the local variable `m`. The function uses a `do-while` loop to ensure that it returns a valid number. The loop iterates as long as the value in variable `m` is less than 2 or greater than `MAX`. The function returns the value in variable `m`.

The function `inputArray`, which is defined in lines 21 through 28, obtains the data for the tested array. The function has two parameters. The open-array parameter `intArr` passes the input values back to the caller of the function. The parameter `n` specifies how many values to obtain for parameter `intArr`. The function uses a `for` loop, which iterates from 0 to n-1, in increments of 1. Each loop iteration prompts you for a value and stores that value in an element of array `intArr`.

> **Note:** The function `inputArray` illustrates that C++ functions treat array parameters as if they are references to their arguments because these parameters affect the values in the arguments beyond the scope of the functions. In reality, the C++ compiler passes a copy of the address of the array argument to the function when dealing with an array parameter. Armed with the address of the array, C++ functions can then alter the values of the array beyond the scope of these functions. This feature is possible because the function is working with the original array and not a copy.

The function `showArray`, which is defined in lines 30 through 37, displays the meaningful data in an array. The function has two parameters. The open-array parameter `intArr` passes the array values to be displayed by the function. The parameter `n` specifies how many array elements to display in `intArr` (remember that not all of the array elements are used to store your data). The function uses a `for` loop, which iterates from 0 to n-1, in increments of 1. Each loop iteration displays the value in an array element. The array elements appear on the same line.

The function `sortArray`, which is defined in lines 39 through 57, sorts the elements of an array using the Comb sort method. The function has two parameters. The open-array parameter `intArr` passes the array values to be sorted by the function. The parameter `n` specifies how many array elements to sort. The statements in the function `sortArray` implement the Comb sort method outlined earlier.

> **Note:** The function `sortArray` illustrates how array parameters can pass data to and from a function. The function `sortArray` receives an unordered array, sorts it, and passes the ordered array to the function's caller. The compiler supports this feature by passing a copy of the address of the array to the function. Thus, the function need not explicitly return the array because it is working with the original data and not a copy.

The function `main` performs the various program tasks by calling the functions mentioned earlier. The function declares the array `arr` and the simple variable `n` in lines 61 and 62, respectively. The statement in line 64 calls function `obtainNumData` to obtain the number of data you want to store in the array. The statement assigns the result of the function `obtainNumData` to variable `n`. The statement in line 65 calls the function `inputArray` to prompt you for the data. The function call passes the arguments `arr` and `n`. The output statement in line 66 displays a message which indicates that the program is about to display the elements of the unordered array. The statement in line 67 calls `showArray` and passes it the arguments `arr` and `n`. This function call displays the elements of the array `arr` on one line. The statement in line 68 calls the function `sortArray` to sort the first `n` elements in array `arr`. The output statement in line 69 displays a message which indicates that the program is about to display the elements of the sorted array. The statement in line 70 calls `showArray` and passes the arguments `arr` and `n`. This function call displays the elements of the ordered array `arr` on one line.

Searching Arrays

Searching arrays is another important nonnumerical operation. Because arrays can be sorted or unordered, there is a general category of search methods for each. The simplest search method for unordered arrays is the linear search method. The simplest search method for sorted arrays is the versatile binary search method. The search methods for unordered arrays can also be applied to sorted arrays. However, they do not take advantage of the array order.

NEW TERM The *linear search* method sequentially examines the array elements, looking for an element that matches the search value. If the sought value is not in the array, the linear search method examines the entire array's elements.

NEW TERM The *binary search* method takes advantage of the order in the array. The method searches for a matching value by using the shrinking intervals approach. The initial search interval includes all the array elements (which contain meaningful data). The method compares the median element of the interval with the search value. If the two match, the search stops. Otherwise, the method determines which subinterval to use as the next search interval. Consequently, each search interval is half the size of the previous one. If the search value has no match in the examined array, the binary method makes far fewer examinations than the linear search method. The binary search method is the most efficient general-purpose search method for sorted arrays.

DO **DON'T**

DO use the unordered-array search method when you are not sure that the array is sorted.

DON'T use sorted-array search methods with unordered arrays. The results of such searches are not reliable.

Let's look at a program that sorts an array of integers. Listing 7.6 shows the source code for program ARRAY6.CPP. I created this program by adding functions and operations to program ARRAY5.CPP. The program performs the following tasks:

- Prompts you to enter the number of data points
- Prompts you to enter the integer values for the array
- Displays the elements of the unordered array
- Asks you if you want to search for data in the unordered array (if you type characters other than Y or y, the program resumes at step 8)
- Prompts you for a search value
- Displays the search outcome (if the program finds a matching element, it displays the index of that element; otherwise, the program tells you that it found no match for the search value)
- Resumes at step 4
- Displays the elements of the sorted array
- Asks you if you want to search for data in the unordered array (if you type characters other than Y or y, the program ends)
- Prompts you for a search value
- Displays the search outcome (if the program finds a matching element, it displays the index of that element; otherwise, the program tells you that it found no match for the search value)
- Resumes at step 9

Type Listing 7.6. Source code for the program ARRAY6.CPP.

```
// C++ program that searches arrays using the linear
// and binary search methods

#include <iostream.h>

const int MAX = 10;
const int TRUE = 1;
const int FALSE = 0;
const int NOT_FOUND = -1;

int obtainNumData()
{
  int m;
  do { // obtain number of data points
    cout << "Enter number of data points [2 to "
         << MAX << "] : ";
    cin >> m;
    cout << "\n";
  } while (m < 2 ¦¦ m > MAX);
  return m;
}

void inputArray(int intArr[], int n)
{
  // prompt user for data
  for (int i = 0; i < n; i++) {
    cout << "arr[" << i << "] : ";
    cin >> intArr[i];
  }
}

void showArray(int intArr[], int n)
{
  for (int i = 0; i < n; i++) {
    cout.width(5);
    cout << intArr[i] << " ";
  }
  cout << "\n";
}

void sortArray(int intArr[], int n)
// sort the first n elements of array intArr
// using the Comb sort method
{
  int offset, temp, inOrder;

  offset = n;
  do {
    offset = (8 * offset) / 11;
    offset = (offset == 0) ? 1 : offset;
    inOrder = TRUE;
    for (int i = 0, j = offset; i < (n - offset); i++, j++) {
      if (intArr[i] > intArr[j]) {
```

continues

Listing 7.6. continued

```
        inOrder = FALSE;
        temp = intArr[i];
        intArr[i] = intArr[j];
        intArr[j] = temp;
      }
    }
  } while (!(offset == 1 && inOrder == TRUE));
}

int linearSearch(int searchVal, int intArr[], int n)
// perform linear search to locate the first
// element in array intArr that matches the value
// of searchVal
{
  int notFound = TRUE;
  int i = 0;
  // search through the array elements
  while (i < n && notFound)
    // no match?
    if (searchVal != intArr[i])
      i++; // increment index to compare the next element
    else
      notFound = FALSE; // found a match
  // return search outcome
  return (notFound == FALSE) ? i : NOT_FOUND;
}

int binarySearch(int searchVal, int intArr[], int n)
// perform binary search to locate the first
// element in array intArr that matches the value
// of searchVal
{
  int median, low, high;

  // initialize the search range
  low = 0;
  high = n - 1;
  // search in array
  do {
    // obtain the median index of the current search range
    median = (low + high) / 2;
    // update search range
    if (searchVal > intArr[median])
      low = median + 1;
    else
      high = median - 1;
  } while (!(searchVal == intArr[median] || low > high));
  // return search outcome
  return (searchVal == intArr[median]) ? median : NOT_FOUND;
}

void searchInUnorderedArray(int intArr[], int n)
// manage the linear search test
{
  int x, i;
```

```
  char c;
  // perform linear search
  cout << "Search in unordered array? (Y/N) ";
  cin >> c;
  while (c == 'Y' || c == 'y') {
    cout << "Enter search value : ";
    cin >> x;
    i = linearSearch(x, intArr, n);
    if (i != NOT_FOUND)
      cout << "Found matching element at index " << i << "\n";
    else
      cout << "No match found\n";
    cout << "Search in unordered array? (Y/N) ";
    cin >> c;
  }
}

void searchInSortedArray(int intArr[], int n)
// manage the binary search test
{
  int x, i;
  char c;
  // perform binary search
  cout << "Search in sorted array? (Y/N) ";
  cin >> c;
  while (c == 'Y' || c == 'y') {
    cout << "Enter search value : ";
    cin >> x;
    i = binarySearch(x, intArr, n);
    if (i != NOT_FOUND)
      cout << "Found matching element at index " << i << "\n";
    else
      cout << "No match found\n";
    cout << "Search in sorted array? (Y/N) ";
    cin >> c;
  }
}

main()
{
  int arr[MAX];
  int n;

  n = obtainNumData();
  inputArray(arr, n);
  cout << "Unordered array is:\n";
  showArray(arr, n);
  searchInUnorderedArray(arr, n);
  sortArray(arr, n);
  cout << "\nSorted array is:\n";
  showArray(arr, n);
  searchInSortedArray(arr, n);
  return 0;
}
```

Here is a sample session with the program in Listing 7.6:

Output

```
Enter number of data points [2 to 10] : 5

arr[0] : 85
arr[1] : 41
arr[2] : 55
arr[3] : 67
arr[4] : 48
Unordered array is:
85    41    55    67    48
Search in unordered array? (Y/N) y
Enter search value : 55
Found matching element at index 2
Search in unordered array? (Y/N) y
Enter search value : 41
Found matching element at index 1
Search in unordered array? (Y/N) n

Sorted array is:
41    48    55    67    85
Search in sorted array? (Y/N) y
Enter search value : 55
Found matching element at index 2
Search in sorted array? (Y/N) y
Enter search value : 67
Found matching element at index 3
Search in sorted array? (Y/N) n
```

Analysis

The program in Listing 7.6 declares the functions `obtainNumData`, `inputArray`, `sortArray`, `linearSearch`, `binarySearch`, `searchInUnorderedArray`, `searchInSortedArray`, and `main`. Because the first three functions are identical to those in Listing 7.5, I discuss only the remaining functions.

The `linearSearch` function performs a linear search to find the first element in array `intArr` with a value that matches the one in parameter `searchVal`. The function searches the first `n` elements in array `intArr`. The `linearSearch` function returns the index of the matching element in array `intArr`, or yields the value of the global constant `NOT_FOUND` if no match is found. The function uses a `while` loop to examine the elements in array `intArr`. The search loop iterates while the value in variable `i` is less than that in variable `n` and while the local variable `notFound` stores `TRUE`. The statement in line 78 returns the function result using the conditional operator.

The `binarySearch` function has the same parameters as the `linearSearch` function and returns the same kind of value. The function uses the local variables low and high to store the current search interval. The function initializes the variables low and high using the values 0 and n-1, respectively. The `do-while` loop in lines 92 through 100 calculates the index of the median element and compares the median element with the search value. The `if` statement in line 96 performs this comparison, and its clauses update the value of either variable low or variable high, depending on the outcome of the comparison. The update in either variable shrinks the search interval. The return statement in line 102 yields the function's value based on one last comparison between the search value and the median element of the current search interval.

The function `searchInUnorderedArray` manages the search in the unordered array. The function accesses the unordered array using the open-array parameter `intArr`. The function declares local variables which are used to prompt you for and store the search value. The statement in line 116 calls the function `linearSearch` and passes the arguments `x` (the local variable which stores the search value), `intArr`, and `n`. The statement assigns the result of function `linearSearch` to the local variable `i`. The `if` statement in line 117 determines whether or not the value in variable `i` is not `NOT_FOUND`. If this condition is true, the output statement in line 118 shows the index of the matching element. Otherwise, the output statement in line 120 displays a no-match-found message.

The function `searchInSortedArray` is very similar to the function `searchInUnorderedArray`. The main difference is that the function `searchInSortedArray` deals with ordered arrays and therefore calls the `binarySearch` function to conduct a binary search on the ordered array `intArr`.

The function `main` invokes these functions to support the program tasks that I described earlier.

Multidimensional Arrays

In a multidimensional array, each additional dimension provides you with an additional access attribute. Two-dimensional arrays (or matrices, if you prefer) are the most popular kind of multidimensional arrays. Three-dimensional arrays are used less frequently than matrices, and so on.

NEW TERM *Multidimensional arrays* are supersets of the single-dimensional arrays.

Syntax

Two-Dimensional and Three-Dimensional Arrays

The general syntax for declaring two-dimensional and three-dimensional arrays is

```
type array [size1][size2];
type array [size1][size2][size3];
```

As with simple arrays, each dimension has a lower bound index of 0, and the declaration defines the number of elements in each dimension.

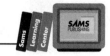

Examples:

```
double matrixA[100][10];
char table[41][22][3];
int index[7][12];
```

It is important to understand how C++ stores the elements of a multidimensional array. Most compilers store the elements of a multidimensional array in a contiguous fashion (that is, as one long array). The run-time code calculates where a sought element is located in that long array. To explain the storage scheme of multidimensional arrays, let me start by employing a convention for referencing the indices of the different dimensions. The following schema specifies the dimension numbering and the concept of high- and low-order dimensions. Here is a six-dimensional array—an extreme case that is a good example:

```
1    2    3    4    5    6  <- dimension number
M [20]  [7]  [5]  [3]  [2]  [2]
higher dimension order ->
```

The first element of the array `M` is `M[0][0][0][0][0][0]` and is stored at the first memory location of array `M`. The array `M` is stored in a contiguous block of 8400 elements. The location in that contiguous block stores the element at index 1 in the highest dimension number, dimension 6 (that is, `M[0][0][0][0][0][1]`). The location of the next elements in the contiguous block stores the subsequent elements in dimension 6 until the upper limit of dimension 6 is reached. Reaching this limit bumps the index of dimension 5 by 1 and resets the index of dimension 6 to 0. This process is repeated until every element in a multidimensional array is accessed. You can depict this storage scheme as looking at a gasoline pump meter when refueling your car: the right digits turn the fastest; the left digits turn the slowest.

Here is another example that uses a three-dimensional array, `M[3][2][2]`:

```
M[0][0][0]     <- the starting memory address
M[0][0][1]     <- 3rd dimension is filled
M[0][1][0]
M[0][1][1]     <- 2nd and 3rd dimensions are filled
M[1][0][0]
M[1][0][1]     <- 3rd dimension is filled
M[1][1][0]
M[1][1][1]     <- 2nd and 3rd dimensions are filled
M[2][0][0]
M[2][0][1]     <- 3rd dimension is filled
M[2][1][0]
M[2][1][1]     <- all dimensions are filled
```

Let's look at a program example that illustrates basic matrix manipulation. Listing 7.7 shows the source code for the MAT1.CPP program. The program manages a matrix that contains up to 10 columns and 30 rows and performs the following tasks:

- Prompts you to enter the number of rows (the program validates your input)
- Prompts you to enter the number of columns (the program validates your input)
- Prompts you to enter the matrix elements
- Calculates and displays the average for each column in the matrix

Type

Listing 7.7. Source code for the program MAT1.CPP.

```
/*
  C++ program that demonstrates the use of two-dimension arrays.
  The average value of each matrix column is calculated.
*/

#include <iostream.h>

const int MAX_COL = 10;
const int MAX_ROW = 30;

main()
{
    double x[MAX_ROW][MAX_COL];
    double sum, sumx, mean;
    int rows, columns;

    // get the number of rows
    do {
      cout << "Enter number of rows [2 to "
           << MAX_ROW << "] : ";
      cin >> rows;
    } while (rows < 2 || rows > MAX_ROW);

    // get the number of columns
    do {
      cout << "Enter number of columns [1 to "
           << MAX_COL << "] : ";
      cin >> columns;
    } while (columns < 1 || columns > MAX_COL);

    // get the matrix elements
    for (int i = 0; i < rows; i++)  {
      for (int j = 0; j < columns; j++)  {
          cout << "X[" << i << "][" << j << "] : ";
          cin >> x[i][j];
      }
      cout << "\n";
    }

    sum = rows;
    // obtain the sum of each column
    for (int j = 0; j < columns; j++)  {
```

continues

Listing 7.7. continued

```
43:        // initialize summations
44:        sumx = 0.0;
45:        for (i = 0; i < rows; i++)
46:          sumx += x[i][j];
47:        mean = sumx / sum;
48:        cout << "Mean for column " << j
49:             << " = " << mean << "\n";
50:      }
51:      return 0;
52: }
```

Here is a sample session with the program in Listing 7.7:

```
Enter number of rows [2 to 30] : 3
Enter number of columns [1 to 10] : 3
X[0][0] : 1
X[0][1] : 2
X[0][2] : 3

X[1][0] : 4
X[1][1] : 5
X[1][2] : 6

X[2][0] : 7
X[2][1] : 8
X[2][2] : 9

Mean for column 0 = 4
Mean for column 1 = 5
Mean for column 2 = 6
```

The program in Listing 7.7 declares the global constants `MAX_COL` and `MAX_ROW` in lines 8 and 9, respectively. These constants define the dimensions of the matrix created in the program. The function `main` declares the matrix `x` to have `MAX_ROW` rows and `MAX_COL` columns. The function also declares other nonarray variables.

The `do-while` loop, in lines 18 through 22, prompts you to enter the number of rows of matrix `x` that will contain your data. The output statement in lines 19 and 20 indicates the range of the valid number of rows. The statement in line 21 stores your input in the variable rows.

The second `do-while` loop, in lines 25 through 29, prompts you to enter the number of columns of matrix `x` that will contain your data. The output statement in lines 26 and 27 indicates the range of the valid number of columns. The statement in line 28 saves your input in the variable columns.

The nested `for` loops, in lines 32 through 38, prompt you for the matrix elements. The outer `for` loop uses the control variable `i` and iterates from 0 to rows -1, in increments of 1. The inner `for` loop uses the control variable `j` and iterates from 0 to columns -1, in increments of 1. The output statement in line 34 displays the index of the matrix element that will receive your input. The statement in line 35 stores your input in the matrix element `x[i][j]`.

The process of obtaining the average of each matrix column starts at line 40. The statement in that line assigns the integer in variable rows to the `double`-typed variable `sum`. The program uses another pair of nested `for` loops in lines 42 through 50. The outer `for` loop uses the control variable `j` and iterates from 0 to columns-1, in increments of 1. This loop processes each column. The first statement inside the outer `for` loop assigns 0 to the variable `sumx`. The inner `for` loop is located at line 45. This loop uses the control variable `i` and iterates from 0 to rows-1, in increments of 1. The inner loop uses the statement in line 46 to add the values of elements `x[i][j]` to the variable `sumx`. The statement in line 47 (which is outside the inner `for` loop) calculates the column average and assigns it to the variable mean. The output statement in lines 48 and 49 displays the column number and its average value.

Note: The `for` loop in line 42 redeclares its control variable `j` (not so with the `for` loop in line 45). Why? The `for` loop in line 33 also declares the control variable `j`. However, the scope of that loop is limited to the scope of the outer `for` loop. Once the first pair of nested loops finishes executing, the loop control variable `j` is removed by the run-time system.

Initializing Multidimensional Arrays

C++ allows you to initialize a multidimensional array in a manner similar to single-dimensional arrays. You need to use a list of values that appear in the same sequence in which the elements of the initialized multidimensional array are stored. Now you realize the importance of understanding how C++ stores the elements of a multidimensional array. I modified the previous C++ program to use an initializing list that internally supplies the program with data. Consequently, the program does not prompt you for any data. Rather, the program displays the values of the matrix and the average for its columns.

Listing 7.8. Source code for the program MAT2.CPP.

```
/*
  C++ program that demonstrates the use of two-dimension arrays.
  The average value of each matrix column is calculated.
*/

#include <iostream.h>

const int MAX_COL = 3;
const int MAX_ROW = 3;

main()
{
    double x[MAX_ROW][MAX_COL] = {
                                 1, 2, 3, // row # 1
                                 4, 5, 6, // row # 2
                                 7, 8, 9  // row # 3
                                 };
    double sum, sumx, mean;
    int rows = MAX_ROW, columns = MAX_COL;

    cout << "Matrix is:\n";
    // display the matrix elements
    for (int i = 0; i < rows; i++)  {
      for (int j = 0; j < columns; j++)  {
          cout.width(4);
          cout.precision(1);
          cout << x[i][j] << "  ";
      }
      cout << "\n";
    }
    cout << "\n";

    sum = rows;
    // obtain the sum of each column
    for (int j = 0; j < columns; j++)  {
      // initialize summations
      sumx = 0.0;
      for (i = 0; i < rows; i++)
        sumx += x[i][j];
      mean = sumx / sum;
      cout << "Mean for column " << j
           << " = " << mean << "\n";
    }
    return 0;
}
```

Here is a sample session with the program in Listing 7.8:

```
Matrix is:
1    2    3
4    5    6
7    8    9
```

```
Mean for column 0 = 4
Mean for column 1 = 5
Mean for column 2 = 6
```

Analysis The program in Listing 7.8 declares the matrix x and initializes it with a list of values. Notice that the program declares the constants MAX_COL and MAX_ROW with values that match the size of the initialized matrix. The declaration statement in lines 13 through 17 shows the elements assigned to each row. The function main also initializes the variables rows and columns with the constants MAX_ROW and MAX_COL, respectively. The function performs this initialization for two reasons: first, the program no longer prompts you to enter values for the variables rows and columns. Second, the program is working with a custom-fit size for matrix x.

The program uses the nested for loops, in lines 21 through 30, to display the elements of the matrix x. The second pair of nested for loops calculates the average for each matrix column. This nested for loop is identical to the one in Listing 7.7.

Multidimensional Array Parameters

C++ allows you to declare function parameters that are multidimensional arrays. As with single-dimensional arrays, C++ allows you to be either specific or general about the size of the array parameter. However, in the latter case, you can only generalize the first dimension of the array. If you wish an array parameter to accept arrays of a fixed dimension, you can specify the size of each dimension of the array in the parameter declaration. By contrast, if you want the array parameter to accept arrays of the same basic type but of different first-dimension sizes, use empty brackets for the first dimension in the array parameter.

Syntax

A Fixed-Array Parameter

The general syntax for declaring a fixed-array parameter is

```
type parameterName[dim1Size][dim2Size]...
```

Examples:

```
int minMatrix(int intMat[100][20], int rows, int cols);
void sort(unsigned mat[23][55],
int rows, int cols, int colIndex);
```

7

Syntax

An Open-Array Parameter

The general syntax for declaring an open-array parameter is

```
type parameterName[][dim2Size]...
```

Examples:

```
int minMat(int intMat[][100], int rows, int cols);
void sort(unsigned mat[][55],
int rows, int cols, int colIndex);
```

Let's look at an example. Listing 7.9 shows the source code for program MAT3.CPP. The program performs the same tasks as program MAT1.CPP in Listing 7.7. I created program MAT3.CPP by editing program MAT1.CPP and placing each program task in a separate function. Thus, program MAT3.CPP is a highly structured version of program MAT1.CPP.

Type

Listing 7.9. Source code for the program MAT3.CPP.

```
/*
  C++ program that demonstrates the use of two-dimension arrays.
  The average value of each matrix column is calculated.
*/

#include <iostream.h>

const int MAX_COL = 10;
const int MAX_ROW = 30;

int getRows()
{
  int n;
  // get the number of rows
  do {
    cout << "Enter number of rows [2 to "
         << MAX_ROW << "] : ";
    cin >> n;
  } while (n < 2 || n > MAX_ROW);
  return n;
}

int getColumns()
{
  int n;
  // get the number of columns
  do {
    cout << "Enter number of columns [1 to "
         << MAX_COL << "] : ";
    cin >> n;
  } while (n < 1 || n > MAX_COL);
  return n;
```

```
}

void inputMatrix(double mat[][MAX_COL],
                 int rows, int columns)
{
  // get the matrix elements
  for (int i = 0; i < rows; i++)  {
    for (int j = 0; j < columns; j++)  {
      cout << "X[" << i << "][" << j << "] : ";
      cin >> mat[i][j];
    }
    cout << "\n";
  }
}

void showColumnAverage(double mat[][MAX_COL],
                       int rows, int columns)
{
  double sum, sumx, mean;
  sum = rows;
  // obtain the sum of each column
  for (int j = 0; j < columns; j++)  {
    // initialize summations
    sumx = 0.0;
    for (int i = 0; i < rows; i++)
      sumx += mat[i][j];
    mean = sumx / sum;
    cout << "Mean for column " << j
         << " = " << mean << "\n";
  }
}

main()
{
    double x[MAX_ROW][MAX_COL];
    int rows, columns;
    // get matrix dimensions
    rows = getRows();
    columns = getColumns();
    // get matrix data
    inputMatrix(x, rows, columns);
    // show results
    showColumnAverage(x, rows, columns);
    return 0;
}
```

Here is a sample session with the program in Listing 7.9:

Output

```
Enter number of rows [2 to 30] : 3
Enter number of columns [1 to 10] : 3
X[0][0] : 10
X[0][1] : 20
X[0][2] : 30

X[1][0] : 40
X[1][1] : 50
```

```
     X[1][2] : 60

     X[2][0] : 70
     X[2][1] : 80
     X[2][2] : 90

     Mean for column 0 = 40
Mean for column 1 = 50
Mean for column 2 = 60
```

Analysis

The program in Listing 7.9 declares the functions `getRows`, `getColumns`, `inputMatrix`, `showColumnAverage`, and `main`. The function `getRows` prompts you for the number of matrix rows that you will be using. The function returns your validated input. Similarly, the function `getColumns` returns the validated number of matrix columns.

The function `inputMatrix` obtains the data for the matrix. The function has three parameters. The parameter `mat` specifies the matrix parameter (with an open first dimension). The parameters `rows` and `columns` specify the number of rows and columns of matrix `mat`, respectively, that will receive input data.

The function `showColumnAverage` calculates and displays the column averages for the matrix parameter `mat`. The parameters `rows` and `columns` specify the number of rows and columns of matrix `mat`, respectively, which contain meaningful data.

This function contains the same statements that appeared in program MAT1.CPP. Program MAT3.CPP uses these functions as shells or wrappers for the statements which perform the various tasks. From a structured programming point of view, program MAT3.CPP is superior to program MAT1.CPP.

The function `main` declares the matrix `x` with `MAX_ROW` rows and `MAX_COL` columns. The function calls the functions `getRows` and `getColumns` to obtain the number of working rows and columns, respectively. The statement in line 73 invokes the function `inputMatrix` and supplies it with the arguments `x`, `rows`, and `columns`. The statement in line 75 calls function `showColumnAverage` and passes it the arguments `x`, `rows`, and `columns`.

Summary

Today's lesson covers various topics that deal with arrays, including single-dimensional and multidimensional arrays. You learn about the following topics:

- Declaring single-dimensional arrays requires you to state the data type of the array elements, the name of the array, and the number of array elements (enclosed in square brackets). All C++ arrays have a 0 lower bound. The upper bound of an array is equal to the number of elements minus 1.

- Using single-dimensional arrays requires you to state the array's name and include a valid index, enclosed in square brackets.
- Initializing single-dimensional arrays can be carried out while declaring them. The initializing list of data is enclosed in braces and contains comma-delimited data. C++ allows you to include fewer data than the size of the array. In this case, the compiler automatically assigns zeros to the elements that you do not explicitly initialize. In addition, C++ allows you to omit the explicit size of the initialized array and instead use the number of initializing items as the number of array elements.
- Declaring single-dimensional arrays as function parameters takes two forms. The first one deals with fixed-array parameters, whereas the second one handles open-array parameters. Fixed-array parameters include the size of the array in the parameter. Arguments for this kind of parameter must match the type and size of the parameter. Open-array parameters use empty brackets to indicate that the arguments for the parameters can be of any size.
- Sorting arrays is an important nonnumerical array operation. Sorting arranges the elements of an array in either ascending or descending order. Sorted arrays are much easier to search. For sorting arrays, the new Comb sort method is very efficient.
- Searching arrays involves locating an array element which contains the same data as the search value. Searching methods are geared toward unordered or ordered arrays. The linear search method is used for unordered arrays and the binary search method is used for sorted arrays.
- Declaring multidimensional arrays requires you to state the data type of the array elements, the name of the array, and the size of each dimension (enclosed in separate brackets). The lower index of each dimension is 0. The upper bound of each dimension in an array is equal to the dimension size minus 1.
- Using multidimensional arrays requires you to state the array's name and include valid indices. Each index must be enclosed in a separate set of brackets.
- Initializing multidimensional arrays can be carried out while declaring them. The initializing list of data is enclosed in braces and contains comma-delimited data. C++ allows you to include fewer data than the total size of the array. In this case, the compiler automatically assigns zeros to the elements that you do not explicitly initialize.
- Declaring multidimensional arrays as function parameters takes two forms. The first one deals with fixed-array parameters, whereas the second one handles

parameters with an open first dimension. Fixed-array parameters include the size of each dimension in the array parameter. Arguments for this kind of parameter must match the type and size of the parameter. Open-array parameters use empty brackets for only the first dimension to indicate that the arguments for the parameters have varying sizes for the first dimensions. The other dimensions of the arguments must match those of the array parameter.

Q&A

Q Does C++ permit me to alter the size of an array?

A No. C++ does not allow you to redimension arrays.

Q Can I declare arrays with the basic type void (for example, `void array[81];`) to create buffers?

A No. C++ does not allow you to use the void type with an array because the type `void` has no defined size. Use the `char` or `unsigned char` type to create an array that works as a buffer.

Q Does C++ allow me to redeclare an array?

A C++ allows you to redeclare an array to change its basic type, number of dimensions, and size if you declare these arrays in nested statement blocks. Here is an example:

```
#include <iostream.h>
const MAX = 100;
const MAX_ROWS = 100;
const MAX_COLS = 20;

main()
{
  // declare variables here?
  {
    double x[MAX];
    // declare other variables?
    // statements to manipulate the single-dimensional
    array x
  }
  {
```

```
    double x[MAX_ROWS][MAX_COLS];
    // declare other variables?
    // statements to manipulate the matrix x
  }
  return 0;
}
```

The function main declares the array x in the first nested statement block. When program execution reaches the end of that block, the run-time system removes the array x and all other variables declared in that block. Then the function redeclares x as a matrix in the second block. When program execution reaches the end of the second block, the run-time system removes the matrix x and all other variables declared in that block.

Q Are arrays limited to the predefined types?

A Not at all. C++ allows you to create arrays using user-defined types (see Day 8).

Workshop

The Workshop provides quiz questions to help you solidify your understanding of the material covered and exercises to provide you with experience in using what you've learned. Try to understand the quiz and exercise answers before continuing on to the next day's lesson. Answers are provided in Appendix B, "Answers."

Quiz

1. What is the output of the following program?

```
#include <iostream.h>
const int MAX = 5;
main()
{
  double x[MAX];
  x[0] = 1;
  for (int i = 1; i < MAX; I++)
    x[i] = i * x[i-1];
  for (i = 0; i < MAX; I++)
    cout << "x[" << i << "] = " << x[i] << "\n";
```

```
  return 0;
}
```

2. What is the output of the following program?

```
#include <iostream.h>
#include <math.h>
const int MAX = 5;
main()
{
  double x[MAX];
  for (int i = 0; i < MAX; I++)
    x[i] = sqrt(double(i));
  for (i = 0; i < MAX; I++)
    cout << "x[" << i << "] = " << x[i] << "\n";
  return 0;
}
```

3. Where is the error in the following program?

```
#include <iostream.h>
const int MAX = 5;
main()
{
  double x[MAX];
  x[0] = 1;
  for (int i = 0; i < MAX; I++)
    x[i] = i * x[i-1];
  for (i = 0; i < MAX; I++)
    cout << "x[" << i << "] = " << x[i] << "\n";
  return 0;
}
```

Exercise

Write the program ARRAY7.CPP by editing program ARRAY6.CPP and replacing the Comb sort method in function `sortArray` with an implementation of the Shell-Metzner method.

WEEK 1 IN REVIEW

Before you proceed to the second week of learning about programming with Visual C++, let's look at a special example that evolves at the end of the next two weeks. The example is a simple number-guessing game, shown in Listing R1.1. The program selects a number, at random, between 0 and 1,000 and prompts you to enter a number in that range. If your input is greater than the secret number, the program tells you that your guess was higher. By contrast, if your input is less than the secret number, the program tells you that your guess was lower. If you guess the secret number, the game ends with your victory. The program allows you up to 11 guesses. You can end the game at any prompt by entering a negative integer. In this case, the program stops the game and displays the secret number.

Type **Listing R1.1. Source code for program GAME1.CPP.**

```
#include <stdlib.h>
#include <iostream.h>
#include <time.h>

// declare a global random number generating function
int random(int maxVal)
{ return rand() % maxVal; }


main()
{
  int n, m;
  int MaxIter = 11;
  int iter = 0;
  int ok = 1;


  // reseed random-number generator
  srand((unsigned)time(NULL));
  n = random(1001);
  m = -1;

  // loop to obtain the other guesses
  while (m != n && iter < MaxIter && ok == 1) {
    cout << "Enter a number between 0 and 1000 : ";
    cin >> m;
    ok = (m < 0) ? 0 : 1;
    iter++;
    // is the user's guess higher?
    if (m > n)
      cout << "Enter a lower guess\n\n";
    else if (m < n)
      cout << "Enter a higher guess\n\n";
    else
      cout << "You guessed it! Congratulations.";
  }
  // did the user guess the secret number
  if (iter >= MaxIter || ok == 0)
    cout << "The secret number is " << n << "\n";

  return 0;
}
```

Here is a sample session with the program in Listing R1.1:

```
Enter a number between 0 and 1000 : 500
Enter a lower guess

Enter a number between 0 and 1000 : 250
Enter a higher guess
```

```
Enter a number between 0 and 1000 : -1
Enter a higher guess

The secret number is 399
```

The program in Listing R1.1 declares the function `random` to return a random number in the range of 0 to 1,000. The program also declares the function `main`, which conducts the guessing game. The function declares a number of local variables in lines 12 through 15. The statement in line 19 reseeds the random number generator. The statement in line 20 assigns the secret number to the variable `n`. The statement in line 21 assigns -1 to the variable `m`, which stores your guesses.

The `while` loop in lines 24 through 36 conducts the game. The `while` loop determines whether or not the following conditions are all true:

- Your guess (stored in variable `m`) does not match the secret number stored in variable `n`
- The number of iterations (stored in variable `iter`) is less than the maximum number of iterations (stored in variable `MaxIter`)
- The variable `ok` stores 1

The first statement in the loop prompts you to enter a number between 0 and 1,000. The statement in line 26 obtains your input and stores it in variable `m`. The statement in line `ok` assigns 0 to the variable `ok` if you entered a negative integer. Otherwise, the statement assigns 1 to variable `ok`. The statement in line 28 increments the variable `iter`.

The multi-alternative `if` statement in lines 30 through 35 compares your input with the secret number and displays the appropriate message reflecting your guess.

The `if` statement in line 38 displays the secret number if you failed to guess it in `MaxIter` iterations or if you entered a negative integer.

WEEK 2 AT A GLANCE

8

9

10

11

12

13

14

This second week continues teaching you about the C++ language. The topics cover the more advanced side of C++. You learn about user-defined data types—especially structures—and about pointers. The week also covers advanced topics on functions and introduces you to object-oriented programming (OOP) in C++. You learn about classes, components, and the rules for using these components. In addition, you learn about basic file I/O using the C++ stream library. The last two days in this week introduce you to the world of Windows programming and the Microsoft Foundation Class (MFC) library. By the end of this week you will write simple, yet functional, Windows programs.

8

User-Defined Types and Pointers

WEEK 2

Creating user-defined data types is one of the features that is expected from modern programming languages. Today's lesson looks at the enumerated data types and structures that allow you to better organize your data. In addition, this lesson discusses using pointers with simple variables, arrays, structures, and dynamic data. Today, you learn about the following topics:

- The type definition using `typedef`
- Enumerated data types
- Structures
- Unions
- Reference variables
- Pointers to existing variables
- Pointers to arrays
- Pointers to structures
- Using pointers to access and manage dynamic data
- Far pointers

Type Definition in C++

C++ offers the `typedef` keyword that enables you to define new data type names as aliases of existing types.

Syntax

The *typedef* Keyword

The general syntax for using `typedef` is

```
typedef knownType newType;
```

Examples:

```
typedef unsigned word;
typedef unsigned char byte;
type unsigned char boolean;
```

The `typedef` keyword defines a new type from a known one. You can use `typedef` to create aliases that shorten the names of existing data types or define names of data types that are more familiar to you (see the previous second example, which `typedef`s a byte type). In addition, the `typedef` statement can define a new type name that better describes how the data type is used. The previous third example illustrates this use of `typedef`. You can also use `typedef` to define the name of an array type.

Syntax

An Array Type Name

The general syntax for defining the name of an array type is

```
typedef baseType arrayTypeName[arraySize];
```

The `typedef` statement defines the *`arrayTypeName`*, whose basic type and size are *`baseType`* and *`arraySize`*, respectively.

Examples:

```
typedef double vector[10];
typedef double matrix[10][30];
```

Thus, the identifiers `vector` and `matrix` are names of data types.

Enumerated Data Types

The rule to follow with enumerated data types is that while the enumerated identifiers must be unique, the values assigned to them are not.

NEW TERM An *enumerated type* defines a list of unique identifiers and associates values with these identifiers.

Syntax

An Enumerated Type

The general syntax for declaring an enumerated type is

```
enum enumType { <list of enumerated identifiers> };
```

Example:

```
enum Boolean { false, true };
num YesNo { no, yes, dontCare, maybe };
enum weekday { Sunday, Monday, Tuesday,
Wednesday, Thursday, Friday, Saturday };
```

Here is an example of declaring an enumerated type:

```
enum CPUtype { i8088, i80286, i80386DX, i80386SX,
               i80486DX, i80486SX };
```

C++ associates integer values with the enumerated identifiers. For example, in this type, the compiler assigns 0 to i8088, 1 to i80286, and so on.

C++ is very flexible in declaring an enumerated type. First, the language allows you to explicitly assign a value to an enumerated identifier. Here is an example:

```
enum weekday { Sunday = 1, Monday, Tuesday, Wednesday,
               Thursday, Friday, Saturday };
```

This declaration explicitly assigns 1 to the enumerated identifier `Sunday`. The compiler then assigns the next integer, `2`, to the next identifier, `Monday`, and so on. C++ allows you to explicitly assign a value to each member of the enumerated list. Moreover, these values need not be unique. Here are some examples of the flexibility in declaring enumerated types in C++:

```
// explicit value assignment for every list member
enum colors { black = 1, red = 2, blue = 3, green = 5,
              yellow = 7, white = 11 };

// intermittent value assignment
enum colors { black = 1, red, blue, green = 5,
              yellow = 7, white = 11 };

// duplicate values
enum CPUtype { i8088 = 1, i80286 = 2,
               i80386DX = 3, i80386SX = 3,
               i80486DX = 4, i80486SX = 4 };

enum choiceType { false, true, dontCare = 0 };
```

In the last example, the compiler associates the identifier `false` with `0` by default. However, the compiler also associates the value `0` with `dontCare` because of the explicit assignment.

C++ allows you to declare variables that have enumerated types in the following ways:

1. The declaration of the enumerated type may include the declaration of the variables of that type. The general syntax is

   ```
   enum enumType { <list of enumerated identifiers> }
                 <list of variables>;
   ```

   Here is an example:

   ```
   enum weekDay { Sun = 1, Mon, Tue, Wed, Thu, Fri, Sat }
        recycleDay, payDay, movieDay;
   ```

2. The separate declaration of the enumerated type and its variables includes multiple statements to declare the type and the associated variables separately. The general syntax is

   ```
   enum enumType { <list of enumerated identifiers> };
   enumType var1, var2, ..., varN;
   ```

Let's look at an example. Listing 8.1 shows the source code for program ENUM1.CPP. The program implements a simple one-line, four-function calculator that performs the following tasks:

- Prompts you to enter a number, an operator (+, -, *, or /), and a number
- Performs the requested operation, if valid
- Displays the operands, the operator, and the result, if the operation was valid; otherwise displays an error message which indicates the kind of error (either you entered a bad operator, or attempted to divide by 0)

Type

Listing 8.1. Source code for the program ENUM1.CPP.

```
/*
  C++ program that demonstrates enumerated types
*/

#include <iostream.h>

enum mathError { noError, badOperator, divideByZero };

void sayError(mathError err)
{
  switch (err) {
    case noError:
      cout << "No error";
      break;
    case badOperator:
      cout << "Error: invalid operator";
      break;
    case divideByZero:
      cout << "Error: attempt to divide by zero";
  }
}

main()
{
  double x, y, z;
  char op;
  mathError error = noError;

  cout << "Enter a number, an operator, and a number : ";
  cin >> x >> op >> y;

  switch (op) {
    case '+':
      z = x + y;
      break;
    case '-':
      z = x - y;
      break;
```

continues

Listing 8.1. continued

```
39:     case '*':
40:       z = x * y;
41:       break;
42:     case '/':
43:       if (y != 0)
44:         z = x / y;
45:       else
46:         error = divideByZero;
47:       break;
48:     default:
49:       error = badOperator;
50:   }
51:
52:   if (error == noError)
53:     cout << x << " " << op << " " << y << " = " << z;
54:   else
55:     sayError(error);
56:   return 0;
57: }
```

Here is a sample session with the program in Listing 8.1:

Output

```
Enter a number, an operator, and a number : 355 / 113
355 / 113 = 3.14159
```

Analysis

The program in Listing 8.1 declares the enumerated type `mathError` in line 7. This data type has three enumerated values: `noError`, `badOperator`, and `divideByZero`.

The program also defines the function `sayError` in lines 9 through 21 to display a message based on the value of the enumerated parameter `err`. The function uses the switch statement in line 11 to display messages that correspond to the various enumerated values.

The function `main` declares the `double`-typed variables `x`, `y`, and `z` to represent the operands and the result, respectively. In addition, the function declares the `char`-typed variable `op` to store the requested operation, and the enumerated variable error to store the error status. The function initializes the variable error with the enumerated value `noError`.

The output statement in line 29 prompts you to enter the operands and the operator. The statement in line 30 stores your input in variables `x`, `op`, and `y`, in that order. The function uses the switch statement in line 32 to examine the value in variable `op` and perform the requested operation. The case labels at lines 33, 36, 39, and 42 provide the values for the four supported math operations. The last case label contains an `if` statement that detects the attempt to divide by zero. If this is true, the `else` clause statement assigns the enumerated value `divideByZero` to the variable error.

The catch-all default clause in line 48 handles invalid operators. The statement in line 49 assigns the enumerated value `badOperator` to the variable error.

The `if` statement in line 52 determines whether or not the variable error contains the enumerated value `noError`. If this condition is true, the program executes the output statement in line 53. This statement displays the operands, the operator, and the result. Otherwise, the program executes the `else` clause statement, which calls the function `sayError` and passes it the argument error. This function call displays a message that identifies the error.

Structures

C++ supports structures, and these members can be predefined types or other structures.

NEW TERM *Structures* enable you to define a new type that logically groups several fields or members.

Syntax

A Structure

The general syntax for declaring a structure is

```
struct structTag {
  < list of members >
};
```

Examples:

```
struct point {
  double x;
  double y;
};

struct rectangle {
  point upperLeftCorner;
  point lowerRightCorner;
  double area;
};

struct circle {
  point center;
  double radius;
  double area;
};
```

Once you define a struct type, you can use that type to declare variables. Here are examples of declarations that use structures that I declared in the syntax box:

```
point p1, p2, p3;
```

You can also declare structured variables when you define the structure itself:

```
struct point {
  double x;
  double y;
} p1, p2, p3;
```

NEW TERM *Untagged structures* allow you to declare structure variables without defining a name for their structures.

Note: Interestingly, C++ permits you to declare untagged structures. For example, the following structure definition declares the variables p1, p2, and p3 but omits the name of the structure:

```
struct {
  double x;
  double y;
} p1, p2, p3;
```

C++ allows you to declare and initialize a structured variable. Here is an example:

```
point pt = { 1.0, -8.3 };
```

Accessing the members of a structure uses the dot operator. Here are a few examples:

```
p1.x = 12.45;
p1.y = 34.56;
p2.x = 23.4 / p1.x;
p2.y = 0.98 * p1.y;
```

Let's look at an example. Listing 8.2 shows the source code for program STRUCT1.CPP. The program prompts you for four sets of coordinates that define four rectangles. Each rectangle is defined by the X and Y coordinates of the upper left and lower right corners. The program calculates the areas of each rectangle, sorts the rectangles by area, and displays the rectangles in the order of their areas.

Listing 8.2. Source code for the program STRUCT1.CPP.

```
/*
  C++ program that demonstrates structured types
*/

#include <iostream.h>
#include <stdio.h>
#include <math.h>

const MAX_RECT = 4;

struct point {
  double x;
  double y;
};

struct rect {
  point ulc; // upper left corner
  point lrc; // lower right corner
  double area;
  int id;
};

typedef rect rectArr[MAX_RECT];

main()
{
  rectArr r;
  rect temp;
  double length, width;

  for (int i = 0; i < MAX_RECT; i++) {
    cout << "Enter (X,Y) coord. for ULC of rect. # "
         << i << " : ";
    cin >> r[i].ulc.x >> r[i].ulc.y;
    cout << "Enter (X,Y) coord. for LRC of rect. # "
         << i << " : ";
    cin >> r[i].lrc.x >> r[i].lrc.y;
    r[i].id = i;
    length = fabs(r[i].ulc.x - r[i].lrc.x);
    width = fabs(r[i].ulc.y - r[i].lrc.y);
    r[i].area = length * width;
  }

  // sort the rectangles by areas
  for (i = 0; i < (MAX_RECT - 1); i++)
    for (int j = i + 1; j < MAX_RECT; j++)
      if (r[i].area > r[j].area) {
        temp = r[i];
        r[i] = r[j];
        r[j] = temp;
      }

```

continues

Listing 8.2. continued

```
53:   // display rectangles sorted by area
54:   for (i = 0; i < MAX_RECT; i++)
55:     printf("Rect # %d has area %5.4lf\n", r[i].id, r[i].area);
56:   return 0;
57: }
```

Here is a sample session with the program in Listing 8.2:

Output

```
Enter (X,Y) coord. for ULC of rect. # 0 : 1 1
Enter (X,Y) coord. for LRC of rect. # 0 : 2 2
Enter (X,Y) coord. for ULC of rect. # 1 : 1.5 1.5
Enter (X,Y) coord. for LRC of rect. # 1 : 3 4
Enter (X,Y) coord. for ULC of rect. # 2 : 1 2
Enter (X,Y) coord. for LRC of rect. # 2 : 5 8
Enter (X,Y) coord. for ULC of rect. # 3 : 4 6
Enter (X,Y) coord. for LRC of rect. # 3 : 8 4
Rect # 0 has area 1.0000
Rect # 1 has area 3.7500
Rect # 3 has area 8.0000
Rect # 2 has area 24.0000
```

Analysis

The program in Listing 8.2 includes the header files IOSTREAM.H, MATH.H, and STDIO.H. The program declares the global constant `MAX_RECT` to specify the maximum number of rectangles. Line 11 contains the declaration of structure point, which is made up of two `double`-typed members, `x` and `y`. This structure models a two-dimensional point. Line 16 contains the declaration of structure `rect`, which models a rectangle. The structure contains two `point`-typed members, `ulc` and `lrc`; the `double`-typed member `area`; and the `int`-typed member `id`. The members `ulc` and `lrc` represent the coordinates for the upper left and lower right corners, which define a rectangle. The member `area` stores the area of the rectangle. The member `id` stores a numeric identification number.

The `typedef` statement in line 23 defines the type `recArr` as an array of `MAX_RECT` elements of structure `rect`.

The function `main` declares the `rectArr`-typed array `r`, the `rect`-typed structure `temp`, and the `double`-typed variables `length` and `width`.

The function `main` uses the `for` loop in lines 31 through 42 to prompt you for the coordinates of the rectangles, calculate their areas, and assign their `id` numbers. The output statements in lines 32 and 33, and in lines 35 and 36, prompt you for the X and Y coordinates of the upper left and lower right corners, respectively. The input statements in lines 34 and 37 store the coordinates you enter in members `r[i].ulc.x`, `r[i].ulc.y`, `r[i].lrc.x`, and `r[i].lrc.y`, respectively. The statement in line 38 stores the value of the loop control variable `i` in member `r[i].id`. The statement in line 39 calculates the length of a rectangle using the `x` members of the `ulc` and `lrc` members in the element `r[i]`. The statement in line 40 calculates the width of a rectangle using the `y` members of the `ulc` and `lrc` members in the element `r[i]`. The statement in line 41 calculates the area of the rectangle and stores it in member `r[i].area`.

The nested loops in lines 44 through 51 sort the elements of array `r` using the member `area`. The loops implement the simple bubble sort method (which is useful for very small arrays). The `if` statement in line 47 compares the areas of elements `r[i]` and `r[j]`. If the area of rectangle `r[i]` is larger than that of rectangle `r[j]`, the statements in lines 48 through 50 swap all the members of `r[i]` and `r[j]`. The swap uses the structure `temp`. This task illustrates that you can assign all the members of a structure to another structure in one statement.

The `for` loop in lines 54 and 55 displays the rectangles sorted according to their areas. The output statement in line 55 uses the `printf` function to display the rectangle `id` numbers and areas.

Unions

The size of a `union` is equal to the size of its largest member.

NEW TERM *Unions* are special structures that store members that are mutually exclusive.

Syntax

Unions

The general syntax for unions is

```
union unionTag {
  type1 member1;
  type2 member2;
...
  typeN memberN;
};
```

Example:

```
union Long {
  unsigned mWord[2];
  long mLong;
};
```

Unions offer an easy alternative for quick data conversion. Unions were more significant in past decades, when the price of memory was much higher and consolidating memory using unions was feasible. Accessing union members involves the dot access operators, just as in structures.

Reference Variables

In Day 2, you learn that you declare reference parameters by placing the `&` symbol after the parameter's type. Recall that a reference parameter becomes an alias to its arguments. In addition, any changes made to the reference parameter affect its argument. In addition to reference parameters, C++ supports reference variables. You can manipulate the referenced variable by using its alias. As a novice C++ programmer, your initial use of reference variables will most likely be limited. On the other hand, you probably are using reference parameters more frequently. As you advance in using C++, you discover how reference variables can implement programming tricks that deal with advanced class design. This book discusses only the basics of reference variables.

NEW TERM Like reference parameters, *reference variables* become aliases for the variables they access.

Syntax

A Reference Variable

The general syntax for declaring a reference variable is

```
type& refVar;
type& refVar = aVar;
```

The `refVar` is the reference variable that can be initialized when declared. You must ensure that a reference variable is initialized or assigned a referenced variable before using the reference variable.

Examples:

```
int x = 10, y = 3;
int& rx = x;
int& ry;
ry = y; // take the reference
```

Here is a simple example that shows a reference variable at work. Listing 8.3 shows the source code for program REFVAR1.CPP. The program displays and alters the values of a variable using either the variable itself or its reference. The program requires no input.

Listing 8.3. Source code for the program REFVAR1.CPP.

```
1: /*
2:   C++ program that demonstrates reference variables
3: */
4:
5: #include <iostream.h>
6:
7: main()
8: {
9:   int x = 10;
10:   int& rx = x;
11:   // display x using x and rx
12:   cout << "x contains " << x << "\n";
13:   cout << "x contains (using the reference rx) "
14:        << rx << "\n";
15:   // alter x and display its value using rx
16:   x *= 2;
17:   cout << "x contains (using the reference rx) "
18:        << rx << "\n";
19:   // alter rx and display value using x
20:   rx *= 2;
21:   cout << "x contains " << x << "\n";
22:   return 0;
23: }
```

Here is a sample session with the program in Listing 8.3:

```
x contains 10
x contains (using the reference rx) 10
x contains (using the reference rx) 20
x contains 40
```

The program in Listing 8.3 declares the `int`-typed variable `x` and the `int`-typed reference variable `rx`. The program initializes the variable `x` with 10 and the reference variable `rx` with the variable `x`.

The output statement in line 12 displays the value in variable `x` using the variable `x`. By contrast, the output statement in line 13 and 14 displays the value in variable `x` using the reference variable `rx`.

The statement in line 16 doubles the integer in variable `x`. The output statement in lines 17 and 18 displays the new value in variable `x` using the reference variable `rx`. As the output shows, the reference variable accurately displays the updated value in variable `x`.

The statement in line 20 doubles the value in variable `x` by using the reference variable `rx`. The output statement in line 21 displays the updated value in variable `x` using variable `x`. Again, the output shows that the variable `x` and reference variable `rx` are synchronized.

Overview of Pointers

Each piece of information, both program and data, in the computer's memory resides at a specific address and occupies a specific number of bytes. When you run a program, your variables reside at specific addresses. With a high-level language such as C++, you are not concerned about the actual address of every variable. That task is handled transparently by the compiler and the run-time system. Conceptually, each variable in your program is a tag for a memory address. Manipulating the data using the tag is much easier than dealing with actual numerical addresses, such as 0F64:01AF4.

NEW TERM An *address* is a memory location. A *tag* is the variable's name.

C++ and its parent C are programming languages that are also used for low-level systems programming. In fact, many regard C as a high-level assembler. Low-level systems programming requires that you frequently work with the address of data. This is where pointers, in general, come into play. Knowing the address of a piece of data enables you to set and query its value.

NEW TERM A *pointer* is a special variable that stores the address of another variable or information.

> **Warning:** Pointers are very powerful language components. They can also be dangerous if used carelessly because they may hang your system! This malfunction occurs when the pointer happens to have a low memory address of some critical data or function.

Pointers to Existing Variables

In this section, you learn how to use pointers to access the values in existing variables. C++ requires that you associate a data type (including `void`) with a declared pointer. The associated data type may be a predefined type or a user-defined structure.

Syntax

A Pointer

The general syntax for declaring a pointer is

```
type* pointerName;
type* pointerName = &variable;
```

The `&` operator is the `address-of` operator and is used to take the address of a variable.

Example:

```
int *intPtr; // pointer to an int
double *realPtr; // pointer to a double
char *aString; // pointer to a character
long lv;
long* lp = &lv;
```

You can also declare nonpointers in the same lines that declare pointers:

```
int *intPtr, anInt;
double *realPtr, x;
char *aString, aKey;
```

Note: C++ permits you to place the asterisk character right after the associated data type. You should not interpret this kind of syntax to mean that every other identifier appearing in the same declaration is automatically a pointer:

```
int* intPtr; // pointer to an int
double* realPtr; // pointer to a double
char* aString; // pointer to a character
int *intP, j; // intP is a pointer to int, j is an int
double *realPtr, *doublePtr;  // both identifiers
// are pointers to a double
```

DO | **DON'T**

DO initialize a pointer before you use it, just as you do with ordinary variables. In fact, the need to initialize pointers is more pressing—using uninitialized pointers invites trouble that leads to unpredictable program behavior or even a system hang!

DON'T assume that uninitialized pointers are harmless!

Once a pointer contains the address of a variable, you can access the value in that variable using the * operator followed by the pointer's name. For example, if px is a pointer to the variable x, you can use *px to access the value in variable x.

DO | **DON'T**

DO include the * operator to the left of a pointer to access the variable whose address is stored in the pointer.

DON'T forget to use the * operator. Without it, a statement ends up manipulating the address in the pointer instead of the data at that address.

Here is a simple example that shows a pointer at work. Listing 8.4 shows the source code for program PTR1.CPP. The program displays and alters the values of a variable using either the variable itself or its pointer. The program requires no input.

Type **Listing 8.4. Source code for the program PTR1.CPP.**

```
/*
  C++ program that demonstrates pointers to existing variables
*/

#include <iostream.h>

main()
{
  int x = 10;
   int* px = &x;
   // display x using x and rx
   cout << "x contains " << x << "\n";
   cout << "x contains (using the pointer px) "
        << *px << "\n";
   // alter x and display its value using *px
   x *= 2;
   cout << "x contains (using the pointer px) "
        << *px << "\n";
   // alter *px and display value using x
   *px *= 2;
   cout << "x contains " << x << "\n";
   return 0;
}
```

Here is a sample session with the program in Listing 8.4:

Output

```
x contains 10
x contains (using the pointer px) 10
x contains (using the pointer px) 20
x contains 40
```

Analysis

The program in Listing 8.4 declares the `int`-typed variable `x` and the `int`-typed pointer `px`. The program initializes the variable `x` with 10 and the pointer `px` with the address of variable `x`.

The output statement in line 12 displays the value in variable `x` using the variable `x`. By contrast, the output statement in lines 13 and 14 displays the value in variable `x` using the pointer `px`. Notice that the statement uses `*px` to access the value in variable `x`.

The statement in line 16 doubles the integer in variable `x`. The output statement in lines 17 and 18 displays the new value in variable `x` using the pointer `px`. As the output shows, the pointer accurately displays the updated value in variable `x`.

The statement in line 20 doubles the value in variable `x` by using the pointer `px`. Notice that the assignment statement uses `*px` on the left side of the `=` operator to access the variable `x`. The output statement in line 21 displays the updated value in variable `x` using variable `x`. Again, the output shows that the variable `x` and the pointer `px` are synchronized.

Pointers to Arrays

C++, and its parent language C, support a special use for the names of arrays. The compiler interprets the name of an array as the address of its first element. Thus, if `x` is an array, the expressions `&x[0]` and `x` are equivalent. In the case of a matrix—call it `mat`—the expressions `&mat[0][0]` and `mat` are also equivalent. This aspect of C++ and C makes them work as high-level assembly languages. Once you have the address of a data item, you've got its number, so to speak. The knowledge of the memory address of a variable or array enables you to manipulate its contents using pointers.

NEW TERM A *program variable* is a label that tags a memory address. Using a variable in a program means accessing the associated memory location by specifying its name (or tag, if you prefer). In this sense, a variable becomes a name that points to a memory location—a pointer.

C++ allows you to use a pointer to access the various elements of an array. When you access the element `x[i]` of an array `x`, the compiled code performs two tasks. First, it obtains the base address of the array `x` (that is, where the first array element is located).

Second, it uses the index `i` to calculate the offset from the base address of the array. This offset equals `i` multiplied by the size of the basic array type:

```
address of element x[i] = address of x + i * sizeof(basicType)
```

Looking at the preceding equation, assume that I have a pointer `ptr` that takes the base address of array `x`:

```
ptr = x; // pointer ptr points to address of x[0]
```

I can now substitute `x` with `ptr` in the equation and come up with the following:

```
address of element x[i] = ptr + i * sizeof(basicType)
```

In order for C++ and C to become high-level assemblers, they simplify the use of this equation by absolving it from having to explicitly state the size of the basic array type. Thus, you can write the following:

```
address of element x[i] = p + i
```

This equation states that the address of element `x[i]` is the expression `(p + i)`.

Let me illustrate the use of pointers to access one-dimensional arrays by presenting the next program, PTR2.CPP (Listing 8.5). This program is a modified version of the program ARRAY1.CPP that calculates the average value for data in an array. The program begins by prompting you to enter the number of data and the data itself. Then the program calculates the average of the data in the array. Next, the program displays the average value.

Type Listing 8.5. Source code for the program PTR2.CPP.

```
/*
   C++ program that demonstrates the use of pointer with
   one-dimension arrays.  Program calculates the average
   value of the data found in the array.
*/

#include <iostream.h>

const int MAX = 30;

main()
{

     double x[MAX];
     // declare pointer and initialize with base
     // address of array x
     double *realPtr = x; // same as = &x[0]
     double sum, sumx = 0.0, mean;
     int n;
```

```
20:     // obtain the number of data points
21:     do {
22:         cout << "Enter number of data points [2 to "
23:              << MAX << "] : ";
24:         cin >> n;
25:         cout << "\n";
26:     } while (n < 2 ¦¦ n > MAX);
27:
28:     // prompt for the data
29:     for (int i = 0; i < n; i++) {
30:         cout << "X[" << i << "] : ";
31:         // use the form *(x+i) to store data in x[i]
32:         cin >> *(x + i);
33:     }
34:
35:     sum = n;
36:     for (i = 0; i < n; i++)
37:     // use the form *(realPtr + i) to access x[i]
38:         sumx += *(realPtr + i);
39:     mean = sumx / sum;
40:     cout << "\nMean = " << mean << "\n\n";
41:     return 0;
42: }
```

Here is a sample session with the program in Listing 8.5:

Output

```
Enter number of data points [2 to 30] : 5

X[0] : 1
X[1] : 2
X[2] : 3
X[3] : 4
X[4] : 5

Mean = 3
```

Analysis The program in Listing 8.5 declares the `double`-typed array `x` to have `MAX` elements. In addition, the program declares the pointer `realPtr` and initializes it using the array `x`. Thus, the pointer `realPtr` stores the address of `x[0]`, the first element in array `x`.

The program uses the pointer for `*(x + i)` in the input statement at line 32. Thus, the identifier `x` works as a pointer to the array `x`. Using the expression `*(x + i)` accesses the element number `i` of array `x`, just as using the expression `x[i]` does.

The program uses the pointer `realPtr` in the `for` loop at lines 37 and 38. The expression `*(realPtr + i)` is the equivalent of `*(x + i)`, which in turn is equivalent to `x[i]`. Thus, the `for` loop uses the pointer `realPtr` with an offset value, `i`, to access the elements of array `x`.

The Pointer Increment/Decrement Method

The previous C++ program maintains the same address in the pointer `realPtr`. Employing pointer arithmetic with the `for` loop index `i`, you can write a new program version that increments the offset to access the elements of array `x`. C++ provides you with another choice that allows you to access sequentially the elements of an array without the help of an explicit offset value. The method merely involves using the increment or decrement operator with a pointer. You still need to initialize the pointer to the base address of an array and then use the ++ operator to access the next array element. Here is a modified version of the last program that uses the pointer increment method. Listing 8.6 shows the source code for the PTR3.CPP program.

Type

Listing 8.6. Source code for the program PTR3.CPP.

```
/*
  C++ program that demonstrates the use of pointers with
  one-dimension arrays.  The average value of the array
  is calculated.  This program modifies the previous version
  in the following way:  the realPtr is used to access the
  array without any help from any loop control variable.
  This is accomplished by 'incrementing' the pointer, and
  consequently incrementing its address.  This program
  illustrates pointer arithmetic that alters the pointer's
  address.

*/

#include <iostream.h>

const int MAX = 30;

main()
{

    double x[MAX];
    double *realPtr = x;
    double sum, sumx = 0.0, mean;
    int i, n;

    do {
        cout << "Enter number of data points [2 to "
             << MAX << "] : ";
        cin >> n;
        cout << "\n";
    } while (n < 2 || n > MAX);

    // loop variable i is not directly involved in accessing
    //  the elements of array x
    for (i = 0; i < n; i++) {
```

```
36:         cout << "X[" << i << "] : ";
37:         // increment pointer realPtr after taking its reference
38:         cin >> *realPtr++;
39:      }
40:
41:      // restore original address by using pointer arithmetic
42:      realPtr -= n;
43:      sum = n;
44:      // loop variable i serves as a simple counter
45:      for (i = 0; i < n; i++)
46:        // increment pointer realPtr after taking a reference
47:         sumx += *(realPtr++);
48:      mean = sumx / sum;
49:      cout << "\nMean = " << mean << "\n\n";
50:      return 0;
51:
52: }
```

Here is a sample session with the program in Listing 8.6:

```
Enter number of data points [2 to 30] : 5

X[0] : 10
X[1] : 20
X[2] : 30
X[3] : 40
X[4] : 50

Mean = 30
```

The program in Listing 8.6 initializes the `realPtr` pointer to the base address of array `x` in line 22. The program uses the `realPtr` pointer in the keyboard input statement in line 38. This statement uses `*realPtr++` to store your input in the currently accessed element of array `x`, and then to increment the pointer to the next element of array `x`. When the input loop terminates, the pointer `realPtr` points past the tail of array `x`. To reset the pointer to the base address of array `x`, the program uses the assignment statement in line 42. This statement uses pointer arithmetic to decrease the current address in pointer `realPtr` by `n` times `sizeof(real)`. The statement resets the address in the pointer `realPtr` to access the array element `x[0]`. The program uses the same incrementing method to calculate the sum of data in the second `for` loop in line 47.

Pointers to Structures

C++ supports declaring and using pointers to structures. Assigning the address of a structured variable to a pointer of the same type uses the same syntax as with simple variables. Once the pointer has the address of the structured variable, it needs to use the -> operator to access the members of the structure.

Accessing Structure Members

The general syntax for accessing the members of a structure by a pointer is

```
structPtr->aMember
```

Example:

```
struct point {
  double x;
  double y;
};

point p;
point* ptr = &p;

ptr->x = 23.3;
ptr->y = ptr->x + 12.3;
```

Here is a sample program that uses pointers to structures. Listing 8.7 shows the source code for program PTR4.CPP. This program is the version of program STRUCT1.CPP, which uses pointers. The program prompts you for four sets of coordinates that define four rectangles. Each rectangle is defined by the X and Y coordinates of the upper left and lower right corners. The program calculates the areas of each rectangle, sorts the rectangles by area, and displays the rectangles in the order of their areas.

Listing 8.7. Source code for the program PTR4.CPP.

```
/*
  C++ program that demonstrates pointers to structured types
*/

#include <iostream.h>
#include <stdio.h>
#include <math.h>

const MAX_RECT = 4;

struct point {
  double x;
  double y;
};

struct rect {
  point ulc; // upper left corner
  point lrc; // lower right corner
  double area;
  int id;
};

typedef rect rectArr[MAX_RECT];
```

```
main()
{
  rectArr r;
  rect temp;
  rect* pr = r;
  rect* pr2;
  double length, width;

  for (int i = 0; i < MAX_RECT; i++, pr++) {
    cout << "Enter (X,Y) coord. for ULC of rect. # "
         << i << " : ";
    cin >> pr->ulc.x >> pr->ulc.y;
    cout << "Enter (X,Y) coord. for LRC of rect. # "
         << i << " : ";
    cin >> pr->lrc.x >> pr->lrc.y;
    pr->id = i;
    length = fabs(pr->ulc.x - pr->lrc.x);
    width = fabs(pr->ulc.y - pr->lrc.y);
    pr->area = length * width;
  }

  pr -= MAX_RECT; // reset pointer
  // sort the rectangles by areas
  for (i = 0; i < (MAX_RECT - 1); i++, pr++) {
    pr2 = pr + 1; // reset pointer pr2
    for (int j = i + 1; j < MAX_RECT; j++, pr2++)
      if (pr->area > pr2->area) {
        temp = *pr;
        *pr = *pr2;
        *pr2 = temp;
      }
  }

  pr -= MAX_RECT - 1; // reset pointer
  // display rectangles sorted by area
  for (i = 0; i < MAX_RECT; i++, pr++)
    printf("Rect # %d has area %5.4lf\n", pr->id, pr->area);
  return 0;
}
```

Here is a sample session with the program in Listing 8.7:

Output

```
Enter (X,Y) coord. for ULC of rect. # 0 : 1 1
Enter (X,Y) coord. for LRC of rect. # 0 : 2 2
Enter (X,Y) coord. for ULC of rect. # 1 : 1.5 1.5
Enter (X,Y) coord. for LRC of rect. # 1 : 3 4
Enter (X,Y) coord. for ULC of rect. # 2 : 1 2
Enter (X,Y) coord. for LRC of rect. # 2 : 5 8
Enter (X,Y) coord. for ULC of rect. # 3 : 4 6
Enter (X,Y) coord. for LRC of rect. # 3 : 8 4
Rect # 0 has area 1.0000
Rect # 1 has area 3.7500
Rect # 3 has area 8.0000
Rect # 2 has area 24.0000
```

Analysis The program in Listing 8.7 declares the pointers `pr` and `pr2` in lines 29 and 30, respectively. These pointers access the structure of type `rect`. The program initializes the pointer `pr` with the base address of array `r`.

The first `for` loop, which begins at line 33, uses the pointer `pr` to access the elements of array `r`. The loop increment part contains the expression `pr++`, which uses pointer arithmetic to make the pointer `pr` access the next element in array `r`. The input statements in lines 36 and 39 use the pointer `pr` to access the members `ulc` and `lrc`. Notice that the statements use the pointer access operator `->` to allow pointer `pr` to access the members `ulc` and `lrc`. The statements in lines 40 through 43 also use the pointer `pr` to access the members `id`, `ulc`, `lrc`, and `area`, using the `->` operator.

The statement in line 46 resets the address stored in pointer `pr` by `MAX_RECT` units (that is `MAX_RECT * sizeof(double)` bytes). The nested loops in lines 48 through 56 use the pointers `pr` and `pr2`. The outer `for` loop increments the address in pointer `pr` by one before the next iteration. The statement in line 49 assigns `pr + 1` to the pointer `pr2`. This statement gives the pointer `pr2` the initial access to the element `i + 1` in array `r`. The inner `for` loop increments the pointer `pr2` by 1 before the next iteration. Thus, the nested `for` loops use the pointers `pr` and `pr2` to access the elements of array `r`. The `if` statement in line 51 uses the pointers `pr` and `pr2` to access the area member in comparing the areas of various rectangles. The statements in line 52 through 54 swap the elements of array `r`, which are accessed by pointers `pr` and `pr2`. Notice that the statements use `*pr` and `*pr2` to access an entire element of array `r`.

The statement in line 58 resets the address in pointer `pr` by subtracting `MAX_RECT -1`. The last `for` loop also uses the pointer `pr` to access and display the members `id` and area of the various elements in array `r`.

This program illustrates that you can completely manipulate an array using pointers only; they are powerful and versatile.

Pointers and Dynamic Memory

The programs presented so far create the space for their variables at compile-time. When the programs start running, the variables have their memory spaces pre-assigned. There are many applications in which you need to create new variables during the program execution. You need to allocate the memory space dynamically for these new variables at run-time. The designers of C++ have chosen to include operators that are not found in C to handle the dynamic allocation and deallocation of memory. These C++ operators are `new` and `delete`. While the C-style dynamic memory functions `malloc`, `calloc`, and `free` are still available, you should use the operators `new` and `delete`. These operators are more aware of the type of dynamic data created than functions `malloc`, `calloc`, and `free`.

Syntax

The *new* and *delete* Operators

The general syntax for using the `new` and `delete` operators in creating dynamic scalar variables is

```
pointer = new type;
delete pointer;
```

The operator `new` returns the address of the dynamically allocated variable. The operator `delete` removes the dynamically allocated memory accessed by a pointer. If the dynamic allocation of operator `new` fails, it returns a `NULL` (equivalent to 0) pointer. Therefore, you need to test for a `NULL` pointer after using the `new` operator if you suspect trouble.

Example:

```
int *pint;
pint = new int;
*pint = 33;
cout << "Pointer pint stores " << *pint;
delete pint;
```

Syntax

A Dynamic Array

To allocate and deallocate a dynamic array, use the following general syntax:

```
arrayPointer = new type[arraySize];
delete [] arrayPointer;
```

The operator `new` returns the address of the dynamically allocated array. If the allocation fails, the operator assigns `NULL` to the pointer. The operator `delete` removes the dynamically allocated array accessed by a pointer.

Example:

```
const int MAX = 10;
int* pint;
pint = new int[MAX];
for (int i = 0; i < MAX; i++)
  *pint[i] = i * i
for (i = 0; i < MAX; i++)
  cout << *(pint + i) << "\n";
delete [] pint;
```

DO	DON'T

DO maintain access to dynamic variables and arrays at all times. Such access does not need the original pointers used to create these dynamic variables and arrays. Here is an example:

```
int* p = new int;
int* q;
*p = 123;
q = p; // q now also points to 123
p = new int; // create another dynamic variable
*p = 345; // p points to 345 whereas q points to 123
cout << *p << " " << *q << " " << (*p + *q) << "\n";
delete p;
delete q;
```

DON'T forget to delete dynamic variables and arrays at the end of their scope.

Using pointers to create and access dynamic data can be illustrated with the next program, PTR5.CPP (Listing 8.8). This program is a modified version of the program ARRAY1.CPP, which calculates the average value for data in an array. The program begins by prompting you to enter the actual number of data and validating your input. Then the program prompts you for the data and calculates the average of the data in the array. Next, the program displays the average value.

Type

Listing 8.8. Source code for the program PTR5.CPP.

```
/*
  C++ program that demonstrates the pointers to manage
  dynamic data
*/

#include <iostream.h>

const int MAX = 30;

main()
{

    double* x;
    double sum, sumx = 0, mean;
    int *n;

    n = new int;
    if (n == NULL)
      return 1;

    do { // obtain number of data points
```

```
22:         cout << "Enter number of data points [2 to "
23:              << MAX << "] : ";
24:         cin >> *n;
25:         cout << "\n";
26:     } while (*n < 2 ¦¦ *n > MAX);
27:     // create tailor-fit dynamic array
28:     x = new double[*n];
29:     if (!x) {
30:       delete n;
31:       return 1;
32:     }
33:     // prompt user for data
34:     for (int i = 0; i < *n; i++) {
35:         cout << "X[" << i << "] : ";
36:         cin >> x[i];
37:     }
38:
39:     // initialize summations
40:     sum = *n;
41:     // calculate sum of observations
42:     for (i = 0; i < *n; i++)
43:         sumx += *(x + i);
44:
45:     mean = sumx / sum; // calculate the mean value
46:     cout << "\nMean = " << mean << "\n\n";
47:     // deallocate dynamic memory
48:     delete n;
49:     delete [] x;
50:     return 0;
51: }
```

Here is a sample session with the program in Listing 8.8:

```
Enter number of data points [2 to 30] : 5

X[0] : 1
X[1] : 2
X[2] : 3
X[3] : 4
X[4] : 5

Mean = 3
```

The program in Listing 8.8 uses two pointers for dynamic allocations. Line 13 declares the first pointer, which is used to allocate and access the dynamic array. Line 15 declares the pointer to create a dynamic variable.

The statement in line 17 uses the operator `new` to allocate the space for a dynamic `int` variable. The statement returns the address of the dynamic data to the pointer `n`. The `if` statement in line 18 determines whether or not the dynamic allocation failed. If so, the function `main` exits and returns an exit code of 1 (to flag an error).

The `do-while` loop in lines 21 through 26 prompts you to enter the number of data points. The statement in line 24 stores your input in the dynamic variable accessed by pointer `n`. The statement uses the pointer reference `*n` for this access. The `while` clause also uses `*n` to access the value in the dynamic variable. In fact, all the statements in the program access the number of data using the pointer reference `*n`.

The statement in line 28 creates a dynamic array using the operator `new`. The statement creates a dynamic `double`-typed array with the number of elements that you specify. This feature shows the advantage of using dynamic allocation to create custom-fit arrays. The `if` statement in line 29 determines whether or not the allocation of the dynamic array was successful. If not, the statements in lines 30 and 31 deallocate the dynamic variable accessed by pointer `n` and exit the function with a return value of 1.

The `for` loop in lines 34 through 37 prompts you to enter values for the dynamic array. The statement in line 36 stores your input to the element `i` of the dynamic array. Notice that the statement uses the expression `x[i]` to access the targeted element. This form resembles that of static arrays. C++ treats the expression `x[i]` as equivalent to `*(x + i)`. In fact, the program uses the latter form in the second `for` loop in lines 42 and 43. The statement in line 43 accesses the elements in the dynamic array using the form `*(x + i)`.

The last statements in function `main` delete the dynamic variable and array. The statement in line 48 deallocates the space for the dynamic variable accessed by pointer `n`. The statement in line 49 deletes the dynamic array accessed by pointer `x`.

Far Pointers

The architecture of processors such as the family of Intel 80x86 uses segmented memory. Each segment is 64K. Using segments has advantages and disadvantages.

NEW TERM This storage scheme supports two kinds of pointers: near pointers and far pointers. Within a segment, you can use *near pointers* to access data in the same segment. The pointers only store the offset address in the segment and thus require fewer bytes to store their addresses. By contrast, *far pointers* store the segment and offset addresses, and thus require more space. Windows applications use far pointers.

To declare far pointers, insert the keyword `far` (or sometimes `_far`) between the pointer's type and the pointer's name.

Summary

Today's lesson introduces you to user-defined data types and covers the following topics:

- You can use the `typedef` statements to create alias types of existing types and define array types. The general syntax for using `typedef` is

```
typedef knownType newType;
```

- Enumerated data types enable you to declare unique identifiers that represent a collection of logically related constants. The general syntax for declaring an enumerated type is

```
enum enumType { <list of enumerated identifiers> };
```

- Structures enable you to define a new type that logically groups several fields or members. These members can be predefined types or other structures. The general syntax for declaring a structure is

```
struct structTag {
  < list of members >
};
```

- Unions are a form of variant structures. The general syntax for `unions` is

```
union unionTag {
  type1 member1;
  type2 member2;
...
  typeN memberN;
};
```

- Reference variables are aliases of the variables that they reference. To declare a reference variable, place the `&` after the data type of the reference variable or to the left of the variable's name.

- Pointers are variables that store the addresses of other variables or data. C++ uses pointers to offer flexible and efficient manipulation of data and system resources.

- Pointers to existing variables use the `&` operator to obtain the addresses of these variables. Armed with these addresses, pointers offer access to the data in their associated variables. To access the value using a pointer, use the `*` operator followed by the name of the pointer.

- Pointers access the elements of arrays by being assigned the base address of a class. C++ considers the name of an array as equivalent to the pointer of the base address. For example, the name of the array `X` is treated as `&X[0]`. Pointers can be used to sequentially traverse the elements of an array to store and/or recall values from these elements.
- Pointers to structures manipulate structures and access their members. C++ provides the `->` operator to allow a pointer access to the members of a structure.
- Pointers can create and access dynamic data using the operators `new` and `delete`. These operators allow you to create dynamic variables and arrays. The `new` operator assigns the address of the dynamic data to the pointer used in creating and accessing the data. The operator `delete` assists in recuperating the space of dynamic data when that information is no longer needed.
- Far pointers are pointers that store both the segment and offset addresses of an item. Near pointers only store the offset address of an item. Far pointers require more storage than near pointers.

Q&A

Q Does C++ support pointers to the predefined type void?

A Yes, `void*` pointers are considered typeless pointers and can be used to copy data.

Q Because C++ pointers have types (even `void*` pointers), can I use typecasting to translate the data accessed by the general-purpose `void*` pointers to non-`void*` pointers?

A Yes, C++ allows you to typecast pointer references. For example:

```
void* p = data;
long *lp = (long*) p;
```

The pointer `lp` uses the typecast to translate the data it accesses.

Q What happens if I delete a dynamic array using the `delete` operator without following it with the empty brackets?

A The run-time system only deletes the first element of the dynamic array. The other elements remain in memory, as inaccessible data.

Q Can a structure contain a pointer to itself?

A Yes. Many structures that model dynamic data structures use this kind of declaration. For example, the following structure models the nodes of a dynamic list with pointer-based links:

```
struct listNode {
  dataType data;
  listNode *next;
};
```

Q Does C++ allow the declaration of a pointer-to-structure type before declaring the structure?

A Yes, this feature makes declaring nodes of dynamic data structure possible.

Q Does C++ allow pointers that access the addresses of other pointers?

A Yes, C++ supports pointers to pointers (also called *double pointers*). To declare such pointers, use two `*` characters, as shown in the example below which declares the double pointer `p`:

```
int x;
int *px = &x;
int **p = &px;
```

Then expression `*p` accesses the pointer `px` and the expression `**p` accesses the variable `x`.

Workshop

The Workshop provides quiz questions to help you solidify your understanding of the material covered and exercises to provide you with experience in using what you've learned. Try to understand the quiz and exercise answers before continuing on to the next day's lesson. Answers are provided in Appendix B, "Answers."

Quiz

1. What is the error in the following statements?

```
enum Boolean { false, true };
enum State { on, off };
enum YesNo { yes, no };
enum DiskDriveStatus { on , off };
```

2. Is the declaration of the following enumerated type incorrect?

```
enum YesNo ( no = 0, No = 0, yes = 1, Yes = 1 };
```

3. What is the problem with the following program?

```
#include <iostream.h>
main()
{
  int *p = new int;
  cout << "Enter a number : ";
  cin >> *p;
  cout << "The square of " << *p << " = " << (*p * *p);
  return 0;
}
```

Exercises

1. Modify program PTR4.CPP to create program PTR6.CPP, which uses the Comb sort method to sort the array of rectangles.
2. Define a structure that can be used to model a dynamic array of integers. The structure should have a member to access the dynamic data and a member to store the size of the dynamic array. Call the structure `intArrStruct`.
3. Define a structure that can be used to model a dynamic matrix. The structure should have a member to access the dynamic data and two members to store the number of rows and columns. Call the structure `matStruct`.

9

Strings

WEEK 2

The examples presented from Day 1 through Day 8 are predominantly numeric, with a few aimed at character manipulation. You may have grown suspicious about the absence of strings in all of these examples. Today's lesson discusses C++ strings. You learn about the following topics:

- Strings in C++
- String input
- Using the standard string library
- Assigning strings
- Getting the length of strings
- Concatenating strings
- Comparing strings
- Converting strings
- Reversing the characters in a string
- Locating characters
- Locating substrings

C++ Strings

C++ (and its parent language C) has no predefined string type. Instead, C++, like C, regards strings as arrays of characters that end with the ASCII 0 null character (`'\0'`).

NEW TERM The `'\0'` character is also called the *null terminator*. Strings that end with the null terminator are sometimes called *ASCIIZ strings*, with the letter Z standing for zero, the ASCII code of the null terminator.

The null terminator must be present in all strings and taken into account when dimensioning a string. When you declare a string variable as an array of characters, be sure to reserve an extra space for the null terminator. The advantage of using the null terminator is that you can create strings that are not restricted by any limit imposed by the C++ implementation. In addition, ASCIIZ strings have very simple structures.

Note: The lesson in Day 8 discusses how pointers can access and manipulate the elements of an array. C and C++ make extensive use of this programming feature in manipulating the characters of a string.

DO | DON'T

DO include an extra space for the null terminator when specifying the size of a string.

DON'T declare a string variable as a single-character array. Such a variable is useless!

9

String Input

The programs that I have presented so far display string literals in output stream statements. Thus, C++ supports stream output for strings as a special case for a non-predefined data type. (You can say the support came by popular demand!) String output using string variables uses the same operator and syntax. With string input, the inserter operator >> does not work well because strings often contain spaces which are ignored by the inserter operator. Instead of the inserter operator, you need to use the `getline` function. This function reads up to a specified number of characters.

Syntax

The *getline* Function

The general syntax for the overloaded `getline` function is

```
istream& getline(signed char* buffer,
                 int size,
                 char delimiter = '\n');

istream& getline(unsigned char* buffer,
                 int size,
              char delimiter = '\n');
```

The parameter `buffer` is a pointer to the string receiving the characters from the stream. The parameter `size` specifies the maximum number of characters to read. The parameter `delimiter` specifies the delimiting character that causes the string input to stop before reaching the number of characters specified by parameter size. The parameter `delimiter` has the default argument of `'\n'`.

Example:

```
#include <iostream.h>
main()
{
  char name[80];
  cout << "Enter your name: ";
  cin.getline(name, sizeof(name)-1);
```

```
    cout << "Hello " << name << ", how are you";
    return 0;
}
```

Using the STRING.H Library

The community of C programmers has developed the standard string library STRING.H that contains the most frequently used string-manipulation functions. The STDIO.H and IOSTREAM.H header file prototype functions also support string I/O. The different C++ compiler vendors have also developed C++-style string libraries. These libraries use classes to model strings (more about classes in Day 11). However, these string libraries are not standard, whereas the C-style string routines in STRING.H are part of the ANSI C standard. In the next subsections I present several, but not all, of the functions which are prototyped in the STRING.H header file.

Some of the string functions in STRING.H have more than one version. The extra versions which append the letters `_f`, `f`, or `_`, work with strings that are accessed using far pointers.

Assigning Strings

C++ supports two methods for assigning strings. You can assign a string literal to a string variable when you initialize it. This method is simple and requires using the = operator and the assigning string.

Syntax

Initializing a String

The general syntax for initializing a string is

```
char stringVar[stringSize] = stringLiteral;
```

Example:

```
char aString[81] = "Visual C++ in 21 days";
char name[] = "Namir Shammas";
```

The second method for assigning one ASCIIZ string to another uses the function `strcpy`. This function assumes that the copied string ends with the null character.

Syntax

The *strcpy* Function

The prototype for the function `strcpy` is

```
char* strcpy(char* target, const char* source)
```

The function copies the characters from string `source` to string `target`. The function *assumes* that the target string accesses enough space to contain the source string.

Example:

```
char name[41];
strcpy(name,"Visual C++");
```

The variable name contains the string `"Visual C++"`.

The function `strdup` allows you to copy the character to another string and allocate required space in the target string.

Syntax

The *strdup* Function

The prototype for the function `strdup` is

```
char* strdup(const char* source)
```

The function copies the characters in the source string and returns a pointer to the duplicate string.

Example:

```
char* string1 = "The reign in Spain";
char* string2;

string2 = strdup(string1);
```

This example copies the contents of `string1` into `string2` after allocating the memory space for `string2`.

The string library also offers the function `strncpy` to support copying a specified number of characters from one string to another.

Syntax

The *strncpy* Function

The prototype for the function `strncpy` is

```
char* strncpy(char* target, const char* source, size_t num);
```

The function copies *num* characters from the source string to the target string. The function performs character truncation or padding, if necessary.

Example:

```
char str1[] = "Pascal";
char str2[] = "Hello there";

strncpy(str1, str2, 6);
```

The variable `str1` now contains the string `"Hello "`.

Note: Using pointers to manipulate strings is new to many novice C++ programmers. In fact, you can use pointers to manipulate the trailing parts of a string by assigning the address of the first character to manipulate. For example, if I declare the string `str1` as follows:

```
char str1[41] = "Hello World";
char str2[41];
char* p = str1;

p += 6; // p now points to substring "World" in str
strcpy(str2, p);
cout << str2 << "\n";
```

The output statement displays the string `"World"`. This example shows how using pointers can incorporate an offset number of characters.

The Length of a String

Many string operations require the number of characters in a string. The STRING.H library offers the function `strlen` to return the number of characters, excluding the null terminator, in a string.

Syntax

The *strlen* Function

The prototype for the function `strlen` is

```
size_t strlen(const char* string)
```

The function strlen returns the number of characters in parameter string. The result type size_t represents a general integer type.

Example:

```
char str[] = "1234567890";
unsigned i;
i = strlen(str);
```

These statements assign 10 to the variable i.

Concatenating Strings

Often, you build a string by concatenating two or more strings. The function strcat allows you to concatenate one string to another.

NEW TERM When you *concatenate* strings, you join or link them together.

Syntax

The *strcat* Function

The prototype for the function strcat is

```
char* strcat(char* target, const char* source)
```

The function appends the contents of the source string to the target string and returns the pointer to the target string. The function assumes that the target string can accommodate the characters of the source strings.

Example:

```
char string[81];
strcpy(string, "Visual");
strcat(string," C++")
```

The variable string now contains "Visual C++".

The function strncat concatenates a specified number of characters from the source string to the target string.

Syntax

The *strncat* Function

The prototype for the function strncat is

```
char* strncat(char* target, const char* source, size_t num)
```

The function appends num characters of the source string to the target string and returns the pointer to the target string.

Example:

```
char str1[81] = "Hello I am ";
char str2[41] = "Thomas Jones";

strncat(str1, str2, 6);
```

The variable str1 now contains "Hello I am Thomas".

DO	DON'T

DO use the function strncat to control the number of concatenated characters when you are unsure of the capacity of the target string.

DON'T assume that the target string is always adequate to store the character in the source string.

Let's look at a program that uses the getline, strlen, and strcat functions. Listing 9.1 contains the source code for the program STRING1.CPP. The program performs the following tasks:

- Prompts you to enter a string (your input should not exceed 40 characters)
- Prompts you to enter a second string (your input should not exceed 40 characters)
- Displays the number of characters in each of the strings you enter
- Concatenates the second string to the first one
- Displays the concatenated strings
- Displays the number of characters in the concatenated strings
- Prompts you to enter a search character
- Prompts you to enter a replacement character
- Displays the concatenated string after translating all the occurrences of the search character with the replacement character

Listing 9.1. Source code for the program STRING1.CPP.

```
/*
  C++ program that demonstrates C-style strings
*/

#include <iostream.h>
#include <string.h>

const unsigned MAX1 = 40;
const unsigned MAX2 = 80;

main()
{

    char smallStr[MAX1+1];
    char bigStr[MAX2+1];
    char findChar, replChar;

    cout << "Enter first string:\n";
    cin.getline(bigStr, MAX2);
    cout << "Enter second string:\n";
    cin.getline(smallStr, MAX1);
    cout << "String 1 has " << strlen(bigStr)
         << " characters\n";
    cout << "String 2 has " << strlen(smallStr)
         << " characters\n";
    // concatenate bigStr to smallStr
    strcat(bigStr, smallStr);
    cout << "Concatenated strings are:\n"
         << bigStr << "\n";
    cout << "New string has " << strlen(bigStr)
         << " characters\n";
    // get the search and replacement characters
    cout << "Enter search character : ";
    cin >> findChar;
    cout << "Enter replacement character : ";
    cin >> replChar;
    // replace characters in string bigStr
    for (unsigned i = 0; i < strlen(bigStr); i++)
      if (bigStr[i] == findChar)
        bigStr[i] = replChar;
    // display the updated string bigStr
    cout << "New string is:\n"
         << bigStr;
    return 0;
}
```

Here is a sample session with the program in Listing 9.1:

Output

```
Enter first string:
The rain in Spain stays
Enter second string:
mainly in the plain
String 1 has 23 characters
String 2 has 20 characters
Concatenated strings are:
The rain in Spain stays mainly in the plain
New string has 43 characters
Enter search character : a
Enter replacement character : A
New string is:
The rAin in SpAin stAys mAinly in the plAin
```

Analysis

The program in Listing 9.1 includes the STRING.H header file for the string manipulation functions. Lines 8 and 9 declare the global constants `MAX1` and `MAX2` used to size a small string and a big string, respectively. The function `main` declares two strings, `smallStr` and `bigStr`. Line 14 declares the variable `smallStr` to store `MAX1+1` characters (the extra space is for the null character). Line 15 declares the variable `bigStr` to store `MAX2+1` characters. Line 16 declares the `char`-typed variables `findChar` and `replChar`.

The output statement in line 18 prompts you to enter the first string. The statement in line 19 uses the stream input function `getline` to obtain your input and to store it in variable `bigStr`. The function `call` specifies that you can enter up to `MAX2` characters. The output statement in line 20 prompts you to enter the second string. The statement in line 21 uses the stream input function `getline` to obtain your input and to store it in variable `smallStr`. The function `call` specifies that you can enter up to `MAX1` characters.

The output statements in lines 22 through 25 display the number of characters in variables `bigStr` and `smallStr`, respectively. Each output statement calls function `strlen` and passes it a string variable.

The statement in line 27 concatenates the string in variable `smallStr` to variable `bigStr`. The output statement in line 28 and 29 displays the updated string `bigStr`. The output statement in lines 30 and 31 displays the number of characters in the updated string variable `bigStr`. This statement also uses the function `strlen` to obtain the number of characters.

The statement in line 33 prompts you to enter the search character. The statement in line 34 obtains your input and stores it in variable `findChar`. The statement in line 35 prompts you to enter the replacement character. The statement in line 36 obtains your input and stores it in variable `replChar`.

The `for` loop in lines 38 through 40 translates the characters in string `bigStr`. The loop uses the control variable `i` and iterates, in increments of 1, from 0 to `strlen(bigstr)-1`. The `if` statement in line 39 determines whether or not character number `i` in `bigStr` matches the character in variable `findChar`. If this condition is true, the program executes the statement in line 40. This statement assigns the character in variable `replChar` to character number `i` in variable `bigStr`. This loop shows how you can manipulate the contents of a string variable by accessing each character in that string.

The output statement in lines 42 and 43 displays the updated string `bigStr`.

9

String Comparison

Because strings are arrays of characters, the STRING.H library provides a set of functions to compare strings. These functions compare the characters of two strings using the ASCII value of each character. The functions are `strcmp`, `stricmp`, `strncmp`, and `strnicmp`.

The function `strcmp` performs a case-sensitive comparison of two strings, using every character possible.

Syntax

The *strcmp* Function

The prototype for the function `strcmp` is

```
int strcmp(const char* str1, const char* str2);
```

The function compares strings *`str1`* and *`str2`*. The integer result indicates the outcome of the comparison:

```
< 0  when str1 is less than str2
= 0  when str1 is equal to str2
> 0  when str1 is greater than str2
```

Example:

```
char string1[] = "Visual C++";
char string2[] = "Visual Basic";
int i;

i = strcmp(string1, string2);
```

The last statement assigns a negative number to the variable `i`, because the string in variable `string1` is less than the string in variable `string2`.

The function `stricmp` performs a case-insensitive comparison between two strings, using every character possible.

Syntax

The *stricmp* Function

The prototype for the function `stricmp` is

```
int stricmp(const char* str1, const char* str2);
```

The function compares the strings *str1* and *str2* without making a distinction between upper- and lowercase characters. The integer result indicates the outcome of the comparison:

```
< 0  when str1 is less than str2
= 0  when str1 is equal to str2
> 0  when str1 is greater than str2
```

Example:

```
char string1[] = "Visual C++";
char string2[] = "VISUAL C++";
int i;

i = stricmp(string1, string2);
```

The last statement assigns 0 to the variable `i`, because the strings in variables `string1` and `string2` differ only in their cases.

The function `strncmp` performs a case-sensitive comparison on specified leading characters in two strings.

Syntax

The *strncmp* Function

The prototype for the function `strncmp` is

```
int strncmp(const char* str1, const char* str2, size_t num);
```

The function compares the *num* leading characters in the two strings *str1* and *str2*. The integer result indicates the outcome of the comparison:

```
< 0  when str1 is less than str2
= 0  when str1 is equal to str2
> 0  when str1 is greater than str2
```

Example:

```
char string1[] = "Visual C++";
char string2[] = "Visual Basic";
int i;

i = strncmp(string1, string2, 8);
```

This assigns a positive number to the variable `i` because `"Visual C"` is greater than `"Visual B"`.

The function `strnicmp` performs a case-insensitive comparison on specified leading characters in two strings.

Syntax

The *strnicmp* Function

The prototype for the function `strnicmp` is

```
int strnicmp(const char* str1, const char* str2, size_t num);
```

The function compares the *num* leading characters in the two strings *str1* and *str2*, regardless of the character case. The integer result indicates the outcome of the comparison:

```
< 0  when str1 is less than str2
= 0  when str1 is equal to str2
> 0  when str1 is greater than str2
```

Example:

```
char string1[] = "Visual C++";
char string2[] = "VISUAL Basic";
int i;

i = strnicmp(string1, string2, 6);
```

This assigns 0 to the variable `i` because the strings `"Visual"` and `"VISUAL"` differ only in the case of their characters.

Let's look at an example that compares strings. Listing 9.2 creates an array of strings and initializes it with data. Then the program displays the unordered array of strings, sorts the array, and displays the sorted array.

Type

Listing 9.2. Source code for the program STRING2.CPP.

```
/*
  C++ program that demonstrates comparing strings
*/

#include <iostream.h>
#include <string.h>

const unsigned STR_SIZE = 40;
const unsigned ARRAY_SIZE = 11;
const int TRUE = 1;
const int FALSE = 0;

main()
{

```

continues

Listing 9.2. continued

```
    char strArr[STR_SIZE][ARRAY_SIZE] =
       { "California", "Virginia", "Alaska", "New York",
         "Michigan", "Nevada", "Ohio", "Florida",
         "Washington", "Oregon", "Arizona" };
    char temp[STR_SIZE];
    unsigned n = ARRAY_SIZE;
    unsigned offset;
    int inOrder;

    cout << "Unordered array of strings is:\n";
    for (unsigned i = 0; i < ARRAY_SIZE; i++)
      cout << strArr[i] << "\n";

    cout << "\nEnter a non-space character and press Enter";
    cin >> temp[0];
    cout << "\n";

    offset = n;
    do {
      offset = (8 * offset) / 11;
      offset = (offset == 0) ? 1 : offset;
      inOrder = TRUE;
      for (unsigned i = 0, j = offset;
           i < n - offset; i++, j++)
        if (strcmp(strArr[i], strArr[j]) > 0) {
          strcpy(temp, strArr[i]);
          strcpy(strArr[i], strArr[j]);
          strcpy(strArr[j], temp);
          inOrder = FALSE;
        }
    } while (!(offset == 1 && inOrder));

    cout << "Sorted array of strings is:\n";
    for (i = 0; i < ARRAY_SIZE; i++)
      cout << strArr[i] << "\n";
    return 0;
}
```

Here is a sample session with the program in Listing 9.2:

Output

```
Unordered array of strings is:
California
Virginia
Alaska
New York
Michigan
Nevada
Ohio
Florida
Washington
Oregon
Arizona
```

```
Enter a non-space character and press Enter
Sorted array of strings is:
Alaska
Arizona
California
Florida
Michigan
Nevada
New York
Ohio
Oregon
Virginia
Washington
```

Analysis

The program in Listing 9.2 declares the global constants `STR_SIZE`, `ARRAY_SIZE`, `TRUE`, and `FALSE` in lines 8 through 11. The constant `STR_SIZE` specifies the size of each string. The constant `ARRAY_SIZE` indicates the number of strings in the array used by the program. The constants `TRUE` and `FALSE` represent the Boolean values employed in sorting the array of strings. The function `main` declares the array `strArr` (actually, the variable `strArr` is a matrix of characters) to have `ARRAY_SIZE` elements and `STR_SIZE` characters per elements. Notice that the declaration states the size of each string in the first dimension and the size of the array in the second dimension. The function also initializes the array `strArr`. The function also declares the variable `temp` as a swap buffer. Lines 21 through 23 declare miscellaneous variables.

The output statement in line 25 displays the title before showing the elements of the unordered array `strArr`. The `for` loop in lines 26 and 27 displays these elements. The loop uses the control variable `i` and iterates, in increments of 1, from 0 to ARRAY_SIZE-1. The output statement in line 27 displays the string at element `i`, using the expression `strArr[i]`.

The output and input statements in lines 29 and 30 prompt you to enter a nonspace character. This input allows you to examine the unordered array before the program sorts the array and displays its ordered elements.

The statements in lines 33 through 46 implement the Comb sort method. Notice that the `if` statement in line 40 uses the function `strcmp` to compare elements number `i` and `j`, accessed using the expressions `strArr[i]` and `strArr[j]`, respectively. The statements in lines 41 through 43 swap the elements `i` and `j` using the function `strcpy` and the swap buffer `temp`.

The output statement in line 48 displays the title before showing the elements of the sorted array. The `for` loop in lines 49 and 50 displays these elements. The loop utilizes the control variable `i` and iterates, in increments of 1, from 0 to `ARRAY_SIZE-1`. The output statement in line 50 displays the string at element `i`, using the expression `strArr[i]`.

Converting Strings

The STRING.H library offers the function `_strlwr` and `_strupr` to convert the characters of a string to lowercase and uppercase, respectively. Note that these functions are more commonly called `strlwr` and `strupr` (without the leading underscore character) in C textbooks.

Syntax

The *_strlwr* Function

The prototype for the function `_strlwr` is

```
char* _strlwr(char* source)
```

The function converts the uppercase characters in string source to lowercase. Other characters are not affected. The function also returns the pointer to the string source.

Example:

```
char str[] = "HELLO THERE";

_strlwr(str);
```

The variable `str` now contains the string `"hello there"`.

Syntax

The *_strupr* Function

The prototype for the function `_strupr` is

```
char* _strupr(char* source)
```

The function converts the lowercase characters in string source to uppercase. Other characters are not affected. The function also returns the pointer to the string source.

Example:

```
char str[] = "Visual C++";
_strupr(str);
```

The variable `str` now contains the string `"VISUAL C++"`.

DO	DON'T

DO make copies for the arguments of functions `_strlwr` and `_strupr` if you need the original arguments later in a program.

DON'T always assume that applying the function `_strlwr` and then the function `_strupr` (or vice versa) to the same variable will succeed in restoring the original characters in that variable.

Reversing Strings

The STRING.H library offers the function `strrev` to reverse the characters in a string.

Syntax

The *strrev* Function

The prototype for the function `strrev` is

```
char* strrev(char* str)
```

The function reverses the order of the characters in string `str` and returns the pointer to the string `str`.

Example:

```
char string[] = "Hello";

strrev(string);
cout << string;
```

This displays `"olleH"`.

Let's look at a program that manipulates the characters in a string. Listing 9.3 shows the source code for the program STRING3.CPP. The program performs the following tasks:

- Prompts you to enter a string
- Displays your input
- Displays the lowercase version of your input
- Displays the uppercase version of your input
- Displays the character you typed in reverse order
- Displays a message that your input has no uppercase character, if this is true
- Displays a message that your input has no lowercase character, if this is true
- Displays a message that your input has symmetrical characters, if this is true

Listing 9.3. Source code for the program STRING3.CPP.

```
/*
  C++ program that demonstrates manipulating the
  characters in a string
*/

#include <iostream.h>
#include <string.h>

const unsigned STR_SIZE = 40;
const int TRUE = 1;
const int FALSE = 0;

main()
{
    char str1[STR_SIZE+1];
    char str2[STR_SIZE+1];
    int isLowerCase;
    int isUpperCase;
    int isSymmetrical;


    cout << "Enter a string : ";
    cin.getline(str1, STR_SIZE);
    cout << "Input: " << str1 << "\n";
    // copy str1 to str2
    strcpy(str2, str1);
    // convert to lowercase
    strlwr(str2);
    isLowerCase = (strcmp(str1, str2) == 0) ? TRUE : FALSE;
    cout << "Lowercase: " << str2 << "\n";
    // convert to uppercase
    strupr(str2);
    isUpperCase = (strcmp(str1, str2) == 0) ? TRUE : FALSE;
    cout << "Uppercase: " << str2 << "\n";
    // copy str1 to str2
    strcpy(str2, str1);
    // reverse characters
    strrev(str2);
    isSymmetrical = (strcmp(str1, str2) == 0) ? TRUE : FALSE;
    cout << "Reversed: " << str2 << "\n";
    if (isLowerCase)
      cout << "Your input has no uppercase letters\n";
    if (isUpperCase)
      cout << "Your input has no lowercase letters\n";
    if (isSymmetrical)
      cout << "Your input has symmetrical characters\n";
    return 0;
}
```

Here is a sample session with the program in Listing 9.3:

Output

```
Enter a string : level
Input: level
Lowercase: level
Uppercase: LEVEL
Reversed: level
Your input has no uppercase letters
Your input has symmetrical characters
```

Analysis

The program in Listing 9.3 declares the string variables `str1` and `str2` in function `main`. Each string stores `STR_SIZE + 1` characters (including the null terminator). The function also declares the flags `isLowerCase`, `isUpperCase`, and `isSymmetrical`.

The output statement in line 22 prompts you to enter a string. The statement in line 23 uses the string input function `getline` to store your input in variable `str1`. The output statement in line 24 echoes your input.

The statement in line 26 copies the characters in variable `str1` to variable `str2`. The statement in line 26 calls the function `strlwr` to convert the characters in variable `str2`. The program manipulates the characters of variable `str2`, while maintaining the original input in variable `str1`. The statement in line 29 calls the function `strcmp` to compare the characters in `str1` and `str2`. The two strings can be equal only if your input has no uppercase characters. The statement uses the conditional operator to assign the constant `TRUE` to the flag `isLowerCase` if the above condition is true. Otherwise, the statement assigns `FALSE` to the flag `isLowerCase`. The output statement in line 30 displays the characters in variable `str2`.

The statement in line 32 calls the function `strupr` and supplies it the argument `str2`. This function `call` converts any lowercase character in variable `str2` into uppercase. The statement in line 33 calls the function `strcmp` to compare the characters in `str1` and `str2`. The two strings can be equal only if your input has no lowercase characters. The statement uses the conditional operator to assign the constant `TRUE` to the flag `isUpperCase` if that is true. Otherwise, the statement assigns `FALSE` to the flag `isUpperCase`. The output statement in line 34 displays the characters in variable `str2`.

To display the original input in reverse order, the program calls the function `strcpy` to copy the characters of variable `str1` to variable `str2` once more. The statement in line 38 calls the function `strrev` and passes it the argument `str2`. The statement in line 39 calls the function `strcmp` to compare the characters in `str1` and `str2`. The two strings can be equal only if your input has symmetrical characters. The statement uses the conditional operator to assign the constant `TRUE` to the flag `isSymmetrical` if the above condition is true. Otherwise, the statement assigns `FALSE` to the flag `isSymmetrical`. The output statement in line 40 displays the characters in variable `str2`.

The program uses the `if` statements in lines 41, 43, and 45 to indicate that your input has special characteristics. The `if` statement in line 41 comments on the fact that your input has no uppercase letter when the value in variable `isLowerCase` is `TRUE`. The `if` statement in line 43 comments on the fact that your input has no lowercase letter when the value in variable `isUpperCase` is `TRUE`. The `if` statement in line 45 comments on the fact that your input has symmetrical characters when the value in variable `isSymmetrical` is `TRUE`.

Locating Characters

The STRING.H library offers a number of functions for locating characters in strings. These functions include `strchr`, `strrchr`, `strspn`, `strcspn`, and `strpbrk`. These functions allow you to search for characters and simple character patterns in strings.

The function `strchr` locates the first occurrence of a character in a string.

Syntax

The *strchr* Function

The prototype for the function `strchr` is

```
char* strchr(const char* target, int c)
```

The function locates the first occurrence of pattern `c` in string *`target`*. The function returns the pointer to the character in string *`target`* which matches the specified pattern `c`. If the character `c` does not occur in the string *`target`*, the function yields a `NULL`.

Example:

```
char str[81] = "Visual C++";
char* strPtr;

strPtr = strchr(str, '+');
```

The pointer `strPtr` points to the substring `"++"` in string `str`.

The function `strrchr` locates the last occurrence of a character in a string.

Syntax

The *strrchr* Function

The prototype for the function `strrchr` is

```
char* strrchr(const char* target, int c)
```

The function locates the last occurrence of pattern `c` in string *`target`*. The function returns the pointer to the character in string *`target`* which matches the specified pattern `c`. If the character `c` does not occur in the string *`target`*, the function yields a `NULL`.

Example:

```
char str[81] = "Visual C++ is here";
char* strPtr;

strPtr = strrchr(str, '+');
```

The pointer `strPtr` points to the substring `"+ is here"` in string `str`.

The function `strspn` yields the number of characters in the leading part of a string that match any character in a pattern of characters.

Syntax

The *strspn* Function

The prototype for the function `strspn` is

```
size_t strspn(const char* target, const char* pattern)
```

The function returns the number of characters in the leading part of string *`target`* that match any character in the string *`pattern`*.

Example:

```
char str[] = "Visual C++ 2.0";
char substr[] = "Vailus ";
int index;

index = strspn(str, substr);
```

This statement assigns 7 to variable `index`, because the characters in `substr` found a match in every one of the first seven characters of `str`.

The function `strcspn` scans a string and yields the number of the leading characters in a string that are totally void of the characters in a substring.

Syntax

The *strcspn* Function

The prototype for the function `strcspn` is

```
size_t strcspn(const char* str1, const char* str2)
```

The function scans *`str1`* and returns the length of the leftmost substring that is totally void of the characters of the substring *`str2`*.

Example:

```
char strng[] = "The rain in Spain";
int i;

i = strcspn(strng," in");
```

This example assigns 8 (the length of `"The rain"`) to the variable `i`.

The function `strpbrk` searches a string for the first occurrence of any character in a pattern of characters.

Syntax

The *strpbrk* Function

The prototype for the function `strpbrk` is

```
char* strpbrk(const char* target, const char* pattern)
```

The function searches the *`target`* string for the first occurrence of *any character* in the characters of string *`pattern`*. If the characters in the pattern do not occur in the string *`target`*, the function yields a `NULL`.

Example:

```
char* str = "Hello there how are you";
char* substr = "hr";
char* ptr;

ptr = strpbrk(str, substr);
cout << ptr << "\n";
```

This displays `"here how are you"`, because the `'h'` is encountered in the string before the `'r'`.

Locating Strings

The STRING.H library offers the function `strstr` to locate a substring in a string.

Syntax

The *strstr* Function

The prototype for the function `strstr` is

```
char* strstr(const char* str, const char* substr);
```

The function scans the string *`str`* for the first occurrence of a string *`substr`*. The function yields the pointer to the first character in string *`str`* which matches the parameter *`substr`*. If the string *`substr`* does not occur in the string *`str`*, the function yields a `NULL`.

Example:

```
char str[] = "Hello there! how are you";
char substr[] = "how";
char* ptr;

ptr = strstr(str, substr);
cout << ptr << "\n";
```

This displays `"how are you"` because the string search matched `"how"`. The pointer `ptr` points to the rest of the original string starting with `"how"`.

DO	DON'T

DO use the function `strrev` before calling function `strstr` if you want to search for the last occurrence of a string.

DON'T forget to reverse both the main and the search strings when using the `strrev` function to locate the last occurrence of the search string.

The string library also provides the function `strtok` (short for **str**ing **tok**ens), which allows you to break down a string into substrings based on a specified set of delimiting characters.

NEW TERM Substrings are sometimes called *tokens*.

Syntax

The *strtok* Function

The prototype for the function `strtok` is

```
char* strtok(char* target, const char* delimiters);
```

The function searches the target string for tokens. A string supplies the set of delimiter characters. The following example shows how this function works in returning the tokens in a string. The function `strtok` modifies the string target by inserting `'\0'` characters after each token. Make sure that you store a copy of the original target string in another string variable.

Example:

```
#include <stdio.h>
#include <string.h>

main()
{
  char* str = "(Base_Cost+Profit) * Margin";
  char* tkn = "+* ()";
  char* ptr = str;

  printf("%s\n", str);
  // the first call looks normal
  ptr = strtok(str, tkn);
  printf("\n\nis broken into: %s",ptr);
```

```
  while (ptr) {
    printf(" ,%s",ptr);
    // must make first argument a NULL character
    ptr = strtok(NULL, tkn);
  }
  printf("\n\n");
}
```

This example displays the following when the program is run:

```
(Base_Cost+Profit) * Margin
```

This is broken into `Base_Cost`, `Profit`, `Margin`.

DO	DON'T

DO remember to supply `NULL` as the first argument to function `strtok` to locate the next token.

DON'T forget to store a copy of the target string in the function `strtok`.

Let's look at an example that searches for characters and strings. Listing 9.4 shows the source code for the program STRING4.CPP. The program performs the following tasks:

- Prompts you to enter the main string
- Prompts you to enter the search string
- Prompts you to enter the search character
- Displays a character ruler and the main string
- Displays the indices where the search string occurs in the main string
- Displays the indices where the search character occurs in the main string

Type

Listing 9.4. Source code for the program STRING4.CPP.

```
/*
  C++ program that demonstrates searching for the
  characters and strings
*/

#include <iostream.h>
#include <string.h>

const unsigned STR_SIZE = 40;

main()
```

```
{
    char mainStr[STR_SIZE+1];
    char subStr[STR_SIZE+1];
    char findChar;
    char *p;
    int index;
    int count;

    cout << "Enter a string : ";
    cin.getline(mainStr, STR_SIZE);
    cout << "Enter a search string : ";
    cin.getline(subStr, STR_SIZE);
    cout << "Enter a search character : ";
    cin >> findChar;

    cout << "          1         2         3         4\n";
    cout << "01234567890123456789012345678901234567890\n";
    cout << mainStr << "\n";
    cout << "Searching for string " << subStr << "\n";
    p = strstr(mainStr, subStr);
    count = 0;
    while (p) {
      count++;
      index = p - mainStr;
      cout << "Match at index " << index << "\n";
      p = strstr(++p, subStr);
    }
    if (count == 0)
      cout << "No match for substring in main string\n";

    cout << "Searching for character " << findChar << "\n";
    p = strchr(mainStr, findChar);
    count = 0;
    while (p) {
      count++;
      index = p - mainStr;
      cout << "Match at index " << index << "\n";
      p = strchr(++p, findChar);
    }
    if (count == 0)
      cout << "No match for search character in main string\n";
    return 0;
}
```

Here is a sample session with the program in Listing 9.4:

Output

```
Enter a string : here, there, and everywhere
Enter a search string : here
Enter a search character : e
1         2         3         4
01234567890123456789012345678901234567890
here, there, and everywhere
Searching for string here
Match at index 0
Match at index 7
```

```
Match at index 23
Searching for character e
Match at index 1
Match at index 3
Match at index 8
Match at index 10
Match at index 17
Match at index 19
Match at index 24
Match at index 26
```

Analysis The program in Listing 9.4 declares the strings `mainStr` and `subStr` to represent the `main` and `search` strings, respectively. The program also declares the variable `findChar` to store the search character. In addition, the program declares the character pointer `p` and the `int`-typed variables `index` and `count`.

The output statement in line 20 prompts you to enter a string. The statement in line 21 calls the stream input function `getline` and stores your input in variable `mainStr`. The output statement in line 22 prompts you to enter the search string. The statement in line 23 calls the stream input function `getline` and saves your input in variable `subStr`. The output statement in line 24 prompts you to enter the search character. The statement in line 25 obtains your input and stores it in variable `findChar`.

The output statements in lines 27 through 29 display a ruler and your input, aligned under the ruler. The output statement in line 30 informs you that the program is searching for the substring you entered. The search begins at the statement in line 31. This statement calls function `strstr` to locate the first occurrence of string `subStr` in the string `mainStr`. The statement in line 32 assigns 0 to the variable count, which keeps track of the number of times the string `mainStr` contains the string `subStr`.

The program uses the `while` loop in lines 33 through 38 to locate all the occurrences of `subStr` in `mainStr`. The condition of the `while` loop examines the address of pointer `p`. If that pointer is not `NULL`, the loop iterates. The first statement inside the loop increments the variable `count`. The statement in line 35 calculates the index of string `mainStr` where the last match occurs. The statement obtains the sought index by subtracting the address of pointer `p` from the address of the first character in variable `mainStr`. (Remember that the expression `&mainStr[0]` is equivalent to the simpler expression `mainStr`.) The statement assigns the result to variable `index`. The output statement in line 36 displays the value in variable `index`.

The statement in line 37 searches for the next occurrence of the string `subStr` in `mainStr`. Notice that this statement calls `strstr` and supplies it the pointer `p` as the first argument. The statement also applies the pre-increment operator to pointer `p` to store the address of the next character. This action ensures that the call to function `strstr` finds the next occurrence, if any, and is not stuck at the last occurrence. The `if` statement outside the `while` loop examines the value in variable `count`. If it contains zero, the program executes the output statement in line 40 to inform you that no match was found for the search string.

The output statement in line 42 informs you that the program is now searching for the character you specified in the main string. The process of searching for the character in `findChar` is very similar to searching for the string `subStr`. The main difference is that searching for a character involves the function `strchr`.

9

Summary

Today's lesson presents C++ strings and discusses string manipulation functions which are exported by the STRING.H header file. You learn about the following topics:

- Strings in C++ are arrays of characters that end with the null character (the ASCII 0 character).
- String input requires the use of the `getline` stream input function. This function requires that you specify the input variable, the maximum number of input characters, and the optional line delimiter.
- The STRING.H header file contains the standard (for the C language) string library. This library contains many versatile functions that support copying, concatenating, converting, reversing, and searching for strings.
- C++ supports two methods for assigning strings. The first method assigns a string to another when you declare the latter string. The second method uses the function `strcpy` to assign one string to another at any stage in the program. The string library also offers the function `strdup` to copy a string and allocate the needed space.
- The function `strlen` returns the length of a string.
- The `strcat` and `strncat` functions permit you to concatenate two strings. The function `strncat` allows you to specify the number of characters to concatenate.
- The functions `strcmp`, `stricmp`, `strncmp`, and `strnicmp` allow you to perform various types of string comparisons. The function `strcmp` performs a case-insensitive comparison of two strings, using every character possible. The `stricmp` is a version of function `strcmp` which performs a case-insensitive comparison. The function `strncmp` is a variant of function `strcmp` which uses a specified number of characters in comparing the strings. The function `strnicmp` is a version of function `strncmp` which performs a case-insensitive comparison.

- The functions strlwr and strupr convert the characters of a string into lowercase and uppercase, respectively.
- The function strrev reverses the order of characters in a string.
- The functions strchr, strrchr, strspn, strcspn, and strpbrk allow you to search for characters and simple character patterns in strings.
- The function strstr searches for a string in another string. The function strtok empowers you to break down a string into small strings which are delimited by a set of characters that you specify.

Q&A

Q Can a statement initialize a pointer using a string literal?

A Yes. The compiler stores the characters of the string literal in memory and assigns its address to that pointer. Here is an example:

```
char* p = "I am a small string";
```

In addition, you can overwrite the characters of the string literal using their pointers. However, keep in mind that the pointer p accesses a string with a fixed number of characters.

Q Can a statement declare a constant pointer to a literal string?

A Yes, this kind of declaration resembles the one I mentioned previously. However, because the statement declares a constant pointer, you cannot overwrite the characters of the initializing string literal. Here is an example:

```
const char* p = "Version 1.0";
```

Use the constant char pointer to store fixed messages and titles.

Q Can a statement declare an array of pointers to a set of string literal strings?

A Yes, this is the easiest method to use an array of pointers to access a collection of messages, titles, or other kinds of fixed strings. Here is an example:

```
char* mainMenu[] = { "File", "Edit", "Search", "View",
                     "Debug", "Options", "Windows", "Help"};
```

Thus the element p[0] accesses the first string, p[1] the second string, and so on.

Q How can I use `strcmp` to compare strings, starting at a specific number of characters?

A Simply add the offset value to the arguments of the function `strcmp`. Here is an example:

```
char s1[41] = "Visual C++";
char s2[41] = "Visual Basic";
int offset = 7;
int i;
i = strcmp(str1 + offset, str2 + offset);
```

Q How can I use `strncmp` to compare a specific number of characters in two strings, starting at a specific character?

A Simply add the offset value to the arguments of the function `strcmp`. Here is an example:

```
char s1[41] = "Visual C++";
char s2[41] = "Visual Basic";
int offset = 7;
int num = 3;
int i;
i = strncmp(str1 + offset, str2 + offset, num);
```

Workshop

The Workshop provides quiz questions to help you solidify your understanding of the material covered, and exercises to provide you with experience in using what you've learned. Try to understand the quiz and exercise answers before continuing on to the next day's lesson. Answers are provided in Appendix B, "Answers."

Quiz

1. Where is the error in the following program?

```
#include <iostream.h>
#include <string.h>
const in MAX = 10;
main()
{
```

```
  char s1[MAX+1];
  char s2[] = "12345678901234567890123456789O";
  strcpy(s1, s2);
  cout << "String 1 is " << s1
       << "\nString 2 is " << s2;
  return 0;
}
```

2. How can you fix the program in the last question using the function `strncpy` instead of `strcpy`?
3. What is the value assigned to variable `i` in the following statements?

```
char s1[] = "Visual C++";
char s2[] = "Visual Basic";
int i;
i = strcmp(s1, s2);
```

4. What is the value assigned to variable `i` in the following statements?

```
char s1[] = "Visual C++";
char s2[] = "Visual Basic";
int offset = strlen("Visual ");
int i;
i = strcmp(s1 + offset, s2 + offset);
```

5. True or false? The following function correctly returns 1 if a string does not contain lowercase characters, and yields 0 if otherwise:

```
int hasNoLowerCase(const char* s)
{
  char s2[strlen(s)+1];
  strcpy(s2, s);
  strupr(s2);
  return (strcmp(s1, s2) == 0) ? 1 : 0);
}
```

Exercises

1. Write your own version of function `strlen`. Use a `while` loop and a character-counting variable to obtain the function result.

2. Write another version of function `strlen`. This time use a `while` loop and a local pointer to obtain the function result.

3. Write the program STRING5.CPP, which uses the function `strtok`, to break down the string `"2*(X+Y)/(X+Z) - (X+10)/(Y-5)"` into three sets of tokens, using the token delimiter strings `"+-*/ ()"`, `"( )"`, and `"+-*/ "`.

10

Advanced Function Parameters

WEEK 2

Functions are the basic building blocks that conceptually extend the C++ language to fit your custom applications. C, the parent language of C++, is more function-oriented than C++. This difference is due to the support for classes, inheritance, and other object-oriented programming features (more about the latter in tomorrow's lesson). Nevertheless, functions still play an important role in C++. In today's lesson, you learn about the following advanced aspects of C++ functions:

- Passing arrays as function arguments
- Passing strings as function arguments
- Passing structures by value
- Passing structures by reference
- Passing structures by pointer
- Recursive functions
- Passing pointers to dynamic structures
- Pointers to functions

Passing Arrays as Arguments

When you write a C++ function that passes an array parameter, you can declare that parameter as a pointer to the basic type of the array.

Syntax

A Pointer-to-Array Parameter

The general syntax for prototyping a function with a pointer-to-array parameter is

```
returnType function(basicType*, <other parameter types>);
```

The general syntax for defining this function is

```
returnType function(basicType *arrParam, <other parameters>)
```

Example:

```
// prototypes
void ShellSort(unsigned *doubleArray, unsigned arraySize);
void QuickSort(unsigned *intArray, unsigned arraySize);
```

In Day 7, I state that C++ allows you to declare open array parameters using a pair of empty brackets. This kind of declaration is equivalent to using a pointer parameter. C++ programmers use the open array form less frequently than the explicit pointer form, even though using the brackets shows the intent of the parameter more clearly.

DO / DON'T

DO use `const` parameters to prevent the host function from altering the arguments.

DON'T forget to include a parameter that specifies the number of array elements to manipulate when the array-typed arguments are only partially filled with meaningful data.

Let's look at an example. Listing 10.1 shows the source code for the program ADVFUN1.CPP. I created this program by performing minor edits to program ARRAY5.CPP (found in Listing 7.5 of Day 7). The program performs the following tasks:

- Prompts you to enter the number of data points
- Prompts you to enter the integer values for the array
- Displays the elements of the unordered array
- Displays the elements of the sorted array

Type

Listing 10.1. Source code for the program ADVFUN1.CPP.

```
// C++ program that sorts arrays using the Comb sort method

#include <iostream.h>

const int MAX = 10;
const int TRUE = 1;
const int FALSE = 0;

int obtainNumData()
{
   int m;
   do { // obtain number of data points
     cout << "Enter number of data points [2 to "
         << MAX << "] : ";
     cin >> m;
     cout << "\n";
   } while (m < 2 || m > MAX);
   return m;
}

void inputArray(int *intArr, int n)
{
   // prompt user for data
   for (int i = 0; i < n; i++) {
```

continues

Listing 10.1. continued

```
    cout << "arr[" << i << "] : ";
    cin >> *(intArr + i);
  }
}

void showArray(const int *intArr, int n)
{
  for (int i = 0; i < n; i++) {
    cout.width(5);
    cout << *(intArr + i) << " ";
  }
  cout << "\n";
}

void sortArray(int *intArr, int n)
{
  int offset, temp, inOrder;

  offset = n;
  do {
    offset = (8 * offset) / 11;
    offset = (offset == 0) ? 1 : offset;
    inOrder = TRUE;
    for (int i = 0, j = offset; i < (n - offset); i++, j++) {
      if (intArr[i] > intArr[j]) {
        inOrder = FALSE;
        temp = intArr[i];
        intArr[i] = intArr[j];
        intArr[j] = temp;
      }
    }
  } while (!(offset == 1 && inOrder == TRUE));
}

main()
{
  int arr[MAX];
  int n;

  n = obtainNumData();
  inputArray(arr, n);
  cout << "Unordered array is:\n";
  showArray(arr, n);
  sortArray(arr, n);
  cout << "\nSorted array is:\n";
  showArray(arr, n);
  return 0;
}
```

Here is a sample session with the program in Listing 10.1:

```
Enter number of data points [2 to 10] : 5

arr[0] : 55
arr[1] : 22
arr[2] : 78
arr[3] : 35
arr[4] : 45
Unordered array is:
55    22    78    35    45

Sorted array is:
22    35    45    55    78
```

The program in Listing 10.1 is almost identical to that in Listing 7.5 of Day 7. The new program uses slightly different parameters in functions `inputArray`, `showArray`, and `sortArray`. The first parameter in these functions is a pointer to the `int` type. The function `showArray` prefixes the pointer type with `const`. Such a declaration tells the compiler that the function `showArray` cannot alter the elements of the arguments for parameter `intArray`.

Using Strings as Arguments

Because C++ treats strings as arrays of characters, the rules for passing arrays as arguments to functions also apply to strings. The next program contains functions that manipulate strings. Listing 10.2 shows the source code for the program ADVFUN2.CPP. The program prompts you to enter a string. Then the program displays the number of characters you typed (the size of the input string) and the uppercase version of your input.

Listing 10.2. Source code for the program ADVFUN2.CPP.

```
/*
  C++ program that declares functions with string parameters
*/

#include <iostream.h>

const unsigned MAX = 40;

char* upperCase(char* str)
{
    int ascii_shift = 'A' - 'a';
    char* p = str;

    // loop to convert each character to uppercase
    while ( *p != '\0') {
        if ((*p  >= 'a' && *p <= 'z'))
           *p += ascii_shift;
        p++;
```

continues

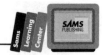

Listing 10.2. continued

```
19:     }
20:     return str;
21: }
22:
23: int strlen(char* str)
24: {
25:   char *p = str;
26:   while (*p++ != '\0');
27:   return -p - str;
28: }
29:
30: main()
31: {
32:     char aString[MAX+1];
33:
34:     cout << "Enter a string: ";
35:     cin.getline(aString, MAX);
36:     cout << "Your string has " << strlen(aString)
37:          << " characters\n";
38:     // concatenate bigStr to aString
39:     upperCase(aString);
40:     cout << "The uppercase version of your input is: "
41:          << aString;
42:     return 0;
43: }
```

Here is a sample session with the program in Listing 10.2:

Output

```
Enter a string: Visual C++ 12.0
Your string has 14 characters
The uppercase version of your input is: VISUAL C++ 12.0
```

Analysis The program in Listing 10.2 declares its own string-manipulating functions: `upperCase` and `strlen`. The function `upperCase` has a single parameter, `str`, which is a pointer to the `char` type. This parameter passes the address of an array of characters. The function converts the characters accessed by the pointer string to uppercase, and returns the pointer to the string. The function declares the local variable `ascii_shift` and the local `char`-pointer `p`. The function also initializes the variable `ascii_shift` with the difference between the ASCII values of the letters `A` and `a`. Thus, the `ascii_shift` variable contains the difference in ASCII codes needed to convert a lowercase character into an uppercase character. The function also initializes the local pointer `p` with the address in parameter `str`.

The `upperCase` function uses the `while` loop in line 15 to traverse the characters of the string argument. The `while` clause determines whether the pointer `p` does not access the null terminator. The `if` statement in line 16 determines if the character accessed by pointer p is a lowercase letter. If this condition is true, the function executes the statement in line 17. This statement adds the value in variable ascii_shift to the character currently accessed by pointer p. This action converts a lowercase character into uppercase. The statement in line 18 increments the address of pointer p to access the next character. The function returns the address of pointer str.

The function strlen returns the number of characters in the string accessed by the char-pointer parameter str. The function declares the local char-pointer p and initializes it with the address of parameter str. The function uses a while loop with an empty loop statement to locate the null terminator in the string accessed by pointer p. The return statement yields the sought value by taking the difference between the addresses of pointers p and str. The return statement first applies the pre-decrement operator to pointer p to adjust the address of that pointer.

The function main declares the string variable aString. The output statement in line 34 prompts you to enter a string. The statement in line 35 calls the stream input function getline to obtain your input and to store it in variable aString. The output statement in line 36 displays the number of characters you typed. The statement calls the function strlen and passes it the argument aString. The statement in line 39 calls the function upperCase and also passes it the argument aString. The output statement in line 40 displays the uppercase version of your input, which is now stored in variable aString.

Using Structures as Arguments

C++ allows you to pass structures either by value or by reference. In this section, I demonstrate passing structures by value. In the next sections, I show you how to pass structures by reference. The structure's type appears in the function prototype and heading in a manner similar to that of predefined types.

Listing 10.3 shows the source code for the program ADVFUN3.CPP. The program performs the following tasks:

- Prompts you for the X and Y coordinates of a first point
- Prompts you for the X and Y coordinates of a second point
- Calculates coordinates of the median point between the two points that you entered
- Displays the coordinates of the median point

Listing 10.3. Source code for the program ADVFUN3.CPP.

```
1: // C++ program which uses a function that passes
2: // a structure by value
3:
4: #include <iostream.h>
5:
6: struct point {
7:   double x;
8:   double y;
9: };
10:
11: // declare the prototype of function getMedian
12: point getMedian(point, point);
13:
14: main()
15: {
16:   point pt1;
17:   point pt2;
18:   point median;
19:
20:   cout << "Enter the X and Y coordinates for point # 1 : ";
21:   cin >> pt1.x >> pt1.y;
22:   cout << "Enter the X and Y coordinates for point # 2 : ";
23:   cin >> pt2.x >> pt2.y;
24:   // get the coordinates for the median point
25:   median = getMedian(pt1, pt2);
26:   // get the median point
27:   cout << "Mid point is (" << median.x
28:        << ", " << median.y << ")\n";
29:   return 0;
30: }
31:
32: point getMedian(point p1, point p2)
33: {
34:   point result;
35:   result.x = (p1.x + p2.x) / 2;
36:   result.y = (p1.y + p2.y) / 2;
37:   return result;
38: };
```

Here is a sample session with the program in Listing 10.3:

```
Enter the X and Y coordinates for point # 1 : 1 1
Enter the X and Y coordinates for point # 2 : 5 5
Mid point is (3, 3)
```

The program in Listing 10.3 declares the structure point, which models a two-dimensional point. This structure has two `double`-typed members, `x` and `y`. Line 12 declares the prototype for the function `getMedian`. The function takes two `point`-typed parameters, which are passed by value.

The function `main` declares the `point`-typed variables `pt1`, `pt2`, and `median` in lines 16 through 18, respectively. The output statement in line 20 prompts you to enter the X and Y coordinates for the first point. The statement in line 21 obtains your input and stores the coordinates in the members `pt1.x` and `pt1.y`. Lines 22 and 23 repeat the same prompting and input process for the second point. The input statement in line 23 stores the values for the second point in members `pt2.x` and `pt2.y`. The statement in line 25 calls function `getMedian` and passes it the arguments `pt1` and `pt2`. The function receives a copy of the arguments `pt1` and `pt2`. The statement assigns the `point`-typed function result to the variable `median`. The output statement in lines 27 and 28 displays the X and Y coordinates of the median point (by displaying the `x` and `y` members of the variable median).

The function `getMedian` declares two `point`-typed parameters, `p1` and `p2`. In addition, the function declares the local `point`-typed variable `result`. The statement in line 35 assigns the average of members `p1.x` and `p2.x` to member `result.x`. The statement in line 36 assigns the average of members `p1.y` and `p2.y` to member `result.y`. Notice that these statements use the dot operator to access the members `x` and `y` of the structures `p1`, `p2`, and `result`. This syntax is used when the function passes a copy or a reference of a structure. The return statement yields the value in the local structure result.

Passing Arguments by Reference

C++ enables you to write functions with parameters that pass arguments by reference. This kind of parameter enables you to change the value of the argument beyond the scope of the function. C++ offers two ways to implement such parameters: with pointers and with formal reference parameters. The following sections present functions that pass various kinds of data types by reference.

Passing Structures by Reference

You can pass structures to functions either by using pointers or by using formal reference. Many C++ programmers consider either approach as more efficient than passing the structure parameters by copy—you save on the overhead of copying the structure-typed arguments.

Note: Passing a structure by reference allows you to use the dot operator with the reference parameters (as with passing by value). The added advantage is that the reference parameters do not create copies of the original arguments. Thus, they are faster and save memory resources. The downside is that because reference parameters become aliases to their arguments, any changes made to the parameters inside the function affect their arguments. One method to prevent this change is to use `const` reference parameters. Such parameters tell the compiler that the function cannot assign new values to the reference parameters.

DO | **DON'T**

DO pass structures either by formal reference or by pointers when both of the following two circumstances apply: the host function does not alter the arguments and the function returns values through these structures.

DON'T pass structures by value unless you need to supply the host function with a copy of the data that will be modified by the function.

Let's look at an example. Listing 10.4 shows the source code for the program ADVFUN4.CPP. The program performs the same tasks as the last program, ADVFUN3.CPP. The new version differs only in its implementation.

Type

Listing 10.4. Source code for the program ADVFUN4.CPP.

```
// C++ program which uses a function that passes
// a structure by reference

#include <iostream.h>

struct point {
  double x;
  double y;
};

// declare the prototype of function getMedian
point getMedian(const point&, const point&);

main()
{
  point pt1;
```

```
   point pt2;
   point median;

   cout << "Enter the X and Y coordinates for point # 1 : ";
   cin >> pt1.x >> pt1.y;
   cout << "Enter the X and Y coordinates for point # 2 : ";
   cin >> pt2.x >> pt2.y;
   // get the coordinates for the median point
   median = getMedian(pt1, pt2);
   // get the median point
   cout << "Mid point is (" << median.x
        << ", " << median.y << ")\n";
   return 0;
}

point getMedian(const point& p1, const point& p2)
{
   point result;
   result.x = (p1.x + p2.x) / 2;
   result.y = (p1.y + p2.y) / 2;
   return result;
};
```

Here is a sample session with the program in Listing 10.4:

Output

```
Enter the X and Y coordinates for point # 1 : 1 1
Enter the X and Y coordinates for point # 2 : 9 9
Mid point is (5, 5)
```

Analysis

The program in Listing 10.4 is very similar to that in Listing 10.3. The new program version uses reference parameters in function `getMedian`. Thus, the prototype and the function's declaration place the `&` character after the structure type `point`. Using reference parameters, the call to function `getMedian` looks very much like the call to the version in Listing 10.3. Likewise, the implementation of function `getMedian` is similar to the one in Listing 10.3—both versions use the dot operator to access the members `x` and `y` in the structure point.

Passing Structures by Pointers

Using pointers is another efficient way to pass structures. As with the reference parameter types, use the `const` declaration to prevent the implementation from changing the structured variables accessed by the pointer parameters.

The next example is, as you might expect, the version of program ADVFUN3.CPP which uses pointer parameters. Listing 10.5 shows the source code for the new version, program ADVFUN5.CPP.

Listing 10.5. Source code for the program ADVFUN5.CPP.

```
1: // C++ program which uses a function that passes
2: // a structure by pointer
3:
4: #include <iostream.h>
5:
6: struct point {
7:   double x;
8:   double y;
9: };
10:
11: // declare the prototype of function getMedian
12: point getMedian(const point*, const point*);
13:
14: main()
15: {
16:   point pt1;
17:   point pt2;
18:   point median;
19:
20:   cout << "Enter the X and Y coordinates for point # 1 : ";
21:   cin >> pt1.x >> pt1.y;
22:   cout << "Enter the X and Y coordinates for point # 2 : ";
23:   cin >> pt2.x >> pt2.y;
24:   // get the coordinates for the median point
25:   median = getMedian(&pt1, &pt2);
26:   // get the median point
27:   cout << "Mid point is (" << median.x
28:        << ", " << median.y << ")\n";
29:   return 0;
30: }
31:
32: point getMedian(const point* p1, const point* p2)
33: {
34:   point result;
35:   result.x = (p1->x + p2->x) / 2;
36:   result.y = (p1->y + p2->y) / 2;
37:   return result;
38: };
```

Here is a sample session with the program in Listing 10.5:

```
Enter the X and Y coordinates for point # 1 : 2 2
Enter the X and Y coordinates for point # 2 : 8 8
Mid point is (5, 5)
```

The program in Listing 10.5 uses pointer parameters in function `getMedian`. The prototype and the implementation of the function uses the `const point*` type for both parameters. The statement in line 25, which calls the function `getMedian`, passes the address of the variable `pt1` and `pt2`, using the `address-of` operator `&`. The implementation of the function `getMedian` uses the `->` operator to access the members `x` and `y` for the pointer parameters `p1` and `p2`.

Recursive Functions

There are many problems that can be solved by breaking them down into simpler and similar problems. Such problems are solved using recursion.

NEW TERM *Recursive functions* are functions which obtain a result and/or perform a task by calling themselves. These recursive calls must be limited to avoid exhausting the memory resources of the computer. Consequently, every recursive function must examine a condition which determines the end of the recursion.

NEW TERM A common example of a recursive function is the *factorial function.* A factorial of a number N is the product of all the integers from 1 to N, with the exclamation point (!) as the mathematical symbol for the factorial function.

The mathematical equation for a factorial is

N! = 1 * 2 * 3 * ... * (N-2) * (N-1) * N

The recursive version of this equation is

N! = N * (N-1)!
(N-1)! = (N-1) * (N-2)!
(N-2)! = (N-2) * (N-3)!
...
2! = 2 * 1!
1! = 1

Recursion entails looping to obtain a result. Most recursive solutions have alternate nonrecursive solutions. In some cases, the recursive solutions are more elegant than the nonrecursive ones. The factorial function is an example of a mathematical function that can be implemented using either recursion or a nonrecursive straightforward loop.

DO	DON'T

DO include a decision-making statement in a recursive function to end the recursion.

DON'T use recursion unless its advantages significantly outweigh the alternate nonrecursive solution.

Let me present an example that implements the recursive factorial function. Listing 10.6 shows the source code for the program ADVFUN6.CPP. The program prompts you to enter two positive integers—the first one must be greater than or equal to the second one. The program displays the number of combinations and permutations obtained from the two integers. The number of combinations is given by the following equation:

```
mCn = m! / ((m - n)! * n!)
```

The number of permutations is given by the following equation:

```
mPn = m! / (m - n)!
```

Type

Listing 10.6. Source code for the program ADVFUN6.CPP.

```
// C++ program which uses a recursive function

#include <iostream.h>

const int MIN = 4;
const int MAX = 30;

double factorial(int i)
{
  if (i > 1)
    return double(i) * factorial(i - 1);
  else
    return 1;
}

double permutation(int m, int n)
{
  return factorial(m) / factorial(m - n);
}

double combination(int m, int n)
{
  return permutation(m, n) / factorial(n);
}

main()
{
  int m, n;

  do {
    cout << "Enter an integer between "
         << MIN << " and " << MAX << " : ";
    cin >> m;
  } while (m < MIN || m > MAX);

  do {
    cout << "Enter an integer between "
         << MIN << " and " << m << ": ";
    cin >> n;
  } while (n < MIN || n > m);
```

```
41:
42:   cout << "Permutations(" << m << ", " << n
43:        << ") = " << permutation(m, n) << "\n";
44:   cout << "Combinations(" << m << ", " << n
45:        << ") = " << combination(m, n) << "\n";
46:
47:   return 0;
48: }
```

Here is a sample session with the program in Listing 10.6:

Output

```
Enter an integer between 4 and 30 : 10
Enter an integer between 4 and 10 : 5
Permutations(10, 5) = 30240
Combinations(10, 5) = 252
```

Analysis The program in Listing 10.6 declares the recursive function `factorial`, and the functions `permutation`, `combination`, and `main`. The program also declares the global constants `MIN` and `MAX` which specify the limits of the first integer you enter.

The function `factorial` has a single parameter, the `int`-typed parameter `i`. The function returns a `double`-typed value. The `if` statement in line 10 compares the value of parameter `i` with 1. This comparison determines whether to make a recursive call, in line 11, or return the value 1 in line 13. The recursive call in line 11 invokes the function `factorial` with the argument `i - 1`. Thus, the recursive call supplies the function with a smaller (or simpler, if you prefer) argument.

The function `permutation` takes two `int`-typed parameters, `m` and `n`. The function calls the recursive function `factorial` twice: once with the argument `m`, and once with the argument `m - n`. The function `permutation` returns the ratio of the two calls to function `factorial`.

The function `combination` also takes two `int`-typed parameters, `m` and `n`. The function calls the function `permutation` and passes it the arguments `m` and `n`. The function also calls the function `factorial` and passes it the argument `n`. The function `combination` returns the ratio of the values returned by functions `permutation` and `factorial`.

The function `main` declares the `int`-typed variable `m` and `n`. The function uses two `do-while` loops to prompt you for integer values. The output statement in the first loop prompts you to enter an integer between `MIN` and `MAX`. The statement in line 33 stores your input in variable `m`. The `while` clause of the `do-while` loop validates your input. The clause determines if your input is less than `MIN` or greater than `MAX`. If this condition is true, the loop iterates again.

The output statement in the second `do-while` loop prompts you to enter an integer between `m` and `MAX`. The statement in line 39 saves your input in variable `n`. The `while` clause validates your input. The clause determines if your input is less than `MIN` or greater than `m`. If this condition is true, the loop iterates again.

The output statement in lines 42 and 43 displays the permutations of the values in variables m and n. The statement calls function permutation and passes it the argument m and n. The output statement in lines 44 and 45 displays the combinations of the values in variables m and n. The statement calls function combination and passes it the arguments m and n.

Passing Pointers to Dynamic Structures

Implementing a binary tree requires functions that—at least—insert, search, delete, and traverse the tree. All these functions access the binary tree through the pointer of its root. Interestingly, operations such as tree insertion and deletion may affect the root itself. In such cases, the address of the root node changes. Consequently, you need to pass a reference to the pointer of the root node. Using a reference to a pointer guarantees that you maintain an updated address of the tree root.

NEW TERM The *binary tree* is among the popular dynamic data structures. Such structures enable you to build ordered collections of data without prior knowledge of the number of data items. The basic building block for a binary tree is a *node*. Every node in a binary tree is the *root* of all subtrees below it. Terminal nodes are the roots of empty subtrees. The binary tree has a special node which is the root of all other nodes. Each node has a *field* (used as a sorting key), optional additional data (called *non-key data*), and two pointers to establish a link with other tree nodes. Dynamic memory allocation enables you to create space for each node and to set up the links between the various nodes dynamically. To learn more about binary tree structure, consult a data structure text book.

DO | **DON'T**

DO declare the parameters handling critical pointers to a data structure using the reference to these pointers. This declaration ensures that the addresses of these parameters are updated outside the scope of the function.

DON'T assume that when a function alters the address of a nonreference pointer parameter, the change also affects the address of the argument.

Let's look at an example that inserts and displays dynamic data in a binary tree. Listing 10.7 shows the source code for the program ADVFUN7.CPP. The program supplies its own set of data (a list of names), inserts the data in a binary tree, then displays the data in ascending order.

Type

Listing 10.7. Source code for the program ADVFUN7.CPP.

```
// C++ program which passes parameter to dynamic data

#include <iostream.h>
#include <string.h>

const unsigned MAX = 30;

typedef struct node* nodeptr;

struct node {
   char value[MAX+1];
   nodeptr left;
   nodeptr right;
};

void insert(nodeptr& root, const char* item)
// Recursively insert element in binary tree
{
  if (!root)  {
    root = new node;
    strncpy(root->value, item, MAX);
    root->left = NULL;
    root->right = NULL;
  }
  else {
    if (strcmp(item, root->value) < 0)
      insert(root->left, item);
    else
      insert(root->right, item);
  }
}

void showTree(nodeptr& root)
{
  if (!root)
    return;

  showTree(root->left);
  cout << root->value << "\n";
  showTree(root->right);
}

main()
{
  char *names[] = { "Virginia", "California", "Maine", "Michigan",
```

continues

Listing 10.7. continued

```
46:                     "New York", "Florida", "Ohio", "Illinois",
47:                     "Alaska", "Arizona", "Oregon", "Vermont",
48:                     "Maryland", "Delaware", "NULL" };
49:   nodeptr treeRoot = NULL;
50:   int i = 0;
51:
52:   // insert the names in the binary tree
53:   while (strcmp(names[i], "NULL") != 0)
54:     insert(treeRoot, names[i++]);
55:
56:   showTree(treeRoot);
57:   return 0;
58: }
```

Here is a sample session with the program in Listing 10.7:

Output

```
Alaska
Arizona
California
Delaware
Florida
Illinois
Maine
Maryland
Michigan
New York
Ohio
Oregon
Vermont
Virginia
```

Analysis

The program in Listing 10.7 declares the global constant `MAX` to specify the maximum number of characters stored by each node in the binary tree. The declaration in line 8 defines the `pointer`-type `nodeptr` based on the structure `node`. The program defines the structure `node` in lines 10 through 14. The structure contains the member value (which stores a string), the pointer to the left node, `left`, and the pointer to the right node, `right`. Both pointers have the `nodeptr` type.

The program declares the recursive function `insert` to insert a string in the binary tree. The function has two parameters: `root` and `item`. The parameter `root` is a reference to a `nodeptr`-typed pointer. This parameter keeps track of the various nodes of the binary tree and updates their addresses as needed. This update occurs when the binary tree inserts a data item.

The `if` statement in line 19 determines whether or not the parameter root is `NULL`. If this condition is true, the function executes the statement in lines 20 through 23. The statement in line 20 allocates a new node using the operator `new`. The statement in line

21 uses the function `strncpy` to copy up to `MAX` characters from the parameter `item` to the member `value`. The statements in lines 22 and 23 assign `NULL`s to the left and right node pointers of the newly created node. The statements in line 20 to 24 not only affect the actual root of the tree, but also alter the pointers to the various nodes. The condition in the `if` statement helps to end the recursive calls.

The `else` clause in line 25 handles the case when the parameter `root` is not `NULL`. The `if` statement in line 26 determines if the string accessed by pointer item is less than the string in the value member of the currently accessed tree node. If this condition is true, the function makes a recursive call passing the argument `root->left` and `item`. This call inserts the new string in the left subtree, whose root is the current node. Otherwise, the function makes a recursive call passing the argument `root->right` and `item`. This call inserts the new string in the right subtree, whose root is the current node.

10

The recursive function `showTree` traverses, in order, the nodes of the tree and subtree whose root is the reference parameter root. The function quickly exits if the current value of the parameter root is `NULL`. This condition indicates that the argument for parameter `root` is a terminal node. Therefore, this condition ends the recursive call. If the argument for parameter `root` is not `NULL`, the function makes a recursive call passing the argument `root->left`. This call allows the function to visit the left subtree whose root is the current node. Once the left subtree of the current node is visited, the function displays the string stored in the member value of the current node. Then the function makes another recursive call, this time passing the argument `root->right`. This call allows the function to visit the right subtree whose root is the current node. Once the right subtree of the current node is visited, the function exits.

The function `main` declares an array of pointers to the internal data, shown in lines 45 through 48. The function also declares the variable `treeRoot` as the root of the binary tree. The declaration of this variable also initializes the variable to `NULL`. The function also declares the `int`-typed variable `i` and initializes it with 0.

The function `main` uses the `while` loop in line 53 to insert the strings in the list of state names. The loop iterates until the current name matches the string `"NULL"`. This string is a special name that I use to track the end of the list. If you modify the program and add more state names, be sure to make the string `"NULL"` the last item in the list. The statement in line 54 calls the function `insert` to insert the element `names[i]` in the binary tree whose root is the pointer `treeRoot`.

The statement in line 56 calls the function `showTree` and supplies it the argument `treeRoot`. The call to this recursive function displays the names of the states in ascending order.

Pointers to Functions

The program compilation process translates the names of variables into memory addresses where data is stored and retrieved. Pointers to addresses can also access these addresses. This translation step holds true for variables and functions alike. The compiler translates the name of a function into the address of executable code. C++ extends the strategy of manipulating variables by using pointers to include functions.

Syntax

A Pointer to a Function

The general syntax for declaring a pointer to a function is

```
returnType (*functionPointer)(<list of parameters>);
```

This form tells the compiler that the `functionPointer` is a pointer to a function that has the `returnType` return type and a list of parameters.

Examples:

```
double (*fx)(int n);
void (*sort)(int* intArray, unsigned n);
unsigned (*search)(int searchKey, int* intArray, unsigned n);
```

The first identifier, `fx`, points to a function that returns a `double` and has a single `int`-typed parameter. The second identifier, `sort`, is a pointer to a function that returns a `void` type and takes two parameters: a pointer to `int` and an `unsigned`. The third identifier, `search`, is a pointer to a function that returns an `unsigned` and has three parameters: an `int`, a pointer to an `int`, and an `unsigned`.

Syntax

An Array of Function Pointers

C++ allows you to declare an array of function pointers. The general syntax is

```
returnType (*functionPointer[arraySize])(<list of parameters>);
```

Examples:

```
double (*fx[3])(int n);
void (*sort[MAX_SORT])(int* intArray, unsigned n);
unsigned (*search[MAX_SEARCH])(int searchKey,
int* intArray, unsigned n);
```

The first identifier, `fx`, points to an array of functions. Each member returns a `double` and has a single `int`-typed parameter. The second identifier, `sort`, is a pointer to an array of functions. Each member returns a `void` type and takes two parameters: a pointer to int and an unsigned. The third identifier, search, is a pointer to an array of functions. Each member returns an unsigned and has three parameters: an int, a pointer to an int, and an unsigned.

As with any pointer, you need to initialize a function pointer before using it. This step is very simple. You merely assign the bare name of a function to the function pointer.

Initializing a Function Pointer

The general syntax for initializing a pointer to a function is

```
functionPointer = aFunction;
```

The assigned function must have the same return type and parameter list as the function pointer. Otherwise, the compiler flags an error.

Example:

```
void (*sort)(int* intArray, unsigned n);
sort = qsort;
```

Assigning a Function to an Element

The general syntax for assigning a function to an element in an array of function pointers is

```
functionPointer[index] = aFunction;
```

Once you assign a function name to a function pointer, you can use the pointer to invoke its associated function. Now it should become evident why the function pointer must have the same return type and parameter list as the accessed function.

Example:

```
void (*sort[2])(int* intArray, unsigned n);
sort[0] = shellSort;
sort[1] = CombSort;
```

The Function Pointer Expression

The general syntax for the expression that invokes function pointers is

```
(*functionPointer)(<argument list>);
(*functionPointer[index])(<argument list>);
```

Examples:

```
(*sort)(&intArray, n);
(*sort[0])(&intArray, n);
```

Let's look at an example. Listing 10.8 shows the source code for the program ADVFUN8.CPP. The program performs linearized regression on two observed variables: the independent variable `X`, and the dependent variable `Y`. The model that relates these two variables is

```
f(Y) = intercept + slope * g(X)
```

The function `f(Y)` transforms the data for the `Y` variable. The function `g(X)` transforms the data for the `X` variable. The functions `f(Y)` and `g(X)` can be linear, logarithmic, exponential, square root, square, or any other mathematical function. When both `f(Y) = Y` and `g(X) = X`, the model becomes this linear regression model:

```
Y = intercept + slope * X
```

The linearized regression (back to the general model) calculates the best values for the slope and intercept for the values of `f(Y)` and `g(X)`. The regression also provides the correlation coefficient statistic which represents the percent (as a fractional number) of the `f(Y)` data that is explained by the variation in `g(X)`. A value of 1 represents a perfect fit, and 0 represents a total lack of any correlation between `f(Y)` and `g(X)` data.

Listing 10.8 performs linear regression and carries out the following tasks:

- Prompts you to enter the number of data (your input must be in the limit indicated by the program)
- Prompts you to enter the observed values of X and Y
- Prompts you to select the function that transforms the observations for variable `X` (the program displays a small itemized menu that shows your options, indicating the linear, logarithmic, square, square root, and reciprocal functions)
- Prompts you to select the function that transforms the observations for variable `Y` (the program displays a small itemized menu that shows your options, indicating the linear, logarithmic, square, square root, and reciprocal functions)
- Performs the regression calculations
- Displays the intercept, slope, and correlation coefficient for the linearized regression
- Prompts you to select another set of transformation functions (if you choose to use another set of functions, the program resumes at step 3)

Listing 10.8. Source code for the program ADVFUN8.CPP.

```
/*
   C++ program that uses pointers to functions to implement
   a linear regression program that supports temporary
   mathematical transformations.
*/

#include <iostream.h>
#include <math.h>

const unsigned MAX_SIZE = 100;

typedef double vector[MAX_SIZE];

struct regression {
   double Rsqr;
   double slope;
   double intercept;
};

// declare function pointer
double (*fx)(double);
double (*fy)(double);

// declare function prototypes
void initArray(double*, double*, unsigned);
double linear(double);
double sqr(double);
double reciprocal(double);
void calcRegression(double*, double*, unsigned, regression&,
                    double (*fx)(double), double (*fy)(double));
int select_transf(const char*);

main()
{
    char ans;
    unsigned count;
    vector x, y;
    regression stat;
    int trnsfx, trnsfy;

    do {
        cout << "Enter array size [2.."
             << MAX_SIZE << "] : ";
        cin >> count;
    } while (count <= 1 || count > MAX_SIZE);

    // initialize array
    initArray(x, y, count);
    // transform data
    do {
      // set the transformation functions
      trnsfx = select_transf("X");
```

continues

Listing 10.8. continued

```
      trnsfy = select_transf("Y");
      // set function pointer fx
      switch (trnsfx) {
       case 0 :
          fx = linear;
          break;
       case 1 :
          fx = log;
          break;
       case 2 :
          fx = sqrt;
          break;
       case 3 :
          fx = sqr;
          break;
       case 4 :
          fx = reciprocal;
          break;
       default :
          fx = linear;
          break;
      }
      // set function pointer fy
      switch (trnsfy) {
       case 0 :
          fy = linear;
          break;
       case 1 :
          fy = log;
          break;
       case 2 :
          fy = sqrt;
          break;
       case 3 :
          fy = sqr;
          break;
       case 4 :
          fy = reciprocal;
          break;
       default :
          fy = linear;
          break;
      }

      /*  call function with functional arguments
                                       ¦    ¦
                                       V    V */
      calcRegression(x, y, count, stat, fx, fy);

      cout << "\n\n"
           << "R-square = " << stat.Rsqr << "\n"
           << "Slope = " << stat.slope << "\n"
           << "Intercept = " << stat.intercept << "\n\n\n";
      cout << "Want to use other transformations? (Y/N) ";
```

```
      cin >> ans;
    } while (ans == 'Y' || ans == 'y');
  return 0;
}

void initArray(double* x, double* y, unsigned count)
// read data for array from the keyboard
{
    for (unsigned i = 0; i < count; i++, x++, y++) {
       cout << "X[" << i << "] : ";
       cin >> *x;
       cout << "Y[" << i << "] : ";
       cin >> *y;
    }
}

int select_transf(const char* var_name)
// select choice of transformation
{

   int choice = -1;
   cout << "\n";
   cout << "select transformation for variable " << var_name
        << "\n"
        << "0) No transformation\n"
        << "1) Logarithmic transformation\n"
        << "2) Square root transformation\n"
        << "3) Square  transformation\n"
        << "4) Reciprocal transformation\n";
   while (choice < 0 || choice > 4) {
      cout << "\nSelect choice by number : ";
      cin >> choice;
   }
   return choice;
}

double linear(double x)
{ return x; }

double sqr(double x)
{ return x * x; }

double reciprocal(double x)
{ return 1.0 / x; }

void calcRegression(double* x,
                    double* y,
                    unsigned count,
                    regression &stat,
                    double (*fx)(double),
                    double (*fy)(double))

{
     double meanx, meany, sdevx, sdevy;
     double sum = (double) count, sumx = 0, sumy = 0;
     double sumxx = 0, sumyy = 0, sumxy = 0;
```

continues

Listing 10.8. continued

```
    double xdata, ydata;

    for (unsigned i = 0; i < count; i++) {
        xdata = (*fx)(*(x+i));
        ydata = (*fy)(*(y+i));
        sumx += xdata;
        sumy += ydata;
        sumxx += sqr(xdata);
        sumyy += sqr(ydata);
        sumxy += xdata * ydata;
    }

    meanx = sumx / sum;
    meany = sumy / sum;
    sdevx = sqrt((sumxx - sqr(sumx) / sum)/(sum-1.0));
    sdevy = sqrt((sumyy - sqr(sumy) / sum)/(sum-1.0));
    stat.slope = (sumxy - meanx * meany * sum) /
                     sqr(sdevx)/(sum-1);
    stat.intercept = meany - stat.slope * meanx;
    stat.Rsqr = sqr(sdevx / sdevy * stat.slope);

}
```

Here is a sample session with the program in Listing 10.8:

Output

```
Enter array size [2..100] : 5
X[0] : 10
Y[0] : 50
X[1] : 25
Y[1] : 78
X[2] : 30
Y[2] : 85
X[3] : 35
Y[3] : 95
X[4] : 100
Y[4] : 212

select transformation for variable X
0) No transformation
1) Logarithmic transformation
2) Square root transformation
3) Square transformation
4) Reciprocal transformation

Select choice by number : 1

select transformation for variable Y
0) No transformation
1) Logarithmic transformation
2) Square root transformation
3) Square transformation
4) Reciprocal transformation
```

```
Select choice by number : 1


R-square = 0.977011
Slope = 0.63039
Intercept = 2.37056


Want to use other transformations? (Y/N) y

select transformation for variable X
0) No transformation
1) Logarithmic transformation
2) Square root transformation
3) Square transformation
4) Reciprocal transformation

Select choice by number : 0

select transformation for variable Y

0) No transformation
1) Logarithmic transformation
2) Square root transformation
3) Square transformation
4) Reciprocal transformation

Select choice by number : 0


R-square = 0.999873
Slope = 1.79897
Intercept = 32.0412


Want to use other transformations? (Y/N) n
```

Analysis The program in Listing 10.8 declares the global constant `MAX_SIZE`, which determines the maximum size of the arrays. The program also declares the type `vector` in line 12. In addition, the program defines the structure `regression` in lines 14 through 18. This structure stores the statistics of a regression. Lines 21 and 22 define the global function pointers `fx` and `fy`. Each pointer deals with a function that takes a `double`-typed argument and returns a `double`-typed value. The program uses these global pointers to store the mathematical transformations that you select.

The program also declares the functions `initArray`, `linear`, `sqr`, `reciprocal`, `calcRegression`, `select_transf`, and `main`. The function `initArray` prompts you to enter the data for the arrays `x` and `y`. The functions `linear`, `sqr`, and `reciprocal` are simple functions that provide the transformations for the data. These functions supplement the mathematical functions, such as `sqrt` and `log`, which are prototyped in the MATH.H header file. Each one of these functions has the same parameter and return type as the function pointers `fx` and `fy`.

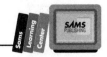

The function `calcRegression` calculates the regression statistics based on the arrays passed by its array parameters `x` and `y`. The function uses the function pointer parameters `fx` and `fy` to transform the data in arrays `x` and `y`. The statements in lines 166 and 167 use the pointers `fx` and `fy` to transform the elements of arrays `x` and `y`, respectively.

The function `select_transf` prompts with a simple itemized menu to select the transformation functions by number. The function returns the value for the transformation code number that you select.

The function `main` declares the arrays `x` and `y`, using the type `vector`. The function also declares the structure `stat`, which stores the regression statistics. The function `main` prompts you to enter the number of data points that you want to process. Then, the function calls function `initArray` to obtain the data for the arrays `x` and `y`. Next, the function invokes the function `select_trans` twice, to select the transformation functions for the data in arrays `x` and `y`. The switch statement in line 55 examines the value in variable `trnsfx`, which contains the index of the transformation value for the array `x`. The various case labels assign the proper function to the pointer `fx`. Some of these functions, such as `log` and `sqrt`, are prototyped in the MATH.H header file. The switch statement in line 76 performs a similar task to assign the proper function to pointer `fy`.

The function `main` then calls the function `calcRegression` and passes the arguments `x`, `y`, `count`, `stat`, the function pointer `fx`, and the function pointer `fy`. The output statement in lines 102 through 105 displays the regression statistics for the current set of transformation functions. The statement in line 106 asks you if you wish to select another set of transformation functions. The statement in line 107 stores your input in variable `ans`. The `while` clause in line 108 determines if the program repeats the process of selecting the transformation functions and calculating the corresponding regression statistics.

Summary

Today's lesson presents simple C++ functions. You learn about the following topics:

- You can pass arrays as function arguments using pointers to the basic types. C++ allows you to declare array parameters using explicit pointer types or using the empty brackets. Such parameters enable you to write general-purpose functions that work with arrays of different sizes. In addition, these pointers access the array by using its address, instead of making a copy of the entire array.
- Passing strings as function arguments follows the same rules as passing arrays, because C++ strings are arrays of characters.

- Passing structures as function arguments enables you to shorten the parameter list by encapsulating various related information in C++ structures. C++ supports passing structures by value. Such parameters pass a copy of their arguments to the host function. Consequently, the changes made to the structure members do not affect the arguments outside the scope of the function.

- Passing reference parameters may use pointers or formal references. The formal references become aliases of their arguments. Any changes made to the parameters affect their arguments outside the function. You can declare a constant reference parameter to ensure that the function does not alter the arguments for the reference parameter. Accessing the members of a structured reference parameter uses the dot operator.

- Passing structures by pointer gives the host function the address of the structure. The pointer parameter needs to use the `->` operator to access the various members of the structure. You can use the `const` prefix with the pointer parameter to prevent the function from changing the members of the structure, which is accessed by the pointer parameters.

- Recursive functions are functions that obtain a result and/or perform a task by calling themselves. These recursive calls must be limited to avoid exhausting the memory resources of the computer. Consequently, every recursive function must examine a condition which determines the end of the recursion.

- Passing pointers to dynamic structures often requires passing the reference to the root or head pointers which manage such structures. Today's lesson illustrates how to create functions to insert data in a binary tree and display its data.

- Pointers to functions store the address of functions. Such pointers need to have the parameter list and return type defined, in order to access functions with the same prototype. Pointers to functions enable you to select which function you wish to invoke at run-time.

Q&A

Q How does using a reference parameter affect the design of a function, compared to a value parameter?

A The reference parameter can also update—unless it is declared as a `const` parameter—the argument. Thus, the function can use reference parameters as an input/output data conduit and also as an output data conduit.

Q How can I distinguish between a pointer that passes an array of value and one used to pass back a value through its argument?

A You need to read the declaration of the function in context. However, you can use a reference parameter to declare a parameter that passes a value back to the caller.

Q What is the memory resource used in managing calls to recursive functions?

A The run-time system uses the stack to store intermediate values, including the ones generated by calls to recursive functions. As with other memory resources, stacks have a limited space. Consequently, recursive calls with long sequence or memory-consuming arguments drain the stack space and cause a run-time error.

NEW TERM A *stack* is a memory location where information is inserted and removed on a Last-In-First-Out (LIFO) priority.

Workshop

The Workshop provides quiz questions to help you solidify your understanding of the material covered and exercises to provide you with experience in using what you've learned. Try to understand the quiz and exercise answers before continuing on to the next day's lesson. Answers are provided in Appendix B, "Answers."

Quiz

1. Can you use the conditional operator to write the recursive factorial function?
2. What is wrong with the following recursive function?

```
double factorial(int I)
{
  switch (i) {
    case 0:
    case 1:
      return 1;
      break;
    case 2:
      return 2;
      break;
```

```
    case 3:
      return 6;
      break;
    case 4:
      return 24;
      break;
    default:
      return double(i) * factorial(i-1);
  }
}
```

3. Convert the following recursive `Fibonacci` function (this function has the sequence `Fib(0) = 0`, `Fib(1) = 1`, `Fib(2) = 1`, `Fib(3) = 2`, `Fib(4) = 3`, and so on) into a nonrecursive version:

```
double Fibonacci(int n)
{
  if (n == 0)
    return 0;
  else if (n == 1 || n == 2)
    return 1;
  else
    return Fibonacci(n - 1) + Fibonacci(n - 2);
}
```

4. True or false? The two versions of the following functions are equivalent:

```
struct stringStruct {
  char source[MAX+1];
  char uprStr[MAX+1];
  char lwrStr[MAX+];
  char revStr[MAX+1];
};

void convertStr2(const char* str, stringStruct& s)
{
  strncpy(s.source, str, MAX);
  strncpy(s.uprStr, str, MAX);
  strncpy(s.lwrStr, str, MAX);
  strncpy(s.revStr, str, MAX);
  _strlwr(s.lwrStr);
```

```
  _strupr(s.uprStr);
  strrev(s.revStr);
}

void convertStr2(const char* str, stringStruct* s)
{
  strncpy(s->source, str, MAX);
  strncpy(s->uprStr, str, MAX);
  strncpy(s->lwrStr, str, MAX);
  strncpy(s->revStr, str, MAX);
  _strlwr(s->lwrStr);
  _strupr(s->uprStr);
  strrev(s->revStr);
}
```

Exercise

Create the program ADVFUN9.CPP from ADVFUN8.CPP by replacing the individual function pointers `fx` and `fy` with the array of function pointers `f`. In addition, replace the two function pointer parameters of function `calcRegression` with a parameter that is an array of function pointers.

11

Object-Oriented Programming and C++ Classes

WEEK 2

Classes provide C++ with object-oriented programming (OOP) constructs. Today's lesson, which marks an important milestone for learning C++, introduces you to building individual classes as well as class hierarchy. You learn about the following topics:

- The basics of object-oriented programming
- Declaring base classes
- Constructors
- Destructors
- Declaring a class hierarchy
- Virtual functions
- Friend functions
- Operators and friend operators

Basics of Object-Oriented Programming

We live in a world of objects. Each object has its attributes and operations. Some objects are more animated than others. You can categorize objects into classes. For example, my CASIO Data Bank watch is an object that belongs to the class of the CASIO Data Bank watches.

NEW TERM *Object-oriented programming (OOP)* uses the notions of real-world objects to develop applications.

You can also relate individual classes in a class hierarchy. The class of CASIO Data Bank watches is part of the watch class hierarchy. The basics of OOP include classes, objects, messages, methods, inheritance, and polymorphism.

NEW TERM A *class* defines a category of objects. Each *object* is an instance of a class.

Classes and Objects

An object shares the same attributes and functionality with other objects in the same class. Typically, an object has a unique state, defined by the current values of its attributes. The functionality of a class determines the operations that are possible for the class instances. C++ calls the attributes of class data members and calls the operations of class member functions. Classes encapsulate data members and member functions.

Going back to the CASIO watch example, the buttons in the watch represent the member functions of the class of CASIO watches, and the display represents a data member. I can press certain buttons to edit the date and/or time. In OOP terms, the member functions alter the state of the object by changing its data members.

Messages and Methods

Object-oriented programming models the interaction with objects as events when messages are sent to an object or between objects. The object receiving a message responds by invoking the appropriate method (that's the member function in C++). C++ does not explicitly foster the notion of messages and methods as other OOP languages such as SmallTalk do. However, I find it easier to discuss invoking member functions using the term "message." The terms "methods" and "member functions" are equivalent.

The *message* is what is done to an object. The *method* is how the object responds to the incoming message.

Inheritance

In object-oriented languages, you can derive a class from another one.

NEW TERM With *inheritance*, the derived class (also called the *descendant class*) inherits the data members and member functions of its *parent* and *ancestor classes.*

Deriving a class refines the parent class by appending new attributes and new operations. The derived class typically declares new data members and new member functions. In addition, the derived class can override inherited member functions when the operations of these functions are not suitable for the derived class.

To apply the concept of inheritance to the CASIO Data Bank watch, consider the following possible scenario. Suppose that the watch manufacturer decides to create a CASIO Data Comm watch that offers the same features of the CASIO Data Bank plus a beeper! Rather than redesigning the new model (that is the new class, in OOP terms) from scratch, the CASIO engineers start with the existing design of the CASIO Data Bank and build on it. This process may well add new attributes and operations to the existing design and alter some existing operations to fit the new design. Thus, the CASIO Data Comm model inherits the attributes and the operations of the CASIO Data Bank model. In OOP terms, the class of CASIO Data Comm watches is a descendant of the class of CASIO Data Bank watches.

Polymorphism

The OOP feature of polymorphism allows the instances of different classes to react in a particular way to a message (or function invocation, in C++ terms). For example, in a hierarchy of graphical shapes (point, line, square, rectangle, circle, ellipse, and so on), each shape has a Draw function that is responsible for properly responding to a request to draw that shape.

NEW TERM *Polymorphism* enables the instances of different classes to respond to the same function in ways that are appropriate to each class.

Declaring Base Classes

C++ enables you to declare a class that encapsulates data members and member functions. These functions alter and/or retrieve the values of the data members as well as perform related tasks.

A Base Class

Syntax

The general syntax for declaring a base class is

```
class className
{
  private:
   <private data members>
   <private constructors>
   <private member functions>
  protected:
   <protected data members>
   <protected constructors>
   <protected member functions>
  public:
   <public data members>
   <public constructors>
   <public destructor>
   <public member functions>
};
```

Example:

```
class point
{
  protected:
   double x;
   double y;
  public:
   point(double xVal, double yVal);
```

```
    double getX();
    double getY();
    void assign(double xVal, double yVal);
    point& assign(point& pt);
};
```

The Sections of a Class

The previous syntax shows that the declaration involves the keyword `class`. C++ classes offer three levels of visibility for the various members (that is, both data members and member functions):

- The private section
- The protected section
- The public section

NEW TERM In the *private section*, only the member functions of the class can access the private members. The class instances are denied access to private members. In the *protected section*, only the member functions of the class and its descendant classes can access protected members. The class instances are denied access to protected members. The *public section* specifies members that are visible to the member functions of the class, class instances, member functions of descendant classes, and their instances.

The following rules apply to the various class sections:

1. The class sections can appear in any order.
2. The class sections may appear more than once.
3. If no class section is specified, the C++ compiler treats the members as protected.
4. You should avoid placing data members in the public section, unless such a declaration significantly simplifies your design. Data members are typically placed in the protected section to allow their access by member functions of descendant classes.
5. Use member functions to set and/or query the values of data members. The members that set the data members assist in performing validation and updating other data members, if need be.
6. The class may have multiple constructors, which are typically located in the public section.

7. The class can have only one destructor, which must be declared in the public section.

8. The member functions (as well as the constructors and destructors) that have multiple statements are defined outside the class declaration. The definition may reside in the same file that declares the class.

NEW TERM *Constructors* are special members that must have the same name as the host class. *Destructors* automatically remove class instances.

In software libraries, the definition of the member functions referred to in rule 8 typically resides in a separate source file. When you define a member function, you must qualify the function name with the class name. The syntax of such a qualification involves using the class name followed by two colons (`::`) and then the name of a function. For example, consider the following class:

```
class point
{
  protected:
   double x;
   double y;
  public:
   point(double xVal, double yVal);
   double getX();
   // other member functions
};
```

The definitions of the constructor and member functions are

```
point::point(double xVal, double yVal)
{
  // statements
}

double point::getX()
{
  // statements
}
```

Once you declare a class, you can use the class name as a type identifier to declare class instances. The syntax resembles declaring variables.

Let's look at an example. Listing 11.1 shows the source code for the program CLASS1.CPP. The program prompts you to enter the length and width of a rectangle (which is an object). The program then displays the length, width, and area of the rectangle you specified.

Type

Listing 11.1. Source code for the program CLASS1.CPP.

```
// C++ program that illustrates a class

#include <iostream.h>

class rectangle
{
  protected:
    double length;
    double width;
   public:
     rectangle() { assign(0, 0); }
     rectangle(double len, double wide) { assign(len, wide); }
     double getLength() { return length; }
     double getWidth() { return width; }
     double getArea() { return length * width; }
     void assign(double len, double wide);
};

void rectangle::assign(double len, double wide)
{
  length = len;
  width = wide;
}

main()
{
  rectangle rect;
  double len, wide;

  cout << "Enter length of rectangle : ";
  cin >> len;
  cout << "Enter width of rectangle : ";
  cin >> wide;
  rect.assign(len, wide);
  cout << "Rectangle length = " << rect.getLength() << "\n"
       << "          width  = " << rect.getWidth() << "\n"
       << "          area   = " << rect.getArea() << "\n";
  return 0;
}
```

Here is a sample session with the program in Listing 11.1:

Output

```
Enter length of rectangle : 10
Enter width of rectangle : 12
Rectangle length = 10
width  = 12
area   = 120
```

Analysis The program in Listing 11.1 declares the class `rectangle`, which models a rectangle. The class has two `double`-typed data members, `length` and `width`, which store the dimension of a rectangle. In addition, the class has two constructors: the default constructor and the nondefault constructor. The class also defines the member functions `getLength`, `getWidth`, `getArea`, and `assign`.

NEW TERM The *default constructor* creates an instance with 0 dimensions, and the *non-default* constructor creates an instance with nonzero dimensions.

The function `getLength`, which is defined in the class declaration, simply returns the value in member `length`. The function `getWidth`, which is also defined in the class declaration, merely returns the value in member `width`. The function `getArea`, which is defined in the class declaration, simply returns the value of the result of multiplying the members `length` and `width`.

The member function `assign`, which is defined outside the class declaration, assigns the arguments for its parameters `len` and `wide` to the data members `length` and `width`, respectively. I simplify the implementation of this function by not checking for negative values.

The function `main` declares `rect` as the instance of class rectangle, and the `double`-typed variables `len` and `wide`. The output statement in line 30 prompts you to enter the length of the rectangle. The statement in line 31 obtains your input and stores it in variable `len`. The output statement in line 32 prompts you to enter the width of the rectangle. The statement in line 33 obtains your input and stores it in variable `wide`.

The function `main` assigns the input values to the instance `rect` using the `assign` member function. In OOP terms, I can say that the function `main` sends the assign message to the object `rect`. The arguments of the message are variables `len` and `wide`. The object `rect` responds by invoking the method (the member function) `rectangle::assign(double, double)`.

The output statement in lines 35 through 37 displays the length, width, and area of the object `rect`. This statement sends the messages `getLength`, `getWidth`, and `getArea` to the object `rect`. In turn, the object `rect` invokes the appropriate methods (or member function, if you prefer) to respond to each one of these messages.

Constructors

C++ constructors and destructors work automatically to guarantee the appropriate creation and removal of class instances.

Syntax

Constructors

The general syntax for constructors is

```
class className
{
```

```
  public:
   className(); // default constructor
   className(className& c); // copy constructor
   className(<parameter list>); // another constructor
};
```

Example:

```
class point
{
  protected:
   double x;
   double y;
  public:
   point();
   point(double xVal, double yVal);
   point(point& pt);
   double getX();
   double getY();
   void assign(double xVal, double yVal);
   point& assign(point& pt);
};
```

NEW TERM A *copy constructor* allows you to create class instances by copying the data from existing instances.

C++ has the following features and rules regarding constructors:

1. The name of the constructor must be identical to the name of its class.
2. You must not include any return type, not even `void`.
3. A class can have any number of constructors, including none. In the latter case, the compiler automatically creates one for that class.
4. The default constructor is the one that either has no parameters or possesses a parameter list where all the parameters use default arguments. Here are two examples:

```
// class use parameterless constructor
class point1
{
    protected:
        double x;
        double y;
    public:
        point1();
        // other member functions
};
```

```
// class use constructor with default arguments
class point2
{
    protected:
        double x;
        double y;
    public:
        point(double xVal = 0, double yVal = 0);
        // other member functions
};
```

5. The copy constructor enables you to create a class instance using an existing instance. Here is an example:

```
class point
{
    protected:
        double x;
        double y;
    public:
        point();
        point(double xVal, double yVal);
        point(point& pt);
        // other member functions
};
```

6. The declaration of a class instance (which includes function parameters and local instances) involves a constructor. Which constructor is called? The answer depends on how many constructors you have declared for the class and how you declared the class instance. For example, consider the following instances of the last version of class `point`:

```
point p1; // involves the default constructor

point p2(1.1, 1.3); // uses the second constructor

point p3(p2); // uses the copy constructor
```

Because instance `p1` specifies no arguments, the compiler uses the default constructor. The instance `p2` specifies two floating-point arguments. Consequently, the compiler uses the second constructor. The instance `p3` has the instance `p2` as an argument. Therefore, the compiler uses the copy constructor to create instance `p3` from instance `p2`.

DO	DON'T

DO declare copy constructors, especially for classes that model dynamic data structures. These constructors perform what is called a deep copy which includes the dynamic data. By default, the compiler creates what are called shallow copy constructors, which copy the data members only.

DON'T rely on the shallow copy constructor to copy instances for classes which have members that are pointers.

Destructors

C++ classes may contain destructors that automatically remove class instances.

Syntax

Destructors

The general syntax for destructors is

```
class className
{
  public:
    className(); // default constructor
   // other constructors
   ~className();
   // other member function
};
```

Example:

```
class String
{
  protected:
   char *str;
   int len;

  public:
   String();
   String(String& s);
   ~String() ;
   // other member functions
};
```

C++ has the following features and rules regarding destructors:

1. The name of the destructor must begin with a tilde (~). The rest of the destructor name must be identical to the name of its class.

2. You must not include any return type, not even `void`.
3. A class can have no more than one destructor. In addition, if you omit the destructor, the compiler automatically creates one for you.
4. The destructor cannot have any parameters.
5. The run-time system automatically invokes a class destructor when the instance of that class is out of scope.

Examples of Constructors and Destructors

Let's look at a program that typifies the use of constructors and destructors. Listing 11.2 contains the source code for the CLASS2.CPP program. The program performs the following tasks:

- Creates a dynamic array (the object)
- Assigns values to the elements of the dynamic array
- Displays the values in the dynamic array
- Removes the dynamic array

Type

Listing 11.2. Source code for the CLASS2.CPP program.

```
// Program demonstrates constructors and destructors

#include <iostream.h>

const unsigned MIN_SIZE = 4;

class Array
{
   protected:
     double *dataPtr;
     unsigned size;

    public:
     Array(unsigned Size = MIN_SIZE);
     ~Array()
       { delete [] dataPtr; }
     unsigned getSize() const
       { return size; }
     void store(double x, unsigned index)
       { dataPtr[index] = x; }
     double recall(unsigned index)
```

```
22:         { return dataPtr[index]; }
23: };
24:
25: Array::Array(unsigned Size)
26: {
27:   size = (Size < MIN_SIZE) ? MIN_SIZE : Size;
28:   dataPtr = new double[size];
29: }
30:
31: main()
32: {
33:   Array Arr(10);
34:   double x;
35:   // assign data to array elements
36:   for (unsigned i = 0; i < Arr.getSize(); i++) {
37:     x = double(i);
38:     x = x * x - 5 * x + 10;
39:     Arr.store(x, i);
40:   }
41:   // display data in the array element
42:   cout << "Array Arr has the following values:\n\n";
43:   for (i = 0; i < Arr.getSize(); i++)
44:     cout << "Arr[" << i << "] = " << Arr.recall(i) << "\n";
45:   return 0;
46: }
```

Here is a sample session with the program in Listing 11.2:

Output

```
Array Arr has the following values:

Arr[0] = 10
Arr[1] = 6
Arr[2] = 4
Arr[3] = 4
Arr[4] = 6
Arr[5] = 10
Arr[6] = 16
Arr[7] = 24
Arr[8] = 34
Arr[9] = 46
```

Analysis

The program in Listing 11.2 declares the global constant `MIN_SIZE`, in line 5, which specifies the minimum size of dynamic arrays. The program also declares the class `Array` in line 7. The class has two data members, `dataPtr` and `size`. The member `dataPtr` is the pointer to the elements' dynamically allocated array. The member `size` stores the number of elements in an instance of class `Array`.

The class declares a default constructor. (The constructor actually has a parameter with the default value `MIN_SIZE`.) The program defines the constructor in lines 25 through 29. The arguments for the parameter `Size` specify the number of array elements. The statement in line 27 assigns the greater value of parameter `Size` and the constant `MIN_SIZE`

to the data member size. The statement in line 28 allocates the dynamic space for the array by using the operator `new`. The statement assigns the base address of the dynamic array to the member `dataPtr`.

The destructor `~Array` removes the dynamic space of the array by applying the operator `delete` to the member `dataPtr`.

The member function `getSize`, which is defined in the class declaration, returns the value in data member `size`.

The function `store`, which is defined in the class declaration, stores the value passed by parameter `x` at the element number specified by the parameter `index`. I simplify the implementation of this function by eliminating the out-of-range index check.

The function `recall`, which is defined in the class declaration, returns the value in the element specified by the parameter `index`. I simplify the implementation of this function by eliminating the out-of-range index check.

The function `main` declares the object `Arr` as an instance of class `Array`. The declaration, located in line 33, specifies that the instance has 10 elements. The function also declares the `double`-typed variable `x`. The `for` loop in lines 36 through 40 stores values in the instance `Arr`. The loop uses the control variable `i` and iterates from 0 to `Arr.getSize() - 1`, in increments of 1. The loop continuation condition sends the `getSize` message to instance `Arr` to obtain the number of elements in the array. The statements in lines 37 and 38 calculate the value to store in an element of instance `Arr`. The statement in line 39 sends the message `store` to instance `Arr` and passes the arguments `x` and `i`. The object `Arr` saves the value in variable `x` at the element number `i`.

The output statement in line 42 comments on the output of the `for` loop in lines 43 and 44. The loop uses the control variable `i` and iterates from 0 to `Arr.getSize() -1`, in increments of 1. The output statement in line 44 displays the element in instance `Arr` by sending the message `recall` to that instance. The message has the argument `i`.

Declaring a Class Hierarchy

The power of the OOP features of C++ comes from the fact that you can derive classes from existing ones. A descendant class inherits the members of its ancestor classes (that is, parent class, grandparent class, and so on) and can also override some of the inherited functions. Inheritance enables you to reuse code in descendant classes.

Syntax

A Derived Class

The general syntax for declaring a derived class is

```
class className : [public] parentClass
{
  <friend classes>

  private:
   <private data members>
   <private constructors>
   <private member functions>

  protected:
   <protected data members>
   <protected constructors>
   <protected member functions>

  public:
   <public data members>
   <public constructors>
   <public destructor>
   <public member functions>

   <friend functions and friend operators>
};
```

Example:

The following example shows the `class cRectangle` and its descendant, `class cBox`:

```
class cRectangle
{
  protected:
   double length;
   double width;
  public:
   cRectangle(double len, double wide);
   double getLength() const;
   double getWidth(); const;
   double assign(double len, double wide);
   double calcArea();
};

class cBox : public cRectangle
{
  protected:
   double height;

  public:
   cBox(double len, double wide, double height);
   double getHeight() const;
   assign(double len, double wide, double height);
   double calcVolume();
};
```

The class lineage is indicated by a colon followed by the optional keyword `public` and then the name of the parent class. When you include the keyword `public`, you allow the instances of the descendant class to access the public members of the parent and other ancestor classes. By contrast, when you omit the keyword `public`, you deprive the instance of the descendant class from accessing the members of the ancestor classes.

A descendant class inherits the data members of its ancestor classes. C++ has no mechanism for removing unwanted inherited data members—you are basically stuck with them. By contrast, C++ allows you to override inherited member functions. More about this topic later in today's lesson. The descendant class declares new data members, new member functions, and overriding member functions. Again, you can place these members in the private, protected, or public sections as you see fit in your class design.

DO | **DON'T**

DO reduce the number of constructors by using default argument parameters.

DO use member functions to access the values in the data members. These member functions allow you to control and validate the values in the data members.

DON'T declare all the constructors of a class protected unless you want to force the client programmers (that is, those programs that use the class) to use the class by declaring its descendants with public constructors.

DON'T declare the data members in the public section.

Let's look at an example that declares a small class hierarchy. Listing 11.3 shows the source code for the CLASS3.CPP program. This program declares classes that contain a hierarchy of two simple geometric shapes: a circle and a cylinder. The program requires no input. Instead, it uses internal data to create the geometric shapes and to display their dimensions, areas, and volume.

Type

Listing 11.3. Source code for the CLASS3.CPP program.

```
// Program that demonstrates a small hierarchy of classes

#include <iostream.h>
#include <math.h>

const double pi = 4 * atan(1);

inline double sqr(double x)
{ return x * x; }
```

```

class cCircle
{
  protected:
    double radius;

  public:
    cCircle(double radiusVal = 0) : radius(radiusVal) {}
    void setRadius(double radiusVal)
      { radius = radiusVal; }
    double getRadius() const
      { return radius; }
    double area() const
      { return pi * sqr(radius); }
    void showData();
};

class cCylinder : public cCircle
{
  protected:
    double height;

  public:
     cCylinder(double heightVal = 0, double radiusVal = 0)
       : height(heightVal), cCircle(radiusVal) {}
     void setHeight(double heightVal)
       { height = heightVal; }
     double getHeight() const
       { return height; }
     double area() const
       { return 2 * cCircle::area() +
                2 * pi * radius * height; }
     void showData();
};

void cCircle::showData()
{
   cout << "Circle radius        = " << getRadius() << "\n"
        << "Circle area          = " << area() << "\n\n";
}

void cCylinder::showData()
{
   cout << "Cylinder radius      = " << getRadius() << "\n"
        << "Cylinder height      = " << getHeight() << "\n"
        << "Cylinder area        = " << area() << "\n\n";
}

main()
{
   cCircle Circle(1);
   cCylinder Cylinder(10, 1);

   Circle.showData();
   Cylinder.showData();
   return 0;
}
```

Output

Here is a sample session with the program in Listing 11.3:

```
Circle radius        = 1
Circle area          = 3.14159

Cylinder radius      = 1
Cylinder height      = 10
Cylinder area        = 69.115
```

Analysis

The program in Listing 11.3 declares the classes `cCircle` and `cCylinder`. The class `cCircle` models a circle, whereas class `cCylinder` models a cylinder.

The `cCircle` class declares a single data member, `radius`, to store the radius of the circle. The class also declares a constructor and a number of member functions. The constructor assigns a value to the data member `radius` when you declare a class instance. Notice that the constructor uses a new syntax to initialize the member `radius`. The functions `setRadius` and `getRadius` serve to set and query the value in member `radius`, respectively. The function `area` returns the area of the circle. The function `showData` displays the radius and area of a class instance.

The class `cCylinder`, a descendant of `cCircle`, declares a single data member, `height`, to store the height of the cylinder. The class inherits the member `radius` needed to store the radius of the cylinder. The `cCylinder` class declares a constructor and a number of member functions. The constructor assigns values to the `radius` and `height` members when creating a class instance. Notice the use of a new syntax to initialize the members—member `height` is initialized, and member `radius` is initialized by invoking the constructor of class `cCircle` with the argument `radiusVal`. The functions `getHeight` and `setHeight` serve to set and query the value in member `height`, respectively. The class uses the inherited functions `setRadius` and `getRadius` to manipulate the inherited member `radius`. The function `area`, which overrides the inherited function `cCircle::area()`, returns the surface area of the cylinder. Notice that this function explicitly invokes the inherited function `cCircle::area()`. The function `showData` displays the radius, height, and area of a class instance.

The function `main` declares the instance `Circle`, of class `cCircle`, and assigns 1 to the circle's radius. In addition, the function also declares the instance `Cylinder`, of class `cCylinder`, and assigns 10 and 1 to the circle's height and radius, respectively. The function then sends the `showData` message to the instances `Circle` and `Cylinder`. Each object responds to this message by invoking the appropriate member function.

Virtual Functions

As I mentioned previously, polymorphism is an important object-oriented programming feature. Consider the following simple classes and the function `main`:

```
#include <iostream.h>
class cA
{
  public:
   double A(double x) { return x * x; }
   double B(double x) { return A(x) / 2; }
};

class cB : public cA
{
  public:
   double A(double x) { return x * x * x; }
};

main()
{
   cB aB;
   cout << aB.B(3) << "\n";
   return 0;
}
```

Class `cA` contains functions `A` and `B`, where function `B` calls function `A`. Class `cB`, a descendant of class `cA`, inherits function `B`, but overrides function `A`. The intent here is to have the inherited function `cA::B` call function `cB::A` in order to support polymorphic behavior. What is the program output? The answer is 4.5 and not 13.5! Why? The answer lies in the fact that the compiler resolves the expression `aB.B(3)` by using the inherited function `cA::B`, which in turn calls function `cA::A`. Therefore, function `cB:A` is left out and the program fails to support polymorphic behavior.

C++ supports polymorphic behavior by offering virtual functions.

NEW TERM *Virtual functions*, which are bound at run-time, are declared by placing the keyword `virtual` before the function's return type.

Once you declare a function virtual, you can override it only with virtual functions in descendant classes. These overriding functions must have the same parameter list. Virtual functions can override nonvirtual functions in ancestor classes.

Syntax

Virtual Functions

The general syntax for declaring virtual functions is

```
class className1
{
```

```
   // member functions
   virtual returnType functionName(<parameter list>);
};

class className2 : public className1
{
   // member functions
   virtual returnType functionName(<parameter list>);
};
```

Example:

This example shows how virtual functions can successfully implement polymorphic behavior in classes `cA` and `cB`:

```
#include <iostream.h>
class cA
{
  public:
   virtual double A(double x) { return x * x; }
   double B(double x) { return A(x) / 2; }
};

class cB : public cA
{
  public:
   virtual double A(double x) { return x * x * x; }
};

main()
{
   cB aB;
   cout << aB.B(3) << "\n";
   return 0;
}
```

This example displays 13.5, the correct result, because the call to the inherited function `cA::B` is resolved at run-time by calling `cB::A`.

DO | **DON'T**

DO use virtual functions when you have a callable function that implements a class-specific behavior. Declaring such a function as virtual ensures that it provides the correct response that is relevant to the associated class.

DON'T declare a member function as virtual by default. Virtual functions have some additional overhead.

Let's look at an example. Listing 11.4 shows the source code for the program CLASS4.CPP. The program creates a square and a rectangle, and displays their dimensions and areas. No input is required.

Listing 11.4. Source code for the program CLASS4.CPP.

```
// Program that demonstrates virtual functions

#include <iostream.h>

class cSquare
{
  protected:
    double length;

  public:
    cSquare(double len) { length = len; }
    double getLength() { return length; }
    virtual double getWidth() { return length; }
    double getArea() { return getLength() * getWidth(); }
};

class cRectangle : public cSquare
{
  protected:
    double width;

  public:
    cRectangle(double len, double wide) :
       cSquare(len), width(wide) {}
    virtual double getWidth() { return width; }
};

main()
{
   cSquare square(10);
   cRectangle rectangle(10, 12);

   cout << "Square has length = " << square.getLength() << "\n"
        << "       and area   = " << square.getArea() << "\n";
   cout << "Rectangle has length = "
        << rectangle.getLength() << "\n"
        << "          and width  = "
        << rectangle.getWidth() << "\n"
        << "          and area   = "
        << rectangle.getArea() << "\n";
   return 0;
}
```

Here is a sample session with the program in Listing 11.4:

Output

```
Square has length = 10
and area    = 100
Rectangle has length = 10
and width   = 12
and area    = 120
```

Analysis

The program in Listing 11.4 declares the classes `cSquare` and `cRectangle` to model squares and rectangles, respectively. The class `cSquare` declares a single data member, `length`, to store the length (and width) of the square. The class declares a constructor with the parameter `len`, which passes arguments to the member `length`. The class also declares the functions `getLength`, `getWidth`, and `getArea`. Both functions `getLength` and `getWidth` return the value in member `length`. Notice that the class declares function `getWidth` as virtual. The function `getArea` returns the area of the rectangle, calculated by calling the functions `getLength` and `getWidth`. I choose to invoke these functions rather than use the data member `length` in order to demonstrate how the virtual function `getWidth` works.

The program declares class `cRectangle` as a descendant of class `cSquare`. The class `cRectangle` declares the data member `width` and inherits the member `length`. These members enable the class to store the basic dimensions of a rectangle. The class constructor has the parameters `len` and `wide`, which pass values to the members `len` and `wide`. Notice that the constructor invokes the constructor `cSquare` and supplies it with the argument `len`. The constructor initializes the data member `width` with the value of parameter `wide`.

The class `cRectangle` declares the virtual function `getWidth`. This version returns the value in data member `width`. The class inherits the member functions `getLength` and `getArea`, because their implementation is adequate for the `cRectangle`.

The function `main` declares the object `square` as an instance of class `cSquare`. The instance square has a length of 10. The function `main` also declares the object `rectangle` as an instance of class `cRectangle`. The instance rectangle has the length of 10 and the width of 12.

The output statement in lines 33 and 34 displays the length and area of the instance square. The statement sends the messages `getLength` and `getArea` to the above instance in order to obtain the sought values. The instance `square` invokes the function `getArea`, which in turn calls the functions `cSquare::getLength` and `cSquare::getWidth`.

The output statement in lines 35 through 40 displays the length, width, and area of the instance `rectangle`. The statement sends the messages `getLength`, `getWidth`, and `getArea` to this instance. The instance responds by calling the inherited function `cSquare::getLength`, the virtual function `cRectangle::getWidth`, and the inherited function cSquare::getArea. The latter function calls the inherited function cSquare::getLength and the virtual function cRectange::getWidth to correctly calculate the area of the rectangle.

DO	DON'T

DO declare your destructor as virtual. This ensures polymorphic behavior in destroying class instances. In addition, it is highly recommended that you declare a copy constructor and an assignment operator for each class.

DON'T forget that you can inherit virtual functions and destructors when appropriate for the descendant class. You need not declare shell functions and destructors that simply call the corresponding member of the parent class.

11

Rules for Virtual Functions

The rule for declaring a virtual function is "once virtual, always virtual." In other words, once you declare a function to be virtual in a class, any subclass that overrides the virtual function must do so using another virtual function (that has the same parameter list). The virtual declaration is mandatory for the descendant classes. At first this rule seems to lock you in. This limitation is certainly true for object-oriented programming languages that support virtual functions but not overloaded functions. In the case of C++, the workaround is interesting. You can declare nonvirtual and overloaded functions that have the same name as the virtual function, but bear a different parameter list. Moreover, you cannot inherit nonvirtual member functions that share the same name with a virtual function. Here is a simple example that illustrates the point:

```
#include <iostream.h>
class cA
{
  public:
   cA() {}
   virtual void foo(char c)
     { cout << "virtual cA::foo() returns " << c << '\n'; }
};

class cB : public cA
{
  public:
   cB() {}
   void foo(const char* s)
      { cout << "cB::foo() returns " << s << '\n'; }
   void foo(int i)
      { cout << "cB::foo() returns " << i << '\n'; }
```

```
   virtual void foo(char c)
      { cout << "virtual cB::foo() returns " << c << '\n'; }
};

class cC : public cB
{
  public:
   cC() {}
   void foo(const char* s)
      { cout << "cC::foo() returns " << s << '\n'; }
   void foo(double x)
      { cout << "cC::foo() returns " << x << '\n'; }
   virtual void foo(char c)
      { cout << "virtual cC::foo() returns " << c << '\n'; }
};

main()
{
   int n = 100;
   cA Aobj;
   cB Bobj;
   cC Cobj;

   Aobj.foo('A');
   Bobj.foo('B');
   Bobj.foo(10);
   Bobj.foo("Bobj");
   Cobj.foo('C');
   // if you uncomment the next statement, program does not compile
   // Cobj.foo(n);
   Cobj.foo(144.123);
   Cobj.foo("Cobj");
   return 0;
}
```

This code declares three classes, `cA`, `cB`, and `cC`, to form a linear hierarchy of classes. Class `cA` declares function `foo(char)` as virtual. Class `cB` also declares its own version of the virtual function `foo(char)`. In addition, class `cB` declares the nonvirtual overloaded functions `foo(const char* s)` and `foo(int)`. Class `cC`, the descendant of class `B`, declares the virtual function `foo(char)` and the nonvirtual and overloaded functions `foo(const char*)` and `foo(double)`. Notice that class `cC` must declare the `foo(const char*)` function if it needs the function, because it cannot inherit the member function `cB::foo(const char*)`. C++ supports a different function inheritance scheme when there is an overloaded and virtual function involved. The function `main` creates an instance for each of the three classes and involves the various versions of the member function `foo`.

Friend Functions

C++ allows member functions to access all the data members of a class. In addition, C++ grants the same privileged access to friend functions. The declaration of friend functions appears in the class and begins with the keyword `friend`. Other than using the special keyword, friend functions look very much like member functions, except they cannot return a reference to the befriended class because this requires returning the self-reference `*this`. However, when you define friend functions outside the declaration of their befriended class, you need not qualify the function names with the name of the class.

NEW TERM *Friend functions* are ordinary functions that have access to all data members of one or more classes.

Syntax

Friend Functions

The general form of friend functions is

```
class className
{
  public:
   className();
   // other constructors

   friend returnType friendFunction(<parameter list>);
};
```

Example:

```
class String
{
  protected:
   char *str;
   int len;

  public:
   String();
   ~String();
   // other member functions
   friend String& append(String& str1, String& str2);
   friend String& append(const char* str1, String& str2);
   friend String& append(String& str1, const char* str2);
};
```

Friend classes are able to accomplish tasks that are awkward, difficult, and even impossible with member functions.

Let's look at a simple example for using friend functions. Listing 11.5 contains the source code for the CLASS5.CPP program. This program internally creates two complex numbers, adds them, stores the result in another complex number, and then displays the operands and resulting complex numbers.

Listing 11.5. Source code for the CLASS5.CPP program.

```
// Program that demonstrates friend functions

#include <iostream.h>

class Complex
{
   protected:
     double x;
     double y;

   public:
     Complex(double real = 0, double imag = 0);
     Complex(Complex& c) { assign; }
     void assign(Complex& c);
     double getReal() const { return x; }
     double getImag() const { return y; }
     friend Complex add(Complex& c1, Complex& c2);
};

Complex::Complex(double real, double imag)
{
  x = real;
  y = imag;
}

void Complex::assign(Complex& c)
{
  x = c.x;
  y = c.y;
}

Complex add(Complex& c1, Complex& c2)
{
  Complex result(c1);

  result.x += c2.x;
  result.y += c2.y;
  return result;
}

main()
{
  Complex c1(2, 3);
  Complex c2(5, 7);
  Complex c3;

  c3.assign(add(c1, c2));
  cout << "(" << c1.getReal() << " + i" << c1.getImag() << ")"
       << " + "
       << "(" << c2.getReal() << " + i" << c2.getImag() << ")"
       << " = "
       << "(" << c3.getReal() << " + i" << c3.getImag() << ")"
```

```
         << "\n\n";
   return 0;
}
```

Here is a sample session with the program in Listing 11.5:

Output

```
(2 + i3) + (5 + i7) = (7 + i10)
```

Analysis

The program in Listing 11.5 declares the class `Complex`, which models complex numbers. This class declares two data members, two constructors, a friend function (the highlight of this example), and a set of member functions. The data members `x` and `y` store the real and imaginary components of a complex number, respectively.

The class has two constructors. The first constructor has two parameters (with default arguments) that allow you to build a class instance using the real and imaginary components of a complex number. Because the two parameters have default arguments, the constructor doubles up as the default constructor. The second constructor, `complex(complex&)`, is the copy constructor.

The `Complex` class declares three member functions. The function `assign` copies a class instance into another one. The functions `getReal` and `getImag` return the value stored in the members `real` and `imag`, respectively.

The `Complex` class declares the friend function `add` to add two complex numbers. To make the program short, I do not implement complementary friend functions that subtract, multiply, and divide class instances. What is so special about the friend function `add`? Why not use an ordinary member function to add a class instance? The following declaration of the alternate add member function answers these questions:

```
complex& add(complex& c)
```

This declaration states that the function treats the parameter `c` as a second operand. Here is how the member function add works:

```
complex c1(3, 4), c2(1.2, 4.5);
c1.add(c2); // adds c2 to c1
```

First, the member function `add` works as an increment and not as an addition function. Second, the targeted class instance is always the first operand. This is not a problem for operations like addition and multiplication, but it is a problem for subtraction and division. That is why the friend function `add` works better by giving you the freedom of choosing how to add the class instances.

The friend function `add` returns a class instance. The function creates a local instance of class `Complex` and returns that instance.

The function `main` uses the member function `assign` and the friend function `add` to perform simple complex operations. In addition, the function `main` invokes the functions `getReal` and `getImag` with the various instances of class `Complex` to display the components of each instance.

Operators and Friend Operators

The last program uses a member function and a friend function to implement complex math operations. The approach is typical in C and Pascal, because these languages do not support user-defined operators. By contrast, C++ allows you to declare operators and friend operators. These operators include +, -, *, /, %, ==, !=, <=, <, >=, >, +=, -=, *=, /=, %=, [], (), <<, and >>. Consult a C++ language reference book for more details on the rules of using these operators. C++ treats operators and friend operators as special member functions and friend functions.

Syntax

Operators and Friend Operators

The general syntax for declaring operators and friend operators is

```
class className
{
  public:
   // constructors and destructor
   // member functions

   // unary operator
   returnType operator operatorSymbol(operand);
   // binary operator
   returnType operator operatorSymbol(firstOperand,
                                      secondOperand);
   // unary friend operator
   friend returnType operator operatorSymbol(operand);
   // binary operator
   friend returnType operator operatorSymbol(firstOperand,
                                      secondOperand);
};
```

Example:

```
class String
{
  protected:
   char *str;
   int len;
```

```
  public:
   String();
   ~String();
   // other member functions
   // assignment operator
   String& operator =(String& s);
   String& operator +=(String& s);
   // concatenation operators
   friend String& operator +(String& s1, String& s2);
   friend String& operator +(const char* s1, String& s2);
   friend String& operator +(String& s1, const char* s2);
   // relational operators
   friend int operator >(String& s1, String& s2);
   friend int operator =>(String& s1, String& s2);
   friend int operator <(String& s1, String& s2);
   friend int operator <=(String& s1, String& s2);
   friend int operator ==(String& s1, String& s2);
   friend int operator !=(String& s1, String& s2);
};
```

The functions you write use the operators and friend operators just like predefined operators. Therefore, you can create operators to support the operations of classes that model, for example, complex numbers, strings, arrays, and matrices. These operators enable you to write expressions that are far more readable than expressions that use named functions.

Let's look at an example. Listing 11.6 contains the source code for the CLASS6.CPP program. I created this program by modifying and expanding Listing 11.5. The new program performs more additions and displays two sets of operands and results.

Type

Listing 11.6. Source code for the CLASS6.CPP program.

```
// Program thatdemonstrates operators and friend operators

#include <iostream.h>

class Complex
{
   protected:
     double x;
     double y;

    public:
      Complex(double real = 0, double imag = 0)
        { assign(real, imag); }
      Complex(Complex& c);
      void assign(double real = 0, double imag = 0);
      double getReal() const { return x; }
      double getImag() const { return y; }
      Complex& operator =(Complex& c);
      Complex& operator +=(Complex& c);
      friend Complex operator +(Complex& c1, Complex& c2);
      friend ostream& operator <<(ostream& os, Complex& c);
```

```
};

Complex::Complex(Complex& c)
{
  x = c.x;
  y = c.y;
}

void Complex::assign(double real, double imag)
{
  x = real;
  y = imag;
}

Complex& Complex::operator =(Complex& c)
{
  x = c.x;
  y = c.y;
  return *this;
}

Complex& Complex::operator +=(Complex& c)
{
  x += c.x;
  y += c.y;
  return *this;
}

Complex operator +(Complex& c1, Complex& c2)
{
  Complex result(c1);

  result.x += c2.x;
  result.y += c2.y;
  return result;
}

ostream& operator <<(ostream& os, Complex& c)
{
  os << "(" << c.x << " + i" << c.y << ")";
  return os;
}

main()
{
  Complex c1(3, 5);
  Complex c2(7, 5);
  Complex c3;
  Complex c4(2, 3);

  c3 = c1 + c2;
  cout << c1 << " + " << c2 << " = " << c3 << "\n";
  cout << c3 << " + " << c4 << " = ";
  c3 += c4;
  cout << c3 << "\n";
  return 0;
}
```

Here is a sample session with the program in Listing 11.6:

Output

```
(3 + i5) + (7 + i5 ) = (10 + i10)
(10 + i10) + (2 + i3) = (12 + i13)
```

Analysis

The new class `Complex` replaces the `assign(Complex&)` member function with the operator =. The class also replaces the friend function `add` with the friend operator +:

```
Complex& operator =(Complex& c);
friend Complex operator +(Complex& c1, Complex& c2);
```

The operator = has one parameter, a reference to an instance of class `Complex`, and also returns a reference to the same class. The friend operator + has two parameters (both are references to instances of class `Complex`) and yields a complex class type.

I also took the opportunity to add two new operators:

```
complex& operator +=(complex& c);
friend ostream& operator <<(ostream& os, complex& c);
```

The operator += is a member of class `Complex`. It takes one parameter, a reference to an instance of class `Complex`, and yields a reference to the same class. The other new operator is the friend operator <<, which illustrates how to write a stream extractor operator for a class. The friend operator has two parameters: a reference to class `ostream` (the output stream class) and a reference to class `Complex`. The operator << returns a reference to class `ostream`. This type of value enables you to chain stream output with other predefined types or other classes (assuming that these classes have a friend operator <<). The definition of friend operator << has two statements. The first one outputs strings and the data members of class `Complex` to the output stream parameter `os`. The friendship status of operator << allows it to access the `real` and `imag` data members of its Complex-typed parameter `c`. The second statement in the operator definition returns the first parameter `os`.

The function `main` declares four instances of class `Complex`: `c1`, `c2`, `c3`, and `c4`. The instances `c1`, `c2`, and `c4` are created with nondefault values assigned to the data members `real` and `imag`. The function tests using the operators =, +, <<, and +=. The program illustrates that you can use operators and friend operators to write code that is more readable and supports a higher level of abstraction.

Summary

Today's lesson introduces you to C++ classes and discusses the following topics:

- The basics of object-oriented programming include classes, objects, messages, methods, inheritance, and polymorphism.

- You declare base classes to specify the various private, protected, and public members. C++ classes contain data members and member functions. The data members store the state of a class instance, and the member functions query and manipulate that state.
- Constructors and destructors support the automatic creation and removal of class instances. Constructors are special members that must have the same name as the host class. You may declare any number of constructors, or none at all. In the latter case, the compiler creates one for you. Each constructor enables you to create a class instance in a different way. There are two special kinds of constructors: the default constructor and the copy constructor. In contrast with constructors, C++ allows you to declare only one parameterless destructor. Destructors automatically remove class instances. The run-time system automatically invokes the constructor and destructor when a class instance comes into and goes out of its scope.
- Declaring a class hierarchy enables you to derive classes from existing ones. The descendant classes inherit the members of their ancestor classes. C++ classes are able to override inherited member functions by defining their own versions. If you override a nonvirtual function, you may declare the new version using a different parameter list. By contrast, you cannot alter the parameter list of an inherited virtual function.
- Virtual member functions enable your classes to support polymorphic behavior. Such behavior offers a response that is suitable for each class in a hierarchy. Once you declare a function virtual, you can override it only with a virtual function in a descendant class. All versions of a virtual function in a class hierarchy must have the same signature.
- Friend functions are special nonmember functions that may access protected and private data members. These functions enable you to implement operations that are more flexible than those offered by member functions.
- Operators and friend operators enable you to support various operations, such as addition, assignment, and indexing. These operators enable you to offer a level of abstraction for your classes. In addition, they assist in making the expressions that manipulate class instances more readable and more intuitive.

Q&A

Q What happens if I declare the default, copy, and other constructors as protected?

A Client programs are unable to create instances of that class. However, client programs can use that class by declaring descendant classes with public constructors.

Q Can I use the constructor for typecasting?

A Yes, you can incorporate this kind of typecasting in the creation of a class instance. For example, if the class `Complex` has the constructor `Complex(double real, double imag)`, you can declare the instance `c` of class `Complex` as follows:

```
Complex c = Complex(1.7, 2.4);
```

Q Can I chain messages to an instance?

A Yes, as long as the chained messages invoke member functions that return a reference to the same class which receives the message. For example, if you have a class `String` with the following member functions

```
String& upperCase();
string& reverse();
String& mapChars(char find, char replace);
```

you can write the following statement for the instance of class `String` `s`:

```
s.upperCase().reverse().mapChar(' ', '+');
```

Q What happens if a class relies on the copy constructor, which is created by the compiler, to copy instances of a class which has pointers?

A These constructors perform a bit-by-bit copy. Consequently, the corresponding pointer members in both instances end up with the address to the same dynamic data. This kind of duplication is a recipe for trouble!

Q Can I create an array of instances?

A Yes; however, the accompanying class must have a default constructor. The instantiation of the array uses the constructor mentioned previously.

Q Can I use a pointer to create an instance of class?

A Yes. You need to use the operators `new` and `delete` to allocate and deallocate the dynamic space for the instance. Here is an example using the class `Complex`:

```
Complex* pC;
pC = new Complex;
// manipulate the instance accessed by pointer pC
delete pC;
```

or

```
Complex* pC = new Complex;
// manipulate the instance accessed by pointer pC
delete pC;
```

Workshop

The Workshop provides quiz questions to help you solidify your understanding of the material covered and exercises to provide you with experience in using what you've learned. Try to understand the quiz and exercise answers before continuing on to the next day's lesson. Answers are provided in Appendix B, "Answers."

Quiz

1. Where is the error in the following class declaration?

```
class String {
        char *str;
        unsigned len;
        String();
        String(String& s);
        String(unsigned size, char = ' ');
        String(unsigned size);
        String& assign(String& s);
        ~String();
        unsigned getLen() const;
        char* getString();
        // other member functions
};
```

2. Where is the error in the following class declaration?

```
class String {
     protected:
        char *str;
```

```
      unsigned len;
    public:
      String();
      String(const char* s);
      String(String& s);
      String(unsigned size, char = ' ');
      String(unsigned size);
      ~String();
      // other member functions
};
```

3. True or false? The following statement, which creates the instance `s`, based on the above declaration of class `String`, is correct:

```
s = String("Hello Visual C++");
```

4. Looking at program CLASS6.CPP, if you change the declarations of the instances in function `main` to the following, will the program still compile?

```
Complex c1 = Complex(3, 5);
Complex c2 = Complex(7, 5);
Complex c3 = c1;
Complex c4 = Complex(2, 3);
```

Exercise

Create program CLASS7.CPP from CLASS6.CPP by replacing the individual instances `c1` to `c4` with `c`, an array of instances.

12

Basic Stream File I/O

WEEK 2

Today's lesson introduces you to file I/O operations using the C++ stream library. Although the STDIO.H library in C has been standardized by the ANSI C committee, the C++ stream library has not. You have a choice of using file I/O functions in the STDIO.H file and those in the C++ stream library. Each of these two I/O libraries offers a lot of power and flexibility. Today's lesson presents basic and practical operations that enable you to read and write data to files. You learn about the following topics:

- Common stream I/O functions
- Sequential stream I/O for text
- Sequential stream I/O for binary data
- Random access stream I/O for binary data

To learn more about the C++ stream library, consult a C++ language reference book, such as Tom Swan's *C++ Primer* (Sams 1992).

The C++ Stream Library

The C++ stream I/O library is made up of a hierarchy of classes that is declared in several header files. The IOSTREAM.H header file that I have used so far is only one of these. Others include IO.H, ISTREAM.H, OSTREAM.H, IFSTREAM.H, OFSTREAM.H, and FSTREAM.H. The IO.H header file declares low-level classes and identifiers. The ISTREAM.H and OSTREAM.H files support the basic input and output stream classes. The IOSTREAM.H file combines the operations of the classes in the previous two header files. Similarly, the IFSTREAM.H and OFSTREAM.H files support the basic file input and output stream classes. The FSTREAM.H file combines the operations of the classes in the previous two header files. There are additional stream library files that offer even more specialized stream I/O. The C++ ANSI committee will define the standard stream I/O library, and this will end any confusion regarding which classes and header files are part of the standard stream library and which ones are not.

Common Stream I/O Functions

In this section, I present stream I/O functions that are common to both sequential and random access I/O. These functions include `open`, `close`, `good`, and `fail`, in addition to the operator `!`.

The open function enables you to open a file stream for input, output, append, and both input and output. The function also permits you to specify whether the related I/O is binary or text.

Syntax

The *open* Function

The prototype for the open function is

```
void open const char* filename,
          int mode,
          int m = filebuf::openprot);
```

The parameter *filename* specifies the name of the file to open. The parameter *mode* indicates the I/O mode. Here is a list of arguments for parameter *mode* that are exported by the IO.H header file:

`in`	Open stream for input.
`out`	Open stream for output.
`ate`	Set stream pointer to the end of the file.
`app`	Open stream for append mode.
`trunc`	Truncate file size to 0 if it already exists.
`nocreate`	Raise an error if the file does not already exist.
`noreplace`	Raise an error if the file already exists.
`binary`	Open in binary mode.

Examples:

```
// open stream for input
fstream f;
f.open("\\AUTOEXEC.BAT", ios::in);

// open stream for output
fstream f;
f.open("\\AUTOEXEC.OLD", ios:out);

// open stream for binary input and output
fstream f;
f.open("INCOME.DAT", ios::in ¦ ios::out ¦ ios::binary);
```

Note: The file stream classes offer constructors that include the action (and have the same parameters) of function open.

The close function closes the stream and recuperates the resources involved. These resources include the memory buffer used in the stream I/O operations.

Syntax

The *close* Function

The prototype for the `close` function is

```
void close();
```

Example:

```
fstream f;
// open stream
f.open("\\AUTOEXEC.BAT", ios::in);
// process file
// now close stream
f.close();
```

The C++ stream library includes a set of basic functions that check the error status of a stream operation. These functions include the following:

1. The `good()` function returns a nonzero value if there is no error in a stream operation. The declaration of function `good` is

   ```
   int good();
   ```

2. The `fail()` function returns a nonzero value if there is an error in a stream operation. The declaration of function `fail` is

   ```
   int fail();
   ```

3. The overloaded operator `!` is applied to a stream instance to determine the error status.

The C++ stream libraries offer additional functions to set and query other aspects and types of stream errors.

Sequential Text Stream I/O

The functions and operators involved in sequential text I/O are simple—you have already been exposed to most of them in earlier lessons. The functions and operators include the following:

1. The stream extractor operator << writes strings and characters to a stream.
2. The stream inserter operator >> reads characters from a stream.
3. The `getline` function reads strings from a stream.

Syntax

The *getline* Function

The prototype for the function `getline` is

```
istream& getline(signed char* buffer,
int size,
char delimiter = '\n');

istream& getline(char* buffer,
int size,
char delimiter = '\n');

istream& getline(unsigned char* buffer,
int size,
char delimiter = '\n');
```

The parameter *buffer* is a pointer to the string receiving the characters from the stream. The parameter *size* specifies the maximum number of characters to read. The parameter *delimiter* specifies the delimiting character, which causes the string input to stop before reaching the number of characters specified by parameter *size*. The parameter *delimiter* has the default argument of `'\n'`.

Example:

```
fstream f;
char textLine[MAX];
f.open("\\CONFIG.SYS", ios::in);
while (!f.eof()) {
   f.getline(textLine, MAX);
   cout << textLine << "\n";
}
f.close();
```

Let's look at an example. Listing 12.1 shows the source code for the IO1.CPP program. The program performs the following tasks:

- Prompts you to enter the name of an input text file
- Prompts you to enter the name of an output text file (the program detects if the names of the input and output files are the same, and if so, reprompts you for a different output filename)
- Reads the lines from the input files and removes any trailing spaces in these lines
- Writes the lines to the output file and also to the standard output window

Listing 12.1. Source code for the IO1.CPP program.

```
// C++ program that demonstrates sequential file I/O

#include <iostream.h>
#include <fstream.h>
#include <string.h>

enum boolean { false, true };

const unsigned LINE_SIZE = 128;
const unsigned NAME_SIZE = 64;

void trimStr(char* s)
{
  int i = strlen(s) - 1;
  // locate the character where the trailing spaces begin
  while (i >= 0 && s[i] == ' ')
    i--;
  // truncate string
  s[i+1] = '\0';
}

void getInputFilename(char* inFile, fstream& f)
{
  boolean ok;

  do {
    ok = true;
    cout << "Enter input file : ";
    cin.getline(inFile, NAME_SIZE);
    f.open(inFile, ios::in);
    if (!f) {
      cout << "Cannot open file " << inFile << "\n\n";
      ok = false;
    }
  } while (!ok);

}

void getOutputFilename(char* outFile, const char* inFile,
                       fstream& f)
{
  boolean ok;

  do {
    ok = true;
    cout << "Enter output file : ";
    cin.getline(outFile, NAME_SIZE);
    if (stricmp(inFile, outFile) != 0) {
      f.open(outFile, ios::out);
      if (!f) {
        cout << "File " << outFile << " is invalid\n\n";
        ok = false;
      }
```

```
54:     }
55:     else {
56:       cout << "Input and output files must be different!\n";
57:       ok = false;
58:     }
59:   } while (!ok);
60: }
61:
62: void processLines(fstream& fin, fstream& fout)
63: {
64:   char line[LINE_SIZE + 1];
65:
66:   // loop to trim trailing spaces
67:   while (fin.getline(line, LINE_SIZE)) {
68:     trimStr(line);
69:     // write line to the output file
70:     fout << line << "\n";
71:     // echo updated line to the output window
72:     cout << line << "\n";
73:   }
74:
75: }
76: main()
77: {
78:
79:   fstream fin, fout;
80:   char inFile[NAME_SIZE + 1], outFile[NAME_SIZE + 1];
81:
82:   getInputFilename(inFile, fin);
83:   getOutputFilename(outFile, inFile, fout);
84:   processLines(fin, fout);
85:   // close streams
86:   fin.close();
87:   fout.close();
88:   return 0;
89: }
```

Here is a sample session with the program in Listing 12.1:

Output

```
Enter input file : sample.txt
Enter output file : sample.out
This is line 1
This is line 2
This is line 3
This is line 4
```

Analysis The program in Listing 12.1 declares no classes and instead focuses on using file streams to input and output text. The program declares the functions `trimStr`, `getInputFilename`, `getOutputFilename`, `processLines`, and `main`.

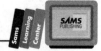

The function `trimStr` shaves the trailing spaces in the strings passed by parameter `s`. The function declares the local variable `i` and assigns it the index of the character just before the null terminator. The function uses the `while` loop in line 13 to perform a backward scan of the characters in string s for the first nonspace character. The statement in line 16 assigns the null terminator character to the character located right after the last nonspace character in the string s.

The function getInputFilename obtains the input filename and opens its corresponding input file stream. The parameter inFile passes the name of the input file to the function caller. The reference parameter f passes the opened input stream to the function caller. The function getInputFilename declares the local flag ok. The function uses the do-while loop in lines 26 through 35 to obtain a valid filename and to open that file for input. Line 27 contains the first statement inside the loop, which assigns the enumerated value true to the local variable ok. The output statement in line 28 prompts you for the input filename. The statement in line 29 calls the stream input function getline to obtain your input and to store it in the parameter inFile. The statement in line 30 opens the input file using the stream parameter f. The open statement uses the ios::in value to indicate that the stream is opened for text input. The if statement in line 31 determines whether or not the stream f is successfully opened. If not, the function executes the statements in lines 32 and 33. These statements display an error message and assign the enumerated value false to the local variable ok. The loop's while clause in line 35 examines the condition !ok. The loop iterates until you supply it a valid filename, which must successfully be opened for input.

The function getOutputFilename complements the function getInputFilename and has three parameters. The parameter outFile passes the output filename of the function caller. The parameter inFile supplies the function with the input filename. The function uses this parameter to ensure that the input and output filenames are not the same. The parameter f passes the output stream to the function caller. The implementation of function getOutputFilename is very similar to that of function getInputFilename. The main difference is that the function getOutputFilename calls the function stricmp to compare the values in parameter inFile and outFile. The function uses the result of stricmp to determine whether the names of the input and output files are identical. If so, the function executes the statements in the else clause at lines 57 and 58. These statements display an error message and assign false to the local variable ok.

The function processLines reads the lines from the input file stream, trims them, and writes them to the output file stream. The parameters fin and fout pass the input and output file streams, respectively. The function declares the local string variable line and uses the while loop in lines 67 through 73 to process the text lines. The while clause contains the call to function getline, which reads the next line in the input stream fin and assigns the input line to variable line. The result of function getline causes the while loop to stop iterating when there are no more input lines. The first statement inside the loop, located at line 68, calls the function `trimStr` and passes it the argument line. This function `call` prunes any existing trailing spaces in the local variable `line`. The statement in line 70 writes the string in variable `line` to the output file stream. The statement in line 72 echoes the string in line to the standard output window. I place this statement in the program so that you can monitor the progress of the program.

The function `main` declares the file streams `fin` and `fout`, and the string variables `inFile` and `outFile`. The statement in line 82 calls function `getInputFilename` and passes it the arguments `inFile` and `fin`. This call obtains the name of the input file and the input stream through the arguments `inFile` and `fin`, respectively. The statement in line 83 calls the function `getOutputFilename` and passes it the arguments `outFile`, `inFile`, and `fout`. This call obtains the name of the output file and the output stream through the arguments `outFile` and `fout`, respectively. The statement in line 84 calls function `processLines` and passes it the arguments `fin` and `fout`. This call processes the lines in the input file stream `fin` and writes the results to the output file stream `fout`. The statements in lines 86 and 87 close the input and output file streams, respectively.

Sequential Binary File Stream I/O

The C++ stream library offers the overloaded stream functions `write` and `read` for sequential binary file stream I/O. The function `write` sends multiple bytes to an output stream. This function can write any variable or instance to a stream.

12

Syntax

The *write* Function

The prototype for the overloaded function `write` is

```
ostream& write(const signed char* buff, int num);
ostream& write(const char* buff, int num);
ostream& write(const unsigned char* buff, int num);
```

The parameter *`buff`* is the pointer to the buffer that contains the data to be sent to the output stream. The parameter *`num`* indicates the number of bytes in the buffer that are sent to the stream.

Example:

```
const MAX = 80;
char buff[MAX+1] = "Hello World!";
int len = strlen(buffer) + 1;
fstream f;
f.open("CALC.DAT", ios::out ¦ ios::binary);
f.write((const unsigned char*)*len, sizeof(len));
f.write((const unsigned char*)buff, len);
f.close();
```

The function read receives multiple bytes from an input stream. This function can read any variable or from a stream.

Syntax

The *read* Function

The prototype for the overloaded function read is

```
istream& read(signed char* buff, int num);
istream& read(char* buff, int num);
istream& read(unsigned char* buff, int num);
```

The parameter *buff* is the pointer to the buffer that receives the data from the input stream. The parameter *num* indicates the number of bytes to read from the stream.

Example:

```
const MAX = 80;
char buff[MAX+1];
int len;
fstream f;
f.open("CALC.DAT", ios::in ¦ ios::binary);
f.read((const unsigned char*)*len, sizeof(len));
f.read((const unsigned char*)buff, len);
f.close();
```

Let's look at an example that performs sequential binary stream I/O. Listing 12.2 shows the source code for the IO2.CPP program. The program declares a class that models dynamic numerical arrays. The stream I/O operations enable the program to read and write both the individual array elements and an entire array in binary files. The program creates the arrays arr1, arr2, and arr3, and then performs the following tasks:

- Assigns values to the elements of array arr1 (this array has 10 elements)
- Assigns values to the elements of array arr3 (this array has 20 elements)
- Displays the values in array arr1
- Writes the elements of array arr1 to the file ARR1.DAT, one element at a time
- Reads the elements of arr1 from the file into the array arr2 (the array arr2 has 10 elements—the same size as array arr1)
- Displays the values in array arr2
- Displays the values in array arr3
- Writes, in one swoop, the elements of array arr3 to file ARR3.DAT
- Reads, in one swoop, the data in file ARR3.DAT and stores them in array arr1

☐ Displays the values in array arr1 (the output shows that array arr1 has the same size and data as array arr3)

Type

Listing 12.2. Source code for the IO2.CPP program.

```
/*
   C++ program that demonstrates sequential binary file I/O
*/

#include <iostream.h>
#include <fstream.h>

const unsigned MIN_SIZE = 10;
const double BAD_VALUE = -1.0e+30;
enum boolean { false, true };

class Array
{
   protected:
     double *dataPtr;
     unsigned size;
     double badIndex;

   public:
     Array(unsigned Size = MIN_SIZE);
     ~Array()
       { delete [] dataPtr; }
     unsigned getSize() const { return size; }
     double& operator [](unsigned index)
     { return (index < size) ? *(dataPtr + index) : badIndex; }
     boolean writeElem(fstream& os, unsigned index);
     boolean readElem(fstream& is, unsigned index);
     boolean writeArray(const char* filename);
     boolean readArray(const char* filename);
};

Array::Array(unsigned Size)
{
  size = (Size < MIN_SIZE) ? MIN_SIZE : Size;
  badIndex = BAD_VALUE;
  dataPtr = new double[size];
}

boolean Array::writeElem(fstream& os, unsigned index)
{
   if (index < size) {
     os.write((unsigned char*)(dataPtr + index), sizeof(double));
     return (os.good()) ? true : false;
   }
   else
     return false;
}

```

continues

Listing 12.2. continued

```
boolean Array::readElem(fstream& is, unsigned index)
{
   if (index < size) {
     is.read((unsigned char*)(dataPtr + index), sizeof(double));
     return (is.good()) ? true : false;
   }
   else
     return false;
}

boolean Array::writeArray(const char* filename)
{
   fstream f(filename, ios::out ¦ ios::binary);

   if (f.fail())
     return false;
   f.write((unsigned char*) &size, sizeof(size));
   f.write((unsigned char*)dataPtr, size * sizeof(double));
   f.close();
   return (f.good()) ? true : false;
}

boolean Array::readArray(const char* filename)
{
   fstream f(filename, ios::in ¦ ios::binary);
   unsigned sz;

   if (f.fail())
     return false;
   f.read((unsigned char*) &sz, sizeof(sz));
   // need to expand the array
   if (sz != size) {
     delete [] dataPtr;
     dataPtr = new double[sz];
     size = sz;
   }
   f.read((unsigned char*)dataPtr, size * sizeof(double));
   f.close();
   return (f.good()) ? true : false;
}

main()
{
  const unsigned SIZE1 = 10;
  const unsigned SIZE2 = 20;
  char* filename1 = "array1.dat";
  char* filename2 = "array3.dat";
  Array arr1(SIZE1), arr2(SIZE1), arr3(SIZE2);
  fstream f(filename1, ios::out ¦ ios::binary);

  // assign values to array arr1
  for (unsigned i = 0; i < arr1.getSize(); i++)
    arr1[i] = 10 * i;
```

```
  // assign values to array arr3
  for (i = 0; i < SIZE2; i++)
    arr3[i] = i;

  cout << "Array arr1 has the following values:\n";
  for (i = 0; i < arr1.getSize(); i++)
    cout << arr1[i] << "  ";
  cout << "\n\n";

  // write elements of array arr1 to the stream
  for (i = 0; i < arr1.getSize(); i++)
    arr1.writeElem(f, i);
  f.close();

  // reopen the stream for input
  f.open(filename1, ios::in | ios::binary);

  for (i = 0; i < arr1.getSize(); i++)
    arr2.readElem(f, i);
  f.close();

  // display the elements of array arr2
  cout << "Array arr2 has the following values:\n";
  for (i = 0; i < arr2.getSize(); i++)
    cout << arr2[i] << "  ";
  cout << "\n\n";

  // display the elements of array arr3
  cout << "Array arr3 has the following values:\n";
  for (i = 0; i < arr3.getSize(); i++)
    cout << arr3[i] << "  ";
  cout << "\n\n";

  // write the array arr3 to file ARRAY3.DAT
  arr3.writeArray(filename2);
  // read the array arr1 from file ARRAY3.DAT
  arr1.readArray(filename2);

    // display the elements of array arr1
  cout << "Array arr1 now has the following values:\n";
  for (i = 0; i < arr1.getSize(); i++)
    cout << arr1[i] << "  ";
  cout << "\n\n";
  return 0;
}
```

Here is a sample session with the program in Listing 12.2:

```
Array arr1 has the following values:
0  10  20  30  40  50  60  70  80  90

Array arr2 has the following values:
0  10  20  30  40  50  60  70  80  90
```

```
Array arr3 has the following values:
0  1  2  3  4  5  6  7  8  9  10  11  12  13  14  15  16  17  18  19

Array arr1 now has the following values:
0  1  2  3  4  5  6  7  8  9  10  11  12  13  14  15  16  17  18  19
```

Analysis The program in Listing 12.2 declares a version of class `Array` that resembles the one in Day 11, Listing 11.2. The main difference is that I use the operator `[]` to replace both the member functions `store` and `recall`. This operator checks for valid indices and returns the value in member `badIndex` if the argument is out of range. In addition to operator `[]`, I add the member functions `writeElem`, `readElem`, `writeArray`, and `readArray` to perform sequential binary file stream I/O.

The function `writeElem`, defined in lines 39 through 47, writes a single array element to an output stream. The parameter `os` represents the output stream. The parameter `index` specifies the array element to write. The function `writeElem` yields true if the argument for the index is valid and if the stream output proceeds without any error. After `writeElem` writes an array element, the internal stream pointer advances to the next location.

The function `readElem`, defined in lines 49 through 57, reads a single array element from an input stream. The parameter `is` represents the input stream. The parameter `index` specifies the array element to read. The function `readElem` returns true if the argument for the index is valid and if the stream input proceeds without any error. After the `readElem` reads an array element, the internal stream pointer advances to the next location.

The functions `writeElem` and `readElem` permit the same class instance to write and read data elements, respectively, from multiple streams.

The function `writeArray`, defined in lines 59 through 69, writes the entire elements of the array to a binary file. The parameter `filename` specifies the name of the output file. The function opens an output stream and writes the value of the data member `size` and then writes the elements of the dynamic array. The `writeArray` function returns `TRUE` if it successfully writes the array to the stream. Otherwise, the function yields `FALSE`. The function opens a local output stream using the stream function `open` and supplies it with the filename and I/O mode arguments. The I/O mode argument is the expression `ios::out | ios::binary`, which specifies that the stream is opened for binary output only. The function makes two calls to the stream function `write`: the first to write the data member size, and the second to write the elements of the dynamic array.

The function `readArray`, defined in lines 71 through 88, reads the entire elements of the array from a binary file. The parameter `filename` specifies the name of the input file. The function opens an input stream and reads the value of the data member `size` and then reads the elements of the dynamic array. The `readArray` function returns `TRUE` if it successfully reads the array to the stream. Otherwise, the function yields `FALSE`. The function opens a local input stream using the stream function `open` and supplies it the filename and I/O mode arguments. The I/O mode argument is the expression `ios::in | ios::binary`, which specifies that the stream is opened for binary input only. The function makes two calls to the stream function `read`: the first to read the data member `size`, and the second to read the elements of the dynamic array. Another feature of function `readArray` is that it resizes the instance of class `Array` to accommodate the data from the binary file. This means that dynamic array accessed by the class instance may either shrink or expand, depending on the size of the array stored on file.

The member functions in Listing 12.2 indicate that the program performs two types of sequential binary stream I/O. The first type of I/O, implemented in functions `readElem` and `writeElem`, involves items that have the same data type. The second type of I/O, implemented in the functions `readArray` and `writeArray`, involves items that have different data types.

The function `main` performs the following relevant tasks:

- ☐ Declares, in line 96, three instances of class `Array`, namely, `arr1`, `arr2`, and `arr3` (the first two instances have the same dynamic array size, specified by the constant `SIZE1`, whereas instance `arr3` has a larger size, specified by the constant `SIZE2`)
- ☐ Declares, in line 97, the file stream `f` and opens it (using a stream constructor) to access file ARR1.DAT in binary output mode
- ☐ Uses the `for` loops in lines 100 and 104 to assign arbitrary values to the instance `arr1` and `arr3`, respectively
- ☐ Displays the elements of instance `arr1` using the `for` loop in line 108
- ☐ Writes the elements of array `arr1` to the output file stream `f`, using the `for` loop in line 113 to send the `writeElem` message to instance `arr1` and to supply the message with the output file stream `f` and the loop control variable `i`
- ☐ Closes the output file stream by sending the close message to the output file stream `f`
- ☐ Opens, in line 118, the file stream `f` to access the data file ARR1.DAT (this time, the message open specifies a binary input mode)
- ☐ Reads the elements of instance `arr2` (which has not yet been assigned any values) from the input file stream `f`, using the `for` loop in line 120 to send the

message `readElem` to instance `arr2` and supply the message with the arguments `f`, the file stream, and `i`, the loop control variable

- Closes the input file stream, in line 122, by sending the close message to the input file stream `f`
- Displays the elements of instance `arr2` using the `for` loop in line 126 (these elements match those of instance `arr1`)
- Displays the elements of instance `arr3` by using the `for` loop in line 132
- Writes the entire instance `arr3` by sending the message `writeArray` to instance `arr3` (the message `writeArray` has the filename argument of ARR3.DAT)
- Reads the array in file ARR3.DAT into instance `arr1`, sending the message `readArray` to instance `arr1` and supplying the message with the filename argument of ARR3.DAT
- Displays the new elements of instance `arr1` using the `for` loop in line 143

Random Access File Stream I/O

Random access file stream operations also use the stream functions `read` and `write` presented in the last section. The stream library offers a number of stream-seeking functions to enable you to move the stream pointer to any valid location. The function `seekg` is one of such functions.

Syntax

The *seekg* Function

The prototype for the overloaded function `seekg` is

```
istream& seekg(long pos);
istream& seekg(long pos, seek_dir dir);
```

The parameter *pos* in the first version specifies the absolute byte position in the stream. In the second version, the parameter *pos* specifies a relative offset based on the argument for parameter *dir*. Here are the arguments for the latter parameter:

`ios::beg`	From the beginning of the file
`ios::cur`	From the current position of the file
`ios::end`	From the end of the file

Example:

```
const BLOCK_SIZE = 80;
char buff[BLOCK_SIZE] = "Hello World!";
```

```
fstream f("CALC.DAT", ios::in ¦ ios::out ¦ ios::binary);
f.seekg(3 * BLOCK_SIZE); // seek block # 4
f.read((const unsigned char*)buff, BLOCK_SIZE);
cout << buff <<< "\n";
f.close();
```

NEW TERM A *virtual array* is a disk-based array that stores fixed-size strings on disk.

Let's look at an example that uses random access file stream I/O. Listing 12.3 shows the source code for the IO3.CPP program and implements a virtual array. The program performs the following tasks:

- Uses an internal list of names to create a virtual array object
- Displays the elements in the unordered virtual array object
- Prompts you to enter a character and press Return
- Sorts the elements of the virtual array object (this process requires random access I/O)
- Displays the elements in the sorted virtual array object

Type

Listing 12.3. Source code for the IO3.CPP program.

```
/*
   C++ program that demonstrates random-access binary file I/O
*/

#include <iostream.h>
#include <fstream.h>
#include <stdlib.h>
#include <string.h>

const unsigned MIN_SIZE = 5;
const unsigned STR_SIZE = 31;
const double BAD_VALUE = -1.0e+30;
enum boolean { false, true };

class VmArray
{
   protected:
     fstream f;
     unsigned size;
     double badIndex;

   public:
     VmArray(unsigned Size, const char* filename);
     ~VmArray()
       { f.close(); }
```


continues

Listing 12.3. continued

```
     unsigned getSize() const
       { return size; }
     boolean writeElem(const char* str, unsigned index);
     boolean readElem(char* str, unsigned index);
     void Combsort();
};

VmArray::VmArray(unsigned Size, const char* filename)
{
  char s[STR_SIZE+1];
  size = (Size < MIN_SIZE) ? MIN_SIZE : Size;
  badIndex = BAD_VALUE;
  f.open(filename, ios::in ¦ ios::out ¦ ios::binary);
  if (f.good()) {
    // fill the file stream with empty strings
    strcpy(s, "");;
    f.seekg(0);
    for (unsigned i = 0; i < size; i++)
      f.write((unsigned char*)s, sizeof(s));
  }
}

boolean VmArray::writeElem(const char* str, unsigned index)
{
   if (index < size) {
     f.seekg(index * (STR_SIZE+1));
     f.write((unsigned char*)str, (STR_SIZE+1));
     return (f.good()) ? true : false;
   }
   else
     return false;
}

boolean VmArray::readElem(char* str, unsigned index)
{
   if (index < size) {
     f.seekg(index * (STR_SIZE+1));
     f.read((unsigned char*)str, (STR_SIZE+1));
     return (f.good()) ? true : false;
   }
   else
     return false;
}

void VmArray::Combsort()
{
   unsigned i, j, gap = size;
   boolean inOrder;
   char strI[STR_SIZE+1], strJ[STR_SIZE+1];

   do {
     gap = (gap * 8) / 11;
     if (gap < 1)
```

```
      gap = 1;
    inOrder = true;
    for (i = 0, j = gap; i < (size - gap); i++, j++) {
      readElem(strI, i);
      readElem(strJ, j);
      if (strcmp(strI, strJ) > 0) {
        inOrder = false;
        writeElem(strI, j);
        writeElem(strJ, i);
      }
    }
  } while (!(inOrder && gap == 1));
}

main()
{
  char* data[] = { "Michigan", "California", "Virginia", "Maine",
                   "New York", "Florida", "Nevada", "Alaska",
                   "Ohio", "Maryland" };
  VmArray arr(10, "arr.dat");
  char str[STR_SIZE+1];
  char c;

  // assign values to array arr
  for (unsigned i = 0; i < arr.getSize(); i++) {
    strcpy(str, data[i]);
    arr.writeElem(str, i);
  }
  // display unordered array
  cout << "Unsorted arrays is:\n";
  for (i = 0; i < arr.getSize(); i++) {
    arr.readElem(str, i);
    cout << str << "\n";
  }
  // pause
  cout << "\nPress any key and then Return to sort the array...";
  cin >> c;
  // sort the array
  arr.Combsort();
  // display sorted array
  cout << "Sorted arrays is:\n";
  for (i = 0; i < arr.getSize(); i++) {
    arr.readElem(str, i);
    cout << str << "\n";
  }
  return 0;
}
```

Here is a sample session with the program in Listing 12.3:

Output

```
Unsorted arrays is:
Michigan
California
Virginia
```

```
Maine
New York
Florida
Nevada
Alaska
Ohio
Maryland

Press any key and then Return to sort the array...d
Sorted arrays is:
Alaska
California
Florida
Maine
Maryland
Michigan
Nevada
New York
Ohio
Virginia
```

Analysis The program in Listing 12.3 declares the class `VmArray`. This class models a disk-based dynamic array that stores all its elements in a random access binary file. Notice that the class declares an instance of class `fstream`, and that there is no pointer to a dynamic array. The class declares a constructor, a destructor, and a number of member functions.

The class constructor has two parameters, namely, `Size` and `filename`. The parameter `Size` specifies the size of the virtual array. The parameter `filename` names the binary file that stores the elements of a class instance. The constructor opens the stream `f` using the stream function `open` and supplies it the argument of parameter `filename` and the I/O mode expression `ios::in | ios::out | ios::binary`. This expression specifies that the stream is opened for binary input and output mode (that is, random access mode). If the constructor successfully opens the file stream, it proceeds with filling the file with zeros. The class destructor performs the simple task of closing the file stream `f`.

The functions `writeElem` and `readElem` support the random access of array elements. These functions use the stream function `seekg` to position the stream pointer at the appropriate array element. The `writeElem` then calls the stream function `write` to store an array element (supplied by the parameter `str`). By contrast, the function `readElem` calls the stream function `read` to retrieve an array element (returned by the parameter `str`). Both functions return Boolean results that indicate the success of the I/O operation.

The `VmArray` class also declares the `Combsort` function to sort the elements of the virtual array. This function uses the `readElem` and `writeElem` member functions to access and swap the array elements.

The function `main` performs the following relevant tasks:

- Declares the instance `arr`, of class `VmArray` (this instance stores 10 strings in the binary file ARR.DAT)
- Assigns random values to the elements of instance `arr`, using the `for` loop in lines 103 through 106 to assign strings accessed by `data[i]` to the variable `str`, then to write the value in `str` to the instance `arr` by sending it the message `writeElem` (the arguments for the message `writeElem` are the string variable, `str`, and the loop control variable, `i`)
- Displays the unsorted elements of instance `arr` using the `for` loop in line 109 (the statement in line 110 sends the message `readElem` to the instance `arr` to obtain an element in the virtual array)
- Sorts the array by sending the message `Combsort` to the instance `arr`
- Displays the sorted elements of instance `arr` using the `for` loop in line 120 (the statement in line 121 sends the message `readElem` to the instance `arr` to obtain an element in the virtual array)

Summary

Today's lesson gives you a brief introduction to the C++ stream I/O library and discusses the following topics:

- Common stream functions include `open`, `close`, `good`, `fail`, and the operator `!`. The function `open` opens a file for stream I/O and supports alternate and multiple I/O modes. The function `close` shuts down a file stream. The functions `good` and `fail` indicate the success or failure, respectively, of a stream I/O operation.
- C++ allows you to perform sequential stream I/O for text, using the operators << and >> as well as the stream function `getline`. The operator << is able to write characters and strings (as well as the other predefined data types). The operator >> is suitable for obtaining characters. The function `getline` enables your applications to read strings from the keyboard or from a text file.
- Sequential stream I/O for binary data uses the stream functions `write` and `read` to write and read data from any kind of variable.

- Random access stream I/O for binary data uses the seekg function in conjunction with the functions read and write. The seekg function enables you to move the stream pointer to either absolute or relative byte locations in the stream.

Q&A

Q How can I emulate the random access of lines in a text file?

A First read the lines in the file as text, obtain the length of the lines (plus the two characters for the end of each line), and store the cumulative length in a special array, call it `lineIndex`. This array stores the byte location where each line starts. The last array element should store the size of the file. To access line number `i`, use the `seek` or `seekg` function to locate the offset value in `lineIndex[i]`. The size of line number `i` is equal to `lineIndex[i+1]-lineIndex[i]`.

Q How do I write a general-purpose routine to copy between an input and an output file stream?

A You need to use the stream function `gcount()` to obtain the number of bytes actually read in the last unformatted stream input. Here is the function `copyStream`:

```
void copyStream(fstream& fin, fstream& fout,
unsigned char* buffer, int buffSize)
{
  int n;
  while (fin.read(buffer, buffSize) {
    n = fin.gcount();
    fout.write(buffer, n);
  }
}
```

Workshop

The Workshop provides quiz questions to help you solidify your understanding of the material covered and exercises to provide you with experience in using what you've learned. Try to understand the quiz and exercise answers before continuing on to the next day's lesson. Answers are provided in Appendix B, "Answers."

Quiz

1. True or false? The stream I/O functions `read` and `write` are able to correctly read and write any data type.
2. True or false? The stream I/O functions `read` and `write` are able to correctly read and write any data type, as long as the type has no pointer members.
3. True or false? The `seek` and `seekg` functions expand the file when you supply them an index that is one byte beyond the current end of file.
4. True or false? The arguments of the functions `seek` and `seekg` require no range checking.

Exercise

Create program IO4.CPP by modifying program IO3.CPP. The class `VmArray` in IO4.CPP should have the function `binSearch`, which conducts a binary search on the members of the sorted array. Add a loop at the end of function `main` to search in the array `arr`, using the unordered data of the initializing list. (The members of this list are accessed using the pointer data.)

13

Programming Windows Using the MFC Library

WEEK 2

The Microsoft Foundation Class (MFC) library provides a powerful tool that assists you in developing Windows applications. Without such a library, coding Windows applications becomes a more difficult, frustrating, and increasingly code-intensive process. The MFC library succeeds in combining object-oriented and event-driven programming concepts, and shows how well these two programming disciplines work together. Today's lesson introduces you to the MFC library and some basic information related to Windows, including creating Windows applications using the MFC library. Today you learn about the following:

- Popular Windows data types
- MFC data-typing conventions
- The MFC hierarchy
- Responding to Windows messages
- Sending messages
- User-defined messages

Although the MFC library provides a good tool for developing Windows applications, you need to know about the underlying Windows API functions.

Popular Windows Data Types

Windows programming comprises a large number of data types. In this section, I focus on the data types that are most relevant for now. Becoming familiar with these data types enables you to better understand the declarations of MFC. The Windows data types include a number of simple ones as well as a group of structures. The simple data types include many that are `typedef`s that declare aliases with more meaningful names. These aliases clarify the declarations of functions and variables. Table 13.1 shows a selection of the most frequently used Windows data types.

Table 13.1. Most frequently used Windows data types.

Data Type	Meaning
`char`	Signed 8-bit character
`int`	Signed 32-bit integer
`long`	Signed 32-bit integer

Data Type	Meaning
`short`	Signed 16-bit integer
`void`	Empty value
`BOOL`	Represents Boolean values
`BOOLEAN`	Represents Boolean values
`BYTE`	Unsigned 8-bit integer
`CHAR`	Windows character
`COLORREF`	32-bit color reference number
`DWORD`	Unsigned 32-bit integer or segment/offset address
`FAR`	Data-type attribute used to create
`FARPROC`	Long pointer to a function
`HANDLE`	General handle
`HDC`	Handle to a display context
`HWND`	Window handler
`LONG`	Same as the `long` type
`LPSTR`	Long pointer to a character string
`LPTSTR`	Long pointer to a character string
`LPARAM`	32-bit message parameter
`LPCTSTR`	Long pointer to a constant character string
`LPVOID`	Long pointer to a `void` type
`LRESULT`	Signed result of message processing
`PWORD`	Pointer to the `WORD` type
`VOID`	Any type (same as `void`)
`UINT`	Unsigned 32-bit integer
`WORD`	Unsigned 16-bit integer
`WPARAM`	32-bit message parameter

In addition to the simple data types shown in Table 13.1, there are many structures that are involved in Windows programming. The `POINT` and `RECT` structures are simple yet important. The `POINT` structure stores the X and Y coordinates of a point and is declared as follows:

```
typedef struct tagPOINT {
     LONG x;
     LONG y;
} POINT;
```

The `RECT` structure defines the coordinates of the upper left and lower right corners of a rectangle, and is declared as follows:

```
typedef struct tagRECT {
     LONG left;
     LONG top;
     LONG right;
     LONG bottom;
} RECT;
```

The `left` and `right` members are the X coordinates for the upper left and lower right corner of the rectangle, respectively. The `top` and `bottom` fields are the Y coordinates for the upper left and lower right corners of the rectangle, respectively.

The MFC library uses the Hungarian prefix naming convention, shown in Table 13.2. The table also shows examples of variables using this naming convention.

NEW TERM With the *Hungarian prefix naming convention*, the prefixes hint at the data type associated with a variable, making your code easier to read.

Table 13.2. Hungarian prefix naming convention.

Prefix	Type	Example	Comment
`ch`	`char`	`chInputChar`	8-bit character
`b`	`BOOL`	`bOk`	Boolean value
`n`	`int`	`nCount`	System-dependent integer
`w`	`WORD`	`wSize`	16-bit unsigned integer
`l`	`LONG`	`lTotalSize`	32-bit signed integer
`dw`	`DWORD`	`dwSumSize`	32-bit unsigned integer
`p`	`*`	`pStr`	Pointer
`lp`	`FAR*`	`lpStr`	Far pointer

Prefix	Type	Example	Comment
`lpsz`	`LPTSTR`	`lpszFilename`	32-bit pointer to a character string
`lpsz`	`LPCTSTR`	`lpszFilename`	32-bit pointer to a constant character string
`h`	`handle`	`hWnd`	Handle to a Windows object
`lpfn`	`callback`	`lpfnHelp`	Far pointer to `CALLBACK` function

The MFC Hierarchy

The MFC hierarchy includes several subhierarchies that manage different aspects of a Windows application. These subhierarchies include Windows classes, GDI classes, miscellaneous Windows classes, Object Linking and Embedding (OLE) classes, file classes, object I/O classes, exceptions classes, collections classes, and miscellaneous support classes.

The *CObject* Class

The `CObject` class is the abstract base class for the MFC library, and is the root class for both the MFC library and the descendants that you create. `CObject` is not a dummy abstract class. Instead, it offers a number of operations that are common to all its descendant classes. These operations include object creation and deletion, support for serialization, diagnostics, and compatibility with collection classes.

The *CMenu* Class

The `CMenu` class, a descendant of `CObject`, manages menus. Menu management includes the creation, update, tracking, and removal of a menu resource associated with a window.

The Document Architecture Subhierarchy

The Document Architecture subhierarchy has the class `CCmdTarget` as its root. This set of classes includes the class `CWinApp`, which is the parent of the custom application classes. Another set of classes in this subhierarchy supports OLE documents.

The Frames Windows Subhierarchy

The Frames Windows subhierarchy has the `CFrameWnd` class as its root. This group of classes models the basic single-document interface (SDI) window or the more complex multiple-document interface (MDI) windows. The Windows Program Manager is an example of an MDI-compliant application. The latter windows use the `CMDIFrameWnd` and `CMDIChildWnd` to model the frame and child windows in an MDI-compliant application.

The Control Bars Subhierarchy

The Control Bars subhierarchy models the tool bar, status bar, dialog bar, and splitter window. (Windows File Manager uses the latter control to display the directory tree and the list of files for the currently selected directory.)

The Views Subhierarchy

The Views subhierarchy has the `CView` class as its root. Views are child windows that can be created inside other windows and provide a special framework for accepting input.

The Dialog Boxes Subhierarchy

The Dialog Boxes subhierarchy includes the general-purpose dialog box class, `CDialog`, as well as the classes that support the common dialog boxes for selecting files, selecting colors, selecting fonts, printing, and finding and replacing text. The `CDialog` class models both model and modeless dialog boxes and is the root of this subhierarchy. Day 20 covers the `CDialog` class.

The Control Subhierarchy

The Control subhierarchy includes classes which model the static text, command buttons, bitmap buttons, list box, combo boxes, scroll bars, edit controls, and VB (Visual Basic) controls. These visual controls provide an important part of the Windows interface. Days 16 through 19 focus on several of these controls.

The Graphical Drawing Subhierarchy

The `CDC` class, a descendant of `CObject`, is the root class for the `CDC` subhierarchy in the MFC library. The class and its descendants support device-context objects. The `CDC` class comes with a large number of member functions ready to do business, so to speak. These functions provide tools such as mapping functions, drawing tools functions, and region functions, to name just a few. The `CDC` class contains member functions that support the functionality offered by the descendants of CDC. Thus, these descendants are basically wrapper classes.

NEW TERM *Regions* are elliptic or polygon areas within a window that can be supplied with a graphical output.

The Graphical Drawing Objects Subhierarchy

The Graphical Drawing Objects subhierarchy models drawing objects such as pens, brushes, fonts, bitmaps, and palettes. If you plan to write Windows applications that draw graphics objects, you need to work with the classes in this hierarchy.

Other MFC Subhierarchies

The MFC library contains other subhierarchies which I do not cover in this book:

1. The Exceptions subhierarchy offers classes which handle various kinds of run-time errors.
2. The File Services subhierarchy presents classes which deal with files as objects.
3. The Collections subhierarchy contains classes which manage dynamic lists and arrays of objects.
4. The OLE 2.0 Support subhierarchy offers classes to support object linking and embedding.
5. The ODBC classes subhierarchy, which supports accessing data sources from databases. This subhierarchy supports swapping data between a C++ recordset object and columns of a table or query result. The ODBC classes support both

dynamic recordsets (dynasets) and snapshots recordsets (snapshots). The database transactions support operations like commit and rollback, as well as common access functions such as adding, changing, and deleting records.

6. The Run-Time Object Model Support subhierarchy provides information about an object or its base class at run-time.
7. The Simple Value Types subhierarchy models commonly used objects, such as strings, time, rectangles, points, and window sizes.
8. The Structures subhierarchy models information related to the status of a file, printing, memory state, and the creation of a window.
9. The Support Classes subhierarchy provides classes that are involved in transferring data to and from dialog boxes, and managing the commands generated by the user interface.

MFC Macros

The MFC library also declares a number of macros that support the `CObject` class and all its descendants:

- The `RUNTIME_CLASS` macro returns the `CRunTimeClass` structure that matches the named class.
- The `DECLARE_DYNAMIC` macro allows access to run-time class data. This macro can be used in each class declaration.
- The `IMPLEMENT_DYNAMIC` macro allows access to run-time class data. This macro is used in the class implementation.
- The `DECLARE_SERIAL` macro allows serialization and access to run-time class data. This macro can be used in each class declaration.
- The `IMPLEMENT_SERIAL` macro allows serialization and access to run-time class data. This macro is used in the class implementation.

Invoking Windows API Functions

The value of the MFC hierarchy comes from the fact that it packages most of the Windows API functions using C++ classes. This section presents two Windows API functions as examples of how you can directly call these functions.

The following code fragment includes the `Polyline`, `MessageBeep`, and `MessageBox` API functions. The code's main purpose is to plot a polygon and involves these tasks:

- Starts a loop that attempts to draw a polygon
- Calls a user-defined routine to obtain a number of points used to create the polygon
- Invokes the Boolean function `Polyline`
- If the result of function `Polyline` is `FALSE`, calls the API function `MessageBeep` to sound a beep, then invokes the `MessageBox` function

The `MessageBox` function pops up an error message box that asks you whether you want to get a new set of points to plot. The message box shows the Yes and No buttons and the lowercase `i` icon.

The code for these steps is

```
const MAX_POINTS = 10;
POINT points[MAX_POINTS];
HDC hDC;
int answer = IDNO;
// other declarations
// other statements
do {
     read_points(points); // get the data for the points
     if (!Polyline(hDC, points, MAX_POINTS)) {
          MessageBeep(0); // beep
         // show error message box
         answer = MessageBox(
               HWindow,                // window handle
               "Error! Try again",     // error message
               "Polygon Plot Error!", // message box title
               MB_YESNO ¦              // message box
                                    // options
               MB_ICONINFORMATION);

     }
} while (answer == IDYES);
// other statements
```

The `Polyline` function is declared as follows:

```
BOOL Polyline(HDC hDC, CONST POINT* lppt, int cPoints);
```

where `hDC` is the handle of the device context. The parameter `lppt` is the pointer to a `POINT`-typed array. The parameter `cPoints` is the number of points in the array that is used to draw the polygon (there must be at least two).

The `MessageBeep` function is a simple function that is declared as follows:

```
void MessageBeep(UINT wType)
```

The argument value of 0 assigned to the `wType` parameter supplies the only required argument.

The `MessageBox` function is an important API function that enables you to communicate with the end-user of your Windows applications. The declaration of the `MessageBox` function is

```
int MessageBox(HWND hwndOwner, LPCTSTR lpszText,
               LPCTSTR lpszTitle, UINT fuStyle)
```

The first parameter is the handle to the parent window. The second and third parameters are the message and caption strings. The last parameter specifies the buttons and the icons that appear in the message box. Table 13.3 shows most of the values for the message box `fuStyle` parameter. In the previous code example, the argument for `fuStyle` is

```
MB_YESNO | MBICONINFORMATION
```

which causes the message box to show the Yes and No buttons and also includes the lowercase `i` icon.

Table 13.3. Most of the values for the message box wType parameter.

Value	Meaning
MB_ABORTRETRYIGNORE	Message box shows three buttons: Abort, Retry, and Ignore.
MB_DEFBUTTON1	First button is the default. If no MB_DEFBUTTONx identifier is specified, the message box makes the first button the default.
MB_DEFBUTTON2	Second button is the default.
MB_DEFBUTTON3	Third button is the default
MB_ICONASTERISK	Message box includes an icon with a lowercase i in a circle; same as MB_ICONINFORMATION
MB_ICONEXCLAMATION	Message box includes an exclamation point icon
MB_ICONHAND	Message box includes a stop sign icon; same as MB_ICONSTOP
MB_ICONINFORMATION	Message box includes an icon with a lowercase i in a circle

Value	Meaning
MB_ICONQUESTION	Message box includes a question mark icon
MB_ICONSTOP	Message box includes a stop sign icon
MB_OK	Message box contains an OK button
MB_OKCANCEL	Message box contains the OK and Cancel buttons
MB_RETRYCANCEL	Message box contains the Retry and Cancel buttons
MB_YESNO	Message box contains the Yes and No buttons
MB_YESNOCANCEL	Message box contains the Yes, No, and Cancel buttons

The `MessageBox` function returns a value that reflects the user's choice. Table 13.3 shows the identifiers that represent the function's values.

The class `CWnd` declares the `MessageBox` member function that is a wrapper for the `MessageBox` API function. The difference between the two functions is that function `CWnd::MessageBox` does not have the `hWndParent` parameter. The `wType` parameter of function `CWnd::MessageBox` also uses the values shown in Table 13.3. The result of the function `CWnd:MessageBox` can also be compared with the values shown in Table 13.4.

Table 13.4. Identifiers representing the values returned by the MessageBox function.

Identifier	Meaning
IDABORT	Abort button was pressed
IDCANCEL	Cancel button was pressed
IDIGNORE	Ignore button was pressed
IDNO	No button was pressed
IDOK	OK button was pressed
IDRETRY	Retry button was pressed
IDYES	Yes button was pressed

The Windows Messages

Windows applications contain various types of objects that interact with each other via messages, in response to events. The Windows metaphor resembles the working office that is made up of employees, managers, departments, and material resources (computers, typewriters, photocopying machines, phones, faxes, and so forth). Each employee (who, for the sake of the discussion, corresponds to a Windows object) has a role to play as defined by his or her job description (which corresponds to a class declaration). The activities of an office are stimulated by events from the outside world, events directed to the outside world, and internal events. To respond to these events, the various employees and departments need to communicate with each other via messages. In a similar manner, the Windows environment and its applications interact with each other and with the outside world (the input and output devices) using messages. These messages can be generated in the following ways:

- A user-generated event, such as typing on the keyboard, moving the mouse, and clicking the mouse button, results in user-generated messages
- A Windows application can call Windows functions and result in Windows sending messages back to the application
- A Windows application can send internal messages aimed at specific program components
- The Windows environment can send messages to a Windows application

Windows has various kinds of message categories, such as:

- Windows management messages
- Initialization messages
- Input messages
- System messages
- Clipboard messages
- System information messages
- Control manipulation messages
- Control notification messages
- Scroll bar notification messages
- Nonclient-area messages
- MDI messages

Windows management messages are sent by Windows to an application when the state of a window is altered. Table 13.5 shows a selection of Windows management messages.

Table 13.5. A selection of Windows management messages.

Message	Meaning
WM_ACTIVATE	Sent when a window becomes active or inactive
WM_CLOSE	Sent when a window is closed
WM_MOVE	Sent when a window is moved
WM_PAINT	Sent when either Windows or an application requests to repaint part of an application's window
WM_QUIT	Request to end an application
WM_SIZE	Sent after a window is resized

Initialization messages are sent by Windows when an application constructs a menu or a dialog box. Table 13.6 shows the initialization messages.

Table 13.6. Initialization messages.

Message	Meaning
WM_INITDIALOG	Sent right before a dialog box is displayed
WM_INITMENU	Request to initialize a menu
WM_INITMENUPOPUP	Sent right before a pop-up menu is displayed

Input messages are emitted by Windows in response to an input through the mouse, keyboard, scroll bars, or system timer. Table 13.7 shows a selection of input messages.

Table 13.7. A selection of input messages.

Message	Meaning
WM_COMMAND	Sent when you select a menu item
WM_HSCROLL	Sent when you click the horizontal scroll bar with the mouse

continues

Table 13.7. continued

Message	Meaning
WM_KEYDOWN	Sent when a nonsystem key is pressed
WM_KEYUP	Sent when a nonsystem key is released
WM_LBUTTTONDBLCLK	Sent when you double-click the left mouse button
WM_LBUTTONDOWN	Sent when you press the left mouse button
WM_LBUTTONUP	Sent when you release the left mouse button
WM_MOUSEMOVE	Sent when you move the mouse
WM_RBUTTONDBLCLK	Sent when you double-click the right mouse button
WM_RBUTTONDOWN	Sent when you press the right mouse button
WM_RBUTTONUP	Sent when you release the right mouse button
WM_TIMER	Sent when the timer limit set for a specific timer has elapsed
WM_VSCROLL	Sent when you click the vertical scroll bar with the mouse

System messages are sent by Windows to an application when you access the Windows Control menu, scroll bars, or size box. Most of the Windows applications do not respond to these messages but rather pass them to the `DefWindowProc` function for default processing.

Clipboard messages are emitted by Windows to an application when other applications attempt to access a window's clipboard.

System information messages are sent by Windows when a system-level change is made that affects other Windows applications. Among such changes are ones that affect the fonts, color palette, system color, time, and contents of the WIN.INI file.

Control manipulation messages are sent by Windows applications to a control object, such as the push-down button, list box, combo box, and edit control. The control messages result in performing a specific task, and also return a value that indicates the outcome.

Control notification messages notify the parent window of the actions that have occurred within a control attached to that window.

Scroll bar notification messages include the WM_HSCROLL and WM_VSCROLL messages. The scroll bars send these messages to their parent windows when you click the bars.

Nonclient-area messages are sent by Windows to create and update the nonclient area. You are seldom required to override the default responses to these messages in your MFC application.

NEW TERM The *nonclient area* is the area outside the working or client area of a window.

MDI messages are sent by an MDI frame window to a child client window. These messages result in operations such as activating, deactivating, creating, removing, arranging, and restoring client windows.

Responding to Messages

The MFC library uses a special mechanism to determine the response of an application to various messages. This mechanism involves a few macros and a language extension. The extension to C++ allows you to declare (or mark, if you prefer) the message response member functions by placing the keyword afx_msg before the return type of the function. The class that contains at least one message response function must declare the macro DECLARE_MESSAGE_MAP(). This macro initializes the message map that is defined in the implementation part of the program. The following is a typical example of declaring message response functions:

```
class CAppWindow : CFrameWnd {
public:
     CAppWindow();
     // handle painting
     afx_msg void OnPaint();
     // handle resizing a window
     afx_msg void OnSize(UINT nType, int cx, int cy);

protected:
     // handle closing the window
     afx_msg void OnClose();

     DECLARE_MESSAGE_MAP();
};
```

The OnPaint, OnSize, and OnClose member functions respond to the predefined messages WM_PAINT, WM_SIZE, and WM_CLOSE, respectively. The class implementation includes the definitions of these member functions as well as the special message map macros START_MESSAGE_MAP() and END_MESSAGE_MAP(). These special macros contain other macros that map the individual member functions and the messages they respond to. The message map macro for the previous class is

```
BEGIN_MESSAGE_MAP(CAppWindow, CFrameWnd)
     ON_WM_PAINT()
     ON_WM_SIZE()
     ON_WM_CLOSE()
END_MESSAGE_MAP()
```

Notice that the BEGIN_MESSAGE_MAP contains two arguments: the application window class and its parent MFC class. Stating the class involved is required, and becomes more important when you have multiple message response maps for multiple classes. Notice the three ON_WM_xxxx macros. The first macro, ON_WM_PAINT(), specifies that the default member function, OnPaint, responds to the message WM_PAINT. In fact, the MFC library has a large set of predefined message mapping macros that relate various class member functions with WM_xxxx messages. The ON_WM_SIZE() and ON_WM_CLOSE() macros are two additional examples. The ON_WM_SIZE() specifies that the OnSize member function responds to the WM_SIZE message, Likewise, the ON_WM_CLOSE() macros ties the OnClose member function with the WM_CLOSE message.

Note: The previous message map declaration has the message macros listed in the same order of declaring the corresponding member functions. This is required by the Microsoft C++ compiler.

Sending Messages

Windows allows your applications to send messages to the application, other applications, or to Windows itself. The Windows API functions SendMessage, PostMessage, and SendDlgItemMessage provide important tools for sending messages. The SendMessage function sends a message to a window and requires that window to handle the emitted message. The SendMessage is declared as follows:

```
LRESULT SendMessage(HWND hWnd, UINT uMsg, WPARAM wParam, LPARAM lParam);
```

The parameter hWnd is the handle of the window receiving the message. The parameter uMsg specifies the message sent. The parameters wParam and lParam designate additional optional information. You can use the SendMessage function to communicate with other windows and controls.

The PostMessage is similar to SendMessage, except it lacks the sense of urgency—the message is posted in the window's message queue. The message is handled later by the targeted window when it is convenient for that window. The declaration of the Boolean PostMessage function is

```
BOOL PostMessage(HWND hWnd, UINT uMsg,WPARAM wParam, LPARAM lParam);
```

The parameter hWnd is the handle of the window receiving the message. The parameter uMsg specifies the message sent. The parameters wParam and lParam designate additional optional information.

The SendDlgItemMessage function sends a message to a particular item in a dialog box. The declaration of the SendDlgItemMessage function is posted next:

```
LRESULT SendDlgItemMessage(HWND hwndDlg, int idControl,
                          UINT uMsg, WPARAM wParam, LPARAM lParam);
```

The parameter hwndDlg is the handle of the dialog box that contains the targeted control. The parameter idDlgItem indicates the integer identifier of the dialog box item that receives the message. The parameter wMsg specifies the message sent. The parameters wParam and lParam designate additional optional information.

The class CWnd declares the SendMessage, PostMessage, and SendDlgItemMessage member functions to send messages to the host window. These member functions are declared as follows:

```
LRESULT SendMessage(UINT message, WPARAM wParam = 0,
                    LPARAM lParam = 0);

BOOL PostMessage(UINT message, WPARAM wParam = 0,
                    LPARAM lParam = 0);

LRESULT SendDlgItemMessage(int nID, UINT message,
                    WPARAM wParam = 0, LPARAM lParam = 0);
```

User-Defined Messages

MFC allows you to define your own messages. The constant WM_USER is associated with the number of the first message (see Table 13.8). You need to declare constants that represent the offset values for your custom messages. For example, you can use the #define directive to define your own messages:

```
#define WM_USER1 (WM_USER + 0)
#define WM_USER2 (WM_USER + 1)
#define WM_USER3 (WM_USER + 2)
```

Table 13.8 shows the range of Windows messages for Windows.

Table 13.8. Ranges of Windows messages.

Constant	Value	Message Range	Meaning
		0x0000-0x03FF	Windows messages
WM_USER	0x0400	0x0400-0x7FFF	Programmer-defined window messages
		0x8000-0xBFFF	Reserved for use by Windows
		0xC000-0xFFFF	String messages for use by applications
		above 0xFFFF	Reserved by Windows

The user-defined messages specify the commands emitted by menu items or keyboard input. The message mapping macro `ON_COMMAND` is used to associate the user-defined command with its response member function. The general form for the `ON_COMMAND` macro is

```
ON_COMMAND(command, command_function)
```

To illustrate how to employ user-defined messages, consider the following messages `CM_CALC` and `CM_STORE` declared in the header file USRMSG.H:

```
#define CM_CALC (WM_USER + 0)
#define CM_STORE (WM_USER + 1)
```

The declaration of the window class that responds to these messages is

```
#include <afxwin.h>
#include "usrmsg.h"

class CAppWindow : CFrameWnd
{
public:
     CAppWindow();

     // handle painting
     afx_msg void OnPaint();

     // handle calculation command
     afx_msg void CMCalc();

     // handle store command
     afx_msg void CMStore();

protected:
```

```
    // handle closing the window
    afx_msg void OnClose();

    DECLARE_MESSAGE_MAP();
};
```

The corresponding message map is

```
BEGIN_MESSAGE_MAP(CAppWindow, CFrameWnd)
    ON_WM_PAINT()
    ON_COMMAND(CM_CALC, CMCalc)
    ON_COMMAND(CM_STORE, CMStore)
    ON_WM_CLOSE()
END_MESSAGE_MAP()
```

The first ON_COMMAND macro specifies that the CMCalc member function responds to the CM_CALC command message. The second ON_COMMAND macro indicates that the CMStore member function responds to the CM_STORE command message. Again, notice the order of the message macros—they match the order of the declarations of message response member functions.

The MFC library has other message mapping macros that will be presented as the need arises.

Summary

Today's lesson presents basic information regarding the Microsoft Foundation Class (MFC) class hierarchy as well as Windows-related information. You learn about the following topics:

- Popular Windows data types include simple data types (such as BYTE, WORD, and LONG) and data structures (such as RECT and POINT).
- The MFC hierarchy presents the various classes that make up the MFC library.
- Windows API functions that can be invoked include MessageBox, MessageBeep, and Polyline.
- There are several categories of Windows messages that you can respond to in your own MFC applications. This is a process that involves declaring descendant MFC classes that contain one or more message response member functions. The latter functions provide the required response.
- You can use a few Windows API functions to send messages.
- You can define your own messages, send these messages, and then respond to them.

Day 14 presents the basics of building an MFC application and attaching menus to such applications.

Q&A

Q Does the MFC library consist of simple wrappers for the various Windows API functions?

A Version 3.0 of the MFC library comes with more sophisticated classes than versions 1.0, 2.0, and 2.5. The new classes have even more functionality built into them. In addition, the MFC 3.0 library makes use of template classes (the template class feature is introduced in Visual C++ 2.0).

Q Is the Hungarian notation required by the Visual C++ compiler?

A No, it is merely a naming convention to make your C++ code clearer. Adapting any naming notation takes time, so try to ease into it.

Q What is the relationship between Windows messages and C++ messages to an instance?

A Both use the object metaphor.

Workshop

The Workshop provides quiz questions to help you solidify your understanding of the material covered and exercises to provide you with experience in using what you've learned. Try to understand the quiz and exercise answers before continuing on to the next day's lesson. Answers are provided in Appendix B, "Answers."

Quiz

1. What `MB_xxxx` constants are needed to create a message box with the Yes, No, and Cancel buttons, and the question mark icon?
2. What `MB_xxxx` constants are needed to create a message box with the O button and the exclamation point icon?
3. What value does the `MessageBox` function return if you click the Yes button in a message dialog box that contains the Yes and No buttons?
4. What value does the `MessageBox` function return if you click the Cancel button in a message dialog box that contains the Yes, No, and Cancel buttons?

Exercise

Familiarize yourself with the MFC hierarchy using the Quick Reference card included in your Visual C++ package.

14

Creating Basic MFC Applications

WEEK 2

Day 13 provides you with a lot of background information regarding the Microsoft Foundation Class library, Windows API functions, and Windows messages. In today's lesson, you start building simple MFC applications. You learn about the following topics:

- Creating a minimal MFC application
- Extending the operations of the application's window
- Adding a menu to an MFC application
- Responding to menu selections
- Alternating between different menus
- Creating multiple instances of an MFC application
- Closing a window

Today's lesson also shows you the power and functionality provided by the MFC library. This functionality includes default characteristics and responses. Building your own MFC application involves extending the basic characteristics and functionality of the MFC.

Creating a Minimal MFC Application

Each MFC application that you create starts with declaring a descendant of class `CWinApp`. This is a step needed by even the most trivial MFC applications. Extending the other MFC library classes relies on the features of your applications. The entry point for a Windows application is the `WinMain` function (which is similar to the function `main()` in a non-Windows C or C++ program). Fortunately, the MFC library supplies a default `WinMain` function that is suitable for most Windows applications. You can define your own version of `WinMain` to supply your application a higher level of customization. The applications in this book use the predefined `WinMain` function. To execute an MFC program, you declare an application instance, as shown in the following general form:

```
_CWindowApp_ _WindowApp_;
```

The `_CWindowApp_` class represents the application class that you derive from `CWinApp`. The `_WindowApp_` variable represents the application instance. This instance is created using the class constructor or the inherited class constructor.

When an MFC application starts running, it invokes the member functions in the following order:

1. Invokes the virtual `InitApplication` member function to initialize the first instances of the MFC application. The code for the member function `CWinApp::InitApplication` is

   ```
   BOOL CWinApp::InitApplication()
   { return TRUE; }
   ```

   This member function performs no task—it's simply a dummy function that you override to carry out a special initialization to the application.

2. Calls the virtual `InitInstance` member function to initialize every other instance of the MFC application. The `CWinApp::InitInstance` member function is also a dummy function like `InitApplication`. Every time you create an instance of an MFC application, these two functions are invoked.

3. Invokes the window class constructor to initialize the main window of each instance.

Note: If you plan to carry out additional steps in initializing the instances of an application, you need to declare your own `InitInstance` in the following general form:

```
BOOL_CWinApp_::InitInstance()
{
  // put statements here
  return boolean_value;
}
```

Syntax

An Application Class

The general syntax for an application class is

```
class _CWindowApp_ : public CWinApp
{
  public:
    // public data members declarations
  protected:
    // protected data members
```

```
    // optional constructor
    _CWindowApp_(const char* pszAppName,    // application name
    _other_params_)           // additional parameter

    // other constructors
    // class destructors
    // other member functions

    // overridable data members
    virtual BOOL InitInstance();
    virtual BOOL InitApplication();  // optional

    // other protected member functions

  private:
    // private data members
    // other private member functions
};
```

This general template shows that your application classes should declare an `InitInstance` member function. The declaration of the member function `InitApplication` is required only to fine-tune the operations of these inherited functions in your MFC application. This fact also applies to declaring other constructor parameters, data members (public, protected, and private), and member functions (public, protected, and private).

Example:

See the program in Listing 14.1.

Let's look at an example. Listing 14.1 shows the source code for the program MINWINAP.CPP. This program is a minimal Windows application. You can move, resize, minimize, and maximize the program's window using either a mouse or the menu selections available in the system menu. To close the window, use the Close selection in the system menu. Other than these operations, the program does nothing! For example, if you click on the mouse, nothing visual happens.

> **Note:** To create any Windows application you need a .DEF file. Listing 14.2 shows the contents of the MINWINAP.DEF file. This file has information that includes the application's name, title, modes of operations, and heap size. All the .DEF files in this book are very similar to MINWINAP.DEF but differ in the application name and title.

To create the MINWINAP.EXE program, create the MINWINAP directory as a child of the \MSVC20\VC21DAY directory. Store the files MINWINAP.CPP and

MINWINAP.DEF in the \MSVC20\VC21DAY\MINWINAP directory. Also use the latter directory to store the MINWINAP.MAK file which is created by the Visual C++ Workbench.

Listing 14.1. Source code in the MINWINAP.CPP file.

```
#include <afxwin.h>

// Define a window class derived from CFrameWnd
class CAppWindow : public CFrameWnd
{
public:
   CAppWindow()
   { Create(NULL, "Minimal MFC Application",
                 WS_OVERLAPPEDWINDOW, rectDefault); }
};

// Define an application class derived from CWinApp
class CWindowApp : public CWinApp
{
public:
 virtual BOOL InitInstance();
};

// Construct the CWindowApp's m_pMainWnd data member
BOOL CWindowApp::InitInstance()
{
  m_pMainWnd = new CAppWindow();
  m_pMainWnd->ShowWindow(m_nCmdShow);
  m_pMainWnd->UpdateWindow();
  return TRUE;
}

// application's constructor initializes and runs the app
CWindowApp WindowApp;
```

Listing 14.2. Contents of the MINWINAP.DEF file.

```
NAME         MinWinAp
DESCRIPTION  'Minimal MFC Windows Application'
CODE         PRELOAD MOVEABLE DISCARDABLE
DATA         PRELOAD MOVEABLE MULTIPLE
HEAPSIZE     1024
```


Figure 14.1 shows a sample session with program MINWINAP.EXE.

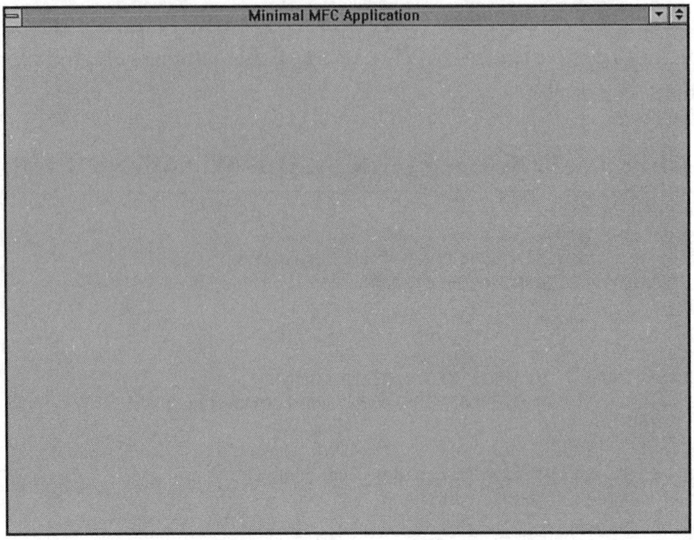

Figure 14.1. *A sample session with program MINWINAP.EXE.*

Analysis

Listing 14.1 shows the source code for a minimal MFC application that uses the template that I presented earlier in today's lesson. The program contains the declaration of an application class `CWindowApp` (a descendant of `CWinApp`), and a window class `CAppWindow` (a descendant of `CWnd`).

Line 1 contains the directive to include the header file AFXWIN.H. This file ensures that all the required Windows and MFC declarations are available to the compiler.

Line 13 contains the declaration of class `CWindowApp` which contains only the member function `InitInstance`. This function creates an instance of `CAppWindow`, which is accessed by the inherited `pointer`-typed data member `m_pMainWnd`.

Line 4 contains the declaration of the window class `CAppWindow`. This class only declares a class constructor to create the class instances using the `CFrameWnd::Create` member function. The member function `CFrameWnd::Create` has the following declaration:

```
BOOL Create(
     const char FAR* lpClassName,        // Windows class
     // registration name
     const char FAR* lpWindowName,       // title
     DWORD dwStyle = WS_OVERLAPPEDWINDOW, // style attribute
     const RECT& rect = rectDefault,     // location and size
     const CWnd* pParentWnd = NULL,      // parent window
     const char FAR* lpMenuName = NULL); // ID of menu
```

The `lpClassName` is the Windows registration class name. This non-OOP name specifies the window category name. The `lpWindowName` parameter specifies the caption or title of the window. The `dwStyle` parameter specifies the style of the created window and has the default value of `WS_OVERLAPPEDWINDOW`. The `rect` parameter defines the location and size of the window and has the default value for `rectDefault`. The `pParentWnd` parameter is the pointer to the parent window and has the default value of `NULL`. The `lpMenuName` parameter defines the name of the menu resource attached to the window. Some menu resources have a numeric ID associated with a constant. To use this kind of menu resource, invoke the macro `MAKEINTRESOURCE` and supply it the numeric ID of the sought menu. This macro translates the numeric ID into a string.

Resources are components that are created and compiled outside a Windows application.

NEW TERM The statement in line 29 declares an application instance. This declaration results in executing the MFC program.

Extending the Window Operations

After building a minimal MFC application, let's write a new application that adds a few operations to the application. The next program performs the following main tasks:

- Responds to the left button mouse click (when the mouse is inside the application window) by displaying a message box with an OK button
- Responds to the right button mouse click by displaying a message box that asks you whether or not you want to close the window
- Supports a menu which includes nested menu selections (the menu items, except for Exit, are dummy ones)

Most Windows applications include menus. The MINWINAP.EXE application has only the System menu. This section shows you how to use a resource file to build a menu that can be attached to the application's window. The example loads a menu from a menu resource while creating a window. The next section illustrates more elaborate menu manipulation.

Applications use resources by loading them. Resources only define the appearance of visual objects. They are not responsible for the behavior of these objects. That is the task of the Windows or MFC application. The advantage of using resources is that you can modify them without recompiling the application. For example, you can change the wording of menu items and alter the location of a button. A more dramatic example is the ability to change the language used in the various menus, dialog boxes, and other controls. This enables a software developer to maintain and update a single version of the application easily, while using different versions of the resources for each language. This approach was applied by Apple Computer in making the Apple Macintosh computer work in different languages, including Arabic.

> **Note:** Appendix A describes the syntax for the menu and dialog box resource scripts. The first section discusses the menu resources.

Listing 14.3 presents the contents of the menu resource file MENU1.RC. The file contains a single menu definition with the OPTIONS name ID. The menu contains three main menu items: File, Edit, and Help. The File and Edit menu items are pop-up menus. The Edit menu options contain the Delete menu item which is also a pop-up menu. The menu items include horizontal separator bars. All the menu names use the ampersand (`&`) to define the corresponding hot-keys.

The various MENUITEM statements contain `CM_xxxx` constants that define the result of selecting the menu items. The `CM_xxxx` constants are defined in the MENU1.H header file, shown in Listing 14.4. Listing 14.5 shows the source code for the MENU1.CPP program.

Create the directory MENU2 as a subdirectory of \MSVC20\VC21DAY and store all the project's files in the new directory. The project's .MAK file should contain the files MENU1.CPP, MENU1.RC, and MENU1.DEF. The latter file resembles file MINWINAP.DEF in Listing 14.2.

Type **Listing 14.3. Script for the MENU1.RC resource file.**

```
#include <afxres.h>
#include "menu1.h"

OPTIONS MENU LOADONCALL MOVEABLE PURE DISCARDABLE
BEGIN
  POPUP "&File"
  BEGIN
    MENUITEM "&New", CM_FILENEW
    MENUITEM "&Open", CM_FILEOPEN
    MENUITEM "&Save", CM_FILESAVE
    MENUITEM "Save&As", CM_FILESAVEAS
    MENUITEM SEPARATOR
    MENUITEM "E&xit", CM_EXIT
  END
```

```
    POPUP "&Edit"
    BEGIN
      MENUITEM "&Undo", CM_EDITUNDO
      MENUITEM SEPARATOR
      MENUITEM "C&ut", CM_EDITCUT
      MENUITEM "C&opy", CM_EDITCOPY
      MENUITEM "&Paste", CM_EDITPASTE
      POPUP "&Delete"
      BEGIN
         MENUITEM "&Line", CM_EDITDELETE
         MENUITEM "&Block", CM_EDITDELETE_BLOCK
      END
      MENUITEM "&Clear", CM_EDITCLEAR
    END
    MENUITEM "&Help", CM_HELP
  END
```

Type Listing 14.4. Source code for the MENU1.H header file.

```
#define CM_FILENEW            (WM_USER + 100)
#define CM_FILEOPEN           (WM_USER + 101)
#define CM_FILESAVE           (WM_USER + 102)
#define CM_FILESAVEAS         (WM_USER + 103)
#define CM_EXIT               (WM_USER + 104)
#define CM_EDITUNDO           (WM_USER + 105)
#define CM_EDITCUT            (WM_USER + 106)
#define CM_EDITCOPY           (WM_USER + 107)
#define CM_EDITPASTE          (WM_USER + 108)
#define CM_EDITDELETE         (WM_USER + 109)
#define CM_EDITDELETE_BLOCK   (WM_USER + 110)
#define CM_EDITCLEAR          (WM_USER + 111)
#define CM_HELP               (WM_USER + 112)
```

Type Listing 14.5. Source code for the MENU1.CPP program.

```
#include <afxwin.h>
#include "menu1.h"

// Define a window class derived from CFrameWnd
class CAppWindow : public CFrameWnd
{
public:
  CAppWindow()
  { Create(NULL, "A Menu-Driven MFC Application",
           WS_OVERLAPPEDWINDOW, rectDefault, NULL, "OPTIONS"); }

protected:
  // handle the left mouse button click
```

continues

Listing 14.5. continued

```
  afx_msg void OnLButtonDown(UINT nFlags, CPoint point);
  // handle the right mouse button click
  afx_msg void OnRButtonDown(UINT nFlags, CPoint point);
  // handle the Exit menu option
  afx_msg void OnExit();

  // message map macro
  DECLARE_MESSAGE_MAP()
};

// Define an application class derived from CWinApp
class CWindowApp : public CWinApp
{
public:
  virtual BOOL InitInstance();
};

void CAppWindow::OnLButtonDown(UINT nFlags, CPoint point)
{
  MessageBox("You clicked the left button!",
             "Mouse Click Event!", MB_OK);
}

void CAppWindow::OnRButtonDown(UINT nFlags, CPoint point)
{
  MessageBeep(0); // beep
  // prompt user if he or she wants to close the application
  if (MessageBox("Want to close this application", "Query",
                 MB_YESNO ¦ MB_ICONQUESTION) == IDYES)
    SendMessage(WM_CLOSE);
}

void CAppWindow::OnExit()
{ SendMessage(WM_CLOSE); }

BEGIN_MESSAGE_MAP(CAppWindow, CFrameWnd)
    ON_WM_LBUTTONDOWN()
    ON_WM_RBUTTONDOWN()
    ON_COMMAND(CM_EXIT, OnExit)
END_MESSAGE_MAP()

// Construct the CWindowApp's m_pMainWnd data member
BOOL CWindowApp::InitInstance()
{
  m_pMainWnd = new CAppWindow();
  m_pMainWnd->ShowWindow(m_nCmdShow);
  m_pMainWnd->UpdateWindow();
  return TRUE;
}

// application's constructor initializes and runs the app
CWindowApp WindowApp;
```

Figure 14.2 shows a sample session with program MENU1.EXE.

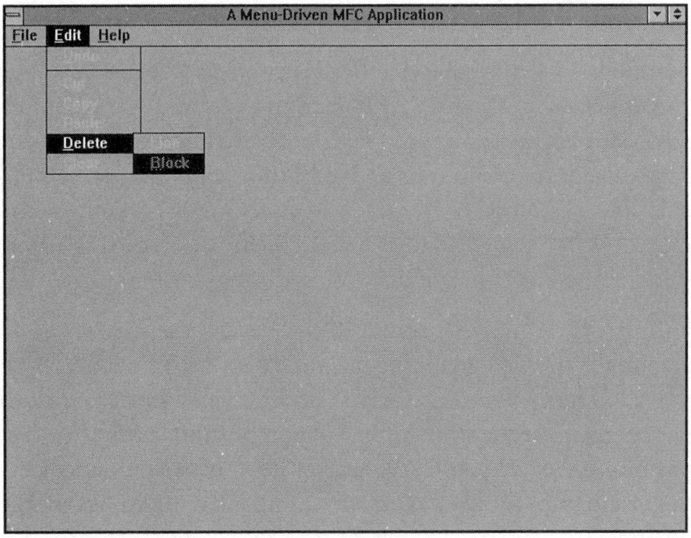

Figure 14.2. *A sample session with program MENU1.EXE.*

Analysis The program in Listing 14.5 declares a descendant of `CFrameWnd` to implement the desired options. Line 5 contains the declaration of class `CAppWindow`, a descendant of `CFrameWnd`. This descendant class declares a constructor, three message response member functions, and the `DECLARE_MESSAGE_MAP` macro. The `CAppWindow` constructor works in a manner similar to that in program MINWINAP.CPP. Notice the call to the function `Create` statement in lines 9 and 10 has a list of arguments that ends with the string `OPTIONS`. This string specifies the name of the menu resource to load. The menu resource name matches the one in line 5 in Listing 14.3. The member functions `OnLButtonDown` and `OnRButtonDown` respond to the Windows messages `WM_LBUTTONDOWN` and `WM_RBUTTONDOWN`, respectively. This response is also echoed in the `BEGIN_MESSAGE_MAP` macro, which specifies the messages handled by the various member functions. The `CAppWindow` class also declares the member function `OnExit` to respond to the Exit menu selection.

Lines 31 through 35 define the member function `OnLButtonDown`. This function merely calls the inherited `CWnd::MessageBox` member function to display the string `You clicked the left button!` in a message box with the caption `Mouse Click Event!`. The box has the OK button that you click to resume program execution.

Lines 46 and 47 define the member function `OnExit`. This function responds to the `CM_EXIT` command generated by the Exit menu selection. This command is associated with the Windows message command `WM_COMMAND`.

Lines 37 through 44 define the member function `OnRButtonDown`. The function first invokes the `MessageBeep` Windows API function to sound a beep. The function then calls the `CWnd::MessageBox` function to display a box with the caption `Query`, the message `Want to close this application`, Yes and No buttons, and a question mark icon. The `if` statement in line 41 compares the result of function `MessageBox` with the predefined constant `IDYES`. When the two values match, the function calls the `CWnd::SendMessage` member function to close the window using the `WM_CLOSE` message.

Lines 49 through 53 define the macros `BEGIN_MESSAGE_MAP` and `END_MESSAGE_MAP`. These macros contain the message-mapping macros `ON_WM_LBUTTONDOWN`, `ON_WM_RBUTTONDOWN`, and `ON_COMMAND`. The first two macros have no arguments and therefore they resort to the default mapping. Consequently, the `OnLButtonDown` and `OnRButtonDown` member functions respond to the `WM_LBUTTONDOWN` and `WM_RBUTTONDOWN` messages, respectively. The `ON_COMMAND` macro traps the `CM_EXIT` menu command and invokes the member function `OnExit` to handle it.

Note: Microsoft has promoted Visual C++ and its Workbench by emphasizing the AppWizard, ClassWizard, and App Studio tools, which make it very easy to develop Windows applications and create resources. These wizard tools are great for automating repetitive work involved in creating MFC-based Windows applications. They build nontrivial Windows applications by generating several kinds of source files. However, if you are a novice, you need to learn the basic components of an MFC application before using AppWizard and ClassWizard. Once you learn to program MFC-based Windows manually, you can then use the AppWizard because you can distinguish between primary and secondary code.

Responding to Menu Selections

The last program demonstrates how to build a nested menu and loads it in an application. However, selecting the menu items (except for Exit) produces no action. This section basically answers the question, "How does an application respond to a menu selection, and can that response load a different menu?"

Let's look at the contents of resource file MENU2.RC, shown in Listing 14.6. The resource file defines two menus, tagged `LONGMENU` and `SHORTMENU`. As the names suggest, the first menu is the longer version of the second one. These menus differ from the ones in MENU1.RC in that they are not as nested and use the `INACTIVE` and `GRAYED` options. Notice that these two options do not appear with every menu item—they are assigned to the menu items which I include but keep inactive. As a result, the names of the menu items appear in a gray color and cannot be selected. From the C++ coding aspect, there are no corresponding message response member functions. By contrast, the menu items that do not have the `INACTIVE` and `GRAYED` options can be selected and will generate a response, albeit a simple one. The `CM_xxxx` constants used by the menu resource are all defined in the MENU2.H header file, shown in Listing 14.7.

The menu items in Listing 14.6 contain two interesting members. The `Short &Menus` item in menu `LONGMENU` results in the `CM_SHORTMENU` command that selects the short menu. The `SHORTMENU` menu has a complementary menu item, `&Long Menu`, that results in the `CM_LONGMENU` command which selects the long menu.

Create the directory MENU2 as a subdirectory of \MSVC20\VC21DAY and store all the project's files in the new directory. The project's .MAK file should contain the files MENU2.CPP, MENU2.RC, and MENU2.DEF. The latter file resembles file MINWINAP.DEF in Listing 14.2. When you run the application, use the Long Menu and Short Menu selections to toggle between the two forms of menus. In addition, select the Help item to get the one-line help message box. Select the Edit Cut, Edit Copy, and Edit Paste items to view the response. Notice the inactive menu items when you navigate through the various menus. The program in Listing 14.8 includes the header file MENU2.H. This inclusion enables the program to use the user-defined `CM_xxxx` constants in the message response member functions. The source code declares the application class `CWindowApp` and the window class `CAppWindow`. The second class has the task of responding to the various Windows messages. The `CAppWindow` class declares a constructor, destructor, and a series of message response member functions. The class constructor creates a window and then creates a `CMenu` instance. The instance is accessed by the `pAppMenu` pointer which is a data member of the `CAppWindow` class. The constructor then loads the `LONGMENU` menu resource, associates the menu object with the window, and invokes the `DrawMenuBar` member function. Consequently, the application's window starts up with the long menu.

Type

Listing 14.6. Resource script in file MENU2.RC.

```
#include <afxres.h>
#include "menu2.h"

LONGMENU MENU LOADONCALL MOVEABLE PURE DISCARDABLE
BEGIN
  POPUP "&File"
  BEGIN
    MENUITEM "&New", CM_FILENEW, INACTIVE, GRAYED
    MENUITEM "&Open", CM_FILEOPEN, INACTIVE, GRAYED
    MENUITEM "&Save", CM_FILESAVE, INACTIVE, GRAYED
    MENUITEM "Save&As", CM_FILESAVEAS, INACTIVE, GRAYED
    MENUITEM SEPARATOR
    MENUITEM "Short &Menus", CM_SHORTMENU
    MENUITEM SEPARATOR
    MENUITEM "E&xit", CM_EXIT
  END
  POPUP "&Edit"
  BEGIN
    MENUITEM "&Undo", CM_EDITUNDO, INACTIVE, GRAYED
    MENUITEM SEPARATOR
    MENUITEM "C&ut", CM_EDITCUT
    MENUITEM "C&opy", CM_EDITCOPY
    MENUITEM "&Paste", CM_EDITPASTE
    MENUITEM "&Delete", CM_EDITDELETE, INACTIVE, GRAYED
    MENUITEM "&Clear", CM_EDITCLEAR, INACTIVE, GRAYED
  END
  MENUITEM "&Help", CM_HELP
END

SHORTMENU MENU LOADONCALL MOVEABLE PURE DISCARDABLE
BEGIN
  POPUP "&File"
  BEGIN
    MENUITEM "&Open", CM_FILEOPEN, INACTIVE, GRAYED
    MENUITEM "Save&As", CM_FILESAVEAS, INACTIVE, GRAYED
    MENUITEM SEPARATOR
    MENUITEM "&Long Menus", CM_LONGMENU
    MENUITEM SEPARATOR
    MENUITEM "E&xit", CM_EXIT
  END
  POPUP "&Edit"
  BEGIN
    MENUITEM "C&ut", CM_EDITCUT
    MENUITEM "C&opy", CM_EDITCOPY
    MENUITEM "&Paste", CM_EDITPASTE
  END
  MENUITEM "&Help", CM_HELP
END
```

Listing 14.7. Contents of the MENU2.H header file.

```
#define CM_FILENEW          (WM_USER + 100)
#define CM_FILEOPEN         (WM_USER + 101)
#define CM_FILESAVE         (WM_USER + 102)
#define CM_FILESAVEAS       (WM_USER + 103)
#define CM_EXIT             (WM_USER + 104)
#define CM_EDITUNDO         (WM_USER + 105)
#define CM_EDITCUT          (WM_USER + 106)
#define CM_EDITCOPY         (WM_USER + 107)
#define CM_EDITPASTE        (WM_USER + 108)
#define CM_EDITDELETE       (WM_USER + 109)
#define CM_EDITDELETE_BLOCK (WM_USER + 110)
#define CM_EDITCLEAR        (WM_USER + 111)
#define CM_HELP             (WM_USER + 112)
#define CM_SHORTMENU        (WM_USER + 113)
#define CM_LONGMENU         (WM_USER + 114)
```

Listing 14.8. Source code in the file MENU2.CPP.

```
#include <afxwin.h>
#include "menu2.h"

// Define a window class derived from CFrameWnd
class CAppWindow : public CFrameWnd
{
public:
    CMenu* pAppMenu;
    CAppWindow();
    ~CAppWindow() { if (pAppMenu) delete pAppMenu; }
protected:
    // handle the left mouse button click
    afx_msg void OnLButtonDown(UINT nFlags, CPoint point);
    // handle the right mouse button click
    afx_msg void OnRButtonDown(UINT nFlags, CPoint point);
    // load the long menu
    afx_msg void OnLongMenu();
    // load the short menu
    afx_msg void OnShortMenu();
    // exit the application
    afx_msg void OnExit();
    // get on-line help
    afx_msg void OnHelp();
    // handle the Cut menu option
    afx_msg void OnEditCut();
    // handle the Copy menu option
    afx_msg void OnEditCopy();
    // handle the Paste menu option
    afx_msg void OnEditPaste();
private:
    // display a message "Feature not implemented"
    void notImplemented();
```


continues

Listing 14.8. continued

```
    // prompt user to quit the application
    void promptToQuit();
    // Assign new menu
    void assignMenu(const char FAR* lpMenuName);
    // message map macro
    DECLARE_MESSAGE_MAP()
};

// Define an application class derived from CWinApp
class CWindowApp : public CWinApp
{
public:
  virtual BOOL InitInstance();
};

CAppWindow::CAppWindow()
{
  Create(NULL, "Multi-Menu Application",
           WS_OVERLAPPEDWINDOW, rectDefault);
  pAppMenu = new CMenu;
  pAppMenu->LoadMenu("LONGMENU");
  SetMenu(pAppMenu);
  DrawMenuBar();
}

void CAppWindow::OnLButtonDown(UINT nFlags, CPoint point)
{
  MessageBox("You clicked the left button!",
             "Mouse Click Event!", MB_OK);
}

void CAppWindow::OnRButtonDown(UINT nFlags, CPoint point)
{ promptToQuit(); }

void CAppWindow::OnLongMenu()
{ assignMenu("LONGMENU"); }

void CAppWindow::OnShortMenu()
{ assignMenu("SHORTMENU"); }

void CAppWindow::OnExit()
{ SendMessage(WM_CLOSE); }

void CAppWindow::OnHelp()
{
  MessageBox("This is a sample one line help",
    "Help", MB_OK | MB_ICONINFORMATION);
}

void CAppWindow::OnEditCut()
{ notImplemented(); }

void CAppWindow::OnEditCopy()
{ notImplemented(); }
```

```

void CAppWindow::OnEditPaste()
{ notImplemented(); }

void CAppWindow::notImplemented()
{
  MessageBox("This feature is not implemented",
             "Information", MB_OK);
}
void CAppWindow::promptToQuit()
{
  MessageBeep(0); // beep
  // prompt user if he or she want to close the application
  if (MessageBox("Want to close this application", "Query",
                 MB_YESNO ¦ MB_ICONQUESTION) == IDYES)
    SendMessage(WM_CLOSE);
}

void CAppWindow::assignMenu(const char FAR* lpMenuName)
{
  SetMenu(NULL);
  pAppMenu->DestroyMenu();
  pAppMenu->LoadMenu(lpMenuName);
  SetMenu(pAppMenu);
  DrawMenuBar();
}

BEGIN_MESSAGE_MAP(CAppWindow, CFrameWnd)
    ON_WM_LBUTTONDOWN()
    ON_WM_RBUTTONDOWN()
    ON_COMMAND(CM_LONGMENU, OnLongMenu)
    ON_COMMAND(CM_SHORTMENU, OnShortMenu)
    ON_COMMAND(CM_EXIT, OnExit)
    ON_COMMAND(CM_HELP, OnHelp)
    ON_COMMAND(CM_EDITCUT, OnEditCut)
    ON_COMMAND(CM_EDITCOPY, OnEditCopy)
    ON_COMMAND(CM_EDITPASTE, OnEditPaste)
END_MESSAGE_MAP()

// Construct the CWindowApp's m_pMainWnd data member
BOOL CWindowApp::InitInstance()
{
  m_pMainWnd = new CAppWindow();
  m_pMainWnd->ShowWindow(m_nCmdShow);
  m_pMainWnd->UpdateWindow();
  return TRUE;
}

// application's constructor initializes and runs the app
CWindowApp WindowApp;
```

Figure 14.3 shows a sample session with program MENU2.EXE.

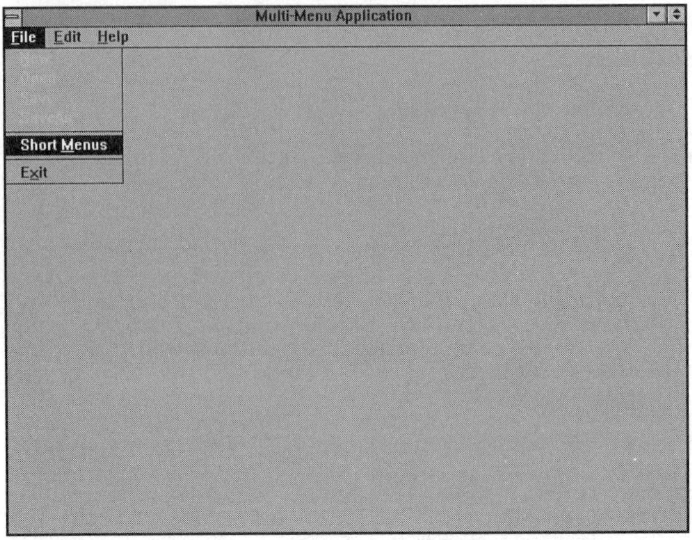

Figure 14.3. *A sample session with program MENU2.EXE.*

The `CAppWindow` class declares three private functions: `notImplemented`, `promptToQuit`, and `assignMenu`. The first function displays a message box that contains the message `This feature is not implemented`. In fact, this is the common response to most menu items. The `promptToQuit` function prompts you to close the application using a message box with Yes and No buttons. The `assignMenu` member function deletes the current menu and loads a new one. The program uses this function to alternate between the short and long menus.

Now let's look at the message response member functions of `CAppWindow`. The first two functions are the same as those in the previous applications—they respond to mouse clicks on the window. The new version of function `OnRButtonDown` merely calls the `promptToQuit` function.

The member function `OnLongMenu` responds to the user-defined `CM_LONGMENU` command. The message map macro `ON_COMMAND(CM_LONGMENU, OnLongMenu)` indicates that the `OnLongMenu` function responds to the `CM_LONGMENU` command message. The `OnLongMenu` calls the `assignMenu` member function with the `"LONGMENU"` argument to load the long menu. The `OnShortMenu` member function is coded similarly and responds to the `CM_SHORTMENU` command to load the short menu.

The `OnExit` member function provides a new response to the Exit menu selection (which generates the `CM_EXIT` command). The function sends the Windows message `WM_CLOSE` using the inherited function `SendMessage`.

The OnHelp member function responds to the user-defined CM_HELP command by providing a one-line help message box. The message box appears with an OK button and an information icon (an i enclosed in a circle).

The member functions OnEditCut, OnEditCopy, and OnEditPaste all invoke the private member function notImplemented. This is the common (and symbolic) response that I provide for the CM_EDITCUT, CM_EDITCOPY, and CM_EDITPASTE commands.

The message loop macros include several ON_COMMAND macros that associate the various CM_xxxx command messages with their corresponding message response member functions.

Creating Multiple Instances

One of the powerful aspects of Windows is the ability to run multiple instances of the same application. This feature is backed by a smart scheme that saves on memory and other system resources by pooling the common code and data segments. Thus, you can load, for example, three instances of a scientific calculator and work with them independently. This section looks at creating multiple instances of an MFC application. To make the example application more interesting, the first instance has a different window title and menu from the other instances. All instances respond the same way to the left and right mouse button clicks. Listing 14.9 shows the resource script file MENU3.RC which defines the menu resources for the various program instances. The file MENU3.RC defines two menu resources, a MAINMENU and a SECONDMENU. These menu resources are similar to the menus LONGMENU and SHORTMENU, found in MENU2.RC, except they do not have the toggle menu items. Listing 14.10 contains the header file MENU3.H. Listing 14.11 shows the source code for the MENU3.CPP MFC application file.

Create the directory MENU3 as a subdirectory of \MSVC20\VC21DAY, and store all the project's files in the new directory. The project's .MAK file should contain the files MENU3.CPP, MENU3.RC, and MENU3.DEF. The latter file resembles file MINWINAP.DEF in Listing 14.2. Run multiple instances of the program MENU3.EXE. The first instance has the window title of Main Window, whereas the other instances have the title of A Secondary Window. In addition, the first instance has more selections in the File menu option than the remaining instances.

Listing 14.9. Resource script in file MENU3.RC.

```
#include <afxres.h>
#include "menu3.h"

MAINMENU MENU LOADONCALL MOVEABLE PURE DISCARDABLE
BEGIN
  POPUP "&File"
  BEGIN
    MENUITEM "&New", CM_FILENEW, INACTIVE, GRAYED
    MENUITEM "&Open", CM_FILEOPEN, INACTIVE, GRAYED
    MENUITEM "&Save", CM_FILESAVE, INACTIVE, GRAYED
    MENUITEM "Save&As", CM_FILESAVEAS, INACTIVE, GRAYED
    MENUITEM SEPARATOR
    MENUITEM "E&xit", CM_EXIT
  END
  POPUP "&Edit"
  BEGIN
    MENUITEM "&Undo", CM_EDITUNDO, INACTIVE, GRAYED
    MENUITEM SEPARATOR
    MENUITEM "C&ut", CM_EDITCUT
    MENUITEM "C&opy", CM_EDITCOPY
    MENUITEM "&Paste", CM_EDITPASTE
    MENUITEM "&Delete", CM_EDITDELETE, INACTIVE, GRAYED
    MENUITEM "&Clear", CM_EDITCLEAR, INACTIVE, GRAYED
  END
  MENUITEM "&Help", CM_HELP
END

SECONDMENU MENU LOADONCALL MOVEABLE PURE DISCARDABLE
BEGIN
  POPUP "&File"
  BEGIN
    MENUITEM "&Open", CM_FILEOPEN, INACTIVE, GRAYED
    MENUITEM "Save&As", CM_FILESAVEAS, INACTIVE, GRAYED
    MENUITEM SEPARATOR
    MENUITEM "E&xit", CM_EXIT
  END
  POPUP "&Edit"
  BEGIN
    MENUITEM "C&ut", CM_EDITCUT
    MENUITEM "C&opy", CM_EDITCOPY
    MENUITEM "&Paste", CM_EDITPASTE
  END
  MENUITEM "&Help", CM_HELP
END
```

Listing 14.10. Source code for the MENU3.H header file.

```
#define CM_FILENEW            (WM_USER + 100)
#define CM_FILEOPEN           (WM_USER + 101)
#define CM_FILESAVE           (WM_USER + 102)
#define CM_FILESAVEAS         (WM_USER + 103)
#define CM_EXIT               (WM_USER + 104)
#define CM_EDITUNDO           (WM_USER + 105)
#define CM_EDITCUT            (WM_USER + 106)
#define CM_EDITCOPY           (WM_USER + 107)
#define CM_EDITPASTE          (WM_USER + 108)
#define CM_EDITDELETE         (WM_USER + 109)
#define CM_EDITDELETE_BLOCK   (WM_USER + 110)
#define CM_EDITCLEAR          (WM_USER + 111)
#define CM_HELP               (WM_USER + 112)
#define CM_SHORTMENU          (WM_USER + 113)
#define CM_LONGMENU           (WM_USER + 114)
```

Listing 14.11. Source code for the file MENU3.CPP.

```
#include <afxwin.h>
#include "menu3.h"

// Define a window class derived from CFrameWnd
class CAppWindow : public CFrameWnd
{
public:
    CAppWindow(BOOL IsMainWindow);

protected:
    // handle the left mouse button click
    afx_msg void OnLButtonDown(UINT nFlags, CPoint point);
    // handle the right mouse button click
    afx_msg void OnRButtonDown(UINT nFlags, CPoint point);
    // exit the application
    afx_msg void OnExit();
    // get on-line help
    afx_msg void OnHelp();
    // handle the Cut menu option
    afx_msg void OnEditCut();
    // handle the Copy menu option
    afx_msg void OnEditCopy();
    // handle the Paste menu option
    afx_msg void OnEditPaste();

private:
    // display a message "Feature not implemented"
    void notImplemented();
    // prompt user to quit the application
    void promptToQuit();
    // message map macro
    DECLARE_MESSAGE_MAP()
```

continues

Listing 14.11. continued

```
};

// Define an application class derived from CWinApp
class CWindowApp : public CWinApp
{
public:
  BOOL IsFirst;
  virtual BOOL InitInstance();
  virtual BOOL InitApplication();
};

CAppWindow::CAppWindow(BOOL IsMainWindow)
{
  if (IsMainWindow)
    Create(NULL, "Main Window",
           WS_OVERLAPPEDWINDOW, rectDefault, NULL, "MAINMENU");
  else
    Create(NULL, "A Secondary Window",
           WS_OVERLAPPEDWINDOW, rectDefault, NULL, "SECONDMENU");
}

void CAppWindow::OnLButtonDown(UINT nFlags, CPoint point)
{
  MessageBox("You clicked the left button!",
             "Mouse Click Event!", MB_OK);
}

void CAppWindow::OnRButtonDown(UINT nFlags, CPoint point)
{ promptToQuit(); }

void CAppWindow::OnExit()
{ SendMessage(WM_CLOSE); }

void CAppWindow::OnHelp()
{
  MessageBox(
    "This a sample one line help",
    "Help", MB_OK | MB_ICONINFORMATION);
}

void CAppWindow::OnEditCut()
{ notImplemented(); }

void CAppWindow::OnEditCopy()
{ notImplemented(); }

void CAppWindow::OnEditPaste()
{ notImplemented(); }

void CAppWindow::notImplemented()
{
  MessageBox("This feature is not implemented",
             "Information", MB_OK);
}
```

```
void CAppWindow::promptToQuit()
{
  MessageBeep(0); // beep

  // prompt user if he or she want to close the application
  if (MessageBox("Want to close this application", "Query",
                 MB_YESNO | MB_ICONQUESTION) == IDYES)
    SendMessage(WM_CLOSE);
}

BEGIN_MESSAGE_MAP(CAppWindow, CFrameWnd)
    ON_WM_LBUTTONDOWN()
    ON_WM_RBUTTONDOWN()
    ON_COMMAND(CM_EXIT, OnExit)
    ON_COMMAND(CM_HELP, OnHelp)
    ON_COMMAND(CM_EDITCUT, OnEditCut)
    ON_COMMAND(CM_EDITCOPY, OnEditCopy)
    ON_COMMAND(CM_EDITPASTE, OnEditPaste)
END_MESSAGE_MAP()

// Construct the CWindowApp's m_pMainWnd data member
BOOL CWindowApp::InitInstance()
{
  m_pMainWnd = new CAppWindow(IsFirst);
  IsFirst = FALSE;
  m_pMainWnd->ShowWindow(m_nCmdShow);
  m_pMainWnd->UpdateWindow();
  return TRUE;
}

// Initialize the application
BOOL CWindowApp::InitApplication()
{
  IsFirst = TRUE;
  return IsFirst;
}

// application's constructor initializes and runs the app
CWindowApp WindowApp;
```

Figure 14.4 shows a sample session with multiple instances of the MENU3.EXE application.

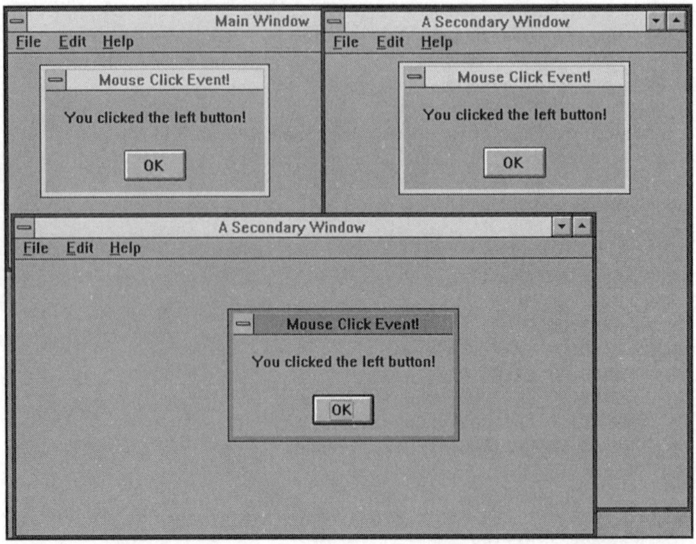

Figure 14.4. *A sample session with the application MENU3.EXE.*

Analysis How does the program in Listing 14.3 create a different first instance? In this case, the first instance has a different window title and menu from all other instances. To implement this feature, the program declares a Boolean data member, `IsFirst`, in the application class `CWindowApp`. The class also declares the `InitApplication` and `InitInstance` member functions. The `CWindowApp::InitApplication` member function, defined in lines 119 through 123, assigns `TRUE` to the `IsFirst` data member. This assignment allows the application to determine if the instance created is the first one. The `CWindowApp::InitInstance` member function, defined in lines 109 through 116, creates a window instance using the argument `IsFirst` (which is initialized with `TRUE`). The function then assigns `FALSE` to member `IsFirst`. This value is not altered by the subsequent instances.

The program declares the `CAppWindow` constructor to have the Boolean parameter `IsMainWindow`. If the argument of parameter `IsMainWindow` is `TRUE`, the constructor creates a window with the `"Main Window"` title and the `MAINMENU` menu resource. Otherwise, the constructor creates a window with the `"A Secondary Window"` title and the `SECONDMENU` menu resource.

Closing a Window

You may recall that programs MENU1.EXE through MENU3.EXE allow you to exit the application and close its window by simply selecting the Exit menu item. These applications use the default response to perform a quick program termination. Although this type of abrupt exit is harmless for the previous programs, it is a feature that, if maintained, drowns software developers with hate letters from application users! Therefore, Windows applications should close their windows only after making sure that the user does not lose data. In addition, the application should make any other appropriate shutdown operations.

> **Note:** Both Windows and MFC offer a sophisticated sequence for carefully closing down an application to include all the child windows. In fact, the process resembles a query of all related objects that can veto closing the target window in response to the `WM_CLOSE` message. By declaring a member function `OnClose` in your custom window classes, you provide your application with an additional say (or vote, if you prefer) in the matter of closing down a window. The `OnClose` member function that you declare focuses on the special closing criteria of your own application. In most cases, you should make sure that the user does not exit the application if there is new and altered data that was not saved. Other criteria might include deallocating special dynamic data.

Let's look at a program that streamlines closing the application's window. Listing 14.12 shows the source code for the program MENU4.CPP. I derived this program from MENU1.CPP. Consequently, the MENU4.H and MENU4.RC files are identical to the MENU1.H and MENU1.RC files, and are therefore not listed.

Create the directory MENU4 as a subdirectory of \MSVC20\VC21DAY and store all the project's files in the new directory. The project's .MAK file should contain the files MENU4.CPP, MENU4.RC, and MENU3.DEF. The latter file resembles file MINWINAP.DEF in Listing 14.2. Run the program and choose the Exit menu selection. The program responds by displaying a message box, with Yes and No buttons, that asks you if you wish to close the application. You obtain the same message box by clicking the right mouse button. Thus, program MENU4.EXE supports consolidated management for exiting an application.

Type

Listing 14.12. Source code for the MENU4.CPP program file.

```
#include <afxwin.h>
#include "menu4.h"

// Define a window class derived from CFrameWnd
class CAppWindow : public CFrameWnd
{
public:
  CAppWindow()
    { Create(NULL, "A Menu-Driven MFC Application",
        WS_OVERLAPPEDWINDOW, rectDefault, NULL, "OPTIONS"); }

protected:
  // handle the left mouse button click
  afx_msg void OnLButtonDown(UINT nFlags, CPoint point);
  // handle the right mouse button click
  afx_msg void OnRButtonDown(UINT nFlags, CPoint point);
  // handle the Exit menu option
  afx_msg void OnExit();
  // handle closing the window
  afx_msg void OnClose();

  // message map macro
  DECLARE_MESSAGE_MAP()
};

// Define an application class derived from CWinApp
class CWindowApp : public CWinApp
{
public:
  virtual BOOL InitInstance();
};

void CAppWindow::OnLButtonDown(UINT nFlags, CPoint point)
{
  MessageBox("You clicked the left button!",
             "Mouse Click Event!", MB_OK);
}

void CAppWindow::OnRButtonDown(UINT nFlags, CPoint point)
{ SendMessage(WM_CLOSE); }

void CAppWindow::OnExit()
{ SendMessage(WM_CLOSE); }

void CAppWindow::OnClose()
{
  if (MessageBox("Want to close this application",
                 "Query", MB_YESNO | MB_ICONQUESTION) == IDYES)
    DestroyWindow();
}

BEGIN_MESSAGE_MAP(CAppWindow, CFrameWnd)
```

```
    ON_WM_LBUTTONDOWN()
    ON_WM_RBUTTONDOWN()
    ON_COMMAND(CM_EXIT, OnExit)
    ON_WM_CLOSE()
END_MESSAGE_MAP()

// Construct the CWindowApp's m_pMainWnd data member
BOOL CWindowApp::InitInstance()
{
  m_pMainWnd = new CAppWindow();
  m_pMainWnd->ShowWindow(m_nCmdShow);
  m_pMainWnd->UpdateWindow();
  return TRUE;
}

// application's constructor initializes and runs the app
CWindowApp WindowApp;
```

Figure 14.5 shows a sample session with the program MENU4.EXE.

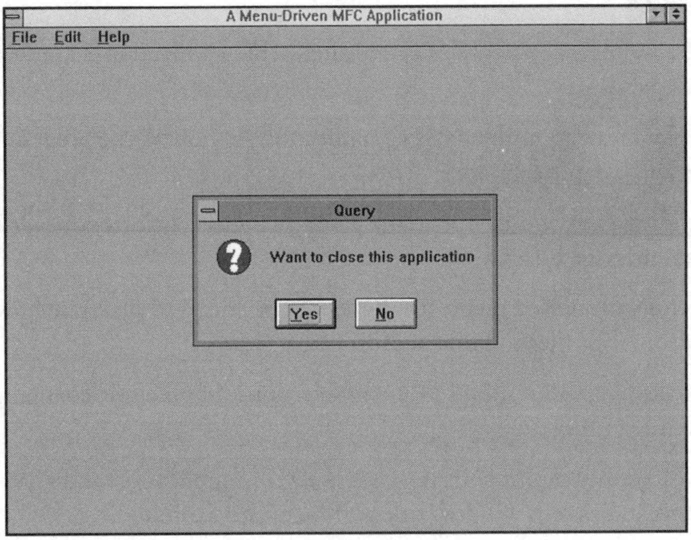

Figure 14.5. *A sample session with the program MENU4.EXE.*

Analysis

The most important difference between programs MENU4.CPP and MENU1.CPP is the declaration of the member function `OnClose` in the custom window class `CAppWindow`:

```
void CAppWindow::OnClose()
{
    if (MessageBox("Want to close this application",
```

```
        "Query", MB_YESNO | MB_ICONQUESTION) == IDYES)
        DestroyWindow();
}
```

The function `OnClose` contains an `if` statement that calls the inherited member function `MessageBox`. The message box displays its querying message along with Yes and No buttons and an information icon. The `OnClose` function compares the result of `MessageBox` with the constant `IDYES`. If the condition is true, the function calls the inherited member function `DestroyWindow`.

Declaring the `OnClose` member function also allows you to rewrite the statement for the `OnRButtonDown` member function. The new version, in lines 41 and 42, has a simple code—one that relies on the `OnClose` function. The `OnRButtonDown` simply sends a `WM_CLOSE` message using the `SendMessage` member function and lets the `OnClose` member function worry about handling that message.

Summary

Today's lesson looks at the basics of creating MFC applications. You learn about the following topics:

- You can create a minimal MFC application that offers the predefined operations and default responses.
- Extending the window operations handles mouse clicks that result in displaying simple message boxes.
- A menu with nested menu structures can be added to illustrate how to use the resource script files to build sophisticated menus.
- There are ways to respond to menu selections that include changing menu structures at run-time.
- You can create multiple instances of an MFC application and give the first instance a different window title and menu structure.
- The `OnClose` member function confirms closing a window.

Today's lesson begins to give you a feel of how MFC models the components of its applications after the employees of a company. The simple interaction provided by each day's programs only scratches the surface of the complex world of Windows and MFC. Tomorrow's lesson focuses more on the window classes and presents applications that place text in the windows.

Q&A

Q What happens if the `Create` member function attempts to load a nonexisting menu resource?

A The runtime system loads the application, whose window may not appear. In addition, the offending application may cause a Windows runtime error.

Q Why are the message-handling member function declarations protected?

A The declarations prohibit the function `CWindowApp::InitInstance` from directly invoking the message-handling function through the pointer `m_pMainWnd`.

Q What are the predefined message response maps?

A The `BEGIN_MESSAGE_MAP` macro may include `ON_WM_XXXX` macros that automatically invoke `OnXxxx` member functions to handle the `WM_XXXX` messages. For example, the `ON_WM_CLOSE` macro maps the `OnClose` function to handle message `WM_CLOSE`.

Q Must the message-mapping macro show the map entries in the same order as declaring the corresponding member functions in the window class?

A No. Such an order is optional.

Workshop

The Workshop provides quiz questions to help you solidify your understanding of the material covered and exercises to provide you with experience in using what you've learned. Try to understand the quiz and exercise answers before continuing on to the next day's lesson. Answers are provided in Appendix B, "Answers."

Quiz

1. True or false? The `ON_WM_CREATE` message map entry associates the function `OnCreate` with the `WM_CREATE` Windows message.
2. True or false? The `ON_WM_ACTIVATE` message map entry associates the function `Onactivate` with the `WM_CREATE` Windows message.
3. True or false? The `ON_COMMAND(CM_CLEAR, OnClear)` message map entry associates the function `OnClear` with the `CM_CLEAR` command Windows message.

4. True or false? In program MENU4.CPP, if I replace line 40 with

```
{ SendMessage(WM_COMMAND, CM_EXIT); }
```

I do not alter the program's interaction.

Exercise

Use App Studio, AppWizard, and ClassWizard to create a program that is similar to MENU1.CPP. Follow the instructions in the Microsoft manuals to use these wizard tools. Notice the difference between the number, size, and contents of the files generated by the wizard tools and the ones in today's lesson.

WEEK 2 IN REVIEW

As you end the second week of learning about programming with Visual C++, let's look at an enhanced version of the number-guessing game. Listing R2.1 shows the source code for the GAME2.CPP program. Although this version interacts with you the same way GAME1.CPP does, it uses a class and an enumerated type.

Listing R2.1. Source code for program GAME2.CPP.

```
#include <stdlib.h>
#include <iostream.h>
#include <time.h>

enum boolean { false, true };

// declare a global random number generating function
int random(int maxVal)
{ return rand() % maxVal; }

class game
{
  protected:
    int n;
    int m;
    int MaxIter;
    int iter;
    boolean ok;
    void prompt();
    void examineInput();

  public:
    game();
    void play();
};

game::game()
{
  MaxIter = 11;
  iter = 0;
  ok = true;

  // reseed random-number generator
  srand((unsigned)time(NULL));
  n = random(1001);
  m = -1;
}

void game::prompt()
{
  cout << "Enter a number between 0 and 1000 : ";
  cin >> m;
  ok = (m < 0) ? false : true;
}

void game::examineInput()
{
  // is the user's guess higher?
  if (m > n)
    cout << "Enter a lower guess\n\n";
  else if (m < n)
    cout << "Enter a higher guess\n\n";
  else
```

```
54:     cout << "You guessed it! Congratulations.";
55: }
56:
57: void game::play()
58: {
59:   // loop to obtain the other guesses
60:   while (m != n && iter < MaxIter && ok) {
61:     prompt();
62:     iter++;
63:     examineInput();
64:   }
65:   // did the user guess the secret number
66:   if (iter >= MaxIter || ok == 0)
67:     cout << "The secret number is " << n << "\n";
68: }
69:
70: main()
71: {
72:   game g;
73:
74:   g.play();
75:   return 0;
76: }
```

Here is a sample session with the program in Listing R2.1:

```
Enter a number between 0 and 1000 : 500
Enter a lower guess

Enter a number between 0 and 1000 : 250
Enter a higher guess

Enter a number between 0 and 1000 : -1
Enter a higher guess

The secret number is 324
```

The program in Listing R2.1 declares the enumerated type `boolean` to model Boolean values. The program also declares the class `game`, which models the number-guessing game. The class has a number of data members, including the Boolean variable `ok`. In addition, the class declares the protected member functions `prompt` and `examineInput`, and the public constructor and member function `play`.

The constructor initializes the data members and reseeds the random-number generator. The member function `prompt`, defined in lines 39 through 44, prompts you for input, obtains your input, and assigns a true/false value to the variable `ok`, based on your input.

The function `examineInput`, defined in lines 46 through 55, compares your guess (stored in the data member `m`) with the secret number (stored in the data member `n`) and displays the appropriate message.

The member function `play`, defined in lines 57 through 68, contains the `while` loop, which plays the game. The loop statements invoke the member functions `prompt` and `examineInput`, and also increment the data member `iter`. In addition, the function contains the `if` statement, which displays the secret number if you fail to guess it or if you quit the game.

The function `main` declares the instance `g` of class `game` and sends the message `play` to that instance.

WEEK 3

AT A GLANCE

15

16

17

18

19

20

21

This last week covers more aspects of creating Windows applications using various classes in the MFC library. You learn how to create scrolling windows. In addition, you learn about using static text controls, edit controls, push buttons, check boxes, radio buttons, group controls, list boxes, scroll bars, combo boxes, dialog boxes, and MDI-compliant windows. These controls make up most of the visual controls that are common to Windows applications. The various chapters in this week include nontrivial applications that illustrate the various features of these controls.

15

Basic Windows

WEEK 3

The most relevant aspect of the Windows environment, as the name suggests, is the use of windows.

NEW TERM Typically, a *window* is a visible part of the screen that contains specific information.

Windows are the placeholders of information. The application is responsible for maintaining that information when you resize, move, or use existing scroll bars. In today's lesson, you learn about the following:

- Creating read-only text windows
- Scrolling through text using scroll bars
- Changing the scroll bar metrics (units, line size, page size, and ranges)
- Optimizing the `OnPaint` member function

Creating a Read-Only Text Window

In Day 14, I present a number of menu-driven MFC applications. However, these programs do not display any information inside their windows. In this section, I present an MFC application which displays read-only text in its windows. The basic notion of the application is similar to that of the read-only on-line help windows.

The purpose of the program is to demonstrate how to display text and maintain that text after one or more of the following has occurred:

- Resizing the window
- Minimizing and then normalizing or maximizing the window
- Moving a modal dialog box over the text area

The main tools to implement the application's features are the member functions `CDC::TextOut` and `CWnd::OnPaint`. The function `TextOut` draws a character string on the specified display. The text appears in the currently selected font and at the specified window coordinates.

Syntax

The *OutText* Function

The declaration for the overloaded member function `OutText` is

```
BOOL TextOut(int X, int Y, char FAR* lpString, int nCount);
BOOL TextOut(int X, int Y, CString& str);
```

The X and Y parameters identify the window location where the first character appears. The lpString parameter points to the string to be displayed in the window. The nCount parameter indicates the leading number of characters of lpString to display. The argument for the last parameter is usually the size of the displayed string argument. In the second version of function TextOut, the str parameter is a reference to a CString instance. The function returns a nonzero value when successful and zero when it fails.

Examples:

```
char s[81] = "Hello";
CString cs = "Bon Jour!";
TextOut(10, 20, s, strlen(s));
TextOut(20, 10, cs);
```

Note: The MFC library offers the class CString, which models string objects. Although the class CString is particular to Visual C++, I encourage you to read about the class in the MFC library reference book that is included in the Visual C++ package.

As expected, the function TextOut displays text once. This means that altering the viewing area of the window or moving another window over the displayed text erases that text. What is needed is a mechanism that updates the display of text in the window. Enter the member function CWnd::OnPaint!. This function enables you to display and maintain the contents of a window (both text and graphics). The versatility of the function Paint comes from the fact that it responds to a WM_PAINT message when the UpdateWindow function is called. This update feature includes the initial creation of the window—after all, it is resized from nothing. Consequently, the versatility of OnPaint includes setting the initial display as well as maintaining it.

Note: You need to declare an OnPaint member function in your window application class. The code you place inside your version of the OnPaint function determines what information appears, remains, and disappears.

In the case of this MFC application, the same information is displayed from start to finish. The general form of the CWnd::OnPaint member function is

```
void _CAppWindow_::OnPaint()
{
```

```
  CPaintDC dc(this);
  // other declarations

  // statements using the TextOut member function
  // e.g.
  //        dc.TextOut(x, y, s, strlen(s));
}
```

The local variable `dc` declares an instance of the `CPaintDC` and is initialized with the argument `this` to point to the application window. This declaration is sufficient to set up the device-context object. The `OnPaint` function can then use `dc.TextOut` function calls as needed. Interestingly, if you come across a C-coded Windows application that uses the `TextOut API` function, you note that a similar text output requires initializing the device-context object and then promptly releasing it once it has finished its task. These steps are automatically performed by the CDC class in an MFC application.

Let's now look at the code for the MFC application. Listing 15.1 shows the WINDOW1.H header file with its single declaration of CM_EXIT. Listing 15.2 contains the script for the resource file WINDOW1.RC. This resource file defines a menu with a single menu item, Exit, to exit the application. Listing 15.3 shows the source code for the WINDOW1.CPP program.

Create the directory WINDOW1 as a subdirectory of \MSVC20\VC21DAY and store all the project's files in the new directory. The project's .MAK file should contain the files WINDOW1.CPP, WINDOW1.RC, and WINDOW1.DEF. The latter file resembles file MINWINAP.DEF in Day 14, Listing 14.2.

Compile and run the application. Notice that the lines of text appear when the window is created. Alter the size of the window by resizing it, minimizing it, and then restoring it back to normal. The lines of text are always visible (or at least a portion of them) as long as the upper left portion of the screen is not obscured by another window. You can also click the left mouse button to display a message box. Drag that message box over the text lines and release the mouse. Then, drag the message box away from the text location. What do you see? The text lines reappear—`OnPaint` is constantly at work.

Type

Listing 15.1. Source code for the WINDOW1.H header file.

```
1: #define CM_EXIT (WM_USER + 100)
```

Type

Listing 15.2. Script for the WINDOW1.RC resource file.

```
#include <afxres.h>
#include "window1.h"

```

```
EXITMENU MENU LOADONCALL MOVEABLE PURE DISCARDABLE
BEGIN
    MENUITEM "E&xit", CM_EXIT
END
```

Type Listing 15.3. Source code for the WINDOW1.CPP program file.

```
#include <afxwin.h>
#include <stdio.h>
#include <string.h>
#include "window1.h"

// Define a window class derived from CFrameWnd
class CAppWindow : public CFrameWnd
{
public:
  CAppWindow()
  { Create(NULL, "A Simple Read-Only Text Window",
           WS_OVERLAPPEDWINDOW, rectDefault, NULL, "EXITMENU"); }

protected:
  // handle the left mouse button click
  afx_msg void OnLButtonDown(UINT nFlags, CPoint point);
  // handle the Exit menu option
  afx_msg void OnExit();
  // handle closing the window
  afx_msg void OnClose();
  // handle painting the window
  afx_msg void OnPaint();

  // message map macro
  DECLARE_MESSAGE_MAP();
};

// Define an application class derived from CWinApp
class CWindowApp : public CWinApp
{
public:
  virtual BOOL InitInstance();

};

void CAppWindow::OnLButtonDown(UINT nFlags, CPoint point)
{
  MessageBox("You clicked the left button!",
             "Mouse Click Event!", MB_OK);
}


void CAppWindow::OnExit()
{ SendMessage(WM_CLOSE); }

void CAppWindow::OnClose()
```

continues

Listing 15.3. continued

```
{
  if (MessageBox("Want to close this application",
                 "Query", MB_YESNO | MB_ICONQUESTION) == IDYES)
    DestroyWindow();
}

void CAppWindow::OnPaint()
{
  const MAX_LINES = 30;
  const LINE_INCR = 20;
  char s[81];
  CPaintDC dc(this);
  BOOL ok = 1;

  for (int i = 0; i < MAX_LINES && ok; i++) {
    sprintf(s, "This is line number %d", i);
    ok = dc.TextOut(0, i * LINE_INCR, s, strlen(s));
  }
}

BEGIN_MESSAGE_MAP(CAppWindow, CFrameWnd)
    ON_WM_LBUTTONDOWN()
    ON_WM_RBUTTONDOWN()
    ON_COMMAND(CM_EXIT, OnExit)
    ON_WM_CLOSE()
    ON_WM_PAINT()
END_MESSAGE_MAP()

// Construct the CWindowApp's m_pMainWnd data member
BOOL CWindowApp::InitInstance()
{
  m_pMainWnd = new CAppWindow();
  m_pMainWnd->ShowWindow(m_nCmdShow);
  m_pMainWnd->UpdateWindow();
  return TRUE;
}

// application's constructor initializes and runs the app
CWindowApp WindowApp;
```

Figure 15.1 shows a sample session with the program WINDOW1.EXE.

Analysis Listing 15.3 shows the source code for the WINDOW1.CPP program file. The part of the program that is relevant to this application is the `CAppWindow` class and its member functions. The window class declares a constructor and three member functions, namely, `OnLButtonDown`, `OnClose`, and `OnPaint`. The constructor creates a window with the title `"A Simple Read-Only Text Window"` that has default size and location, and uses the `EXITMENU` menu resource.

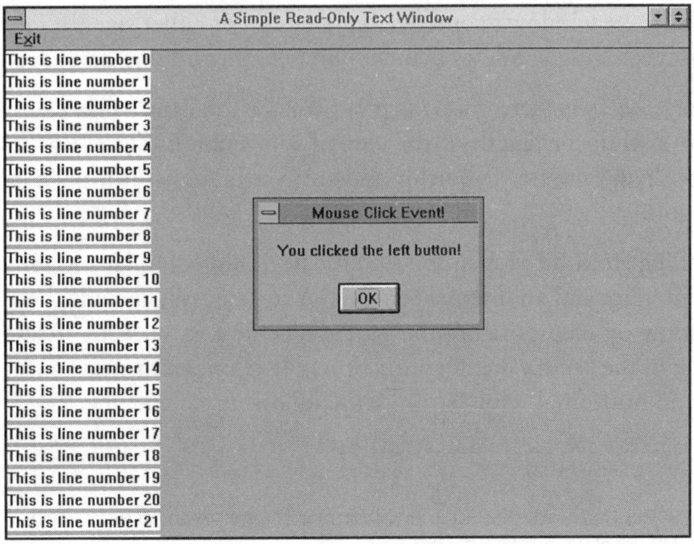

Figure 15.1. *A sample session with the program WINDOW1.EXE.*

The main point of interest is the `OnPaint` function, which is defined in lines 53 through 65. The function declares the two constants `MAX_LINES` and `LINE_INCR`, the string variable `s`, the device-context instance `dc`, and the `BOOL`-typed variable `ok`. The `OnPaint` function displays the lines using the `for` loop in lines 61 through 64. Each loop iteration executes two statements. The first statement, in line 62, calls the `sprintf` function (prototyped in the STDIO.H header file) to create the image of a formatted output and store it in the variable `s`. The statement in line 63 calls the `TextOut` function. Notice the arguments of the `TextOut` function. The first two arguments are `0` (for parameter `X`) and `i * LINE_INCR` (for parameter `Y`). These values result in displaying the text starting with the left margin of the window. The constant `LINE_INCR` represents the total height of a line, taking into account both the height of the displayed characters and the line spacing. The third and fourth arguments are the string variable `s` and its length, `strlen(s)`, respectively.

Scrolling Through Text

One of the versatile features of windows is the ability to scroll information if that information cannot be contained in the current viewing portion of the screen. The scroll bars are the visual components of a window that assist in scrolling through the window's contents. Recall that a window can have a vertical scroll bar, a horizontal scroll bar, or both. A scroll bar has an arrow box at each end and a scroll thumb. The arrow boxes allow you to scroll the window's contents to either end or either side. In today's lesson, you learn about scrolling windows that contain text drawn using device-context objects.

NEW TERM The *scroll thumb* serves two purposes. First, it indicates where you are relative to the entire width or length of the viewed information. Second, when you drag the thumb with the mouse, it quickly moves in or zooms on a portion of the viewed information.

The scrolling effect that I mentioned at the beginning of today's lesson is supported by a visual interface and an internal "engine." You can easily include the visual scroll bars in a window by incorporating the `WS_VSCROLL` and `WS_HSCROLL` styles in the `dwStyle` parameter of the `Create` member function. For example, to create a window with both vertical and horizontal scroll bars, use the following statement:

```
// both vertical and horizontal scroll bars
AStyle = WS_OVERLAPPEDWINDOW ¦ WS_VSCROLL ¦ WS_HSCROLL;
```

The `WS_VSCROLL` and `WS_HSCROLL` constants add the visual aspect of the scroll bars. The functionality is supported by the `OnVScroll`, `OnHScroll`, `OnPaint`, `OnSize`, `SetScrollRange`, `SetScrollPos`, and `ScrollWindow` functions, all inherited from class `CWnd`. Of course, your applications need to override the first four member functions to implement the custom scrolling features.

The `SetScrollRange` member function defines the minimum and maximum range, in device units, for the vertical and horizontal scroll bars. The `SetScrollPos` member function sets the position of the scroll bar. The `ScrollWindow` member function scrolls the contents of a window vertically and/or horizontally. The `OnVScroll` member function responds to the `WM_VSCROLL` message to vertically scroll a scroll bar. The `OnHScroll` member function responds to the `WM_HSCROLL` message to horizontally scroll a scroll bar.

Syntax

The *SetScrollRange* Function

The declaration of the `SetScrollRange` function is

```
void SetScrollRange(int nBar, int nMinPos, int nMaxPos,
                    BOOL bRedraw = TRUE);
```

The `nBar` parameter is a numeric switch that specifies the scroll bar to set. The arguments for the `nBar` parameter can be one of the following predefined values:

- `SB_VERT` to set the range of the vertical scroll bar
- `SB_HORZ` to set the range of the horizontal scroll bar

The nMinPos and nMaxPos parameters define the scroll bar range. If you pass a 0 argument for each of these parameters, you hide the scroll bar. The range of scroll bar values cannot exceed the upper value of the int type, namely, 32767. The Boolean bRedraw parameter indicates whether or not the scroll bar should be redrawn to reflect the new scroll bar range. The default argument value causes the scroll bar to be redrawn. A FALSE value prevents the scroll bar from being redrawn.

Examples:

```
// set range for vertical scroll bar
SetScrollRange(SB_VERT, 0, 250);

// set range for horizontal scroll bar
SetScrollRange(SB_HORZ, 0, 500);
```

Syntax

The *SetScrollPos* Function

The declaration of the SetScrollPos function is

```
int SetScrollPos(int nBar, int nPos, BOOL bRedraw = TRUE);
```

The nBar parameter is a numeric switch that specifies which scroll bar to set. The arguments for the nBar parameter can be one of the following predefined values:

- SB_VERT to set the position of the vertical scroll bar
- SB_HORZ to set the position of the horizontal scroll bar

The nPos parameter specifies the new scroll bar position, which must be within the range of values defined by calling the function SetScrollRange. The Boolean bRedraw parameter indicates whether or not the scroll bar should be redrawn to reflect the new scroll bar range. The default argument value causes the scroll bar to be redrawn. A FALSE value prevents the scroll bar from being redrawn. The SetScrollPos function returns the previous position of the scroll bar.

Example:

```
prevPos = SetScrollPos(SB_VERT, 75);
```

Syntax

The *ScrollWindow* Function

The declaration of the ScrollWindow function is

```
void ScrollWindow(int xAmount, int yAmount,
                  LPRECT lpRect = NULL,
                  LPRECT lpClipRect = NULL);
```

The xAmount indicates the amount of horizontal scrolling. Positive arguments for xAmount scroll the window to the right, and negative arguments scroll it to the left. The yAmount specifies the amount of vertical scrolling. Positive arguments for yAmount scroll the window downward, and negative arguments scroll it upward. The lpRect parameter is a pointer to the CRect or RECT variable that defines the position of the client area to scroll. The default value of NULL causes the entire client area to scroll. The lpClipRect parameter is a pointer to a pointer to a CRect or RECT variable that defines the clipping rectangle to be scrolled. The default value of NULL results in scrolling the entire window. Calling the ScrollWindow function results in generating a WM_PAINT message, which is handled by the OnPaint member function. You must define the OnPaint member function in your MFC application.

Example:

```
ScrollWindow(nDeltaX, nDeltaY);
```

Syntax

The *OnVScroll* Function

The declaration of the OnVScroll function is

```
void OnVScroll(UINT nSBCode, UINT nPos, CWnd* pScrollBar);
```

The nSBCode is an integer code that specifies the vertical scrolling request. Table 15.1 shows the predefined constants for the various scrolling requests. The nPos parameter specifies the position of the thumb box when the argument for nSBCode is either SB_THUMBPOSITION or SB_THUMBTRACK. The pScrollBar parameter is a pointer to the control that has sent the WM_VSCROLL message.

Example:

```
OnVScroll(SB_LINEDOWN, 23, NULL);
```

Table 15.1. Predefined constants for vertical scrolling requests.

Value	Meaning
SB_BOTTOM	Scroll to the bottom
SB_ENDSCROLL	End scroll
SB_LINEDOWN	Scroll one line down
SB_LINEUP	Scroll one line up
SB_PAGEDOWN	Scroll one page down

Value	Meaning
SB_PAGEUP	Scroll one page up
SB_THUMBPOSITION	Scroll to the nPos position
SB_THUMBTRACK	Drag the scroll thumb box to the nPos position
SB_TOP	Scroll to the top

Syntax

The *OnHScroll* Function

The declaration of the OnHScroll function is

```
void OnHScroll(UINT nSBCode, UINT nPos, CWnd* pScrollBar);
```

The nSBCode is an integer code that specifies the horizontal scrolling request. Table 15.2 shows the predefined constants for the various scrolling requests. The nPos parameter specifies the position of the thumb box when the argument for nSBCode is SB_THUMBPOSITION. The pScrollBar parameter is a pointer to the control that has sent the WM_HSCROLL message.

Example:

```
OnHScroll(SB_LINEDOWN, 14, NULL);
```

Table 15.2. Predefined constants for horizontal scrolling requests.

Value	Meaning
SB_LEFT	Scroll to the left end
SB_ENDSCROLL	End scroll
SB_LINELEFT	Scroll one line to the left
SB_LINERIGHT	Scroll one line to the right
SB_PAGELEFT	Scroll one page left
SB_PAGERIGHT	Scroll one page right
SB_THUMBPOSITION	Scroll to the nPos position
SB_THUMBTRACK	Drag the scroll thumb box to the nPos position
SB_RIGHT	Scroll to the right end

The `OnSize` member function responds to the `WM_SIZE` message sent when a window is resized. The `OnSize` function has the task of updating the scrolling parameter (or metrics).

Syntax

The *OnSize* Function

The declaration of the `OnSize` function is

```
void OnSize(UINT nType, int nCx, int nCy);
```

The `nType` parameter indicates the type of resizing request. Table 15.3 shows the predefined values for the various sizing requests. The `nCx` and `nCy` parameters specify the new width and height of the client area.

Example:

```
OnSize(SIZEFULLSCREEN, 13, 55);
```

Table 15.3. Predefined values for sizing requests.

Value	Meaning
`SIZE_MAXIMIZED`	Window is maximized
`SIZE_MINIMIZED`	Window is minimized
`SIZE_RESTORED`	Window is normal
`SIZE_MAXHIDE`	Message is sent to pop-up windows when another window is maximized
`SIZE_MAXSHOW`	Message is sent to pop-up windows when another window is restored to its prior size

The parameterless `OnPaint` member function responds to the `WM_PAINT` message that requests the repainting of the window client area. The `OnPaint` function is responsible for displaying the updated contents of the window.

A Scrolling Window

This section presents a program that defines general scrollable windows. WINDOW2.EXE has two main menu items, Exit and Char Sets. The second menu item is a pop-up menu that has three selections: Set 1, Set 2, and Set 3. These options produce text lines that have a different line spacing and different maximum number of lines. The text fonts are the same for all three sets. Initially, the client area of the application window is clear. Therefore, you must select one of the three character sets. The application also supports the cursor movement keys to scroll the text. The Home and End keys scroll vertically to the top and bottom, respectively. The PageUp and PageDown keys scroll one page up or down, respectively. The up and down arrow keys scroll one line up or down, respectively. The left and right arrow keys scroll horizontally one page left and right, respectively.

This program illustrates two main aspects of scrolling windows:

1. Declaring a scrolling window class with additional member functions that manage the assignment, access, and use of scrolling-related data.
2. Using assigned values to control vertical scrolling, and relying on the current window metrics to control the horizontal scrolling.

Let's look at the code for the general text-scroller window application. Listings 15.4 and 15.5 show the header file WINDOW2.H and the resource file WINDOW2.RC, respectively. Listing 15.6 contains the source code for the WINDOW2.CPP program.

Create the directory WINDOW2 as a subdirectory of \MSVC20\VC21DAY and store all the project's files in the new directory. The project's .MAK file should contain the files WINDOW2.CPP, WINDOW2.RC, and WINDOW2.DEF. The latter file resembles file MINWINAP.DEF in Day 14, Listing 14.2.

Type **Listing 15.4. Source code for the WINDOW2.H header file.**

```
#define CM_EXIT (WM_USER + 100)
#define CM_SET1 (WM_USER + 101)
#define CM_SET2 (WM_USER + 102)
#define CM_SET3 (WM_USER + 103)
```

Type **Listing 15.5. Script for the resource file WINDOW2.RC.**

```
#include <afxres.h>
#include "window2.h"

MAINMENU MENU LOADONCALL MOVEABLE PURE DISCARDABLE
BEGIN
    MENUITEM "E&xit", CM_EXIT
    POPUP "&Char Sets"
    BEGIN
      MENUITEM "Set &1", CM_SET1
      MENUITEM "Set &2", CM_SET2
```

continues

Listing 15.5. continued

```
        MENUITEM "Set &3", CM_SET3
    END
END
```

Listing 15.6. Source code for the WINDOW2.CPP program file.

```
#include <afxwin.h>
#include <stdio.h>
#include <stdlib.h>
#include <string.h>
#include "window2.h"

// declare the initial arguments for the window class constructor
const DefYMax = 100;
const DefXLine = 1;
const DefYLine = 1;
const DefXPage = 5;

// Define a window class derived from CFrameWnd
class CAppWindow : public CFrameWnd
{
public:
    CAppWindow();

protected:
    // declare data members to store character and page metrics
    int nCharWidth;
    int nCharHeight;
    int nXLine;
    int nYLine;
    int nXPage;
    int nYPage;
    int nVScrollMax;
    int nHScrollMax;
    int nVScrollPos;
    int nHScrollPos;
    int nxClient;
    int nyClient;
    BOOL bNoPaint;
    BOOL bNoInitPaint;

    // handle vertical scrolling
    afx_msg void OnVScroll(UINT nSBCode, UINT nPos,
                           CScrollBar* pScrollBar);
    // handle horizontal scrolling
    afx_msg void OnHScroll(UINT nSBCode, UINT nPos,
                           CScrollBar* pScrollBar);
    // handle pressing keys
    afx_msg void OnKeyDown(UINT nChar, UINT nRepCnt, UINT Flags);
    // handle selecting character set # 1
    afx_msg void OnSet1();
    // handle selecting character set # 2
```

```
     afx_msg void OnSet2();
     // handle selecting character set # 3
     afx_msg void OnSet3();
     // handle the Exit menu option
     afx_msg void OnExit();
     // member functions to set the scroll parameters
     void SetCharHeight(int nCharHeightVal);
     void SetLineSize(int nXLineVal, int nYLineVal);
     void SetVScrollMax(int nVScrollMaxVal);
     void SetPageSize(int nXPageVal);
     // member functions to get the scroll parameters
     void GetCharHeight(int& nCharWidth, int& nCharHeightVal);
     void GetLineSize(int& nXLineVal, int& nYLineVal);
     void GetScrollMaxSize(int& nHScrollMaxVal,
                           int& nVScrollMaxVal);
     void GetPageSize(int& nXPageVal, int& nYPageVal);
     // handle closing the window
     afx_msg void OnClose();
     // handle resizing the window
     afx_msg void OnSize(UINT nTypes, int nCx, int nCy);
     // handle painting the window
     afx_msg void OnPaint();

private:
    void makeSet(int nX, int nY);
    int GetVScrollPos(int nVpos)
    { return int(long(nVpos) * long(nyClient) / nVScrollMax);}

    // message map macro
    DECLARE_MESSAGE_MAP();
};

// Define an application class derived from CWinApp
class CWindowApp : public CWinApp
{
public:
     virtual BOOL InitInstance();
};

CAppWindow::CAppWindow()
{
  DWORD AttrStyle = WS_OVERLAPPEDWINDOW ¦ WS_VSCROLL
                    ¦ WS_HSCROLL;
  UINT ClassStyle = CS_VREDRAW ¦ CS_HREDRAW;
  const char FAR* lpszClassName;
  HBRUSH hColor = (HBRUSH)(COLOR_HIGHLIGHTTEXT + 1);

  // disable initial painting
  bNoInitPaint = TRUE;
  // get the registration class name
  lpszClassName = AfxRegisterWndClass(ClassStyle, NULL, hColor,
                                      NULL);
  // create the window
   Create(lpszClassName, "A General Text Scroller Window",
          AttrStyle, rectDefault, NULL, "MAINMENU");
   // set the vertical and horizontal line heights
   SetLineSize(DefXLine, DefYLine);
```

Listing 15.6. continued

```
}

void CAppWindow::OnVScroll(UINT nSBCode, UINT nPos,
                           CScrollBar* pScrollBar)
{
  short nScrollInc;
  int nNewPos;

  switch (nSBCode) {
    case SB_TOP: // move to the top
     nScrollInc = -nVScrollPos;
     break;
    case SB_BOTTOM: // move to the bottom
      nScrollInc = nVScrollMax - nVScrollPos;
     break;
    case SB_LINEUP: // move one line up
        nScrollInc = -nYLine;
     break;
    case SB_LINEDOWN: // move one line down
        nScrollInc = nYLine;
     break;
    case SB_PAGEUP: // move one page up
        nScrollInc = -nYPage;
     break;
    case SB_PAGEDOWN: // move one page down
        nScrollInc = nYPage;
     break;
    case SB_THUMBPOSITION: // track the thumb box
     nScrollInc = nPos - nVScrollPos;
     break;
    default:
     nScrollInc = 0;
  }
  // calculate new vertical thumb position so that:
  //      0 <= nNewPos <= nVScrollMax
  nNewPos = max(0, min(nVScrollPos + nScrollInc, nVScrollMax));
  // adjust scroll increment
  nScrollInc = nNewPos - nVScrollPos;
  // is nScrollInc not zero?
  if (nScrollInc) {
    nVScrollPos = nNewPos; // update vertical thumb position
    // scroll the window
    ScrollWindow(0, -nScrollInc * nCharHeight);
    // move the thumb box
    SetScrollPos(SB_VERT, GetVScrollPos(nVScrollPos));
    // repaint the window
    UpdateWindow();
  }
}

void CAppWindow::OnHScroll(UINT nSBCode, UINT nPos,
                           CScrollBar* pScrollBar)
{
  short nScrollInc;
```

```
  int nNewPos;

  switch (nSBCode) {
    case SB_LINELEFT: // move to the left by one character
        nScrollInc = -nXLine;
     break;
    case SB_LINERIGHT: // move to the right by one character
        nScrollInc = nXLine;
     break;
    case SB_PAGELEFT: // move to the left
        nScrollInc = -nXPage;
     break;
    case SB_PAGERIGHT: // move to the right
        nScrollInc = nXPage;
     break;
    case SB_THUMBPOSITION: // track the thumb box
     nScrollInc = nPos - nHScrollPos;
     break;
    default:
     nScrollInc = 0;
  }
  // calculate new horizontal thumb position so that:
  //      0 <= nNewPos <= nHScrollMax
  nNewPos = max(0, min(nHScrollPos + nScrollInc, nHScrollMax));
  // adjust scroll increment
  nScrollInc = nNewPos - nHScrollPos;
  // is nScrollInc not zero?
  if (nScrollInc) {
    nHScrollPos = nNewPos; // update thumb position
    // scroll window
    ScrollWindow(-nScrollInc * nCharWidth, 0);
    // set the thumb box position
    SetScrollPos(SB_HORZ, nHScrollPos * nCharWidth);
    // repaint the window
    UpdateWindow();
  }
}

void CAppWindow::OnKeyDown(UINT nChar, UINT nRepCnt, UINT Flags)
{
  switch(nChar) {
    case VK_HOME:
       OnVScroll(SB_TOP, 0, NULL);
       break;
    case VK_END:
       OnVScroll(SB_BOTTOM, 0, NULL);
       break;
    case VK_PRIOR:
       OnVScroll(SB_PAGEUP, 0, NULL);
       break;
    case VK_NEXT:
       OnVScroll(SB_PAGEDOWN, 0, NULL);
       break;
    case VK_UP:
       OnVScroll(SB_LINEUP, 0, NULL);
       break;
```

continues

Listing 15.6. continued

```
      case VK_DOWN:
         OnVScroll(SB_LINEDOWN, 0, NULL);
         break;
      case VK_LEFT:
         OnHScroll(SB_PAGEUP, 0, NULL);
         break;
      case VK_RIGHT:
         OnHScroll(SB_PAGEDOWN, 0, NULL);
         break;
   }
}

void CAppWindow::OnSet1()
{ makeSet(0, DefYMax); }

void CAppWindow::OnSet2()
{ makeSet(-5, 2 * DefYMax); }

void CAppWindow::OnSet3()
{ makeSet(-10, DefYMax / 2); }

void CAppWindow::makeSet(int nX, int nY)
{
  // enable painting
  bNoInitPaint = FALSE;
  // set default character height
  SetCharHeight(nX);
  // set maximum vertical scrolling range
  SetVScrollMax(nY);
  // set the page size
  SetPageSize(DefXPage);
  // clear the window client area
  InvalidateRect(NULL, TRUE);
}

void CAppWindow::OnExit()
{ SendMessage(WM_CLOSE); }

void CAppWindow::SetCharHeight(int nCharHeightVal)
{
  TEXTMETRIC tm;
  CRect r;
  CDC* dc = GetDC();

  // get the text metrics
  dc->GetTextMetrics(&tm);
  ReleaseDC(dc);
  // get the client area coordinates
  GetWindowRect(&r);
  nxClient = r.right - r.left;
  nyClient = r.bottom - r.top;
  // obtain the character height
  if (nCharHeightVal == 0)
    nCharHeight = tm.tmHeight + tm.tmExternalLeading;
```

```
  else if (nCharHeightVal > 0)
    nCharHeight = nCharHeightVal;
  else
    nCharHeight = tm.tmHeight + tm.tmExternalLeading -
                      nCharHeightVal;
  // set the range of the vertical scroll bar
  SetScrollRange(SB_VERT, 0, nyClient, TRUE);
  // get the character width
  nCharWidth =  tm.tmAveCharWidth;
  // set the range of the horizontal scroll bar
  SetScrollRange(SB_HORZ, 0, nxClient, TRUE);
}

void CAppWindow::SetLineSize(int nXLineVal, int nYLineVal)
{
  // set the vertical and horizontal line heights
  nXLine = nXLineVal;
  nYLine = nYLineVal;
}

void CAppWindow::SetVScrollMax(int nVScrollMaxVal)
{
  // set the vertical and horizontal limits
  nVScrollMax = nVScrollMaxVal;
  // set the initial line position
  nVScrollPos = 0;
  // set the position of the vertical scroll bar
  SetScrollPos(SB_VERT, 0, TRUE);
  // calculate the maximum number of characters
  nHScrollMax = nxClient / nCharWidth;
  // set the initial column position
  nHScrollPos = 0;
  // set the position of the horizontal scroll bar
  SetScrollPos(SB_HORZ, 0, TRUE);
  UpdateWindow();
}

void CAppWindow::SetPageSize(int nXPageVal)
{
  // set the vertical and horizontal page up/down sizes
  nXPage = nXPageVal;
  nYPage = nyClient / nCharHeight;
}

void CAppWindow::GetCharHeight(int& nCharHeightVal,
                          int& nCharWidthVal)
{
  nCharHeightVal = nCharHeight;
  nCharWidthVal = nCharWidth;
}

void CAppWindow::GetLineSize(int& nXLineVal, int& nYLineVal)
{
  nXLineVal = nXLine;
  nYLineVal = nYLine;
}

```

continues

Listing 15.6. continued

```
void CAppWindow::GetScrollMaxSize(int& nHScrollMaxVal,
                                  int& nVScrollMaxVal)
{
  nHScrollMaxVal = nHScrollMax;
  nVScrollMaxVal = nVScrollMax;
}

void CAppWindow::GetPageSize(int& nXPageVal, int& nYPageVal)
{
  nXPageVal = nXPage;
  nYPageVal = nYPage;
}

void CAppWindow::OnClose()
{
  if (MessageBox("Want to close this application",
      "Query", MB_YESNO ¦ MB_ICONQUESTION) == IDYES)
    DestroyWindow();
}

void CAppWindow::OnSize(UINT nTypes, int nCx, int nCy)
{
   // disable painting?
  bNoPaint = nTypes == SIZEICONIC ¦¦ nTypes == SIZEZOOMHIDE;
  // exit if painting is disabled
  if (bNoPaint ¦¦ bNoInitPaint) return;

  // update the client area
  nxClient = nCx;
  nyClient = nCy;
  // update the vertical page size
  nYPage = nyClient / nCharHeight;
  // set the new vertical scroll bar range
  SetScrollRange(SB_VERT, 0, nyClient,  FALSE);
  // set the new vertical thumb box position
  SetScrollPos(SB_VERT, GetVScrollPos(nVScrollPos), TRUE);
  // calculate the new maximum width
  nHScrollMax = max(1, nxClient / nCharWidth);
  //  set the new horizontal scroll bar range
  nHScrollPos = min(nHScrollPos, nHScrollMax);
  // set the new horizontal scroll bar range
  SetScrollRange(SB_HORZ, 0, nxClient, FALSE);
  // set the new horizontal thumb box position
  SetScrollPos(SB_HORZ,  nHScrollPos * nCharWidth, TRUE);
  // clear and repaint the window
  Invalidate(TRUE);
}

void CAppWindow::OnPaint()
{
  CPaintDC dc(this);
  char aStr[80];
  char* pStr;

```

```
379:   // exit if OnPaint is disabled
380:   if (bNoPaint || bNoInitPaint) return;
381:
382:   // draw lines of text
383:   for (int i = 0, j = i + nVScrollPos;
384:        i < nYPage && j < nVScrollMax;
385:        i++, j++) {
386:     sprintf(aStr, "This is line number %d   ", j+1);
387:     // is the line visible?
388:     if (nHScrollPos < (int)(strlen(aStr))) {
389:       pStr = aStr + nHScrollPos;
390:       dc.TextOut(0, i * nCharHeight, pStr, strlen(pStr));
391:     }
392:   }
393: }
394:
395: BEGIN_MESSAGE_MAP(CAppWindow, CFrameWnd)
396:     ON_WM_VSCROLL()
397:     ON_WM_HSCROLL()
398:     ON_WM_KEYDOWN()
399:     ON_COMMAND(CM_SET1, OnSet1)
400:     ON_COMMAND(CM_SET2, OnSet2)
401:     ON_COMMAND(CM_SET3, OnSet3)
402:     ON_COMMAND(CM_EXIT, OnExit)
403:     ON_WM_CLOSE()
404:     ON_WM_SIZE()
405:     ON_WM_PAINT()
406: END_MESSAGE_MAP()
407:
408: // Construct the CWindowApp's m_pMainWnd data member
409: BOOL CWindowApp::InitInstance()
410: {
411:   m_pMainWnd = new CAppWindow();
412:   m_pMainWnd->ShowWindow(m_nCmdShow);
413:   m_pMainWnd->UpdateWindow();
414:   return TRUE;
415: }
416:
417: // application's constructor initializes and runs the app
418: CWindowApp WindowApp;
```

Figure 15.2 shows a sample session with the program WINDOW2.EXE.

Analysis The program in Listing 15.6 declares a set of global constants that serve as default (or initial) values to some of the character and page metrics. The program declares two classes: an application class and a window class. The latter is by far the most relevant one.

The `CAppWindow` window class declares a number of data members and member functions (public, protected, and private). The data members, which appear in lines 20 through 34, manage the display of text and can be divided into the following subgroups:

- The `nCharHeight` and `nCharWidth` members store the character height and width, respectively. Basically, these members obtain their data from the

Windows text metrics. However, the program is coded to include additional line spacing to the `nCharHeight` data member. Consequently, the window class allows you to influence the character height.

- The `nXLine` and `nYLine` members store the number of characters and lines used in horizontal and vertical line scrolling, respectively. Each of these data members is assigned 1, the typical value.
- The `nXPage` and `nYPage` members store the number of characters and lines used in horizontal and vertical page scrolling, respectively. The `nXPage` member is assigned a value, and the `nYPage` member obtains its value by dividing the client window height by the character height. Consequently, the vertical page size depends on the size of the window, the character height, and the character spacing.
- The `nVScrollMax` and `nHScrollmax` members store the vertical and horizontal maximum scroll bar ranges, respectively. The member `nVScrollMax` is assigned a value. By contrast, the `nHScrollMax` has its value calculated as the ratio between the client window width and the character width.
- The `nVScrollPos` and `nHScrollPos` members store the vertical and horizontal scroll bar positions, respectively. The values stored in these members change with scrolling their respective bars.
- The `nCxClient` and `nCyClient` members store the width and height of the client area, respectively. The values of these members are updated by the `OnSize` member function.
- The Boolean `bNoPaint` member is used as a flag to prevent repainting the window when the window is either minimized or hidden by another window that is maximized.
- The Boolean `bNoInitPaint` member disables painting before you select any character from the Char Sets menu.

The class constructor, which appears in lines 86 through 104, performs the following tasks that initialize and build the application's window:

- Declares a number of initialized variables that assist in the window class (read as category) registration process
- Assigns the value `TRUE` to the Boolean data member `bNoInitPaint`, initially disabling painting

- Obtains the registration class (read as category) name by calling the global function `AfxRegisterWndClass`, enabling you to fine-tune the creation of a window
- Creates a window instance
- Sets the line sizes by calling the `SetLineSize` member function

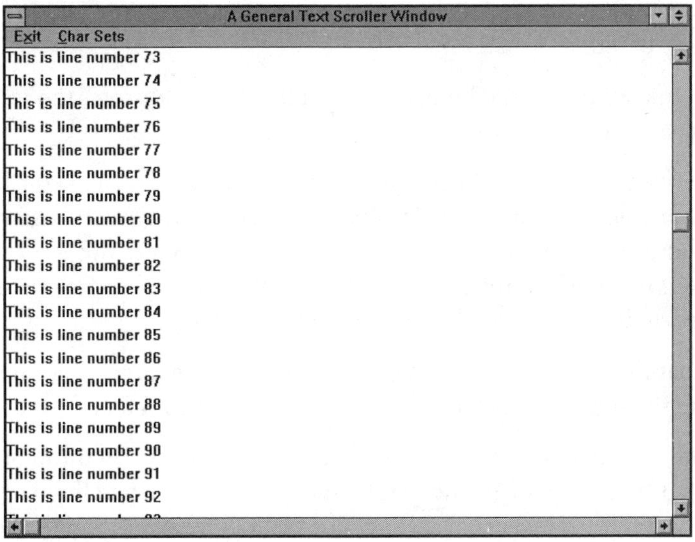

Figure 15.2. *A sample session with the program WINDOW2.EXE.*

Note: The CAppWindow class declares the private inline member function `GetVScrollPos`. This function, which appears in lines 72 and 73, converts the number of the first line displayed into device units. This function is important in correctly positioning the scroll bar thumb box. Keep in mind that the text drawn in the window and the vertical thumb box do not scroll by the same number of device units.

The member function `OnVScroll`, which is defined in lines 106 through 152, responds to the `WM_VSCROLL` message and moves the vertical scroll bar. The function declares two local variables, `nScrollInc` and `nNewPos`. The `nScrollInc` variable stores the number of lines to scroll, and the nNewPos stores the anticipated new scroll bar position. The OnVScroll function carries out the following tasks:

- Uses a switch statement to determine the kind of vertical scroll request (notice that the line and page scroll requests now use the nYLine and nYPage data members rather than literal constants)
- Calculates the anticipated new scroll bar position, using the min and max functions (declared in stdlib.h) to ensure that the new position lies in the range of 0 to nVScrollMax
- Calculates the adjusted number of scrolled lines and stores the result in nScrollInc
- Vertically scrolls the window if the adjusted value of nScrollInc is not zero (the if statement assigns the new value for nVScrollPos, vertically scrolls the window by calling the ScrollWindow function, updates the vertical scroll bar position by calling the SetScrollPos and GetVScrollPos functions, and repaints the window by calling the UpdateWindow function)

Notice that the window is vertically scrolled by (-nScrollInc * nCharHeight) device units, and the vertical scroll bar is moved to the position GetVScrollPos(nVScrollPos).

The member function OnHScroll, which is defined in lines 154 through 194, responds to the WM_HSCROLL message and scrolls the window horizontally. The code for this function is similar to that of OnVScroll. The main difference is that the horizontal scroll bar is moved to the (nHScrollPos * nCharWidth) position. This value is calculated using an expression that is quite different from that in function OnVScroll.

The member function OnKeyDown, which is defined in lines 196 through 224, handles the WM_KEYDOWN message to determine if and how to respond to keyboard input. The function uses a switch statement to handle the Home, End, PageUp, PageDown, up arrow, down arrow, left arrow, and right arrow keys. The statements in the various case labels invoke either function OnVScroll or function OnHScroll. These calls use the predefined SB_xxxx constants to determine the kind of scroll requests. All the calls supply 0 and NULL to the nPos and pScrollBar parameters of functions OnVScroll and OnHScroll.

The window class declares three similar member functions, OnSet1, OnSet2, and OnSet3, to load different sets of lines. These functions, which are defined in lines 226 through 233, in turn, call member function makeSet, with different arguments, to perform the required tasks. The makeSet function, which is defined in lines 235 through 247, performs the following tasks:

- Enables painting by assigning FALSE to bNoInitPaint

- Sets the character height
- Sets the maximum limit for the vertical scroll bar
- Sets the horizontal page size, using the same arguments for all three `OnSetx` functions
- Clears the window and requests repainting the client window area

The member function `SetCharHeight`, which is defined in lines 252 through 279, sets the character height and updates the character width. The function has one parameter, `nCharHeightVal`, because you are allowed to set or influence only the character height. The character width is computed based on current text metrics. The function carries out the following tasks:

- Obtains the text metrics by calling the `GetTextMetrics` function and passing the reference argument `tm`, which obtains the current text metrics
- Obtains the window width and height and stores them in the `nCxClient` and `nCyClient` members, respectively
- Obtains the character height
- Sets the vertical scroll bar range as 0 to `nCyClient`
- Calculates the character width using the related data given by the `tm` structure
- Sets the horizontal scroll bar range as 0 to `nCxClient`

There are three possibilities when `SetCharHeight` obtains the character height. If the argument for `nCharHeightVal` is zero, the function calculates the value for `nCharHeight` using only the text metrics data obtained by the local structure `tm`. If the argument for `nCharHeightVal` is positive, the function simply assigns `nCharHeightVal` to member `nCharHeight`. If the argument for `nCharHeightVal` is negative, the function adds that argument value to the height of the character obtained by the `tm` structure. In other words, negative arguments for `nCharHeightVal` are interpreted as additional line spacing, in device units.

Warning: Be careful if you experiment with the program! If the argument for `nCharHeightVal` is positive, the function assigns `nCharHeightVal` to member `nCharHeight`.

The member function `SetLineSize`, which is defined in lines 281 through 286, sets the sizes of the vertical and horizontal lines. The values passed to the function's parameters are assigned to their corresponding data members.

The member function `SetVScrollMax`, which is defined in lines 288 through 303, sets the maximum range for the vertical and horizontal scroll bars and resets these scroll bars to the 0 position. The function has one parameter, `nVScrollMaxVal`, indicating that the caller can assign a new value only to data member `nVScrollMax`. The function carries out the following tasks:

- Assigns the argument of the `nVScrollMaxVal` to the `nVScrollMax` data member
- Assigns 0 to the data member `nVScrollPos`
- Scrolls the vertical scroll bar to the position 0
- Calculates the maximum range for the horizontal scroll bar and stores the result in member `nHScrollMax`
- Assigns 0 to the data member `nHScrollPos`
- Scrolls the horizontal scroll bar to the position 0

The member function `SetPageSize`, which is defined in lines 305 through 310, sets the size of the vertical and horizontal page sizes. The function has one parameter, `nXPageVal`, indicating that a caller can assign a value only to the `nXPage` data member. The new value for the `nYPage` member is calculated as the ratio between the client window height and the character height (including any additional spacing).

The window class declares the member functions `GetCharHeight`, `GetLineSize`, `GetScrollMax`, and `GetPageSize` in lines 312 through 336. These functions use reference parameters to return the various queried data members. Although the program does not use these functions, I have included them for the sake of the example—your own scrolling windows may well need such functions.

The member function `OnSize`, which is defined in lines 345 through 371, handles the `WM_SIZE` request and updates the scroll bar ranges and positions. The `OnSize` function performs the following tasks:

- Verifies that the window can be painted, using the `bNoPaint` member to store the no-paint state (the function exits if either the `bNoPaint` or `bNoInitPaint` data member is `TRUE`)
- Assigns the width and height of the resized client area (passed by the arguments of parameters `nCx` and `nCy`) to the data members `nCxClient` and `nCyClient`, respectively

- Updates the value of vertical page size, stored in `nYPage` (the new value is calculated as the ratio between the client window height and the character height)
- Sets the new vertical scroll bar range as 0 to `nCyClient`
- Sets the new vertical scroll bar position by calling the `SetScrollPos` function, using the `GetVScrollPos` member function to convert vertical lines into device units
- Sets the new vertical scroll bar position by calling the `SetScrollPos` function
- Calculates the new maximum width as the greater value of 1 and the ratio between the client area width and the character width
- Sets the new horizontal scroll bar position member, `nHScrollPos`, as the least of the old position and the maximum number of characters
- Sets the new horizontal scroll bar range as 0 to `nCxClient` by calling the `SetScrollPos` function
- Sets the new horizontal scroll bar position by calling the `SetScrollPos` function
- Clears and repaints the client area by calling the `Invalidate` function

The member function `OnPaint`, which is defined in lines 373 through 393, responds to the `WM_PAINT` message requesting to repaint the window. The code for function `OnPaint` is simple, short, and needs no statements that obtain the current number of visible lines. That information is readily available from the `nYPage` data member. Notice that the loop termination condition uses the data member `nVScrollMax`.

Summary

Today's lesson discusses the mechanics of creating windows which show fixed and scrollable text, and includes the following topics:

- Read-only text windows that display information are the basis of help screens.
- You can write text in a window using the versatile `CDC::TextOut` member function.
- Scrollable windows can be created with vertical and horizontal scroll bars. These windows scroll using either the mouse or the cursor control keys. The classes of scrollable windows use the member functions `OnVScroll`, `OnHScroll`, `OnPaint`, and `OnSize`, as well as other functions to manage the text metrics.

Q&A

Q Does the MFC library have a scrollable window class?

A Yes, the MFC library has the `CScrollView` class, which implements a scrollable view—a child window that can scroll its contents.

Q Is the member function `OnPaint` needed to maintain windows with visual controls like command buttons?

A No. You need only to write the function `OnPaint` to maintain windows that draw text and graphics. In the case of windows with controls, you need not declare your own version of function `OnPaint`.

Workshop

The Workshop provides quiz questions to help you solidify your understanding of the material covered and exercises to provide you with experience in using what you've learned. Try to understand the quiz and exercise answers before continuing on to the next day's lesson. Answers are provided in Appendix B, "Answers."

Quiz

1. True or false? The member function `OnPaint` redraws the window only when needed.
2. True or false? The inherited `CWnd::OnVScroll` and `CWnd::OnHScroll` member functions offer default scrolling features.
3. True or false? If you declare the `OnPaint` member function in your window class, you must also declare the `OnSize` member function.
4. True or false? Omitting the `OnKeyDown` member function in program WINDOW2.CPP disables the vertical scrolling feature altogether.

Exercise

Experiment with modifying the WINDOW2.CPP program by altering the arguments of the member functions `OnSet1`, `OnSet2`, and `OnSet3`. In addition, you can experiment with adding more OnSetx menu selections and the corresponding member functions.

16

MFC Controls

WEEK 3

Interacting with Windows applications often involves dialog boxes that contain various types of controls, such as the list box, the edit control (also called edit box), and the pushbutton. These controls can be included in windows or, more frequently, in dialog boxes. Today's lesson and the next three look at the controls as they appear in windows and focus on the basic properties of these controls. Day 20 presents dialog boxes and views how the controls work with these boxes. Today, you learn about the following topics:

- Static text control
- Edit control
- Pushbutton control

Understanding the various controls and mastering how they behave and interact enables you to implement highly interactive Windows applications. Today's lesson and the two that follow discuss the constructors and relevant member functions for the control classes.

The Static Text Control

The static text control provides a window or a dialog box with static text. The `CStatic` class implements the static text control. Let's look at the class constructor and members.

NEW TERM

Static text is text that the application user cannot easily and readily change. Static text does not necessarily mean text etched in stone! In fact, static text controls allow your MFC applications to alter the text at will. You can still specify that the text be permanent and unchangeable. The choice is ultimately yours.

The `CStatic` class, a descendant of `CWnd`, offers static text that is defined by a display area, text to display, and text attributes. Of these three components, you can alter only the displayed text during run-time.

Syntax

The *Create* Function

The declaration of the `Create` member function is

```
BOOL Create(LPCSTR lpText,             // control text
         DWORD dwStyle,           // control style
         const RECT& rect,        // control area
         CWnd* pParentWnd,        // parent window
         UINT nID = 0xffff);      // control ID
```

The `lpText` parameter specifies the text for the static text control. The `dwStyle` parameter designates the control style. The arguments for style typically include the `WS_CHILD` and

WS_VISIBLE styles. Table 16.1 shows the set of SS_xxxx static text styles. The creation of static text control includes one or more of these styles. The rect parameter specifies the rectangular area occupied by the control. The pParentWnd parameter is the pointer to the parent window. The nID parameter specifies the control's ID. The Create function assigns a default parameter of 0xffff, because a static text control typically does not send notification messages to its parent window. The Create function returns TRUE if it succeeds and yields FALSE if it fails.

Example:

```
CStatic* pText;
// create control...

pText->Create("Operand 1", SS_SIMPLE, r, NULL);
```

Table 16.1. Values for static text styles.

Value	Meaning
SS_BLACKFRAME	Designates a box with a frame drawn with the color matching that of the window frame (black in the default Windows color scheme)
SS_BLACKRECT	Specifies a rectangle filled with the color matching that of the window frame (black in the default Windows color scheme)
SS_CENTER	Centers the static text characters; text is wrappable
SS_GRAYFRAME	Specifies a box with a frame that has the same color as the screen background (gray in the default Windows color scheme)
SS_GRAYRECT	Selects a rectangle filled with the same color as the screen background (gray in the default Windows color scheme)
SS_LEFT	Indicates left-justified text; text is wrappable
SS_LEFTNOWORDWRAP	Indicates left-justified text that cannot be wrapped

continues

Table 16.1. continued

Value	Meaning
`SS_NOPREFIX`	Specifies that the ampersand character (`&`) in the static text string should not be a hotkey designator character, but rather part of the static text character
`SS_RIGHT`	Selects right-justified text that is wrappable
`SS_SIMPLE`	Indicates that the static text characters cannot be altered at run-time and that the static text is displayed on a single line with line breaks ignored
`SS_GRAYFRAME`	Specifies a box with a frame that has the same color as the window background (white in the default Windows color scheme)
`SS_GRAYRECT`	Selects a rectangle filled with the same color as the window background (white in the default Windows color scheme)

The string accessed by the `lpText` pointer in the `Create` function may include the ampersand (`&`) to visually specify a hotkey—to actually support the hotkey your application needs to load accelerator keys. The hotkey character appears as an underlined character. The ampersand should be placed before the hotkey character. If the string contains multiple ampersand characters, only the last occurrence is effective. The other occurrences of the ampersand are not displayed and are ignored. To display the `&` character, you need to specify the `SS_NOPREFIX` style. The price to pay for using this style is the inability to display a hotkey character.

Now, let's focus on the component of the static text control that you can change during run-time, namely, the text itself. If you specify the `SS_SIMPLE` style during the creation of a `CStatic` instance, you cannot alter its text. In this sense, the instance of `CStatic` is indeed etched in stone. The `CStatic` class allows you to set, query, and clear the characters of the static text using the functions `GetWindowTextLength`, `GetWindowText`, and `SetWindowText`, inherited from class `CWnd`.

Syntax

The *GetWindowTextLength* Function

The parameterless `GetWindowTextLength` member function returns the length of the control's text:

```
int GetWindowTextLength();
```

Example:

```
int nLen;
CStatic* pText;
// create control...

nLen = pText->GetWindowTextLength();
```

Syntax

The *GetWindowText* Function

The `GetWindowText` member function allows you to access the static text characters. The declaration of the `GetWindowText` function is

```
int GetWindowText(LPSTR lpString, int nMaxCount) const;
```

The `lpString` parameter is a pointer to the string that receives a copy of the static text characters. The `nMaxCount` parameter specifies the maximum number of static text characters to copy. The function result returns the actual number of characters copied to the string accessed by the pointer `lpString`.

Example:

```
const int MAX_LEN = 80;
char s[MAX_LEN+1];
int nLen;
CStatic* pText;
// create control...

nLen = pText->GetWindowText(s, MAX_LEN);
```

Syntax

The *SetWindowText* Function

The `SetWindowText` member function overwrites the current static text characters with those of a new string. The declaration of the `SetWindowText` function is

```
void SetWindowText(const char FAR* lpString);
```

The `lpString` parameter is the pointer to the new text for the control. If the new text is an empty string, the `SetWindowText` function call simply clears the text in the static text control instance.

Example:

```
char s[81] = "New window text";
CStatic* pText;
// create control...

pText->SetWindowText(s);
```

The Edit Control

Microsoft Foundation Class offers the `CEdit` class, which implements an edit control. You have encountered this control in some of the earlier programs that use the input dialog box. The edit control allows you to type in and edit the text in the input dialog box. In this section, I discuss the functionality of class `CEdit` in more detail, because implementing customized text editors in your MFC application requires you to become quite familiar with the `CEdit` member functions.

The *CEdit* Class

The `CEdit` class, a child of class `CWnd`, implements a versatile edit control that supports single-line and multiline text, as well as the ability to cut, paste, copy, delete, and clear text. The edit control can also undo the last text changes and exchange text with the clipboard. The `CEdit` class has a constructor and a `Create` member function used in building the various class instances.

Syntax

The *Create* Function

The declaration of the `Create` function is

```
BOOL Create(DWORD dwStyle,          // control style
         const RECT& rect,        // control area
         CWnd* pParentWnd,        // parent window
         UINT nID);               // control ID
```

The `dwStyle` parameter designates the control style. The arguments for style typically include the `WS_CHILD` and `WS_VISIBLE` styles. Table 16.2 shows the set of `ES_xxxx` edit control styles. The creation of edit control includes one or more of these styles. The `rect` parameter specifies the rectangular area occupied by the control. The `pParentWnd` parameter is the pointer to the parent window. The `nID` parameter specifies the control's ID. The `Create` function returns `TRUE` if it succeeds and yields `FALSE` if it fails.

Example:

```
const ID_EDIT_TXT;
dwEditStyle = WS_CHILD ¦ WS_VISIBLE ¦ WS_TABSTOP ¦ WS_BORDER
                  ¦ WS_LEFT ¦ ES_AUTOHSCROLL;
Crect r = Crect(100, 30);
CEdit* pEdit;

pEdit->Create(dwEditStyle, r, this, IS_EDIT_TXT);
```

The typical styles for `CEdit` instances are `WS_CHILD`, `WS_VISIBLE`, `WS_TABSTOP`, `ES_LEFT`, `ES_AUTOHSCROLL`, and `WS_BORDER`. These styles produce an edit control that has a frame and shows left-justified text that can be scrolled horizontally if the entire text does not fit in the frame. When you create multiline edit controls, you need to include the following styles: `ES_MULTILINE`, `ES_AUTOVSCROLL`, `WS_HSCROLL`, and `WS_VSCROLL`. These additional default styles support multiple text lines, make the text scroll vertically, and include vertical and horizontal scroll bars.

Table 16.2. Values for edit control styles.

Value	Meaning
`ES_AUTOHSCROLL`	Enables the text to automatically scroll to the right by 10 characters when the user enters a character at the end of the line; when the user presses the Enter key, text scrolls back to the left
`ES_AUTOVSCROLL`	Permits the text to scroll up by one page when the user presses the Enter key on the last visible line
`ES_CENTER`	Centers the text in a multiline edit control
`ES_LEFT`	Justifies the text to the left
`ES_LOWERCASE`	Converts all the letters that the user types into lowercase
`ES_MULTILINE`	Specifies a multiline edit control that recognizes line breaks (designated by the sequence of carriage-return and line-feed characters)

continues

Table 16.2. continued

Value	Meaning
`ES_NOHIDESEL`	By default, hides the selected text when it loses focus and shows the selection when it gains focus again; prevents edit control from restoring the selected text
`ES_RIGHT`	Justifies the text to the right
`ES_UPPERCASE`	Converts all the letters that the user types into uppercase

Clipboard-Related Editing Functions

The `CEdit` class includes a set of member functions that handle clipboard-related text-editing commands. These commands are available in typical menu options: Cut, Copy, Paste, Clear, Undo, and Delete. Table 16.3 shows the `CEdit` member functions and their purposes. These functions work with the clipboard in the `CF_TEXT` format.

Table 16.3. `CEdit` member functions that support clipboard-related editing menu commands.

Member Function	Purpose
`Cut`	Deletes the current selection in the edit control and copies the text to the clipboard
`Copy`	Copies the current selection to the clipboard
`Paste`	Inserts the text from the clipboard to the current cursor position in the edit control
`Clear`	Deletes the current selection; does not affect the clipboard
`Undo`	Undoes the last change made to the text of the edit control

Query of Edit Controls

The `CEdit` class has a family of text-query member functions. These functions enable you to retrieve either the entire control text or parts of it, or permit you to obtain information on the text statistics (number of lines, length of lines, and so on). The relevant query member functions are

- The parameterless `GetWindowTextLength` member function returns the length of the control's text. This member function is inherited from the parent class, `CWnd`.
- The `GetWindowText` member function allows you to access the edit control characters. This function is also inherited from the parent class.
- The `GetLineCount` member function returns the number of lines in a multiline edit control.
- The `LineFromChar` member function returns the line number of a specified character index.
- The `LineIndex` member function returns the character index of a specific line. The character index is also the size of the text in the edit control up to the specified line number.
- The `LineLength` member function returns the length of a line for a specific character index.
- The `GetSel` member function returns the starting and ending character positions of the selected text. The starting character position is the index of the first selected character. The ending position is the index of the first character after the selected text.
- The overloaded `GetLine` member function returns a line from a multiline edit control.

Syntax

The *GetWindowText* Function

The declaration of the `GetWindowText` function is

```
int GetWindowText(LPSTR lpString, int nMaxCount) const;
```

The `lpString` parameter is a pointer to the string that receives a copy of the static text characters. The `nMaxCount` parameter specifies the maximum number of static text characters to copy. The function `result` returns the actual number of characters copied to the string accessed by the pointer `lpString`.

Example:

```
const MAX_SIZE = 80;
char s[MAX_SIZE+1];
int nLen;
CEdit* pEdit;
// create control...
nLen = pEdit->GetWindowText(s, MAX_SIZE);
```

Syntax

The *GetLineCount* Function

The declaration of the `GetLineCount` function is

```
int GetLineCount() const;
```

Example:

```
CEdit* pEdit;
// create control...
nLineCount = pEdit->GetLineCount();
```

Note: In the case of multiline edit controls, take into account the characters involved in either the soft or hard line breaks. Hard line breaks use pairs of carriage return and line-feed characters at the end of each line. Soft line breaks use two carriage returns and a line feed at line breaks. This information is relevant when you are counting the number of characters to process.

Syntax

The *LineFromChar* Function

The declaration of the `LineFromChar` function is

```
int LineFromChar(int nIndex = -1) const;
```

The function returns the line number for character `nIndex`. The default argument value of `-1` is interpreted as a request to return either of these values:

- If there is selected text, the function yields the line number where the first selected character is located.
- If there is no selected text, the function returns the line number where character insertion occurs.

Example:

```
int nIdx = 3;
int nLineNum;
CEdit* pEdit;
// create control...

nLineNum = pEdit->LineFromChar(nIdx);
```

Syntax

The *LineIndex* Function

The declaration of the `LineIndex` function is

```
int LineIndex(int nLine = -1) const;
```

The `nLine` parameter specifies the line index. The `-1` argument indicates the current line. The function returns the number of characters from the first line and up to the specified line. If the argument of `nLine` is greater than the actual number of lines, the function yields `-1`.

Example:

```
CEdit* pEdit;
// create control...

nCharIndex = pEdit->LineIndex();
```

Syntax

The *LineLength* Function

The declaration of the `LineLength` function is

```
int LineLength(int nLine = -1) const;
```

The `nLine` parameter specifies the character index. A `-1` argument results in returning the length of the current line. In the case of a single-line edit control, the `LineLength` function yields the total number of characters in the control.

Example:

```
int nLineNum = 1;
int nLen;
CEdit* pEdit;
// create control...

nLen = pEdit->LineLength(nLineNum);
```

Syntax

The *GetSel* Function

The declaration of the overloaded `GetSel` function is

```
DWORD GetSel() const;
void GetSel(int& nStartChar, int& nEndChar) const;
```

The first function returns a 32-bit integer that contains the starting position in the low word and the ending position in the high word. Use the predefined `HIWORD` and `LOWORD` macros to extract the high and low words, respectively. If these two words are equal, there is no selected text, because both words are the character indices to the current insertion point. The second function uses the reference parameters `nStartChar` and `nEndChar` to obtain the indices of the characters which define the selected text.

Example:

```
DWORD dwSelPos;
CEdit* pEdit;
// create control...
dwSelPos = pEdit->GetSel();
int nStartPos, nEndPos;
CEdit* pEdit;
// create control...
pEdit->GetSel(nStartPos, nEndPos);
```

Syntax

The *GetLine* Function

The declaration of the two versions of the `GetLine` function is

```
int GetLine(int nIndex, LPTSTR lpszBuffer) const;
int GetLine(int nIndex, LPTSTR lpszBuffer, int nMaxLength) const;
```

The `nIndex` parameter specifies the index of the line to retrieve. The `lpszBuffer` is a buffer that stores the retrieved line. The first two bytes of `lpBuffer` contain the length of the line. The `nMaxLength` parameter specifies the maximum number of bytes to copy to the buffer `lpBuffer`. When the second version of `GetLine` is used, it copies the argument of `nMaxLength` to the first two bytes of `lpBuffer`.

Example:

```
const MAX_STR = 80;
int nLineIndex;
int nNumChars;
char s[MAX_STR+1];
CEdit* pEdit;
// create control...
nNumChars = pEdit->GetLine(nLineIndex, s, MAX_STR);
```

Note: Because `lpBuffer` is *not* an ASCIIZ string, you might prefer writing another version of `GetLine` that returns an ASCIIZ string. Of course, the new version of `GetLine` must be added to a descendant class of `CEdit`.

16

Altering the Edit Controls

Let's now focus on the member functions of `CEdit` that alter the edit control text. The operations of these member functions include writing new text to the control, selecting text, and replacing the selected text:

- The `SetWindowText` member function, which is inherited from the parent class, overwrites the current edit control characters with those of a new string.
- The overloaded `SetSel` member function defines a block of characters as the new selected text.
- The `ReplaceSel` member function replaces the selected text with new characters.

Syntax

The *SetWindowText* Function

The declaration of the `SetWindowText` function is

```
void SetWindowText(const char FAR* lpString);
```

The `lpString` parameter is the pointer to the new text for the control. If the new text is an empty string, the `SetWindowText` call simply clears the text in the edit control instance.

Example:

```
CEdit* pEdit;
// create control...
pEdit->SetWindowText("Calculate");
```

Syntax

The *SetSel* Function

The declaration of the `SetSel` function is

```
void SetSel(DWORD dwSelection);
void SetSel(int nStartChar, int nEndChar, BOOL bNoScroll = FALSE);
```

The `dwSelection` parameter contains the starting position in its low word and the ending position in its high word. The parameters `nStartChar` and `nEndChar` define the range of characters that make up the new selected text. In either version of `SetSel`, if the starting and ending positions are 0 and -1, respectively, the entire text in the edit control is selected. The parameter `bNoScroll` indicates if the caret should be scrolled into view. When this parameter has the argument `FALSE`, the caret is scrolled into view.

Example:

```
int nStart = 10, nEnd = 20;
CEdit* pEdit;
// create control...
pEdit->SetSel(nStart, nEnd);
```

Syntax

The *ReplaceSel* Function

The declaration of the `ReplaceSel` function is

```
void ReplaceSel(LPCTSTR lpszNewText);
```

The `lpszNewText` parameter is the pointer to the new selected text that replaces the current selection. If there is no selected text, the function simply inserts the text accessed by `lpNewText` at the current insertion point.

Example:

```
CEdit* pEdit;
// create control...
pEdit->ReplaceSel("New text");
```

Note: You can use the `ReplaceSel` function to delete parts of the edit control text by first selecting that part and then replacing it with an empty string.

The Pushbutton Control

The pushbutton control is perhaps psychologically the most powerful control (you never hear about the nuclear list box or the nuclear check box). In a sense, the pushbutton control represents the fundamental notion of a control—you click on the control and something happens.

NEW TERM The pushbutton is also known as the *command button.*

Note: The MFC library implements the `CButton` class, whose instances create pushbutton controls, group boxes, check boxes, and radio buttons. These controls are created by specifying the button style. This multiplicity is considered by many practicing OOP programmers as an odd (or poor) design. The reason for the current form of class `CButton` is that the MFC library is an OOP shell around the Windows API functions.

The rest of today's lesson focuses on the aspects of class `CButton` that deal with the pushbutton controls. Day 17 presents the aspects of `CButton` that are related to the group box, check box, and radio button controls.

NEW TERM There are basically two types of pushbutton controls: *default buttons* and *nondefault buttons*. Default buttons have slightly thicker edges than nondefault buttons. Pressing the Enter key is equivalent to clicking on the default button in a dialog box. There can be only one default button in a group. You can select a new default button by pressing the Tab key. This feature works only when the buttons are in a dialog box. If a nondialog box window owns pushbutton control, it can only visually display a default button—the functionality is not supported.

The *CButton* Class

The `CButton` class, a descendant of `CWnd`, declares a rather small number of member functions. The following are `CButton` member functions that are relevant to the pushbutton controls:

- The `Create` member function works with the class constructor to create a pushbutton instance.
- The `GetButtonStyle` and `SetButtonStyle` member functions allow you to query and set the style of a pushbutton. These functions enable you to determine whether or not, for example, a button is a default pushbutton.

Syntax

The *Create* Function

The declaration of the `Create` function is

```
BOOL Create(LPCTSTR lpszCaption,      // button label
        DWORD dwStyle,                // style
        const RECT& rect,             // area
        CWnd* pParentWnd,             // parent window
        UINT nID);                    // control ID
```

The `lpszCaption` parameter specifies the button's label or caption. The `dwStyle` parameter determines the exact type of button. This parameter plays a more important role in class `CButton`'s `Create` function than in the `Create` function of any other class. Typical styles for pushbuttons include `WS_CHILD`, `WS_VISIBLE`, `BS_PUSHBTTON` (or `BS_DEFPUSHBUTTON`), and `WS_TABSTOP` (when the parent window is a dialog box). The `rect` parameter specifies the area and location of the control. The `pParent` parameter is the pointer to the owner window, which can be either a window or a dialog box. The `nID` parameter specifies a unique control ID.

Example:

```
CButton* pBtn;
dwBtnStyle = WS_CHILD | WS_VISIBLE | BS_PUSHBTTON;
pBtn->Create("Calc", dwBtnStyle, rect, NULL, ID_CALC_BTN);
```

Syntax

The *GetButtonStyle* and *SetButtonStyle* Functions

The declarations for the `GetButtonStyle` and `SetButtonStyle` functions are

```
UINT GetButtonStyle() const;
void SetButtonStyle(UINT nStyle, BOOL bRedraw = TRUE);
```

The `nStyle` parameter specifies the new style of the `CButton` instance. The Boolean `bRedraw` parameter indicates whether or not to redraw the control.

Example:

```
UNIT nBtnStyle;
CButton* pBtn1;
CButton* pBtn2;
// create controls...
nBtnStyle = pBtn1->GetButtonStyle();
pBtn2->SetButtonStyle(nBtnStyle);
```

Handling Button Messages

When you click on a button, the control sends the `BN_CLICKED` notification message to its parent window. The parent window responds to this message by invoking a message response member function based on the ID of the button. For example, if you have a button that was created with an ID of ID_EXIT_BTN, the message handler function is

```
// other declarations
afx_msg void HandleExitBtn();
// other declarations

BEGIN_MESSAGE_LOOP(_CAppWindow_, CFrameWnd)
  // other possible message mapping macros
  ON_BN_CLICKED(ID_EXIT_BTN, HandleExitBtn)
  // other possible message mapping macros
END_MESSAGE_LOOP()
```

This example shows that the message map macro ON_BN_CLICKED is used to map the ID_EXIT_BTN notification message with the HandleExitBtn member function.

Manipulating Buttons

You can disable, enable, show, and hide a button by using the CWnd::EnableWindow function. A disabled button has a faded gray caption and does not respond to mouse clicks. The CWnd::EnableWindow function allows you to enable or disable a button. The function accepts a single argument, a Boolean argument that specifies whether the button is enabled (when the argument is TRUE) or disabled (when the argument is FALSE). Sample calls to the EnableWindow function are

```
AButton->EnableWindow(FALSE); // disable button
AButton->EnableWindow(TRUE);  // enable button
```

You can query the enabled state of a button by using the Boolean CWnd::IsWindowEnabled function, which takes no arguments. A sample call to IsEnabledWindow is

```
// toggle the enabled state of a button
if (AButton->IsWindowEnabled()
  AButton->EnableWindow(FALSE); // disable button
else
  AButton->EnableWindow(TRUE); // enable button
```

You can also hide and show a button using the CWnd::ShowWindow function. The function takes one argument: either the SW_HIDE constant to hide the button or the SW_SHOW constant to show the button. The Boolean CWnd::IsWindowVisible function queries the visibility of a button. This function takes no arguments. A sample call to the ShowWindow and IsWindowVisible functions is

```
// toggle the visibility of a button
if (AButton->IsWindowVisible()
  ABUtton->ShowWindow(SW_HIDE); // hide button
else
  AButton->ShowWindow(SW_SHOW); // show button
```

The Command-Line Calculator

Let's look at an application that uses static text, single-line edit controls, multiline edit controls, and pushbuttons—the *Command-Line Calculator Application (COCA)*. This nontrivial application implements a floating-point calculator that uses edit controls instead of buttons. This type of interface is somewhat visually inferior to the typical button-populated calculator Windows applications. However, this interface can support more mathematical functions without requiring the addition of the buttons for these extra functions. In COCA, the calculator is made up of the following controls:

- Two edit controls for the first and second operands accept integers, floating-point numbers, and the names of single-letter variables, A to Z.
- One edit control for the operator supports the calculator's four basic math operations and the exponentiation (using a caret, ^).
- One edit control displays the result of the math operation.
- One edit control displays any error messages.
- One multiline edit control enables you to store a number in the Result edit control in one of 26 single-letter variables, A to Z. The multiline edit displays the current values stored in these variables and allows you to view and edit these numbers. You can use the vertical scroll bar to inspect the values in the different variables.
- Multiple static text controls serve to label the various edit controls. Of particular interest is the static control for the Error Message box. If you click on the accompanying static text, the Error Message is cleared of any text.
- A menu has the single Exit option.
- A pushbutton with the caption `Calc` performs the operation specified in the Operator edit control, using the operands in the operand edit controls.
- A pushbutton with the caption `Store` stores the contents of the resulting edit control in the currently selected line of the multiline edit control.
- A pushbutton with the caption `Exit` exits the application after asking you for a confirmation.

The program supports the following special features for the Store button control:

- The Store pushbutton is disabled if the application attempts to execute an invalid operator. This feature illustrates an example of disabling a pushbutton when a certain condition arises (in this case, a specific calculation error).

- The Store pushbutton is enabled if you click on the Error Message static text. The same button is enabled when you successfully execute a math operation.

The calculator application demonstrates the following tasks:

- Using single-line edit controls for simple input
- Using a multiline edit control to view and edit information
- Accessing and editing line-oriented text
- Simulating static text that responds to mouse clicks
- Writing custom `GetLine` and `GetLineLength` member functions
- Extending the `CEdit` class to accommodate the previous two member functions
- Using pushbuttons
- Disabling and enabling pushbuttons
- Associating accelerator keys with pushbuttons (this feature allows the program to use keys)

Create the directory CTLBTN1 as a subdirectory of \MSVC20\VC21DAY and store all the project's files in the new directory. The project's .MAK file should contain the files CTLBTN1.CPP, CTLBTN1.RC, and CTLBTN1.DEF. The latter file resembles file MINWINAP.DEF in Day 14, Listing 14.2.

First, compile and run the application to get a good feel of how the calculator application works. Experiment with typing different numeric operands and the supported operators and click on the `Calc` button. Each time, the result appears in the Result box, overwriting the previous result. Try dividing a number by zero to experiment with the error-handling features.

Using the single-letter variables is easy. All these variables are initialized with 0. Therefore, the first step to using them is to store a nonzero value. Perform an operation and then click inside the Variables edit box. Select the first line that contains the variable A. Now click the Store button (or press Alt+S) and watch the number in the Result box appear in the first line of the Variables edit box. The name of the variable and the colon and space characters that follow reappear with the new text line. Now replace the contents of the Operand1 edit box with the variable `A`, and then click the `Calc` button. The Result edit box displays the result of the latest operation.

Listing 16.1 shows the source code for the CTLBTN1.H header file. The header file declares the command constants for the menu item and the pushbutton accelerator keys. These accelerator keys associate the Alt+C, Alt+S, and Alt+E keys with their respective

pushbutton IDs. Listing 16.2 contains the script for the CTLBTN1.RC resource file. Listing 16.3 contains the source code for the CTLBTN1.CPP program file.

Type

Listing 16.1. Source code for the CTLBTN1.H header file.

```
#define CM_EXIT  (WM_USER + 100)

#define ID_CALC_BTN  107
#define ID_STORE_BTN 108
#define ID_EXIT_BTN  109
```

Type

Listing 16.2. Script for the CTLBTN1.RC resource file.

```
#include <afxres.h>
#include "ctlbtn1.h"

BUTTONS ACCELERATORS
BEGIN
  "c", ID_CALC_BTN, ALT
  "s", ID_STORE_BTN, ALT
  "e", ID_EXIT_BTN, ALT
END

EXITMENU MENU LOADONCALL MOVEABLE PURE DISCARDABLE
BEGIN
    MENUITEM "E&xit", CM_EXIT
END
```

Type

Listing 16.3. Source code for the CTLBTN1.CPP program file.

```
#include <stdlib.h>
#include <ctype.h>
#include <stdio.h>
#include <math.h>
#include <string.h>
#include <afxwin.h>
#include "ctlbtn1.h"

// declare the constants that represent the sizes of the controls
const Wlbl = 100;
const Hlbl = 20;
const LblVertSpacing = 5;
const LblHorzSpacing = 40;
const Wbox = 100;
const Hbox = 30;
const BoxVertSpacing = 40;
const BoxHorzSpacing = 40;
const WLongbox = 4 * (Wbox + BoxHorzSpacing);
```

```
const Wvarbox = 2 * Wbox;
const Hvarbox = 3 * Hbox;
const Hbtn = 30;
const Wbtn = 80;
const BtnHorzSpacing = 30;
const MaxEditLen = 30;
const MAX_MEMREG = 26;

// declare the ID_XXXX constants for the edit boxes
#define ID_OPERAND1_EDIT 101
#define ID_OPERATOR_EDIT 102
#define ID_OPERAND2_EDIT 103
#define ID_RESULT_EDIT 104
#define ID_ERRMSG_EDIT 105
#define ID_VARIABLE_EDIT 106

class CxButton : public CButton
{
public:

   BOOL Create(const char FAR* lpCaption, const RECT& rect,
               CWnd* pParentWnd, UINT nID, BOOL bIsDefault);
   6p 42: };

class CxEdit : public CEdit
{
public:
  // get an ASCIIZ string from a line
  BOOL GetLine(LPSTR lpString, int nStrSize, int nLineNumber);
  // get the line length given a line number
  int GetLineLength(int nLineNumber);

};

class CWindowApp : public CWinApp
{
public:
    virtual BOOL InitInstance();
};

// expand the functionality of CFrameWnd by deriving
// class CAppWindow
class CAppWindow : public CFrameWnd
{
public:

  CAppWindow();

  ~CAppWindow();

protected:
  // declare the pointers to the various controls
  // first, the edit box controls
  CEdit* Operand1Box;
  CEdit* OperatorBox;
```

continues

Listing 16.3. continued

```
CEdit* Operand2Box;
CEdit* ResultBox;
CEdit* ErrMsgBox;
CxEdit* VariableBox;
// then the static text controls
CStatic* Operand1Txt;
CStatic* OperatorTxt;
CStatic* Operand2Txt;
CStatic* ResultTxt;
CStatic* ErrMsgTxt;
CStatic* VariableTxt;
// then the pushbuttons
CxButton* CalcBtn;
CxButton* StoreBtn;
CxButton* ExitBtn;
// math error flag
BOOL bInError;
// coordinates for the Error Message static text area
int nXulc, nYulc, nXlrc, nYlrc;

// handle clicking the left mouse button
afx_msg void OnLButtonDown(UINT nFlags, CPoint point);
// handle the calculation
afx_msg void HandleCalcBtn();
// handle the calculation
afx_msg void CMCalc() { HandleCalcBtn(); }
// handle storing the result in a variable
afx_msg void HandleStoreBtn();
// handle storing the result in a variable
afx_msg void CMStore() { HandleStoreBtn(); }
// handle exiting the application
afx_msg void HandleExitBtn()
  { SendMessage(WM_CLOSE); }
// handle exiting the application
afx_msg void CMExit() { SendMessage(WM_CLOSE); }
// handle exiting the application
afx_msg void OnExit() { SendMessage(WM_CLOSE); }
// enable a pushbutton control
virtual void EnableButton(CxButton* pBtn)
  { pBtn->EnableWindow( TRUE); }
// disable a pushbutton control
virtual void DisableButton(CxButton* pBtn)
  { pBtn->EnableWindow(FALSE); }
// handle creating the controls
afx_msg int OnCreate(LPCREATESTRUCT lpCS);
// handle keydown events
afx_msg void OnKeyDown(UINT nChar, UINT nRepCnt, UINT nFlags);
// handle closing the window
afx_msg void OnClose();
// return a reference to member r based on individual
// coordinates and dimensions
void makeRect(int X, int Y, int W, int H, CRect& r);
// obtain a number of a Variable edit box line
double getVar(int lineNum);
```

```
  // store a number in the selected text of
  // the Variable edit box line
  void putVar(double nX);

  // declare message map macro
  DECLARE_MESSAGE_MAP();
};

BOOL CxButton::Create(const char FAR* lpCaption, const RECT& rect,
                      CWnd* pParentWnd, UINT nID, BOOL bIsDefault)

{
  DWORD dwBtnStyle = (bIsDefault == TRUE) ?
                  BS_DEFPUSHBUTTON : BS_PUSHBUTTON;

  return CButton::Create(lpCaption, WS_CHILD | WS_VISIBLE |
                         WS_TABSTOP | dwBtnStyle, rect, pParentWnd, nID);
}

BOOL CxEdit::GetLine(LPSTR lpString, int nStrSize,
                     int nLineNumber)
{
  int nCopyCount;
  BOOL bResult;

  if (nStrSize <= 0)
    return FALSE;
  bResult = (nStrSize >= GetLineLength(nLineNumber) + 1) ? TRUE
                                                          : FALSE;
  if (nStrSize == 1)
  {
    lpString[0] = '\0';
    return bResult;
  }
  ((WORD FAR *)lpString)[0] = nStrSize;
  nCopyCount = (WORD)(SendMessage(EM_GETLINE, nLineNumber,
                 long(lpString)));
  if (nCopyCount)
  {
    // Windows returns non-null-terminated string
    lpString[nCopyCount] = '\0';
    return bResult;
  }
  return FALSE;
}

int CxEdit::GetLineLength(int nLineNumber)
{
  int nStartPos = -1;

  if (nLineNumber > -1)
    nStartPos = LineIndex(nLineNumber);
  return (WORD) SendMessage(EM_LINELENGTH, nStartPos);
}

```

continues

Listing 16.3. continued

```
CAppWindow::CAppWindow()
{
  // load accelerator resources
  LoadAccelTable("BUTTONS");
  // create the window
  Create(NULL,
    "Command-Oriented Calculator Application (COCA)",
      WS_OVERLAPPEDWINDOW ¦ WS_MAXIMIZE,
          rectDefault, NULL, "EXITMENU");
  // clear the bInError flag
  bInError = FALSE;
}   6p196:    6p197: int CAppWindow::OnCreate(LPCREATESTRUCT lpCS)
{
  char s[81];
  char bigStr[6 * MAX_MEMREG + 1];
  char chC;
  int nX0 = 20;
  int nY0 = 30;
  int nX = nX0, nY = nY0;
  CRect r;
  DWORD dwStaticStyle = WS_CHILD ¦ WS_VISIBLE ¦ SS_LEFT;
  DWORD dwBoxStyle = WS_CHILD ¦ WS_VISIBLE ¦ WS_TABSTOP ¦
                     WS_BORDER ¦ ES_LEFT ¦ ES_AUTOHSCROLL ¦
                     ES_UPPERCASE;

  // create the first set of labels for the edit boxes
  makeRect(nX, nY, Wlbl, Hlbl, r);
  Operand1Txt = new CStatic();
  Operand1Txt->Create("Operand1", dwStaticStyle, r, this);
  strcpy(s, "Operator");
  nX += Wlbl + LblHorzSpacing;
  makeRect(nX, nY, Wlbl, Hlbl, r);
  OperatorTxt = new CStatic();
  OperatorTxt->Create(s, dwStaticStyle, r, this);
  nX += Wlbl + LblHorzSpacing;
  makeRect(nX, nY, Wlbl, Hlbl, r);
  Operand2Txt = new CStatic();
  Operand2Txt->Create("Operand2", dwStaticStyle, r, this);
  nX += Wlbl + LblHorzSpacing;
  makeRect(nX, nY, Wlbl, Hlbl, r);
  ResultTxt = new CStatic();
  ResultTxt->Create("Result", dwStaticStyle, r, this);
  // create the operand1, operator, operand2, and result
  // edit boxes
  nX = nX0;
  nY += Hlbl + LblVertSpacing;
  makeRect(nX, nY, Wbox, Hbox, r);
  Operand1Box = new CEdit();
  Operand1Box->Create(dwBoxStyle, r, this, ID_OPERAND1_EDIT);
  Operand1Box->LimitText(); // set no limit for text
  nX += Wbox + BoxHorzSpacing;
  makeRect(nX, nY, Wbox, Hbox, r);
  OperatorBox = new CEdit();
  OperatorBox->Create(dwBoxStyle, r, this, ID_OPERATOR_EDIT);
```

```
OperatorBox->LimitText(); // set no limit for text
nX += Wbox + BoxHorzSpacing;
makeRect(nX, nY, Wbox, Hbox, r);
Operand2Box = new CEdit();
Operand2Box->Create(dwBoxStyle, r, this, ID_OPERAND2_EDIT);
Operand2Box->LimitText(); // set no limit for text
nX += Wbox + BoxHorzSpacing;
makeRect(nX, nY, Wbox, Hbox, r);
ResultBox = new CEdit();
ResultBox->Create(dwBoxStyle, r, this, ID_RESULT_EDIT);
ResultBox->LimitText(); // set no limit for text
// create the static text and edit box for the error message
nX = nX0;
nY += Hbox + BoxVertSpacing;
// store the coordinates for the static text area
nXulc = nX;
nYulc = nY;
nXlrc = nX + Wlbl;
nYlrc = nY + Hlbl;
makeRect(nX, nY, Wlbl, Hlbl, r);
ErrMsgTxt = new CStatic();
ErrMsgTxt->Create("Error Message", dwStaticStyle, r, this);
nY += Hlbl + LblVertSpacing;
makeRect(nX, nY, WLongbox, Hbox, r);
ErrMsgBox = new CEdit();
ErrMsgBox->Create(dwBoxStyle, r, this, ID_ERRMSG_EDIT);
ErrMsgBox->LimitText(); // set no limit for text
// create the static text and edit box for the single-letter
// variable selection
nY += Hbox + BoxVertSpacing;
makeRect(nX, nY, Wlbl, Hlbl, r);
VariableTxt = new CStatic();
VariableTxt->Create("Variables", dwStaticStyle, r, this);
nY += Hlbl + LblVertSpacing;
bigStr[0] = '\0';
// build the initial contents of the Variable edit box
for (chC = 'A'; chC <= 'Z'; chC++) {
  sprintf(s, "%c: 0\r\n", chC);
  strcat(bigStr, s);
}
makeRect(nX, nY, Wvarbox, Hvarbox, r);
VariableBox = new CxEdit();
VariableBox->Create(dwBoxStyle | ES_MULTILINE | WS_HSCROLL
                | WS_VSCROLL | ES_AUTOVSCROLL,
                     r, this, ID_VARIABLE_EDIT);
VariableBox->LimitText(); // set no limit for text
VariableBox->SetWindowText(bigStr);
// create the Calc pushbutton
nX += Wvarbox + BtnHorzSpacing;
CalcBtn = new CxButton();
makeRect(nX, nY, Wbtn, Hbtn, r);
CalcBtn->Create("&Calc", r, this, ID_CALC_BTN, TRUE);
// create the Store Btn
nX += Wbtn + BtnHorzSpacing;
makeRect(nX, nY, Wbtn, Hbtn, r);
```

continues

Listing 16.3. continued

```
  StoreBtn = new CxButton();
  StoreBtn->Create("&Store", r, this, ID_STORE_BTN, FALSE);
  // Create the Exit Btn
  nX += Wbtn + BtnHorzSpacing;
  makeRect(nX, nY, Wbtn, Hbtn, r);
  ExitBtn = new CxButton();
  ExitBtn->Create("&Exit", r, this, ID_EXIT_BTN, FALSE);
  return CFrameWnd::OnCreate(lpCS);
}

CAppWindow::~CAppWindow()
{
  // delete the controls 6p308:   delete Operand1Box;
  delete OperatorBox;
  delete Operand2Box;
  delete ResultBox;
  delete ErrMsgBox;
  delete VariableBox;
  delete Operand1Txt;
  delete OperatorTxt;
  delete Operand2Txt;
  delete ResultTxt;
  delete ErrMsgTxt;
  delete VariableTxt;
  delete CalcBtn;
  delete StoreBtn;
  delete ExitBtn;
}   6p324:
void CAppWindow::OnLButtonDown(UINT nFlags, CPoint point)
{
  int nX = point.x;
  int nY = point.y;

  if (nX >= nXulc && nX <= nXlrc &&
      nY >= nYulc && nY <= nYlrc) {
      ErrMsgBox->SetWindowText("");
      EnableButton(StoreBtn);
  }
}

void CAppWindow::HandleCalcBtn()
{
  double x, y, z;
  char opStr[MaxEditLen+1];
  char s[MaxEditLen+1];

  // obtain the string in the Operand1 edit box
  Operand1Box->GetWindowText(s, MaxEditLen);
  // does the Operand1Box contain the name
  // of a single-letter variable?
  if (isalpha(s[0]))
    // obtain value from the Variable edit control
    x = getVar(s[0] - 'A');
  else
```

```
  // convert the string in the edit box
  x = atof(s);

// obtain the string in the Operand2 edit box
Operand2Box->GetWindowText(s, MaxEditLen);
// does the Operand2Box contain the name
// of a single-letter variable?
if (isalpha(s[0]))
  // obtain value from the Variable edit control
  y = getVar(s[0] - 'A');
else
   // convert the string in the edit box
  y = atof(s);

// obtain the string in the Operator edit box
OperatorBox->GetWindowText(opStr, MaxEditLen);
// clear the error message box
ErrMsgBox->SetWindowText("");
bInError = FALSE;
// determine the requested operation
if (strcmp(opStr, "+") == 0)
  z = x + y;
else if (strcmp(opStr, "-") == 0)
  z = x - y;
else if (strcmp(opStr, "*") == 0)
  z = x * y;
else if (strcmp(opStr, "/") == 0) {
  if (y != 0)
    z = x / y;
  else {
    z = 0;
    bInError = TRUE;
    ErrMsgBox->SetWindowText("Division-by-zero error");
  }
}
else if (strcmp(opStr, "^") == 0) {
  if (x > 0)
    z = exp(y * log(x));
  else {
    bInError = TRUE;
    ErrMsgBox->SetWindowText(
      "Cannot raise the power of a negative number");
  }
}
else {
  bInError = TRUE;
  ErrMsgBox->SetWindowText("Invalid operator");
}
// display the result if no error has occurred
if (!bInError) {
  sprintf(s, "%g", z);
  ResultBox->SetWindowText(s);
  // enable the Store button
  EnableButton(StoreBtn);
}
```

continues

Listing 16.3. continued

```
  else
    // disable the Store button
    DisableButton(StoreBtn);
}

void CAppWindow::HandleStoreBtn()
{
  char result[MaxEditLen+1];

  // get the string in the Result edit box
  ResultBox->GetWindowText(result, MaxEditLen);
  // store the result in the selected text of
  // the Variable edit box
  putVar(atof(result));
}

void CAppWindow::makeRect(int nX, int nY, int nW,
                          int nH, CRect& r)
{
  r.top = nY;
  r.left = nX;
  r.bottom = nY + nH;
  r.right = nX + nW;
}

double CAppWindow::getVar(int nLineNum)
{
  int nLineSize;
  char s[MaxEditLen+1];

  if (nLineNum >= MAX_MEMREG) return 0;
  // get the size of the target line
  nLineSize = VariableBox->GetLineLength(nLineNum);
  // get the line
  VariableBox->GetLine(s, nLineSize, nLineNum);
  // delete the first three characters
  strcpy(s, (s+3));
  // return the number stored in the target line
  return atof(s);
}

void CAppWindow::putVar(double x)
{
  DWORD dwSelPos;
  WORD wStartPos, wEndPos;
  int nLineNum;
  int nLineSize;
  char s[MaxEditLen+1];

  // locate the character position of the cursor
  dwSelPos = VariableBox->GetSel();
  wStartPos = LOWORD(dwSelPos);
  wEndPos = HIWORD(dwSelPos);
  // turn off the selected text
```

```
  if (wStartPos != wEndPos) {
    dwSelPos = MAKELONG(wStartPos, wStartPos);
    VariableBox->SetSel(dwSelPos);
  }
  // get the line number where the cursor is located
  nLineNum = VariableBox->LineFromChar(-1);
  // get the line size of line lineNum
  nLineSize = VariableBox->GetLineLength(nLineNum);
  // obtain the text of line lineNum
  VariableBox->GetLine(s, nLineSize, nLineNum);
  // build the new text line
  sprintf(s, "%c: %g", s[0], x);
  // get the character positions for the deleted line
  wStartPos = (WORD) (VariableBox->LineIndex(-1));
  wEndPos = (WORD) (wStartPos + VariableBox->LineLength(-1));
  // select the current line
  dwSelPos = MAKELONG(wStartPos, wEndPos);
  VariableBox->SetSel(dwSelPos);
  // replace the current line with the new line
  VariableBox->ReplaceSel(s);
}

void CAppWindow::OnKeyDown(UINT nChar, UINT nRepCnt, UINT nFlags)
{
  if (nFlags & 0x2000 == 1)
    switch (nChar) {
      case 'c':
        HandleCalcBtn();
        break;
      case 's':
        HandleStoreBtn();
        break;
      case 'e':
        HandleExitBtn();
        break;
      default:
        MessageBeep(0);
    }
}

void CAppWindow::OnClose()
{
  if (MessageBox("Want to close this application",
                 "Query", MB_YESNO | MB_ICONQUESTION) == IDYES)
    DestroyWindow();               6p505: }

BEGIN_MESSAGE_MAP(CAppWindow, CFrameWnd)
    ON_WM_LBUTTONDOWN()
    ON_BN_CLICKED(ID_CALC_BTN, HandleCalcBtn)
    ON_COMMAND(ID_CALC_BTN, CMCalc)
    ON_BN_CLICKED(ID_STORE_BTN, HandleStoreBtn)
    ON_COMMAND(ID_STORE_BTN, CMStore)
    ON_BN_CLICKED(ID_EXIT_BTN, HandleExitBtn)
    ON_COMMAND(ID_EXIT_BTN, CMExit)
    ON_COMMAND(CM_EXIT, OnExit)
```

continues

Listing 16.3. continued

```
516:      ON_WM_CREATE()
517:      ON_WM_KEYDOWN()
518:      ON_WM_CLOSE()
519: END_MESSAGE_MAP()
520:
521: // Construct the CWindowApp's m_pMainWnd data member
522: BOOL CWindowApp::InitInstance()
523: {
524:   m_pMainWnd = new CAppWindow();
525:   m_pMainWnd->ShowWindow(m_nCmdShow);
526:   m_pMainWnd->UpdateWindow();
527:   return TRUE;
528: }
529:
530: // application's constructor initializes and runs the app
531: CWindowApp WindowApp;
```

Figure 16.1 shows a sample session with the program CTLBTN1.EXE.

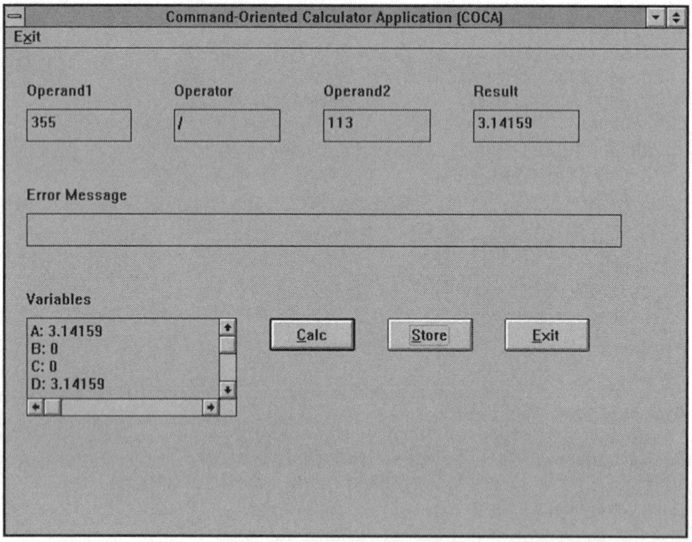

Figure 16.1. *A sample session with the program CTLBTN1.EXE.*

Analysis

The program in Listing 16.3 contains three sets of constants in lines 10 through 33. The first set, in lines 10 through 23, declares the constants for height, width, vertical spacing, and horizontal spacing that are used to dimension the various controls. The second set of constants, in lines 24 and 25, declares maximum characters in the edit control and the number of variables in the multiline edit control. The third set of constants, in lines 28 through 33, declares the ID_xxxx values used in creating the various edit-control instances. The ID_xxxx for the pushbutton controls are declared in the header file CTLBTN1.H, which is included in the program.

The COCA program declares the application class, CWindowApp; the window class, CAppWindow; the extended button class, CxButton; and the extended edit box class, CxEdit.

16

Note: The program declares class CxButton, which in turn declares a more specialized version of function Create. This version creates a normal or default pushbutton control by specifying the typical pushbutton styles. Assigning these styles makes it easier for client windows or dialog boxes to create pushbutton controls.

The CxEdit class is a descendant of CEdit and declares the GetLine and GetLineLength member functions. The GetLine function works with ASCIIZ arguments. The function is declared as follows:

```
BOOL GetLine(LPSTR lpString, int nStrSize, int nLineNumber);
```

The lpString is the pointer to an ASCIIZ string. The nStrSize parameter specifies the maximum number of characters to copy. The nLineNumber parameter designates the target line number. The function returns TRUE if it succeeds, and yields FALSE if it fails.

The GetLineLength member function returns the length of a specified line. The declaration of the GetLineLength function is

```
int GetLineLength(int nLineNumber);
```

The nLineNumber parameter specifies the number of the line whose length is sought.

The CAppWindow window class is the owner of the static text and edit controls. The class declares a number of data members and member functions.

The CAppWindow contains the following groups of data members:

- Pointers to the various CStatic, CEdit, CxEdit, and CxButton instances (each pointer accesses one of the edit controls that appear in the program)
- The Boolean data member bInError, which flags any error

- The data members `nXulc`, `nYulc`, `nXlrc`, and `nYlrc`, which store the coordinates for the rectangle that contains the Error Message static text (the mouse-click response member function `OnLButtonDown` examines whether the mouse is clicked inside that rectangle, and if so, clears the Error Message edit control text)

The `CAppWindow` class contains a constructor, a destructor, and a number of message-response member functions that handle the mouse click and respond to the menu options.

The window class constructor performs the following tasks:

- Loads the menu resource by invoking the `LoadAccelTable` function and specifying the `BUTTONS` accelerator resource
- Builds the window instance by invoking the `Create` member function
- Assigns `FALSE` to the `bInError` data member

The call to `Create` specifies the window title, the `WS_OVERLAPPEDWINDOW` and `WS_MAXIMIZE` styles, and the `EXITMENU` menu resource. The `WS_MAXIMIZE` style produces a maximized window. The call to function `Create` also creates the instances for the static text, edit box, and pushbuttons.

The `EnableButton` and `DisableButton` member functions enable and disable a pushbutton, respectively, by calling the `CWnd::EnableWindow` function. The functions are called by other member functions with the `StoreBtn` argument.

The `makeRect` member function produces the values for the rectangular area occupied by a control, given the following values:

- The coordinates of the upper left corner of the rectangular area
- The width of the rectangle
- The height of the rectangle

The `OnCreate` member function responds to the `WM_CREATE` message and builds the various controls attached to the window. The function carries out the following tasks:

- Creates the static text controls that label the operands, operator, and the resulting edit controls by invoking the `CStatic` constructor
- Creates the edit boxes for the operands, operator, and result
- Creates the `CxButton` instances, each with a unique ID and caption

- Calculates the upper left corner and lower right corner of the rectangle containing the Error Message static text, and stores them in the `nXulc`, `nYulc`, `nXlrc`, and `nYlrc` data members
- Creates the error-message static text control and edit control
- Creates the variables multiline edit control by building the contents of the Variables box using the string variable `bigStr`
- Returns the expression `CFrameWnd::OnCreate(lpCS)`

The member function `OnCreate` uses the style `WS_CHILD ¦ WS_VISIBLE ¦ SS_LEFT` in creating the static text controls. The creation of the controls involves the private member function `makeRect`, which generates the required `CRect` object. The local variable `nX` is increased by `(Wlbl + LblHorzSpacing)` to calculate the X-coordinate for the next static text control. This approach allows you to systematically increment the X- and/or Y-coordinates for the control's area.

The instances for the edit boxes for the operands, operator, and result are accessed by the `Operand1Box`, `OperatorBox`, `Operand2Box`, and `ResultBox` data members, respectively. Each `CEdit` instance is created with its own `ID_xxxx` constant and an empty edit box. The edit boxes have the same size. The styles of the edit controls include the `ES_UPPERCASE` style. This style results in automatically converting into uppercase the single-letter variable names that you type in these edit controls.

The caption for the `CxButton` instance uses the ampersand character to underline the hot key. The first pushbutton is created as the default control, by making the last argument of `CxButton:Create` a `TRUE`. The other two buttons are created as normal controls by specifying a `FALSE` argument to the last parameter of function `Create`. Consequently, the `Calc` button appears as the default pushbutton. However, appearances can be deceiving—the `Calc` button totally lacks the functionality of a default button because its owner is a window and not a dialog box.

The Variables edit control is created with the additional styles of `ES_MULTILINE`, `WS_HSCROLL`, `WS_VSCROLL`, and `ES_AUTOVSCROLL`. These styles produce an edit control with fully functioning vertical and horizontal scroll bars. The `OnCreate` function writes the contents of `bigStr` in the edit control by calling the `SetWindowText` function.

The `OnLButtonDown` member function performs a simple task. It checks whether or not the mouse click occurs in the rectangle occupied by the error-message static text control. If this condition is true, the function performs the following tasks:

- Clears the error-message box by invoking the function `SetWindowText`
- Enables the Store button by invoking the function `EnableButton`

The HandleCalcBtn member function responds to the notification message emitted by the Calc button. The corresponding message map macro uses the message ID of ID_CALC_BTN. The latter is the ID of the Calc button that is also used in creating the Calc button instance. The function performs the following tasks:

- Obtains the first operand from the Operand1 edit box
- Obtains the second operand in a manner identical to the first one (the function stores the actual (numeric) second operand in variable y)
- Copies the text in the Operator edit box into the local variable opStr
- Clears the error message text box and sets the bInError data member to FALSE
- Determines the requested operation by using a series of if and if-else statements—operators supported are +, -, *, /, and ^ (power)-and, if the function detects an error, sets the bInError data member to TRUE and displays a message in the error-message box
- Displays the result in the Result box if the bInError data member is FALSE (first converting the result from double to a string and then writing to the Result box using the SetWindowText function), and systematically enables the Store button (if member bInError is TRUE, it disables the Store pushbutton by calling the member function DisableButton)

When the member function HandleCalcBtn obtains the first operand from the Operand1 edit box, the control may contain the name of a single-letter variable (A to Z) or a floating-point number. The function uses the GetWindowText function to store a copy of the edit-control text in the local variable s. The function then examines the first character in variable s. If that character is a letter, the first operand is a single-letter variable. Consequently, the function calls the protected member function getVar to obtain the value associated with that variable. If the first character is not a letter, the function uses the atof function to convert the contents of variable s into a double-typed number. In both cases, the function stores the actual (numeric) first operand in variable x.

The CMCalcBtn member function handles the command messages emitted by the Alt+C accelerator key. The corresponding macro message ID is specified as ID_CALC_BTN, the ID associated with the Alt+C in the resource file (which is also the ID for the Calc button). The CMCalcBtn function simply invokes the HandleCalcBtn member function to execute the requested calculation.

The HandleStoreBtn member function stores the contents of the Result box in a single-letter variable. The function first obtains the string in the Result edit box by calling the GetWindowText function. Then, the function invokes the protected member function `putVar` to actually store the result string at the current insertion point in the Variables edit box.

The `CMStore` member function intercepts the Alt+S hot key in the form of the command message with the ID number `ID_STORE_BTN`. The `CMStore` function merely calls the `HandleStoreBtn` member function.

The `getVar` member function returns the number stored at line number `lineNum` of the Variables edit box. The function performs the following tasks:

- Exits and returns `0` if the `lineNum` is greater than or equal to the constant `MAX_MEMREG`
- Obtains the size of the target line by making the `GetLineLength(nLineNum)` call
- Retrieves the strings of line number `nLineNum` by calling the `GetLine` function
- Deletes the first three characters of the retrieved line (this step should leave the string with the number stored in the target line)
- Returns the `double`-typed number obtained by calling the `atof` function and supplying it argument `s`

The `putVar` member function stores the number in the Result box in the variable that is located on the same line that contains the text insert position. The function performs the following tasks:

- Locates the character position of the cursor by calling the `GetSel` function, which returns the start and end character positions in the local `dwSelPos`, and then uses the predefined macros `HIWORD` and `LOWORD` to store the starting and ending positions in the local variables `wStartPos` and `wEndPos`
- Turns off any selected text, comparing the values in the variables `wStartPos` and `wEndPos` and, if they do not match, calculating a new value for variable `dwSelPos` so that the low and high words are both `wStartPos` (the function then invokes the `SetSel` function and supplies it with the variable `dwSelPos` to turn off the selected text)
- Obtains the line number where the cursor is located using the `GetLineFromChar` function
- Obtains the size of the target line using the `GetLineLength` function
- Retrieves the text in the target line by calling the `GetLine` function
- Builds the new text line

- Obtains the starting and ending character positions for the line to be replaced
- Selects the line to be replaced using the `SetSel` function
- Replaces the current line with a new line

The `HandleExitBtn` member function responds to the notification message of the Exit button. The function sends the `WM_CLOSE` message to the parent window. The `CMExit` member function intercepts the Alt+E hot key in the form of a command message with the ID number `ID_EXIT_BTN`. The `CMExit` function also sends a `WM_CLOSE` message to the parent window.

Summary

Today's lesson looks at the static text, edit box, and pushbutton controls. Using these and other controls animate the Windows applications and provide a more consistent user interface. You learn about the following topics:

- You can create static text controls and manipulate their text at run-time.
- Single-line and multiline edit box controls allow you to type and edit the text in the input dialog box.
- The two types of pushbutton controls—default and nondefault—give you instant power.

On Day 17, I present the grouped controls: the classes for group, check box, and radio controls. These controls are used to fine-tune the execution of a specific task, such as searching and replacing text in a text editor.

Q&A

Q How do I create a string for a multiline static text control?

A You build a multiline string, such as `"This is\na multiline"` (notice the imbedded \n character, which breaks the line) and pass it as the first argument to the `CStatic::Create` member function.

Q How important is selecting the correct control style?

A Very important. The style fine-tunes the control appearance, optional components, and behavior.

Q Why does program CTLBTN1.CPP use local variables such as `nX` and `nY` to specify the location of a control? Why not replace these variables with numeric constants?

A Using variables, such as `nX` and `nY`, allows you to specify the location of the controls relative to one another. This method enables you to shift controls very easily. By contrast, using numeric constants specifies the absolute values for the control locations. Shifting controls, in this case, means plugging in a new set of numbers!

Workshop

The Workshop provides quiz questions to help you solidify your understanding of the material covered and exercises to provide you with experience in using what you've learned. Try to understand the quiz and exercise answers before continuing on to the next day's lesson. Answers are provided in Appendix B, "Answers."

Quiz

1. True or false? The text for all static text controls is unchangeable.
2. True or false? The `SS_CENTER` centers each line of a multiline static text control.
3. True or false? A static text control needs an accompanying pointer to access only when the program needs to set or query the text in the control.
4. True or false? Every edit control needs an accompanying pointer to access it.
5. True or false? The API Windows functions `EnableWindow` and `DisableWindow` can disable any control.
6. True or false? The Windows messages emitted by a pushbutton can be mapped using the `ON_COMMAND` map.

Exercises

1. Experiment with the program CTLBTN1.CPP to add trigonometric functions, inverse trigonometric functions, hyperbolic functions, and inverse hyperbolic functions.
2. Experiment with a copy of program CTLBTN1.CPP by changing values assigned to the constants that specify the size and spacing of the various controls.

17

Grouped Controls

WEEK
3

Windows supports check box and radio button controls that act as software switches. These controls appear in typical search-and-replace dialog boxes and influence certain aspects of the text search or replacement. These aspects include the scope, direction, and case-sensitivity of searching or replacing text. In today's lesson, you learn about the following topics:

- The check box control
- The radio button control
- The group box control

Today's lesson also shows you how to respond to the messages emitted by these controls, as well as how to use the `ForEach` iterators to manipulate the check box and radio button controls.

NEW TERM The *group box control* is a special control that visually and logically groups the check box and radio button controls.

The Check Box Control

The check box control is a special button that toggles a check mark. The control instances appear with a small rectangular button and a title that appears, by default, to the right side of the square. When you click on the square, you toggle the control's check mark. Think of the check box as a binary digit that can be either set or cleared. The instances of a check box can appear inside or outside a group box and are mutually nonexclusive—toggling any check box does not affect the check state of other check boxes.

> **Note:** Placing check boxes inside groups (inside a dialog box) serves two purposes. First, the group box provides a visual grouping that clarifies the purpose of the check boxes to the application user. Second, you can streamline the notification messages emitted by the check boxes in a group to detect any change in the checked state of the check boxes.

NEW TERM Windows allows you to specify a check box with three states: checked, unchecked, and *grayed.* Table 5.1 in Day 5 shows the styles for the check box control. The grayed state fills the control's rectangular button with a gray color. This third state can serve to indicate that the check box control is in an indeterminate (or call it "don't care") state.

The *CButton* Class and Check Boxes

Microsoft Foundation Class offers the `CButton` class, a descendant of `CWnd`, as the class that provides the instances of check box controls (as well as other controls). Day 16 introduces you to the `CButton` class and discusses the aspects of that class that are related to the pushbutton controls. In this section I focus on the aspects of class `CButton` that are relevant to the check box controls. Of course, the check box instances need the class constructor and the `Create` member function to come to life. The check box styles shown in Table 17.1 indicate that there are two basic modes for managing the check state of a check box control: automatic and nonautomatic (manual, if you prefer). In automatic mode (specified by `BS_AUTOCHECK` and `BS_AUTO3STATE`), Windows toggles the check state when you click on the control. In manual mode, your application code is responsible for managing the check state of the check box.

17

Table 17.1. Check box control styles.

Style	Meaning
`BS_CHECKBOX`	Specifies a check box with the title to the right of the rectangular button
`BS_AUTOCHECKBOX`	Same as `BS_CHECKBOX`, except the button is automatically toggled when you click on it
`BS_3STATE`	Same as `BS_CHECKBOX`, except that the control has three states: checked, unchecked, and grayed
`BS_AUTO3STATE`	Same as `BS_3STATE`, except the button is automatically toggled when you click on it
`BS_LEFTTEXT`	Sets the control's title to the left of the button

The `CButton` class provides member functions to set and query the state of the check box. The `GetCheck` member function returns a state of the check box control and is declared as follows:

```
int GetCheck() const;
```

The function returns an `int`-typed value that represents the check state. A value of 0 indicates that the control is not checked. A value of 1 signals that the control is checked. A value of 2 indicates that the control is in an indeterminate state. The latter value is valid for the `BS_3STATE` and `BS_AUTO3STATE` styles.

Note: To enhance the readability of the code, I recommend that you declare constants, such as `BF_UNCHECKED`, `BF_CHECKED`, and `BF_GRAYED`, to represent the three states of the check box controls.

The `SetCheck` member function allows you to set the check state of a check box control. The declaration of the `SetCheck` function is

```
void SetCheck(int nCheck);
```

The `nCheck` parameter specifies the new state of the check box control.

Responding to Check Box Messages

Because check boxes are instances of `CButton` with a `BS_CHECKBOX` or `BS_AUTOCHECKBOX` style, your MFC application responds to the messages emitted by check boxes in a manner similar to the pushbuttons. The `BN_CLICKED` macro maps the message sent by the check box control with the member function that responds to that message.

The Radio Button Control

Radio button controls typically allow you to select an option from two or more options. This kind of control comes with a circular button and a title that appears, by default, to the right of the button. When you check a radio button, a tiny filled circle appears inside the circular button. Radio buttons need to be placed in group boxes that visually and logically group them. In each group of radio buttons, only one button can be selected. Therefore, radio buttons are mutually exclusive.

The *CButton* Class and Radio Buttons

The MFC applications use the `CButton` class to create radio button controls by specifying the `BS_RADIOBUTTON` or `BS_AUTORADIOBUTTON`. Table 17.2 contains the radio button styles. The constructor creates a radio button with the `BS_AUTORADIOBUTTON` style. Creating these controls involves the class constructor and the `Create` member function. Like the check box controls, the radio buttons use the `GetCheck` and `SetCheck` member functions to query and set the state. Unlike the check box, the radio button has only two states: checked and unchecked.

Table 17.2. Radio button control styles.

Style	Meaning
`BS_RADIOBUTTON`	Specifies a radio button with the title to the right of the circular button
`BS_AUTORADIOBUTTON`	Same as `BS_RADIOBUTTON`, except the button is automatically toggled when you click on it
`BS_LEFTTEXT`	Sets the control's title to the left of the button

The radio button controls send the same type of notification messages to their parent windows as do the check box controls. Handling of these messages for radio buttons is identical to that of check box and pushbutton controls.

The Group Box Control

The group box control encloses radio buttons and check boxes. The group box performs the following tasks:

- Visually groups radio buttons and/or check boxes, which makes relating these controls to each other clearer for the application user
- Logically groups multiple radio buttons so that when you select one radio button, the other buttons in the same group are automatically deselected

NEW TERM The group box control is a special type of control known as a *container control.* You can code your MFC application so that the controls inside a group box notify the parent of the group box that you have changed the state of its controls.

The *CButton* Class and Group Boxes

Your MFC applications can create group boxes by specifying the `BS_GROUPBOX` style when creating a `CButton` instance. Unlike the check box, radio button, and pushbutton controls, there is no state for the group box controls. In addition, group boxes do not send messages.

The Updated Calculator Application

The operations of the calculator application that are presented on Day 16 can be expanded to include trigonometric functions. Using trigonometric functions frequently offers you the choice of angle modes: radians, degrees, or gradians (100 gradians equal 90 degrees). Using a group box that contains angle mode radio buttons seems suitable to illustrate the operations of these controls. Check boxes are added to fine-tune other operational aspects of the calculator. More about this later in this section.

Create the directory CTLGRP1 as a subdirectory of \MSVC20\VC21DAY and store all the project's files in the new directory. The project's .MAK file should contain the files CTLGRP1.CPP, CTLGRP1.RC, and CTLGRP1.DEF. The latter file resembles file MINWINAP.DEF in Day 14, Listing 14.2.

> **Note:** I choose to present nontrivial applications to illustrate nontrivial features that involve the radio button, check box, and edit text controls. Although the program in Listing 17.3 is long, you can create it by starting with a copy of program CTLBTN1.CPP and adding the new functions and statements.

The Illustrated Aspects

The updated calculator application (COCA version 2) illustrates the following:

- The basic use of check box controls
- The basic use of radio buttons
- Responding to radio button notification messages
- Echoing the changes in the selected radio button control to the group box control
- Using a check box control to alter the action of a response message function (this function handles the group box response to select a new radio button)
- Manipulating multiple check boxes and edit boxes using the `ForEach` iterator
- Making initial check box selections

- Making initial radio button selections

The new version of the calculator application contains the following controls:

- The single-line edit controls labeled Operand1, Operator, Operand2, Result, and Error Message
- The multiline edit control labeled Variables
- The static text controls that label these edit boxes
- The Calc, Store, and Exit pushbuttons
- The Angle Mode group box that contains the Radians, Degrees, and Gradians radio buttons
- The Substitute variable name check box that replaces the names of the single-letter variables appearing in either operand edit box with their values (the replacement occurs after you click the Calc pushbutton)
- The Echo Group box message check box that permits the group notification message handler to display a message box when you select another radio button
- The menu that contains the Exit and Clear main menu items

The Clear pop-up menu has the Edit Controls and Check Boxes menu items. The Edit Controls menu item clears the contents of the edit controls, except the Variables edit box. The Check Boxes menu item unchecks the three check boxes.

Experimenting with the Application

Listing 17.1 contains the source code for the CTLGRP1.H header file, and Listing 17.2 shows the script for the CTLGRP1.RC resource file. The resource file contains the accelerator keys and the menu resources. Listing 17.3 contains the source code for the CTLGRP1.CPP program file. The program contains `#include` statements; declarations of constants; iterated functions; and the classes for the application, its window, and its controls.

Compile and run the calculator application to get a good feel for the features supported by the radio buttons, check boxes, and the group box. When the application's window appears, maximize it to get a full view. The Angle Mode group box shows the initial selection of the Degrees radio button. The current application version supports the `SIN`, `COS`, `TAN`, `ASIN`, `ACOS`, and `ATAN` trigonometric functions that you can enter in the Operator edit box. Enter the number 45 in the Operand1 edit box and type `TAN` in the Operator edit box. Click the Calc button to obtain the tangent of 45 degrees in the Result edit box (a value of 1). Store the result in variable A by clicking the Store button. Now replace the number 45 with the # character in the Operand1 edit box. Then insert an A before the string TAN in the Operator box, and click the Calc button. The # character is replaced by 1, the previous number in the Result edit box. The Result edit box now shows the number 45, the arctangent of 1. Using the # character is a new feature that I added to the program—the ability to use the result from the previous calculation in either or both operand edit boxes by typing in the # character. Next, click the Store button again. The application stores the number 45 in variable A, overwriting the previous result. Now, the number in the Result edit box is stored in multiple variables.

Check the Echo Group message box check box and then click on any radio button. The application displays a message box that contains information on converting between different angles. Selecting a different radio button yields a different message. These messages are responses to the Angle Mode group notification message.

Experiment with selecting different angle modes. Each time, enter a value in the Operand1 edit box and type in a trigonometric function. Observe how the results differ for the same arguments although the angle mode varies. Keep in mind that the inverse sine and cosine functions accept arguments between -1 and 1. The application detects invalid arguments for these two functions and displays error messages.

Finally, use the Clear | Edit Control and Clear | Check Boxes menu items to clear the edit boxes (except the Variables edit box) and the check boxes.

I omit the feature that clears the error message and enables the Store button when you click on the Error Message label. This omission should shorten the program a bit.

Type **Listing 17.1. Source code for the CTLGRP1.H header file.**

```
#define CM_EXIT     (WM_USER + 100)
#define CM_CLEARBOX (WM_USER + 101)
#define CM_CLEARCHK (WM_USER + 102)

#define ID_CALC_BTN  107
#define ID_STORE_BTN 108
#define ID_EXIT_BTN  109
```

Type **Listing 17.2. Script for the CTLGRP1.RC resource file.**

```
#include <afxres.h>
#include "ctlgrp1.h"

BUTTONS ACCELERATORS
BEGIN
```

```
  "c", ID_CALC_BTN, ALT
  "s", ID_STORE_BTN, ALT
  "e", ID_EXIT_BTN, ALT
END

EXITMENU MENU LOADONCALL MOVEABLE PURE DISCARDABLE
BEGIN
    MENUITEM "E&xit", CM_EXIT
    POPUP "C&lear"
    BEGIN
      MENUITEM "&Edit Controls", CM_CLEARBOX
      MENUITEM "&Check Boxes", CM_CLEARCHK
    END
END
```

Type Listing 17.3. Source code for the CTLGRP1.CPP program file.

```
#include <stdlib.h>
#include <ctype.h>
#include <stdio.h>
#include <math.h>
#include <string.h>
#include <afxwin.h>
#include "ctlgrp1.h"

// declare the constants that represent the sizes of the controls
const Wlbl = 100;
const Hlbl = 20;
const LblVertSpacing = 5;
const LblHorzSpacing = 40;
const Wbox = 100;
const Hbox = 30;
const BoxVertSpacing = 10;
const BoxHorzSpacing = 40;
const WLongbox = 4 * (Wbox + BoxHorzSpacing);
const Wvarbox = 2 * Wbox;
const Hvarbox = 3 * Hbox;
const Hbtn = 30;
const Wbtn = 80;
const BtnHorzSpacing = 30;
const BtnVertSpacing = 10;
const Hgrp = 150;
const Wgrp = 180;
const GrpHorzSpacing = 30;
const GrpVertSpacing = 10;
const Hchk = 30;
const Wchk = 200;
const ChkHorzSpacing = 30;
const ChkVertSpacing = 10;
const Hrbt = 30;
const Wrbt = 80;
const RbtHorzSpacing = 30;
```

continues

Listing 17.3. continued

```
const RbtVertSpacing = 30;
const RbtLeftMargin = 30;
// non-ctrol related constants
const MaxEditLen = 30;
const MAX_MEMREG = 26;
// declare the ID_XXXX constants for the various controls
// (except the pushbuttons)
#define ID_OPERAND1_EDIT 101
#define ID_OPERATOR_EDIT 102
#define ID_OPERAND2_EDIT 103
#define ID_RESULT_EDIT 104
#define ID_ERRMSG_EDIT 105
#define ID_VARIABLE_EDIT 106
#define ID_SUBST_CHK 110
#define ID_ECHO_CHK 111
#define ID_ANGLE_GRP 112
#define ID_RADIAN_RBT 113
#define ID_DEGREE_RBT 114
#define ID_GRADIAN_RBT 115
// declare constants for the check box and radio button states
const BF_CHECKED = 1;
const BF_UNCHECKED = 0;
// declare angle-related constants
const double pi = 4 * atan(1);
const double DegToRad = pi / 180;
const double GradToRad = 0.9 * DegToRad;

// declare extended button class
class CxButton : public CButton
{
public:

   BOOL Create(const char FAR* lpCaption, const RECT& rect,
               CWnd* pParentWnd, UINT nID)
   {
       return CButton::Create(lpCaption,
                              WS_CHILD ¦ WS_VISIBLE ¦
                              WS_TABSTOP ¦ BS_PUSHBUTTON,
                              rect, pParentWnd, nID);
   }
};

// declare check box class
class CCheckBox : public CButton
{
public:
   BOOL Create(const char FAR* lpCaption, const RECT& rect,
               CWnd* pParentWnd, UINT nID)
   {
       return CButton::Create(lpCaption,
                              WS_CHILD ¦ WS_VISIBLE ¦
                              WS_TABSTOP ¦ BS_AUTOCHECKBOX,
                              rect, pParentWnd, nID);
   }
```

```
    // check control
    void Check() { SetCheck(BF_CHECKED); }
    // uncheck control
    void UnCheck() { SetCheck(BF_UNCHECKED); }
};

// declare radio button class
class CRadioButton : public CButton
{
public:
    BOOL Create(const char FAR* lpCaption, const RECT& rect,
                CWnd* pParentWnd, UINT nID)
    {
        return CButton::Create(lpCaption,
                               WS_CHILD | WS_VISIBLE |
                               WS_TABSTOP |
                               BS_AUTORADIOBUTTON,
                               rect, pParentWnd, nID);
    }
    // check control
    void Check() { SetCheck(BF_CHECKED); }
    // uncheck control
    void UnCheck()
      { SetCheck(BF_UNCHECKED); }
};

// declare group box class
class CGroupBox : public CButton
{
public:
    BOOL Create(const char FAR* lpCaption, const RECT& rect,
                CWnd* pParentWnd, UINT nID)
    {
        return CButton::Create(lpCaption,
                               WS_CHILD | WS_VISIBLE |
                               WS_TABSTOP | BS_GROUPBOX,
                               rect, pParentWnd, nID);
    }
};


class CxEdit : public CEdit
{
public:

  BOOL GetLine(LPSTR ATextString, int nStrSize, int nLineNumber);
  int GetLineLength(int nLineNumber);
};

class CWindowApp : public CWinApp
{
public:
     virtual BOOL InitInstance();
};
// expand the functionality of CFrameWnd by deriving class
// CAppWindow
```

17

continues

Listing 17.3. continued

```
class CAppWindow : public CFrameWnd
{
public:

  CAppWindow();
  ~CAppWindow();

protected:
  // declare the pointers to the various controls
  // first, the edit box controls
  CEdit* Operand1Box;
  CEdit* OperatorBox;
  CEdit* Operand2Box;
  CEdit* ResultBox;
  CEdit* ErrMsgBox;
  CxEdit* VariableBox;
  // then the static text controls
  CStatic* Operand1Txt;
  CStatic* OperatorTxt;
  CStatic* Operand2Txt;
  CStatic* ResultTxt;
  CStatic* ErrMsgTxt;
  CStatic* VariableTxt;
  // then the pushbuttons
  CxButton* CalcBtn;
  CxButton* StoreBtn;
  CxButton* ExitBtn;
  // then the angle group box
  CGroupBox* AngleModeGrp;
  // then the radio buttons
  CRadioButton* RadianRbt;
  CRadioButton* DegreeRbt;
  CRadioButton* GradianRbt;
  // then the check boxes
  CCheckBox* AutoVarSubstChk;
  CCheckBox* EchoGroupChk;
  // math error flag
  BOOL bInError;
  // the factor that converts between angles the
  // currently selected angle mode and radians
  double angleFactor;

  // handle clearing the edit controls
  afx_msg void CMClearBox();
  // handle clearing the check box controls
  afx_msg void CMClearChk();
  // handle the calculation
  afx_msg void HandleCalcBtn();
  // handle the calculation
  afx_msg void CMCalc() { HandleCalcBtn(); }
  // handle storing the result in a variable
  afx_msg void HandleStoreBtn();
  // handle storing the result in a variable
  afx_msg void CMStore() { HandleStoreBtn(); }
```

```
  // handle exiting the application
  afx_msg void HandleExitBtn() { SendMessage(WM_CLOSE); }
  // handle exiting the application
  afx_msg void CMExit() { SendMessage(WM_CLOSE); }
  // handle exiting the application
  afx_msg void OnExit() { SendMessage(WM_CLOSE); }
  // handle the Angle Mode group box message
  // this member is called only by the radio button
  // controls; it therefore need not be included in the
  // message map
  void HandleAngleModeGrp();
  // handle selecting the Radians radio button
  afx_msg void HandleRadianRbt();
  // handle selecting the Degrees radio button
  afx_msg void HandleDegreeRbt();
  // handle selecting the Gradians radio button
  afx_msg void HandleGradianRbt();
  // enable a pushbutton control
  virtual void EnableButton(CxButton* pBtn)
    { pBtn->EnableWindow( TRUE); }
  // disable a pushbutton control
  virtual void DisableButton(CxButton* pBtn)
    { pBtn->EnableWindow(FALSE); }
  // handle creating the controls
  afx_msg int OnCreate(LPCREATESTRUCT lpCS);
  // handle closing the window
  afx_msg void OnClose();
  // initialize the instances of CAppWindow
  virtual void InitAppWindow();
  // return a reference to member r based on individual
  // coordinates and dimensions
  void makeRect(int nX, int nY, int nW, int nH, CRect& r);
  // obtain a number of a Variable edit box line
  double getVar(int nLineNum);
  // store a number in the selected text of
  // the Variable edit box line
  void putVar(double x);
  // declare the iterator for the check boxes
  void ForEachCheckBox(void (FAR *f)(CCheckBox*));
  // declare the iterator for the edit controls
  void ForEachEditCtl(void (FAR *f)(CEdit*));

  // declare message map macro
  DECLARE_MESSAGE_MAP();
};

// declare an iterated function to clear all edit controls
// except the Variables edit control
void FAR ClearEditControls(CEdit* P)
{ P->SetWindowText(""); }

// declare the iterated function to clear the check boxes
void FAR ClearCheckBoxes(CCheckBox* P)
{ P->UnCheck(); }

BOOL CxEdit::GetLine(LPSTR ATextString, int nStrSize,
```

continues

Listing 17.3. continued

```
                          int nLineNumber)
{
  int nBytesCopied;
  BOOL bSuccess;

  if (nStrSize <= 0)
    return FALSE;
  bSuccess = (nStrSize >= GetLineLength(nLineNumber) + 1) ? TRUE
                                                          : FALSE;
  if (nStrSize == 1)
  {
    ATextString[0] = '\0';
    return bSuccess;
  }

  ((WORD FAR *)ATextString)[0] = nStrSize;

  nBytesCopied = (WORD)(SendMessage(EM_GETLINE, nLineNumber,
                                    long(ATextString)));
  if (nBytesCopied)
  {
    // Windows returns non-null-terminated string
    ATextString[nBytesCopied] = '\0';
    return bSuccess;
  }
  else
    return FALSE;
}

int CxEdit::GetLineLength(int nLineNumber)
{
  int nStartPos = -1;

  if (nLineNumber > -1)
    nStartPos = LineIndex(nLineNumber);
  return (WORD) SendMessage(EM_LINELENGTH, nStartPos);
}

CAppWindow::CAppWindow()
{
  // load accelerator resources
  LoadAccelTable("BUTTONS");
  // create the window
  Create(NULL,
    "Command-Oriented Calculator Application (COCA) Version 2",
      WS_OVERLAPPEDWINDOW | WS_MAXIMIZE,
        rectDefault, NULL, "EXITMENU");
  // perform initialization
  InitAppWindow();
  // clear the bInError flag
  bInError = FALSE;
}

CAppWindow::~CAppWindow()
```

```
{
  // delete the controls
  delete Operand1Box;
  delete OperatorBox;
  delete Operand2Box;
  delete ResultBox;
  delete ErrMsgBox;
  delete VariableBox;
  delete Operand1Txt;
  delete OperatorTxt;
  delete Operand2Txt;
  delete ResultTxt;
  delete ErrMsgTxt;
  delete VariableTxt;
  delete CalcBtn;
  delete StoreBtn;
  delete ExitBtn;
  delete AngleModeGrp;
  delete RadianRbt;
  delete DegreeRbt;
  delete GradianRbt;
  delete AutoVarSubstChk;
  delete EchoGroupChk;
}

int CAppWindow::OnCreate(LPCREATESTRUCT lpCS)
{
  char s[81];
  char bigStr[6 * MAX_MEMREG + 1];
  char chC;
  int nX0 = 20;
  int nY0 = 30;
  int nX = nX0, nY = nY0;
  int nX1, nY1;
  CRect r;
  DWORD StatStyle = WS_CHILD ¦ WS_VISIBLE ¦ SS_LEFT;
  DWORD BoxStyle = WS_CHILD ¦ WS_VISIBLE ¦ WS_TABSTOP ¦ WS_BORDER
                   ¦ ES_LEFT ¦ ES_AUTOHSCROLL ¦ ES_UPPERCASE;

  // create the first set of labels for the edit boxes
  makeRect(nX, nY, Wlbl, Hlbl, r);
  Operand1Txt = new CStatic();
  Operand1Txt->Create("Operand1", StatStyle, r, this, -1);
  nX += Wlbl + LblHorzSpacing;
  makeRect(nX, nY, Wlbl, Hlbl, r);
  OperatorTxt = new CStatic();
  OperatorTxt->Create("Operator", StatStyle, r, this, -1);
  nX += Wlbl + LblHorzSpacing;
  makeRect(nX, nY, Wlbl, Hlbl, r);
  Operand2Txt = new CStatic();
  Operand2Txt->Create("Operand2", StatStyle, r, this, -1);
  nX += Wlbl + LblHorzSpacing;
  makeRect(nX, nY, Wlbl, Hlbl, r);
  ResultTxt = new CStatic();
  ResultTxt->Create("Result", StatStyle, r, this, -1);

```

continues

Listing 17.3. continued

```
// create the operand1, operator, operand2, and result
// edit boxes
nX = nX0;
nY += Hlbl + LblVertSpacing;
makeRect(nX, nY, Wbox, Hbox, r);
Operand1Box = new CEdit();
Operand1Box->Create(BoxStyle, r, this, ID_OPERAND1_EDIT);
Operand1Box->LimitText(); // set no limit for text
nX += Wbox + BoxHorzSpacing;
makeRect(nX, nY, Wbox, Hbox, r);
OperatorBox = new CEdit();
OperatorBox->Create(BoxStyle, r, this, ID_OPERATOR_EDIT);
OperatorBox->LimitText(); // set no limit for text
nX += Wbox + BoxHorzSpacing;
makeRect(nX, nY, Wbox, Hbox, r);
Operand2Box = new CEdit();
Operand2Box->Create(BoxStyle, r, this, ID_OPERAND2_EDIT);
Operand2Box->LimitText(); // set no limit for text
nX += Wbox + BoxHorzSpacing;
makeRect(nX, nY, Wbox, Hbox, r);
ResultBox = new CEdit();
ResultBox->Create(BoxStyle, r, this, ID_RESULT_EDIT);
ResultBox->LimitText(); // set no limit for text
// create the static text and edit box for the error message
nX = nX0;
nY += Hbox + BoxVertSpacing;
makeRect(nX, nY, Wlbl, Hlbl, r);
ErrMsgTxt = new CStatic();
ErrMsgTxt->Create("Error Message", StatStyle, r, this, -1);
nY += Hlbl + LblVertSpacing;
makeRect(nX, nY, WLongbox, Hbox, r);
ErrMsgBox = new CEdit();
ErrMsgBox->Create(BoxStyle, r, this, ID_ERRMSG_EDIT);
ErrMsgBox->LimitText(); // set no limit for text
// create the static text and edit box for the single-letter
// variable selection
nY += Hbox + BoxVertSpacing;
makeRect(nX, nY, Wlbl, Hlbl, r);
VariableTxt = new CStatic();
VariableTxt->Create("Variables", StatStyle, r, this, -1);
nY += Hlbl + LblVertSpacing;
bigStr[0] = '\0';
// build the initial contents of the Variable edit box
for (chC = 'A'; chC <= 'Z'; chC++) {
  sprintf(s, "%c: 0\r\n", chC);
  strcat(bigStr, s);
}
makeRect(nX, nY, Wvarbox, Hvarbox, r);
VariableBox = new CxEdit();
VariableBox->Create(BoxStyle ¦ ES_MULTILINE ¦ WS_HSCROLL
               ¦ WS_VSCROLL ¦ ES_AUTOVSCROLL,
                     r, this, ID_VARIABLE_EDIT);
VariableBox->LimitText(); // set no limit for text
VariableBox->SetWindowText(bigStr);
```

```
    // create the Calc pushbutton
    nX += Wvarbox + BtnHorzSpacing;
    nX1 = nX;
    nY1 = nY;
    makeRect(nX, nY, Wbtn, Hbtn, r);
    CalcBtn = new CxButton();
    CalcBtn->Create("&Calc", r, this, ID_CALC_BTN);

    // create the Store Btn
    nX += Wbtn + BtnHorzSpacing;
    makeRect(nX, nY, Wbtn, Hbtn, r);
    StoreBtn = new CxButton();
    StoreBtn->Create("&Store", r, this, ID_STORE_BTN);

    // create the Exit Btn
    nX += Wbtn + BtnHorzSpacing;
    makeRect(nX, nY, Wbtn, Hbtn, r);
    ExitBtn = new CxButton();
    ExitBtn->Create("&Exit", r, this, ID_EXIT_BTN);

    // create the "Substitute variable name" check box
    nX = nX0;
    nY += Hvarbox + BoxVertSpacing;
    makeRect(nX, nY, Wchk, Hchk, r);
    AutoVarSubstChk = new CCheckBox();
    AutoVarSubstChk->Create("Substitute variable name", r,
                            this, ID_SUBST_CHK);

    // create the "Echo Group box message" check box
    nY += Hchk + ChkVertSpacing;
    makeRect(nX, nY, Wchk, Hchk, r);
    EchoGroupChk = new CCheckBox();
    EchoGroupChk->Create("Echo Group box message", r,
                         this, ID_ECHO_CHK);

    // create the Angle Mode group box
    nY = nY1 + Hbtn + BtnVertSpacing;
    nX = nX1;
    makeRect(nX, nY, Wgrp, Hgrp, r);
    AngleModeGrp = new CGroupBox();
    AngleModeGrp->Create(" Angle Mode ", r, this, ID_ANGLE_GRP);

    // create the Radians radio button
    nY += RbtVertSpacing;
    makeRect(RbtLeftMargin + nX, nY, Wrbt, Hrbt, r);
    RadianRbt = new CRadioButton();
    RadianRbt->Create("Radians", r, this, ID_RADIAN_RBT);

    // create the Degrees radio button
    nY += RbtVertSpacing;
    makeRect(RbtLeftMargin + nX, nY, Wrbt, Hrbt, r);
    DegreeRbt = new CRadioButton();
    DegreeRbt->Create("Degrees", r, this, ID_DEGREE_RBT);

    // create the Gradians radio button
```

continues

Listing 17.3. continued

```
  nY += RbtVertSpacing;
  makeRect(RbtLeftMargin + nX, nY, Wrbt, Hrbt, r);
  GradianRbt = new CRadioButton();
  GradianRbt->Create("Gradians", r, this, ID_GRADIAN_RBT);

  return CFrameWnd::OnCreate(lpCS);
}

void CAppWindow::InitAppWindow()
{

  // disable the Store button control
  EnableButton(StoreBtn);

  // check the Degrees radio button
  DegreeRbt->Check();
  angleFactor = DegToRad;

  // check the "Echo Group message box" check button
  EchoGroupChk->Check();
}

void CAppWindow::CMClearBox()
{
  ForEachEditCtl(ClearEditControls);
}

void CAppWindow::CMClearChk()
{
  ForEachCheckBox(ClearCheckBoxes);
}

void CAppWindow::HandleCalcBtn()
{
  double x, y, z, result;
  char opStr[MaxEditLen+1];
  char s[MaxEditLen+1];

  // convert the string in the Result box to a double
  ResultBox->GetWindowText(s, MaxEditLen);
  result = atof(s);

  // obtain the string in the Operand1 edit box
  Operand1Box->GetWindowText(s, MaxEditLen);
  // does the Operand1Box contain the name
  // of a single-letter variable?
  if (isalpha(s[0])) {
    // obtain value from the Variable edit control
    x = getVar(s[0] - 'A');
    // substitute the variable name with its value
    if (AutoVarSubstChk->GetCheck() == BF_CHECKED) {
      sprintf(s, "%g", x);
      Operand1Box->SetWindowText(s);
    }
```

```
  }
  // translate the # character into the value in the Result box
  else if (s[0] == '#')
    x = result;
  else
    // convert the string in the edit box
    x = atof(s);

  // obtain the string in the Operand2 edit box
  Operand2Box->GetWindowText(s, MaxEditLen);
  // does the Operand2Box contain the name
  // of a single-letter variable?
  if (isalpha(s[0])) {
    // obtain value from the Variable edit control
    y =getVar(s[0] - 'A');
    // substitute the variable name with its value
    if (AutoVarSubstChk->GetCheck() == BF_CHECKED) {
      sprintf(s, "%g", y);
      Operand2Box->SetWindowText(s);
    }
  }
  // translate the # character into the value in the Result box
  else if (s[0] == '#')
    y = result;
  else
     // convert the string in the edit box
    y = atof(s);

  // obtain the string in the Operator edit box
  OperatorBox->GetWindowText(opStr, MaxEditLen);

  // clear the error message box
  ErrMsgBox->SetWindowText("");
  bInError = FALSE;

  // determine the requested operation
  if (strlen(opStr) == 1) {
    if (strcmp(opStr, "+") == 0)
      z = x + y;
    else if (strcmp(opStr, "-") == 0)
      z = x - y;
    else if (strcmp(opStr, "*") == 0)
      z = x * y;
    else if (strcmp(opStr, "/") == 0) {
      if (y != 0)
        z = x / y;
      else {
        z = 0;
        bInError = TRUE;
        ErrMsgBox->SetWindowText("Division-by-zero error");
      }
    }
    else if (strcmp(opStr, "^") == 0) {
      if (x > 0)
        z = exp(y * log(x));
      else {
```

continues

Listing 17.3. continued

```
        bInError = TRUE;
        ErrMsgBox->SetWindowText(
          "Cannot raise the power of a negative number");
      }
    }
    else {
      bInError = TRUE;
      ErrMsgBox->SetWindowText("Invalid operator");
    }
  }
  else if (strcmp(opStr, "SIN") == 0) {
    z = sin(angleFactor * x);
  }
  else if (strcmp(opStr, "COS") == 0) {
    z = cos(angleFactor * x);
  }
  else if (strcmp(opStr, "TAN") == 0) {
    z = tan(angleFactor * x);
  }
  else if (strcmp(opStr, "ASIN") == 0) {
    if (fabs(x) <= 1)
      z = asin(x) / angleFactor;
    else {
      bInError = TRUE;
      ErrMsgBox->SetWindowText(
          "Invalid argument for the asin(x)  function");
    }
  }
  else if (strcmp(opStr, "ACOS") == 0) {
    if (fabs(x) <= 1)
      z = acos(x) / angleFactor;
    else {
      bInError = TRUE;
      ErrMsgBox->SetWindowText
                     ("Invalid argument for the acos(x) function");
    }
  }
  else if (strcmp(opStr, "ATAN") == 0) {
    z = atan(x) / angleFactor;
  }
  else {
    bInError = TRUE;
    ErrMsgBox->SetWindowText("Invalid math function");
  }

  // display the result if no error has occurred
  if (!bInError) {
    sprintf(s, "%g", z);
    ResultBox->SetWindowText(s);
    // enable the Store button
    EnableButton(StoreBtn);
  }
  else
    // disable the Store button
```

```
    DisableButton(StoreBtn);
}

void CAppWindow::HandleStoreBtn()
{
  char result[MaxEditLen+1];

  // get the string in the Result edit box
  ResultBox->GetWindowText(result, MaxEditLen);

  // store the result in the selected text of
  // the Variable edit box
  putVar(atof(result));
}

void CAppWindow::HandleAngleModeGrp()
{
  char angleStr[81];

  // exit if the EchoGroup check box is not checked
  if (EchoGroupChk->GetCheck() != BF_CHECKED) return;
  // build the text of the message
  if (DegreeRbt->GetCheck() == BF_CHECKED)
    sprintf(angleStr, "1 radian = %g degrees", 1 / DegToRad);
  else if (GradianRbt->GetCheck() == BF_CHECKED)
    sprintf(angleStr, "1 radian = %g gradians", 1 / GradToRad);
  else
    sprintf(angleStr, "1 radian = %g degrees = %g gradians",
            1 / DegToRad, 1 / GradToRad);
  MessageBox(angleStr, "Group Box Message",
             MB_OK | MB_ICONINFORMATION);
}

void CAppWindow::HandleRadianRbt()
{
  angleFactor = 1;
  HandleAngleModeGrp();
}

void CAppWindow::HandleDegreeRbt()
{
  angleFactor = DegToRad;
  HandleAngleModeGrp();
}

void CAppWindow::HandleGradianRbt()
{
  angleFactor = GradToRad;
  HandleAngleModeGrp();
}

void CAppWindow::makeRect(int X, int Y, int W, int H, CRect& r)
{
  r.top = Y;
  r.left = X;
  r.bottom = Y + H;
```

continues

Listing 17.3. continued

```
  r.right = X + W;
}

double CAppWindow::getVar(int nLineNum)
{
  int nLineSize;
  char s[MaxEditLen+1];

  if (nLineNum >= MAX_MEMREG) return 0;
  // get the size of the target line
  nLineSize = VariableBox->GetLineLength(nLineNum);
  // get the line
  VariableBox->GetLine(s, nLineSize, nLineNum);
  // delete the first three characters
  strcpy(s, (s+3));
  // return the number stored in the target line
  return atof(s);
}

void CAppWindow::putVar(double x)
{
  DWORD dwSelPos;
  WORD wStartPos, wEndPos;
  int nLineNum;
  int nLineSize;
  char s[MaxEditLen+1];

  // locate the character position of the cursor
  dwSelPos = VariableBox->GetSel();
  wStartPos = LOWORD(dwSelPos);
  wEndPos = HIWORD(dwSelPos);
  // turn off the selected text
  if (wStartPos != wEndPos) {
    dwSelPos = MAKELONG(wStartPos, wStartPos);
    VariableBox->SetSel(dwSelPos);
  }
  // get the line number where the cursor is located
  nLineNum = VariableBox->LineFromChar(-1);
  // get the line size of line nLineNum
  nLineSize = VariableBox->GetLineLength(nLineNum);
  // obtain the text of line nLineNum
  VariableBox->GetLine(s, nLineSize, nLineNum);
  // build the new text line
  sprintf(s, "%c: %g", s[0], x);
  // get the character positions for the deleted line
  wStartPos = (WORD) (VariableBox->LineIndex(-1));
  wEndPos = (WORD) (wStartPos + VariableBox->LineLength(-1));
  // select the current line
  dwSelPos = MAKELONG(wStartPos, wEndPos);
  VariableBox->SetSel(dwSelPos);
  // replace the current line with the new line
  VariableBox->ReplaceSel(s);
}

void CAppWindow::OnClose()
{
```

```
  if (MessageBox("Want to close this application",
                 "Query", MB_YESNO | MB_ICONQUESTION) == IDYES)
    DestroyWindow();
}

void CAppWindow::ForEachCheckBox(void (FAR *f)(CCheckBox*))
{
  CCheckBox* P;

  for (int nID = ID_SUBST_CHK; nID <= ID_ECHO_CHK; nID++) {
     // get the pointer to the next button
     P = (CCheckBox*) (this->GetDlgItem(nID));
     // process the button
     (*f)(P);
  }
}

void CAppWindow::ForEachEditCtl(void (FAR *f)(CEdit*))
{
  CEdit* P;

  for(int nID = ID_OPERAND1_EDIT; nID <= ID_ERRMSG_EDIT; nID++) {
     // get the pointer to the next button
     P = (CEdit*) (this->GetDlgItem(nID));
     // process the button
     (*f)(P);
  }
}

BEGIN_MESSAGE_MAP(CAppWindow, CFrameWnd)
    ON_COMMAND(CM_CLEARBOX, CMClearBox)
    ON_COMMAND(CM_CLEARCHK, CMClearChk)
    ON_BN_CLICKED(ID_CALC_BTN, HandleCalcBtn)
    ON_COMMAND(ID_CALC_BTN, CMCalc)
    ON_BN_CLICKED(ID_STORE_BTN, HandleStoreBtn)
    ON_COMMAND(ID_STORE_BTN, CMStore)
    ON_BN_CLICKED(ID_EXIT_BTN, HandleExitBtn)
    ON_COMMAND(ID_EXIT_BTN, CMExit)
    ON_COMMAND(CM_EXIT, OnExit)
    ON_BN_CLICKED(ID_RADIAN_RBT, HandleRadianRbt)
    ON_BN_CLICKED(ID_DEGREE_RBT, HandleDegreeRbt)
    ON_BN_CLICKED(ID_GRADIAN_RBT, HandleGradianRbt)
    ON_WM_CREATE()
    ON_WM_KEYDOWN()
    ON_WM_CLOSE()
END_MESSAGE_MAP()

// Construct the CWindowApp's m_pMainWnd data member
BOOL CWindowApp::InitInstance()
{
  m_pMainWnd = new CAppWindow();
  m_pMainWnd->ShowWindow(m_nCmdShow);
  m_pMainWnd->UpdateWindow();
  return TRUE;
}

// application's constructor initializes and runs the app
CWindowApp WindowApp;
```

Figure 17.1 shows a sample session with program CTRLGRP1.EXE.

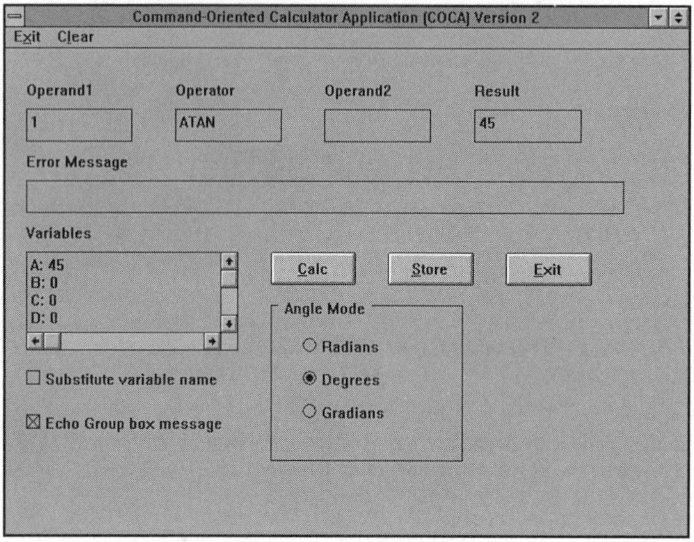

Figure 17.1. *A sample session with program CTLGRP1.EXE.*

Analysis

The application declares the following sets of controls:

- A set of constants, in lines 10 through 37, specifies the sizes and spacings between the various controls.
- The macro-based constants, in lines 43 through 54, define the IDs of the various controls.
- The constants, in lines 56 and 57, are for the check box and radio button states.
- The last set of constants, in lines 59 through 61, specifies the value of pi and the angle conversion factors between radians and degrees and between radians and gradians.

The CTLGRP1.CPP program declares the following classes:

- The `CxButton` class, a descendant of `CButton`, to model pushbutton controls (the declaration for this class starts at line 64).
- The `CCheckBox` class, a descendant of `CButton`, to model check box controls (the declaration for this class starts at line 79).

- The CRadioButton class, a descendant of CButton, to model radio button controls (the declaration for this class starts at line 97).
- The CGroupBox class, a descendant of CButton, to model group box controls (the declaration for this class starts at line 117).
- The CxEdit class, a descendant of CEdit, to model an enhanced version of the edit controls (the declaration for this class starts at line 131).
- The CWindowApp application class (the declaration for this class starts at line 139).
- The CAppWindow window class (the declaration for this class starts at line 146).

17

The CCheckBox and CRadioButton classes declare the member functions Check and UnCheck to set and clear the check state of these controls.

The CAppWindow window class contains a good number of data members in lines 156 through 186. Most of these members are pointers to the instances of the various controls used by the application. The application adds the angleFactor data member to store the angle conversion factor between the currently selected angle mode and radians.

The CAppWindow class declares a constructor, a destructor, and a number of member functions to support the nontrivial program operations and special initialization. The constructor loads the menu resource and creates the various controls, with the help of member function OnCreate. Of interest are the statements in function OnCreate that create the check boxes, the group box, and the radio buttons. Each instance of CCheckBox involves a unique control ID, title, and coordinates. These CCheckBox instances are created without the WS_GROUP style to indicate that each check box is created outside a group box. The group box instance is created with its own ID, title, and coordinates. Each radio button control is created with a unique ID, title, and coordinates. Notice that these radio buttons have the main window as their parent and not the group box, even though they are visually located inside the group box.

The CAppWindow class declares the various member functions needed to implement the program's operations. The CMClearBox function clears the text in all the edit controls, except the Variables edit control. The function uses the ForEachEditCtl member function as the iterator to perform the required task. Similarly, the CMClearChk member function clears the check boxes by invoking the ForEachCheckBox member function as the iterator.

The HandleCalcBtn member function performs the calculations and any character substitution. The member function performs the following tasks:

- Converts the string in the Result edit control to a double and stores that value in the local variable result.
- Obtains the value for the first operand stored in variable `x`; the Operand1 edit control contains either a string image of a number, the name of a single-letter variable, or the `#` character:
  - The statements that support the first option determine whether or not the Operand1 box contains a letter. If this condition is true, the statements invoke the `getVar` member function and assign the result to variable `x`. In addition, the code checks whether the Substitute variable name check box is checked. If so, the name of the variable in the Operand1 box is replaced with its value.
  - The statements that support the second option compare the first character in the Operand1 box with the `#` character. If the two characters match, the value stored in the local variable result is assigned to the variable `x`.
  - The statements that support the third option simply convert the string in the Operand1 edit box to a double and assign it to the local variable `x`.
- Obtains the second operand in a manner very similar to the first one (the second operand is stored in the local variable `y`).
- Acquires the operator or function from the Operator edit box.
- Performs the requested operation or function evaluation, with a set of `if` statements used to determine the requested operation (the statements also include argument error checking, and if there is any error, the function assigns `TRUE` to the `bInError` data member and displays an error message in the error message edit box).
- Displays the result in the Result edit box if no error has occurred.

The member functions `CMCalcBtn`, `HandleStoreBtn`, `CMStoreBtn`, `HandleExitBtn`, `CMExitBtn`, `putVar`, and `getVar` are the same as in the second version of the COCA program file CTLBTN1.CPP.

The `HandleAngleModeGrp` member function, defined in lines 655 through 671, is called by the response message functions of the radio buttons. The function first verifies whether the Echo Group message check box is not checked. If this condition is true, the member function simply exits. Otherwise, the function determines which radio button is checked and accordingly builds an angle-conversion message. The function then invokes the `MessageBox` function to display this message.

The `HandleRadianRbt`, `HandleDegreeRbt`, and `HandleGradianRbt` member functions, defined in lines 673 through 689, respond to the individual notification messages sent by the three radio buttons. Each member function assigns an angle-conversion factor to the `angleFactor` data member and then calls function `HandleAngleModeGrp`. Using these member functions is more efficient than systematically examining the check states of the radio buttons in the `HandleCalcBtn` member function. This approach alters the value in `angleFactor` only when you select a new angle mode.

Note: When you run the application and select another radio button, the previous radio button is automatically unchecked. It seems that the MFC library regards the radio buttons that are owned by a window as a single group. Therefore, deselecting the previous radio button requires no code within the program.

The `CAppWindow` class includes the `InitAppWindow` member function that initializes the following controls:

- Disables the Store button
- Checks the Degrees radio button
- Checks the Echo Group message box check box

Note: The window class also defines two iterator functions, namely, `ForEachEditCtl` and `ForEachCheckBox` in lines 757 through 779. Both functions use a `for` loop to iterate over the range of the target control ID. Each loop iteration obtains the pointer to the control based on its ID and then applies the iterated function to that control. The iterated (nonmember) functions themselves are `ClearEditControls` and `ClearCheckBoxes`, defined in lines 248 through 253. Each function has one statement that performs the sought task. This example shows that specialized iterators offer more control and require iterated functions with short code. The comparison is made with a C++ compiler sold by another major vendor.

Summary

Today's lesson discusses the special switch controls: check box, radio button, and group box. You learn about the following:

- Check box and radio button controls act as software switches.
- You can set and query the check state for the check box and radio button controls.
- You can respond to notification messages sent by these controls to their parent window.
- Group box controls enclose radio buttons and check boxes.
- Switch controls can be selectively manipulated.

Day 18 presents the scroll bar, list box, and combo box controls. These controls are value selectors because they enable you to select from a list or range of values.

Q&A

Q The check box has the states `BF_UNCHECKED`, `BF_CHECKED`, and `BF_GRAYED`. What can I use the third state for?

A You can use the `BF_GRAYED` state as a "don't care" or undetermined state.

Q Should I use the classes `CxButton`, `CRadioButton`, and `CCheckBox` that appear in program CTLGRP1.CPP? Why are such classes not part of the MFC library?

A Using these classes enhances the readability of your programs because you can readily tell what kind of controls they generate. Such classes are not part of the MFC library because of a design decision. The developers of MFC wanted to consolidate multiple controls in the class `CButton`.

Q Does it make any difference if I place check box controls in a group control?

A Placing check box controls in a group control affects the logical grouping of such controls. Consequently, this enhances the interface for the user.

Workshop

The Workshop provides quiz questions to help you solidify your understanding of the material covered and exercises to provide you with experience in using what you've learned. Try to understand the quiz and exercise answers before continuing on to the next day's lesson. Answers are provided in Appendix B, "Answers."

Quiz

1. True or false? A check box can replace any two radio buttons in a group control.
2. True or false? You should use radio buttons in a group control when you have three or more options.
3. True or false? A set of check boxes parallels the bits in a byte or word.
4. True or false? Radio buttons, in a group control, are mutually nonexclusive.

Exercise

Expand on program CTLGRP1.CPP by adding more mathematical functions, such as the hyperbolic functions `sinh`, `cosh`, and `tanh`, and their inverse functions.

18

List Boxes

WEEK
3

List controls are input tools that conveniently provide you with the items to choose. This feature makes list controls popular because they absolve you from remembering the list members—especially when computer programs expect exact spelling. Experience with DOS programs has shown that the various DOS utilities which display lists of files and directories are far easier and friendlier to use than their counterparts that assume you know all the names of your files and directories. Using list controls has gradually become a routine method for retrieving information. Today's lesson discusses the single-selection and multiple-selection list boxes. You learn about the following topics:

- The list box control
- Handling single-selection list boxes
- Handling multiple-selection list boxes

The List Box Control

List boxes are typically framed and include a vertical scroll bar. When you select an item by clicking on it, the selection is highlighted. Microsoft suggests the following guidelines for making a selection:

- Use a single mouse click to select a new or an additional item. A separate button control retrieves the selected item.
- Use a double-click as a shortcut for selecting an item and retrieving it.

NEW TERM The *list box* is an input control that permits the application user to select from a list of items.

A list box control supports multiple selections only if you specify the multiple-selection style when you create the control. Making multiple selections is convenient when you want to process the selected items in a similar manner. For example, selecting multiple files for deletion speeds up the process and reduces the effort you have to make.

The *CListBox* Class

The Microsoft Foundation Class library offers the `CListBox` class, a descendant of `CWnd`, to implement list box controls. The `CListBox` class has a set of member functions that enable you to easily manipulate and query both the contents of the list box as well as the selected item. As with many other classes in the MFC library, the class `CListBox` uses a default constructor and the `Create` member function to create list box instances.

Syntax

The *Create* Function

The declaration of the `Create` function is

```
BOOL Create(DWORD dwStyle,       // control style
            const RECT& rect,    // location and dimensions
            CWnd* pParentWnd,    // pointer to parent window
            UINT nID);           // control ID
```

The `dwStyle` parameter specifies the style of the list box control. The list box styles include the usual `WS_xxxx` window styles as well as the special `LBS_xxxx` list box styles (shown in Table 18.1). The `rect` parameter specifies the location and dimensions of the control. The `pParentWnd` parameter is the pointer to the parent window. The `nID` parameter specifies the unique ID of the scroll bar instance.

Example:

```
CListBox* pList;
pList->Create(LBS_STANDARD, rectDefault, this, ID_FILES_LST);
```


Note: The `LBS_STANDARD` style is equivalent to the `WS_BORDER`, `WS_VSCROLL`, `LBS_SORT`, and `LBS_NOTIFY` styles. You can remove the `LBS_SORT` style from the list box controls to maintain a list of items that is not automatically sorted. Such a list allows you to maintain items in a chronological fashion. You can also use this type of list to maintain the items sorted in descending order. Of course, you are responsible for maintaining the list items in that order. Removing the `WS_VSCROLL` style gives you a list box without the vertical scroll bar. The next section presents a demonstration program that uses this type of list box to implement the synchronized scrolling of multiple list boxes.

Table 18.1. List box control styles.

Style	Meaning
`LBS_EXTENDESEL`	Allows the extension of multiple-selections in the list box by using the Shift key
`LBS_MULTICOLUMN`	Designates a multicolumn list box that scrolls horizontally, and requires the use of Windows API functions (the number of columns is set by sending the message `LB_SETCOLUMNWIDTH`)

continues

Table 18.1. continued

Style	Meaning
`LBS_MULTIPLESEL`	Supports multiple selections in a list box
`LBS_NOINTEGRALHEIGHT`	Suppresses showing parts of an item
`LBS_NOREDRAW`	Prevents the list box from being updated when the selection is changed (the message `WM_SETREDRAW` alters this style at will)
`LBS_NOTIFY`	Notifies the parent window when you click or double-click in the list box
`LBS_SORT`	Specifies that the items inserted in the list box be automatically sorted in ascending order
`LBS_STANDARD`	Sets the `WS_BORDER`, `WS_VSCROLL`, `LBS_SORT`, and `LBS_NOTIFY` styles
`LBS_HASSTRINGS`	Specifies an owner-draw list box which contains items which themselves contain strings
`LBS_USETABSTOPS`	Permits a list box to detect an expand tab characters when daring strings
`LBS_DISABLENOSCROLL`	The list box shows a disabled vertical scroll bar when the list box does not hold enough items to scroll
`LBS_WANTKEYBOARDINPUT`	Permits the list box owner to receive `WM_VKEYTOITEM` or `WM_CHARTOITEM` messages when a key is pressed while the list box has the focus (allows the application to manipulate the items in the list box)

The `CListBox` class allows you to refer to the items in a list box by index. The index of the first item is 0. The `CListBox` class offers the following member functions to set and query ordinary and selected list members:

- The `AddString` member function adds a string to the list box.
- The `DeleteString` member function removes a list member from a specified position.

- The parameterless `ResetContent` member function clears the list of strings in the list box control in one swoop. This function serves to reset the contents of a list box before building up a new list.
- The `FindString` member function performs a case-insensitive search for an item in the list box. This function matches a partial string items in the list box.
- The `FindStringExact` member function performs a case-insensitive search for an item in the list box. This function matches a whole string item in the list box.
- The parameterless `GetCount` member function returns the number of items in the list box. The function returns the `LB_ERR` value if there is an error.
- The parameterless `GetCurSel` member function returns the position of the selected item in a single-selection list box. If there is no selected item, the function yields a negative value. This function is aimed at single-selection list boxes only.
- The `GetSel` member function returns the selection state of a list box item, specified by index.
- The parameterless `GetSelCount` member function returns the number of selected items in the list box. For single-selection list boxes, the function returns `LB_ERR`.
- The `GetSelItems` member function returns the number and positions of the selected items in a multiple-selection list box.
- The overloaded `GetText` member function obtains an item in a list box by specifying its index.
- The `GetTextLen` member function returns the length of a list item specified by its position in the list.
- The parameterless `GetTopIndex` member function returns the index of the first visible list box item.
- The `InsertString` member function inserts a string in a list box.
- The `SelectString` member function selects a list box item that matches a search string.
- The `SelItemRange` member function is another function that allows you to select a range of items in one call.

- The `SetCurSel` member function chooses a list item as the new selection in a single-selection list box.
- The `SetSel` member function makes or clears a selection in a multiple-selection list box.
- The `SetTopIndex` member function selects the list box that becomes the first visible item in the list box control.
- The `Dir` member function is a special member function that allows you to insert filenames in a list box.

Syntax

The *AddString* Function

The declaration of the `AddString` member function is

```
int AddString(LPCTSTR lpszItem);
```

The `lpszItem` parameter is the pointer to the added string. The function also returns the position of the added string in the control. If there is any error in adding the string, the function yields an `LB_ERR` or `LB_ERRSPACE` value (out-of-memory error). If the `LBS_SORT` style is set, the string is inserted so that the list order is maintained. If the `LBS_SORT` style is not set, the added string is inserted at the end of the list.

Example:

```
CListBox* pList;
// create control...
pList->AddString("MS-DOS");
```

Syntax

The *DeleteString* Function

The declaration of the `DeleteString` member function is

```
int DeleteString(UINT nIndex);
```

The `nIndex` parameter specifies the position of the item to delete. The function returns the number of remaining list members. If an error occurs, `DeleteString` yields the value `LB_ERR`.

Example:

```
CListBox* pList;
// create control...
// add names to the list...
pList->DeleteString(0);
```

Syntax

The *FindString* Function

The declaration of the `FindString` function is

```
int FindString(int nStartAfter, LPCTSTR lpszItem) const;
```

The `nStartAfter` parameter specifies the index of the first list box member to be searched. The `lpszItem` parameter is the pointer to the searched string. The function searches the entire list, beginning with position `nStartAfter` and resuming at the beginning of the list if needed. The function looks for a partial string item which matches the search string. The search stops when either a list member matches the search string or the entire list is searched. Passing an argument of `-1` to `nStartAfter` forces the function to start searching from the beginning. The function returns the position of the matching list item, or yields the `LB_ERR` value if no match is found or when an error occurs.

Example:

```
CListBox* pList;
int nIdx;
// create control...
// add names to the list...
nIdx = pList->FindString(-1, "MS-DOS");
```


Note: The interesting search method used by `FindString` enables you to speed up the search by specifying a position that comes closely before the most likely location for a match. The beauty of this method is that if you specify a position that is actually beyond that of the string you seek, you cannot miss finding that string because the function resumes searching at the beginning of the list. Another benefit of `FindString` is its ability to find duplicate strings.

Syntax

The *FindStringExact* Function

The declaration of the `FindStringExact` function is

```
int FindStringExact(int nStartAfter, LPCTSTR lpszFind) const;
```

The `nStartAfter` parameter specifies the index of the first list box member to be searched. The `lpszFind` parameter is the pointer to the searched string. The function searches the entire list, beginning with position `nStartAfter` and resuming at the beginning of the list if needed. The function looks for a whole string item which matches the search string. The search stops when either a list member matches the search string or the entire list is searched. Passing an argument of -1 to nStartAfter forces the function to start searching from the beginning. The function returns the position of the matching list item, or yields the LB_ERR value if no match is found or when an error occurs.

Example:

```
CListBox* pList;
int nIdx;
// create control...
// add names to the list...
nIdx = pList->FindStringExact(-1, "MS-DOS");
```

Syntax

The *GetSel* Function

The declaration of the function GetSel is

```
int GetSel(int nIndex) const;
```

The nIndex parameter specifies the index of the queried list box item. The function returns a positive number if the item is selected, yields 0 if the item is not selected, and returns LB_ERR if an error occurs.

Example:

```
CListBox* pList;
// create control...
// add names to the list...
if (pList->GetSel(0))
  // process information
```

Syntax

The *GetSelItems* Function

The declaration of the GetSelItems function is

```
int GetSelItems(int nMaxItems, LPINT rgIndex) const;
```

The nMaxItems parameter specifies the size of the array accessed by the rgIndex pointer. The rgIndex parameter is the pointer to an array of integers that stores the positions of the selected items. The function returns the current number of selections. The function yields LB_ERR with single-selection list boxes.

Example:

```
const int MAX_ARRAY = 100;
CListBox* pList;
int intArr[MAX_ARRAY];
int nCount;
// create control...
// add names to the list...
nCount = pList->GetSelItems(MAX_ARRAY, intArr);
```

Syntax

The *GetText* Function

The declaration of the `GetText` function is

```
int GetText(int nIndex, LPTSTR lpszBuffer) const;
void GetText(int nIndex, CString& rString) const;
```

The `nIndex` parameter specifies the index of the retrieved items. The first list box item has the index of 0. The `lpBuffer` parameter points to a buffer that receives the retrieved item. You are responsible for ensuring that the buffer has enough space for the retrieved item. The `rString` parameter is a reference to the `CString` object that receives a copy of the list box item. The first form of the function returns the number of characters retrieved from the list box.

Example:

```
const STR_SIZE = 80;
char s[STR_SIZE+1];
CListBox* pList;
// create control...
// add names to the list...
if (pList->GetText(0, s) > 0)
  MessageBox(s, MB_OK, "Information");
```

18

Syntax

The *GetTextLen* Function

The declaration of the `GetTextLen` function is

```
int GetTextLen(int nIndex) const;
```

The parameter `nIndex` specifies the index of the target list item. The function returns the length of the target item, or the `LB_ERR` result if an error occurs.

Example:

```
int nLen;
CListBox* pList;
// create control...
// add names to the list...
nLen = pList->GetTextLen(0);
```

Syntax

The *InsertString* Function

The declaration of the `InsertString` function is

```
int InsertString(int nIndex, LPCTSTR lpszItem);
```

The `nIndex` parameter specifies the requested insertion position. The `lpszItem` parameter is the pointer to the inserted string. The function returns the actual insertion position, or yields the LB_ERR value if an error occurs. If the argument for Index is -1, the string is simply appended to the end of the list.

Example:

```
CListBox* pList;
// create control...
// add names to the list...
if (pList->InsertString(0, "Windows") == 0)
      MessageBox("Inserted at index 0", MB_OK, "Information");
```

Warning: In general, do not use the InsertString member function with list boxes that have the LBS_SORT style set. Using this function with ordered list boxes will most likely corrupt the sort order of the list.

Syntax

The *SelectString* Function

The declaration of the SelectString function is

```
int SelectString(int nStartAfter, LPCTSTR lpszItem);
```

The parameters and search mechanism of SelectString are identical to those of FindString. The difference is that SelectString selects the list box item that matches the string accessed by parameter lpszItem.

Example:

```
CListBox* pList;
int nIdx;
// create control...
// add names to the list...
nIdx = pList->SelectString(-1, "MS-DOS");
```

Syntax

The *SelItemRange* Function

The declaration of the SelItemRange function is

```
int SelItemRange(BOOL bSelect, int nFirstItem, int nLastItem);
```

The bSelect parameter acts as a switch used to select or deselect the range of list box items defined by parameters nFirstItem and nLastItem.

Example:

```
CListBox* pList;
int nNumSel;
```

```
// create control...
// add names to the list...
nNumSel = pList->SelectItemRange(TRUE, 0, 10);
```

Syntax

The *SetCurSel* Function

The declaration of the `SetCurSel` function is

```
int SetCurSel(int nSelect);
```

The parameter `nSelect` specifies the position of the new selection. To clear a list box from any selection, pass a -1 argument to the `nSelect` parameter. The function returns `LB_ERR` if an error occurs.

Example:

```
CListBox* pList;
// create control...
// add names to the list...
pList->SetCurSel(-1); // clear current selection
```

Syntax

The *SetSel* Function

The declaration of the `SetSel` function is

```
int SetSel(int nIndex, BOOL bSelect = TRUE);
```

The `nIndex` parameter specifies the list box item to either select, if `bSelect` is `TRUE`, or deselect, if `bSelect` is `FALSE`. The function returns `LB_ERR` if an error occurs. The function result serves only to flag a selection/deselection error. You can use the `SetSel` function to toggle the selection of multiple items in a multiple-selection list box, one at a time.

Example:

```
CListBox* pList;
// create control...
// add names to the list...
pList->SetSel(0, TRUE); // select first item in list
```

Syntax

The *SetTopIndex* Function

The declaration of the function `SetTopIndex` is

```
int SetTopIndex(int nIndex);
```

The `nIndex` parameter specifies the index of the list box item that becomes the first visible item. This selection scrolls the list box, unless item `nIndex` is already the first visible item. The function returns `LB_ERR` if an error occurs. Otherwise, the result is meaningless.

Example:

```
CListBox* pList;
int nIdxTop;
// create control...
// add names to the list...
nIdxTop = pList->SetTopIndex(10); // select 11th item
if (nIdxTop != 10)
  MessageBox("Selection failed!", MB_OK, "Error!");
```

Syntax

The *Dir* Function

The declaration of the `Dir` function is

```
int Dir(UINT attr, LPCTSTR lpszWildCard);
```

The `attr` parameter specifies the combination of attributes, shown in Table 18.2. The table also shows the equivalent file attribute constants that are declared in the DOS.H header file. The `lpszWildCard` parameter is the pointer to the filename wildcard, such as `*.*`, `L*.EXE`, or `A???.CPP`.

Example:

```
int nNumFiles;
CListBox* pList;
// create control...
// get all CTL*.CPP files
nNumFiles = pList->Dir(_A_ARCH, "CTL*.CPP");
```

Table 18.2. Attributes for the `attr` parameter in the `Dir` member function.

Attribute Value	Equivalent Constant in DOS.H Header File	Meaning
0x0000	`_A_NORMAL`	File can be used for input and output
0x0001	`_A_RDONLY`	File is read only
0x0002	`_A_HIDDEN`	File is hidden
0x0004	`_A_SYSTEM`	File is system file
0x0010	`_A_SUBDIR`	Name indicated by parameter `lpWildCard` also supplies the directory
0x0020	`_A_ARCH`	File has the archive bit set

Attribute Value	Equivalent Constant in DOS.H Header File	Meaning
0x4000		Include all the drives that match the filename supplied by `lpWildCard`
0x8000		Exclusive flag (prevents normal files from being included with specified files)

Responding to List Box Notification Messages

The list box control emits various types of messages, shown in Table 18.3. The table also shows the message-mapping macros that are associated with the various command and notification messages. Each type of command or notification message requires a separate member function declared in the control's parent window class.

18

Table 18.3. List box notification messages.

Message	Macro	Meaning
`WS_COMMAND`	`ON_COMMAND`	A Windows command message
`LBN_CHANGE`	`ON_LBN_SELCHANGE`	A list item is selected with a mouse click
`LBN_DBLCLK`	`ON_LBN_DBLCLK`	A list item is selected with a mouse double-click
`LBN_SETFOCUS`	`ON_LBN_SETFOCUS`	The list box has gained focus
`LBN_KILLFOCUS`	`ON_LBN_KILLFOCUS`	The list box has lost focus
`LBN_ERRSPACE`	`ON_LBNERRSPACE`	The list box cannot allocate more dynamic memory to accommodate new list items

The List Manipulation Tester

The next program demonstrates how to set and query normal and selected strings, and how to set and query the current selection in a single-selection list box—a simple list manipulation tester. This program focuses on illustrating how to use most of the `CListBox` member functions presented earlier in this section. The program contains the following controls that offer the indicated test features:

- A list box control
- A String Box edit control that allows you to type in and retrieve a list member
- An Index Box edit control that enables you to key in and retrieve the position of the current selection
- An Add String pushbutton to add the content of the String Box to the list box (the program does not allow you to add duplicate names, and, if you attempt to do so, the program displays a warning message)
- A Delete String pushbutton to delete the current selection in the list box (the program automatically selects another list member)
- The Get Selected String pushbutton that copies the current list selection to the String Box
- The Set Selected String pushbutton that overwrites the current selection with the string in the String Box
- The Get Selected Index pushbutton that writes the position of the current selection in the Index Box
- The Set Selected Index pushbutton that uses the integer value in the Index Box as the position of the new list box selection
- The Get String button that copies the string whose position appears in the Index Box into the String Box
- The Exit pushbutton

These controls exercise various aspects of manipulating a sorted list box and its members. The program is coded to retain a current selection and to prevent the insertion of duplicate names.

Listings 18.1, 18.2, and 18.3 show the header file CTLLST1.H, the script for the CTLLST1.RC resource file, and the source code for the CTLLST1.CPP program file, respectively. The resource file contains a single-item menu resource. I purposely avoid using accelerator keys to make the program a bit shorter.

Create the directory CTLLST1 as a subdirectory of \MSVC20\VC21DAY and store all the project's files in the new directory. The project's .MAK file should contain the files CTLLST1.CPP, CTLLST1.RC, and CTLLST1.DEF. The latter file resembles file MINWINAP.DEF in Day 14, Listing 14.2.

Compile and run the program. When the program starts running, it places a set of names in the list box. Experiment with the various push button controls to add, delete, and obtain strings. The program is straightforward and easy to run.

Listing 18.1. Source code for the CTLLST1.H header file.

```
#define CM_EXIT (WM_USER + 100)
```

Listing 18.2. Script for the CTLLST1.RC resource file.

```
#include <afxres.h>
#include "ctllst1.h"

EXITMENU MENU LOADONCALL MOVEABLE PURE DISCARDABLE
BEGIN
MENUITEM "E&xit", CM_EXIT
END
```


Listing 18.3. Source code for the CTLLST1.CPP program file.

```
#include <stdio.h>
#include <string.h>
#include <afxwin.h>
#include "ctllst1.h"

// declare constants for the size and spacing of controls
const LowVertSpacing = 5;
const HiVertSpacing = 25;
const HorzSpacing = 50;
const Wctl = 150;
const Hctl = 30;
const Wbox = 2 * Wctl + HorzSpacing;
const Hlst = Hctl + LowVertSpacing + 4 * (Hctl + HiVertSpacing);
const MaxEditLen = 10;

// declare the ID constants for the various controls
#define ID_STRING_LST 101
#define ID_STRING_EDIT 102
#define ID_INDEX_EDIT 103
#define ID_ADDSTR_BTN 104
```

continues

Listing 18.3. continued

```
#define ID_DELSTR_BTN 105
#define ID_GETSELSTR_BTN 106
#define ID_SETSELSTR_BTN 107
#define ID_GETSELIDX_BTN 108
#define ID_SETSELIDX_BTN 109
#define ID_EXIT_BTN 110
#define ID_GETSTR_BTN 111

class CxButton : public CButton
{
public:

   BOOL Create(const char FAR* lpCaption, const RECT& rect,
               CWnd* pParentWnd, UINT nID)
   {
     return CButton::Create(lpCaption,
            WS_CHILD | WS_VISIBLE | BS_PUSHBUTTON,
            rect, pParentWnd, nID);
   }
};

class CWindowApp : public CWinApp
{
public:
    virtual BOOL InitInstance();
};

// expand the functionality of CFrameWnd by deriving
// class CAppWindow
class CAppWindow : public CFrameWnd
{
public:

  CAppWindow();
  ~CAppWindow();

protected:
  // handle creating the controls
  // declare the pointers to the controls
  CStatic* StringListTxt;
  CStatic* StringBoxTxt;
  CStatic* IndexBoxTxt;
  CListBox* StringLst;
  CEdit* StringBox;
  CEdit* IndexBox;
  CxButton* AddStrBtn;
  CxButton* DelStrBtn;
  CxButton* GetSelStrBtn;
  CxButton* SetSelStrBtn;
  CxButton* GetSelIdxBtn;
  CxButton* SetSelIdxBtn;
  CxButton* GetStrBtn;
  CxButton* ExitBtn;
  char dataStr[MaxEditLen+1];  // string for StringBox
```

```
   char indexStr[MaxEditLen+1]; // string for IndexBox

   afx_msg int OnCreate(LPCREATESTRUCT lpCS);
   // initialize the String list box
   void InitStringLst();
   // handle adding a string to the list box
   afx_msg void HandleAddStrBtn();
   // handle deleting a string from the list box
   afx_msg void HandleDelStrBtn();
   // handle getting the selected text
   afx_msg void HandleGetSelStrBtn();
   // handle setting the selected text
   afx_msg void HandleSetSelStrBtn();
   // handle getting the index of the selected text
   afx_msg void HandleGetSelIdxBtn();
   // handle setting the index of the selected text
   afx_msg void HandleSetSelIdxBtn();
   // handle getting a string from the list box
   afx_msg void HandleGetStrBtn();
   // handle setting a string in the list box
   afx_msg void HandleExitBtn()
     { SendMessage(WM_CLOSE); }
   // handle exiting the application
   afx_msg void OnExit()
     { SendMessage(WM_CLOSE); }
  // handle closing the window
  afx_msg void OnClose();
  void makeRect(int nX, int nY, int nW, int nH, CRect& r);

  // declare message map macro
  DECLARE_MESSAGE_MAP();
};

CAppWindow::CAppWindow()
{
  // create the window
  Create(NULL, "Simple List Box Tester Application",
      WS_OVERLAPPEDWINDOW | WS_MAXIMIZE,
      rectDefault, NULL, "EXITMENU");
  // insert the initial list of names
  InitStringLst();
}

CAppWindow::~CAppWindow()
{
  delete StringListTxt;
  delete StringBoxTxt;
  delete IndexBoxTxt;
  delete StringLst;
  delete StringBox;
  delete IndexBox;
  delete AddStrBtn;
  delete DelStrBtn;
  delete GetSelStrBtn;
  delete SetSelStrBtn;
  delete GetSelIdxBtn;
```

continues

Listing 18.3. continued

```
  delete SetSelIdxBtn;
  delete GetStrBtn;
  delete ExitBtn;
}

int CAppWindow::OnCreate(LPCREATESTRUCT lpCS)
{
  int nX0 = 30;
  int nX1 = nX0 + Wctl + HorzSpacing;
  int x2 = nX1 + Wctl + HorzSpacing;
  int nY0 = 10;
  int nX = nX0;
  int nY = nY0;
  int nY1;
  DWORD dwStaticStyle = WS_CHILD | WS_VISIBLE | SS_LEFT;
  DWORD dwEditStyle = WS_CHILD | WS_VISIBLE | ES_LEFT |
                      WS_BORDER;
  DWORD dwScrollStyle = WS_CHILD | WS_VISIBLE | SBS_VERT;
  DWORD dwListBoxStyle = WS_CHILD | WS_VISIBLE | WS_VSCROLL |
                         LBS_STANDARD;
  CRect r;

  // create the list box and its label
  makeRect(nX, nY, Wctl, Hctl, r);
  StringListTxt = new CStatic();
  StringListTxt->Create("List Box", dwStaticStyle, r, this);
  nY += Hctl + LowVertSpacing;
  makeRect(nX, nY, Wctl, Hlst, r);
  StringLst = new CListBox();
  StringLst->Create(dwListBoxStyle, r, this, ID_STRING_LST);

  // create the edit boxes and their labels
  nX = nX1;
  nY = nY0;
  makeRect(nX, nY, Wctl, Hctl, r);
  StringBoxTxt = new CStatic();
  StringBoxTxt->Create("String Box", dwStaticStyle, r, this);
  nY += Hctl + LowVertSpacing;
  makeRect(nX, nY, Wbox, Hctl, r);
  StringBox = new CEdit();
  StringBox->Create(dwEditStyle, r, this, ID_STRING_EDIT);

  nY += Hctl + HiVertSpacing;
  makeRect(nX, nY, Wctl, Hctl, r);
  IndexBoxTxt = new CStatic();
  IndexBoxTxt->Create("Index Box", dwStaticStyle, r, this);
  nY += Hctl + LowVertSpacing;
  makeRect(nX, nY, Wbox, Hctl, r);
  IndexBox = new CEdit();
  IndexBox->Create(dwEditStyle, r, this, ID_INDEX_EDIT);

  // create the button controls
  nY += Hctl + HiVertSpacing;
  nY1 = nY;
```

```
  makeRect(nX, nY, Wctl, Hctl, r);
  AddStrBtn = new CxButton();
  AddStrBtn->Create("Add String", r, this, ID_ADDSTR_BTN);

  nY += Hctl + HiVertSpacing;
  makeRect(nX, nY, Wctl, Hctl, r);
  DelStrBtn = new CxButton();
  DelStrBtn->Create("Delete String", r, this, ID_DELSTR_BTN);

  nY += Hctl + HiVertSpacing;
  makeRect(nX, nY, Wctl, Hctl, r);
  GetSelStrBtn = new CxButton();
  GetSelStrBtn->Create("Get Selected String", r, this,
                       ID_GETSELSTR_BTN);

  nY += Hctl + HiVertSpacing;
  makeRect(nX, nY, Wctl, Hctl, r);
  SetSelStrBtn = new CxButton();
  SetSelStrBtn->Create("Set Selected String", r, this,
                       ID_SETSELSTR_BTN);

  // create the second row of buttons
  nY  = nY1;
  nX = x2;
  makeRect(nX, nY, Wctl, Hctl, r);
  GetSelIdxBtn = new CxButton();
  GetSelIdxBtn->Create("Get Selected Index", r, this,
                       ID_GETSELIDX_BTN);

  nY += Hctl + HiVertSpacing;
  makeRect(nX, nY, Wctl, Hctl, r);
  SetSelIdxBtn = new CxButton();
  SetSelIdxBtn->Create("Set Selected Index", r, this,
                       ID_SETSELIDX_BTN);

  nY += Hctl + HiVertSpacing;
  makeRect(nX, nY, Wctl, Hctl, r);
  GetStrBtn = new CxButton();
  GetStrBtn->Create("Get String by Index", r, this,
                    ID_GETSTR_BTN);

  nY += Hctl + HiVertSpacing;
  makeRect(nX, nY, Wctl, Hctl, r);
  ExitBtn = new CxButton();
  ExitBtn->Create("Exit", r, this, ID_EXIT_BTN);

  return CFrameWnd::OnCreate(lpCS);

}

void CAppWindow::HandleAddStrBtn()
{
  int nIdx;
  // get the string in the String box
  StringBox->GetWindowText(dataStr, MaxEditLen);
  // exit if the string is empty?
```

continues

Listing 18.3. continued

```
  if (dataStr[0] == '\0') return;
  // add the string if it is not already in the list box
  if (StringLst->FindString(-1, dataStr) < 0) {
    // add the string and store the position of the new string
    nIdx = StringLst->AddString(dataStr);
    // make the added string the new selection
    StringLst->SetCurSel(nIdx);
  }
  else
    // handle the duplicate-data error
    MessageBox("Cannot add duplicate names", "Bad Data", MB_OK);
}

void CAppWindow::HandleDelStrBtn()
{
  // get the index of the currently selected list member
  int nIdx = StringLst->GetCurSel();
  // delete the currently selected list member
  StringLst->DeleteString(nIdx);
  // select another list member
  StringLst->SetCurSel((nIdx > 0) ? (nIdx-1) : 0);
}

void CAppWindow::HandleGetSelStrBtn()
{
  // get the selected list item
  StringLst->GetText(StringLst->GetCurSel(), dataStr);
  /// store it in the String box
  StringBox->SetWindowText(dataStr);
}

void CAppWindow::HandleSetSelStrBtn()
{
  // get the index of the currently selected list member
  int nIdx = StringLst->GetCurSel();
  // get the string to replace the currently selected
  // list item
  StringBox->GetWindowText(dataStr, MaxEditLen);
  // is the candidate string not in the list?
  if (StringLst->FindString(-1, dataStr) < 0) {
    // delete the current selection
    StringLst->DeleteString(nIdx);
    // insert the new selection
    nIdx = StringLst->AddString(dataStr);
    // select the inserted string
    StringLst->SetCurSel(nIdx);
  }
  else
    MessageBox("Cannot add duplicate names", "Bad Data", MB_OK);
}

void CAppWindow::HandleGetSelIdxBtn()
{
  sprintf(indexStr, "%d", StringLst->GetCurSel());
```

```
  IndexBox->SetWindowText(indexStr);
}

void CAppWindow::HandleSetSelIdxBtn()
{
  IndexBox->GetWindowText(indexStr, MaxEditLen);
  StringLst->SetCurSel(atoi(indexStr));
}

void CAppWindow::HandleGetStrBtn()
{
  int nIdx;
  // get the index from the Index box
  IndexBox->GetWindowText(indexStr, MaxEditLen);
  nIdx = atoi(indexStr);
  // get the target string from the list box
  StringLst->GetText(nIdx, dataStr);
  // write the list member in the String box
  StringBox->SetWindowText(dataStr);
}

void CAppWindow::OnClose()
{
  if (MessageBox("Want to close this application",
           "Query", MB_YESNO | MB_ICONQUESTION) == IDYES)
    DestroyWindow();
}

void CAppWindow::InitStringLst()
{
  // add data in the list box
  StringLst->AddString("Edward");
  StringLst->AddString("John");
  StringLst->AddString("Anne");
  StringLst->AddString("Elaine");
  StringLst->AddString("Joseph");
  StringLst->AddString("Clement");
  StringLst->AddString("Daisy");
  StringLst->AddString("Tony");
  // select the second item
  StringLst->SetCurSel(1);
}

void CAppWindow::makeRect(int nX, int nY, int nW, int nH,
                          CRect& r)
{
  r.top = nY;
  r.left = nX;
  r.bottom = nY + nH;
  r.right = nX + nW;
}

BEGIN_MESSAGE_MAP(CAppWindow, CFrameWnd)
  ON_WM_CREATE()
  ON_BN_CLICKED(ID_ADDSTR_BTN, HandleAddStrBtn)
  ON_BN_CLICKED(ID_DELSTR_BTN, HandleDelStrBtn)
```

continues

Listing 18.3. continued

```
   ON_BN_CLICKED(ID_GETSELSTR_BTN, HandleGetSelStrBtn)
   ON_BN_CLICKED(ID_SETSELSTR_BTN, HandleSetSelStrBtn)
   ON_BN_CLICKED(ID_GETSELIDX_BTN, HandleGetSelIdxBtn)
   ON_BN_CLICKED(ID_SETSELIDX_BTN, HandleSetSelIdxBtn)
   ON_BN_CLICKED(ID_GETSTR_BTN, HandleGetStrBtn)
   ON_BN_CLICKED(ID_EXIT_BTN, HandleExitBtn)
   ON_COMMAND(CM_EXIT, OnExit)
   ON_WM_CLOSE()
END_MESSAGE_MAP()

// Construct the CWindowApp's m_pMainWnd data member
BOOL CWindowApp::InitInstance()
{
   m_pMainWnd = new CAppWindow();
   m_pMainWnd->ShowWindow(m_nCmdShow);
   m_pMainWnd->UpdateWindow();
   return TRUE;
}

// application's constructor initializes and runs the app
CWindowApp WindowApp;
```

Figure 18.1 shows a sample session with the CTLLST1.EXE application.

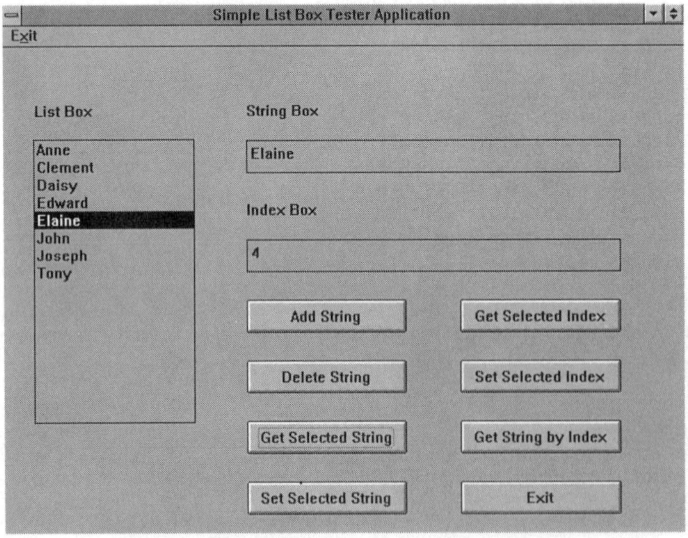

Figure 18.1. *A sample session with the CTLLST1.EXE application.*

Analysis The program in Listing 18.3 declares two sets of constants. The first, declared in lines 7 through 14, specifies the dimensions and sizes of the various controls used. The second set of constants, declared in lines 17 through 27, specifies the ID for the various controls.

The program declares the application class, `CWindowApp`; the window class, `CAppWindow`; and the button class, `CxButton`. The class `CAppWindow` declares a number of data members, in lines 60 through 73, that are pointers to the controls owned by the main window. The class also declares two strings to handle the contents of the String Box and Index Box edit controls. The `CAppWindow` class also declares a constructor, a destructor, and a number of member functions that respond to the notification messages emitted by the various push button controls.

The `CAppWindow` constructor performs two tasks:

- Invokes the member function `Create` to build the application window
- Calls the `InitStringLst` member function to initialize the Names list box with data

The member function `OnCreate`, defined in lines 136 through 233, creates the controls using the appropriate styles. For example, the list box control appears with a vertical scroll bar and automatically maintains a sorted list of strings.

The member function `HandleAddStrBtn`, defined in lines 235 through 252, adds the string of the String Box in the list box control. The function performs the following tasks:

- Obtains the string in the String Box edit control and stores it in the `dataStr` data member
- Exits if the `dataStr` member stores an empty string
- Verifies that the added string does not already exist in the list box, using the `FindString` function to detect an attempt to add duplicate strings (if `FindString` returns a negative number, `HandleAddStrBtn` resumes with the subsequent tasks; and if it doesn't return a negative number, `HandleAddStrBtn` displays a message informing you that you cannot add duplicate strings in the list box)
- Adds the string of the `dataStr` member to the list box and assigns the position of the string to the local variable `nIdx`, using the `AddString` member
- Makes the added string the current selection by invoking the `SetCurSel` function with the argument `nIdx`

The member function `HandleDelStrBtn`, defined in lines 254 through 262, deletes the current selection by carrying out the following tasks:

- Obtains the position of the current selection by invoking the `GetCurSel` function, and stores the selection position in the local variable `nIdx`
- Deletes the selection by calling the `DeleteString` function and supplying it the argument `nIdx`
- Selects another list item as the new selection at position `nIdx -1` (if the variable `nIdx` already contains `0`, the new first list item becomes the new selection)

The member function `HandleGetSelStrBtn`, defined in lines 264 through 270, copies the current selection to the String Box edit control. The function performs the following tasks:

- Copies the current selection to the `dataStr` member by calling the `GetText` and `GetCurSel` functions
- Overwrites the contents of the String Box with the characters of the `dataStr` member

The member function `HandleSetSelStrBtn`, defined in lines 272 through 290, overwrites the current selection with the string in the String Box edit control. Because the list maintains sorted items, the replacement string likely has a different position than the original selection. The function performs the following tasks:

- Obtains the position of the current selection, using the `GetCurSel` function, and assigns that value to the local variable `nIdx`
- Copies the text in the String Box to the `dataStr` member
- Verifies that the string in `dataStr` does not already exist in the list box, using the `FindString` function (if the string in `dataStr` is new to the list, the function uses the `DeleteString` function to delete the current selection, uses the `AddString` function to add the `dataStr`, and then uses the `SetCurSel` function to select the added string)

If the string in `dataStr` has a matching list item, the function displays a message informing you that you cannot add duplicate strings in the list box. This warning also appears if you attempt to overwrite the current selection with the same string!

The member function `HandleGetSelIdxBtn`, defined in lines 292 through 296, writes the position of the current selection to the Index Box edit box. The function uses the `GetCurSel` function to obtain the sought position.

The member function `HandleSetSelIdxBtn`, defined in lines 298 through 302, reads the value in the Index Box edit control and uses that value to set the new current selection. The function uses the `SetCurSel` function to make the new selection.

The member function `HandleGetStrBtn`, defined in lines 304 through 314, enables you to retrieve the list item whose position appears in the Index Box edit control. The function performs the following tasks:

- Copies the characters of the Index Box to the `indxStr` data member
- Converts the string in `indexStr` to the `int`-typed local variable `nIdx`
- Copies the characters of the list item at position `nIdx` to the `dataStr` member
- Writes the characters of `dataStr` in the String Box edit control

Handling Multiple-Selection Lists

This section demonstrates the use of multiple-selection lists and focuses on getting and setting the selection strings and their indices. There are two modes for making multiple selections in a list box. These modes depend on whether or not you set the `LBS_EXTENDEDSEL` style when you create a `CListBox` instance. Setting this style enables you to quickly extend the range of selected items by holding down the Shift key and clicking the mouse. The disadvantage for this style is that you are committed to selecting blocks of contiguous items in the list box manually (that is, using the mouse or cursor keys). Using the `SetSel` or `SetItemRange` member functions, you can make your program select noncontiguous items. However, this approach requires extra effort on behalf of the application user and a few extra controls. By contrast, if you do not set the `LBS_EXTENDEDSEL` style, you can make dispersed selections easily by clicking the mouse button on the individual items that you want to select. The disadvantage of this selection mode is that you must click on every item to select it, including neighboring items. Choose the selection mode that you feel best meets the user-interface requirements for your MFC applications.

The Multiple-Selection List Tester

Figure 18.2 shows a sample session with the CTLLST2.EXE application—a program that demonstrates how to set and query multiple selections in a list box—and also conveys the controls used by that application. The controls used by the test program and the operation they support are

- A multiple-selection list that has the `LBS_MULTIPLESEL` style selected, but not the `LBS_EXTENDEDSEL` style (the strings in the list box are sorted in ascending order)

- A multiline edit box control labeled Names Box that contains the names of the selected strings
- A pushbutton with the caption Get Names to copy the list box selections in the Names Box edit control (each selection appears on a separate line in the edit box, and every time you click this button you lose the previous contents of the Names Box edit control)
- A pushbutton with the caption Set Names to select, or deselect, the list box items that match those in the Names Box edit control (the match need not be exact, but the Names Box strings must match the leading characters of the list items)
- A multiline edit box control labeled Indices Box that contains the indices of the selected strings
- A pushbutton with the caption Get Indices to copy the indices of the list box selections in the Indices Box edit control (the index of each selection appears on a separate line in the edit box, and every time you click this button you lose the previous contents of the Indices Box edit control)
- A pushbutton with the caption Set Indices to select, or deselect, the list box items using the values in the Indices Box edit control
- A check box control with the caption Deselect mode that determines whether the Set Names and Set Indices buttons select or deselect list items
- The static text controls that label the list and edit boxes

The multiple-selection list tester application basically drills the `GetSelIndexes`, `GetSelStrings`, `SetSelIndexes`, and `SetSelStrings` member functions of class `CListBox`. Listings 18.4, 18.5, and 18.6 contain the source code for the CTLLST2.H, CTLLST2.RC, and CTLLST2.CPP files, respectively.

Create the directory CTLLST2 as a subdirectory of \MSVC20\VC21DAY and store all the project's files in the new directory. The project's .MAK file should contain the files CTLLST2.CPP, CTLLST2.RC, and CTLLST2.DEF. The latter file resembles file MINWINAP.DEF in Day 14, Listing 14.2.

Compile and run the program. The application initializes the list box with many names. This feature saves you the time and effort needed to enter the names yourself. Select a few list items and click on the Get Names and Get Indices pushbuttons. The selected strings and indices appear in the Names Box and Indices Box edit controls. Now edit the lines on the Names Box by deleting one or two trailing characters from each line to create partial names. Click on the Set Names pushbutton. What do you see? The selections have not changed because the strings in the Names Box still match the same list box selection. Type in a new set of indices in the Indices Box and click the Set Indices pushbutton. The program now displays a new set of selected items in the list box. You can also make a new selection by deleting the text in the Names Box and typing in names that are found in the list box. Now click the Set Names button and view the new list box selections. When you are finished experimenting with the program, click on the Exit menu item or press Alt+X.

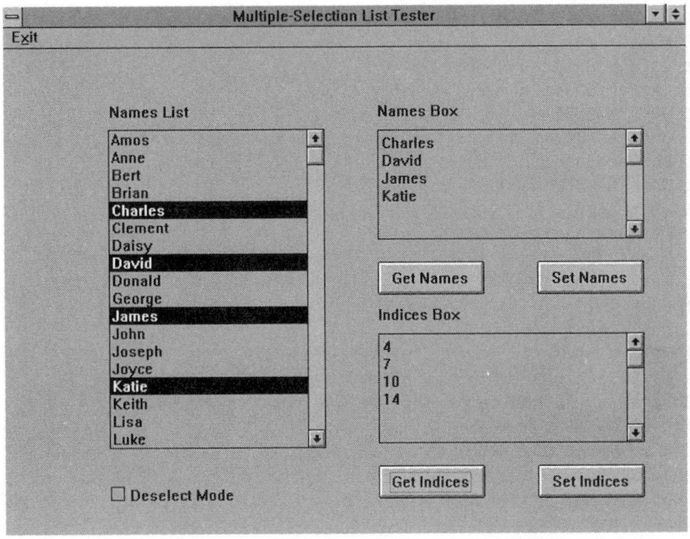

Figure 18.2. *A sample session with the CTLLST2.EXE application.*

Type Listing 18.4. Source code for the CTLLST2.H header file.

```
#define CM_EXIT (WM_USER + 100)
```

Type Listing 18.5. Script for the CTLLST2.RC resource file.

```
#include <afxres.h>
#include "ctllst2.h"

EXITMENU MENU LOADONCALL MOVEABLE PURE DISCARDABLE
BEGIN
    MENUITEM "E&xit", CM_EXIT
END
```

Listing 18.6. Source code for the CTLLST2.CPP program file.

```
#include <stdio.h>
#include <string.h>
#include <afxwin.h>
#include "ctllst2.h"

// declare the constants for the dimensions and spacing
// of the various controls
const Wtxt = 100;
const Htxt = 20;
const TxtVertSpacing = 5;
const Wlst = 200;
const Hlst = 300;
const LstHorzSpacing = 50;
const LstVertSpacing = 20;
const Wbox = 250;
const Hbox = 100;
const BoxVertSpacing = 20;
const Wbtn = 100;
const Hbtn = 30;
const BtnHorzSpacing = 50;
const BtnVertSpacing = 10;
const Wchk = 200;
const Hchk = 20;
// miscellaneous constants
const MaxString = 40;
const MaxSelections = 35; // maximum number of selections
// declare the ID constants for the various controls
#define ID_NAMES_LST 101
#define ID_NAMES_EDIT 102
#define ID_INDICES_EDIT 103
#define ID_GETNAMES_BTN 104
#define ID_SETNAMES_BTN 105
#define ID_GETINDICES_BTN 106
#define ID_SETINDICES_BTN 107
#define ID_SELECT_CHK 108
// declare constants for the check box and radio button states
const BF_CHECKED = 1;
const BF_UNCHECKED = 0;

// declare extended edit control class
class CxEdit : public CEdit
{
public:

  BOOL GetLine(LPSTR lpString, int nStrSize, int nLineNumber);
  int GetLineLength(int nLineNumber);
  int GetNumOfLines();
};

// declare the extended button class
class CxButton : public CButton
{
public:
```

```

   BOOL Create(const char FAR* lpCaption, const RECT& rect,
               CWnd* pParentWnd, UINT nID)
   {
       return CButton::Create(lpCaption,
                       WS_CHILD | WS_VISIBLE |
                       WS_TABSTOP | BS_PUSHBUTTON,
                       rect, pParentWnd, nID);
   }
};

// declare the check box class
class CCheckBox : public CButton
{
public:
   BOOL Create(const char FAR* lpCaption, const RECT& rect,
               CWnd* pParentWnd, UINT nID)
   {
       return CButton::Create(lpCaption,
                          WS_CHILD | WS_VISIBLE |
                          WS_TABSTOP | BS_AUTOCHECKBOX,
                          rect, pParentWnd, nID);
   }

};


// expand the functionality of CFrameWnd by deriving
// class CAppWindow
class CAppWindow : public CFrameWnd
{
public:

  CAppWindow();
  ~CAppWindow();

protected:
  // declare pointers to controls
  CStatic* NamesListTxt;
  CStatic* NamesBoxTxt;
  CStatic* IndicesBoxTxt;
  CListBox* NamesLst;
  CxEdit* NamesBox;
  CxEdit* IndicesBox;
  CxButton* GetNamesBtn;
  CxButton* SetNamesBtn;
  CxButton* GetIndicesBtn;
  CxButton* SetIndicesBtn;
  CCheckBox* SelectChk;
  // declare edit control insertion buffer
  CString insertBuffer;
  // array of string pointers
  LPSTR names[MaxSelections];
  // array of integers to store the selection indices
  int indices[MaxSelections];

```


continues

Listing 18.6. continued

```
  // handle creating the controls
  afx_msg int OnCreate(LPCREATESTRUCT lpCS);
  // initialize the list box
  void InitNamesLst();
  // handle getting the selections
  afx_msg void HandleGetNamesBtn();
  // handle setting the selections
  afx_msg void HandleSetNamesBtn();
  // handle getting the selection indices
  afx_msg void HandleGetIndicesBtn();
  // handle setting the selection indices
  afx_msg void HandleSetIndicesBtn();
  // handle exiting the application
  afx_msg void OnExit()
    { SendMessage(WM_CLOSE); }
  // handle closing the window
  virtual void OnClose();
  void resetSelections();
  void makeRect(int nX, int nY, int nW, int nH, CRect& r);

  // declare message map macro
  DECLARE_MESSAGE_MAP();
};

class CWindowApp : public CWinApp
{
public:
    virtual BOOL InitInstance();
};

BOOL CxEdit::GetLine(LPSTR lpString, int nStrSize,
                      int nLineNumber)
{
  int nCopyCount;
  BOOL bResult;

  if (nStrSize <= 0)
    return FALSE;
  bResult = (nStrSize >= GetLineLength(nLineNumber) + 1) ? TRUE
                                                           : FALSE;
  if (nStrSize == 1) {
    lpString[0] = '\0';
    return bResult;
  }
  ((WORD FAR *)lpString)[0] = nStrSize;
  nCopyCount = (WORD)(SendMessage(EM_GETLINE, nLineNumber,
                                  long(lpString)));
  if (nCopyCount) {
    // Windows returns non-null terminated string
    lpString[nCopyCount] = '\0';
    return bResult;
  }
  else
    return FALSE;
```

```
}

int CxEdit::GetLineLength(int nLineNumber)
{
  int nStartPos = -1;

  if (nLineNumber > -1)
    nStartPos = LineIndex(nLineNumber);
  return (WORD) SendMessage(EM_LINELENGTH, nStartPos);
}

int CxEdit::GetNumOfLines()
{
  // get the size of the text in the edit control
  int nSize = GetWindowTextLength();
  // initialize the function's result
  int nCount = (nSize == 0) ? 0 : 1;
  // return 0 if the edit box is empty
  if (nSize == 0)
    return 0;
  // create a string object of the same nSize
  CString s(' ', nSize);
  // copy the text in the edit control to the string object
  GetWindowText(s.GetBuffer(nSize), nSize);
  s.ReleaseBuffer(); // release any extra space
  // loop to nCount the number of lines by counting the number
  // of '\n' characters (assuming they only occur at a line
  // break)
  for (int i = 0; i < s.GetLength();)
    if (s[i++] == '\r' && s[i] == '\n') {
     nCount++;
     i++;
    }
  return nCount;
}

CAppWindow::CAppWindow()
{
  // create the window
  Create(NULL, "Multiple-Selection List Tester",
        WS_OVERLAPPEDWINDOW ¦ WS_MAXIMIZE,
        rectDefault, NULL, "EXITMENU");
  // insert the initial names in the lists
  InitNamesLst();
}

CAppWindow::~CAppWindow()
{
  delete NamesListTxt;
  delete NamesBoxTxt;
  delete IndicesBoxTxt;
  delete NamesLst;
  delete NamesBox;
  delete IndicesBox;
  delete GetNamesBtn;
  delete SetNamesBtn;
```

continues

Listing 18.6. continued

```
  delete GetIndicesBtn;
  delete SetIndicesBtn;
  delete SelectChk;
  // deallocate the dynamic string space
  for (int i = 0; i < MaxSelections; i++)
    delete names[i];
}

int CAppWindow::OnCreate(LPCREATESTRUCT lpCS)
{
  int nX0 = 100;
  int nY0 = 10;
  int nX = nX0;
  int nY = nY0;
  DWORD dwStaticStyle = WS_CHILD ¦ WS_VISIBLE ¦ SS_LEFT;
  DWORD dwEditStyle = WS_CHILD ¦ WS_VISIBLE ¦ WS_TABSTOP ¦
                      WS_BORDER ¦ WS_VSCROLL ¦ ES_LEFT ¦
                      ES_AUTOHSCROLL ¦ ES_AUTOVSCROLL ¦
                      ES_MULTILINE;
  DWORD dwListBoxStyle = WS_CHILD ¦ WS_VISIBLE ¦ LBS_STANDARD ¦
                         LBS_MULTIPLESEL;
  CRect r;

  // create the name list box and its label
  makeRect(nX, nY, Wtxt, Htxt, r);
  NamesListTxt = new CStatic();
  NamesListTxt->Create("Names List", dwStaticStyle, r, this);
  nY += Htxt + TxtVertSpacing;
  makeRect(nX, nY, Wlst, Hlst, r);
  NamesLst = new CListBox();
  NamesLst->Create(dwListBoxStyle, r, this, ID_NAMES_LST);
  // create the Deselect Mode check box
  nY += Hlst + LstVertSpacing;
  makeRect(nX, nY, Wchk, Hchk, r);
  SelectChk = new CCheckBox();
  SelectChk->Create("Deselect Mode", r, this, ID_SELECT_CHK);
  nX0 += Wlst + LstHorzSpacing;
  nX = nX0;
  nY = nY0;
  // creates the multiline Names Box edit control and its label
  makeRect(nX, nY, Wtxt, Htxt, r);
  NamesBoxTxt = new CStatic();
  NamesBoxTxt->Create("Names Box", dwStaticStyle, r, this);
  nY += Htxt + TxtVertSpacing;
  makeRect(nX, nY, Wbox, Hbox, r);
  NamesBox = new CxEdit();
  NamesBox->Create(dwEditStyle, r, this, ID_NAMES_EDIT);
  // create the Get Names button
  nY += Hbox + BoxVertSpacing;
  makeRect(nX, nY, Wbtn, Hbtn, r);
  GetNamesBtn = new CxButton();
  GetNamesBtn->Create("Get Names", r, this, ID_GETNAMES_BTN);
  // create the Set Names button
  nX += Wbtn + BtnHorzSpacing;
```

```
  makeRect(nX, nY, Wbtn, Hbtn, r);
  SetNamesBtn = new CxButton();
  SetNamesBtn->Create("Set Names", r, this, ID_SETNAMES_BTN);
  nX = nX0;
  nY += Hbtn + BtnVertSpacing;
  // create the multi-line Indices Box edit control and its label
  makeRect(nX, nY, Wtxt, Htxt, r);
  IndicesBoxTxt = new CStatic();
  IndicesBoxTxt->Create("Indices Box", dwStaticStyle, r, this);
  nY += Htxt + TxtVertSpacing;
  makeRect(nX, nY, Wbox, Hbox, r);
  IndicesBox = new CxEdit();
  IndicesBox->Create(dwEditStyle, r, this, ID_INDICES_EDIT);
  // create the GetIndices button
  nY += Hbox + BoxVertSpacing;
  makeRect(nX, nY, Wbtn, Hbtn, r);
  GetIndicesBtn = new CxButton();
  GetIndicesBtn->Create("Get Indices", r, this,
                        ID_GETINDICES_BTN);
  // create the Set Indices button
  nX += Wbtn + BtnHorzSpacing;
  makeRect(nX, nY, Wbtn, Hbtn, r);
  SetIndicesBtn = new CxButton();
  SetIndicesBtn->Create("Set Indices", r, this,
                        ID_SETINDICES_BTN);
  // allocate the dynamic space for the array of strings accessed
  // by the array of pointers names
  for (int i = 0; i < MaxSelections; i++)
    names[i] = new char[MaxString + 1];
  return CFrameWnd::OnCreate(lpCS);
}

void CAppWindow::InitNamesLst()
{
  char* p[] = { "John", "Ribert", "Melody", "Charles", "Olivia",
                "Richard", "James", "Anne", "Keith", "Brian",
                "Lisa", "Margie", "Thomas", "Joseph", "Donald",
                "Bert", "George", "Ronald", "Katie", "Susan",
                "Joyce", "David", "Paul", "Mark", "Luke",
                "Amos", "Matthew", "Mary", "Patrick", "Clement",
                "Daisy", "EOL" };
  for (int i = 0; stricmp(p[i], "EOL") != 0; i++)
    NamesLst->AddString(p[i]);
}

void CAppWindow::HandleGetNamesBtn()
{
  char s[MaxString+1];
  // get the indices of the selected strings
  int n = NamesLst->GetSelItems(MaxSelections, indices);

  // exit if n is not positive
  if (n <= 0) return;
  // clear the insertion buffer
  insertBuffer = "";
  // concatenate the selected strings in the insertion buffer
```

Listing 18.6. continued

```
  for (int i = 0; i < n; i++) {
    NamesLst->GetText(indices[i], names[i]);
    sprintf(s, "%s\r\n", names[i]);
    insertBuffer += s;
  }
  // copy the insertion buffer to the Names Box edit control
  NamesBox->SetWindowText((const char*) insertBuffer);
}

void CAppWindow::HandleSetNamesBtn()
{
  char s[MaxString+1];
  int j;
  // get the number of lines in the Names Box edit control
  int n = NamesBox->GetNumOfLines();
  // get the select status from the Deselect Mode check box
  BOOL bShouldSet =
    (SelectChk->GetCheck() == BF_UNCHECKED) ? TRUE : FALSE;

  resetSelections();
  // read the lines from the Names Box control
  for (int i = 0; i < n; i++) {
    // get the i'th name from the Names Box edit control
    NamesBox->GetLine(s, MaxString, i);
    // find its match in the list box
    j = NamesLst->FindString(-1, s);
    // select the matching element
    if (j != LB_ERR)
      NamesLst->SetSel(j, bShouldSet);
  }
}

void CAppWindow::HandleGetIndicesBtn()
{
  char s[MaxString+1];
  // get the selected indices
  int n = NamesLst->GetSelItems(MaxSelections, indices);

  // exit if n is not positive
  if (n <= 0) return;
  // initialize the insertion buffer
  insertBuffer = "";
  // concatenate the selected indices in the insertion buffer
  for (int i = 0; i < n; i++) {
    sprintf(s, "%d\r\n", indices[i]);
    insertBuffer += s;
  }
  // copy the insertion buffer to the Names edit control
  IndicesBox->SetWindowText((const char*) insertBuffer);
}

void CAppWindow::HandleSetIndicesBtn()
{
  char s[MaxString + 1];
```

```
  int j;

  resetSelections();
  // get the number of lines in the Indices Box edit control
  int n = IndicesBox->GetNumOfLines();
  // get the select status from the Deselect Mode check box
  BOOL bShouldSet =
    (SelectChk->GetCheck() == BF_UNCHECKED) ? TRUE : FALSE;

  // read the lines from the Names Box control and set the
  // corresponding names in the list box
  for (int i = 0; i < n; i++) {
    IndicesBox->GetLine(s, MaxString, i);
    j = atoi(s);
    NamesLst->SetSel(j, bShouldSet);
  }
}

void CAppWindow::OnClose()
{
  if (MessageBox("Want to close this application",
                 "Query", MB_YESNO | MB_ICONQUESTION) == IDYES)
    DestroyWindow();
}

void CAppWindow::resetSelections()
{
  int n = NamesLst->GetSelItems(MaxSelections, indices);

  for (int i = 0; i < n; i++)
      NamesLst->SetSel(indices[i], FALSE);
}

void CAppWindow::makeRect(int nX, int nY, int nW, int nH,
                          CRect& r)
{
  r.top = nY;
  r.left = nX;
  r.bottom = nY + nH;
  r.right = nX + nW;
}

BEGIN_MESSAGE_MAP(CAppWindow, CFrameWnd)
  ON_WM_CREATE()
  ON_BN_CLICKED(ID_GETNAMES_BTN, HandleGetNamesBtn)
  ON_BN_CLICKED(ID_SETNAMES_BTN, HandleSetNamesBtn)
  ON_BN_CLICKED(ID_GETINDICES_BTN, HandleGetIndicesBtn)
  ON_BN_CLICKED(ID_SETINDICES_BTN, HandleSetIndicesBtn)
  ON_COMMAND(CM_EXIT, OnExit)
  ON_WM_CLOSE()
END_MESSAGE_MAP()

// Construct the CWindowApp's m_pMainWnd data member
BOOL CWindowApp::InitInstance()
{
  m_pMainWnd = new CAppWindow();
```

continues

Listing 18.6. continued

```
440:    m_pMainWnd->ShowWindow(m_nCmdShow);
441:    m_pMainWnd->UpdateWindow();
442:    return TRUE;
443: }
444:
445: // application's constructor initializes and runs the app
446: CWindowApp WindowApp;
```

The program in Listing 18.6 declares the following sets of constants:

- The set in lines 8 through 23 specifies the dimensions and spacing for the various application controls.
- The set in lines 25 and 26 declares the maximum string size and maximum number of selections.
- The set in lines 28 through 35 establishes the ID numbers for the various controls.
- The set in lines 37 and 38 declares the check box state constants, `BF_CHECKED` and `BF_UNCHECKED`.

The test program declares the application class, `CWindowApp`; the window class, `CAppWindow`; the edit control class, `CxEdit`; the button class, `CxButton`; and the check box class, `CCheckBox`. The last three classes extend the `CEdit` and `CButton` classes in a manner similar to that shown in previous programs. The current implementation of class `CxEdit` introduces an additional member function, `GetNumOfLines`. This function counts the number of lines in an edit control. This result is required by the application to read individual lines in a multiline edit control.

The `CAppWindow` class declares two sets of data members. The first set represents pointers to the various controls used in the application. The second set of data members contains the array of string pointers, `Names`, and the array of integers, `Indices`. Both arrays have `MaxSelections` members.

The `CAppWindow` class declares a class constructor, a destructor, and a collection of member functions. The class destructor removes the dynamic control instances and the dynamic strings.

The `CAppWindow` constructor invokes the `Create` function and calls the `InitNamesLst` function to initialize the Names list box.

The member function `OnCreate`, defined in lines 228 through 304, creates the various controls and creates the array of dynamic strings. The function sets the style for `CListBox` instance to include the LBS_MULTIPLESEL style. If you want to make the application extend the list box selections with the Shift key, add | LBS_EXTENDEDSEL to the expression that initializes the local variable dwListBoxStyle.

The member function HandleGetNamesBtn, defined in lines 319 through 337, responds to the notification message sent by clicking the Get Names pushbutton. The function performs the following tasks:

- Invokes the GetSelItems function to obtain the list box selections, which are copied to the array of indices accessed by the Indices array of pointers, and specifies that up to MaxSelections indices can be copied (the function result is assigned to the local variable n)
- Exits the function if the variable n stores a negative value
- Initializes the insertion buffer insertBuffer
- Uses a loop to append the strings accessed by the names array to the insertion buffer insertBuffer
- Copies the contents of the insertion buffer to the Names Box control

The member function HandleSetNamesBtn, defined in lines 339 through 360, responds to the notification message of the Set Names pushbutton control. The function carries out the following tasks:

- Obtains the number of lines in the Names Box control
- Obtains the check state of the Deselect Mode check box and assigns a Boolean value, equivalent to the check state, to the local variable shouldSet
- Calls the resetSelections member function to deselect the current selections
- Copies the lines of the Names Box control to the string array accessed by the array of pointer names
- Uses a loop to read each line from the Names Box control and then selects that line (this involves using the FindString function to locate the index of the matching list box item and the SetSel function to select or deselect the matching element, based on the value stored in the local variable shouldSet)

The member function HandleGetIndicesBtn, defined in lines 362 through 379, responds to the notification message sent by the Get Indices pushbutton control. The function performs the following tasks:

- Invokes the `GetSelItems` function to obtain the list box selections, copies these selections to the integer array indices, and specifies that up to `MaxSelections` indices can be copied (the function result is assigned to the local variable `n`)
- Exits the function if the variable `n` stores a negative value
- Initializes the insertion buffer `insertBuffer` with an empty string
- Uses a loop to convert the selection indices to their string images and concatenate these strings in the insertion buffer
- Copies the string of the insertion buffer to the Indices Box edit control

The member function `HandleSetIndicesBtn`, defined in lines 381 through 400, responds to the notification message of the Set Indices pushbutton control. The function carries out the following tasks:

- Obtains the number of lines in the Indices Box control, using the `CxEdit::GetNumOfLines()` member function
- Obtains the check state of the Deselect Mode check box, assigning a Boolean value equivalent to the check state to the local variable `shouldSet`
- Copies each line of the Indices Box control to a temporary string, converts that string into an `int` value, and stores that integer in a member of the indices array
- Uses a loop to read each line from the Indices Box control, convert that line into an index, and then use that index to select (or deselect, depending on the value of the local variable `shouldSet`) a list box item

Summary

Today's lesson presents the list box control, which allows an application user to choose from a fixed collection of values. You learn about the following topics:

- The single-selection list box control provides you with a list of items to select from. This kind of list box allows you to select only one item at a time.
- The multiple-selection list box permits you to select multiple items in a list box for collective processing. Setting the `LBS_EXTENDEDSEL` style when you create the list box enables you to quickly extend the range of selected items by holding down the Shift key and clicking the mouse.

Q&A

Q Can the argument for the `lpWildCard` parameter in function `CListBox::Dir` contain multiple wildcards such as `*.CPP *.H`?

A No, the argument for `lpWildCard` is limited to one filename wildcard.

Q Does the MFC library support intercepting the messages related to the movement of the thumb box in a list box control?

A No.

Q What is the general approach to implementing a program with two list boxes that scroll simultaneously?

A The general approach is to create the two list boxes with hidden scroll bars and then add a scroll bar control (see Day 19). The list boxes then are made to scroll in sync with the scroll bar control, because you can handle the messages emitted by this control and scroll the lists accordingly. You cannot intercept the messages sent by the scroll bars that are part of the list box itself.

Q Should I use `InsertString` in a list box created with the `LBS_SORT` style?

A No, because the `LBS_SORT` style maintains the list box items in order. Using `InsertString` corrupts the order in the list box. Instead, use the `AddString` member function.

18

Workshop

The Workshop provides quiz questions to help you solidify your understanding of the material covered and exercises to provide you with experience in using what you've learned. Try to understand the quiz and exercise answers before continuing on to the next day's lesson. Answers are provided in Appendix B, "Answers."

Quiz

1. True or false? The list box notification message `LBN_SETFOCUS` is suitable for optional initializing related to selecting a list box control.
2. True or false? The list box notification message `LBN_KILLFOCUS` is suitable for optional validation after you deselect a list box control.

3. True or false? The list box allows you to detect only the final selection, using the LBN_KILLFOCUS notification.
4. True or false? You should use LBN_CHANGE with a special flag to detect mouse double-clicks on a list box item.
5. True or false? LBS_STANDARD creates a list box control with unordered items.

Exercise

Write a program that displays a list of files (in a list box) which match the filename wildcard that appears in a text box.

19

Scroll Bars and Combo Boxes

WEEK 3

Day 18 presents list box controls. Today's lesson presents two somewhat similar controls, the scroll bar and the combo box. The scroll bar control allows you to select a numeric value quickly, usually in a wide range of values. The combo box control combines the edit control and the list box, allowing the user to select a value from the list box component or enter a new value in the edit control part. You learn about the following topics:

- The scroll bar control
- The combo box control in its various styles

The Scroll Bar Control

Windows allows the scroll bar to exist as a separate control as well as to be incorporated in windows, lists, and combo boxes. The scroll bar control appears and behaves much like the scroll bar of a window. The control has a thumb box that keeps track of the current value and allows mouse clicks to move it by either single lines or by pages. This thumb box mechanism is supported by the `OnVScroll` or `OnHScroll` member functions. In addition, the scroll bar responds to cursor control keys, such as Home, End, PageUp, and PageDown. This feature is supported by the `OnKeyDown` member function. The main purpose of the scroll bar control is to enable you to quickly and efficiently select an integer value in a predefined range of values. Windows, for example, uses scroll bars to fine-tune the color palette, the keyboard rate, and the mouse sensitivity.

The *CScrollBar* Class

Microsoft Foundation Class offers `CScrollBar`, a descendant of `CWnd`, as the class that models the scroll bar controls. The `CScrollBar` class declares a class constructor and a number of member functions to set and query the control's current position and range of values.

The class constructor, like other MFC classes, has no parameters. To create a scroll bar control, you first invoke the constructor and then call the `Create` member function.

Syntax

The *Create* Function

The declaration of the function `Create` is

```
BOOL Create(DWORD dwStyle,       // control style
         const RECT& rect,    // location and dimensions
         CWnd* pParentWnd,    // pointer to parent window
         UINT nID);           // control ID
```

The `dwStyle` parameter specifies the style of the scroll bar control. Scroll bar styles include the `WS_xxxx` window styles as well as the special `SBS_xxxx` scroll bar styles. Table 19.1 shows the `SBS_xxxx` styles and indicates that you can make the `CScrollBar` instances as size boxes by specifying the `SBS_SIZEBOX` style. The `rect` parameter specifies the location and dimensions of the control. The `pParentWnd` parameter is the pointer to the parent window. The `nID` parameter specifies the unique ID of the scroll bar instance.

Example:

```
CScrollBar* pSB;
pSB->Create(SBS_HORZ, rectDefault, this, ID_SB_SCR);
```

Table 19.1. SBS_xxxx styles for the scroll bar control.

Value	Meaning
`SBS_BOTTOMALIGN`	Specifies a style used with `SBS_HORZ` to align the bottom of the scroll bar with the bottom edge of the rectangle specified in function `Create`
`SBS_HORZ`	Specifies a horizontal scroll bar whose location, width, and height are specified by the parameter `rect` in function `Create`, if neither `SBS_BOTTOMALIGN` nor `SBS_TOPALIGN` is specified
`SBS_LEFTALIGN`	Specifies a style used with the `SBS_VERT` to align the left edge of the scroll bar with the left edge of the rectangle specified in function `Create`
`SBS_RIGHTALIGN`	Specifies a style used with `SBS_VERT` to align the right edge of the scroll bar with the right edge of the rectangle specified in function `Create`
`SBS_SIZEBOX`	Specifies a size box whose location, width, and parameter rect in function `Create`, if neither one of the next two `SBS_xxxx` styles is specified

continues

Table 19.1. continued

Value	Meaning
`SBS_SIZEBOXBOTTOMRIGHTALIGN`	Specifies a style used with `SBS_SIZEBOX` to align the lower right corner of the size box with the lower right corner of the rectangle specified in the function `Create`
`SBS_SIZEBOXTOPLEFTALIGN`	Specifies a style used with the `SBS_SIZEBOX` style to align the upper left corner of the size box with the upper left corner of the rectangle specified in the function `Create`
`SBS_TOPALIGN`	Specifies a style used with `SBS_HORZ` to align the top of the scroll bar with the top edge of the rectangle specified in function `Create`
`SBS_VERT`	Specifies a vertical scroll bar whose location, width, and height are specified by parameter rect in function `Create`, if neither `SBS_RIGHTALIGN` nor `SBS_LEFTALIGN` is specified

The `CScrollBar` declares a number of member functions. The following are the relevant functions:

- The first member function that you most likely will use after creating a `CScrollBar` instance is `SetScrollRange`. This function allows you to set the range of values for the scroll bar.
- The `GetScrollRange` member function enables you to query the current range of values for the scroll bar.
- The parameterless `GetScrollPos` member function returns the current position of the thumb box.
- The `SetScrollPos` member function moves the thumb box to the specified position. You are responsible for ensuring that the new thumb position is within the current scroll bar range.

Syntax

The *SetScrollRange* Function

The declaration of the `SetScrollRange` function is

```
void SetScrollRange(int nMinPos, int nMaxPos,
                    BOOL bRedraw = TRUE);
```

The arguments for the `nMinPos` and `nMaxPos` parameters designate the new range of values for the scroll bar control. The Boolean parameter `bRedraw` indicates whether or not to redraw the scroll bar instance using the new range.

Example:

```
int nMin = 1, nMax = 100;
CScrollBar* pSB;
// create control...
pSB->SetScrollRange(nMin, nMax);
```

Syntax

The *GetScrollRange* Function

The declaration of the `GetScrollRange` function is

```
void GetScrollRange(LPINT lpMinPos, LPINT lpMaxPos) const;
```

The parameters `lpMinPos` and `lpMaxPos` point to the current range of values for the scroll bar control.

Example:

```
int nMin, nMax;
CScrollBar* pSB;
// create control...
pSB->GetScrollRange(&nMin, &nMax);
```

Syntax

The *SetScrollPos* Function

The declaration of the member function `SetScrollPos` is

```
void SetScrollPos(int nPos, BOOL bRedraw = TRUE);
```

The parameter `nPos` specifies the new thumb box position. The Boolean parameter `bRedraw` indicates whether or not to redraw the scroll bar instance using the new position.

Example:

```
CScrollBar* pSB;
// create control...
pSB->SetScrollPos(nMedianValue);
```

Responding to Scroll Bar Notification Messages

The instances of `CScrollBar` that implement scroll bar controls rely on the `CWnd::OnVScroll` or `CWnd::OnHScroll` member functions to support the actual scrolling of the thumb box. The MFC library requires you to declare the scrolling functions as members of the parent window. How is the connection made between the scroll bar and the parent window? The answer lies in the parameters of the `OnVScroll` and `OnHScroll` member functions:

```
afx_msg void OnVScroll(UINT nSBCode, UINT nPos,
                       CScrollBar* pScrollBar);
afx_msg void OnHScroll(UINT nSBCode, UINT nPos,
                        CScrollBar* pScrollBar);
```

The `pScrollBar` parameter is the pointer to the scroll bar control that is clicked by the user. In the scrolling windows examples in Day 15's lesson, I use the `OnVScroll` and `OnHScroll` functions but do not employ the `pScrollBar` parameter in the functions' statements. When you write an `OnVScroll` or `OnHScroll` member function to handle a scroll bar control, you must use the `pScrollBar` parameter along with other `CScrollBar` member functions. The run-time message-handling system makes the connection between the scroll bar control and the `OnVScroll` or `OnHScroll` member functions of the parent window. You need not be concerned about that aspect. The next example shows how this method works.

The Count-Down Timer

The count-down timer application contains the following controls:

- The Timer Input Box edit control that accepts input for the timer and displays the current timer value
- The Static text control that labels the edit box
- The Start button that triggers the count-down timer
- The Exit Button
- The timer scroll bar control that has a default range of 0 to 600 seconds
- The static text controls that label the range of values for the timer scroll bar

You can set the number of seconds in one of two ways: type in that value in the edit box or use the scroll bar. When you move the scroll bar thumb box, the current thumb position appears in the edit box. To trigger the count-down process, click the Start button or press the Alt-S keys. The count-down process takes the value stored in the edit box and converts it into the maximum number of seconds to count down. If the edit box is empty, contains 0, or has nonnumeric text, the program assigns a default of 15 seconds. The program also assigns that value to the static text that specifies the maximum scroll bar value. During the count-down, the application decrements the number of seconds in the edit box and moves the scroll bar's thumb box upward. When the count-down ends, the program sounds a beep, restores the maximum limit of the scroll bar, and restores the maximum limit static text.

The count-down timer application illustrates the following scroll bar manipulations:

- Setting and altering the scroll bar range of values
- Moving and changing the scroll bar thumb box position (the program illustrates how these tasks are performed internally or with the mouse)
- Using the scroll bar to supply a value

Listing 19.1 shows the source code for the CTLSCRL1.H header file. Listing 19.2 shows the script for the CTLSCRL1.RC resource file. The resource file contains the accelerator keys and menu resources. Listing 19.3 shows the source code for the CTLSCRL1.CPP program file. The program uses a menu with the single menu item Exit.

Type Listing 19.1. Source code for the CTLSCRL1.H header file.

```
#define CM_EXIT      (WM_USER + 100)
#define ID_START_BTN (WM_USER + 101)
#define ID_EXIT_BTN  (WM_USER + 102)
#define ID_INPUT_BOX (WM_USER + 103)
#define ID_TIMER_SCR (WM_USER + 104)
```

Type Listing 19.2. Script for the CTLSCRL1.RC resource file.

```
#include <afxres.h>
#include "ctlscrl1.h"

BUTTONS ACCELERATORS
BEGIN
  "s", ID_START_BTN, ALT
  "e", ID_EXIT_BTN, ALT
END

EXITMENU MENU LOADONCALL MOVEABLE PURE DISCARDABLE
BEGIN
    MENUITEM "E&xit", CM_EXIT
END
```

Type

Listing 19.3. Source code for the CTLSCRL1. CPP program file.

```
#include <stdio.h>
#include <string.h>
#include <afxwin.h>
#include "ctlscrl1.h"

// current timer limit is 10 minutes
const MaxTimer = 600; // seconds
const MaxEditLen = 10;
const PageSize = 100;

class CxButton : public CButton
{
public:

   BOOL Create(const char FAR* lpCaption, const RECT& rect,
               CWnd* pParentWnd, UINT nID)
   {
     return CButton::Create(lpCaption,
                 WS_CHILD ¦ WS_VISIBLE ¦ BS_PUSHBUTTON,
                 rect, pParentWnd, nID);
   }
};

class CWindowApp : public CWinApp
{
public:
    virtual BOOL InitInstance();
};

// expand the functionality of CFrameWnd by deriving
// class CAppWindow
class CAppWindow : public CFrameWnd
{
public:

  CAppWindow();
  ~CAppWindow();

protected:
  // declare the pointers to the various controls
  CEdit* InputBox;
  CxButton* StartBtn;
  CxButton* ExitBtn;
  CScrollBar* TimerScr;
  CStatic* InputTxt;
  CStatic* Timer1Txt;
  CStatic* Timer2Txt;
  // handle creating the controls
  afx_msg int OnCreate(LPCREATESTRUCT lpCS);
  // handle the vertical scrolling of the scroll bar
  afx_msg void OnVScroll(UINT nSBCode, UINT nPos,
                CScrollBar* pScrollBar);
  // handle starting the timer
  afx_msg void HandleStartBtn();
```

```
  // handle starting the timer
  afx_msg void CMStartBtn()
    { HandleStartBtn(); }
  // handle exiting the program
  afx_msg void HandleExitBtn()
    { SendMessage(WM_CLOSE); }
  // handle exiting the program
  afx_msg void CMExitBtn()
    { SendMessage(WM_CLOSE); }
  // handle moving the scroll bar
  void HandleTimerScr();
  // handle exiting the application
  afx_msg void OnExit()
    { SendMessage(WM_CLOSE); }
  // handle closing the window
  afx_msg void OnClose();
  void makeRect(int nX, int nY, int nW, int nH, CRect& r);

private:
  // delay the program for about ms milliseconds
  void delay(DWORD dwMs);

  // declare message map macro
  DECLARE_MESSAGE_MAP();
};

CAppWindow::CAppWindow()
{
  // load accelerator resources
  LoadAccelTable("BUTTONS");
  // create the window
  Create(NULL, "CountDown Timer", WS_OVERLAPPEDWINDOW,
      rectDefault, NULL, "EXITMENU");
}

CAppWindow::~CAppWindow()
{
  delete InputBox;
  delete StartBtn;
  delete ExitBtn;
  delete TimerScr;
  delete InputTxt;
  delete Timer1Txt;
  delete Timer2Txt;
}

int CAppWindow::OnCreate(LPCREATESTRUCT lpCS)
{
  char s[81];
  int nX = 50, nY = 50;
  DWORD dwStaticStyle = WS_CHILD | WS_VISIBLE | SS_LEFT;
  DWORD dwEditStyle = WS_CHILD | WS_VISIBLE | ES_LEFT |
                      WS_BORDER;
  DWORD dwScrollStyle = WS_CHILD | WS_VISIBLE | SBS_VERT;
  CRect r;

```

continues

Listing 19.3. continued

```
  // create the timer input box and its label
  makeRect(nX, nY, 150, 30, r);
  InputTxt = new CStatic();
  InputTxt->Create("Timer Input Box", dwStaticStyle, r, this);
  nY += 30 + 5;
  makeRect(nX, nY, 150, 30, r);
  InputBox = new CEdit();
  InputBox->Create(dwEditStyle, r, this, ID_INPUT_BOX);
  InputBox->LimitText(MaxEditLen);
  // create the Start button
  nY += 30 + 20;
  makeRect(nX, nY, 60, 40, r);
  StartBtn = new CxButton();
  StartBtn->Create("&Start", r, this, ID_START_BTN);
  // create the Exit button
  nX += 60 + 20;
  makeRect(nX, nY, 60, 40, r);
  ExitBtn  = new CxButton();
  ExitBtn->Create("&Exit", r, this, ID_EXIT_BTN);
  // create the timer scroll bar
  nX = 300;
  nY = 100;
  makeRect(nX, nY, 20, 150, r);
  TimerScr = new CScrollBar();
  TimerScr->Create(dwScrollStyle, r, this, ID_TIMER_SCR);
  // create the static text controls that label the
  // minimum and maximum values
  nX += 20 + 10;
  makeRect(nX, nY, 80, 20, r);
  Timer1Txt = new CStatic();
  Timer1Txt->Create("0", dwStaticStyle, r, this);
  nY += 130;
  makeRect(nX, nY, 80, 20, r);
  sprintf(s, "%d", MaxTimer);
  Timer2Txt = new CStatic();
  Timer2Txt->Create(s, dwStaticStyle, r, this);
  // initialize the timer range
  TimerScr->SetScrollRange(0, MaxTimer);
  return CFrameWnd::OnCreate(lpCS);
}

void CAppWindow::HandleStartBtn()
{
  char s[MaxEditLen+1];
  int nX;

  // get the text in the edit box
  InputBox->GetWindowText(s, MaxEditLen);
  // convert the string into an integer
  nX = atoi(s);
  // if nX is 0 assign it 15
  nX = (nX != 0) ? nX : 15;
  // set the maximum timer static text
  sprintf(s, "%d", nX);
```

```
  Timer2Txt->SetWindowText(s);
  // set the new range
  TimerScr->SetScrollRange(0, nX);
  // set the thumb position to the maximum position
  TimerScr->SetScrollPos(nX);
  // countdown loop
  while (nX-- > 0) {
    delay(980);
    // update the thumb position
    TimerScr->SetScrollPos(TimerScr->GetScrollPos() - 1);
    sprintf(s, "%d", nX);
    // echo thumb position in the edit box
    InputBox->SetWindowText(s);
    InputBox->UpdateWindow();
  }
  MessageBeep(0); // beep
  // restore the default timer limits
  sprintf(s, "%d", MaxTimer);
  TimerScr->SetScrollRange(0, MaxTimer);
  TimerScr->SetScrollPos(MaxTimer);
  Timer2Txt->SetWindowText(s);
}

void CAppWindow::OnVScroll(UINT nSBCode, UINT nPos,
                           CScrollBar* pScrollBar)
{
  short nScrollInc;
  int nNewPos;
  int nVScrollMin, nVScrollMax;
  int nVScrollPos = pScrollBar->GetScrollPos();

  // get the scroll bar range
  pScrollBar->GetScrollRange(&nVScrollMin, &nVScrollMax);
  switch (nSBCode) {
    case SB_TOP: // move to the top
        nScrollInc = -nVScrollPos;
        break;
    case SB_BOTTOM: // move to the bottom
         nScrollInc = nVScrollMax - nVScrollPos;
        break;
    case SB_LINEUP: // move one line up
        nScrollInc = -1;
        break;
    case SB_LINEDOWN: // move one line down
        nScrollInc = 1;
        break;
    case SB_PAGEUP: // move one page up
        nScrollInc = -PageSize;
        break;
    case SB_PAGEDOWN: // move one page down
        nScrollInc = PageSize;
        break;
    case SB_THUMBPOSITION: // track the thumb box
        nScrollInc = nPos - nVScrollPos;
        break;
    default:
```

continues

Listing 19.3. continued

```
      nScrollInc = 0;
  }
  // calculate new vertical thumb position so that:
  //              0 <= nNewPos <= nVScrollMax
  nNewPos = max(0, min(nVScrollPos + nScrollInc, nVScrollMax));
  // adjust scroll increment
  nScrollInc = nNewPos - nVScrollPos;
  // is nScrollInc not zero?
  if (nScrollInc) {
    // move the thumb box
    pScrollBar->SetScrollPos(nNewPos);
    // scroll the list boxes
    HandleTimerScr();
  }
}

void CAppWindow::HandleTimerScr()
{
  int nX = TimerScr->GetScrollPos();
  char s[MaxEditLen+1];
  // convert the thumb position into a string
  sprintf(s, "%d", nX);
  // insert the string in the edit box
  InputBox->SetWindowText(s);
}

void CAppWindow::OnClose()
{
  if (MessageBox("Want to close this application",
           "Query", MB_YESNO ¦ MB_ICONQUESTION) == IDYES)
    DestroyWindow();
}

void CAppWindow::delay(DWORD dwMs)
{
  DWORD dwTime = GetTickCount();
  do { ; } while ((GetTickCount() - dwTime) < dwMs);
}

void CAppWindow::makeRect(int nX, int nY, int nW, int nH,
                          CRect& r)
{
  r.top = nY;
  r.left = nX;
  r.bottom = nY + nH;
  r.right = nX + nW;
}

BEGIN_MESSAGE_MAP(CAppWindow, CFrameWnd)
  ON_WM_CREATE()
  ON_WM_VSCROLL()
  ON_BN_CLICKED(ID_START_BTN, HandleStartBtn)
  ON_COMMAND(ID_START_BTN, CMStartBtn)
  ON_BN_CLICKED(ID_EXIT_BTN, HandleExitBtn)
```

```
  ON_COMMAND(ID_EXIT_BTN, CMExitBtn)
  ON_COMMAND(CM_EXIT, OnExit)
  ON_WM_CLOSE()
END_MESSAGE_MAP()

// Construct the CWindowApp's m_pMainWnd data member
BOOL CWindowApp::InitInstance()
{
  m_pMainWnd = new CAppWindow();
  m_pMainWnd->ShowWindow(m_nCmdShow);
  m_pMainWnd->UpdateWindow();
  return TRUE;
}

// application's constructor initializes and runs the app
CWindowApp WindowApp;
```

Figure 19.1 shows a sample session with the CTLSCRL1.EXE application.

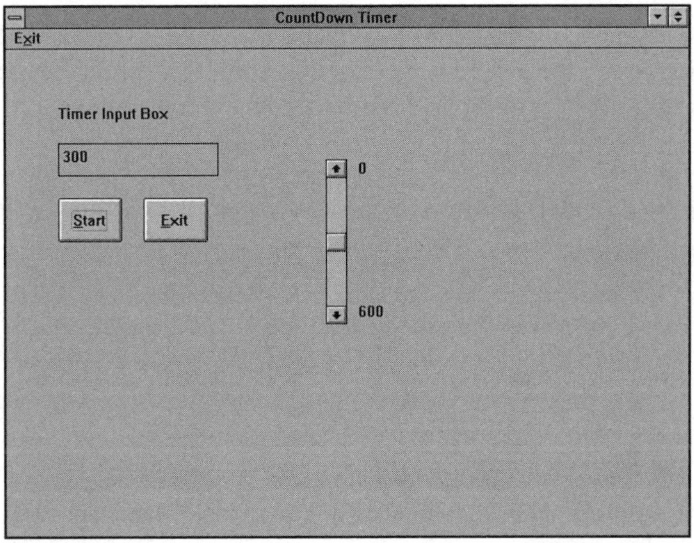

Figure 19.1. *A sample session with the CTLSCRL1.EXE application.*

Analysis The program in Listing 19.3 contains the declaration for the application class, `CWindowApp`; the window class, `CAppWindow`; and the button control class, `CxButton`. The window class `CAppWindow` declares a number of data members that are pointers to the application's controls. The class `CAppWindow` declares a constructor, a destructor, and 10 member functions.

The `CAppWindow` class constructor creates the application window and performs the following tasks:

- ☐ Loads the accelerator keys resource
- ☐ Creates the application window, specifying a title, a default size, a default location, and the `EXITMENU` menu resource

The member function `OnCreate`, defined in lines 101 through 150, creates the various controls used by the application. The function carries out the following tasks:

- ☐ Creates the timer edit box and the static text that labels it
- ☐ Creates the push button controls marked Start and Exit
- ☐ Creates the timer scroll bar control (the function `CScrollBar::Create` specifies a vertical scroll using the `SBS_VERT` style, and assigns the argument `ID_TIMER_SCR` as the control's ID)
- ☐ Creates the static text controls that label the range of scroll bar values, the lower always `0` and the upper initially set using the global constant `MaxTimer` (the program changes the upper limit for the count-down process)
- ☐ Returns the function's result

The member function `HandleStartBtn`, defined in lines 152 through 186, implements the functionality that triggers the timer count-down. The function carries out the following tasks:

- ☐ Retrieves the text in the edit box and stores it in the local variable `s`
- ☐ Converts the characters in variable `s` into an int type and stores the result in the local variable `x`
- ☐ Examines the value of `x` (if it is zero, the function assigns 15 to variable `x`)
- ☐ Sets the maximum timer limit static text to the string image of the value in variable `x`
- ☐ Sets the range of the timer scroll bar by invoking the `CScrollBar::SetScrollRange` member function with the arguments of `0` and `x`
- ☐ Moves the thumb position all the way to the bottom of the scroll bar by using the `CScrollBar::SetScrollPos` member function (the argument for that function call is `x`)
- ☐ Starts the count-down loop, which invokes the delay function; requests that the program wait for 980 milliseconds; changes the thumb box position by moving

it one value upward (using the member functions `CScrollBar::GetScrollPos` and `CScrollBar::SetScrollPos`); and writes the string image of the current thumb box position in the edit box (this simulates the edit box showing the count-down time in seconds)

- Beeps when the previous loop terminates
- Restores the default upper range of the scroll bar timer to 600 and updates the maximum limit static text accordingly

The `CMStartBtn` member function traps the command message generated by the Alt-S keys. The function merely calls the `HandleStartBtn` member function.

The `HandleExitBtn` and `CMExitBtn` member functions send a `WM_CLOSE` message to the application window.

Note: The member function `OnVScroll`, defined in lines 188 through 235, has the task of vertically scrolling the thumb box of the scroll bar control. The statements in the function use the `pScrollBar` parameter to query and set the thumb box position, and also to query the current scroll bar range.

19

The member function `HandleTimerScr`, defined in lines 237 through 245, is called by the `OnVScroll` member function. The function converts the current thumb box position into a string and writes it in the edit box. Thus, function `HandleTimerScr` is responsible for updating the contents of the edit box when you move the thumb box.

The delay member function uses the `GetTickCount` API function to simulate the requested delay.

The Combo Box Control

Windows supports the combo box control, which combines an edit box with a list box. Thus, a combo box allows you to select either an item in the list box component (or part, if you prefer) or type in your own input. In a sense, the list box part of the combo box contains convenient or frequently used selections. A combo box, unlike a list box, does not confine you to choosing items in the list box. There are three kinds of combo boxes: simple, drop-down, and drop-down list.

NEW TERM The *simple combo box* includes the edit box and the list box that is always displayed. The *drop-down combo box* differs from the simple type by the fact that the list box appears only when you click on the down scroll arrow. The *drop-down list combo box* provides a drop-down list that appears when you click on the down scroll arrow. There is no edit box in this kind of combo box!

The *CComboBox* Class

MFC offers the `CComboxBox` class, a descendant of `CWnd`, to support the combo box controls. The `CComboBox` class declares a constructor and a rich set of member functions to support both the list box and edit control components. The `Create` member function assists the class constructor in building class instances.

Syntax

The *Create* Function

The declaration of the `Create` function is

```
BOOL Create(DWORD dwStyle,         // control style
            const RECT& rect,      // location and dimensions
            CWnd* pParentWnd,      // pointer to parent window
            UINT nID);             // control ID
```

The `dwStyle` parameter specifies the style of the list box control. The list box styles include the usual `WS_xxxx` window styles as well as the special `CBS_xxxx` combo box styles (shown in Table 19.2). The `rect` parameter specifies the location and dimensions of the control. The `pParentWnd` parameter is the pointer to the parent window. The `nID` parameter specifies the unique ID of the scroll bar instance.

Example:

```
DWORD dwStyle = WS_CHILD ¦ WS_VISIBLE ¦ WS_GROUP ¦ WS_TABSTOP
                ¦ CBS_SORT ¦ CBS_AUTOHSCROLL ¦ WS_VSCROLL;
CComboBox pCB;
pCB->Create(dwStyle, rectDefault, this, ID_CTL_CMB);
```

The arguments in the `dwStyle` parameter may include either `CBS_SIMPLE` for a simple combo box, `CBS_DROPDOWN` for a drop-down combo box, or `CBS_DROPDOWNLIST` for a drop-down list combo box. Typical instances of `CComboBox` are created with styles `WS_CHILD`, `WS_VISIBLE`, `WS_GROUP`, `WS_TABSTOP`, `CBS_SORT`, `CBS_AUTOHSCROLL`, and `WS_VSCROLL`.

Table 19.2. Common combo box control styles.

Style	Meaning
CBS_AUTOHSCROLL	Automatically scrolls the text in the edit control to the right when you enter a character at the end of the line (removing this style limits the text to the characters that fit inside the rectangular boundary of the edit control)
CBS_DROPDOWN	Specifies a drop-down combo box
CBS_DROPDOWNLIST	Specifies a drop-down list combo box
CBS_SIMPLE	Specifies a simple combo box
CBS_SORT	Automatically sorts the items in the list box

The `CComboBox` class declares member functions to manage the list box and the edit control components. Most of these functions are similar to members of the `CEdit` and `CListBox` classes. Because the MFC library does not declare the `CComboBox` as a descendant of the `CListBox` and `CEdit` (using multiple inheritance), these functions must be redeclared.

Among the functions that handle the list box components are the following:

- The parameterless `GetCount` member function returns the number of items in the list box.
- The parameterless `GetCurSel` member function yields the index of the current selection. If there is no current selection, the function returns `CB_ERR`.
- The `SetCurSel` member function selects the current selection.
- The overloaded `GetLBText` member function is similar to the function `CListBox::GetText`. The function returns the item of the list box.
- The `GetLBTextLen` member function returns the length of list box items specified by an index.
- The `ShowDropDown` member function shows or hides the list box components of a combo box control.
- The `AddString` member function adds a string to the list box component of a combo box control.
- The `DeleteString` member function removes an item from the list box.

- The `InsertString` member function inserts a string at a specified location in the list box.
- The parameterless `ResetContent` member function clears the list box components of a combo box control.
- The `Dir` member function is a special member function that allows you to insert filenames in the list box component.
- The `FindString` member function performs a case-insensitive search for an item in the list box. This function matches a partial string item in the list box part of the control.
- The `FindStringExact` member function performs a case-insensitive search for an item in the list box. This function matches a whole string item in the list box part of the control.
- The `SelectString` member function selects a list box item that matches a search string.

Syntax

The *SetCurSel* Function

The declaration of the `SetCurSel` function is

```
int SetCurSel(int nSelect);
```

The `nSelect` parameter specifies the index of the new selection in the list box. The function returns the index of the selected item or yields `CB_ERR` if there is an error.

Example:

```
CComboBox* pCB;
// create control...
pCB->SetCurSel(0); // select the first item
```

Syntax

The *GetLBText* Function

The declaration of the `GetLBText` function is

```
int GetLBText(int nIndex, LPSTR lpszText) const;
void GetLBText(int nIndex, CString& rString) const;
```

The `nIndex` parameter specifies the index of the retrieved item. The `lpszText` parameter is the pointer to the buffer (which must be large enough) that receives the list box item. The `rString` parameter is the reference to a `CString` object that receives a copy of the list box item. The first form of the function returns the length of the retrieved list box item or yields `CB_ERR` if there is an error.

Example:

```
char* s[81];
CComboBox* pCB;
// create control...
pCB->GetLBText(0, s); // get string in first list box item
```

Syntax

The *GetLBTextLen* Function

The declaration of the function `GetLBTextLen` is

```
int GetLBTextLen(int nIndex) const;
```

The `nIndex` parameter specifies the list box item. The function returns the length of the sought list box item or yields `CB_ERR` if the argument for `nIndex` is not valid. Use `GetLBTextLen` to ensure that the buffer used with function `GetLBText` is large enough.

Example:

```
int nLen;
CComboBox* pCB;
// create control...
nLen = pCB->GetLBTextLen(0); // get length of first item
```

Syntax

The *ShowDropDown* Function

The declaration of the function `ShowDropDown` is

```
void ShowDropDown(BOOL bShowIt = TRUE);
```

The Boolean `bShowIt` parameter is a switch that is used to show (when `TRUE`) or hide (when `FALSE`) the drop-down list box. Use the `ShowDropDown` member function when you want to toggle the visibility of the drop-down list box from within a program.

Example:

```
CComboBox* pCB;
// create control...
pCB->ShowDropDown();
```

Syntax

The *AddString* Function

The declaration of the `AddString` function is

```
int AddString(LPCTSTR lpszString);
```

The `lpszString` parameter is the pointer to the added string. The function returns the index of the inserted item, when successful. Otherwise, the function yields the negative `CB_ERR` value. If the `CBS_SORT` style is set, the added string is placed in the appropriate location to maintain a sorted list. Otherwise, the string is added at the end of the list.

Example:

```
CComboBox* pCB;
// create control...
pCB->AddString("MS-DOS");
```

Syntax

The *DeleteString* Function

The declaration of the `DeleteString` function is

```
int DeleteString(int nIndex);
```

The `nIndex` parameter specifies the index of the deleted list box item. The function returns the number of remaining strings if the deletion is successful. Otherwise, the function yields the negative `CB_ERR` value.

Example:

```
CComboBox* pCB;
// create control...
// add strings to control...
pCB->DeleteString(0); // delete first item
```

Syntax

The *InsertString* Function

The declaration of the `InsertString` function is

```
int InsertString(int nIndex, LPCTSTR lpszString);
```

The `nIndex` parameter specifies the insertion index. The `lpszString` parameter is the pointer to the inserted string. Do not use `InsertString` while the `CBS_SORT` style is set, unless you are inserting an item so that the order of the list box is not corrupted. The function returns the index of the inserted string, or yields `CB_ERR` if an error occurs. If the list box runs out of memory space, the function returns `CB_ERRSPACE`.

Example:

```
CComboBox* pCB;
// create control...
// add strings to control...
pCB->InsertString(0, "Windows"); // insert as new first item
```

Syntax

The *Dir* Function

The declaration of the `Dir` function is

```
int Dir(UINT attr, LPCTSTR lpszWildCard);
```

The attr parameter specifies the combination of attributes. The file attributes are the same ones for the CListBox::Dir function, shown in Day 18, Table 18.2. The lpszWildCard parameter is the pointer to the filename wildcard, such as *.*, L*.EXE, or A???.CPP.

Example:

```
int nNumFiles;
CComboBox* pCB;
// create control...
nNumFiles = pCB->Dir(_A_ARCH, "*.*");
```

Syntax

The *FindString* Function

The declaration of the FindString function is

```
int FindString(int nStartAfter, LPCTSTR lpszString) const;
```

The nStartAfter parameter specifies the index of the first list box member to be searched. The lpszString parameter is the pointer to the searched string. The function searches the *entire* list, beginning with position nStartAfter and resuming at the beginning of the list if needed. The function matches a partial string item in the list box part of the control. The search stops when either a list member matches the search string or the entire list is searched. Passing an argument of -1 to nStartAfter forces the function to start searching from the beginning. The function returns the position of the matching list item or LB_ERR if no match is found or when an error occurs.

Example:

```
int nIndex;
CComboBox* pCB;
// create control...
// add strings to control...
nIndex = pCB->FindString(-1, "MS-DOS");
```

Syntax

The *FindStringExact* Function

The declaration of the FindStringExact function is

```
int FindStringExact(int nStartAfter, LPCTSTR lpszFind) const;
```

The nStartAfter parameter specifies the index of the first list box member to be searched. The lpszFind parameter is the pointer to the searched string. The function searches the *entire* list beginning with position nStartAfter and resuming at the beginning of the list if needed. The function matches a whole string item in the list box part of the control. The search stops when either a list member matches the search string or the entire list is

Syntax

searched. Passing an argument of -1 to nStartAfter forces the function to start searching from the beginning. The function returns the position of the matching list item or LB_ERR if no match is found or when an error occurs.

Example:

```
int nIndex;
CComboBox* pCB;
// create control...
// add strings to control...
nIndex = pCB->FindStringExact(-1, "MS-DOS");
```

The *SelectString* Function

The declaration of function SelectString is

```
int SelectString(int nStartAfter, LPCTSTR lpszString);
```

The parameters and search mechanism of SelectString are identical to those of FindString. The difference is that SelectString selects the list box item that matches the string accessed by parameter lpItem.

Example:

```
CComboBox* pCB;
// create control...
// add strings to control...
pCB->SelectString(-1, "MS-DOS");
```

The following are among the functions that manage the edit control component:

- The parameterless GetEditSel member function returns a DWORD value containing the starting and ending character positions for the selected text. The lower word contains the starting character position (that is, the index of the first selected character) and the higher word contains the ending character position (that is, the index of the first character that is not in the selected text).
- The LimitText member function limits the number of characters that you can type in the edit box of a combo box control.
- The parameterless Clear member function clears the selected text.
- The parameterless Copy member function copies the selected text to the clipboard.
- The Cut member function clears the selected text and copies it to the clipboard.
- The Paste member function copies the contents of the clipboard to the current insertion point of the edit box.

Syntax

The *LimitText* Function

The declaration of the `LimitText` function is

```
BOOL LimitText(int nMaxChars);
```

The parameter `nMaxChars` specifies the limit of the text in the edit box. The function returns `TRUE` if successful and yields `FALSE` otherwise.

Example:

```
const int MAX_STR_SIZE = 81;
CComboBox* pCB;
// create control...
pCB->LimitText(MAX_STR_SIZE);
```

Responding to Combo Box Notification Messages

The combo box control emits various types of messages, shown in Table 19.3. The table also shows the message-mapping macros that are associated with the various command and notification messages. Each type of command or notification message requires a separate member function declared in the control's parent window class.

Table 19.3. Combo box notification messages.

Message	Macro	Meaning
WS_COMMAND	ON_COMMAND	A Windows command message
CBN_SELCHANGE	ON_CBN_SELCHANGE	A combo item is selected with a mouse click
CBN_DBLCLK	ON_CBN_DBLCLK	A combo item is selected with a mouse double-click
CBN_SETFOCUS	ON_CBN_SETFOCUS	The combo box has gained focus
CBN_KILLFOCUS	ON_CBN_KILLFOCUS	The combo box has lost focus
CBN_ERRSPACE	ON_CBN_ERRSPACE	The combo box cannot allocate more dynamic memory to accommodate new list items

continues

Table 19.3. continued

Message	Macro	Meaning
`CBN_EDITCHANGE`	`ON_CBN_EDITCHANGE`	The contents of the edit box are changed
`CBN_EDITUPDATE`	`ON_CBN_EDITUPDATE`	The contents of the edit box are updated

Combo Boxes as History List Boxes

A combo box can also be a history list box. History list boxes typically follow these rules of operations:

1. The combo list box removes the `CBS_SORT` style to insert the list items in a chronological fashion. New items are inserted at position `0`, pushing the older items farther down the list. The oldest item is the one at the bottom of the list.
2. History boxes usually have a limit on the number of items you can insert, to prevent bleeding memory. This conservative scheme requires that the oldest list items be removed once the number of list items reaches a maximum limit.
3. If the edit control contains a string that does not have an exact match in the accompanying list box, the edit control string is inserted as a new member at position `0`.
4. If the edit control contains a string that has an exact match in the accompanying list box, the matching list member is moved to position `0`, the top of the list. Of course, this process involves first deleting the matching list member from its current position and then reinserting it at position `0`.

NEW TERM A *history list box* is a special combo box that inserts new edit control strings in the list box in chronological order.

A history list box is really a combo box that manipulates its edit control and list box items in a certain way. There is no need to derive a descendant of `CComboBox` to add new member functions.

NEW TERM The history list box behaves like a *queue data structure*, with new items inserted at position `0`, pushing the older items farther down the list.

The COCA Version 3 Application

Let me present the calculator application (COCA). This new version is actually derived from the second version, not the third one (except that the feature of substituting the # character in the operand controls with the previous result is also included). Figure 19.2 shows a sample session with the CTLCOMB1.EXE application and indicates the controls that are used:

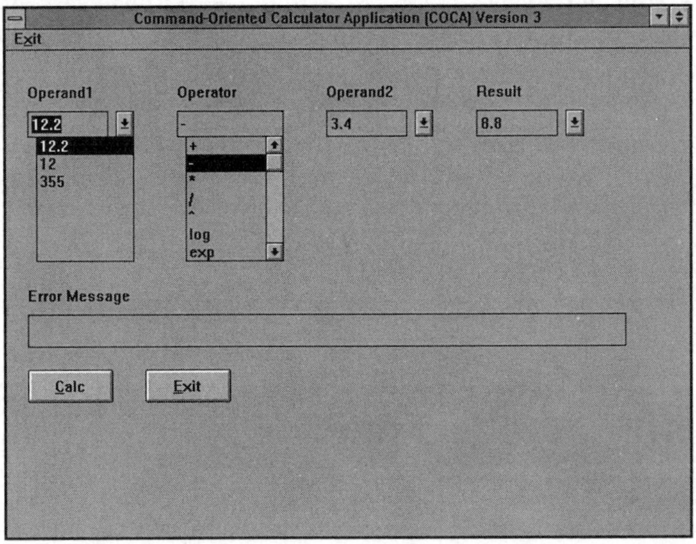

Figure 19.2. *A sample session with the CTLCOMB1.EXE application.*

- An Operand1 drop-down combo box that operates like a history list box
- An Operator simple combo box that contains the list of supported operators and functions `log`, `exp`, and `sqrt` (the program handles the `LBN_KILLFOCUS` notification messages sent by this control to select these functions by typing in the letters `l`, `e`, and `s`, respectively)
- An Operand2 drop-down combo box that operates like a history list box
- A Result drop-down combo box that operates like a history list box
- The error message edit box
- The Calc pushbutton control
- The Exit pushbutton control

Compile and run the program. Experiment with entering and executing numbers and operators or functions. Notice that combo boxes for the operands and the result enter in their accompanying list boxes in a chronological order. The operand combo boxes remember the last 30 different operands you entered. The Result combo box remembers the last 30 different results calculated. In a way, the Result combo box acts as a temporary transient memory.

Listing 19.4 shows the source code for the CTLCOMB1.H header file. Listing 19.5 shows the script for the CTLCOMB1.RC resource file. Listing 19.6 contains the source code for the CTLCOMB1.CPP program file. The resource file defines the accelerator keys and menu resources.

Type

Listing 19.4. Source code for the CTLCOMB1.H header file.

```
#define CM_EXIT (WM_USER + 100)
#define ID_CALC_BTN 110
#define ID_EXIT_BTN 111
```

Type

Listing 19.5. Script for the CTLCOMB1.RC resource file.

```
#include <afxres.h>
#include "ctlcomb1.h"

BUTTONS ACCELERATORS
BEGIN
  "s", ID_START_BTN, ALT
  "e", ID_EXIT_BTN, ALT
END

EXITMENU MENU LOADONCALL MOVEABLE PURE DISCARDABLE
BEGIN
    MENUITEM "E&xit", CM_EXIT
END
```

Type

Listing 19.6. Source code for the CTLCOMB1.CPP program file.

```
#include <stdlib.h>
#include <ctype.h>
#include <stdio.h>
#include <math.h>
#include <string.h>
#include <afxwin.h>
#include "ctlcomb1.h"
```

```
// declare the constants that represent the sizes of the controls
const Wlbl = 100;
const Hlbl = 20;
const LblVertSpacing = 5;
const LblHorzSpacing = 40;
const Wbox = 100;
const Hbox = 30;
const BoxVertSpacing = 20;
const BoxHorzSpacing = 40;
const WLongbox = 4 * (Wbox + BoxHorzSpacing);
const Hbtn = 30;
const Wbtn = 80;
const BtnHorzSpacing = 30;
const BtnVertSpacing = 10;
const Wcmb = 100;
const Hcmb = 150;
const CmbVertSpacing = 10;
const CmbHorzSpacing = 40;
// declare maximum size of text in edit control
const MaxEditLen = 30;
// maximum number of items in a combo box that doubles up as
// history list box
const MaxHistory = 30;
// declare the ID_XXXX constants for the edit boxes
#define ID_OPERAND1_CMB 101
#define ID_OPERATOR_CMB 102
#define ID_OPERAND2_CMB 103
#define ID_RESULT_CMB 104
#define ID_ERRMSG_EDIT 105

class CxButton : public CButton
{
public:

   BOOL Create(const char FAR* lpCaption, const RECT& rect,
               CWnd* pParentWnd, UINT nID)
   {  return CButton::Create(lpCaption,
                    WS_CHILD | WS_VISIBLE | WS_TABSTOP,
                    rect, pParentWnd, nID);
   }
};

// expand the functionality of CFrameWnd by deriving
// class CAppWindow
class CAppWindow : public CFrameWnd
{
public:

  CAppWindow();
  ~CAppWindow();

protected:
  // declare the pointers to the controls
  CStatic* Operand1Txt;
  CStatic* OperatorTxt;
```

continues

Listing 19.6. continued

```
  CStatic* Operand2Txt;
  CStatic* ResultTxt;
  CStatic* ErrMsgTxt;
  CComboBox* Operand1Cmb;
  CComboBox* OperatorCmb;
  CComboBox* Operand2Cmb;
  CComboBox* ResultCmb;
  CEdit* ErrMsgBox;
  CxButton* CalcBtn;
  CxButton* ExitBtn;
  // math error flag
  BOOL bInError;

  // handle notification messages from the Operator combo box
  afx_msg void HandleOperatorCmb();
  // handle the calculation
  afx_msg void HandleCalcBtn();
  // handle the accelerator key for the Calculate button
  afx_msg void CMCalcBtn()
    { HandleCalcBtn(); }
  // handle exiting the application
  afx_msg void HandleExitBtn()
    { SendMessage(WM_CLOSE); }
  // handle the accelerator key for the Exit button
  afx_msg void CMExitBtn()
    { SendMessage(WM_CLOSE); }
  // handle exiting the application
  afx_msg void OnExit()
    { SendMessage(WM_CLOSE); }
  // handle creating the controls
  afx_msg int OnCreate(LPCREATESTRUCT lpCS);
  // initialize the instances of CAppWindow
  void InitAppWindow();
  // handle closing the window
  afx_msg void OnClose();
  // return a reference to member r based on individual
  // coordinates and dimenions
  void makeRect(int nX, int nY, int nW, int nH, CRect& r);
  // update the combo box with the text in the
  // accompanying edit box, assuming that the text
  // is not already in the box
  void updateComboBox(CComboBox* pComboBox);

  // declare message map macro
  DECLARE_MESSAGE_MAP();
};

class CWindowApp : public CWinApp
{
public:
    virtual BOOL InitInstance();
};

CAppWindow::CAppWindow()
```

```
{
  // load accelerator resources
  LoadAccelTable("BUTTONS");
  // create the window
  Create(NULL,
    "Command-Oriented Calculator Application (COCA) Version 3",
      WS_OVERLAPPEDWINDOW | WS_MAXIMIZE,
         rectDefault, NULL, "EXITMENU");
  // clear the bInError flag
  bInError = FALSE;
  // initialize application
  InitAppWindow();
}

CAppWindow::~CAppWindow()
{
  // delete the controls
  delete Operand1Txt;
  delete OperatorTxt;
  delete Operand2Txt;
  delete ResultTxt;
  delete ErrMsgTxt;
  delete Operand1Cmb;
  delete OperatorCmb;
  delete Operand2Cmb;
  delete ResultCmb;
  delete ErrMsgBox;
  delete CalcBtn;
  delete ExitBtn;
}

int CAppWindow::OnCreate(LPCREATESTRUCT lpCS)
{
  int nX0 = 20;
  int nY0 = 30;
  int nX = nX0, nY = nY0;
  DWORD dwStaticStyle = WS_CHILD | WS_VISIBLE | SS_LEFT;
  DWORD dwEditStyle = WS_CHILD | WS_VISIBLE | WS_BORDER |
                      ES_LEFT | ES_AUTOHSCROLL | ES_UPPERCASE;
  DWORD dwComboStyle = WS_CHILD | WS_VISIBLE | WS_VSCROLL;
  CRect r;

  // create the first set of labels for the edit boxes
  makeRect(nX, nY, Wlbl, Hlbl, r);
  Operand1Txt = new CStatic();
  Operand1Txt->Create("Operand1", dwStaticStyle, r, this);
  nX += Wlbl + LblHorzSpacing;
  makeRect(nX, nY, Wlbl, Hlbl, r);
  OperatorTxt = new CStatic();
  OperatorTxt->Create("Operator", dwStaticStyle, r, this);
  nX += Wlbl + LblHorzSpacing;
  makeRect(nX, nY, Wlbl, Hlbl, r);
  Operand2Txt = new CStatic();
  Operand2Txt->Create("Operand2", dwStaticStyle, r, this);
  nX += Wlbl + LblHorzSpacing;
  makeRect(nX, nY, Wlbl, Hlbl, r);
```

Listing 19.6. continued

```
    ResultTxt = new CStatic();
    ResultTxt->Create("Result", dwStaticStyle, r, this);
    // create the Operand1, Operator, Operand2, and Result
    // combo list boxes
    nX = nX0;
    nY += Hlbl + LblVertSpacing;
    makeRect(nX, nY, Wcmb, Hcmb, r);
    Operand1Cmb = new CComboBox();
    Operand1Cmb->Create(dwComboStyle | CBS_DROPDOWN, r,
                        this, ID_OPERAND1_CMB);
    // create the Operator combo box
    nX += Wcmb + CmbHorzSpacing;
    makeRect(nX, nY, Wcmb, Hcmb, r);
    OperatorCmb = new CComboBox();
    OperatorCmb->Create(dwComboStyle | CBS_SIMPLE, r,
                        this, ID_OPERATOR_CMB);
    nX += Wcmb + CmbHorzSpacing;
    makeRect(nX, nY, Wcmb, Hcmb, r);
    Operand2Cmb = new CComboBox();
    Operand2Cmb->Create(dwComboStyle | CBS_DROPDOWN, r,
                        this, ID_OPERAND2_CMB);
    nX += Wcmb + CmbHorzSpacing;
    makeRect(nX, nY, Wcmb, Hcmb, r);
    ResultCmb = new CComboBox();
    ResultCmb->Create(dwComboStyle | CBS_DROPDOWN, r,
                      this, ID_RESULT_CMB);
    // create the static text and edit box for the error message
    nX = nX0;
    nY += Hcmb + CmbVertSpacing;
    makeRect(nX, nY, Wlbl, Hlbl, r);
    ErrMsgTxt = new CStatic();
    ErrMsgTxt->Create("Error Message", dwStaticStyle, r, this);
    nY += Hlbl + LblVertSpacing;
    makeRect(nX, nY, WLongbox, Hbox, r);
    ErrMsgBox = new CEdit();
    ErrMsgBox->Create(dwEditStyle, r, this, ID_ERRMSG_EDIT);
    // create the Calc push button
    nY += Hbox + BoxVertSpacing;
    makeRect(nX, nY, Wbtn, Hbtn, r);
    CalcBtn = new CxButton();
    CalcBtn->Create("&Calc", r, this, ID_CALC_BTN);
    // Create the Exit Btn
    nX += Wbtn + BtnHorzSpacing;
    makeRect(nX, nY, Wbtn, Hbtn, r);
    ExitBtn = new CxButton();
    ExitBtn->Create("&Exit", r, this, ID_EXIT_BTN);
    // clear the bInError flag
    bInError = FALSE;
    return CFrameWnd::OnCreate(lpCS);
  }

  void CAppWindow::InitAppWindow()
  {
    char* p[] = { "+", "-", "*", "/", "^",
```

```
                      "log", "exp", "sqrt", "EOL" };

  // add the operators in the Operator combo box
  for (int i = 0; stricmp(p[i], "EOL") != 0; i++)
    OperatorCmb->AddString(p[i]);
}

void CAppWindow::HandleOperatorCmb()
{
  char s[MaxEditLen+1];

  // get the text in the Operator combo box edit area
  OperatorCmb->GetWindowText(s, MaxEditLen);
  // use it to search for a matching list item
  OperatorCmb->SelectString(-1, s);
}

void CAppWindow::HandleCalcBtn()
{
  int nOpIndex;
  double x, y, z;
  char opStr[MaxEditLen+1];
  char s[MaxEditLen+1];

  // obtain the string in the Operand1 combo box
  Operand1Cmb->GetWindowText(s, MaxEditLen);
  // convert the string in the edit box area
  x = atof(s);
  // obtain the string in the Operand2 combo box
  Operand2Cmb->GetWindowText(s, MaxEditLen);
  // convert the string in the edit box area
  y = atof(s);
  // obtain the string in the Operator combo box
  OperatorCmb->GetWindowText(opStr, MaxEditLen);
  // clear the error message box
  ErrMsgBox->SetWindowText("");
  bInError = FALSE;
  // determine the requested operation using the FindString
  // member function of CListBox
  nOpIndex = OperatorCmb->FindString(-1, opStr);
  switch (nOpIndex) {
    case 0: // + operator
      z = x + y;
      break;
    case 1: // - operator
      z = x - y;
      break;
    case 2: // * operator
      z = x * y;
      break;
    case 3: // / operator
      if (y != 0)
        z = x / y;
      else {
        z = 0;
        bInError = TRUE;
```

continues

Listing 19.6. continued

```
        ErrMsgBox->SetWindowText("Division-by-zero error");
      }
      break;
    case 4: // ^ operator
      if (x > 0)
        z = exp(y * log(x));
      else {
        bInError = TRUE;
         ErrMsgBox->SetWindowText(
          "Cannot raise the power of a negative number");
      }
      break;
    case 5: // the natural logarithm function
      if (x > 0)
        z = log(x);
      else {
        bInError = TRUE;
         ErrMsgBox->SetWindowText(
          "Invalid argument for the log(x) function");
      }
      break;
    case 6: // the exponential function
      if (x < 230)
        z = exp(x);
      else {
        bInError = TRUE;
         ErrMsgBox->SetWindowText(
          "Invalid argument for the exp(x) function");
      }
      break;
    case 7: // the square root function
      if (x >= 0)
        z = sqrt(x);
      else {
        bInError = TRUE;
         ErrMsgBox->SetWindowText(
          "Invalid argument for the sqrt(x) function");
      }
      break;
    default:
      bInError = TRUE;
      ErrMsgBox->SetWindowText("Invalid operator");
      break;
  }
  // display the result if no error has occurred
  if (!bInError) {
    sprintf(s, "%g", z);
    ResultCmb->SetWindowText(s);
    updateComboBox(ResultCmb);
  }
  // update the operand combo boxes
  updateComboBox(Operand1Cmb);
  updateComboBox(Operand2Cmb);
}
```

```
void CAppWindow::makeRect(int nX, int nY, int nW, int nH,
                          CRect& r)
{
  r.top = nY;
  r.left = nX;
  r.bottom = nY + nH;
  r.right = nX + nW;
}

void CAppWindow::updateComboBox(CComboBox* pComboBox)
{
  char s[MaxEditLen+1];
  int nIdx;

  pComboBox->GetWindowText(s, MaxEditLen);
  // is string s in the combo list
  nIdx = pComboBox->FindString(-1, s);
  if (nIdx == 0) return;
  else if (nIdx < 0) {
    pComboBox->InsertString(0, s);
    // delete extra history list members?
    while (pComboBox->GetCount() >= MaxHistory)
      pComboBox->DeleteString(pComboBox->GetCount()-1);
  }
  else {
    // delete the current selection
    pComboBox->DeleteString(nIdx);
    // insert the string s at the first position
    pComboBox->InsertString(0, s);
    // select the first combo box item
    pComboBox->SetCurSel(0);
  }
}

void CAppWindow::OnClose()
{
  if (MessageBox("Want to close this application",
                 "Query", MB_YESNO | MB_ICONQUESTION) == IDYES)
    DestroyWindow();
}

BEGIN_MESSAGE_MAP(CAppWindow, CFrameWnd)
    ON_CBN_EDITUPDATE(ID_OPERATOR_CMB, HandleOperatorCmb)
    ON_BN_CLICKED(ID_CALC_BTN, HandleCalcBtn)
    ON_COMMAND(ID_CALC_BTN, CMCalcBtn)
    ON_BN_CLICKED(ID_EXIT_BTN, HandleExitBtn)
    ON_COMMAND(ID_EXIT_BTN, CMExitBtn)
    ON_COMMAND(CM_EXIT, OnExit)
    ON_WM_CREATE()
    ON_WM_CLOSE()
END_MESSAGE_MAP()

// Construct the CWindowApp's m_pMainWnd data member
BOOL CWindowApp::InitInstance()
```

continues

Listing 19.6. continued

```
394: {
395:   m_pMainWnd = new CAppWindow();
396:   m_pMainWnd->ShowWindow(m_nCmdShow);
397:   m_pMainWnd->UpdateWindow();
398:   return TRUE;
399: }
400:
401: // application's constructor initializes and runs the app
402: CWindowApp WindowApp;
```

Analysis The program in Listing 19.6 declares three sets of constants. The first set specifies the dimensions and spacing for the various application controls. The second set of constants declares the maximum string size and maximum number of selections. The third set of constants establishes the ID numbers for the various controls.

The calculator program declares the application class, `CWindowApp`; the window class, `CAppWindow`; and the button class, `CxButton`. The `CAppWindow` class declares two sets of data members. The first set represents pointers to the various controls used in the application. The second set of members merely contains the `bInError` data member that flags any computational errors.

The `CAppWindow` class declares a constructor, a destructor, and a collection of member functions to handle the various messages. The `CAppWindow` constructor performs the following tasks:

- Loads the accelerator keys resource
- Invokes the `Create` function to create the application window (the window is maximized and uses the `EXITMENU` resource menu)
- Assigns `FALSE` to the `bInError` data member
- Calls the `InitAppWindow` function to initialize the application

The member function `OnCreate`, defined in lines 149 through 223, creates the instances for the various controls. The operand and result combo boxes are created with the `CBS_DROPDOWN` style. These same combo boxes avoid including the `CBS_SORT` style to enable them to work as history list boxes. The function creates the Operator combo box with the `CBS_SIMPLE` style and maintains the ordered items in the accompanying list box.

The member function `InitAppWindow`, defined in lines 225 through 233, initializes the window instance by adding the supported operators and math functions in the list box component of the Operator combo box. This task uses a `for` loop that invokes the member function `AddString`.

The member function `HandleOperatorCmb`, defined in lines 235 through 243, responds to the `CBN_EDITUPDATE` notification message sent by the Operator combo box. The function carries out the following tasks:

- Obtains the text from the edit box using the `GetText` function
- Invokes the `SelectString` function to search for a list box member that matches the retrieved string (if it finds a match, the matching item appears as selected text in the edit control area of the combo box)

The member function `HandleCalcBtn`, defined in lines 245 through 337, responds to the notification message of the `Calc` button and performs the requested calculation. The function performs these subsequent tasks:

- Retrieves the string in the edit box of the Operand1 combo box
- Converts this retrieved string into a numeric value and stores this value in the local variable `x`
- Retrieves the string in the edit box of the Operand2 combo box
- Converts this retrieved string into a numeric value and stores this value in the local variable `y`
- Obtains the string in the edit control of the Operator combo box
- Clears the Error Message edit control and assigns `FALSE` to the `bInError` data member
- Finds the position of the invoked operator or math function in the Operator combo box list, using the member function `CComboBox::FindString`
- Uses a switch statement to determine the requested operation or math function evaluation, then performs the requested task and assigns the result to variable `z`, or flags an error (this is the first time a version of the COCA program uses the switch statement, which should execute faster than the cascaded if statements that use the `strcmp` function found in earlier versions)
- If no error occurs, displays the result of the operation or function evaluation in the edit control box of the Result combo box, then inserts the new result in the list box of the Result combo box by calling the `updateComboBox` member function

- Inserts the new operands in the list boxes of their respective combo boxes, calling the `updateComboBox` member function twice to update both operand combo boxes (this update occurs regardless of the error condition and, if you request to evaluate a math function, the list box of the Operand2 combo box remains unchanged unless you enter a new and superfluous operand in that combo box)

The function `CMCalcBtn` responds to the command message invoked by the Alt-C accelerator key. The function merely calls the `HandleCalcBtn` member function to provide the needed response.

The member function `updatedComboBox`, defined in lines 349 through 372, inserts the string of the edit control part in the list box part. This insertion occurs only if the string is not already in the list box part. In this case, the string is inserted at index `0` and becomes the new top-of-the-list item. If the targeted string is already in the list box part, the function deletes the existing item in the list box and reinserts it at index `0`. Thus, the targeted string appears to have moved up to the top of the list box part.

The `HandleExitBtn` and `CMExitBtn` member functions offer the same response to the messages sent by the Exit button and the Alt-E accelerator key. Both functions send the `WM_CLOSE` message to the parent window.

Summary

Today's lesson presents the scroll bar and combo box controls. These controls share the common factor of being input objects. You learn about the following topics:

- The scroll bar control enables you to select quickly from a wide range of integers.
- There are various types of combo box controls: simple, drop-down, and drop-down list. You can use the `CBN_EDITUPDATE` notification message to make the combo boxes more interactive.
- You can make a history list box out of a drop-down combo box.

Q&A

Q Do the scroll bars strictly select integers?

A Yes. However, these integers can be indices to arrays, items in list box controls, and other integer codes to various attributes, such as colors. Therefore, in a sense, the scroll bar can be used to select nonintegers.

Q Can I create a scroll bar control with an excluded subrange of values?

A No. You may want to use a list box control instead and have that control list the value numbers.

Workshop

The Workshop provides quiz questions to help you solidify your understanding of the material covered, and exercises to provide you with experience in using what you've learned. Try to understand the quiz and exercise answers before continuing on to the next day's lesson. Answers are provided in Appendix B, "Answers."

Quiz

1. True or false? If you do not include the `CBS_AUTOHSCROLL` style in creating a combo list box, you limit the text to the characters that fit inside the rectangular boundary of the edit control.
2. True or false? You can handle the `CBN_SELCHANGE` notification message to monitor every keystroke in the edit control of a combo box.
3. True or false? Setting `CBS_SORT` creates a combo box whose list box items are sorted and unique.
4. True or false? To emulate a history list box, a combo box must be created without the `CBS_SORT` style.
5. True or false? A history list may have duplicate items.
6. True or false? CTLSCRL1.CPP demonstrates how to implement a two-way connection between the current value of a scroll bar control and the numeric value in a text box.
7. True or false? The range of values for a scroll bar control are fixed when you create the control.

Exercises

1. Modify the CTLCOMB1.CPP program by adding a Variables multiline box and a Store pushbutton.
2. Modify the CTLCOMB1.CPP program by adding a Variables list box and a Store pushbutton.

20

Dialog Boxes

WEEK 3

Dialog boxes are special child windows that contain controls serving to display information or to input data. Windows applications use dialog boxes to exchange information with the user. Today's lesson looks at the modal and modeless dialog boxes supported by Windows.

NEW TERM *Modal dialog boxes* require you to close them before you can proceed any further with the application, because they are meant to perform a critical exchange of data. In fact, modal dialog boxes disable their parent windows while they have the focus. *Modeless dialog boxes* do need to be closed to continue using the application.

Today you learn about the following topics:

- Constructing instances of class `CDialog`
- Executing a modal dialog box
- Transferring control data
- Transferring data for modal dialog boxes
- Transferring data for modeless dialog boxes

Constructing Dialog Boxes

The MFC library declares the `CDialog` class to support both modeless and modal dialog boxes. The `CDialog` class, a descendant of `CWnd`, has a class constructor and a number of member functions, including the `Create` function. The `CDialog` constructor is declared as a protected member to force you to create your own modeless dialog box classes. These derived classes can declare either set of members to supplement your custom dialog box classes:

- Declare only a public constructor that invokes the `CDialog::Create` member function. This approach creates dialog box instances in one step.
- Declare both a public constructor and a `Create` member function. This scheme creates dialog box instances in two steps, by first calling the class constructor and then invoking the `Create` member function.

The declaration of the overloaded `CDialog::Create` member function is

```
BOOL Create(LPCSTR lpTemplateName, CWnd* pParentWnd = NULL);
BOOL Create(UINT nIDTemplate, CWnd* pParentWnd = NULL);
```

The `lpTemplateName` and `nIDTemplate` parameters are the dialog box resource name and ID, respectively. The `pParentWnd` parameter is the pointer to the parent window. You can use the default argument when the dialog box instance is also the main application window.

> **Note:** Using resources to define dialog boxes and their controls allows you to define the location, dimensions, style, and caption of a control outside the Windows application source code. Thus, you can change the resource file, recompile it, and then incorporate it in the .EXE application file without recompiling the source file itself. This approach enables you to develop different resource versions with varying colors, styles, and even languages while maintaining a single copy of the application code.

> **Note:** The Visual C++ package includes the App Studio that enables you to create dialog boxes by drawing the controls in the dialog boxes, Visual Basic style. The App Studio creates .RC resource files that are then bound in your Windows applications. If you are a novice Windows programmer, first learn about the .RC file and its script. Using the App Studio is very easy and intuitive. Knowing about the .RC resource script makes working with the output of the App Studio even easier.

Executing Modal Dialog Boxes

Typically, modal dialog boxes are created and removed more frequently than modeless dialog boxes and much more frequently than windows. Executing modal dialog boxes involves the following steps:

1. Create a dialog box instance by using the dialog box class constructor.
2. Call the `DoModal()` member function, declared in class `CDialog`, to bring up the dialog box. Typically, dialog boxes contain the OK and Cancel pushbuttons, with the OK button as the default button. The OK and Cancel buttons have the predefined ID of `IDOK` and `IDCANCEL`, respectively. You may use pushbutton controls with different captions than OK and Cancel. However, you should still use the `IDOK` and `IDCANCEL` with these renamed buttons. Using these IDs allows you to take advantage of the automatic response to `IDOK` and `IDCANCEL`

provided by the `OnOK` and `OnCancel` member functions defined in your dialog box class. Clicking OK or pressing the Enter key usually signals your acceptance of the current (that is, the default and/or edited) data in the dialog box. By contrast, clicking the Cancel button signals your dissatisfaction with the current data. The declaration of the `DoModal()` function is

```
virtual DoModal();
```

The function returns an integer that represents the outcome. Typical outcome values are `IDOK` or `IDCANCEL`.

3. Compare the result of the `DoModal` function with `IDOK` (or, less frequently, `IDCANCEL`). The outcome of this comparison determines the steps to take. Such steps usually involve accessing data that you entered in the dialog box controls.

The `OnInitDialog` (inherited from class `CDialog`), `OnOK`, and `OnCancel` member functions support the execution of the modal dialog boxes. These parameterless functions are declared as virtual, requiring that overriding functions be void of any parameters. The `OnInitDialog` member function serves to initialize the dialog box and its controls. The declaration of the `OnInitDialog` is

```
virtual BOOL OnInitDialog();
```

The function returns a Boolean result to indicate the success of the dialog box initialization. Typically, the `OnInitDialog` function initializes the controls of the dialog box. This initialization usually involves copying data from buffers or data members.

The `OnOK` member function handles pressing the OK button. The declaration of the `OnOK` function is

```
virtual void OnOK();
```

The `OnOK` function serves to copy data from the dialog box controls to data members or buffers. Using the `EndDialog` member function, the `OnOk` function is able to provide the `DoModal` function with its return value. Usually, the last statement in the `OnOK` member function definition is `EndDialog(IDOK)`. The latter function call causes the `DoModal` function to return `IDOK`.

The `OnCancel` member function handles pressing the Cancel button. The declaration of the `OnCancel` function is

```
virtual void OnCancel();
```

The `OnCancel` function serves to clean up before the dialog box is closed, which may involve closing data files, for example. Usually, the last statement in the `OnCancel` member function definition is `EndDialog(IDCANCEL)`. The latter function call causes the `DoModal` function to return `IDCANCEL`.

The next example is a simple MFC program that uses a dialog box defined in resource files. It also uses resource files to create alternate forms of the same dialog box—the first uses modern English and the second uses old English. The application is simple and is made up of an empty window with a single menu item, Exit. When you click the Exit menu item (or press the Alt+X keys) you get a dialog box that asks you whether or not you want to exit the application. The dialog box has a title, a message, and the two buttons (in fact, I purposely made it to resemble the dialog boxes spawned by the `CWnd::MessageBox` function). The program alternates between the two versions of the dialog box. When you first click the Exit menu, you get the modern English version (with OK and Cancel buttons), shown in Figure 20.1. If you click on the Cancel button and then click the Exit menu again, you get the old English version of the dialog box (with Yea and Nay buttons), shown in Figure 20.2. Every time you select the Cancel or Nay button and then click the Exit menu, you toggle between the two versions of the dialog box. To exit the application, click on the OK or Yes button, depending on the current dialog box version.

Listing 20.1 shows the DIALOG1.H header file. Listing 20.2 contains the script for the DIALOG1.RC resource file. Listing 20.3 shows the source code for the DIALOG1.CPP program.

Type **Listing 20.1. Source code for the DIALOG1.H header file.**

```
#define CM_EXIT (WM_USER + 100)
```

Type **Listing 20.2. Script for the DIALOG1.RC resource file.**

```
#include <afxres.h>
#include "dialog1.h"

EXITMENU MENU LOADONCALL MOVEABLE PURE DISCARDABLE
BEGIN
    MENUITEM "E&xit", CM_EXIT
END

NEW DIALOG DISCARDABLE LOADONCALL PURE MOVEABLE 30, 50, 200, 100
STYLE WS_POPUP | DS_MODALFRAME
CAPTION "Message"
BEGIN
  CTEXT "Exit the application?", 1, 10, 10, 170, 15
  CONTROL "OK", IDOK, "BUTTON", WS_CHILD | WS_VISIBLE |
    WS_TABSTOP | BS_DEFPUSHBUTTON, 20, 50, 70, 15
  CONTROL "Cancel", IDCANCEL, "BUTTON", WS_CHILD | WS_VISIBLE |
    WS_TABSTOP | BS_PUSHBUTTON, 110, 50, 70, 15
END
```

continues

Listing 20.2. continued

```

OLD DIALOG DISCARDABLE LOADONCALL PURE MOVEABLE 30, 50, 200, 100
STYLE WS_POPUP | DS_MODALFRAME
CAPTION "A Word With Thou"
BEGIN
  CTEXT "Thou leavest now?", 1, 10, 10, 170, 15
  CONTROL "Yea", IDOK, "BUTTON", WS_CHILD | WS_VISIBLE |
    WS_TABSTOP | BS_DEFPUSHBUTTON, 20, 50, 70, 15
  CONTROL "Nay", IDCANCEL, "BUTTON", WS_CHILD | WS_VISIBLE |
    WS_TABSTOP | BS_PUSHBUTTON, 110, 50, 70, 15
END
```

Type Listing 20.3. Source code for the DIALOG1.CPP program file.

```
#include <afxwin.h>
#include "dialog1.h"

class CWindowApp : public CWinApp
{
public:
    virtual BOOL InitInstance();
};
// expand the functionality of CFrameWnd by deriving
// class CAppWindow
class CAppWindow : public CFrameWnd
{
public:

  CAppWindow();

protected:
  // handle exiting the application
  afx_msg void OnExit()
    { SendMessage(WM_CLOSE); }
  // Handle closing the window
  afx_msg void OnClose();

  DECLARE_MESSAGE_MAP();

};

CAppWindow::CAppWindow()
{
  // create the window
  Create(NULL, "A Bare-Bones Dialog Box Tester",
         WS_OVERLAPPEDWINDOW, rectDefault, NULL, "EXITMENU");

}

void CAppWindow::OnClose()
{
  static BOOL bFlag = FALSE;
```

```
  CDialog* pDialogBox;
  BOOL bCloseIt;

  // toggle flag that selects alternate dialog box resources
  bFlag = (bFlag == TRUE) ? FALSE : TRUE;
  if (bFlag) {
    pDialogBox = new CDialog("NEW", this);
    // use Modern English dialog box
    bCloseIt = (pDialogBox->DoModal() == IDOK) ? TRUE : FALSE;
  }
  else {
    pDialogBox = new CDialog("OLD", this);
    // use Old English dialog box
    bCloseIt = (pDialogBox->DoModal() == IDOK) ? TRUE : FALSE;
  }
  if (bCloseIt)
     DestroyWindow();
}

BEGIN_MESSAGE_MAP(CAppWindow, CFrameWnd)
  ON_COMMAND(CM_EXIT, OnExit)
  ON_WM_CLOSE()
END_MESSAGE_MAP()

// Construct the CWindowApp's m_pMainWnd data member
BOOL CWindowApp::InitInstance()
{
  m_pMainWnd = new CAppWindow();
  m_pMainWnd->ShowWindow(m_nCmdShow);
  m_pMainWnd->UpdateWindow();
  return TRUE;
}

// application's constructor initializes and runs the app
CWindowApp WindowApp;
```


Listing 20.2 shows the script for the DIALOG1.RC resource file, which defines the following resources:

- The menu resource, `EXITMENU`, displays a single menu with the single item Exit.
- The dialog box resource, `NEW`, has a defined style, caption, and list of child controls. The specified style indicates that the dialog box is a modal pop-up child window. The caption specified is the string `Message`. The dialog box contains three controls: a centered static text (for the dialog box message), a default OK pushbutton, and an ordinary Cancel button. The OK button has the resource ID of the predefined `IDOK` constant. The Cancel button has the resource ID of the predefined `IDCANCEL` constant.
- The dialog box resource, `OLD`, is similar to the `NEW` dialog box resource, except it uses old English wording. The Yea button has the resource ID of the predefined `IDOK` constant. The Nay button has the resource ID of the predefined

IDCANCEL constant. These buttons are examples of exit buttons with atypical captions.

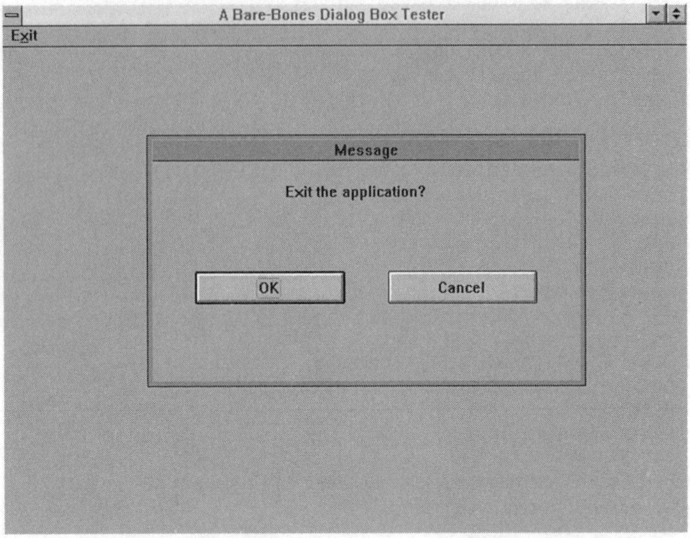

Figure 20.1. *A sample session with the DIALOG1.EXE application showing the dialog box with modern English wording.*

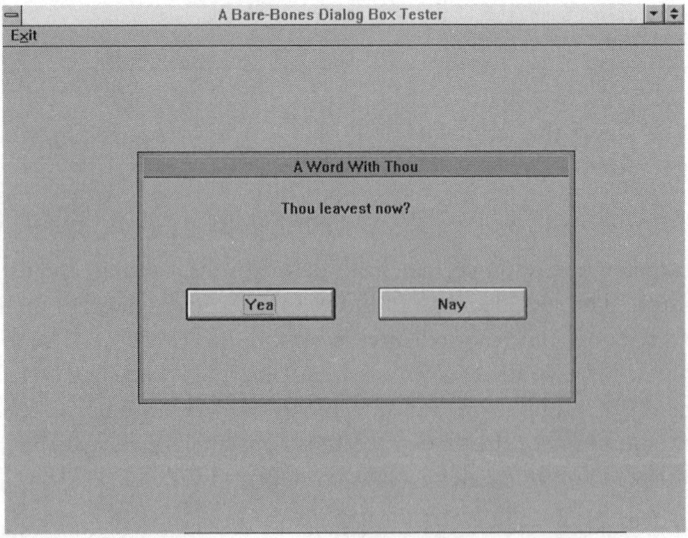

Figure 20.2. *A sample session with the DIALOG1.EXE application showing the dialog box with old English wording.*

The resource definition of the dialog box and controls may be new to you. Appendix A discusses the resource files for dialog boxes and their controls in more detail. The `CTEXT` is a keyword that specifies centered text. The `CONTROL` keyword allows you to define any control and requires the caption, ID, control class, control style, location, and dimensions of the control.

Listing 20.3 shows the source code for the DIALOG1.CPP program file. The source code declares two classes: an application class and a window class. The application uses the `CDialog` class, because no additional dialog box functionality is required.

The most relevant member function is `CAppWindow::OnClose` which responds to the `WM_CLOSE` command message sent by the Exit menu item. The function uses the Boolean static local variable, flag, to toggle between the two dialog box resources `NEW` and `OLD`. The new English dialog box is invoked in the following statement:

```
pDialogBox = new CDialog("NEW", this);
```

The dialog box is executed using the `DoModal` function, disabling the parent window until you click on either pushbutton control. The value returned by the `DoModal` member function is compared with the `IDOK` constant to assign either `TRUE` or `FALSE` to the local Boolean variable `bCloseIt`. The `OnClose` function examines the value in `bCloseIt` to determine whether or not to close the application window.

The instance of the old English version of the dialog box is similarly created, as shown in the following statement:

```
pDialogBox = new CDialog("OLD", this);
```

The `CDialog::OnOK` member function responds to the `IDOK` command by closing the dialog boxes and returning the `IDOK` result.

Transferring Control Data

Dialog boxes serve mainly as pop-up windows to request input from the application user. This input often includes a variety of settings that use radio buttons, check boxes, and edit boxes. Because dialog boxes are frequently created, it makes sense to preserve the latest values in the dialog's controls for the next time it appears. Search and Replace dialog boxes that are found in many Windows editors are typical examples. These dialog boxes remember the settings of all or some of their controls from the last time the dialog box was executed.

To implement this feature in dialog boxes, you need a data transfer mechanism between the dialog box and a buffer. This buffer is usually a data member of the parent window.

Therefore, the first step in supporting data transfer is to define a transfer buffer type. The buffer declares the data fields to buffer the controls that transfer their data. These controls typically include the static text, edit box, list box, combo box, scroll bar, check box, and radio button. The group box and pushbutton controls have no data to transfer and therefore do not enter in the declaration of the data transfer buffer type. A sample data buffer type that includes a single instance of each allowable control is

```
struct TAppTransferBuffer {
     char StaticText[MaxStaticLen];
     char EditBox[MaxEditLen];
     CListBoxData ListBoxData;      // user-defined class
     CComboBoxData ComboBoxData;    // user-defined class
     CScrollBarData ScrollBarData;  // user-defined class
     int CheckBox;
     int RadioButton;
};
```

The buffer structure needs only to include the controls that participate in the data transfer. You do not need to declare the fields of the buffer structure in any particular order. This sample buffer type includes three special user-defined classes that transfer data between dialog boxes and list boxes, combo boxes, and scroll bars. More about these classes later in this section.

Note: The MFC library declares the class `CDataExchange` to support dialog data exchange and dialog data validation routines used by the MFC library. You can use the `CDataExchange` class instead of the method presented in this book. To learn more about the `CDataExchange`, read Technical Note 26 in the directory \MSVC20\HELP\MFCNOTES.HLP.

Let's look at the various members of the data transfer buffer type:

- The `StaticText` member helps in transferring data between a static text control and the data buffer. The data member defines a character array that should be equal to or greater than the number of characters in the static text control.
- The `EditBox` member assists in moving data between the edit box control and the data buffer. The data member defines a character array that should be equal to or greater than the number of characters in the edit box control.
- The `ListBoxData` member helps to transfer data between a list box control and the data buffer. The `ListBoxData` is an instance of the class that you declare to manage the data transfer between a dialog box and a list box. Why use a special

data transfer class? Such a class successfully encapsulates the data and operations related to the transferred data. A typical declaration for the CListBoxData class is

```
class CListBox
{
   public:
   // array of CString to store the list box items
   StringArray DataList;
   ListBoxData();
   // transfer data to the buffer
   void GetListBoxData(CListBox* pListBox);
   // transfer data to the list box
   void SetListBoxData(CListBox* pListBox);
};
```

- The DataList member is a dynamic array of CString objects that stores the list box items. The MFC library declares the CStringArray class and provides adequate operations to manipulate the array of strings. The absence of a data member to keep track of the number of list box items is justified by the fact that the CStringArray class offers the GetSize member function to provide the number of string objects in a CStringArray instance.
- The GetListBoxData and SetListBoxData member functions provide the two-way data transfer between a list box control and the data buffer.
- The ComboBoxData member helps to move data between a combo box control and the data buffer. The ComboBoxData is an instance to the CComboBoxData class that you declare. Here is a typical declaration for class CComboBoxData:

```
class CComboBox
{
   public:
   // the combo box selection
   CString Selection;
   // array of CString to store the list box items
   CStringArray DataList;
   CComboBoxData();
   // transfer data to the buffer
   void GetComboBoxData(CListBox* pComboBox);
   // transfer data to the combo box
   void SetComboBoxData(CListBox* pComboBox);
};
```

- The suggested declaration of class CComboBoxData is similar to that of class CListBoxData. The class ComboBoxData has an additional data member, Selection, to store the combo box selection located in its edit control.

- The `ScrollBarData` member assists in transferring data between a scroll bar control and the data buffer. This member has the suggested `CScollBarData` class, defined as follows:

```
class CScrollBarData
{
   public:
   int LowValue;
   int HighValue;
   int Position;
   CScrollBarData();
   // move data to the buffer
   void GetScrollBarData(CScrollBar* pScrollBar);
   // move data to the scroll bar
   void SetScrollBarData(CScrollBar* pScrollBar);
};
```

- The `LowValue`, `HighValue`, and `Position` members store the scrollbar range and the current thumb position.
- The `CheckBox` member stores the current check state of a check box in an `int` type.
- The `RadioButton` member stores the current check state of a radio button in an `int` type.

Data Transfer for Modal Dialog Boxes

The next application is a simple example of transferring data between the controls of a modal dialog box and a buffer. It creates a typical dialog box that is used in replacing characters in a text editor. The dialog box contains the following controls:

- The Find edit box
- The Replace edit box
- The Scope group box that contains the Global and Selected Text radio button controls
- The Case-Sensitive check box
- The Whole Word check box
- The OK pushbutton control
- The Cancel pushbutton control

The application has a main menu with the Exit and Dialog menu items. To invoke the dialog box, click on the Dialog menu item or press the Alt+D keys. When you invoke the dialog box for the first time, the controls have the following initial values and states:

- The Find edit box contains the string DOS.
- The Replace edit box has the string Windows.
- The Global radio button is checked.
- The Case-Sensitive check box is checked.
- The Whole Word check box is checked.

Type in new strings in the edit box and alter the check states of the radio buttons and check boxes. Now, click on the OK button (or press the Alt+O keys) to close the dialog box. Invoke the Dialog menu item again to pop up the dialog box. Notice that the controls of the dialog box have the same values and states as when you last closed the dialog box.

Listing 20.4 shows the source code for the DIALOG2.H header file. Listing 20.5 contains the script for the DIALOG2.RC resource file. Listing 20.6 shows the source code for the DIALOG2.CPP program file.

Type

Listing 20.4. Source code for the DIALOG2.H header file.

```
#define CM_EXIT   (WM_USER + 100)
#define CM_DIALOG (WM_USER + 101)

#define ID_FIND_TXT       201
#define ID_FIND_EDIT      202
#define ID_REPLACE_TXT    203
#define ID_REPLACE_EDIT   204
#define ID_SCOPE_GRP      205
#define ID_GLOBAL_RBT     206
#define ID_SELTEXT_RBT    207
#define ID_CASE_CHK       208
#define ID_WHOLEWORD_CHK 209
```

Type

Listing 20.5. Script for the DIALOG2.RC resource file.

```
#include <afxres.h>
#include "dialog2.h"

BUTTONS ACCELERATORS
BEGIN
  "o", IDOK, ALT
  "c", IDCANCEL, ALT
```

continues

Listing 20.5. continued

```
END

SEARCH DIALOG DISCARDABLE LOADONCALL PURE MOVEABLE 10, 10,
                                                   200, 150
STYLE WS_POPUP | WS_CLIPSIBLINGS | WS_CAPTION | WS_SYSMENU |
      DS_MODALFRAME
CAPTION "Controls Demo"
BEGIN
  CONTROL "Find", ID_FIND_TXT, "STATIC", WS_CHILD | WS_VISIBLE |
    SS_LEFT, 20, 10, 100, 15
  CONTROL "", ID_FIND_EDIT, "EDIT", WS_CHILD | WS_VISIBLE |
    WS_BORDER | WS_TABSTOP, 20, 25, 100, 15
  CONTROL "Replace", ID_REPLACE_TXT, "STATIC", WS_CHILD |
    WS_VISIBLE | SS_LEFT, 20, 45, 100, 15
  CONTROL "", ID_REPLACE_EDIT, "EDIT", WS_CHILD | WS_VISIBLE |
    WS_BORDER | WS_TABSTOP, 20, 60, 100, 15
  CONTROL " Scope ", ID_SCOPE_GRP, "BUTTON", WS_CHILD | WS_VISIBLE
    | WS_GROUP | BS_GROUPBOX, 20, 80, 90, 50
  CONTROL "Global", ID_GLOBAL_RBT, "BUTTON", WS_CHILD | WS_VISIBLE
    | WS_TABSTOP | BS_AUTORADIOBUTTON, 30, 90, 50, 15
  CONTROL "Selected Text", ID_SELTEXT_RBT, "BUTTON", WS_CHILD |
    WS_VISIBLE | WS_TABSTOP | BS_AUTORADIOBUTTON, 30, 105, 60, 15
  CONTROL "Case Sensitive", ID_CASE_CHK, "BUTTON", WS_CHILD |
    WS_VISIBLE | WS_TABSTOP | BS_AUTOCHECKBOX, 20, 130, 80, 15
  CONTROL "Whole Word", ID_WHOLEWORD_CHK, "BUTTON", WS_CHILD |
    WS_VISIBLE | WS_TABSTOP | BS_AUTOCHECKBOX, 100, 130, 80, 15
  CONTROL, "&OK", IDOK, "BUTTON", WS_CHILD | WS_VISIBLE |
    WS_TABSTOP | WS_GROUP | BS_DEFPUSHBUTTON, 120, 90, 30, 20
  CONTROL "&Cancel", IDCANCEL, "BUTTON", WS_CHILD | WS_VISIBLE |
    WS_TABSTOP | WS_GROUP | BS_PUSHBUTTON, 160, 90, 30, 20
END

MAINMENU MENU LOADONCALL MOVEABLE PURE DISCARDABLE
BEGIN
    MENUITEM "E&xit", CM_EXIT
    MENUITEM "&Dialog", CM_DIALOG
END
```

Type Listing 20.6. Source code for the DIALOG2.CPP program file.

```
#include <string.h>
#include <afxwin.h>
#include "dialog2.h"

// declare constants
const MaxEditLen = 30;
const BF_CHECKED = 1;
const BF_UNCHECKED = 0;
```

```
// declare the application buffer
struct TAppTransferBuf {
  char FindBoxBuff[MaxEditLen+1];
  char ReplaceBoxBuff[MaxEditLen+1];
  int GlobalRbtBuff;
  int SelTextRbtBuff;
  int CaseChkBuff;
  int WholeWordChkBuff;
};

class CWindowApp : public CWinApp
{
public:
    virtual BOOL InitInstance();
};

// expand the functionality of CDialog by
// deriving class CAppDialog
class CAppDialog : public CDialog
{
public:

  CAppDialog(const char FAR* lpTemplateName,
          CWnd* pParentWnd = NULL) :
          CDialog(lpTemplateName, pParentWnd) {}

protected:

  // handle initializing the dialog box
  virtual BOOL OnInitDialog();
  // handle pressing the OK button
  virtual void OnOK();
  // pointer to data buffer in parent window
  TAppTransferBuf* pAppBuffer;
};

// expand the functionality of CFrameWnd by deriving class CAppWindow
class CAppWindow : public CFrameWnd
{

  friend CAppDialog;

public:

  // declare data transfer buffer
  TAppTransferBuf AppBuffer;

  CAppWindow();
  // handle the dialog command
  afx_msg void CMDialog();
  // handle exiting the application
  afx_msg void OnExit()
    { SendMessage(WM_CLOSE); }

protected:

```


continues

Listing 20.6. continued

```
  // handle closing the window
  afx_msg void OnClose();

  // declare message map macro
  DECLARE_MESSAGE_MAP();

};

BOOL CAppDialog::OnInitDialog()
{
  CAppWindow* pW = (CAppWindow*)(GetParent());
  pAppBuffer = &pW->AppBuffer;
  // copy data from the buffer to the dialog box controls
  SetDlgItemText(ID_FIND_EDIT, pAppBuffer->FindBoxBuff);
  SetDlgItemText(ID_REPLACE_EDIT, pAppBuffer->ReplaceBoxBuff);
  CButton* pBtn = (CButton*)(GetDlgItem(ID_GLOBAL_RBT));
  pBtn->SetCheck(pAppBuffer->GlobalRbtBuff);
  pBtn = (CButton*)(GetDlgItem(ID_SELTEXT_RBT));
  pBtn->SetCheck(pAppBuffer->SelTextRbtBuff);
  pBtn = (CButton*)(GetDlgItem(ID_CASE_CHK));
  pBtn->SetCheck(pAppBuffer->CaseChkBuff);
  pBtn = (CButton*)(GetDlgItem(ID_WHOLEWORD_CHK));
  pBtn->SetCheck(pAppBuffer->WholeWordChkBuff);
  return TRUE;
}

void CAppDialog::OnOK()
{
  // copy data from the dialog box controls to the buffer
  GetDlgItemText(ID_FIND_EDIT, pAppBuffer->FindBoxBuff,
                 MaxEditLen);
  GetDlgItemText(ID_REPLACE_EDIT, pAppBuffer->ReplaceBoxBuff,
                 MaxEditLen);
  CButton* pBtn = (CButton*)(GetDlgItem(ID_GLOBAL_RBT));
  pAppBuffer->GlobalRbtBuff = pBtn->GetCheck();
  pBtn = (CButton*)(GetDlgItem(ID_SELTEXT_RBT));
  pAppBuffer->SelTextRbtBuff = pBtn->GetCheck();
  pBtn = (CButton*)(GetDlgItem(ID_CASE_CHK));
  pAppBuffer->CaseChkBuff = pBtn->GetCheck();
  pBtn = (CButton*)(GetDlgItem(ID_WHOLEWORD_CHK));
  pAppBuffer->WholeWordChkBuff = pBtn->GetCheck();
  // return dialog box value
  EndDialog(IDOK);
}

CAppWindow::CAppWindow()
{
  // load the accelerator keys resource
  LoadAccelTable("BUTTONS");

  // create the window
  Create(NULL, "Modal Dialog Box Data Transfer Tester",
         WS_OVERLAPPEDWINDOW, rectDefault, NULL, "MAINMENU");

```

```
  // fill buffer with 0's
  memset(&AppBuffer, 0x0, sizeof(AppBuffer));
  strcpy(AppBuffer.FindBoxBuff, "DOS");
  strcpy(AppBuffer.ReplaceBoxBuff, "Windows");
  AppBuffer.GlobalRbtBuff = BF_CHECKED;
  AppBuffer.CaseChkBuff = BF_CHECKED;
  AppBuffer.WholeWordChkBuff = BF_CHECKED;
};

void CAppWindow::CMDialog()
{
  CString msgStr;
  CAppDialog* pDlg = new CAppDialog("SEARCH", this);

  if (pDlg->DoModal() == IDOK) {
    msgStr = "Find String: ";
    msgStr += AppBuffer.FindBoxBuff;
    msgStr += "\n\nReplace String:";
    msgStr += AppBuffer.ReplaceBoxBuff;
    MessageBox((const char*) msgStr, "Dialog Box Data", MB_OK);
  }
}

void CAppWindow::OnClose()
{
  if (MessageBox("Want to close this application",
                 "Query", MB_YESNO ¦ MB_ICONQUESTION) == IDYES)
    DestroyWindow();
}

BEGIN_MESSAGE_MAP(CAppWindow, CFrameWnd)
  ON_COMMAND(CM_DIALOG, CMDialog)
  ON_COMMAND(CM_EXIT, OnExit)
  ON_WM_CLOSE()
END_MESSAGE_MAP()

// Construct the CWindowApp's m_pMainWnd data member
BOOL CWindowApp::InitInstance()
{
  m_pMainWnd = new CAppWindow();
  m_pMainWnd->ShowWindow(m_nCmdShow);
  m_pMainWnd->UpdateWindow();
  return TRUE;
}

// application's constructor initializes and runs the app
CWindowApp WindowApp;
```

Figure 20.3 shows a sample session with the DIALOG2.EXE program.

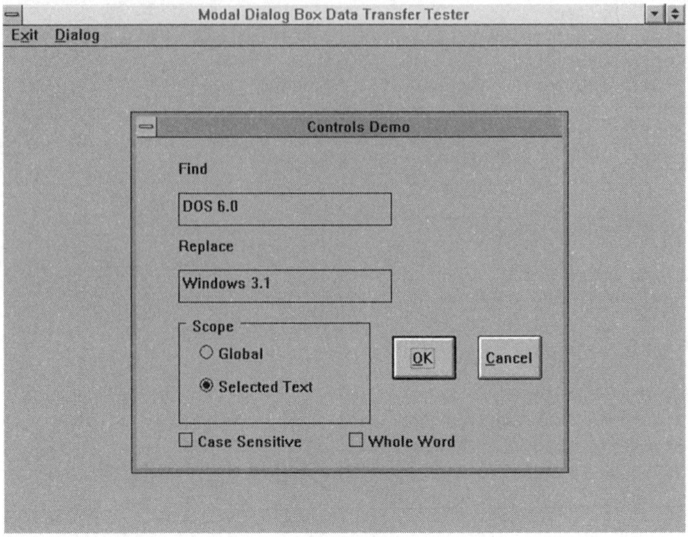

Figure 20.3. *A sample session with the DIALOG2.EXE application.*

Analysis Listing 20.5 contains the script for the DIALOG2.RC resource file. This file defines the resources for the accelerator keys, the menu, and the dialog box, including its controls. In the dialog box resource definition, the OK and Cancel pushbuttons have the predefined `IDOK` and `IDCANCEL` IDs, respectively. The OK button has the default pushbutton style, and the Cancel button has the normal pushbutton style. The group box, radio buttons, and check boxes have the `BUTTON` class name. The styles associated with these controls determine their final form. Appendix A gives you more details about declaring the resources for controls that are owned by dialog boxes.

Listing 20.6 shows the source code for the DIALOG2.CPP program file. The program declares the data transfer type `TAppTransferBuf` and includes members for the edit boxes, radio buttons, and check boxes.

The program listing declares three classes: an application class, a window class, and a modal dialog box class.

The application's dialog box class `CAppDialog` declares a class constructor, a few member functions, and the `pAppBuffer` data member. This data member is the pointer to the data buffer `AppBuffer`, a member of the parent window. This is a data-hiding scheme applied to manage the data buffer. You can simplify the code by declaring the transfer buffer as a global variable. Keep in mind that this approach makes the buffer accessible (and also vulnerable) to all sorts of objects in a full-blown Windows application. The class constructor creates the instances by invoking the parent class constructor.

The `OnInitDialog` member function, defined in lines 73 through 89, initializes the dialog box by performing the following tasks:

- Assigns the address of the parent window to the local pointer `pW`
- Uses the `pW` pointer to have the data member `pAppBuffer` point to the parent window's `AppBuffer` member
- Obtains the data from the buffer to the controls of the modal dialog box, using the `CWnd::SetDlgItemText` function and a local pointer, `pBtn`, to access the various pushbutton controls (the `pBtn` pointer and the `SetCheck()` function set the check state for the various radio button and check box controls)

The `OnOK` member function, defined in lines 91 through 108, transfers data from the dialog box to the data buffer. The transfer takes place using the `CWnd::GetDlgItemText` function and a local pointer, `pBtn`, to the pushbutton controls. The `pBtn` pointer and the `GetCheck()` function obtain the check state for the various radio button and check box controls.

The application window class, `CAppWindow`, declares a public data transfer buffer, `AppBuffer`, a class constructor, and three member functions. The class also declares class `CAppDialog` to be a friend. Making the `AppBuffer` member public and making `CAppDialog` a friend are steps necessary to give the dialog box member functions access to the `AppBuffer` member.

The `CAppWindow` constructor creates the window (which also loads the menu resource) and then initializes the data buffer. The call to the `memset` function fills the `AppBuffer` member with zeros. I recommend that you systematically call the `memset` function to perform a basic initialization of the buffer before assigning specific values to its controls. The constructor then assigns the `"DOS"` and `"Windows"` strings to the Find and Replace edit box buffers, respectively. The constructor also assigns the constant `BF_CHECKED` to the `GlobalRbtBuff`, `CaseChkBuff`, and `WholeWordChkBuf` members.

The `CAppWindow` class defines the `CMDialog` member function, in lines 128 through 140, to handle the command message emitted by the Dialog menu item. This function invokes an instance of the dialog box using the `DoModal` member function and compares the result of that function with `IDOK`. If the two items match, the `CMDialog` function builds and displays a message string that reflects the current Find and Replace text.

Transferring Data for Modeless Dialog Boxes

This section presents an MFC application that transfers data for a modeless dialog box. Thus, the program shows how to create a modeless dialog box and how to transfer data at will by using a special pushbutton control. The next application uses a modified version of program DIALOG2.CPP. This new version, DIALOG3.EXE, is very similar to that presented in DIALOG2.EXE but differs in the following aspects:

- The dialog box is modeless.
- The dialog box has an extra Send pushbutton.
- The main window has two edit boxes labeled Find and Replace.

When you click the Send button, the dialog box copies the text in its Find and Replace edit boxes to the edit boxes in the parent window that are also labeled Find and Replace.

When you click the Dialog menu item in the program, the application pops up a modeless dialog box. The dialog box has the `"DOS"` and `"Windows"` strings appearing in the Find and Replace edit boxes, respectively. The Global radio button, Case-Sensitive check box, and Selected check box are all initially selected. Type in new text in either or both edit boxes and click the OK pushbutton. This action closes the dialog box and echoes the text of the dialog box in the edit boxes of the window. Reinvoke the dialog box to check that it retains your last input. Now type in new text in both edit boxes and then click the Send button. Watch the text echoed in the window's edit boxes.

Listing 20.7 shows the source code for the DIALOG3.H header file. Listing 20.8 contains the script for the DIALOG3.RC resource file. Listing 20.9 shows the source code for the DIALOG3.CPP program file.

Type

Listing 20.7. Source code for the DIALOG3.H header file.

```
#define CM_EXIT   (WM_USER + 100)
#define CM_DIALOG (WM_USER + 101)
#define ID_FIND_TXT      201
#define ID_FIND_EDIT     202
#define ID_REPLACE_TXT   203
#define ID_REPLACE_EDIT  204
#define ID_SCOPE_GRP     205
#define ID_GLOBAL_RBT    206
#define ID_SELTEXT_RBT   207
#define ID_CASE_CHK      208
#define ID_WHOLEWORD_CHK 209
#define ID_FIND_BOX      301
#define ID_REPLACE_BOX   302
#define ID_SEND_BTN      303
```

Listing 20.8. Script for the DIALOG3.RC resource file.

```
#include <afxres.h>
#include "dialog3.h"

BUTTONS ACCELERATORS
BEGIN
  "o", IDOK, ALT
  "c", IDCANCEL, ALT
  "s", ID_SEND_BTN, ALT
END

SEARCH DIALOG DISCARDABLE LOADONCALL PURE MOVEABLE 10, 10,
                                                   200, 150
STYLE WS_POPUP | WS_CLIPSIBLINGS | WS_CAPTION | WS_SYSMENU |
      WS_DLGFRAME | WS_VISIBLE
CAPTION "Controls Demo"
BEGIN
  CONTROL "Find", ID_FIND_TXT, "STATIC", WS_CHILD | WS_VISIBLE |
    SS_LEFT, 20, 10, 100, 15
  CONTROL "", ID_FIND_EDIT, "EDIT", WS_CHILD | WS_VISIBLE |
    WS_BORDER | WS_TABSTOP, 20, 25, 100, 15
  CONTROL "Replace", ID_REPLACE_TXT, "STATIC", WS_CHILD |
    WS_VISIBLE | SS_LEFT, 20, 45, 100, 15
  CONTROL "", ID_REPLACE_EDIT, "EDIT", WS_CHILD | WS_VISIBLE |
    WS_BORDER | WS_TABSTOP, 20, 60, 100, 15
  CONTROL " Scope ", ID_SCOPE_GRP, "BUTTON", WS_CHILD |
    WS_VISIBLE | WS_GROUP | BS_GROUPBOX, 20, 80, 90, 50
  CONTROL "Global", ID_GLOBAL_RBT, "BUTTON", WS_CHILD |
    WS_VISIBLE | WS_TABSTOP | BS_AUTORADIOBUTTON, 30, 90, 50, 15
  CONTROL "Selected Text", ID_SELTEXT_RBT, "BUTTON", WS_CHILD |
    WS_VISIBLE | WS_TABSTOP | BS_AUTORADIOBUTTON, 30, 105, 60, 15
  CONTROL "Case Sensitive", ID_CASE_CHK, "BUTTON", WS_CHILD |
    WS_VISIBLE | WS_TABSTOP | BS_AUTOCHECKBOX, 20, 130, 80, 15
  CONTROL "Whole Word", ID_WHOLEWORD_CHK, "BUTTON", WS_CHILD |
    WS_VISIBLE | WS_TABSTOP | BS_AUTOCHECKBOX, 100, 130, 80, 15
  CONTROL, "&OK", IDOK, "BUTTON", WS_CHILD | WS_VISIBLE |
    WS_TABSTOP | BS_DEFPUSHBUTTON, 120, 90, 30, 20
  CONTROL "&Cancel", IDCANCEL, "BUTTON", WS_CHILD | WS_VISIBLE |
    WS_TABSTOP | BS_PUSHBUTTON, 160, 90, 30, 20
  CONTROL "&Send", ID_SEND_BTN, "BUTTON", WS_CHILD | WS_VISIBLE |
    WS_TABSTOP | BS_PUSHBUTTON, 160, 60, 30, 20
END



MAINMENU MENU LOADONCALL MOVEABLE PURE DISCARDABLE
BEGIN
    MENUITEM "E&xit", CM_EXIT
    MENUITEM "&Dialog", CM_DIALOG
END
```

Listing 20.9. Source code for the DIALOG3.CPP program file.

```
#include <string.h>
#include <afxwin.h>
#include "dialog3.h"

// declare constants for sizing and dimensioning the
// application window's controls
const Wtxt = 200;
const Htxt = 20;
const TxtVertSpacing = 10;
const Wbox = 200;
const Hbox = 30;
const BoxHorzSpacing = 40;
// declare other constants
const MaxEditLen = 30;
const BF_CHECKED = 1;
const BF_UNCHECKED = 0;

// declare the application buffer
struct TAppTransferBuf {
  char FindBoxBuff[MaxEditLen+1];
  char ReplaceBoxBuff[MaxEditLen+1];
  int GlobalRbtBuff;
  int SelTextRbtBuff;
  int CaseChkBuff;
  int WholeWordChkBuff;
};

class CWindowApp : public CWinApp
{
public:
    virtual BOOL InitInstance();
};

// expand the functionality of CDialog by
// deriving class CAppDialog
class CAppDialog : public CDialog
{
public:

  CAppDialog(const char FAR* lpTemplateName,
          CWnd* pParentWnd);
  // handle pressing the OK button
  afx_msg void OnOK();
  afx_msg void CMOK() { OnOK(); }
  // handle pressing the Cancel button
  afx_msg void OnCancel();
  afx_msg void CMCancel() { OnCancel(); }
  // handle sending data without closing the modal dialog box
  afx_msg void HandleSendBtn();
  afx_msg void CMSendBtn() { HandleSendBtn(); }

protected:

```

```
  // pointer to data buffer in parent window
  TAppTransferBuf* pAppBuffer;

  // handle initializing the dialog box
  virtual BOOL OnInitDialog();
  // transfer data from the controls to the buffer
  void TransferData();

  // declare message map macro
  DECLARE_MESSAGE_MAP();
};

// expand the functionality of CFrameWnd by deriving
// class CAppWindow
class CAppWindow : public CFrameWnd
{
public:

  // declare data transfer buffer
  TAppTransferBuf AppBuffer;
  // flag to indicate whether or not the
  // modeless dialog box is active
  BOOL bDialogActive;

  CAppWindow();
  ~CAppWindow();
  // handle the dialog command
  afx_msg void CMDialog();
  // handle a message sent by the Send button of
  // the dialog box
  afx_msg void HandleSendBtn();
  // handle exiting the application
  afx_msg void OnExit()
    { SendMessage(WM_CLOSE); }

protected:

  // declare the pointers to the window's controls
  // and the modeless dialog box
  CStatic* FindTxt;
  CEdit* FindBox;
  CStatic* ReplaceTxt;
  CEdit* ReplaceBox;
  CAppDialog* pDlg;

  // handle creating the controls
  afx_msg int OnCreate(LPCREATESTRUCT lpCS);
  // handle closing the window
  afx_msg void OnClose();
  // return a reference to member r based on individual
  // coordinates and dimenions
  void makeRect(int nX, int nY, int nW, int nH, CRect& r);

  // declare message map macro
  DECLARE_MESSAGE_MAP();

```

continues

Listing 20.9. continued

```
};

CAppDialog::CAppDialog(const char FAR* lpTemplateName,
                       CWnd* pParentWnd)
{
  Create(lpTemplateName, pParentWnd);
}

BOOL CAppDialog::OnInitDialog()
{
  CAppWindow* pW = (CAppWindow*)(GetParent());
  pAppBuffer = &pW->AppBuffer;
  // copy data from the buffer to the dialog box controls
  SetDlgItemText(ID_FIND_EDIT, pAppBuffer->FindBoxBuff);
  SetDlgItemText(ID_REPLACE_EDIT, pAppBuffer->ReplaceBoxBuff);
  CButton* pBtn = (CButton*)(GetDlgItem(ID_GLOBAL_RBT));
  pBtn->SetCheck(pAppBuffer->GlobalRbtBuff);
  pBtn = (CButton*)(GetDlgItem(ID_SELTEXT_RBT));
  pBtn->SetCheck(pAppBuffer->SelTextRbtBuff);
  pBtn = (CButton*)(GetDlgItem(ID_CASE_CHK));
  pBtn->SetCheck(pAppBuffer->CaseChkBuff);
  pBtn = (CButton*)(GetDlgItem(ID_WHOLEWORD_CHK));
  pBtn->SetCheck(pAppBuffer->WholeWordChkBuff);
  return TRUE;
}

void CAppDialog::OnOK()
{
  CAppWindow* pParent = (CAppWindow*)(GetParent());
  // transfer data to the buffer
  TransferData();
  // notify parent of transfer
  pParent->SendMessage(WM_COMMAND, ID_SEND_BTN);
  // clear active dialog flag
  pParent->bDialogActive = FALSE;
  // close the modeless dialog box
  DestroyWindow();
}

void CAppDialog::OnCancel()
{
  CAppWindow* pParent = (CAppWindow*)(GetParent());
  // clear active dialog flag
  pParent->bDialogActive = FALSE;
  // close the modeless dialog box
  DestroyWindow();
}

void CAppDialog::HandleSendBtn()
{
  CAppWindow* pParent = (CAppWindow*)(GetParent());

  // transfer data to the buffer
  TransferData();
```

```
  // notify parent of transfer
  pParent->SendMessage(WM_COMMAND, ID_SEND_BTN);
}

void CAppDialog::TransferData()
{
  // copy data from the dialog box controls to the buffer
  GetDlgItemText(ID_FIND_EDIT, pAppBuffer->FindBoxBuff,
                 MaxEditLen);
  GetDlgItemText(ID_REPLACE_EDIT, pAppBuffer->ReplaceBoxBuff,
           MaxEditLen);
  CButton* pBtn = (CButton*)(GetDlgItem(ID_GLOBAL_RBT));
  pAppBuffer->GlobalRbtBuff = pBtn->GetCheck();
  pBtn = (CButton*)(GetDlgItem(ID_SELTEXT_RBT));
  pAppBuffer->SelTextRbtBuff = pBtn->GetCheck();
  pBtn = (CButton*)(GetDlgItem(ID_CASE_CHK));
  pAppBuffer->CaseChkBuff = pBtn->GetCheck();
  pBtn = (CButton*)(GetDlgItem(ID_WHOLEWORD_CHK));
  pAppBuffer->WholeWordChkBuff = pBtn->GetCheck();
}

CAppWindow::CAppWindow()
{
  // load the accelerator keys resource
  LoadAccelTable("BUTTONS");

  // create the window
  Create(NULL, "Modeless Dialog Box Data Transfer Tester",
         WS_OVERLAPPEDWINDOW, rectDefault, NULL, "MAINMENU");

  // fill buffer with 0's
  memset(&AppBuffer, 0x0, sizeof(AppBuffer));
  strcpy(AppBuffer.FindBoxBuff, "DOS");
  strcpy(AppBuffer.ReplaceBoxBuff, "Windows");
  AppBuffer.GlobalRbtBuff = BF_CHECKED;
  AppBuffer.CaseChkBuff = BF_CHECKED;
  AppBuffer.WholeWordChkBuff = BF_CHECKED;
  // clear the active dialog flag
  bDialogActive = FALSE;
};

CAppWindow::~CAppWindow()
{
  delete FindTxt;
  delete FindBox;
  delete ReplaceTxt;
  delete ReplaceBox;
}

int CAppWindow::OnCreate(LPCREATESTRUCT lpCS)
{
  int nX0 = 30;
  int nY0 = 20;
  int nX = nX0;
  int nY = nY0;

```

continues

Listing 20.9. continued

```
  CRect r;
  DWORD dwStaticStyle = WS_CHILD | WS_VISIBLE | SS_LEFT;
  DWORD dwEditStyle = WS_CHILD | WS_VISIBLE | WS_BORDER |
                 ES_LEFT | ES_AUTOHSCROLL;
  // create Find static text
  makeRect(nX, nY, Wtxt, Htxt, r);
  FindTxt = new CStatic();
  FindTxt->Create("Find", dwStaticStyle, r, this);
  // create Find edit control
  nY += Htxt + TxtVertSpacing;
  makeRect(nX, nY, Wbox, Hbox, r);
  FindBox = new CEdit();
  FindBox->Create(dwEditStyle, r, this, ID_FIND_BOX);
  // create Replace static text
  nX += Wbox + BoxHorzSpacing;
  nY = nY0;
  makeRect(nX, nY, Wtxt, Htxt, r);
  ReplaceTxt = new CStatic();
  ReplaceTxt->Create("Replace", dwStaticStyle, r, this);
  // create Replace edit control
  nY += Htxt + TxtVertSpacing;
  makeRect(nX, nY, Wbox, Hbox, r);
  ReplaceBox = new CEdit();
  ReplaceBox->Create(dwEditStyle, r, this, ID_REPLACE_BOX);
  return CFrameWnd::OnCreate(lpCS);
}

void CAppWindow::CMDialog()
{
  if (bDialogActive) return;
  pDlg = new CAppDialog("SEARCH", this);
  bDialogActive = TRUE;
  pDlg->SendMessage(WM_INITDIALOG);
}

void CAppWindow::HandleSendBtn()
{
  FindBox->SetWindowText(AppBuffer.FindBoxBuff);
  ReplaceBox->SetWindowText(AppBuffer.ReplaceBoxBuff);
}

void CAppWindow::OnClose()
{
  if (MessageBox("Want to close this application",
                 "Query", MB_YESNO | MB_ICONQUESTION) == IDYES)
    DestroyWindow();
}

void CAppWindow::makeRect(int nX, int nY, int nW, int nH,
                          CRect& r)
{
  r.top = nY;
  r.left = nX;
  r.bottom = nY + nH;
  r.right = nX + nW;
}
```

```
BEGIN_MESSAGE_MAP(CAppDialog, CDialog)
  ON_BN_CLICKED(IDOK, OnOK)
  ON_COMMAND(IDOK, CMOK)
  ON_BN_CLICKED(IDCANCEL, OnCancel)
  ON_COMMAND(IDCANCEL, CMCancel)
  ON_BN_CLICKED(ID_SEND_BTN, HandleSendBtn)
  ON_COMMAND(ID_SEND_BTN, CMSendBtn)
END_MESSAGE_MAP()

BEGIN_MESSAGE_MAP(CAppWindow, CFrameWnd)
  ON_COMMAND(CM_DIALOG, CMDialog)
  ON_COMMAND(ID_SEND_BTN, HandleSendBtn)
  ON_COMMAND(CM_EXIT, OnExit)
  ON_WM_CREATE()
  ON_WM_CLOSE()
END_MESSAGE_MAP()

// Construct the CWindowApp's m_pMainWnd data member
BOOL CWindowApp::InitInstance()
{
  m_pMainWnd = new CAppWindow();
  m_pMainWnd->ShowWindow(m_nCmdShow);
  m_pMainWnd->UpdateWindow();
  return TRUE;
}

// application's constructor initializes and runs the app
CWindowApp WindowApp;
```

Figure 20.4 shows a sample session with the DIALOG3.EXE application.

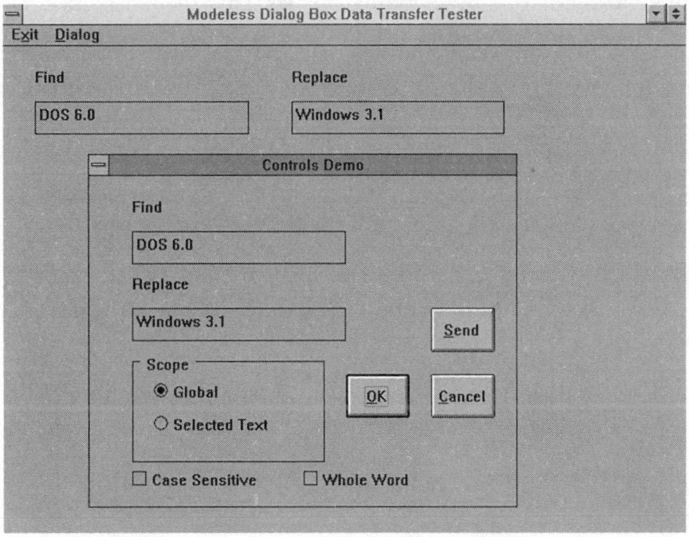

Figure 20.4. *A sample session with the DIALOG3.EXE application.*

Analysis Listing 20.8 shows the script for the DIALOG3.RC resource file. The resource file defines the resources for the accelerator keys, menu, and modeless dialog box.

Listing 20.9 contains the source code for the DIALOG3.CPP program file. The listing declares a group of constants for sizing and spacing the controls in the window application. The listing also contains the declaration of the data transfer buffer type—which is identical to that shown in program DIALOG2.EXE.

The application declares three classes: the application class, the window class, and the dialog box class. The `CAppDialog` constructor simply invokes the inherited `Create` function to build a dialog box. The `CAppDialog` class declares member functions to handle each pushbutton. The dialog class declares the `TransferData` member function to transfer data from the dialog box controls to the buffer. This function is called by the `OnOK` and `HandleSendBtn` member functions.

The virtual `OnOK` member function, defined in lines 136 through 147, responds to the `IDOK` notification message emitted by the OK button. The function performs the following tasks:

- Transfers the data from the controls to the buffer by calling the `TransferData` member function
- Sends an `ID_SEND_BTN` message to the parent window using the `SendMessage` function
- Sets the parent window data member, `bDialogActive`, to `FALSE`
- Closes the dialog box by invoking the `DestroyWindow` function

The `OnCancel` member function, defined in lines 149 through 156, handles the `IDCANCEL` notification message sent by the Cancel button. The function performs the following two tasks:

- Sets the parent window data member, `bDialogActive`, to `FALSE`
- Closes the dialog box by invoking the `DestroyWindow` function

The `HandleSendBtn` member function, defined in lines 255 through 259, handles the `ID_SEND_BTN` notification message emitted by the Send button. The function carries out the following tasks:

- Transfers the data from the controls to the buffer by calling the `TransferData` member function
- Sends an `ID_SEND_BTN` message to the parent window using the `SendMessage` function

The CMSendBtn member function handles the ID_SEND_BTN command message generated by the accelerator key Alt+S. The function simply calls the HandleSendBtn member function.

The application window class CAppWindow declares two public data members, five protected data members, a constructor, a destructor, and six member functions. The Boolean bDialogActive data member indicates whether or not the dialog box instance exists. Using this flag ensures that there is one instance of the modeless dialog box. The AppBuffer data member is the data transfer buffer. The window class declares five protected pointers. The FindBox and ReplaceBox pointers access the edit box instances. The pDlg pointer is the pointer to the dialog box instance.

The CAppWindow constructor performs the following tasks:

- Loads the menu resource
- Creates the application window by calling the Create function
- Initializes the buffer by filling it with zeros
- Assigns values to the edit box buffers, the check box buffers, and the Global radio button buffer
- Sets the bDialogActive data member to FALSE

The OnCreate member function, defined in lines 213 through 245, actually creates the controls that are attached to the application window. The function carries out the following tasks:

- Creates the static text instance that labels the Find edit box
- Creates the Find edit box
- Creates the static text instance that labels the Replace edit box
- Creates the Replace edit box
- Returns the function value

The application window class declares the CMDialog member function to create a modeless dialog box. The function carries out these subsequent tasks:

- Exits if the bDialogActive member is TRUE
- Creates a CAppDialog instance that is accessed by the pDlg pointer
- Sets the bDialogActive data member to TRUE

- Brings up the modeless dialog box on the screen by sending it a `WM_INITDIALOG` message (this task involves using the `pDlg` pointer to make the dialog box receive the intended message)

The `HandleSendBtn` member function, defined in lines 255 through 259, responds to the message sent by the Send button in the dialog box by copying the `FindBoxBuff` and `ReplaceBoxBuff` buffer members to the Find and Replace edit boxes in the window.

Summary

Today's lesson presents you with powerful dialog boxes that serve as input tools. You learn about the following topics:

- You can construct instances of class `CDialog` to create modeless or modal dialog boxes.
- Modal dialog boxes are executed with the `DoModal` member function.
- The basics of transferring control data include declaring the data transfer buffer type, declaring the buffer, creating the controls in a sequence that matches their buffers, and establishing the buffer link.
- The first step in supporting data transfer is to define a transfer buffer type. You can transfer data for modal dialog boxes and modeless dialog boxes.

Q&A

Q Does MFC support specialized dialog boxes?

A Yes. The MFC library has a set of classes that implement dialog boxes for selecting files, selecting colors, selecting fonts, printing, and searching/replacing text. The classes that model these dialog boxes are all descendants of class `CDialog`.

Q Does the MFC version 1.0 implement dialog box classes differently?

A Yes, version 1.0 implements the `CModalDialog` box as a descendant of class `CDialog`. Version 2 uses class `CDialog` for both kinds of dialog boxes. The compiler is aware of class `CModialDialog` and treats listings where it appears as though it were `CDialog`.

Q Can I create a set of modeless dialog boxes followed by a modal dialog box?

A Yes. Interestingly, the modal dialog box allows you to select the modeless dialog boxes created before it. However, you cannot create any additional modeless dialog boxes until you close the modal dialog box.

Q Is the data transfer buffer necessary for modeless dialog boxes?

A Not always. You can have an application that pops up multiple modeless dialog boxes and have them communicate with each other directly, without the need of a data transfer buffer.

Q Are there any advantages to writing my own .RC resource files now that a tool such as App Studio is available?

A Yes. The .RC resource file documents the exact dimensions, styles, and other attributes of the controls in a dialog box or any kind of resource.

Q What do .RC resource files compile into?

A The resource compiler, RC.EXE, compiles .RC files into .RES files.

Workshop

The Workshop provides quiz questions to help you solidify your understanding of the material covered and exercises to provide you with experience in using what you've learned. Try to understand the quiz and exercise answers before continuing on to the next day's lesson. Answers are provided in Appendix B, "Answers."

Quiz

1. True or false? You must compile all the .RC files into .RES before or during the creation of the application.
2. True or false? The OK and Cancel buttons in a dialog box are optional.
3. True or false? You can create a dialog box with buttons labeled Yes and No.
4. True or false? Nested dialog boxes are not allowed by Windows.
5. True or false? Dialog boxes must always have a non-dialog window parent.

Exercises

1. Create a version of the Command-Line Calculator Application (COCA) that uses a dialog box as a stand-alone window.
2. Use the Studio App to create the dialog box resources for program DIALOG2.CPP.
3. Use the Studio App to create the dialog box resources for program DIALOG3.CPP.

21

MDI Windows

WEEK
3

Recall that many Windows applications, such as the Windows Program Manager, Windows File Manager, and many Windows text editors, implement a special windows interface—the Multiple Document Interface (MDI). The MDI standard is also part of the Common User Access (CUA) standard set by IBM. Each MDI-compliant application allows you to open child windows for file-specific tasks such as editing text, managing a database, and working with a spreadsheet. In today's lesson, you learn about the following topics relative to managing MDI windows and objects:

- Basic features and components of an MDI-compliant application
- Building an MDI-compliant application
- The `CMDIFrameWnd` class
- Building MDI frame windows
- The `CMDIChildWnd` class
- Building MDI child windows

MDI Application Features and Components

An MDI-compliant application is made up of the following objects:

- The MDI frame window is an instance of class `CMDIFrameWnd` or its descendants. Each MDI application has one MDI frame window.
- The MDI client window is created by the `CreateClient` member function. Each MDI application has one MDI client window.
- The MDI child window is an instance of `CMDIChildWNd` or its descendant. An MDI application dynamically creates and removes multiple instances of MDI child windows. At any given time (and while there is at least one MDI child window), there is only one active MDI child window.

NEW TERM The visible *MDI frame window* contains all other MDI objects. The invisible *MDI client window* performs underlying management of the MDI child windows that are dynamically created and removed. The dynamic and visible *MDI child window* is located, moved, resized, maximized, and minimized inside the area defined by the MDI frame window.

When you maximize an MDI child window, it occupies the area defined by the MDI frame window. When you minimize an MDI child window, the icon of that window appears at the bottom of the MDI frame window.

> **Note:** The MDI frame window has a menu that manipulates the MDI child windows and their contents. The MDI child windows cannot have menus, but may contain controls. The MFC library supports the ability to change the menu attached to the MDI frame window when you select a different MDI child window. This feature supports MDI child windows that have different uses and data.

Building an MDI Application

In the last section, you learned that the basic ingredients for an MDI application are the `CMDIFrameWnd` and `CMDIChildWnd` classes. The `CMDIFrameWnd` class supports the following tasks:

- Creating and handling the MDI client window
- Creating and handling the MDI child windows
- Managing menu selections

The *CMDIFrameWnd* Class

MFC offers the `CMDIFrameWnd` class, a descendant of `CFrameWnd`, to implement the MDI frame window of an MDI application.

The `CMDIFrameWnd` class declares a constructor, a `Create` function, and a number of member functions to manipulate MDI child windows.

The class constructor and the inherited `Create` function work together in creating the instances of class `CMDIFrameWnd`. The `Create` function takes a number of arguments that define the Windows class (a `WNDCLASS` structure), the MDI window title, the window style, the window location and position (specified using the `CRect` parameter), the pointer to the parent window, and the name of the associated menu resource. When the

MDI frame window is the top-level window, the argument for the parent pointer is `NULL`.

The `CreateClient` member function has the role of creating the invisible MDI client window. The function takes two arguments: an `LPCREATESTRUCT` parameter and a `CMenu*` menu pointer parameter.

The member functions of `CMDIFrameWnd` support a number of operations for the MDI child windows. These operations include the following:

- Activating an MDI child window with the `MDIActive` member function
- Obtaining the pointer to the currently active MDI child window, using the `MDIGetActive` member function
- Maximizing and restoring an MDI child window, using the `MDIMaximize` and `MDIRestore` member functions, respectively
- Cascading and tiling MDI child windows, using the `MDICascade` and `MDITile` member functions, respectively
- Selecting the next MDI child window (the one right behind the currently active MDI child window)

Building MDI Frame Windows

The usual approach for creating the objects that make up an MFC application is to create the application instance and then its main window instance. In the case of an MDI-compliant application, the application's main window is typically a descendant of class `CMDIFrameWnd`. The `InitInstance` member function of the application class creates this window. The constructor of the MDI frame window class, together with the `Create` function, builds the MDI frame and MDI client windows. It is also possible to create an initial or default MDI child window. For example, some Windows text editors open the last edited file (if possible), and other editors display an empty MDI child window.

The *CMDIChildWnd* Class

MFC offers the `CMDIChildWnd` class, a descendant of `CFrameWnd`, to implement the MDI child windows. The `CMDIChildWnd` class declares a constructor, a `Create` function, a set of member functions, and a data member. The member functions allow you to destroy, activate, maximize, restore, and obtain the pointer to the parent window.

Building MDI Child Windows

Building MDI child windows is similar to building application windows in the previous programs in this book, with the following differences:

- An MDI child window is an instance of `CMDIChildWnd` or its descendants.
- An MDI child window cannot have its own menu. The menu of the MDI frame window is the one that manipulates the currently active MDI child window or all of the MDI child windows.
- An MDI child window can have controls—unusual but certainly allowed.

Managing MDI Messages

The message loop directs the command messages first to the active MDI child window to allow it to respond. If that window does not respond, the message is then sent to the parent MDI frame window. Of course, the active MDI child window responds to the notification messages sent by its controls, just as any window or dialog box would.

A Simple Text Viewer

Let's look at a simple MDI-compliant application. MDI applications are frequently used as text viewers and text editors. This application emulates a simple text viewer—the application actually displays random text rather than text that you can retrieve from a file. This approach keeps the program simple and helps you focus on implementing the various MDI objects. The MDI application has a simple menu containing the Exit and MDI Children menu items.

Compile and run the application. Experiment with creating MDI children. Notice that the text in odd-numbered MDI child windows is static, and the text in even-numbered windows can be edited. This feature illustrates how to create a simple form of text viewer and text editor (with no load and save options, to keep the example short). Try to tile, cascade, maximize, and minimize these windows. Also test closing individual MDI child windows as well as closing all the MDI children.

Listing 21.1 shows the source code for the MDIWIN1.H header file. Listing 21.2 contains the script for the MDIWIN1.RC resource file. Listing 21.3 shows the source code for the MDIWIN1.CPP program.

Listing 21.1. Source code for the MDIWIN1.H header file.

```
#define CM_EXIT            (WM_USER + 100)
#define CM_COUNTCHILDREN   (WM_USER + 101)
#define CM_CREATECHILD     (WM_USER + 102)
#define CM_CASCADECHILDREN (WM_USER + 103)
#define CM_TILECHILDREN    (WM_USER + 104)
#define CM_ARRANGEICONS    (WM_USER + 105)
#define CM_CLOSECHILDREN   (WM_USER + 106)
#define WM_CHILDDESTROY    (WM_USER + 200)

#define ID_TEXT_EDIT     100
```

Listing 21.2. Script for the MDIWIN1.RC resource file.

```
#include <afxres.h>
#include "mdiwin1.h"

MAINMENU MENU LOADONCALL MOVEABLE PURE DISCARDABLE
BEGIN
  MENUITEM "E&xit", CM_EXIT
  POPUP "&MDI Children"
  BEGIN
    MENUITEM  "C&reate", CM_CREATECHILD
    MENUITEM  "&Cascade", CM_CASCADECHILDREN
    MENUITEM  "&Tile", CM_TILECHILDREN
    MENUITEM  "Arrange &Icons", CM_ARRANGEICONS
    MENUITEM  "C&lose All", CM_CLOSECHILDREN
    MENUITEM  "C&ount Children", CM_COUNTCHILDREN
  END
END
```

Listing 21.3. Source code for the MDIWIN1.CPP program file.

```
#include <stdlib.h>
#include <stdio.h>
#include <string.h>
#include <afxwin.h>
#include "mdiwin1.h"

const char* MenuRezName = "MAINMENU";
const Hctl = 200;
const Wctl = 400;
const MaxWords = 200;
const WordsPerLine = 10;
const NumWords = 10;
char* Words[NumWords] = { "The ", "man ", "ate ", "the ",
                          "food ", "in ", "hurry ", "girl ",
```

```
                            "cake ", "bread " };
// declare a global random-number generating function
int random(int maxVal)
{ return rand() % maxVal; }

// declare global function to calculate the size and
// location of a control
void makeRect(int nX, int nY, int nW, int nH, CRect& r)
{
  r.top = nY;
  r.left = nX;
  r.bottom = nY + nH;
  r.right = nX + nW;
}

// Define an application class derived from CWinApp
class CWindowApp : public CWinApp
{
public:

  virtual BOOL InitInstance();
};

class CAppMDIChild : public CMDIChildWnd
{
public:
  int nChildNum;
  // pointer to the edit box control
  CEdit* TextBox;
  CStatic* TextTxt;

  CAppMDIChild();
  ~CAppMDIChild();
  BOOL Create(LPSTR szTitle, int nChildNum);

protected:
  // handle closing the MDI child window
  afx_msg void OnClose();
  // handle destroying an MDI child window
  afx_msg void OnDestroy();
  afx_msg int OnCreate(LPCREATESTRUCT lpCS);

  // declare message map macro
  DECLARE_MESSAGE_MAP()
};

class CAppMDIFrame : public CMDIFrameWnd
{
  //DECLARE_DYNCREATE(CAppMDIFrame)
public:
  // flag to quickly close all MDI children windows
  BOOL bExpressClose;
  int nLastMDIChild;

  CAppMDIFrame();
```


continues

Listing 21.3. continued

```
  ~CAppMDIFrame() { delete pMenu; }
  // create a new client window area
  afx_msg int OnCreate(LPCREATESTRUCT lpCS);
  // create an MDI child window
  afx_msg void CMCreateChild();
  // cascade MDI children
  afx_msg void CMCascadeChildren() { MDICascade(); }
  // tile MDI children
  afx_msg void CMTileChildren() { MDITile(); }
  // arrange MDI children icons
  afx_msg void CMArrageIcons() { MDIIconArrange(); }
  // close all MDI children
  afx_msg void CMCloseChildren();
  // get the number of MDI children
  int GetChildCount() { return nNumMDIChildren; }
  // handle the command for counting the MDI children
  afx_msg void CMCountChildren();
  // handle the child destroy message
  afx_msg LONG OnChildDestroy(UINT wParam, LONG lParam);
  // handle exiting the application
  afx_msg void OnExit()
    { SendMessage(WM_CLOSE); }

protected:
  CMenu* pMenu;
  int nNumMDIChildren;
  // handle closing the MDI frame window
  virtual void OnClose();

  // declare message map macro
  DECLARE_MESSAGE_MAP();
};

CAppMDIChild::CAppMDIChild()
{
  TextBox = NULL;
  TextTxt = NULL;
}

CAppMDIChild::~CAppMDIChild()
{
  if (TextBox)
    delete TextBox;
  else
    delete TextTxt;
}

BOOL CAppMDIChild::Create(LPSTR szTitle, int nChildNumber)
{
  nChildNum = nChildNumber;
  return CMDIChildWnd::Create(NULL, szTitle);
}

CAppMDIChild::OnCreate(LPCREATESTRUCT lpCS)
```

```
{
  CString s;
  CRect r;
  DWORD dwStaticStyle = WS_CHILD | WS_VISIBLE | SS_LEFT;
  DWORD dwEditStyle = WS_CHILD | WS_VISIBLE | ES_LEFT |
                ES_MULTILINE | ES_AUTOHSCROLL |
                ES_AUTOVSCROLL;

  // randomize seed for the random-number generator
  srand((unsigned)time(NULL));
  // build the list of random words
  for (int i = 0; i < MaxWords; i++) {
    if (i > 0 && i % WordsPerLine == 0)
      s += "\r\n";
    s += Words[random(NumWords)];
  }
  // obtain the size and location of the control to create
  makeRect(10, 10, Wctl, Hctl, r);
  // create a static text object in the child window if the
  // nChildNum variable stores an odd number.  Otherwise,
  // create an edit box control
  if (nChildNum % 2 == 0) {
    // create the edit box
    TextBox = new CEdit();
    TextBox->Create(dwEditStyle, r, this, ID_TEXT_EDIT);
    TextBox->SetWindowText((const char*) s);
  }
  else {
    // create static text
    TextTxt = new CStatic();
    TextTxt->Create((const char*)s, dwStaticStyle, r,  this);
  }
  return 0;
}

void CAppMDIChild::OnClose()
{
  CAppMDIFrame* pParent = (CAppMDIFrame*)(GetParentFrame());

  // return TRUE if the bExpressClose member of the
  // is the express-close flag of the parent window set?
  if (pParent->bExpressClose == TRUE)
    return;
  else
    // prompt the user and return the prompt result
    if (MessageBox("Close this MDI window?",
             "Query", MB_YESNO | MB_ICONQUESTION) == IDYES) {
      MDIDestroy();
  }
}

void CAppMDIChild::OnDestroy()
{
  CAppMDIFrame* pParent = (CAppMDIFrame*)(GetParentFrame());
  pParent->SendMessage(WM_CHILDDESTROY, (UINT)m_hWnd, 0);
```


continues

Listing 21.3. continued

```
}

CAppMDIFrame::CAppMDIFrame()
{
   Create(NULL, "MDI Text Viewer",
          WS_OVERLAPPEDWINDOW ¦ WS_MAXIMIZE, rectDefault,
      NULL, MenuRezName);
   // clear the express-close flag
   bExpressClose = FALSE;
   // initialize the number of MDI children
   nLastMDIChild = 0;
   nNumMDIChildren = 0;
}

int CAppMDIFrame::OnCreate(LPCREATESTRUCT lpCS)
{
  pMenu = new CMenu();
  pMenu->LoadMenu(MenuRezName);
  CreateClient(lpCS, pMenu->GetSubMenu(0));
  return 0;
}

void CAppMDIFrame::CMCreateChild()
{
  char s[81];
  CRect r;
  CAppMDIChild* pChild = new CAppMDIChild();
  makeRect(10 * nNumMDIChildren, 10 * nNumMDIChildren,
           Wctl, Hctl, r);
  nLastMDIChild++;
  sprintf(s, "Child # %d", nLastMDIChild);
  if (!pChild->Create(s, nLastMDIChild)) {
    delete pChild;
    nLastMDIChild-; // decrement highest child index
    return;
  }
  nNumMDIChildren++;
  // show the new MDI child window
  pChild->ShowWindow(SW_SHOW);
}

void CAppMDIFrame::CMCloseChildren()
{
  CAppMDIChild* pChild = (CAppMDIChild*) MDIGetActive();

  // set the bExpressClose flag
  bExpressClose = TRUE;
  while (pChild) {
    // close the active MDI child
    pChild->MDIDestroy();
    MDINext; // get the next MDI child
    pChild = (CAppMDIChild*) MDIGetActive();
  }
  // clear the bExpressClose flag
```

```
  bExpressClose = FALSE;
}

//  display a message box which shows the number of children
void CAppMDIFrame::CMCountChildren()
{
  char msgStr[81];

  sprintf(msgStr, "There are %d MDI children", nNumMDIChildren);
  MessageBox(msgStr, "Information", MB_OK | MB_ICONINFORMATION);
}

LONG CAppMDIFrame::OnChildDestroy(UINT wParam, LONG lParam)
{
  nNumMDIChildren--;
  // reset nLastMDIChild to 0, if there are no MDI children
  nLastMDIChild = (nNumMDIChildren == 0) ? 0 : nLastMDIChild;
  return 0;
}

void CAppMDIFrame::OnClose()
{
  if (MessageBox("Want to close this application",
                 "Query", MB_YESNO | MB_ICONQUESTION) == IDYES)
    DestroyWindow();
}

BEGIN_MESSAGE_MAP(CAppMDIChild, CMDIChildWnd)
  ON_WM_CREATE()
  ON_WM_CLOSE()
  ON_WM_DESTROY()
END_MESSAGE_MAP()

BEGIN_MESSAGE_MAP(CAppMDIFrame, CMDIFrameWnd)
  ON_WM_CREATE()
  ON_COMMAND(CM_CREATECHILD, CMCreateChild)
  ON_COMMAND(CM_CASCADECHILDREN, CMCascadeChildren)
  ON_COMMAND(CM_TILECHILDREN, CMTileChildren)
  ON_COMMAND(CM_ARRANGEICONS, CMArrageIcons)
  ON_COMMAND(CM_CLOSECHILDREN, CMCloseChildren)
  ON_COMMAND(CM_COUNTCHILDREN, CMCountChildren)
  ON_MESSAGE(WM_CHILDDESTROY, OnChildDestroy)
  ON_COMMAND(CM_EXIT, OnExit)
  ON_WM_CLOSE()
END_MESSAGE_MAP()

// Construct the CWindowApp's m_pMainWnd data member
BOOL CWindowApp::InitInstance()
{
  m_pMainWnd = new CAppMDIFrame();
  m_pMainWnd->ShowWindow(m_nCmdShow);
  m_pMainWnd->UpdateWindow();
  return TRUE;
}

// application's constructor initializes and runs the app
CWindowApp WindowApp;
```

Listing 21.2 contains the script for the MDIWIN1.RC resource file. The file defines the menu resource required by the MDI frame window. The menu has two menu items, Exit and MDI Children. The latter menu item is a pop-up menu with several options. These options include creating a new MDI child window, cascading the MDI child windows, tiling the MDI child windows, arranging the icons for the MDI child windows, closing all MDI child windows, and displaying the number of MDI child windows.

Listing 21.3 shows the source code for the MDIWIN1.CPP program file. The program listing declares the following sets of constants:

- The `MenuRezName` constant defines the name of the menu resource used in calling the `Create` and `CreateClient` functions.
- The `Hctl` and `Wctl` constants are used to size up the static text and edit controls that are attached to the MDI child windows.
- The constants `MaxWords`, `WordsPerLine`, and `NumWords` are used in generating the random text in each MDI child window.

The global array of pointers, `Words`, contains the program's rather limited vocabulary. The listing also declares the global functions `random` and `makeRect`. The `random` function generates the random number between 0 and `maxVal` (the function's only parameter). The `makeRect` function is similar to the `makeRect` member functions that are used in many examples shown in previous Days in this book. Because both MDI frame and child window classes need this function, I made it global rather than declaring in each class.

The program listing declares three classes: the application class `CWindowApp`, the MDI frame class `CAppMDIFrame`, and the MDI child window class `CAppMDIChild`.

The code for the application class looks very much like the ones in previous programs, with one exception. The `InitInstance` member function creates an instance of the MDI frame class `CAppMDIFrame`.

The `CAppMDIFrame` class, a descendant of `CMDIFrameWnd`, declares four data members, a constructor, a destructor, and a group of member functions. There are two public and two protected data members. The public data members are `bExpressClose` and `nLastMDIChild`. The Boolean data member `bExpressClose` assists in quickly closing all the windows—this process bypasses the confirmation normally requested when you close an individual MDI child window. The `nLastMDIChild` member stores the highest index of an MDI child window. The protected data members are `pMenu` and `nNumMDIChildren`. The `pMenu` member is the pointer to the menu attached to the MDI frame window. The `nNumMDIChildren` member stores the current number of MDI child windows.

The class constructor invokes the Create member function to specify the window title, style (maximized and overlapped), and the MAINMENU menu resource (using the global constant MenuRezName). The constructor also initializes the bExpressClose, nLastMDIChild, and nNumMDIChildren data members. The class destructor deletes the dynamic menu accessed by the pMenu pointer.

The member function OnCreate, defined in lines 193 through 199, responds to the WM_CREATE message sent by the Create function (which itself is called by the class constructor). The function performs the following tasks:

- Creates a new instance of CMenu, the menu class, and links that instance with the pMenu data member
- Attaches the resource menu MAINMENU to the MDI frame window by calling the CMenu::LoadMenu function, using the pMenu pointer
- Creates the invisible MDI client window by calling the CreateClient member function (the first argument of the CreateClient function is the parameter of the OnCreate function itself; the second argument of the CreateClient function is the pointer to the first menu item, accessed by the expression pMenu->GetSubMenu(0))
- Returns zero as the function result

The member function CMCreateChild, defined in lines 201 through 218, creates an MDI child window. The function carries out the following tasks:

- Creates a new instance of class CAppMDIChild and accesses that instance with the local pointer pChild
- Calculates the size and location of the MDI child window by calling the global function makeRect
- Increments the nLastMDIChild data member
- Builds the MDI child window title, using the value stored in nLastMDIChild, and stores the title in the local string s
- Builds the MDI child window by calling the member function CAppMDIFrame::Create (the function call supplies the MDI child window title and child number; if the Create function returns FALSE, the CMCreateChild function deletes the dynamic instance of CAppMDIChild, decrements the nLastMDIChild member, and then exits)
- Increments the number of current MDI child windows that is stored in data member nNumMDIChildren

- Displays the new MDI child window by invoking the `ShowWindow` function

The member function `CMCloseChildren`, defined in lines 220 through 234, closes all the MDI child windows. The function performs the following tasks:

- Obtains the pointer to the currently active MDI child window by calling the `MDIGetActive` member function (the local pointer `pChild` accesses the active window)
- Assigns `TRUE` to the data member `bExpressClose`
- Uses a `while` loop statement to close each MDI child window, starting with the currently active window (using the `pChild` pointer, the loop statements close the currently active window by calling the `MDIDestroy` function; then, the loop selects the next MDI child by calling the `MDINext` function, and uses the `MDIGetActive` function to assign the address of the new active child to pointer `pChild`)
- Assigns `FALSE` to the `bExpressClose` data member

When the `while` loop closes all MDI child windows, the `MDIGetActive` function assigns a `NULL` to the `pChild` pointer. This `NULL` value ends the loop iteration.

The member function `CMCountChildren`, defined in lines 237 through 243, displays the current number of MDI child windows in a message box. The function converts the value stored in the `nNumMDIChildren` into a formatted string displayed by a message box.

The member function `OnChildDestroy`, defined in lines 245 through 251, responds to the messages sent by an MDI child window when it is destroyed. The function decrements the value stored in member `nNumMDIChildren` and resets the value of member `nLastMDIChild` to 0 if `nNumMDIChildren` is 0. Therefore, when you close all the MDI child windows, the next MDI child window you create has a `Child #1` caption.

The member functions `CMCascadeChildren`, `CMTileChldren`, and `CMArrangeIcons` invoke the inherited member functions `MDICascade`, `MDITile`, and `MDIIconArrange`, respectively.

The `CAppMDIChild` class declares two public members, `TextBox` and `TextTxt`, and a protected member, `nChildNum`. The `TextBox` and `TextTxt` members are pointers to the edit control and static text control that are created (the instances of `CAppMDIChild` create either one but not both). The class also declares a constructor, a destructor, a `Create` function, and a number of member functions. The `nChildNum` data member stores the child number of an MDI child window for self-identification.

The class constructor assigns NULL values to the TextBox and TextTxt pointers. The class destructors delete the dynamic instance of the control accessed by either TextBox or TextTxt.

The member function Create, defined in lines 117 through 121, is a short version of the inherited Create function, and has two parameters: szText and nChildNumber. The function assigns the argument of nChildNumber to the member nChildNum and then calls the Create member function of the parent class.

The member function OnCreate, defined in lines 123 through 157, responds to the WM_CREATE message emitted by the Create function. The OnCreate function carries out the following tasks:

- Randomizes the seed for the random-number generator
- Builds the list of random words using the CString object s (this task uses a for loop statement and inserts a line break after generating each WordsPerLine random word)
- Calculates the size and location of the edit control or static text control to be created in the next task
- Creates an edit control accessed by member TextBox if the value stored in nChildNum is even; otherwise, creates a static text control accessed by member TextTxt
- Returns zero as the function value

The member function OnClose, defined in lines 159 through 173, closes an MDI child window with or without user confirmation. The function uses the local pointer pParent to access the parent MDI frame window. This access allows the function to then obtain the Boolean value of bExpressClose and, depending on that value, determines whether or not to prompt the user before closing the window.

The member function OnDestroy, defined in lines 175 through 179, sends the parent MDI frame window a WM_CHILDDESTROY message when an MDI child window is removed. This allows the parent MDI frame window to take appropriate action, which in this case is the decrement of the nNumMDIChildren member.

Summary

Today's lesson presents the Multiple Document Interface (MDI), which is an interface standard in Windows. You learn about the following subjects:

- The basic features and components of an MDI-compliant application include the MDI frame window, the invisible MDI client window, and the dynamically created MDI child window.
- The basic ingredients for an MDI application are the `CMDIFrameWnd` and `CMDIChildWnd` classes.
- The `CMDIFrameWnd` class manages the MDI client window, the MDI child window, and the execution of the menu commands.
- You can build MDI frame windows as objects that are owned by the application and that own the MDI children.
- The `CMDIChildWnd` class is used in building MDI child windows.

Q&A

Q Should each MDI child window have an ID?

A Yes. Associating each MDI child window with an ID gives you more control over managing these windows, especially if they vary in relevance. Thus, you can use the ID to exclude special MDI child windows from collective operations.

Q Can I hide MDI child windows?

A Yes, you can use the inherited member function `CWnd::ShowWindow` to show and hide one or more MDI child windows.

Workshop

The Workshop provides quiz questions to help you solidify your understanding of the material covered, and exercises to provide you with experience in using what you've learned. Try to understand the quiz and exercise answers before continuing on to the next day's lesson. Answers are provided in Appendix B, "Answers."

Quiz

1. True or false? MDI child windows can have their own menus.
2. True or false? MDI child windows can be moved outside the area of the frame window.
3. True or false? The MFC library supports nested MDI child windows.
4. True or false? This is the last quiz question in this book.

Exercise

Experiment with program MDIWIN1.CPP by adding command buttons in each MDI child window. Make these command buttons toggle the case of the text in the static text or edit controls associated with each MDI child window.

WEEK 3 IN REVIEW

As you end the last week of learning about programming with Visual C++, let's look at a Windows version of the number-guessing game. Listing R3.1 shows the source code for the INPUTDIA.H header file. Listing R3.2 contains the script for the INPUTDIA.RC resource file. Listing R3.3 shows the source code for the GAME3.H header file. Listing R3.4 contains the script for the GAME3.RC resource file. Listing R3.5 shows the source code for the GAME3.CPP program file. Create the GAME3.MAK project file in the directory \MSVC20\VC21DAY\GAME3 and include the files GAME3.CPP, GAME3.DEF (which resembles the MINWINAP.DEF file in Day 14, Listing 14.2), and GAME3.RC. The INPUTDIA.RC is automatically included with file GAME3.RC using the `rcinclude` statement in the latter file.

Listing R3.1. Source code for the INPUTDIA.H header file.

```
#define ID_INPUT_TXT 100
#define ID_INPUT_EDIT 101
```

Listing R3.2. Script for the INPUTDIA.RC resource file.

```
#include <afxres.h>
#include "inputdia.h"

GAME DIALOG 44, 34, 200, 80
STYLE DS_MODALFRAME | WS_CAPTION | WS_VISIBLE | WS_SYSMENU
CAPTION "Hi-Lo Guessing Game"
BEGIN
    LTEXT "Enter a string:", ID_INPUT_TXT, 20, 10, 160, 12,
          NOT WS_GROUP
    EDITTEXT ID_INPUT_EDIT, 20, 25, 160, 12, ES_AUTOHSCROLL
    DEFPUSHBUTTON "OK", IDOK, 20, 45, 65, 14, WS_GROUP
    PUSHBUTTON "Cancel", IDCANCEL, 110, 45, 65, 14, WS_GROUP
END
```

Listing R3.3. Source code for the GAME3.H header file.

```
#define CM_EXIT (WM_USER + 100)
#define CM_GAME (WM_USER + 101)
```

Listing R3.4. Script for the GAME3.RC resource file.

```
#include <afxres.h>
#include "game3.h"

MAINMENU MENU LOADONCALL MOVEABLE PURE DISCARDABLE
BEGIN
    MENUITEM "E&xit", CM_EXIT
    MENUITEM "&Game", CM_GAME
END

rcinclude inputdia.rc
```

Listing R3.5. Source code for the GAME3.CPP program file.

```
#include <stdlib.h>
#include <stdio.h>
#include <string.h>
#include <afxwin.h>
```

```
#include "game3.h"
#include "inputdia.h"

const MaxBuffer = 81;

// declare a global random number generating function
int random(int maxVal)
{ return rand() % maxVal; }

class CWindowApp : public CWinApp
{
public:
    virtual BOOL InitInstance();
};

// expand the functionality of CFrameWnd by deriving
// class CAppWindow
class CAppWindow : public CFrameWnd
{
public:

  CAppWindow();

protected:
  // handle the Game menu item
  afx_msg void CMGame();
  afx_msg void OnExit()
    { SendMessage(WM_CLOSE); }
  // handle closing the window
  afx_msg void OnClose();

  // declare message map macro
  DECLARE_MESSAGE_MAP();
};

// declare a class for the line input dialog box
class CInputDialog : public CDialog
{
public:
  CInputDialog(CWnd* pParent) : CDialog("GAME", pParent) {}
  // handle invoking the dialog box
  int DoModal(CString& Message, CString& Text);
  // handle initializing the dialog box
  virtual BOOL OnInitDialog();
  // handle the OK button
  virtual void OnOK();
  // access input
  CString& GetInput() { return szText; }

protected:
  CString szText;
  CString szMessage;
};

int CInputDialog::DoModal(CString& Message, CString& Text)
```

continues

Listing R3.5. continued

```
{
  // copy parameters to data members
  szText = Text;
  szMessage = Message;
  return CDialog::DoModal();
}

BOOL CInputDialog::OnInitDialog()
{
  // assign the message a default input to the dialog
  // box static and edit box controls
  SetDlgItemText(ID_INPUT_TXT, (const char*) szMessage);
  SetDlgItemText(ID_INPUT_EDIT, (const char*) szText);
  return TRUE;
}

void CInputDialog::OnOK()
{
    // obtain the user's input
    GetDlgItemText(ID_INPUT_EDIT, szText.GetBuffer(MaxBuffer),
                   MaxBuffer);
    szText.ReleaseBuffer();
    EndDialog(IDOK);
}

CAppWindow::CAppWindow()
{
  // create the window
  Create(NULL, "Hi-Lo Game", WS_OVERLAPPEDWINDOW,
         rectDefault, NULL, "MAINMENU");
}

void CAppWindow::CMGame()
{
  CString Message = "Enter a number between 0 and 1000";
  CString Input = "500";
  int nNum, nGuess;
  int MaxIter = 11;
  int nIter = 0;
  BOOL bOk = TRUE;
  CInputDialog GameDlg(this);


  // reseed random-number generator
  srand((unsigned)time(NULL));
  nNum = random(1001);
  // execute the opening dialog box
  if (GameDlg.DoModal(Message, Input) == IDOK) {
       Input = GameDlg.GetInput();
       nGuess = atoi((const char*) Input);
       nIter++;
       // loop to obtain the other guesses
       while (nGuess != nNum && nIter < MaxIter && bOk ==            TRUE) {
```

```
            // is the user's guess higher?
            Message = (nGuess > nNum) ? "Enter a lower guess" :
                                        "Enter a higher guess";
            bOk = (GameDlg.DoModal(Message, Input) == IDOK) ?
TRUE :

            FALSE;
            Input = GameDlg.GetInput();
            nGuess = atoi((const char*) Input);
            nIter++;
          }

          // did the user guess the secret number
          if (nIter < MaxIter && bOk == TRUE) {
            MessageBeep(0);
            MessageBeep(0);
            MessageBox("You guessed it!", "Congratulations!",
                       MB_OK);
          }
          else {
             sprintf(Message.GetBuffer(MaxBuffer),
                     "The secret number is %d", nNum);
             Message.ReleaseBuffer();
             MessageBox((const char*) Message, "Sorry!", MB_OK);
          }
    }
}

void CAppWindow::OnClose()
{
  if (MessageBox("Want to close this application",
                 "Query", MB_YESNO | MB_ICONQUESTION) ==
                 IDYES)
    DestroyWindow();
}

BEGIN_MESSAGE_MAP(CAppWindow, CFrameWnd)
  ON_COMMAND(CM_GAME, CMGame)
  ON_COMMAND(CM_EXIT, OnExit)
  ON_WM_CLOSE()
END_MESSAGE_MAP()

// Construct the CWindowApp's m_pMainWnd data member
BOOL CWindowApp::InitInstance()
{
  m_pMainWnd = new CAppWindow();
  m_pMainWnd->ShowWindow(m_nCmdShow);
  m_pMainWnd->UpdateWindow();
  return TRUE;
}

// application's constructor initializes and runs the app
CWindowApp WindowApp;
```

Analysis Listings R3.1 and R3.2 contribute in defining the GAME dialog box resource used to prompt you for a guess. Listings R3.3 and R3.4 define the menu resource used by the main window.

The program in Listing R3.5 declares the application class, `CWindowApp`; the window class, `CAppWindow`; and the input dialog box class, `CInputDialog`.

The input dialog box class, `CInputDialog`, declares a constructor, a number of member functions, and two `CString` data members. The member functions include `DoModal`, `OnInitDialog`, `OnOK`, and `GetInput`.

The member function `DoModal`, defined in lines 59 through 65, has two `CString` reference parameters: `Message` and `Text`. The function assigns the parameters `Text` and `Message` to the data members `szText` and `szMessage`. The function returns the value of the inherited `CDialog::DoModal` member function.

The member function `OnInitDialog`, defined in lines 67 through 74, calls the function `SetDlgItemText` twice. The first call assigns the string in member `szMessage` to the static text control of the input dialog box. The second call assigns the string in member `szText` to the edit control in the input dialog box. The Boolean function then returns `TRUE`.

The member function `OnOK`, defined in lines 76 through 83, copies the text in the edit control to the data member `szText`.

The member function `GetInput` returns the contents of the data member `szText`.

The class `CAppWindow` declares the member functions `CMGame`, `OnExit`, and `OnClose`. The function `CMGame` plays the number-guessing game and performs the following tasks:

- Declares and initializes a number of local variables and instances of classes `CString` and `CInputDialog`
- Reseeds the random-number generator
- Generates the secret number and stores it in the variable `nNum`
- Executes the modal dialog box instance `GameDlg`. When the examined condition in the `if` statement of line 107 is true, the function performs the following subtasks:

  Obtains the input text by sending the `GetInput` message to instance `GameDlg` (the result is stored in the string `Input`)

  Converts the string in variable `Input` into an integer and stores the integer in variable `nGuess`

Increments the iteration counter, variable `nIter`

Executes a `while` loop that redisplays the input dialog box and performs these subtasks

- Displays a congratulatory message if the user guesses the secret number; if the user does not guess the secret number, displays the secret number in a message dialog box

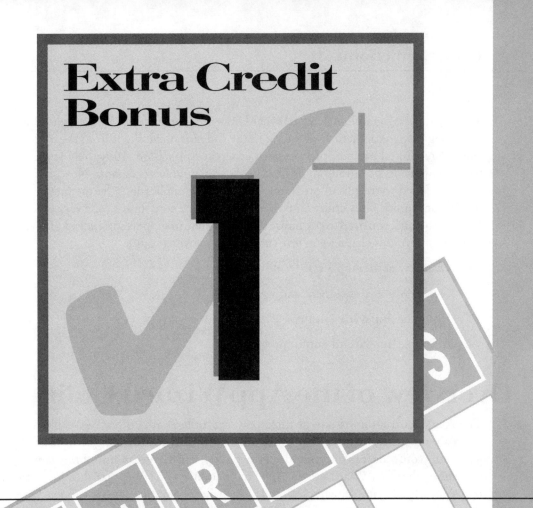

Extra Credit Bonus

1

Working with AppWizard

The Windows programming chapters that I presented earlier created the various source files using the typical method of typing in the code (or obtaining it from the optional companion disk). I had purposely avoided using the AppWizard utility to show you the basic components of various kinds of MFC-based Windows programs. Now that you have developed your skills in programming Windows applications, let me present the AppWizard utility. This utility empowers you to create core source code very quickly. I say core because you need to customize the source code to support specific tasks for your applications. In this chapter you learn about the following topics:

- Overview of the AppWizard utility
- Overview of the document and view classes
- Using the AppWizard utility
- A Sample AppWizard output program

Overview of the AppWizard Utility

The AppWizard utility is one of three powerful utilities (the other two utilities are ClassWizard and App Studio) that empowers you to automate creating source code by generating core code (or skeleton code, if you prefer), which you can customize manually or by using the ClassWizard and the App Studio utilities. The AppWizard emits a series of resource, header, implementation, and bitmap files. These files contain various classes that make up the application. The ClassWizard (which I discuss in the next chapter) empowers you to customize the code emitted by the AppWizard utility. The App Studio utility also permits you to customize the various resources of the files generated by the AppWizard utility. Due to space limitation, I do not cover App Studio. Note, however, that using this resource-managing utility is very easy.

The Document and View Classes

The AppWizard utility generates the source code files for a special kind of MFC-based Windows programs. These programs use the document/view classes instead of the descendants of the frame window class `CFrameWnd`. What's the conceptual difference between these classes? The frame window classes that I presented on Day 14 possess both the underlying information and offer the view to display that information. The document/view design supports a more sophisticated scheme of storing, viewing, and entering data. The document class has the primary role of storing the information using data members and manipulating this information (if necessary) using member functions.

The view classes have the primary tasks of displaying and entering the data in a document class. The document/view design works by having a single document class with one or more view classes. In the case of multiple view classes, each view class supports accessing some or all of the document's data in a specific fashion. For example, you can have a document class store the lines of a text file. The associated view classes can display these lines either as ASCII characters or as hexadecimal integers. Both view classes rely on the document class to store and manage the displayed information.

The next subsections introduce you to the various classes that support the document/view design. I do not present the declarations of these classes. Instead, I present the relevant class members when I present the sample programs in this chapter and in the next one.

The Document Template Classes

The MFC library uses a special set of classes to help Windows applications assemble (or coordinate, if you like) the components of an application that uses documents and views. These classes are

- The class `CDocTemplate` is the base for all the other document template classes. This class coordinates the creation of the instances of frame window, document, and view classes.
- The class `CSingleDocTemplate`, a descendant of class `CDocTemplate`, supports an SDI-compliant application that has one document open at a time.
- The class `CMultiDocTemplate`, a descendant of class `CDocTemplate`, supports an MDI-compliant application that has multiple documents open at one time.

The *CDocument* Class

The MFC library offers the class `CDocument` to store the viewed data and any other supporting data. Typically, you derive a descendant of class `CDocument` and declare the data members for the viewed data as public. Why declare these members public when such a practice is against C++ programming practices? Because the views need to access these data members in order to store and recall data. You can certainly accomplish this purpose using member functions that store and recall the sought information. However, these member functions add an overhead to the application and further complicate the expressions that access the document's data members.

The View Classes

The MFC library declares the view classes to support viewing, entering, and editing data. The AppWizard utility creates view classes that are descendants of one of the following view classes:

- The class `CView` is the base of the view classes subhierarchy. The class `CView` displays data and accepts input from the user.
- The class `CScrollView`, a descendant of class `CView`, supports scrolling views.
- The class `CFormView`, a descendant of class `CScrollView`, supports a form (which greatly resembles a dialog box) defined in a form resource. Forms are views which contain various controls that display and input data. You can use the App Studio to quickly and easily create a form resource.
- The class `CEditView`, a descendant of class `CView`, has text editing features. These features include typical text editing, finding, replacing, and scrolling.

Using the AppWizard Utility

You invoke the AppWizard when you choose, in the New Project dialog box, to create a new project which is an AppWizard application. The AppWizard uses several dialog boxes to create an application. Figure B1.1 shows the New Project dialog box that appears when you choose to create a new project. The New Project dialog box contains the following controls:

- The **Project Name** edit control, in which you type the name of the project.
- The **Project Type** dropdown combo box, which allows you to select the kind of project. You must select the MFC AppWizard (exe) option to create an MFC-based AppWizard application.
- The **New Subdirectory** edit control, in which you enter a name that is different from the default subdirectory name. The default subdirectory name is based on the project name.
- The **Platforms** group box, which specifies the various platforms supported by Visual C++.
- The **Project Path** static text control, which displays the current location of the project subdirectory.

- The **Directory** list box, which displays the location of the project subdirectory. You can select the directory that becomes the parent of the new project subdirectory.
- The **Drive** drop-down list box, which allows you to access any other on-line drive.
- The **Help** pushbutton, which offers on-line help.
- The **Cancel** pushbutton, which cancels the creation of a new project.
- The **Create...** pushbutton, which begins the process of generating a new subdirectory project, all of the related source code files, and the related subdirectories.

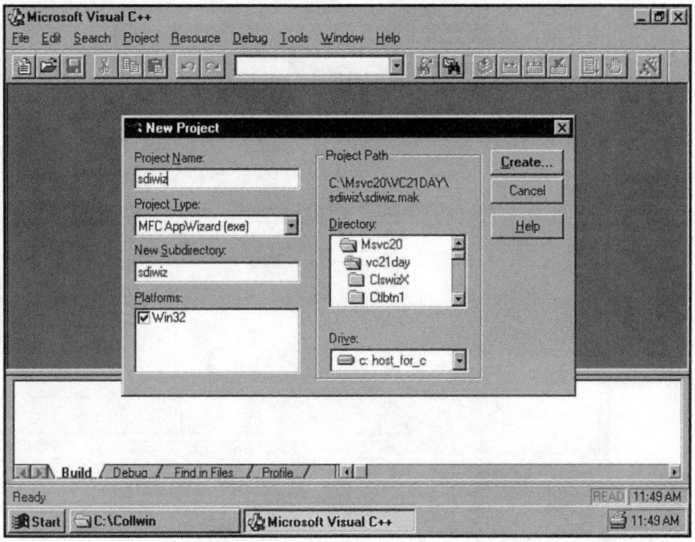

Figure B1.1. *The New Project dialog box.*

The SDI View Example

Let's create a minimal AppWizard program. The steps involved are as follows:

1. Invoke the **File | New** command and select to create a new project.
2. When the Workbench invokes the New Project dialog box, type **`sdiwiz`** as the name of the project and select the directory \MSVC20\VC21DAY as the parent for the new project.

3. Click the **Create...** pushbutton. This button brings up the MFC AppWizard - Step 1 dialog box, which is similar to the one shown in Figure B1.2. This dialog box is the first in a sequence of dialog boxes which allow you to fine-tune the various aspects of the application. This dialog box has the check boxes Single document, Multiple documents, and Dialog-based. By default, the Multiple documents check box is selected. Click on the Single document check box (the resulting dialog box should match the one in Figure B1.2.). The bottom of this dialog box (and the rest of the MFC AppWizard dialog boxes) contains the **Help**, **Cancel**, **< Back, Next >**, and **Finish** pushbuttons. The **Back** and **Next** buttons allows you to navigate back and forth through various AppWizard dialog boxes.

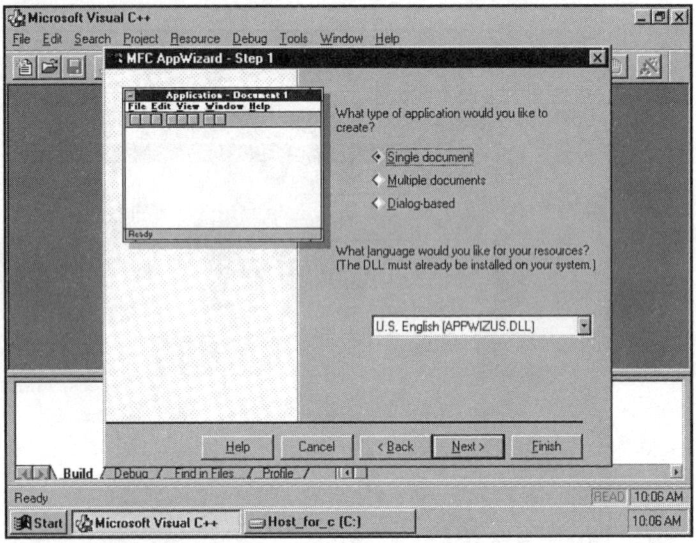

Figure B1.2. *The MFC AppWizard - Step 1 dialog box while creating project SDIWIZ.*

4. Click the **Next >** pushbutton in the MFC AppWizard - Step 1 dialog box. AppWizard displays the MFC AppWizard - Step 2 of 6 dialog box, shown in Figure B1.3. This dialog box allows you to include database support by clicking on the appropriate check box. By default, the Non check box is selected. Since I do not want to include any database support in the minimal application, accept the default choice.

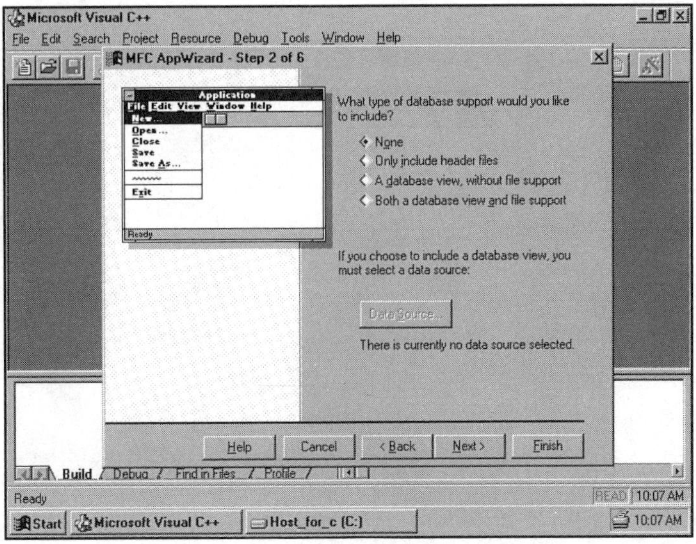

Figure B1.3. *The MFC AppWizard - Step 2 of 6 dialog box while creating project SDIWIZ.*

5. Click the **Next >** pushbutton. This action pops up the MFC AppWizard - Step 3 of 6 dialog box, which allows you to select OLE support (see Figure B1.4). The check boxes permit you to create an application with no OLE support (the default), as an OLE container, as an OLE mini-server, as an OLE full-sever, and as an OLE container/server. Since I do not want to include any OLE support in the minimal application, accept the default choice.

6. Click the **Next >** pushbutton. This action pops up the MFC AppWizard - Step 4 of 6 dialog box, which allows you to adjust the visual interface of the application. The check boxes permit you to create an application with a dockable toolbar, initial status bar, support for printing and print previewing, support for context-sensitive help, and support for 3D controls. Clear the check marks for the check boxes associated with the above options. You should end up with a dialog box that looks like Figure B1.5. The dialog box also allows you to select the number of most recently used (MRU) files. The default is 4.

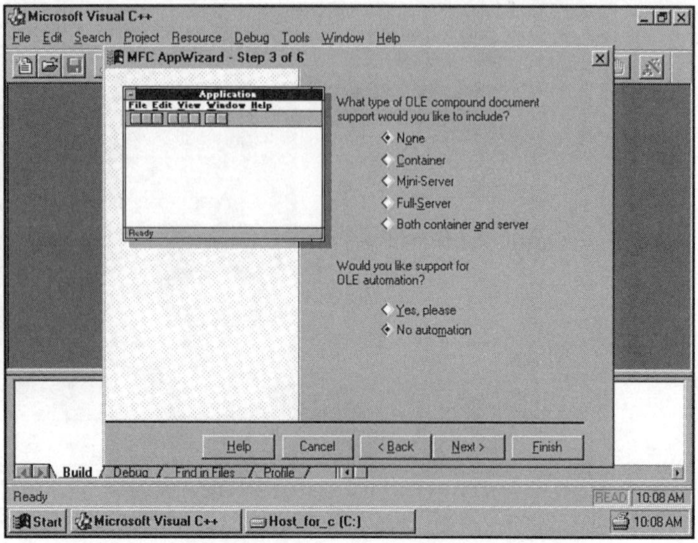

Figure B1.4. *The MFC AppWizard - Step 3 of 6 dialog box while creating project SDIWIZ.*

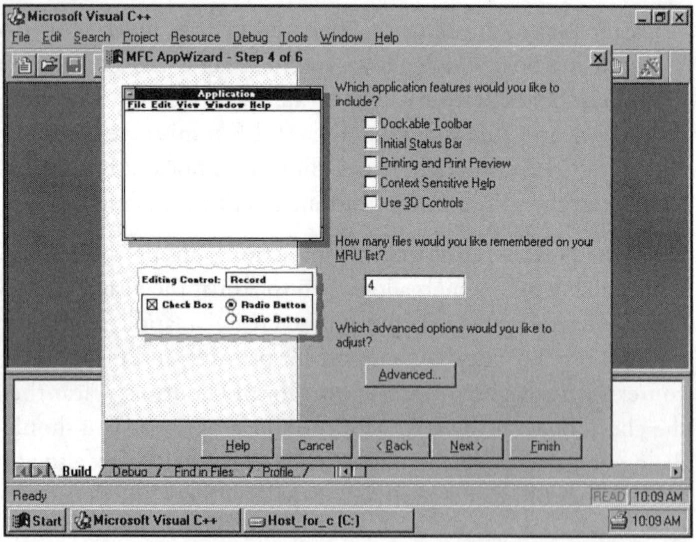

Figure B1.5. *The MFC AppWizard - Step 4 of 6 dialog box while creating project SDIWIZ.*

6. Click the **Next >** pushbutton. This action pops up the MFC AppWizard - Step 5 of 6 dialog box, shown in Figure B1.6. The dialog box has three sets of choices, each using two check boxes. The first set of choices allows you to determine whether or not to include comments in the AppWizard-generated source code. The second set of options allows you to select the kind of make file for your project—the choice is between the Visual C++ make file (the default) and the external makefile. The third set of options permits you to select linking your code using the MFC in a static library or in a shared DLL (Dynamic Link Library). For all of these options, accept the default settings.

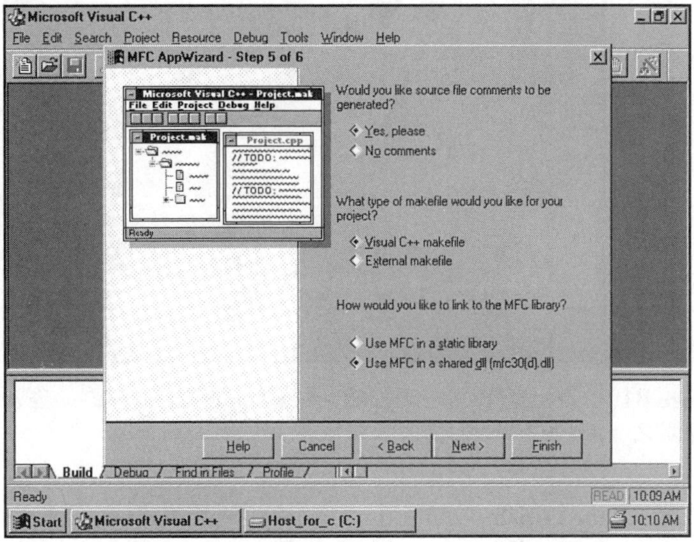

Figure B1.6. *The MFC AppWizard - Step 5 of 6 dialog box while creating project SDIWIZ.*

7. Click the **Next >** pushbutton. This action pops up the MFC AppWizard - Step 6 of 6 dialog box, shown in Figure B1.7. This dialog box lists the following project classes:

   - The class `CSdiwizApp`, which models the MFC application
   - The class `CMainFrame`, which supports the SDI frame window
   - The class `CSdiwizDoc`, which models the application's document
   - The class `CSdiwizView`, which represents the application's view

The Classes dialog box contains edit boxes that display the names of the currently selected class, its header file, its implementation file, and its base class. If you select the document class, the dialog box also displays the file extension and type name for the documents created by your application.

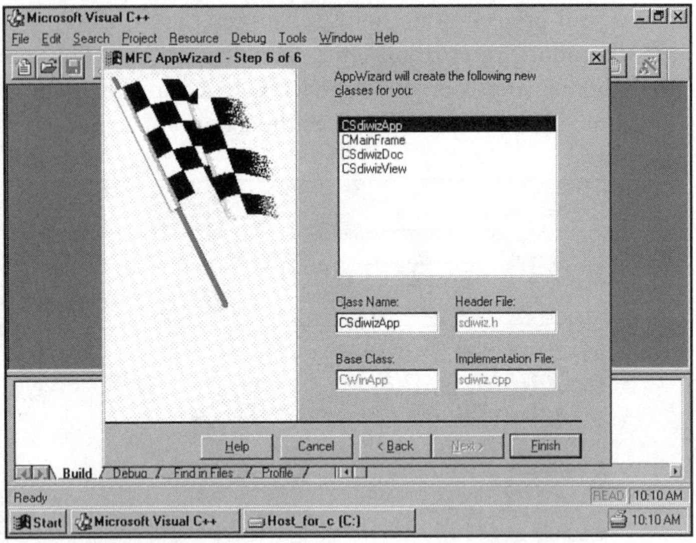

Figure B1.7. *The MFC AppWizard - Step 6 of 6 dialog box while creating project SDIWIZ.*

8. Click the **Finish** pushbutton. The AppWizard displays the New Project Information dialog box, shown in Figure B1.8. The dialog box summuraizes the information related to the application type, classes to be created, and features supported.

9. Click the **OK** pushbutton in the New Project Information dialog box to generate the source code files for the SDIWIZ project.

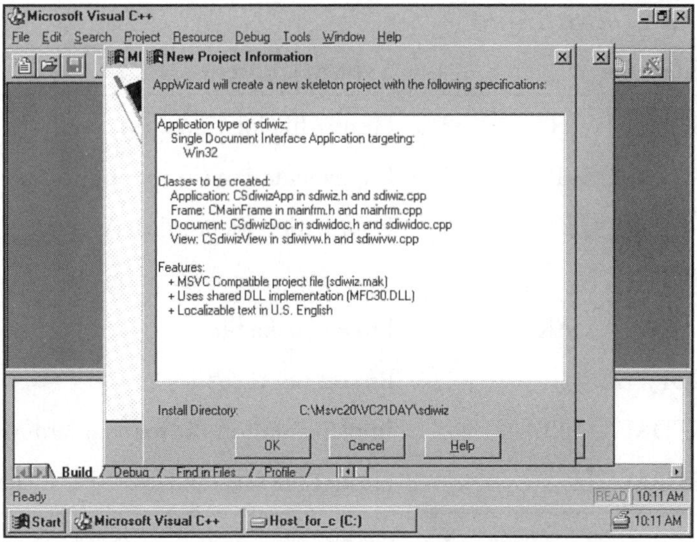

Figure B1.8. *The New Project Information dialog box while creating project SDIWIZ.*

Once the preceding process ends, you can list the files by clicking the **Project Files** button in the toolbar (the first one to the left). Table B1.1 shows the source code files generated in the directory \MSVC20\VC21DAY\SDIWIZ. The AppWizard utility also generates the directory \MSVC20\VC21DAY\SDIWIZ\RES and places resource files and resource script files.

Table B1.1. The source code files generated in the directory \MSVC20\VC21DAY\SDIWIZ.

Filename	Type of Contents
MAINFRM.CPP	Implementation file for window frame class
MAINFRM.H	Header file for window frame class
RESOURCE.H	Header file for standard resources
SDIWIDOC.CPP	Implementation file for document class
SDIWIDOC.H	Header file for document class
SDIWIVW.CPP	Implementation file for view class

continues

Table B1.1. continued

Filename	Type of Contents
SDIWIVW.H	Header file for view class
SDIWIZ.CPP	Implementation file for application class
SDIWIZ.CLW	Information file for ClassWizard
SDIWIZ.H	Header file for application class
SDIWIZ.MAK	Project make file
SDIWIZ.RC	Project resource file
STDAFX.CPP	Implementation file for standard MFC includes
STDAFX.H	Header file for standard MFC includes

Thus, the AppWizard generates files for the application, frame window, document, and views classes, as well as the resource (including icon and bitmap files), definition, and project make files.

Note: I edited some of the source code listings generated by AppWizard so that they fit the page margin.

Build and run the SDIWIZ.EXE program file using the **Execute** option in the **Project** menu selection. The program has a menu with the selections **File**, **Edit**, and **Help**. The **Edit** menu selection has disabled options of **Undo**, **Cut**, **Copy**, and **Paste**. The **File** menu selection has the options **New**, **Open...**, **Save**, **Save As...**, and **Exit**. Only the **Exit** option is fully functioning. The other options are partially operational. For example, the **Open...** option pops up the Open dialog box (shown in Figure B1.9) and allows you to select a file. However, nothing actually happens with the file, except that it becomes part of the window title.

In the next subsections, I discuss the various source code files generated by the AppWizard tool.

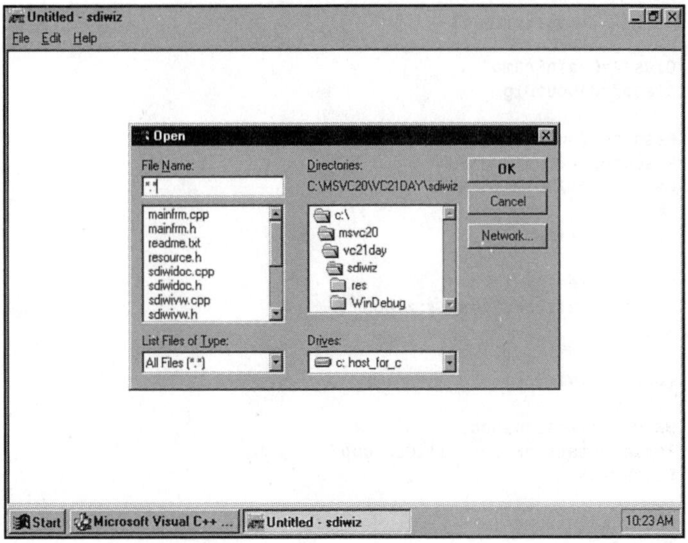

Figure B1.9. *The options of the Open File menu selection in the SDIWIZ.EXE program.*

The File SDIWIZ.CLW

Listing B1.1 shows the contents of the SDIWIZ.CLW information file for the ClassWizard utility. The file contains several sections whose names are enclosed in square brackets (much like .INI files). These sections describe various kinds of information which permit the ClassWizard utility to add more classes and member functions.

Type

Listing B1.1. The contents of the SDIWIZ.CLW definition file.

```
; CLW file contains information for the MFC ClassWizard

[General Info]
Version=1
LastClass=CSdiwizView
LastTemplate=CDialog
NewFileInclude1=#include "stdafx.h"
NewFileInclude2=#include "sdiwiz.h"
LastPage=0

ClassCount=8
Class1=CSdiwizApp
Class2=CSdiwizDoc
Class3=CSdiwizView
```

continues

Listing B1.1. continued

```
Class4=CMainFrame
Class7=CAboutDlg

ResourceCount=7
Resource1=IDD_ABOUTBOX
Resource2=IDR_MAINFRAME

[CLS:CSdiwizApp]
Type=0
HeaderFile=sdiwiz.h
ImplementationFile=sdiwiz.cpp
Filter=N

[CLS:CSdiwizDoc]
Type=0
HeaderFile=sdiwidoc.h
ImplementationFile=sdiwidoc.cpp
Filter=N

[CLS:CSdiwizView]
Type=0
HeaderFile=sdiwivw.h
ImplementationFile=sdiwivw.cpp
Filter=C

[CLS:CMainFrame]
Type=0
HeaderFile=mainfrm.h
ImplementationFile=mainfrm.cpp
Filter=T



[CLS:CAboutDlg]
Type=0
HeaderFile=sdiwiz.cpp
ImplementationFile=sdiwiz.cpp
Filter=D

[DLG:IDD_ABOUTBOX]
Type=1
ControlCount=4
Control1=IDC_STATIC,static,1342177283
Control2=IDC_STATIC,static,1342308352
Control3=IDC_STATIC,static,1342308352
Control4=IDOK,button,1342373889
Class=CAboutDlg

[MNU:IDR_MAINFRAME]
Type=1
Class=CMainFrame
Command3=ID_FILE_NEW
Command4=ID_FILE_OPEN
Command5=ID_FILE_SAVE
```

```
Command6=ID_FILE_SAVE_AS
Command10=ID_FILE_MRU_FILE1
Command11=ID_APP_EXIT
Command12=ID_EDIT_UNDO
Command13=ID_EDIT_CUT
Command14=ID_EDIT_COPY
Command15=ID_EDIT_PASTE
Command28=ID_APP_ABOUT
CommandCount=28

[ACL:IDR_MAINFRAME]
Type=1
Class=CMainFrame
Command1=ID_FILE_NEW
Command2=ID_FILE_OPEN
Command3=ID_FILE_SAVE
Command5=ID_EDIT_UNDO
Command6=ID_EDIT_CUT
Command7=ID_EDIT_COPY
Command8=ID_EDIT_PASTE
Command9=ID_EDIT_UNDO
Command10=ID_EDIT_CUT
Command11=ID_EDIT_COPY
Command12=ID_EDIT_PASTE
Command13=ID_NEXT_PANE
Command14=ID_PREV_PANE
CommandCount=17
```

The File RESOURCE.H

The header file RESOURCE.H, shown in Listing B1.2, contains a set of `#define` statements that define the IDs for the About dialog box (the macro `IDD_ABOUTBOX`) and the main menu (using the macro `IDR_MAINFRAME`). The other `_APS_NEXT_XXXX` constants are not directly used in the other source code files.

Type

Listing B1.2. The source code for the RESOURCE.H header file.

```
//{{NO_DEPENDENCIES}}
// Microsoft Visual C++ generated include file.
// Used by SDIWIZ.RC
//
#define IDR_MAINFRAME                        128
#define IDD_ABOUTBOX                         100

// Next default values for new objects
//
#ifdef APSTUDIO_INVOKED
```

continues

Listing B1.2. continued

```
#ifndef APSTUDIO_READONLY_SYMBOLS
#define _APS_NEXT_RESOURCE_VALUE130
#define _APS_NEXT_CONTROL_VALUE 1000
#define _APS_NEXT_SYMED_VALUE          101
#define _APS_NEXT_COMMAND_VALUE 32771
#endif
#endif
```

The File SDIWIZ.H

The header file SDIWIZ.H, shown in Listing B1.3, has the declaration of the application class `CSdiwizApp`. This class is a descendant of class `CWinApp` and declares (in line 15) a constructor, the overridden member function `InitInstance` (in line 24), and the member function `OnAppAbout` (in line 30). The AppWizard includes the latter member function in a special comment that it uses to generate the message response table.

Type Listing B1.3. The contents of the SDIWIZ.H header file.

```
 1: // sdiwiz.h : main header file for the SDIWIZ application
 2: //
 3:
 4: #ifndef __AFXWIN_H__
 5:   #error include 'stdafx.h' before including this file for PCH
 6: #endif
 7:
 8: #include "resource.h"       // main symbols
 9:
10: /////////////////////////////////////////////////////////////////
11: // CSdiwizApp:
12: // See sdiwiz.cpp for the implementation of this class
13: //
14:
15: class CSdiwizApp : public CWinApp
16: {
17: public:
18:      CSdiwizApp();
19:
20: // Overrides
21:      // ClassWizard generated virtual function overrides
22:      //{{AFX_VIRTUAL(CSdiwizApp)
23:      public:
24:      virtual BOOL InitInstance();
25:      //}}AFX_VIRTUAL
26:
27: // Implementation
28:
29:      //{{AFX_MSG(CSdiwizApp)
30:      afx_msg void OnAppAbout();
```

```
    // NOTE - the ClassWizard will add and remove member functions here.
    //    DO NOT EDIT what you see in these blocks of generated code !
       //}}AFX_MSG
       DECLARE_MESSAGE_MAP()
};


/////////////////////////////////////////////////////////////////////
```

The File STDAFX.H

The header file STDAFX.H, whose contents appear in Listing B1.4, merely includes the MFC header files AFXWIN.H and AFXEXT.H in lines 6 and 7, respectively. These `#include` directives permit the application to utilize both the standard and extended MFC classes.

Type **Listing B1.4. The source code for the STDAFX.H header file.**

```
1:  // stdafx.h : include file for standard system include files,
2:  //  or project specific include files that are used frequently,
3:  //      but are changed infrequently
4:  //
5:
6:  #include <afxwin.h>         // MFC core and standard components
7:  #include <afxext.h>         // MFC extensions
```

The File MAINFRM.H

The header file MAINFRM.H, shown in Listing B1.5, contains the declaration of the frame window class, `CMainFrame`, in line 5. The file declares this class as a descendant of `CFrameWnd`, since the application is SDI-compliant. The class `CMainFrame` declares a protected constructor (line 8), a public destructor (line 24), and the debug-related functions `AssertValid` and `Dump` (lines 26 and 27). The class also declares a message map, and the listing contains comments that act as placeholders for message-response member functions that you may elect to add using the ClassWizard.

Type **Listing B1.5. The source code for the MAINFRM.H header file.**

```
1:  // mainfrm.h : interface of the CMainFrame class
2:  //
```

continues

Listing B1.5. continued

```
////////////////////////////////////////////////////////////////////

class CMainFrame : public CFrameWnd
{
protected: // create from serialization only
        CMainFrame();
        DECLARE_DYNCREATE(CMainFrame)

// Attributes
public:

// Operations
public:

// Overrides
      // ClassWizard generated virtual function overrides
      //{{AFX_VIRTUAL(CMainFrame)
      //}}AFX_VIRTUAL

// Implementation
public:
      virtual ~CMainFrame();
#ifdef _DEBUG
      virtual void AssertValid() const;
      virtual void Dump(CDumpContext& dc) const;
#endif

// Generated message map functions
protected:
      //{{AFX_MSG(CMainFrame)
// NOTE - the ClassWizard will add and remove member functions here.
//    DO NOT EDIT what you see in these blocks of generated code!
      //}}AFX_MSG
      DECLARE_MESSAGE_MAP()
};

/////////////////////////////////////////////////////////////////////////////
```

The File SDIWIVW.H

The header file SDIWIVW.H, shown in Listing B1.6, contains the declaration of the view class `CSdiwizView`. The listing declares this class as a descendant of class `CView` and includes a protected constructor (line 8), the public member function `GetDocument` (line 13), a public destructor (line 29), the member function `OnDraw` (line 22), and the debug-related functions `Assert` and `Dump` (lines 31 and 32). The listing declares the message map and contains a comment-based placeholder that can include any added message-handling member functions. The listing contains an inline implementation of function `GetDocument`, enclosed in an `#ifndef` compiler directive.

Listing B1.6. The source code for the SDIWIVW.H header file.

```
// sdiwivw.h : interface of the CSdiwizView class
//
/////////////////////////////////////////////////////////////////

class CSdiwizView : public CView
{
protected: // create from serialization only
     CSdiwizView();
     DECLARE_DYNCREATE(CSdiwizView)

// Attributes
public:
     CSdiwizDoc* GetDocument();

// Operations
public:

// Overrides
     // ClassWizard generated virtual function overrides
     //{{AFX_VIRTUAL(CSdiwizView)
     public:
     virtual void OnDraw(CDC* pDC);  // overridden to draw
                                     // this view
     protected:
     //}}AFX_VIRTUAL

// Implementation
public:
     virtual ~CSdiwizView();
#ifdef _DEBUG
     virtual void AssertValid() const;
     virtual void Dump(CDumpContext& dc) const;
#endif

protected:

// Generated message map functions
protected:
     //{{AFX_MSG(CSdiwizView)
// NOTE - the ClassWizard will add and remove member functions here.
//    DO NOT EDIT what you see in these blocks of generated code !
     //}}AFX_MSG
     DECLARE_MESSAGE_MAP()
};

#ifndef _DEBUG  // debug version in sdiwivw.cpp
inline CSdiwizDoc* CSdiwizView::GetDocument()
   { return (CSdiwizDoc*)m_pDocument; }
#endif

/////////////////////////////////////////////////////////////////
```

The File SDIWIDOC.H

The header file SDIWIDOC.H, shown in Listing B1.7, declares the document class `CSdiwizDoc` as a descendant of class `CDocument`, in line 5. The derived class includes a protected constructor (line 8), a public destructor (line 26), the public member function `Serialize` (line 27), the message-handling function `OnNewDocument` (line 21), and the debug-related functions `AssertValid` and `Dump` (lines 30 and 31).

Type

Listing B1.7. The source code for the SDIWIDOC.H header file.

```
 1: // sdiwidoc.h : interface of the CSdiwizDoc class
 2: //
 3: /////////////////////////////////////////////////////////////////
 4:
 5: class CSdiwizDoc : public CDocument
 6: {
 7: protected: // create from serialization only
 8:         CSdiwizDoc();
 9:         DECLARE_DYNCREATE(CSdiwizDoc)
10:
11: // Attributes
12: public:
13:
14: // Operations
15: public:
16:
17: // Overrides
18:      // ClassWizard generated virtual function overrides
19:      //{{AFX_VIRTUAL(CSdiwizDoc)
20:      public:
21:      virtual BOOL OnNewDocument();
22:      //}}AFX_VIRTUAL
23:
24: // Implementation
25: public:
26:      virtual ~CSdiwizDoc();
27:      virtual void Serialize(CArchive& ar); // overridden for
28:                                            // document i/o
29: #ifdef _DEBUG
30:      virtual void AssertValid() const;
31:      virtual void Dump(CDumpContext& dc) const;
32: #endif
33:
34: protected:
35:
36: // Generated message map functions
37: protected:
38:      //{{AFX_MSG(CSdiwizDoc)
39: // NOTE - the ClassWizard will add and remove member functions here.
40: //    DO NOT EDIT what you see in these blocks of generated code !
41:      //}}AFX_MSG
```

```
        DECLARE_MESSAGE_MAP()
};

/////////////////////////////////////////////////////////////////////////////
```

The File SDIWIZ.RC

The resource file SDIWIZ.RC, whose contents appear in Listing B1.8, shows the resource script used in building program SDIWIZ.EXE. The resource file contains resources for strings, the program menu selections, menu options, accelerators (that is, the hot keys and shortcut keys), and the About SDIWIZ dialog box. Lines 59 to 84 define the main menu resource `IDR_MAINFRAME`. Lines 95 to 110 define the accelerators for the various menu options. Lines 121 to 130 define the About dialog box.

Type

Listing B1.8. The script for the SDIWIZ.RC resource file.

```
 1: //Microsoft Visual C++ generated resource script.
 2: //
 3: #include "resource.h"
 4:
 5: #define APSTUDIO_READONLY_SYMBOLS
 6: /////////////////////////////////////////////////////////////////////////////
 7: //
 8: // From TEXTINCLUDE 2
 9: //
10: #include "afxres.h"
11:
12: /////////////////////////////////////////////////////////////////////////////
13: #undef APSTUDIO_READONLY_SYMBOLS
14:
15: #ifdef APSTUDIO_INVOKED
16:
17: /////////////////////////////////////////////////////////////////////////////
18: //
19: // TEXTINCLUDE
20: //
21:
22: 1 TEXTINCLUDE DISCARDABLE
23: BEGIN
24:     "resource.h\0"
25: END
26:
27: 2 TEXTINCLUDE DISCARDABLE
28: BEGIN
29:     "#include ""afxres.h""\r\n"
30:     "\0"
31: END
32:
```

continues

Listing B1.8. continued

```
3 TEXTINCLUDE DISCARDABLE
BEGIN
    "#include ""res\\sdiwiz.rc2""  // non-Microsoft Visual
                                   // C++ edited resources\r\n"
    "\r\n"
    "#include ""afxres.rc""     // Standard components\r\n"
    "\0"
END

/////////////////////////////////////////////////////////////////
#endif    // APSTUDIO_INVOKED


/////////////////////////////////////////////////////////////////
//
// Icon
//

IDR_MAINFRAME           ICON    DISCARDABLE    "res\\sdiwiz.ico"


/////////////////////////////////////////////////////////////////
//
// Menu
//

IDR_MAINFRAME MENU PRELOAD DISCARDABLE
BEGIN
  POPUP "&File"
  BEGIN
    MENUITEM "&New\tCtrl+N",       ID_FILE_NEW
    MENUITEM "&Open...\tCtrl+O",   ID_FILE_OPEN
    MENUITEM "&Save\tCtrl+S",      ID_FILE_SAVE
    MENUITEM "Save &As...",        ID_FILE_SAVE_AS
    MENUITEM SEPARATOR
    MENUITEM "Recent File",        ID_FILE_MRU_FILE1,GRAYED
    MENUITEM SEPARATOR
    MENUITEM "E&xit",              ID_APP_EXIT
  END
  POPUP "&Edit"
  BEGIN
    MENUITEM "&Undo\tCtrl+Z",      ID_EDIT_UNDO
    MENUITEM SEPARATOR
    MENUITEM "Cu&t\tCtrl+X",       ID_EDIT_CUT
    MENUITEM "&Copy\tCtrl+C",      ID_EDIT_COPY
    MENUITEM "&Paste\tCtrl+V",     ID_EDIT_PASTE
  END
  POPUP "&Help"
  BEGIN
    MENUITEM "&About sdiwiz...",   ID_APP_ABOUT
  END
END
```

```
//////////////////////////////////////////////////////////////////
//
// Accelerator
//

IDR_MAINFRAME ACCELERATORS PRELOAD MOVEABLE
BEGIN
    "N",            ID_FILE_NEW,            VIRTKEY,CONTROL
    "O",            ID_FILE_OPEN,           VIRTKEY,CONTROL
    "S",            ID_FILE_SAVE,           VIRTKEY,CONTROL
    "Z",            ID_EDIT_UNDO,           VIRTKEY,CONTROL
    "X",            ID_EDIT_CUT,            VIRTKEY,CONTROL
    "C",            ID_EDIT_COPY,           VIRTKEY,CONTROL
    "V",            ID_EDIT_PASTE,          VIRTKEY,CONTROL
    VK_BACK,        ID_EDIT_UNDO,           VIRTKEY,ALT
    VK_DELETE,      ID_EDIT_CUT,            VIRTKEY,SHIFT
    VK_INSERT,      ID_EDIT_COPY,           VIRTKEY,CONTROL
    VK_INSERT,      ID_EDIT_PASTE,          VIRTKEY,SHIFT
    VK_F6,          ID_NEXT_PANE,           VIRTKEY
    VK_F6,          ID_PREV_PANE,           VIRTKEY,SHIFT
END

//////////////////////////////////////////////////////////////////
//
// Dialog
//

IDD_ABOUTBOX DIALOG DISCARDABLE  34, 22, 217, 55
CAPTION "About sdiwiz"
STYLE DS_MODALFRAME ¦ WS_POPUP ¦ WS_CAPTION ¦ WS_SYSMENU
FONT 8, "MS Sans Serif"
BEGIN
  ICON            IDR_MAINFRAME,IDC_STATIC,11,17,20,20
  LTEXT           "sdiwiz Version 1.0",IDC_STATIC,40,10,119,8
  LTEXT           "Copyright \251 1994",IDC_STATIC,40,25,119,8
  DEFPUSHBUTTON   "OK",IDOK,176,6,32,14,WS_GROUP
END

//////////////////////////////////////////////////////////////////
//
// String Table
//

STRINGTABLE PRELOAD DISCARDABLE
BEGIN
  IDR_MAINFRAME  "sdiwiz\n\nSdiwiz\n\n\nSdiwiz.Document\nSdiwiz Document"
END
```

Listing B1.8. continued

```
STRINGTABLE PRELOAD DISCARDABLE
BEGIN
     AFX_IDS_APP_TITLE       "sdiwiz"
     AFX_IDS_IDLEMESSAGE     "Ready"
END
STRINGTABLE DISCARDABLE
BEGIN
  ID_INDICATOR_EXT        "EXT"
  ID_INDICATOR_CAPS       "CAP"
  ID_INDICATOR_NUM        "NUM"
  ID_INDICATOR_SCRL       "SCRL"
  ID_INDICATOR_OVR        "OVR"
  ID_INDICATOR_REC        "REC"
END
STRINGTABLE DISCARDABLE
BEGIN
  ID_FILE_NEW        "Create a new document\nNew"
  ID_FILE_OPEN       "Open an existing document\nOpen"
  ID_FILE_CLOSE      "Close the active document\nClose"
  ID_FILE_SAVE       "Save the active document\nSave"
  ID_FILE_SAVE_AS    "Save the active document with a new name\nSave As"
  ID_APP_ABOUT       "Display program information, version number and
                    ➥copyright\nAbout"
  ID_APP_EXIT        "Quit the application; prompts to save documents\nExit"
  ID_FILE_MRU_FILE1  "Open this document"
  ID_FILE_MRU_FILE2  "Open this document"
  ID_FILE_MRU_FILE3  "Open this document"
  ID_FILE_MRU_FILE4  "Open this document"
  ID_NEXT_PANE       "Switch to the next window pane\nNext Pane"
  ID_PREV_PANE       "Switch back to the previous window pane\nPrevious Pane"
  ID_WINDOW_SPLIT    "Split the active window into panes\nSplit"
  ID_EDIT_CLEAR      "Erase the selection\nErase"
  ID_EDIT_CLEAR_ALL  "Erase everything\nErase All"
  ID_EDIT_COPY       "Copy the selection and put it on the Clipboard\nCopy"
  ID_EDIT_CUT        "Cut the selection and put it on the Clipboard\nCut"
  ID_EDIT_FIND       "Find the specified text\nFind"
  ID_EDIT_PASTE      "Insert Clipboard contents\nPaste"
  ID_EDIT_REPEAT     "Repeat the last action\nRepeat"
  ID_EDIT_REPLACE    "Replace specific text with different text\nReplace"
  ID_EDIT_SELECT_ALL "Select the entire document\nSelect All"
  ID_EDIT_UNDO       "Undo the last action\nUndo"
  ID_EDIT_REDO       "Redo the previously undone action\nRedo"
END

STRINGTABLE DISCARDABLE
BEGIN
  AFX_IDS_SCSIZE          "Change the window size"
  AFX_IDS_SCMOVE          "Change the window position"
  AFX_IDS_SCMINIMIZE      "Reduce the window to an icon"
  AFX_IDS_SCMAXIMIZE      "Enlarge the window to full size"
  AFX_IDS_SCNEXTWINDOW    "Switch to the next document window"
  AFX_IDS_SCPREVWINDOW    "Switch to the previous document window"
  AFX_IDS_SCCLOSE         "Close the active window and prompts to save the
                         ➥documents"
```

```
  AFX_IDS_SCRESTORE        "Restore the window to normal size"
  AFX_IDS_SCTASKLIST       "Activate Task List"
END

/////////////////////////////////////////////////////////////////
//
// Version
//

#include "winver.h"

VS_VERSION_INFO     VERSIONINFO
  FILEVERSION       1,0,0,1
  PRODUCTVERSION    1,0,0,1
  FILEFLAGSMASK     VS_FFI_FILEFLAGSMASK
#ifdef _DEBUG
  FILEFLAGS         VS_FF_DEBUG
#else
  FILEFLAGS         0 // final version
#endif
  FILEOS            VOS__WINDOWS32
  FILETYPE          VFT_APP
  FILESUBTYPE       0   // not used
BEGIN
  BLOCK "StringFileInfo"
  BEGIN
    BLOCK "040904B0" // Lang=US English, CharSet=Unicode
    BEGIN
      VALUE "CompanyName",      "\0"
      VALUE "FileDescription", "SDIWIZ MFC Application\0"
      VALUE "FileVersion",      "1, 0, 0, 1\0"
      VALUE "InternalName",     "SDIWIZ\0"
      VALUE "LegalCopyright",   "Copyright \251 1994\0"
      VALUE "LegalTrademarks", "\0"
      VALUE "OriginalFilename","SDIWIZ.EXE\0"
      VALUE "ProductName",      "SDIWIZ Application\0"
      VALUE "ProductVersion",   "1, 0, 0, 1\0"
    END
  END
  BLOCK "VarFileInfo"
  BEGIN
    VALUE "Translation", 0x409, 1200
    // English language (0x409) and the Unicode codepage (1200)
  END
END

#ifndef APSTUDIO_INVOKED
/////////////////////////////////////////////////////////////////
//
// From TEXTINCLUDE 3
//

#include "res\sdiwiz.rc2"  // non-Microsoft Visual
                           // C++ edited resources

#include "afxres.rc"  // Standard components
```

continues

Listing B1.8. continued

```

////////////////////////////////////////////////////////////////////
#endif    // not APSTUDIO_INVOKED
```

The File SDIWIZ.RC2

The directory \MSVC20\VC21DAY\SDIWIZ\RES contains the additional resource file SDIWIZ.RC2, shown in Listing B1.9. This resource file, which is not modified by App Studio, contains resources which you manually insert.

Listing B1.9. The script for the SDIWIZ.RC2 resource file.

```
//
// SDIWIZ.RC2 - resources Microsoft Visual C++ does not edit
//              directly
//

#ifdef APSTUDIO_INVOKED
  #error this file is not editable by Microsoft Visual C++
#endif //APSTUDIO_INVOKED


////////////////////////////////////////////////////////////////////
// Add manually edited resources here...

////////////////////////////////////////////////////////////////////
```

The File SDIWIZ.CPP

The implementation file SDIWIZ.CPP, shown in Listing B1.10, contains the implementation and message map for the application class `CSdiwizApp` in lines 19 to 28. In addition, the listing includes the declaration, implementation, and message map for the About dialog box class, `CAboutDlg`.

The listing contains the message map for class `CSdiwizApp`, which links the following member functions and Windows messages:

1. The message `ID_APP_ABOUT` with the member function `OnAppAbout`. This message map allows the program to respond to the **About SDIWIZ...** menu option in the **Help** menu selection.

2. The message ID_FILE_NEW with the member function CWinApp::OnFileNew. This message map permits the program to respond to the **New** option in the **File** menu selection. As you can see, the program actually relies on the member function OnFileNew in the parent class for a response.

3. The message ID_FILE_OPEN with the member function CWinApp::OnFileOpen. This message map permits the program to respond to the **Open...** option in the **File** menu selection. Again, the program depends on the member function OnFileOpen in the parent class for a response.

The source file contains the implementation for the following class members:

1. The constructor in lines 33 to 37. This member has no statements, and instead contains comments that indicate the location of any constructor code you want to include.

2. The member function InitInstance in lines 47 to 80. This function initializes the instances of class CSDIwizApp by carrying out the following tasks:
   - Loads the options from the standard .INI file.
   - Registers the application, window frame, and view classes in the application's document template. This task uses the document template class CSingleDocTemplate. The registration involves the document, window frame, and view classes.
   - Creates a new, empty document. This task involves sending the C++ message (as opposed to a Window message) OnFileNew to the class instance.
   - Offers minimal code to process command-line arguments.
   - Returns the Boolean value TRUE.

3. The member function OnAppAbout in lines 125 to 129. This function invokes the About dialog box. The function contains two statements. The first statement declares the instance of class CAboutDlg, aboutDlg; the second statement sends the C++ message DoModal to the object aboutDlg.

The implementation file declares the dialog class CAboutDlg as a descendant of class CDialog. The dialog box class declares the local untagged enumerated type with the single value IDD (which is initialized with the dialog box resource ID of IDD_ABOUTBOX). The class also declares a constructor and the member function DoDataExchange. The constructor CAboutDlg (shown in lines 102 to 106) merely invokes the constructor of the parent class and passes the enumerated value IDD to invoke the dialog box resource

IDD_ABOUTBOX. The code contains comments that define a placeholder for additional code you may need to insert. The function DoDataExchange (shown in lines 111 to 116) simply calls the function CDialog::DoDataExchange and offers a comment-based placeholder for possible additional code. The listing file defines the message map for the dialog box class in lines 118 to 122. This map is empty and uses a comment-based placeholder for any possible map entries that you may add.

Type

Listing B1.10. The source code for the SDIWIZ.CPP implementation file.

```
1:  // sdiwiz.cpp : Defines the class behaviors for the application.
2:  //
3:
4:  #include "stdafx.h"
5:  #include "sdiwiz.h"
6:
7:  #include "mainfrm.h"
8:  #include "sdiwidoc.h"
9:  #include "sdiwivw.h"
10:
11: #ifdef _DEBUG
12: #undef THIS_FILE
13: static char BASED_CODE THIS_FILE[] = __FILE__;
14: #endif
15:
16: /////////////////////////////////////////////////////////////////////////////
17: // CSdiwizApp
18:
19: BEGIN_MESSAGE_MAP(CSdiwizApp, CWinApp)
20:     //{{AFX_MSG_MAP(CSdiwizApp)
21:     ON_COMMAND(ID_APP_ABOUT, OnAppAbout)
22: // NOTE - the ClassWizard will add and remove mapping macros here.
23: //    DO NOT EDIT what you see in these blocks of generated code!
24:     //}}AFX_MSG_MAP
25:     // Standard file based document commands
26:     ON_COMMAND(ID_FILE_NEW, CWinApp::OnFileNew)
27:     ON_COMMAND(ID_FILE_OPEN, CWinApp::OnFileOpen)
28: END_MESSAGE_MAP()
29:
30: /////////////////////////////////////////////////////////////////////////////
31: // CSdiwizApp construction
32:
33: CSdiwizApp::CSdiwizApp()
34: {
35:     // TODO: add construction code here,
36:     // Place all significant initialization in InitInstance
37: }
38:
39: /////////////////////////////////////////////////////////////////////////////
40: // The one and only CSdiwizApp object
41:
42: CSdiwizApp theApp;
```

```

///////////////////////////////////////////////////////////////////
// CSdiwizApp initialization

BOOL CSdiwizApp::InitInstance()
{
  // Standard initialization
  // If you are not using these features and wish to reduce the
  // size of your final executable, you should remove from the
  // following the specific initialization routines you do not
  // need.

  LoadStdProfileSettings();  // Load standard INI file options
                             // (including MRU)

  // Register the application's document templates.  Document
  // templates serve as the connection between documents,
  // frame windows and views.

  CSingleDocTemplate* pDocTemplate;
  pDocTemplate = new CSingleDocTemplate(
                    IDR_MAINFRAME,
                    RUNTIME_CLASS(CSdiwizDoc),
                    RUNTIME_CLASS(CMainFrame), // main SDI frame
                                               // window
                    RUNTIME_CLASS(CSdiwizView));
  AddDocTemplate(pDocTemplate);

  // create a new (empty) document
  OnFileNew();

  if (m_lpCmdLine[0] != '\0')
  {
    // TODO: add command line processing here
  }

  return TRUE;
}

///////////////////////////////////////////////////////////////////
// CAboutDlg dialog used for App About

class CAboutDlg : public CDialog
{
public:
    CAboutDlg();

// Dialog Data
    //{{AFX_DATA(CAboutDlg)
    enum { IDD = IDD_ABOUTBOX };
    //}}AFX_DATA

// Implementation
protected:
```

continues

Listing B1.10. continued

```
  virtual void DoDataExchange(CDataExchange* pDX); // DDX/DDV
                                                   // support
  //{{AFX_MSG(CAboutDlg)
    // No message handlers
  //}}AFX_MSG
  DECLARE_MESSAGE_MAP()
};

CAboutDlg::CAboutDlg() : CDialog(CAboutDlg::IDD)
{
    //{{AFX_DATA_INIT(CAboutDlg)
    //}}AFX_DATA_INIT
}

void CAboutDlg::DoDataExchange(CDataExchange* pDX)
{
    CDialog::DoDataExchange(pDX);
    //{{AFX_DATA_MAP(CAboutDlg)
    //}}AFX_DATA_MAP
}

BEGIN_MESSAGE_MAP(CAboutDlg, CDialog)
    //{{AFX_MSG_MAP(CAboutDlg)
          // No message handlers
    //}}AFX_MSG_MAP
END_MESSAGE_MAP()

// App command to run the dialog
void CSdiwizApp::OnAppAbout()
{
     CAboutDlg aboutDlg;
     aboutDlg.DoModal();
}

/////////////////////////////////////////////////////////////////
// CSdiwizApp commands
```

The File STDAFX.CPP

The implementation file merely contains a single `#include` directive to include the header file STDAFX.H.

Type **Listing B1.11. The source code for the STDAFX.CPP implementation file.**

```
// stdafx.cpp : source file that includes just the standard
//   includes
//   sdiwiz.pch will be the pre-compiled header
//   stdafx.obj will contain the pre-compiled type information
```

```
#include "stdafx.h"
```

The File MAINFRM.CPP

The file MAINFRM.CPP, shown in Listing B1.12, contains the minimal implementation of the window frame class `CMainFrame`. The listing shows in lines 19 to 24 a message map with no map entries—only a comment-based placeholder for possible map entries. The class offers a *dummy* implementation for the constructor and destructor. I say *dummy* because neither member has any statement and neither member calls the corresponding member of the parent class. The listing contains the implementation for the member functions `AssertValid` and `Dump`. Each of these functions invokes the version of that function defined in the parent class.

Type

Listing B1.12. The source code for the MAINFRM.CPP implementation file.

```
1:  // mainfrm.cpp : implementation of the CMainFrame class
2:  //
3:
4:  #include "stdafx.h"
5:  #include "sdiwiz.h"
6:
7:  #include "mainfrm.h"
8:
9:  #ifdef _DEBUG
10: #undef THIS_FILE
11: static char BASED_CODE THIS_FILE[] = __FILE__;
12: #endif
13:
14: /////////////////////////////////////////////////////////////////////////////
15: // CMainFrame
16:
17: IMPLEMENT_DYNCREATE(CMainFrame, CFrameWnd)
18:
19: BEGIN_MESSAGE_MAP(CMainFrame, CFrameWnd)
20:     //{{AFX_MSG_MAP(CMainFrame)
21: // NOTE - the ClassWizard will add and remove mapping macros here.
22: //    DO NOT EDIT what you see in these blocks of generated code !
23:       //}}AFX_MSG_MAP
24: END_MESSAGE_MAP()
25:
26: /////////////////////////////////////////////////////////////////////////////
27: // CMainFrame construction/destruction
28:
29: CMainFrame::CMainFrame()
```

continues

Listing B1.12. continued

```
{
     // TODO: add member initialization code here

}

CMainFrame::~CMainFrame()
{
}

/////////////////////////////////////////////////////////////////////////////
// CMainFrame diagnostics

#ifdef _DEBUG
void CMainFrame::AssertValid() const
{
     CFrameWnd::AssertValid();
}

void CMainFrame::Dump(CDumpContext& dc) const
{
     CFrameWnd::Dump(dc);
}

#endif //_DEBUG

/////////////////////////////////////////////////////////////////////////////
// CMainFrame message handlers
```

The File SDIWIVW.CPP

The file SDIWIVW.CPP, whose contents appear in Listing B1.13, offers the implementation of the view class `CSdiAppView`. The listing shows a message map (in lines 20 to 25) with no map entries—only a comment-based placeholder for possible map entries. The class offers a dummy implementation for the constructor and destructor—neither member has any statement and neither member calls the corresponding member of the parent class. The listing offers a minimal implementation for the member function `OnDraw`, shown in lines 43 to 49. The function declares the instance `pDoc` as a pointer to the application's document. The listing also offers the implementation for the member functions `AssertValid` and `Dump`. Each of these functions invokes the version of that function declared in the parent class.

Listing B1.13. The source code for the SDIWIVW.CPP implementation file.

```
1:  // sdiwivw.cpp : implementation of the CSdiwizView class
2:  //
```

```

#include "stdafx.h"
#include "sdiwiz.h"

#include "sdiwidoc.h"
#include "sdiwivw.h"

#ifdef _DEBUG
#undef THIS_FILE
static char BASED_CODE THIS_FILE[] = __FILE__;
#endif

/////////////////////////////////////////////////////////////////
// CSdiwizView

IMPLEMENT_DYNCREATE(CSdiwizView, CView)

BEGIN_MESSAGE_MAP(CSdiwizView, CView)
    //{{AFX_MSG_MAP(CSdiwizView)
// NOTE - the ClassWizard will add and remove mapping macros here.
//    DO NOT EDIT what you see in these blocks of generated code!
    //}}AFX_MSG_MAP
END_MESSAGE_MAP()

/////////////////////////////////////////////////////////////////
// CSdiwizView construction/destruction

CSdiwizView::CSdiwizView()
{
     // TODO: add construction code here

}

CSdiwizView::~CSdiwizView()
{
}

/////////////////////////////////////////////////////////////////
// CSdiwizView drawing

void CSdiwizView::OnDraw(CDC* pDC)
{
     CSdiwizDoc* pDoc = GetDocument();
     ASSERT_VALID(pDoc);

     // TODO: add draw code for native data here
}

/////////////////////////////////////////////////////////////////
// CSdiwizView diagnostics

#ifdef _DEBUG
void CSdiwizView::AssertValid() const
{
```

continues

Listing B1.13. continued

```
        CView::AssertValid();
}

void CSdiwizView::Dump(CDumpContext& dc) const
{
        CView::Dump(dc);
}

CSdiwizDoc* CSdiwizView::GetDocument() // non-debug version is
                                       // inline
{
        ASSERT(m_pDocument->IsKindOf(RUNTIME_CLASS(CSdiwizDoc)));
        return (CSdiwizDoc*)m_pDocument;
}
#endif //_DEBUG

/////////////////////////////////////////////////////////////////
// CSdiwizView message handlers
```

The File SDIWIDOC.CPP

The file SDIWIDOC.CPP, shown in Listing B1.14, provides the implementation for the document class `CSdiwizDoc`. The listing shows a message map (in lines 19 to 24) with no map entries—only a comment-based placeholder for possible map entries. The class offers a dummy implementation for the constructor and destructor—neither member has any statement and neither member calls the corresponding member of the parent class. The listing offers the implementations for the following member functions:

1. The Boolean function `OnNewDocument` in lines 39 to 48. This function invokes the parent's `OnNewDocument` function and ends up returning the Boolean value of the invoked function. The function has comment-based placeholders for additional code.
2. The function `Serialize` in lines 53 to 63. This minimal function supports persistent objects.
3. The debug-related function `AssertValid` in lines 69 to 72. This function simply invokes the parent's version.
4. The debug-related function `Dump` in lines 74 to 77. This function merely calls the parent's version.

Type

Listing B1.14. The source code for the SDIWIDOC.CPP implementation file.

```
1:  // sdiwidoc.cpp : implementation of the CSdiwizDoc class
2:  //
```

```

#include "stdafx.h"
#include "sdiwiz.h"

#include "sdiwidoc.h"

#ifdef _DEBUG
#undef THIS_FILE
static char BASED_CODE THIS_FILE[] = __FILE__;
#endif

/////////////////////////////////////////////////////////////////
// CSdiwizDoc

IMPLEMENT_DYNCREATE(CSdiwizDoc, CDocument)

BEGIN_MESSAGE_MAP(CSdiwizDoc, CDocument)
     //{{AFX_MSG_MAP(CSdiwizDoc)
// NOTE - the ClassWizard will add and remove mapping macros here.
//    DO NOT EDIT what you see in these blocks of generated code!
     //}}AFX_MSG_MAP
END_MESSAGE_MAP()

/////////////////////////////////////////////////////////////////
// CSdiwizDoc construction/destruction

CSdiwizDoc::CSdiwizDoc()
{
     // TODO: add one-time construction code here

}

CSdiwizDoc::~CSdiwizDoc()
{
}

BOOL CSdiwizDoc::OnNewDocument()
{
      if (!CDocument::OnNewDocument())
            return FALSE;

     // TODO: add reinitialization code here
     // (SDI documents will reuse this document)

     return TRUE;
}

/////////////////////////////////////////////////////////////////
// CSdiwizDoc serialization

void CSdiwizDoc::Serialize(CArchive& ar)
{
     if (ar.IsStoring())
     {
```

continues

Listing B1.14. continued

```
            // TODO: add storing code here
        }
        else
        {
            // TODO: add loading code here
        }
}

/////////////////////////////////////////////////////////////////////////////
// CSdiwizDoc diagnostics

#ifdef _DEBUG
void CSdiwizDoc::AssertValid() const
{
        CDocument::AssertValid();
}

void CSdiwizDoc::Dump(CDumpContext& dc) const
{
        CDocument::Dump(dc);
}
#endif //_DEBUG

/////////////////////////////////////////////////////////////////////////////
// CSdiwizDoc commands
```

Summary

This chapter introduces you to the AppWizard utility and shows you how to create a minimal SDI-compliant Windows program. The chapter covers the following topics:

- The AppWizard utility assists in quickly generating the skeleton code for MFC-based Windows applications that use the document/view classes.
- The AppWizard utility runs from the Visual Workshop by selecting to create a new project whose type is an AppWizard application. The AppWizard uses a series of dialog boxes that support various kinds of features, including OLE and ODBC.
- The document and view classes support a special visual interface that uses the document class as a container of data to be viewed and modified by the user. The view classes provide the visual interface with the users, allowing them to

view the data in specific ways and edit that information. The MFC library offers a subhierarchy for the view classes. These include classes `CView`, `CScrollView`, `CFormView`, and `CEditView`. The MFC library offers class `CDocument` to support the document class.

- The chapter creates a minimal SDI-compliant program and presents its relevant headers, resource, and implementation files.

Q&A

Q Can the view of project SDIWIZ have controls?

A No, you need to derive the project's view class from class `CFormView` instead of class `CView`. The class `CFormView` uses a form resource that specifies the controls on that form.

Q Does the AppWizard utility support VBX Visual Basic controls?

A No. While Visual C++ 1.5 did support VBX controls, version 2.0 does not since the emphasis has recently shifted to the more versatile OLE controls (OCX).

Q Can I make the application's view class a descendant of class `CFrameWnd`?

A No, the AppWizard utility requires that you derive your application's view class from class `CView` or its MFC descendants.

Q Should I store AppWizard generated files in separate directories?

A Yes, because some of the names of the header files are not derived from the project name. By storing these files in separate directories, you avoid erroneous multiple-project use of the same header files.

Exercises

1. Create an SDI-compliant application which has the toolbar and the speed bar (check the **Dockable Toolbar** check box in the MFC AppWizard - Step 4 of 6 dialog box). Examine the .H and .CPP files generated by AppWizard. Compile and run the program to exercise its (minimal) features.

2. Create an SDI-compliant application that has print-related features (check the **Printing and Print Preview** check box in the MFC AppWizard - Step 4 of 6 dialog box). Examine the .H and .CPP files generated by AppWizard. Compile and run the program to exercise its (minimal) features.
3. Create an MDI-compliant application that has the toolbar and the speed bar (check the **Multiple documents** check box in MFC AppWizard - Step 1 and the **Dockable Toolbar** check box in the MFC AppWizard - Step 4 of 6 dialog box). Examine the .H and .CPP files generated by AppWizard. Compile and run the program to exercise its (minimal) features.

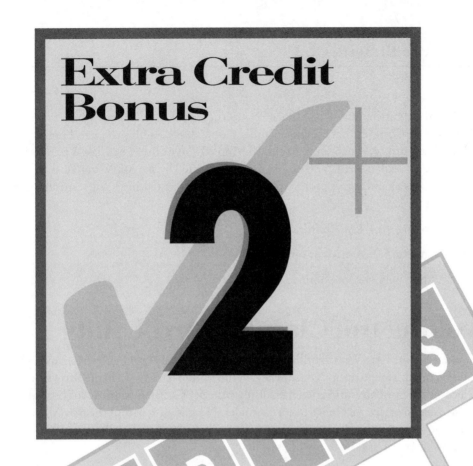

Extra Credit Bonus

2

Working with ClassWizard

In the preceding chapter, I introduce you to the AppWizard utility, which generates Windows applications that use the document/view classes. In this chapter, I present the ClassWizard utility, which supplements the AppWizard utility. The ClassWizard utility enables you to expand, edit, and extend the code emitted by the AppWizard utility. This chapter offers a hands-on approach to using the ClassWizard utility. You learn about the following topics:

- Invoking the ClassWizard utility
- Using the Message Maps options
- Adding member functions to a view

Invoking the ClassWizard Utility

You can run the ClassWizard utility from within the Visual Workbench by invoking the **ClassWizard...** menu option (the hot key for this option is Ctrl+W) in the **Browse** menu selection. The Visual Workbench then displays the MFC Class Wizard dialog box, which has a visual interface that looks like a file folder. (This look is part of the new Microsoft dialog box interface used in various new Microsoft products such as Word for Windows 6.) This interface has the following sets of options:

- The Message Maps tab offers options which manage binding messages to member functions.
- The Member Variables tab presents options which deal with the data member for the controls in dialog boxes and form views.
- The OLE Automation tab offers features to support OLE 2.0.
- The OLE Events tab provides options that define OLE events which are supported by OLE objects.
- The Class Info tab has options to manage binding messages to member functions.

I focus on the Message Maps tab options. The other options are either more advanced or more involved—either way, they are beyond the scope of this book.

The Message Maps Options

The ClassWizard utility automatically selects the Message Maps options in the MFC Class Wizard dialog box. These options permit you to add a member function in order to handle a message, delete a message-handling member function, and edit a message-handling member function. The Message Maps options display the following controls, which also appear in Figure B2.1:

- The **Class Name** drop-down combo box allows you to select a class in the current project.
- A static text control states the names of the header and implementation files that contain the declaration and implementation of the selected file, respectively.
- The **Object IDs** list box lists the name of the currently selected class, as well as the IDs of the menu options.
- The **Messages** list box lists the available messages for the currently selected item in the **Object IDs** list box. The **Messages** list box displays a hand icon to the left of a message; the message includes an associated member function.
- The **Member Functions** list box lists the current set of member functions for the currently selected item in the **Object IDs** list box.
- The **Description** static text explains the task of the currently selected item in the **Messages** list box.
- The **Add Class...** pushbutton adds a new class to the project. The new class must be related to a dialog box or a view.
- The **Add Function** pushbutton adds a new message-handling member function in the **Member Functions** list box. This new member function corresponds to the currently selected message in the **Messages** list box.
- The **Delete Function** pushbutton deletes the currently selected item in the **Member Functions** list box.
- The **Edit Code** pushbutton edits the currently selected item in the **Member Functions** list box. This control causes the Visual Workbench to close the MFC Class Wizard dialog box and to open the source code window containing the targeted member function. In addition, the Visual Workbench highlights the name of that member function.
- The **OK**, **Cancel**, and **Help** pushbuttons.

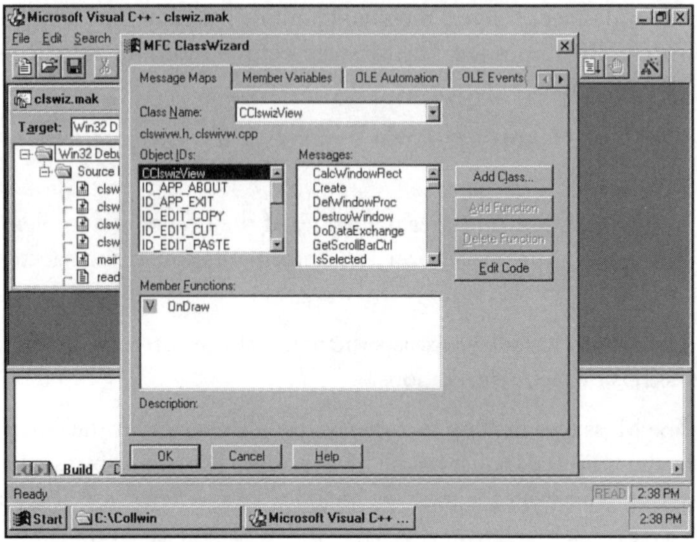

Figure B2.1. *A sample session with the MFC ClassWizard dialog box displaying the Message Maps options.*

Adding Member Functions to the View Class

In this section, I use the next example, project CLSWIZ, to explain the process of adding new member functions to the source code files. The process of creating this example encompasses several stages. The first stage involves the AppWizard utility, which creates the skeleton source code. The second stage involves the ClassWizard, which customizes the skeleton code by adding declarations and statements to support message-handling member functions. The last stage involves the manual insertion of code.

Before I discuss the various program-building stages, let me present the features of the program. This program is built using a minimal SDI-compliant AppWizard output, equivalent to the program I presented in the last chapter. It adds the following features:

- The program displays the current mouse coordinates in the upper left corner of the view.

- The program echoes keyboard input to a string (which I'll call the *input string*) that appears below the mouse coordinates. The input string has a limited capacity. When you reach that limit, the program wraps further keyboard input. You can delete the last input by clicking the left mouse button while holding down the Shift key. You can also erase the entire input string by clicking the right mouse button while holding down the Shift key. (See Table B2.1 for a summary of the supported mouse clicks.)
- The program displays the current date and time when you click the right mouse button. If you hold down the Ctrl key while clicking the right mouse button, the current time is displayed.
- The program supports a simple timer. To start the timer, click the left mouse button. To view the elapsed time, click the same mouse button. To view the elapsed time and reset the timer, click the left mouse button while holding down the Ctrl key.

Table B2.1 shows a summary of the program's features that use the mouse button clicks.

Table B2.1. The features of the sample program that use the mouse button clicks.

Mouse Button Clicked	Control Key	Purpose
Left		Starts timer or displays elapsed time
Left	Ctrl	Displays elapsed time and resets timer
Left	Shift	Deletes the last character in the input string
Right		Displays the date and time
Right	Ctrl	Displays the time
Right	Shift	Clears the input string

Now that you understand the program's features, let's look at the first stage of building the program.

Using the AppWizard Utility

The first stage creates the application's files using the AppWizard utility. Follow these steps:

1. Invoke the **File | New** command to create an AppWizard application.
2. Type **clswiz** as the name of the project that should be created in a directory attached to the directory \MSVC20\VC21DAY.
3. Click the **Single document** check box in the MFC AppWizard - Step 1 dialog box.
4. Click the **Next >** pushbutton to reach the MFC AppWizard - Step 4 of 6 dialog box. Clear the check marks in the check boxes of this dialog box.
5. Click the **Next >** pushbutton until you reach the MFC AppWizard - Step 6 of 6 dialog box.
6. Click the **Finish** pushbutton in the MFC AppWizard - Step 6 of 6 dialog box.
7. Click the **OK** pushbutton in the New Project Information dialog box.

The preceding steps create a minimal MFC-based Windows viewer application. The files for this project are similar to those of project SDIWIZ, which is covered in the preceding chapter. The differences lie in the names of the classes; everything else is identical. This similarity allows me to bypass presenting and discussing the various files generated by the AppWizard utility. If you would like to refresh your memory, look at the header and implementation files for the document and view classes.

Using the ClassWizard Utility

The second stage of building the program involves using the ClassWizard utility. Invoke the ClassWizard utility and select the class `CClswizView` from the **Class Name** combo box. Now select the ID `CClswizView` from the **Object IDs** list box. The latter selection shows the set of possible messages that can be handled by the view class. Choose the message `WM_MOUSEMOVE` from the **Messages** list box, and then click the **Add Function** pushbutton. This step displays the name of the member function `OnMouseMove` in the **Member Functions** list box. Repeat the message selection and function addition steps for the messages `WM_LBUTTONDOWN`, `WM_RBUTTONDOWN`, and `WM_CHAR`. Figure B2.2 shows the MFC Class Wizard dialog box after adding the four targeted member functions. Click the **OK** pushbutton to close the MFC Class Wizard dialog box.

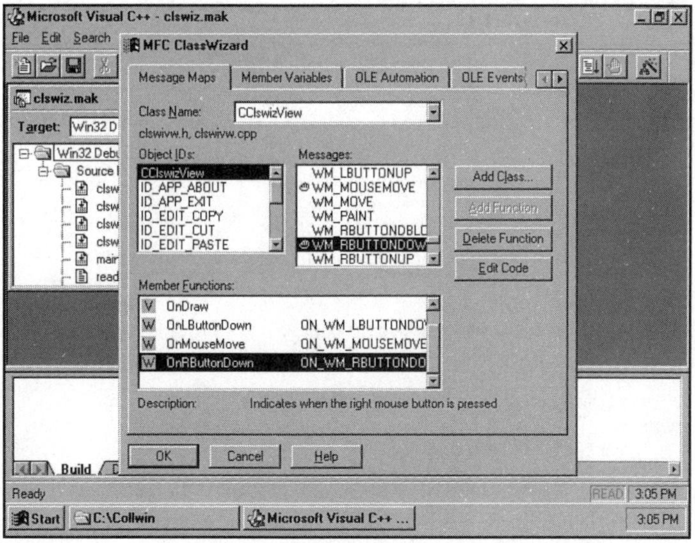

Figure B2.2. *The MFC ClassWizard dialog box after adding the four targeted member functions.*

Listing B2.1 shows the source code for the CLSWIDOC.H header file as generated by the AppWizard utility. Listing B2.2 contains the source code for the CLSWIDOC.CPP implementation file as generated by the AppWizard utility. These files are not affected by the ClassWizard utility. I am presenting them here because later I manually add some code to these files.

Listing B2.3 shows the source code for the CLSWIVW.H header file as generated by the AppWizard utility and modified by the ClassWizard utility. Listing B2.4 holds the source code for the CLSWIVW.CPP implementation file as generated by the AppWizard utility and modified by the ClassWizard utility.

Type

Listing B2.1. The source code for the CLSWIDOC.H header file as generated by the AppWizard utility.

```
// clswidoc.h : interface of the CClswizDoc class
//
/////////////////////////////////////////////////////////////////

class CClswizDoc : public CDocument
{
protected: // create from serialization only
     CClswizDoc();
     DECLARE_DYNCREATE(CClswizDoc)
```

continues

Listing B2.1. continued

```
10:
11:  // Attributes
12:  public:
13:
14:  // Operations
15:  public:
16:
17:  // Overrides
18:       // ClassWizard generated virtual function overrides
19:       //{{AFX_VIRTUAL(CClswizDoc)
20:       public:
21:       virtual BOOL OnNewDocument();
22:       //}}AFX_VIRTUAL
23:
24:  // Implementation
25:  public:
26:       virtual ~CClswizDoc();
27:       virtual void Serialize(CArchive& ar);   // overridden for
28:                                               // document i/o
29:  #ifdef _DEBUG
30:       virtual void AssertValid() const;
31:       virtual void Dump(CDumpContext& dc) const;
32:  #endif
33:
34:  protected:
35:
36:  // Generated message map functions
37:  protected:
38:       //{{AFX_MSG(CClswizDoc)
39:  // NOTE - the ClassWizard will add and remove member functions here.
40:  //    DO NOT EDIT what you see in these blocks of generated code !
41:       //}}AFX_MSG
42:       DECLARE_MESSAGE_MAP()
43:  };
44:
37:  ///////////////////////////////////////////////////////////////////////////
```

The header file CLSWIDOC.H, shown in Listing B2.1, declares the document class `CClswizDoc` as a descendant of class `CDocument` (see line 5). The derived class includes a protected constructor, a public destructor, the public member function `Serialize`, the message-handling function `OnNewDocument`, and the debug-related functions `AssertValid` and `Dump`.

Type Listing B2.2. The source code for the CLSWIDOC.CPP implementation file as generated by the AppWizard utility.

```
// clswidoc.cpp : implementation of the CClswizDoc class
//

#include "stdafx.h"
```

```
#include "clswiz.h"

#include "clswidoc.h"

#ifdef _DEBUG
#undef THIS_FILE
static char BASED_CODE THIS_FILE[] = __FILE__;
#endif

/////////////////////////////////////////////////////////////////////////////
// CClswizDoc

IMPLEMENT_DYNCREATE(CClswizDoc, CDocument)

BEGIN_MESSAGE_MAP(CClswizDoc, CDocument)
	//{{AFX_MSG_MAP(CClswizDoc)
// NOTE - the ClassWizard will add and remove mapping macros here.
//    DO NOT EDIT what you see in these blocks of generated code!
	//}}AFX_MSG_MAP
END_MESSAGE_MAP()

/////////////////////////////////////////////////////////////////////////////
// CClswizDoc construction/destruction

CClswizDoc::CClswizDoc()
{
	// TODO: add one-time construction code here

}

CClswizDoc::~CClswizDoc()
{
}

BOOL CClswizDoc::OnNewDocument()
{
	if (!CDocument::OnNewDocument())
		return FALSE;

	// TODO: add reinitialization code here
	// (SDI documents will reuse this document)

	return TRUE;
}

/////////////////////////////////////////////////////////////////////////////
// CClswizDoc serialization

void CClswizDoc::Serialize(CArchive& ar)
{
	if (ar.IsStoring())
	{
		// TODO: add storing code here
	}
	else
```

continues

Listing B2.2. continued

```
60:         {
61:             // TODO: add loading code here
62:         }
63:     }
64:
65:     /////////////////////////////////////////////////////////////////////////////
66:     // CClswizDoc diagnostics
67:
68:     #ifdef _DEBUG
69:     void CClswizDoc::AssertValid() const
70:     {
71:         CDocument::AssertValid();
72:     }
73:
74:     void CClswizDoc::Dump(CDumpContext& dc) const
75:     {
76:         CDocument::Dump(dc);
77:     }
78:     #endif //_DEBUG
79:
80:     /////////////////////////////////////////////////////////////////////////////
81:     // CClswizDoc commands
```

The file CLSWIDOC.CPP, shown in Listing B2.2, provides the implementation for the document class `CClswizDoc`. The listing shows a message map (in lines 19 to 24) with no map entries—only a comment-based placeholder for possible map entries. The class offers a dummy implementation for the constructor and destructor; neither member has any statement and neither member calls the corresponding member of the parent class. The listing offers the implementations for the following member functions:

1. The Boolean function `OnNewDocument` in lines 39 to 48. This function invokes the parent's `OnNewDocument` function and ends up returning the Boolean value of the invoked function. The function has comment-based placeholders for additional code.

2. The function `Serialize` in lines 53 to 63. This minimal function supports persistent objects.

3. The debug-related function `AssertValid` in lines 69 to 72. This function simply invokes the parent's version.

4. The debug-related function `Dump` in lines 74 to 77. This function merely calls the parent's version.

Type

Listing B2.3. The source code for the CLSWIVW.H header file as generated by the AppWizard utility and modified by the ClassWizard utility.

```
// clswivw.h : interface of the CClswizView class
//
/////////////////////////////////////////////////////////////////

class CClswizView : public CView
{
protected: // create from serialization only
     CClswizView();
     DECLARE_DYNCREATE(CClswizView)

// Attributes
public:
     CClswizDoc* GetDocument();

// Operations
public:

// Overrides
     // ClassWizard generated virtual function overrides
     //{{AFX_VIRTUAL(CClswizView)
     public:
     virtual void OnDraw(CDC* pDC);  // overridden to draw
                                     // this view
     protected:
     //}}AFX_VIRTUAL

// Implementation
public:
     virtual ~CClswizView();
#ifdef _DEBUG
     virtual void AssertValid() const;
     virtual void Dump(CDumpContext& dc) const;
#endif

protected:

// Generated message map functions
protected:
     //{{AFX_MSG(CClswizView)
     afx_msg void OnChar(UINT nChar, UINT nRepCnt, UINT nFlags);
     afx_msg void OnLButtonDown(UINT nFlags, CPoint point);
     afx_msg void OnMouseMove(UINT nFlags, CPoint point);
     afx_msg void OnRButtonDown(UINT nFlags, CPoint point);
     //}}AFX_MSG
     DECLARE_MESSAGE_MAP()
};

#ifndef _DEBUG  // debug version in clswivw.cpp
inline CClswizDoc* CClswizView::GetDocument()
   { return (CClswizDoc*)m_pDocument; }
#endif
```

continues

Listing B2.3. continued

```
52:
53: ////////////////////////////////////////////////////////////////////
```

Listing B2.3 shows the header file for the view class. Lines 40 to 43 show the declarations for the member functions `OnChar`, `OnLButtonDown`, `OnMouseMove`, and `OnRButtonDown`. The ClassWizard utility inserted the declarations for these member functions. The rest of the code was created by the AppWizard utility.

Listing B2.4. The source code for the CLSWIVW.CPP implementation file as generated by the AppWizard utility and modified by the ClassWizard utility.

```
// clswivw.cpp : implementation of the CClswizView class
//

#include "stdafx.h"
#include "clswiz.h"

#include "clswidoc.h"
#include "clswivw.h"

#ifdef _DEBUG
#undef THIS_FILE
static char BASED_CODE THIS_FILE[] = __FILE__;
#endif

/////////////////////////////////////////////////////////////////////////////
// CClswizView

IMPLEMENT_DYNCREATE(CClswizView, CView)

BEGIN_MESSAGE_MAP(CClswizView, CView)
    //{{AFX_MSG_MAP(CClswizView)
    ON_WM_CHAR()
    ON_WM_LBUTTONDOWN()
    ON_WM_MOUSEMOVE()
    ON_WM_RBUTTONDOWN()
    //}}AFX_MSG_MAP
END_MESSAGE_MAP()

/////////////////////////////////////////////////////////////////////////////
// CClswizView construction/destruction

CClswizView::CClswizView()
{
    // TODO: add construction code here

}

```

```
CClswizView::~CClswizView()
{
}

/////////////////////////////////////////////////////////////////
// CClswizView drawing

void CClswizView::OnDraw(CDC* pDC)
{
    CClswizDoc* pDoc = GetDocument();
    ASSERT_VALID(pDoc);

    // TODO: add draw code for native data here
}

/////////////////////////////////////////////////////////////////
// CClswizView diagnostics

#ifdef _DEBUG
void CClswizView::AssertValid() const
{
    CView::AssertValid();
}

void CClswizView::Dump(CDumpContext& dc) const
{
    CView::Dump(dc);
}

CClswizDoc* CClswizView::GetDocument() // non-debug version
                                       // is inline
{
    ASSERT(m_pDocument->IsKindOf(RUNTIME_CLASS(CClswizDoc)));
    return (CClswizDoc*)m_pDocument;
}
#endif //_DEBUG

/////////////////////////////////////////////////////////////////
// CClswizView message handlers

void CClswizView::OnChar(UINT nChar, UINT nRepCnt, UINT nFlags)
{
  // TODO: Add your message handler code here and/or call default

  CView::OnChar(nChar, nRepCnt, nFlags);
}

void CClswizView::OnLButtonDown(UINT nFlags, CPoint point)
{
  // TODO: Add your message handler code here and/or call default

  CView::OnLButtonDown(nFlags, point);
}

void CClswizView::OnMouseMove(UINT nFlags, CPoint point)
```

continues

Listing B2.4. continued

```
 93:  {
 94:    // TODO: Add your message handler code here and/or call default
 95:
 96:    CView::OnMouseMove(nFlags, point);
 97:  }
 98:
 99:  void CClswizView::OnRButtonDown(UINT nFlags, CPoint point)
100:  {
101:    // TODO: Add your message handler code here and/or call default
102:
103:    CView::OnRButtonDown(nFlags, point);
104:  }
```

Listing B2.4 shows the implementation file for the view class. Lines 20 to 27 contain the definition of the message map. The entries in lines 22 to 25 correspond to the four member functions added by the ClassWizard utility. This utility also inserted the message map entries for the preceding four member functions.

ClassWizard also added the minimal definitions for the new message-handling member functions. Lines 78 to 83 contain the definition of member function `OnChar`; this definition simply invokes the function `CView::OnChar`. Lines 85 to 90 contain the definition of member function `OnLButtonDown`; this definition calls the function `CView::OnLButtonDown`. Lines 92 to 97 contain the definition of member function `OnMouseMove`; this definition invokes the function `CView::OnMouseMove`. Lines 99 to 104 contain the definition of member function `OnRButtonDown`; this definition invokes the function `CView::OnRButtonDown`.

Fine-Tuning the Code

The last stage of building the program entails manual coding to fine-tune the source code. This process involves the STDAFX.H header file, the CLSWIDOC.H header file, the CLSWIDOC.CPP implementation file, and the CLSWIVW.CPP implementation file. If you are using this example and my approach, you will not need to modify the CLSWIVW header file. You can easily recode the example to add members to the view class.

> **Note:** Please note that in this chapter, manually inserted code appears in boldface text in the listings.

Listing B2.5. The modified source code for the STDAFX.H header file.

```
// stdafx.h : include file for standard system include files,
//  or project specific include files that are used frequently,
//      but are changed infrequently
//

#include <afxwin.h>         // MFC core and standard components
#include <afxext.h>         // MFC extensions

// **** START MANUALLY INSERTED CODE ****
const MaxStringLen = 30;
// **** END MANUALLY INSERTED CODE ****
```

Listing B2.5 holds the modified source code for the STDAFX.H header file. I simply added the declaration of constant `MaxStringLen`. I also surrounded the added line with special comments.

Listing B2.6. The modified source code for CLSWIDOC.H header file.

```
// clswidoc.h : interface of the CClswizDoc class
//
/////////////////////////////////////////////////////////////////////////////

class CClswizDoc : public CDocument
{
protected: // create from serialization only
     CClswizDoc();
     DECLARE_DYNCREATE(CClswizDoc)

// Attributes
public:
  // **** START MANUALLY INSERTED CODE ****
  CTime timeObj;
  long lInitTimer;
  int nIndex;
  BOOL bIsTimerOn;
  BOOL bIsStringNew;
  char szInputStr[MaxStringLen+1];
  // **** END MANUALLY INSERTED CODE ****

// Operations
public:

// Overrides
     // ClassWizard generated virtual function overrides
     //{{AFX_VIRTUAL(CClswizDoc)
     public:
     virtual BOOL OnNewDocument();
```

continues

Listing B2.6. continued

```
30:         //}}AFX_VIRTUAL
31:
32: // Implementation
33: public:
34:         virtual ~CClswizDoc();
35:         virtual void Serialize(CArchive& ar);   // overridden for
36:                                                 // document i/o
37: #ifdef _DEBUG
38:         virtual void AssertValid() const;
39:         virtual void Dump(CDumpContext& dc) const;
40: #endif
41:
42: protected:
43:
44: // Generated message map functions
45: protected:
46:         //{{AFX_MSG(CClswizDoc)
47: // NOTE - the ClassWizard will add and remove member functions here.
48: //    DO NOT EDIT what you see in these blocks of generated code !
49:         //}}AFX_MSG
50:         DECLARE_MESSAGE_MAP()
51: };
52:
53: ///////////////////////////////////////////////////////////////
```

Listing B2.6 shows the modified source code for CLSWIDOC.H header file. I inserted the declarations for the following data members (in lines 14 to 20) into the class `CClswizDoc`:

- The data member `timeObj`, which is an instance of the MFC class `CTime`. This class allows the program to easily retrieve the current system date and time using a member function of class `CTime`.
- The data member `lInitTimer` stores the initial tick count—the number of milliseconds since Windows has been running. The timer feature uses this data member.
- The data member `nIndex` specifies where the next input character is stored in the input string.
- The Boolean data member `bIsTimerOn` is the flag for the on/off state of the timer.
- The Boolean data member `bIsStringNew` is the flag for wrapping the keyboard input in the input string.
- The data member `szInputStr` stores the characters of the input string.

Listing B2.7. The modified source code for the CLSWIDOC.CPP implementation file.

```
// clswidoc.cpp : implementation of the CClswizDoc class
//

#include "stdafx.h"
#include "clswiz.h"

#include "clswidoc.h"

#ifdef _DEBUG
#undef THIS_FILE
static char BASED_CODE THIS_FILE[] = __FILE__;
#endif

/////////////////////////////////////////////////////////////////
// CClswizDoc

IMPLEMENT_DYNCREATE(CClswizDoc, CDocument)

BEGIN_MESSAGE_MAP(CClswizDoc, CDocument)
     //{{AFX_MSG_MAP(CClswizDoc)
// NOTE - the ClassWizard will add and remove mapping macros here.
//    DO NOT EDIT what you see in these blocks of generated code!
     //}}AFX_MSG_MAP
END_MESSAGE_MAP()

/////////////////////////////////////////////////////////////////
// CClswizDoc construction/destruction

CClswizDoc::CClswizDoc()
{
    // TODO: add one-time construction code here
  // **** START MANUALLY INSERTED CODE ****
  nIndex = 0;
  szInputStr[0] = '\0';
  bIsTimerOn = FALSE;
  bIsStringNew = TRUE;
  // **** END MANUALLY INSERTED CODE ****
}

CClswizDoc::~CClswizDoc()
{
}

BOOL CClswizDoc::OnNewDocument()
{
     if (!CDocument::OnNewDocument())
           return FALSE;

     // TODO: add reinitialization code here
     // (SDI documents will reuse this document)

```

continues

Listing B2.7. continued

```
52:         return TRUE;
53:  }
54:
55:  ////////////////////////////////////////////////////////////////////
56:  // CClswizDoc serialization
57:
58:  void CClswizDoc::Serialize(CArchive& ar)
59:  {
60:         if (ar.IsStoring())
61:         {
62:              // TODO: add storing code here
63:         }
64:         else
65:         {
66:              // TODO: add loading code here
67:         }
68:  }
69:
70:  ////////////////////////////////////////////////////////////////////
71:  // CClswizDoc diagnostics
72:
73:  #ifdef _DEBUG
74:  void CClswizDoc::AssertValid() const
75:  {
76:         CDocument::AssertValid();
77:  }
78:
79:  void CClswizDoc::Dump(CDumpContext& dc) const
80:  {
81:         CDocument::Dump(dc);
82:  }
83:  #endif //_DEBUG
84:
85:  ////////////////////////////////////////////////////////////////////
86:  // CClswizDoc commands
```

Listing B2.7 shows the modified source code for the CLSWIDOC.CPP implementation file. I inserted the following initialization statements into the constructor `CClswizDoc` (in lines 33 to 36):

- The statement in line 33 assigns `0` to the member `nIndex`.
- The statement in line 34 assigns the null character to the first element of member `szInputStr`.
- The statement in line 35 assigns `FALSE` to the timer flag, member `bIsTimerOn`.
- The statement in line 36 assigns `FALSE` to the text wrap flag, member `bIsStringNew`.

Listing B2.8. The modified source code for the CLSWIVW.CPP implementation file.

```
// clswivw.cpp : implementation of the CClswizView class
//

#include "stdafx.h"
#include "clswiz.h"

#include "clswidoc.h"
#include "clswivw.h"

// **** START MANUALLY INSERTED CODE ****
#include <stdio.h>
#include <string.h>

const X0 = 10;
const X1 = 10;
const Y0 = 10;
const Y1 = 30;
// **** END MANUALLY INSERTED CODE ****

#ifdef _DEBUG
#undef THIS_FILE
static char BASED_CODE THIS_FILE[] = __FILE__;
#endif

/////////////////////////////////////////////////////////////////
// CClswizView

IMPLEMENT_DYNCREATE(CClswizView, CView)

BEGIN_MESSAGE_MAP(CClswizView, CView)
    //{{AFX_MSG_MAP(CClswizView)
    ON_WM_CHAR()
    ON_WM_LBUTTONDOWN()
    ON_WM_MOUSEMOVE()
    ON_WM_RBUTTONDOWN()
    //}}AFX_MSG_MAP
END_MESSAGE_MAP()

/////////////////////////////////////////////////////////////////
// CClswizView construction/destruction

CClswizView::CClswizView()
{
    // TODO: add construction code here

}

CClswizView::~CClswizView()
{
}

/////////////////////////////////////////////////////////////////
// CClswizView drawing
```

continues

Listing B2.8. continued

```

void CClswizView::OnDraw(CDC* pDC)
{
    CClswizDoc* pDoc = GetDocument();
    ASSERT_VALID(pDoc);

    // TODO: add draw code for native data here
}

/////////////////////////////////////////////////////////////////////////////
// CClswizView diagnostics

#ifdef _DEBUG
void CClswizView::AssertValid() const
{
    CView::AssertValid();
}

void CClswizView::Dump(CDumpContext& dc) const
{
    CView::Dump(dc);
}

CClswizDoc* CClswizView::GetDocument() // non-debug version
                                       // is inline
{
    ASSERT(m_pDocument->IsKindOf(RUNTIME_CLASS(CClswizDoc)));
    return (CClswizDoc*)m_pDocument;
}
#endif //_DEBUG

/////////////////////////////////////////////////////////////////////////////
// CClswizView message handlers

void CClswizView::OnChar(UINT nChar, UINT nRepCnt, UINT nFlags)
{
  // **** START MANUALLY INSERTED CODE ****
  CClswizDoc* pDoc = GetDocument();
  CClientDC dc(this);

  if (pDoc->nIndex < MaxStringLen) {
    pDoc->szInputStr[pDoc->nIndex++] = char(nChar);
    if (pDoc->bIsStringNew)
      pDoc->szInputStr[pDoc->nIndex] = '\0';
  }
  else { // reached the end
    pDoc->nIndex = 0;
    pDoc->bIsStringNew = FALSE;
    pDoc->szInputStr[pDoc->nIndex++] = char(nChar);
  }
  CString tempStr(pDoc->szInputStr);
  tempStr += CString(' ',
                   2 * (MaxStringLen - strlen(pDoc->szInputStr)));
  dc.TextOut(X1, Y1, tempStr);
```

```
  // **** END MANUALLY INSERTED CODE ****
}

void CClswizView::OnLButtonDown(UINT nFlags, CPoint point)
{
  // **** START MANUALLY INSERTED CODE ****
  CClswizDoc* pDoc = GetDocument();
  char szStr[MaxStringLen+1];
  int n;
  CClientDC dc(this);

  if (nFlags & MK_CONTROL) {
    // read and reset timer
    if (pDoc->bIsTimerOn) {
      pDoc->bIsTimerOn = FALSE;
      sprintf(szStr, "%3.3lf seconds elapsed",
              (GetTickCount() - pDoc->lInitTimer) / 1000.0);
      MessageBox(szStr, "Timer Event",
                 MB_OK | MB_ICONINFORMATION);
    }
  }
  else if (nFlags & MK_SHIFT) {
     n = strlen(pDoc->szInputStr);
     if (n > 0) {
       pDoc->szInputStr[n-1] = '\0';
       if (pDoc->nIndex > 0)
         pDoc->nIndex--;
       CString tempStr(pDoc->szInputStr);
       tempStr += CString(' ', 2 * (MaxStringLen - n - 1));
       dc.TextOut(X1, Y1, tempStr);
     }
  }
  else {
    if (pDoc->bIsTimerOn) {
      sprintf(szStr, "%3.3lf seconds elapsed",
              (GetTickCount() - pDoc->lInitTimer) / 1000.0);
      MessageBox(szStr, "Timer Event",
                 MB_OK | MB_ICONINFORMATION);
    }
    else {
      pDoc->bIsTimerOn = TRUE;
      pDoc->lInitTimer = GetTickCount();
      MessageBox("Timer is now On!", "Timer Event",
                 MB_OK | MB_ICONEXCLAMATION);
    }
  }
  // **** END MANUALLY INSERTED CODE ****
}

void CClswizView::OnMouseMove(UINT nFlags, CPoint point)
{
  // **** START MANUALLY INSERTED CODE ****
  CClswizDoc* pDoc = GetDocument();
  char szStr[MaxStringLen+1];
  CClientDC dc(this);

```

continues

Listing B2.8. continued

```
164:    sprintf(szStr, "[%03d, %03d]", point.x, point.y);
165:    dc.TextOut(X0, Y0, szStr, strlen(szStr));
166:    // **** END MANUALLY INSERTED CODE ****
167:  }
168:
169:  void CClswizView::OnRButtonDown(UINT nFlags, CPoint point)
170:  {
171:    // **** START MANUALLY INSERTED CODE ****
172:    CClswizDoc* pDoc = GetDocument();
173:    char szStr[MaxStringLen+1];
174:    CClientDC dc(this);
175:
176:    if (nFlags & MK_CONTROL) {
177:      // show the time
178:      pDoc->timeObj = CTime::GetCurrentTime();
179:      sprintf(szStr, "Time is %02d:%02d:%02d",
180:              pDoc->timeObj.GetHour(),
181:              pDoc->timeObj.GetMinute(),
182:              pDoc->timeObj.GetSecond());
183:       MessageBox(szStr, "Current Date/Time",
184:                  MB_OK | MB_ICONINFORMATION);
185:
186:    }
187:    else if (nFlags & MK_SHIFT) {
188:      CString tempStr(' ', 2 * MaxStringLen);
189:      pDoc->szInputStr[0] = '\0';
190:      pDoc->nIndex = 0;
191:      pDoc->bIsStringNew = TRUE;
192:      dc.TextOut(X1, Y1, tempStr);
193:    }
194:    else {
195:      pDoc->timeObj = CTime::GetCurrentTime();
196:      sprintf(szStr, "Date is %02d/%02d/%4d, Time is %02d:%02d:%02d",
197:              pDoc->timeObj.GetMonth(), pDoc->timeObj.GetDay(),
198:              pDoc->timeObj.GetYear(),  pDoc->timeObj.GetHour(),
199:              pDoc->timeObj.GetMinute(), pDoc->timeObj.GetSecond());
200:       MessageBox(szStr, "Current Date/Time",
201:                  MB_OK | MB_ICONINFORMATION);
202:
203:    }
204:    // **** END MANUALLY INSERTED CODE ****
205:  }
```

Listing B2.8 contains the modified source code for the CLSWIVW.CPP implementation file. I added the `#include` directives in lines 11 and 12 to include the STDIO.H and STRING.H header files, respectively. I also added the declarations of global constants `X0`, `X1`, `Y0`, and `Y1` in lines 14 to 17.

In addition, I inserted the code for the following message-handling member functions:

1. The member function `OnChar` responds to the Windows message `WM_CHAR` (which echoes keyboard input) by performing the following tasks:
   - ☐ Declares the pointer-to-document `pDoc`.
   - ☐ Declares the device context **dc**.
   - ☐ Determines whether the document's data member `nIndex` has a value that is less than that of global constant `MaxStringLen`. If this condition is true, the function performs the following subtasks:
     - ☐ Assigns the input character (obtained using the expression `char(nChar)`) to the next character of the input string. This task also increments the document's data member `nIndex`.
     - ☐ Assigns a null character to the character `pDoc->nIndex` if the text wrap flag is `TRUE`.
     - ☐ If the document's data member `nIndex` is equal to or greater than the constant `MaxStringLen`, the function performs the following subtasks:
     - ☐ Assigns 0 to the document's data member `nIndex` to reset the character insertion index.
     - ☐ Assigns `FALSE` to the document's data member `bIsStringNew` to clear the wrap text flag.
     - ☐ Assigns the input character to the next character in the document's data member `szInputStr`.
   - ☐ Creates a temporary `CString` object, `tempStr`, by using the document's data member `szInputStr`.
   - ☐ Appends space characters to the `tempStr` object.
   - ☐ Displays the `tempStr` object by sending the C++ message TextOut to the object `dc`.
2. The member function `OnLButtonDown` responds to the left mouse click. The function declares the pointer-to-document `pDoc` to access the public data members of class `CClswizDoc`. The function also declares a device context instance, `dc`, as well as the local string variable `szStr`, and integer variable `n`.

The function has a set of `if` statements to handle the cases when you hold down the Ctrl or Shift key while clicking the left mouse button. The function detects holding down the Ctrl key using the expression `nFlags & MK_CONTROL`. This expression performs a bitwise `AND` operation between the parameter `Flags` and the predefined constant `MK_CONTROL`. If the expression yields a non-zero value, the function performs the following tasks to display the elapsed time and reset the (virtual) timer:

- Verifies that the timer is on by examining the Boolean value in the document's data member `bIsTimerOn`. The function uses the local pointer-to-document `pDoc` to access the document's public data members (including member `bIsTimerOn`). If the tested expression is non-zero, the `if` statement performs the remaining tasks.
- Assigns `FALSE` to the document's data member `bIsTimerOn` to logically turn off the timer. (This action has no effect on Windows timers.)
- Creates a string image for the elapsed time. This task involves using the function `sprintf`. The function calculates the number of elapsed seconds using the expression `(GetTickCount() - pDoc->lInitTimer) / 1000.0`. The Windows API function `GetTickCount` obtains the tick count.
- Displays the number of elapsed seconds in a message dialog box.

The function detects holding down the Shift key by using the expression `nFlags & MK_SHIFT`. This expression performs a bitwise `AND` operation between the parameter `Flags` and the predefined constant `MK_SHIFT`. If the expression yields a non-zero value, the function performs the following tasks to delete the last character in the input string:

- Stores the current length of the string in the local variable `n`.
- Verifies that the variable `n` stores a positive integer. If this condition is true, the outer `if` statement performs the remaining tasks.
- Assigns the null character to the index `n-1` of the document's data member `szInputStr`.
- Decrements the document's data member `nIndex` if that member stores a positive value.
- Creates the local `CString` instance `tempStr` using the input string.
- Appends extra space characters to the `tempStr` object. The function specifies `2 * (MaxStringLen - n - 1)` to be doubly sure that the output covers all the characters. (These extra spaces provide a quick solution to the problem of displaying characters in a proportional font.)

- Displays the tempStr object by sending the C++ message TextOut to the device context object dc.

The else clause in the function OnLButtonDown performs the following tasks to trigger the timer (or read the elapsed time without resetting the timer):

- If the document's data member bIsTimerOn is TRUE, the function creates a string image of the elapsed time and then displays that image in a message dialog box. Otherwise, the function assigns TRUE to the document's data member bIsTimerOn to logically turn on the timer, assigns the result of the Windows API function GetTickCount to the document's data member lInitTimer, and brings up a message box dialog to let you know that the timer is on.

3. The member function OnMouseMove displays the current mouse coordinates in the upper left corner of the view. The function responds to the Windows message WM_MOUSEMOVE by performing the following tasks:
   - Declares the local pointer-to-document pDoc.
   - Declares the local string variable szStr.
   - Declares the device context object dc.
   - Creates a string image of the current mouse coordinates using the function sprintf. The members x and y of the parameter point provide the sought mouse coordinates.
   - Displays the string image by sending the C++ message TextOut to the object dc. The arguments for this message are constant X0, constant Y0, local variable szStr, and the expression strlen(szStr).
4. The member function OnRButtonDown responds to the right mouse click. The function declares the pointer-to-document pDoc to access the public data members of class CClswizDoc. The function also declares a device context instance, dc, as well as the local string variable szStr. The function has a set of if statements to handle the cases when you hold down the Ctrl or Shift key while clicking the right mouse button. The function detects holding down the Ctrl key using the expression nFlags & MK_CONTROL. If the expression yields a non-zero value, the function performs the following tasks to display the current system time:
   - Obtains the current system date and time by invoking the static member function CTime::GetCurrentTime. This static function returns a CTime object, which is assigned to the document's data member timeObj.

- Creates a string image for the current time. This task uses the function `sprintf` and the results of sending the C++ messages `GetHour`, `GetMinute`, and `GetSecond` to the document's data member `timeObj`.
- Displays the string image of the current time in a message dialog box.

The function detects holding down the Shift key using the expression `nFlags & MK_SHIFT`. This expression performs a bitwise `AND` between the parameter Flags and the predefined constant `MK_SHIFT`. If the expression yields a non-zero value, the function performs the following tasks to delete all the characters in the input string:

- Creates a `CString` instance `tempStr` that contains `2 * MaxStringLen` space characters.
- Assigns the null character to the first element of the input string.
- Assigns `0` to the document's data member `nIndex` to reset the character index.
- Assigns `TRUE` to the text wrap flag `bIsStringNew`.
- Displays the `tempStr` object by sending the C++ message `TextOut` to the device context object `dc`.

The `else` clause in the function `OnLButtonDown` performs the following tasks to display the current system date and time:

- Obtains the current system date and time by invoking the static member function `CTime::GetCurrentTime`. This static function returns a `CTime` object that is assigned to the document's data member `timeObj`.
- Creates a string image for the current date and time. This task uses the function `sprintf` and the results of sending the C++ messages `GetMonth`, `GetDay`, `GetYear`, `GetHour`, `GetMinute`, and `GetSecond` to the document's data member `timeObj`.
- Displays the string image of the current time in a message dialog box.

Compile and run the CLSWIZ.EXE program. Experiment with moving the mouse, typing text, editing the text (using the special mouse clicks), and displaying the current date/time and elapsed time. Figure B2.3 shows a sample session displaying the mouse cursor location, input text, and the current date/time message box. Figure B2.4 shows another sample session with the elapsed time and part of the input string (in Figure B2.3) deleted.

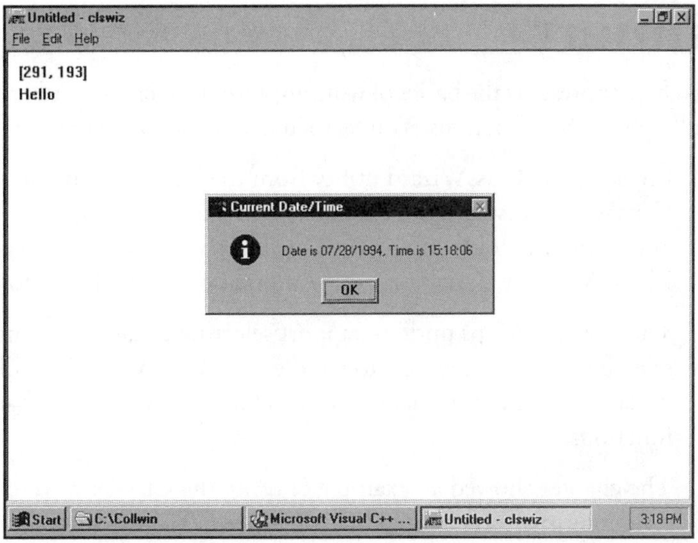

Figure B2.3. *A sample session with CLSWIZ.EXE displaying the mouse cursor location, input text, and the current date/time message box.*

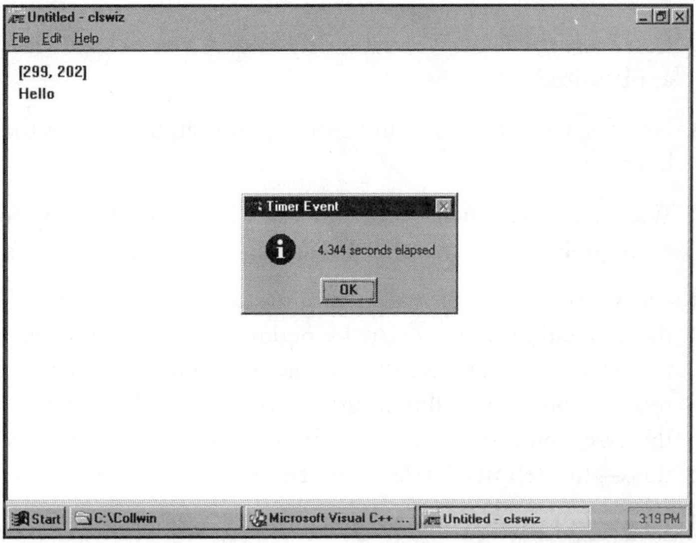

Figure B2.4. *A sample session with program CLSWIZ.EXE displaying the elapsed time and part of the input string (in Figure B2.3) deleted.*

Summary

This chapter presents the basics of working with the ClassWizard utility to add message-handling member functions. You learned about the following:

- Invoking the ClassWizard utility from the **Tools** menu selection. The ClassWizard displays the MFC Class Wizard dialog box, which includes the new Windows folder interface. This interface allows you to access the Message Maps, Member Variables, OLE Automation, and Class Info options.
- The Message Maps options support selecting a class or a control, and then selecting a related message to handle. The ClassWizard handles creating the declarations and minimal definitions for the new message handler member functions.
- The chapter showed an example of using the ClassWizard to add member functions to a view created by AppWizard. The example shows how to handle the Windows messages related to moving the mouse, clicking the left and right mouse buttons, and typing characters from the keyboard.

Q&A

Q Can I use the ClassWizard utility to add a nonvisual class to an application?

A No. The ClassWizard utility only supports adding classes that model dialog boxes or views.

Q What happens when I reinvoke the ClassWizard utility to delete a message-handling member function?

A The ClassWizard utility displays a message box telling you that it has removed the declarations of the deleted function but not its implementation. This means that you have to remove the function's definition manually. One advantage of this method is the ability to easily recover from deleting the wrong function! In this case, you can add the previously deleted function to restore its declarations—the definition already exists!

Q How can I modify the document and view files for project CLSWIZ?

A Because CLSWIZ has a single view, you can move the document's member functions to the view class. This approach still makes the program work, but defeats the purpose of having the document class as the repertoire of the viewed data.

Exercises

1. Alter the member function `CClswizView:OnChar` to automatically translate lowercase characters into uppercase.

2. Alter the member functions `CClswizView::OnLButtonDown` and `CClswizView::OnRButtonDown` so that the `if(Flags & MK_SHIFT)` statements convert the input string characters into lowercase and uppercase, respectively.

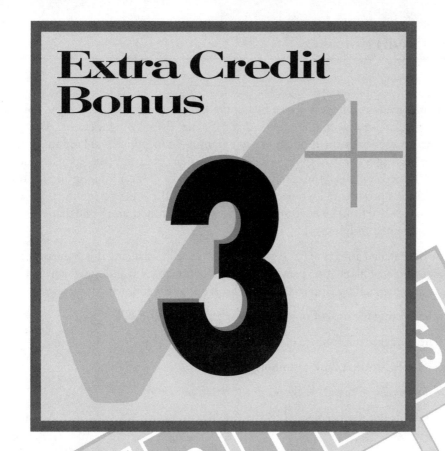

Extra Credit Bonus

3

Introduction to OLE 2.0

The Windows environment is driven by hundreds of API functions. The MFC library, and any similar library, builds classes that tap into these API functions. The API functions are essentially the product of programming in C, which was used to develop Windows 1.*x* through 4.0. Many developers believe that the future versions of Windows will be influenced by object-oriented technology (OOT). Object Linking and Embedding (OLE) is a product of an object-oriented design. OLE will provide the bridge for Windows to evolve from an environment driven by API functions to one that is driven by object-oriented technology.

Because the detailed aspects of OLE are highly advanced, discussing this topic is worthy of an entire book. This chapter provides an introduction to OLE and shows you an OLE application generated by AppWizard. You learn about the following topics:

- The existing features of object-oriented technology (OOT)
- The fundamental features of OLE 2.0
- The MFC-related OLE terminology
- An overview of the OLE classes in the MFC library
- A sample program generated by the AppWizard utility

Existing OOT Features

The evolution of Windows into a complete object-oriented environment is a gradual process. Already Windows offers features influenced by object-oriented technology. For example, Windows stores in the WIN.INI file a list of file extensions which are associated with the applications that manage them. An example of this kind of association is the default link between .TXT files and the Windows notepad editor. If you click a .TXT file from the File Manager (or any compatible shell) you invoke the notepad, which loads the targeted .TXT file. This association is based on the object-oriented notion of an object (the .TXT file) and its owner, the notepad text editor. In simple OLE terms, the .TXT is a type of client object and the notepad editor is a type of server—because it serves to edit the .TXT file.

Fundamental OLE 2.0 Features

The basic notions of OLE developed as a cross between object-oriented technology and application integration. In the mid-eighties, several major software vendors launched integrated applications that included word processors, databases, spreadsheets, communication programs, and so on. These integrated packages offered the feature of moving data from one application to another within the package. The problem was that each application was a subset of rival full-blown commercial products. Consequently, power users stayed away from these integrated applications. During this time, however, application users dreamed of the ability to interlink major applications, such as inserting a spreadsheet or a graphics image into a word processor document without pacifying the inserted document. These dreams lead to the birth of OLE.

So what is object linking and embedding, you might ask? Object linking empowers a document to include another document (also called an object) that is stored outside the host document. For example, you can link a .PCX graphics file in a Word for Windows document. Moreover, you can have several Word documents (or documents for other word processors) link the same .PCX file. This capability has two advantages. First, a linked object reduces storage requirement because there is only one copy of the object. Second, if you edit the linked object using its server application, you automatically update the object for the documents that include it. Object embedding, as the name suggests, allows a document to include another document that is stored with the host document. Here the sole ownership of the nested document is relevant, because the host document monopolizes the embedded object.

What about editing the linked or embedded objects? Under OLE 1.0, when you edit an embedded or linked document, Windows brings up the server application. Consequently, you are aware that you are changing applications. OLE 2.0 has made the process much smoother by allowing the server application to interact transparently with the current application.

The MFC-Related OLE Terminology

Let's look at the OLE terms used by MFC. These terms label the roles of the various host and nested documents. The MFC library uses the following terms:

- The *item* indicates an OLE object that supports a special protocol. This term allows you to distinguish easily between C++ objects and OLE objects. A wide variety of OLE items exists: spreadsheets, databases, word processor documents, graphics images, and sounds.
- The *compound document* includes native data in addition to linked or embedded OLE items. For example, you can have a Word for Windows document that embeds sound items, perhaps representing special audio comments from the document's author.

- The *client application* is a program that access, displays, and stores diverse kinds of OLE items. Examples of client applications include Word for Windows and Excel.
- The *server application* is a program that edits or manipulates an OLE item, as requested by the client application. Examples of server applications include Word for Windows and Excel. You can develop an application to be a client and a server.
- The *mini-server application* is an OLE server application that only edits embedded OLE items. In addition, a mini-server application cannot run on its own. Instead, it serves to edit and save embedded OLE items.
- The *full-server application* is an OLE server that edits and stores embedded items, and typically offers these same features for linked OLE items. A full-server application is also a stand-alone program, such as Write, that you can launch from the File Manager.

Overview of OLE Classes

The MFC offers several classes to support the sophisticated dynamics of OLE 2.0. Here is a partial list of the OLE classes, categorized by class type:

- The OLE Base Classes
  - `COleDocument`
  - `CDocItem`
- The OLE Client Classes
  - `COleClientDoc` (This is really an alias for class `COleDocument`. Class `COleClientDoc` was declared in the earlier version of MFC for the support of OLE 1.0.)
  - `COleClientItem`
- The OLE Server Classes
  - `COleObjectFactory`
  - `COleServerDoc`
  - `COleServerItem`
  - `COleTemplateServer`

- The OLE In-Place Frame Window
  - `COleIPFrameWnd`
- The OLE Exception Class
  - `COleException`

The MFC contains more OLE-related classes that offer auxiliary support. The preceding list introduces you to the most relevant OLE classes, based on the scope of this chapter.

The class `COleDocument` supports the client document that manages the client items. Your applications must derive its client document classes from `COleDocument`. The class is also the ancestor of class `COleServerDoc`, which I discuss later in this section.

The class `CDocItem` models an item that comprises an OLE document. This class is an abstract class that is the parent for the classes `COleClientItem` and `COleServerItem`.

The class `COleClientDoc` is an alias (in Visual C++ 1.5) to class `COleDocument`. The header file `AFXOLE.H` uses a `#define` statement to define the identifier `COleClient` as an alias to `COleDocument`.

The class `COleClientItem` models a client item class. This class represents and manages the client's side of the association with an embedded or linked OLE item. Your applications need to derive their client item classes from `COleClientItem`.

The class `COleObjectFactory` is a server application class that creates and manages server documents.

The class `COleServerDoc` is a server document class responsible for creating and handling server items. Your applications must derive their server document classes from class `COleServerDoc`.

The class `COleServerItem` is a server item class that supports the server's side of the association with an embedded or linked item. Your applications must derive their server document classes from class `COleServerItem`.

The class `COleTemplateServer` provides the document templates needed to manage OLE documents. Your application can use this class to support an OLE document template.

The class `COleIPFrameWnd`, a descendant of class `CFrameWnd`, handles the in-place frame that displays an OLE item.

The class `COleException` deals with OLE-related run-time errors. You can use this class to trap and handle such errors without resorting to traditional defensive programming methods. Instead, you can use the exception mechanism supported by Visual C++. Consult my book, *Secrets of the Visual C++ Masters*, to learn more about the Visual C++ exception mechanism.

The Sample OLE Program

The preceding section presents a brief overview of the relevant OLE classes; this section presents an OLE program generated by the AppWizard utility. Interestingly, the AppWizard utility generates enough code to make the OLE program useful for cataloging various OLE items. To create the OLEWIZ project, follow these steps:

1. Invoke the New Project dialog box to create an AppWizard application. Enter the project name `olewiz`. In addition, select the directory \MSVC20\VC21DAY to be the parent directory for the OLEWIZ project.
2. Click the **Create...** pushbutton in the New Project dialog box to edit the project options. The Visual Workbench displays the MFC AppWizard - Step 1 dialog box, shown in Figure B3.1. Accept the default selection which creates an MDI-compliant application.
3. Click the **Next >** pushbutton until you reach the MFC AppWizard - Step 3 of 6 dialog box.
4. Click the **Container** radio button of the MFC AppWizard - Step 3 of 6 dialog box (see Figure B3.2).
5. Click the **Next >** pushbutton until you reach the MFC AppWizard - Step 6 of 6 dialog box, shown in Figure B3.3.
6. Click the **Finish** pushbutton.
7. The Visual WorkBench displays the New Project Information dialog box, shown in Figure B3.4.
8. Click the **OK** pushbutton in the New Project Information dialog to generate the source files for the OLEWIZ project.

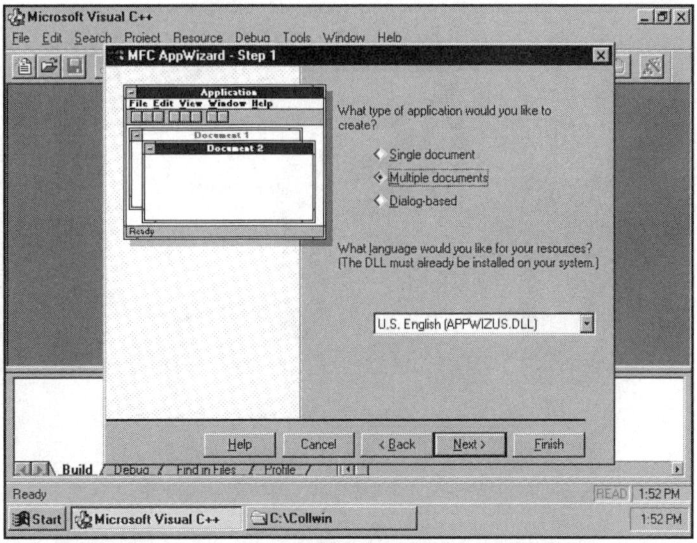

Figure B3.1. *The MFC AppWizard - Step 1 dialog box during the creation of project* `olewiz`.

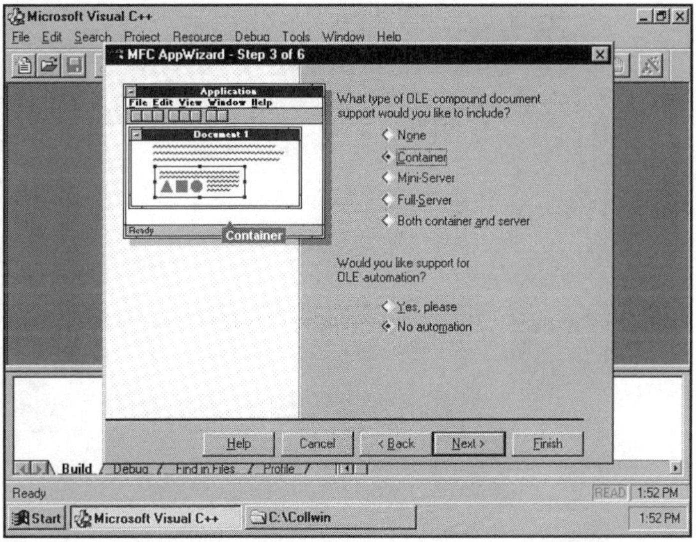

Figure B3.2. *The MFC AppWizard - Step 3 of 6 dialog box during the creation of project* `olewiz`.

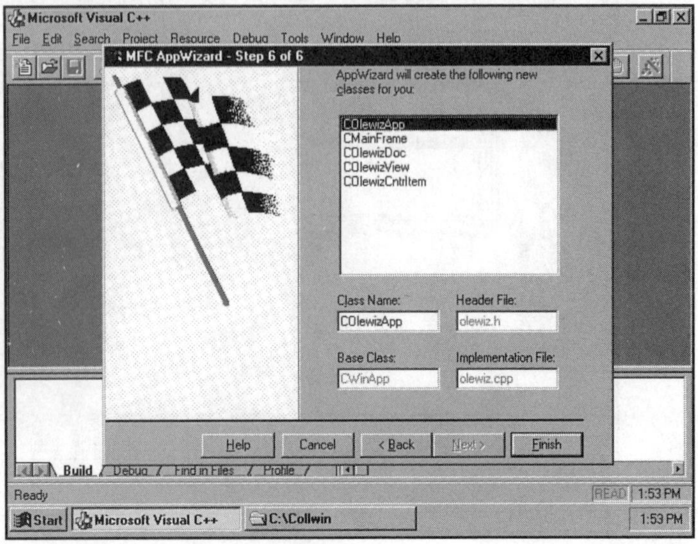

Figure B3.3. *The MFC AppWizard - Step 6 of 6 dialog box during the creation of project* `olewiz`.

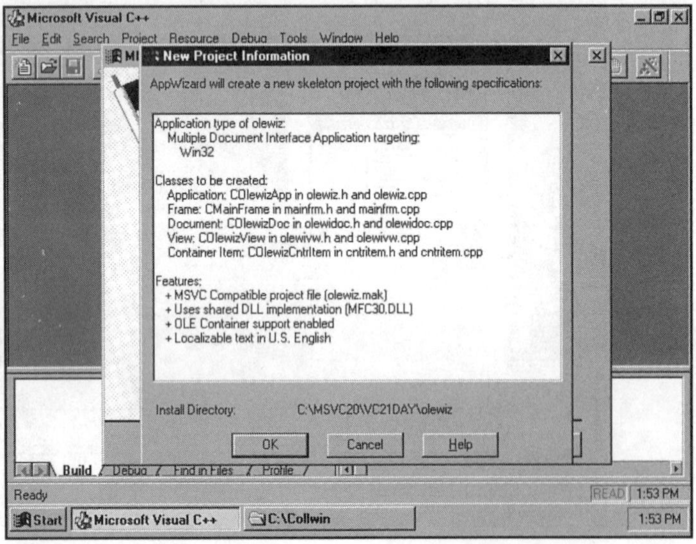

Figure B3.4. *The New Project Information dialog box during the creation of project* `olewiz`.

Compile and run the OLEWIZ.EXE program. Keep in mind that each MDI child view holds only one OLE item. Test inserting the following OLE items:

1. Choose **Insert New Object...** from the **Edit** menu. The program displays the Insert Object dialog box, which lists the available OLE objects. Select the **Paintbrush Picture** item and click the **OK** pushbutton. The program then invokes the Paintbrush program. Draw lines and/or shapes in the Paintbrush client area, and then choose **Update** from the **File** menu. The **Update** menu option appears especially for the case when Paintbrush (or any other OLE-aware application) is invoked as an OLE server. After you choose **Update**, the program displays the shapes you draw in the MDI child window and the caption `Olewiz1`. Figure B3.5 shows the MDI child window Olewiz1 and Paintbrush after I made further changes in Paintbrush. Close Paintbrush by choosing **Exit & Return to Olewiz1** from the **File** menu.

2. Choose **New...** from the **File** menu. This step displays the new MDI child window titled `Olewiz2`. Next, choose **Insert New Object...** from the **Edit** menu. The program displays the Insert Object dialog box, which lists the available OLE objects. Choose the **Media Clip** item and click the **OK** pushbutton. The program then invokes the Media Player program. Choose **Open...** from the **File** menu to load the file CHIMES.WAV in the Windows directory, and then choose the **Update** menu option.

   The **Update** menu option appears especially for the case when Media Player (another OLE-aware application) is invoked as an OLE server. After you invoke the **Update** menu option, the program displays the Media Player graphics (with the title CHIMES.WAV) in the MDI child window; you see the caption `Olewiz2`. To close the Media Player dialog box, choose **Exit** from the **File** menu.

3. Choose **New...** from the **File** menu; this step displays the MDI child window titled `Olewiz3`. Then choose **Insert New Object...** from the **Edit** menu. The program displays the Insert Object dialog box, which lists the available OLE objects. Choose the Sound item and click the **OK** pushbutton; the program then invokes the Sound Recorder program.

   To load the file CHIMES.WAV in the Windows directory, choose **Open...** from the **File** menu, and then invoke the **Update** menu option. After you invoke the **Update** menu option, the program displays the sound graphics in the MDI child window with the caption `Olewiz3`. To close the Sound Recorder dialog box, choose **Exit** from the **File** menu.

You can save and load the OLE items in the MDI child windows, and you can also edit the OLE item by choosing the appropriate option from the **Edit** menu. I say "appropriate" because some of the options of the **Edit** menu are context sensitive and vary in order to accommodate the OLE object in the current active MDI child window.

Figure B3.5 shows a sample session with the OLEWIZ.EXE application. When you finish experimenting, choose **Exit** from the **File** menu to close the OLEWIZ.EXE program.

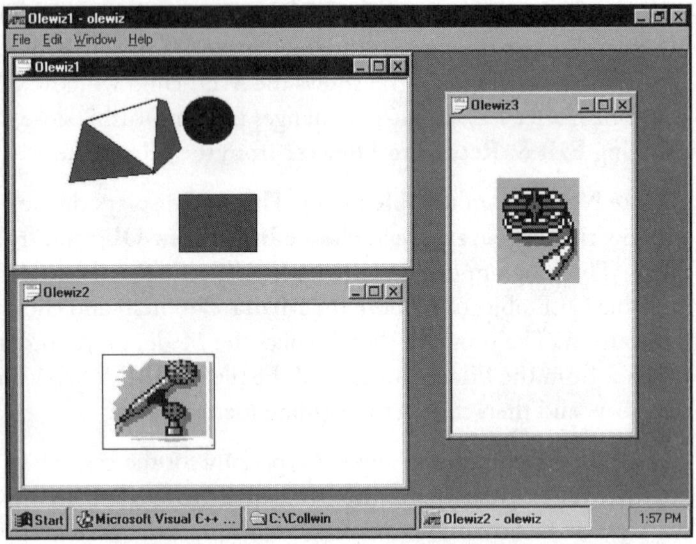

Figure B3.5. *A sample session with program OLEWIZ.EXE.*

The Program's Source Code

Let's focus on the .H and .CPP files generated by the AppWizard utility. In this section, I discuss these files to give you an idea of the OLE-related code.

Listing B3.1. The source code for the RESOURCE.H header file.

```
//{{NO_DEPENDENCIES}}
// Microsoft Visual C++ generated include file.
// Used by OLEWIZ.RC
//
#define IDR_MAINFRAME                   128
```

```
#define IDR_OLEWIZTYPE                  129
#define IDR_OLEWIZTYPE_CNTR_IP          6
#define IDD_ABOUTBOX                    100
#define IDP_OLE_INIT_FAILED             100
#define IDP_FAILED_TO_CREATE            102
#define ID_CANCEL_EDIT_CNTR             32768

// Next default values for new objects
//
#ifdef APSTUDIO_INVOKED
#ifndef APSTUDIO_READONLY_SYMBOLS
#define _APS_NEXT_RESOURCE_VALUE        130
#define _APS_NEXT_CONTROL_VALUE         1000
#define _APS_NEXT_SYMED_VALUE           101
#define _APS_NEXT_COMMAND_VALUE         32771
#endif
#endif
```

Listing B3.1 shows the contents of the RESOURCE.H header file. This file contains the definitions of various resources used by the program, including menu resources, the About dialog box resource, and several OLE-related resources.

Type Listing B3.2. The source code for the STDAFX.H header file.

```
// stdafx.h : include file for standard system include files,
//  or project specific include files that are used frequently, but
//      are changed infrequently
//

#include <afxwin.h>         // MFC core and standard components
#include <afxext.h>         // MFC extensions
#include <afxole.h>         // MFC OLE classes
#include <afxodlgs.h>       // MFC OLE dialog classes
```

Listing B3.2 holds the source code for the STDAFX.H header file. This file contains a series of `#include` directives to include the required header files for the core MFC, MFC extensions, OLE classes, and OLE dialog classes.

Type Listing B3.3. The source code for the OLEWIZ.H header file.

```
// olewiz.h : main header file for the OLEWIZ application
//

```

continues

Listing B3.3. continued

```
#ifndef __AFXWIN_H__
      #error include 'stdafx.h' before including this file for PCH
#endif

#include "resource.h"       // main symbols

/////////////////////////////////////////////////////////////////////////////
// COlewizApp:
// See olewiz.cpp for the implementation of this class
//

class COlewizApp : public CWinApp
{
public:
      COlewizApp();

// Overrides
      // ClassWizard generated virtual function overrides
      //{{AFX_VIRTUAL(COlewizApp)
      public:
      virtual BOOL InitInstance();
      //}}AFX_VIRTUAL

// Implementation

      //{{AFX_MSG(COlewizApp)
      afx_msg void OnAppAbout();
       // NOTE - the ClassWizard will add and remove member functions here.
       //    DO NOT EDIT what you see in these blocks of generated code !
      //}}AFX_MSG
      DECLARE_MESSAGE_MAP()
};


/////////////////////////////////////////////////////////////////////////////
```

Listing B3.3 contains the source code for the OLEWIZ.H header file. This file declares the application class `COlewizApp` as a descendant of class `CWinApp`. The class also declares a constructor, the member function `InitInstance`, the member function `OnAppAbout`. All the member functions in the class `COlewizApp` are public.

Listing B3.4. The source code for the OLEWIDOC.H header file.

```
// olewidoc.h : interface of the COlewizDoc class
//
/////////////////////////////////////////////////////////////////////////////

class COlewizDoc : public COleDocument
{
```

```
protected: // create from serialization only
	COlewizDoc();
	DECLARE_DYNCREATE(COlewizDoc)

// Attributes
public:

// Operations
public:

// Overrides
	// ClassWizard generated virtual function overrides
	//{{AFX_VIRTUAL(COlewizDoc)
	public:
	virtual BOOL OnNewDocument();
	//}}AFX_VIRTUAL

// Implementation
public:
	virtual ~COlewizDoc();
	virtual void Serialize(CArchive& ar);   // overridden for document i/o
#ifdef _DEBUG
	virtual void AssertValid() const;
	virtual void Dump(CDumpContext& dc) const;
#endif

protected:

// Generated message map functions
protected:
	//{{AFX_MSG(COlewizDoc)
	// NOTE - the ClassWizard will add and remove member functions here.
	//    DO NOT EDIT what you see in these blocks of generated code !
	//}}AFX_MSG
	DECLARE_MESSAGE_MAP()
};

/////////////////////////////////////////////////////////////////////////////
```

Listing B3.4 shows the source code for the OLEWIDOC.H header file. This class declares the application's document class `COlewizDoc` as a descendant of `COleDocument` (instead of class `CDocument`, as is the case with non-OLE-aware programs). The class declares a protected constructor; a public destructor; the member function `OnNewDocument`; and the public member functions `Serialize`, `OnGetEmbeddedItem`, `AssertValid`, and `Dump`.

Listing B3.5. The source code for the MAINFRM.H header file.

```
// mainfrm.h : interface of the CMainFrame class
//
/////////////////////////////////////////////////////////////////////////////

class CMainFrame : public CMDIFrameWnd
{
     DECLARE_DYNAMIC(CMainFrame)
public:
     CMainFrame();

// Attributes
public:

// Operations
public:

// Overrides
     // ClassWizard generated virtual function overrides
     //{{AFX_VIRTUAL(CMainFrame)
     //}}AFX_VIRTUAL

// Implementation
public:
     virtual ~CMainFrame();
#ifdef _DEBUG
     virtual void AssertValid() const;
     virtual void Dump(CDumpContext& dc) const;
#endif

// Generated message map functions
protected:
     //{{AFX_MSG(CMainFrame)
      // NOTE - the ClassWizard will add and remove member functions here.
      //    DO NOT EDIT what you see in these blocks of generated code!
     //}}AFX_MSG
     DECLARE_MESSAGE_MAP()
};

/////////////////////////////////////////////////////////////////////////////
```

Listing B3.5 shows the source code for the MAINFRM.H header file. This file declares the MDI frame window class, `CMainFrame`, as a descendant of class `CMDIFrameWnd`. The class declares a constructor, a destructor, and the public member functions `AssertValid` and `Dump`.

Type Listing B3.6. The source code for the OLEWIVW.H header file.

```
// olewivw.h : interface of the COlewizView class
//
/////////////////////////////////////////////////////////////////////////////

class COlewizCntrItem;

class COlewizView : public CView
{
protected: // create from serialization only
     COlewizView();
     DECLARE_DYNCREATE(COlewizView)

// Attributes
public:
     COlewizDoc* GetDocument();
     // m_pSelection holds the selection to the current COlewizCntrItem.
     // For many applications, such a member variable isn't adequate to
     //  represent a selection, such as a multiple selection or a selection
     //  of objects that are not COlewizCntrItem objects.  This selection
     //  mechanism is provided just to help you get started.

     // TODO: replace this selection mechanism with one appropriate to your app.
     COlewizCntrItem* m_pSelection;

// Operations
public:

// Overrides
     // ClassWizard generated virtual function overrides
     //{{AFX_VIRTUAL(COlewizView)
     public:
     virtual void OnDraw(CDC* pDC);  // overridden to draw this view
     protected:
     virtual void OnInitialUpdate(); // called first time after construct
     virtual BOOL IsSelected(const CObject* pDocItem) const;// Container support
     //}}AFX_VIRTUAL

// Implementation
public:
     virtual ~COlewizView();
#ifdef _DEBUG
     virtual void AssertValid() const;
     virtual void Dump(CDumpContext& dc) const;
#endif

protected:

// Generated message map functions
protected:
```

continues

Listing B3.6. continued

```
        //{{AFX_MSG(COlewizView)
        // NOTE - the ClassWizard will add and remove member functions here.
        //    DO NOT EDIT what you see in these blocks of generated code !
        afx_msg void OnSetFocus(CWnd* pOldWnd);
        afx_msg void OnSize(UINT nType, int cx, int cy);
        afx_msg void OnInsertObject();
        afx_msg void OnCancelEditCntr();
        //}}AFX_MSG
        DECLARE_MESSAGE_MAP()
};

#ifndef _DEBUG  // debug version in olewivw.cpp
inline COlewizDoc* COlewizView::GetDocument()
   { return (COlewizDoc*)m_pDocument; }
#endif

/////////////////////////////////////////////////////////////////////////////
```

Listing B3.6 holds the source code for the OLEWIVW.H header file. This file declares the view class, `COlewizView`, as a descendant of class `CView`. The class declares the data member `m_pSelection`, a constructor; destructor; the public member functions `GetDocument` (which returns a pointer to class `COlewizDoc`), `OnDraw`, `AssertValid`, and `Dump`; and the protected member functions `OnInitialUpdate`, `IsSelected`, `OnSetFocus`, `OnSize`, `OnInsertObject`, and `OnCancelEdit`. The member functions `OnXXXX` handle main options, including the one used to insert a new OLE item.

Type Listing B3.7. The source code for the CNTRITEM.H header file.

```
// cntritem.h : interface of the COlewizCntrItem class
//

class COlewizDoc;
class COlewizView;

class COlewizCntrItem : public COleClientItem
{
        DECLARE_SERIAL(COlewizCntrItem)

// Constructors
public:
        COlewizCntrItem(COlewizDoc* pContainer = NULL);
    // Note: pContainer is allowed to be NULL to enable IMPLEMENT_SERIALIZE.
    //  IMPLEMENT_SERIALIZE requires the class have a constructor with
    //  zero arguments.  Normally, OLE items are constructed with a
    //  non-NULL document pointer.

// Attributes
```

```
public:
     COlewizDoc* GetDocument()
          { return (COlewizDoc*)COleClientItem::GetDocument(); }
     COlewizView* GetActiveView()
          { return (COlewizView*)COleClientItem::GetActiveView(); }

     // ClassWizard generated virtual function overrides
     //{{AFX_VIRTUAL(COlewizCntrItem)
     public:
     virtual void OnChange(OLE_NOTIFICATION wNotification, DWORD dwParam);
     protected:
     virtual void OnGetItemPosition(CRect& rPosition);
     virtual void OnDeactivateUI(BOOL bUndoable);
     virtual BOOL OnChangeItemPosition(const CRect& rectPos);
     //}}AFX_VIRTUAL

// Implementation
public:
     ~COlewizCntrItem();
#ifdef _DEBUG
     virtual void AssertValid() const;
     virtual void Dump(CDumpContext& dc) const;
#endif
     virtual void Serialize(CArchive& ar);
};

/////////////////////////////////////////////////////////////////////////////
```

Listing B3.7 shows the source code for the CNTRITEM.H header file. This file declares the OLE client item class, `COlewizCntrItem`, as a descendant of class `COleClientItem`. The class declares a constructor; a destructor; the public member functions `GetDocument`, `GetActiveView`, `AssertValid`, `Dump`, `Serialize`, `OnChange`, `OnGetItemPosition`, and `OnDeactivateUI`, and `OnChangeItemPosition`. The last three member functions are protected.

Listing B3.8. The source code for the STDAFX.CPP implementation file.

```
// stdafx.cpp : source file that includes just the standard includes
//     olewiz.pch will be the pre-compiled header
//     stdafx.obj will contain the pre-compiled type information

#include "stdafx.h"
```

Listing B3.8 shows the source code for the STDAFX.CPP implementation file. The file simply includes the STDAFX.H header file.

Listing B3.9. The source code for the OLEWIZ.CPP implementation file.

```
// olewiz.cpp : Defines the class behaviors for the application.
//

#include "stdafx.h"
#include "olewiz.h"

#include "mainfrm.h"
#include "olewidoc.h"
#include "olewivw.h"

#ifdef _DEBUG
#undef THIS_FILE
static char BASED_CODE THIS_FILE[] = __FILE__;
#endif

/////////////////////////////////////////////////////////////////////////////
// COlewizApp

BEGIN_MESSAGE_MAP(COlewizApp, CWinApp)
    //{{AFX_MSG_MAP(COlewizApp)
    ON_COMMAND(ID_APP_ABOUT, OnAppAbout)
    // NOTE - the ClassWizard will add and remove mapping macros here.
    //    DO NOT EDIT what you see in these blocks of generated code!
    //}}AFX_MSG_MAP
    // Standard file based document commands
    ON_COMMAND(ID_FILE_NEW, CWinApp::OnFileNew)
    ON_COMMAND(ID_FILE_OPEN, CWinApp::OnFileOpen)
END_MESSAGE_MAP()

/////////////////////////////////////////////////////////////////////////////
// COlewizApp construction

COlewizApp::COlewizApp()
{
    // TODO: add construction code here,
    // Place all significant initialization in InitInstance
}

/////////////////////////////////////////////////////////////////////////////
// The one and only COlewizApp object

COlewizApp theApp;

/////////////////////////////////////////////////////////////////////////////
// COlewizApp initialization

BOOL COlewizApp::InitInstance()
{
    // Initialize OLE libraries
    if (!AfxOleInit())
    {
        AfxMessageBox(IDP_OLE_INIT_FAILED);
        return FALSE;
```

```
    }

    // Standard initialization
    // If you are not using these features and wish to reduce the size
    //  of your final executable, you should remove from the following
    //  the specific initialization routines you do not need.

    LoadStdProfileSettings();  // Load standard INI file options (including MRU)

    // Register the application's document templates.  Document templates
    //  serve as the connection between documents, frame windows and views.

    CMultiDocTemplate* pDocTemplate;
    pDocTemplate = new CMultiDocTemplate(
        IDR_OLEWIZTYPE,
        RUNTIME_CLASS(COlewizDoc),
        RUNTIME_CLASS(CMDIChildWnd),        // standard MDI child frame
        RUNTIME_CLASS(COlewizView));
    pDocTemplate->SetContainerInfo(IDR_OLEWIZTYPE_CNTR_IP);
    AddDocTemplate(pDocTemplate);

    // create main MDI Frame window
    CMainFrame* pMainFrame = new CMainFrame;
    if (!pMainFrame->LoadFrame(IDR_MAINFRAME))
        return FALSE;
    m_pMainWnd = pMainFrame;

    // create a new (empty) document
    OnFileNew();

    if (m_lpCmdLine[0] != '\0')
    {
        // TODO: add command line processing here
    }

    // The main window has been initialized, so show and update it.
    pMainFrame->ShowWindow(m_nCmdShow);
    pMainFrame->UpdateWindow();

    return TRUE;
}

/////////////////////////////////////////////////////////////////////////////
// CAboutDlg dialog used for App About

class CAboutDlg : public CDialog
{
public:
    CAboutDlg();

// Dialog Data
    //{{AFX_DATA(CAboutDlg)
    enum { IDD = IDD_ABOUTBOX };
    //}}AFX_DATA
```

continues

Listing B3.9. continued

```

// Implementation
protected:
    virtual void DoDataExchange(CDataExchange* pDX);  // DDX/DDV support
    //{{AFX_MSG(CAboutDlg)
        // No message handlers
    //}}AFX_MSG
    DECLARE_MESSAGE_MAP()
};

CAboutDlg::CAboutDlg() : CDialog(CAboutDlg::IDD)
{
    //{{AFX_DATA_INIT(CAboutDlg)
    //}}AFX_DATA_INIT
}

void CAboutDlg::DoDataExchange(CDataExchange* pDX)
{
    CDialog::DoDataExchange(pDX);
    //{{AFX_DATA_MAP(CAboutDlg)
    //}}AFX_DATA_MAP
}

BEGIN_MESSAGE_MAP(CAboutDlg, CDialog)
    //{{AFX_MSG_MAP(CAboutDlg)
    // No message handlers
    //}}AFX_MSG_MAP
END_MESSAGE_MAP()

// App command to run the dialog
void COlewizApp::OnAppAbout()
{
    CAboutDlg aboutDlg;
    aboutDlg.DoModal();
}

/////////////////////////////////////////////////////////////////////////////
// COlewizApp commands
```

Listing B3.9 contains the source code for the OLEWIZ.CPP implementation file. The file includes the message map macros to support the commands for creating a new MDI child window, loading an existing MDI child window, and invoking the About dialog box. The file contains the definitions for the following relevant member functions:

1. The definition of the constructor is an empty shell in which you insert code to further customize the application.

2. The member function `InitInstance` initializes the application by performing the following tasks:

- Initializes the OLE 2.0 libraries by invoking the function `AfxOleInit`.
- Performs typical initialization, which sets up the background color and the standard .INI file options.
- Registers the application's document templates. This registration involves the local pointer `pDocTemplate` (which points to the class `CMultiDocTemplate`) to associate the document, view, and MDI child window classes. The registration also involves specifying the server and client information.
- Creates the main MDI frame window.
- Creates a new, empty MDI child window.
- Displays the main window.

The file also contains the definitions of the member functions for class `CAboutDlg`.

Listing B3.10. The source code for the OLEWIDOC.CPP implementation file.

```
// olewidoc.cpp : implementation of the COlewizDoc class
//

#include "stdafx.h"
#include "olewiz.h"

#include "olewidoc.h"
#include "cntritem.h"

#ifdef _DEBUG
#undef THIS_FILE
static char BASED_CODE THIS_FILE[] = __FILE__;
#endif

/////////////////////////////////////////////////////////////////////////////
// COlewizDoc

IMPLEMENT_DYNCREATE(COlewizDoc, COleDocument)

BEGIN_MESSAGE_MAP(COlewizDoc, COleDocument)
     //{{AFX_MSG_MAP(COlewizDoc)
     // NOTE - the ClassWizard will add and remove mapping macros here.
     //    DO NOT EDIT what you see in these blocks of generated code!
     //}}AFX_MSG_MAP
     // Enable default OLE container implementation
ON_UPDATE_COMMAND_UI(ID_EDIT_PASTE, COleDocument::OnUpdatePasteMenu)
ON_UPDATE_COMMAND_UI(ID_EDIT_PASTE_LINK, COleDocument::OnUpdatePasteLinkMenu)
```

continues

Listing B3.10. continued

```
    ON_UPDATE_COMMAND_UI(ID_OLE_EDIT_LINKS, COleDocument::OnUpdateEditLinksMenu)
    ON_COMMAND(ID_OLE_EDIT_LINKS, COleDocument::OnEditLinks)
    ON_UPDATE_COMMAND_UI(ID_OLE_VERB_FIRST, COleDocument::OnUpdateObjectVerbMenu)
    ON_UPDATE_COMMAND_UI(ID_OLE_EDIT_CONVERT, COleDocument::OnUpdateObjectVerbMenu)
    ON_COMMAND(ID_OLE_EDIT_CONVERT, COleDocument::OnEditConvert)
END_MESSAGE_MAP()

/////////////////////////////////////////////////////////////////////////////
// COlewizDoc construction/destruction

COlewizDoc::COlewizDoc()
{
    // For most containers, using compound files is a good idea.
    EnableCompoundFile();

    // TODO: add one-time construction code here

}

COlewizDoc::~COlewizDoc()
{
}

BOOL COlewizDoc::OnNewDocument()
{
    if (!COleDocument::OnNewDocument())
        return FALSE;

    // TODO: add reinitialization code here
    // (SDI documents will reuse this document)

    return TRUE;
}

/////////////////////////////////////////////////////////////////////////////
// COlewizDoc serialization

void COlewizDoc::Serialize(CArchive& ar)
{
    if (ar.IsStoring())
    {
        // TODO: add storing code here
    }
    else
    {
        // TODO: add loading code here
    }

    // Calling the base class COleDocument enables serialization
    //  of the container document's COleClientItem objects.
    COleDocument::Serialize(ar);
}

/////////////////////////////////////////////////////////////////////////////
```

```
// COlewizDoc diagnostics

#ifdef _DEBUG
void COlewizDoc::AssertValid() const
{
     COleDocument::AssertValid();
}

void COlewizDoc::Dump(CDumpContext& dc) const
{
     COleDocument::Dump(dc);
}
#endif //_DEBUG

/////////////////////////////////////////////////////////////////////////////
// COlewizDoc commands
```


Listing B3.10 shows the source code for the OLEWIDOC.CPP implementation file. This file contains the message map macros for the OLE-related menu options, such as **Paste**, **Paste Link**, **Edit**, and **Convert**.

The file contains the definitions for the following member functions of the document class. The constructor initializes the document class by enabling compound files.

Type

Listing B3.11. The source code for the MAINFRM.CPP implementation file.

```
// mainfrm.cpp : implementation of the CMainFrame class
//

#include "stdafx.h"
#include "olewiz.h"

#include "mainfrm.h"

#ifdef _DEBUG
#undef THIS_FILE
static char BASED_CODE THIS_FILE[] = __FILE__;
#endif

/////////////////////////////////////////////////////////////////////////////
// CMainFrame

IMPLEMENT_DYNAMIC(CMainFrame, CMDIFrameWnd)

BEGIN_MESSAGE_MAP(CMainFrame, CMDIFrameWnd)
     //{{AFX_MSG_MAP(CMainFrame)
          // NOTE - the ClassWizard will add and remove mapping macros here.
          //    DO NOT EDIT what you see in these blocks of generated code !
```

continues

Listing B3.11. continued

```
        //}}AFX_MSG_MAP
END_MESSAGE_MAP()

/////////////////////////////////////////////////////////////////////////////
// CMainFrame construction/destruction

CMainFrame::CMainFrame()
{
        // TODO: add member initialization code here

}

CMainFrame::~CMainFrame()
{
}

/////////////////////////////////////////////////////////////////////////////
// CMainFrame diagnostics

#ifdef _DEBUG
void CMainFrame::AssertValid() const
{
        CMDIFrameWnd::AssertValid();
}

void CMainFrame::Dump(CDumpContext& dc) const
{
        CMDIFrameWnd::Dump(dc);
}

#endif //_DEBUG

/////////////////////////////////////////////////////////////////////////////
// CMainFrame message handlers
```

Listing B3.11 contains the source code for the MAINFRM.CPP implementation file. The file contains empty-shell definitions for the constructor and destructor of class `CMainFrame`. In addition, the file presents minimal definitions for the member function `AssertValid` and `Dump`.

Listing B3.12. The source code for the OLEWIVW.CPP implementation file.

```
// olewivw.cpp : implementation of the COlewizView class
//

#include "stdafx.h"
#include "olewiz.h"

#include "olewidoc.h"
```

```
#include "cntritem.h"
#include "olewivw.h"

#ifdef _DEBUG
#undef THIS_FILE
static char BASED_CODE THIS_FILE[] = __FILE__;
#endif

/////////////////////////////////////////////////////////////////////////////
// COlewizView

IMPLEMENT_DYNCREATE(COlewizView, CView)

BEGIN_MESSAGE_MAP(COlewizView, CView)
    //{{AFX_MSG_MAP(COlewizView)
    // NOTE - the ClassWizard will add and remove mapping macros here.
    //    DO NOT EDIT what you see in these blocks of generated code!
    ON_WM_SETFOCUS()
    ON_WM_SIZE()
    ON_COMMAND(ID_OLE_INSERT_NEW, OnInsertObject)
    ON_COMMAND(ID_CANCEL_EDIT_CNTR, OnCancelEditCntr)
    //}}AFX_MSG_MAP
END_MESSAGE_MAP()

/////////////////////////////////////////////////////////////////////////////
// COlewizView construction/destruction

COlewizView::COlewizView()
{
    // TODO: add construction code here

}

COlewizView::~COlewizView()
{
}

/////////////////////////////////////////////////////////////////////////////
// COlewizView drawing

void COlewizView::OnDraw(CDC* pDC)
{
    COlewizDoc* pDoc = GetDocument();
    ASSERT_VALID(pDoc);

    // TODO: add draw code for native data here
    // TODO: also draw all OLE items in the document

    // Draw the selection at an arbitrary position.  This code should be
    //  removed once your real drawing code is implemented.  This position
    //  corresponds exactly to the rectangle returned by COlewizCntrItem,
    //  to give the effect of in-place editing.

```

continues

Listing B3.12. continued

```
    // TODO: remove this code when final draw code is complete.

    if (m_pSelection == NULL)
    {
         POSITION pos = pDoc->GetStartPosition();
         m_pSelection = (COlewizCntrItem*)pDoc->GetNextClientItem(pos);
    }
    if (m_pSelection != NULL)
        m_pSelection->Draw(pDC, CRect(10, 10, 210, 210));
}

void COlewizView::OnInitialUpdate()
{
    CView::OnInitialUpdate();

    // TODO: remove this code when final selection model code is written
    m_pSelection = NULL;    // initialize selection

}

/////////////////////////////////////////////////////////////////////////////
// OLE Client support and commands

BOOL COlewizView::IsSelected(const CObject* pDocItem) const
{
    // The implementation below is adequate if your selection consists of
    //  only COlewizCntrItem objects.  To handle different selection
    //  mechanisms, the implementation here should be replaced.

    // TODO: implement this function that tests for a selected OLE client item

    return pDocItem == m_pSelection;
}

void COlewizView::OnInsertObject()
{
    // Invoke the standard Insert Object dialog box to obtain information
    //  for new COlewizCntrItem object.
    iCOleInsertDialog dlg;
    if (dlg.DoModal() != IDOK)
         return;

    BeginWaitCursor();

    COlewizCntrItem* pItem = NULL;
    TRY
    {
         // Create new item connected to this document.
         COlewizDoc* pDoc = GetDocument();
         ASSERT_VALID(pDoc);
         pItem = new COlewizCntrItem(pDoc);
         ASSERT_VALID(pItem);

         // Initialize the item from the dialog data.
```

```
        if (!dlg.CreateItem(pItem))
            AfxThrowMemoryException();  // any exception will do
        ASSERT_VALID(pItem);

        // If item created from class list (not from file) then launch
        //  the server to edit the item.
        if (dlg.GetSelectionType() == COleInsertDialog::createNewItem)
            pItem->DoVerb(OLEIVERB_SHOW, this);

        ASSERT_VALID(pItem);

         // As an arbitrary user interface design, this sets the selection
       //  to the last item inserted.

       // TODO: reimplement selection as appropriate for your
       // application
        m_pSelection = pItem;   // set selection to last inserted item
        pDoc->UpdateAllViews(NULL);
    }
    CATCH(CException, e)
    {
        if (pItem != NULL)
        {
            ASSERT_VALID(pItem);
            pItem->Delete();
        }
        AfxMessageBox(IDP_FAILED_TO_CREATE);
    }
    END_CATCH

    EndWaitCursor();
}

// The following command handler provides the standard keyboard
//  user interface to cancel an in-place editing session.  Here,
//  the container (not the server) causes the deactivation.
void COlewizView::OnCancelEditCntr()
{
    // Close any in-place active item on this view.
    COleClientItem* pActiveItem = GetDocument()->GetInPlaceActiveItem(this);
    if (pActiveItem != NULL)
    {
        pActiveItem->Close();
    }
    ASSERT(GetDocument()->GetInPlaceActiveItem(this) == NULL);
}

// Special handling of OnSetFocus and OnSize are required for a container
//  when an object is being edited in-place.
void COlewizView::OnSetFocus(CWnd* pOldWnd)
{
    COleClientItem* pActiveItem = GetDocument()->GetInPlaceActiveItem(this);
    if (pActiveItem != NULL &&
        pActiveItem->GetItemState() == COleClientItem::activeUIState)
```

continues

Listing B3.12. continued

```
    {
        // need to set focus to this item if it is in the same view
        CWnd* pWnd = pActiveItem->GetInPlaceWindow();
        if (pWnd != NULL)
        {
            pWnd->SetFocus();   // don't call the base class
            return;
        }
    }

    CView::OnSetFocus(pOldWnd);
}

void COlewizView::OnSize(UINT nType, int cx, int cy)
{
    CView::OnSize(nType, cx, cy);
    COleClientItem* pActiveItem = GetDocument()->GetInPlaceActiveItem(this);
    if (pActiveItem != NULL)
        pActiveItem->SetItemRects();
}

/////////////////////////////////////////////////////////////////////////////
// COlewizView diagnostics

#ifdef _DEBUG
void COlewizView::AssertValid() const
{
    CView::AssertValid();
}

void COlewizView::Dump(CDumpContext& dc) const
{
    CView::Dump(dc);
}

COlewizDoc* COlewizView::GetDocument() // non-debug version is inline
{
    ASSERT(m_pDocument->IsKindOf(RUNTIME_CLASS(COlewizDoc)));
    return (COlewizDoc*)m_pDocument;
}
#endif //_DEBUG

/////////////////////////////////////////////////////////////////////////////
// COlewizView message handlers
```

Listing B3.12 shows the source code for the OLEWIVW.CPP implementation file. The listing contains the message map macros for the messages that resize, set focus, insert a new object, and cancel editing an object. The listing contains the definitions for the following relevant members:

1. The definition of the constructor `COlewizView` is an empty shell.
2. The definition of the destructor is an empty shell.
3. The member function `OnDraw` draws an OLE item using arbitrarily assigned values.
4. The member function `OnInitialUpdate` (lines 73 to 79) updates the MDI child views by first invoking the function `OnInitialUpdate` of the parent class, and then assigning `NULL` to the member `m_pSelection`.
5. The Boolean member function `IsSelected` (lines 84 to 93) returns the value of the Boolean expression `pDocItem == m_pSelection`. The `pDocItem` is a pointer to the view's OLE item. The `m_pSelection` is the pointer to the currently selected item.
6. The member function `OnInsertObject` (lines 95 to 146) responds to the menu option, which inserts a new OLE object. The function performs the following tasks:
   - ☐ Invokes the standard Insert Object dialog box to get the user to select an OLE item. This task involves the OLE dialog box class `COleInsertDialog`. The function declares the instance `dlg` for that class.
   - ☐ Creates a new OLE item and associates it with the document. This task involves getting the address of the document, and then creating a dy namic instance of class `COlewizCntrItem`. (The function assigns the address of this instance to pointer `pItem`.) This task only creates the OLE item; it does not initialize the item.
   - ☐ Initializes the OLE item by sending the C++ message `CreateItem` to the object `dlg`. The argument for this message is the pointer `pItem`.
   - ☐ Launches the server if the item was created from the class list.
   - ☐ Sets the selection to the last inserted OLE item.
   - ☐ Updates all the views.
7. The member function `OnCancelEdit` (lines 151 to 160) cancels editing an OLE item. The function obtains the pointer to that item and then sends it the C++ message `Close`.

Listing B3.13. The source code for the CNTRITEM.CPP implementation file.

```
// cntritem.cpp : implementation of the COlewizCntrItem class
//

#include "stdafx.h"
#include "olewiz.h"

#include "olewidoc.h"
#include "cntritem.h"

#ifdef _DEBUG
#undef THIS_FILE
static char BASED_CODE THIS_FILE[] = __FILE__;
#endif

/////////////////////////////////////////////////////////////////////////////
// COlewizCntrItem implementation

IMPLEMENT_SERIAL(COlewizCntrItem, COleClientItem, 0)

COlewizCntrItem::COlewizCntrItem(COlewizDoc* pContainer)
    : COleClientItem(pContainer)
{
    // TODO: add one-time construction code here

}

COlewizCntrItem::~COlewizCntrItem()
{
    // TODO: add cleanup code here

}

void COlewizCntrItem::OnChange(OLE_NOTIFICATION nCode, DWORD dwParam)
{
    ASSERT_VALID(this);

    COleClientItem::OnChange(nCode, dwParam);

    // When an item is being edited (either in-place or fully open)
    //  it sends OnChange notifications for changes in the state of the
    //  item or visual appearance of its content.

    // TODO: invalidate the item by calling UpdateAllViews
    //  (with hints appropriate to your application)

    GetDocument()->UpdateAllViews(NULL);
        // for now just update ALL views/no hints
}

BOOL COlewizCntrItem::OnChangeItemPosition(const CRect& rectPos)
{
    ASSERT_VALID(this);

```

```
    // During in-place activation COlewizCntrItem::OnChangeItemPosition
    //  is called by the server to change the position of the in-place
    //  window.  Usually, this is a result of the data in the server
    //  document changing such that the extent has changed or as a result
    //  of in-place resizing.
    //
    // The default here is to call the base class, which will call
    //  COleClientItem::SetItemRects to move the item
    //  to the new position.

    if (!COleClientItem::OnChangeItemPosition(rectPos))
         return FALSE;

    // TODO: update any cache you may have of the item's rectangle/extent

    return TRUE;
}

void COlewizCntrItem::OnGetItemPosition(CRect& rPosition)
{
    ASSERT_VALID(this);

  // During in-place activation, COlewizCntrItem::OnGetItemPosition
  //  will be called to determine the location of this item.  The default
  //  implementation created from AppWizard simply returns a hard-coded
  //  rectangle.  Usually, this rectangle would reflect the current
  //  position of the item relative to the view used for activation.
  //  You can obtain the view by calling COlewizCntrItem::GetActiveView.

  // TODO: return correct rectangle (in pixels) in rPosition

    rPosition.SetRect(10, 10, 210, 210);
}

void COlewizCntrItem::OnDeactivateUI(BOOL bUndoable)
{
    COleClientItem::OnDeactivateUI(bUndoable);

    // Close an in-place active item whenever it removes the user
    //  interface.  The action here should match as closely as possible
    //  to the handling of the escape key in the view.

    Deactivate();   // nothing fancy here — just deactivate the object
}

void COlewizCntrItem::Serialize(CArchive& ar)
{
    ASSERT_VALID(this);

    // Call base class first to read in COleClientItem data.
    // Since this sets up the m_pDocument pointer returned from
    //  COlewizCntrItem::GetDocument, it is a good idea to call
    //  the base class Serialize first.
    COleClientItem::Serialize(ar);
```

continues

Listing B3.13. continued

```
108:
109:      // now store/retrieve data specific to COlewizCntrItem
110:      if (ar.IsStoring())
111:      {
112:           // TODO: add storing code here
113:      }
114:      else
115:      {
116:           // TODO: add loading code here
117:      }
118:  }
119:
120:  /////////////////////////////////////////////////////////////////////////////
121:  // COlewizCntrItem diagnostics
122:
123:  #ifdef _DEBUG
124:  void COlewizCntrItem::AssertValid() const
125:  {
126:      COleClientItem::AssertValid();
127:  }
128:
129:  void COlewizCntrItem::Dump(CDumpContext& dc) const
130:  {
131:      COleClientItem::Dump(dc);
132:  }
133:  #endif
134:
135:  /////////////////////////////////////////////////////////////////////////////
```

Listing B3.13 shows the source code for the CNTRITEM.CPP implementation file. The listing contains the definitions of the following relevant members:

1. The constructor merely calls the constructor of the parent class. The body of the constructor contains no executable statements.
2. The definition of the destructor is an empty shell.
3. The member function `OnChange` (lines 33 to 48) handles editing an OLE item. The function first invokes `COleClientItem::OnChange`, and then sends the C++ message `UpdateAllViews` to the document.
4. The Boolean member function `OnChangeItemPosition` (lines 50 to 70) returns a Boolean value to indicate whether the edited OLE item changed positions during editing. The function relies on the function `COleClientItem::OnChangeItemPosition` to determine the returned Boolean value.

5. The member function `OnGetItemPosition` (lines 72 to 86) returns the position of the edit OLE item during in-place activation. The function simply sends the C++ message `SetRect` to the member `rPosition`. The arguments for this message are the arbitrary values `10`, `10`, `210`, and `210`.

6. The member function `OnDeactivateUI` (lines 88 to 97) handles deactivating an OLE item. The function invokes the parent's function `OnDeactivateUI`, and then invokes the function `Deactivate`.

Summary

This chapter introduces you to programming OLE 2.0 applications. It covers the following topics:

- The existing features of object-oriented technology (OOT), which includes the ability to launch applications that are associated with various data files. The WIN.INI file lists the association between these files and the application that creates and edits them.
- The fundamental features of OLE 2.0, which enable you to link or embed an OLE item in a host document. The term *client* refers to the host document that contains OLE items. The term *server* refers to the application that creates and edits the OLE items.
- The MFC-related OLE terminology. You learned about compound documents, client applications, server applications, mini-server applications, and full-server applications.
- An overview of the OLE classes in the MFC library, which includes the OLE base classes, the OLE client classes, the OLE server classes, and the OLE exception classes. The MFC library also contains many other OLE-related classes to support the sophisticated OLE 2.0 mechanisms.
- A sample program generated by the AppWizard utility. This program works as a repertoire for OLE items, enabling you to create, edit, save, and load these items.

Q&A

Q Does OLE 2.0 replace the DDE (dynamic data exchange) mechanism promoted by Microsoft?

A Yes, OLE 2.0 has features that include and superset those of DDE. In fact, DDE has reached a dead end as far as developers are concerned. The future is with OLE Version 2.0 and beyond.

Q Where do I learn more about OLE?

A Several advanced Visual C++ programming and Windows programming books, which discuss OLE 2.0 programming in more detail.

Exercises

1. Create the project OLEWIZ2 by following the same steps as in project OLEWIZ, except check the **Automation support** radio button in the MFC AppWizard - Step 3 of 6 dialog box. Compare the output files for project OLWWIZ2 with those of OLEWIZ. What is the difference in the new program's behavior?
2. Create the project OLEWIZ3 by following the same steps as in project OLEWIZ, except check the **Full container and server** radio button in the OLE Options dialog box. Compare the output files for project OLWWIZ2 with those of OLEWIZ. What is the difference in the new program's behavior?

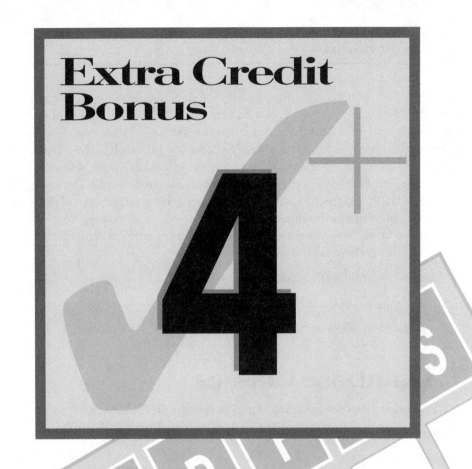

Extra Credit Bonus

4

Using the Database Features

Starting with version 1.5, Visual C++ offers new MFC classes to support the Open Database Connectivity (ODBC) features. This means that you can develop Visual C++ database applications that can access database files for Microsoft Access, Microsoft FoxPro, Borland dBASE, Borland Paradox, Btrieve, Microsoft Excel, Microsoft SQL Server, Oracle, and Text (text files containing comma-delimited records). Discussing the details of the ODBC and the MFC classes that support it is beyond the scope of this book. Nevertheless, the topic is important and does deserve an overview. This chapter introduces you to the MFC database classes and uses an example to demonstrate these classes. This chapter discusses the following topics:

- An overview of the MFC database classes
- Running the ENROLL.EXE sample program
- An overview of the source code files for the ENROLL.EXE program

MFC Database Classes

The MFC library offers the following classes to support ODBC drivers:

- `CDatabase`
- `CRecordset`
- `CFieldExchange`
- `CRecordView`
- `CLongBinary`
- `CDBException`

The class `CDatabase`, a descendant of class `CObject`, provides the bridge to access a data source (located in a database file). The class provides members to open, close, and fine-tune the modes of operating on the data source. For example, the class provides member functions to start and end a series of reversible transactions, to reverse the transactions, and to execute SQL (pronounced *sequel*) statements.

The class `CRecordset`, a descendant of class `CObject`, models a collection of database records known as *recordsets*. The instances of class `CRecordset` support two kinds of recordsets: *snapshots* and *dynasets*. A *snapshot* is a static recordset that represents the state of the database at the instance the snapshot was created. The *dynaset* is a dynamic recordset that remains updated by the transactions of the database users. The class `CRecordset` supports the following kinds of operations:

- Scrolling through records
- Updating (adding, deleting, and editing) records and designating a locking mode
- Filtering the recordset to pick specific records
- Sorting the records in the recordset
- Parameterizing the recordset to customize its selection with data only available at runtime

The class `CFieldExchange` provides member functions to assist the record field exchange (RFX) process involving the other MFC database classes. The class supports swapping data between the field data members or the parameter data members of a recordset instance and the associated table columns on the data source.

The class `CRecordView`, a descendant of class `CFormView`, models a view that shows the database record inside controls. An instance of class `CRecordView` is a special form view that is attached to a `CRecordSet` instance. The record view automatically exchanges data with the recordset using the dialog box exchange (DDX) and record field exchange (RFX) mechanisms. The class `CRecordView` also provides member functions to move to the first, last, next, and previous records, as well as to query whether the current record is either the first or last in the recordset.

B4

The class `CLongBinary`, a descendant of class `CObject`, assists in handling sizable binary data objects, called *BLOBs (Binary Large Objects)*, that exist in a database. A bitmap is a good example of a BLOB.

The class `CDBException`, a descendant of class `CException`, models the exception raised by a database class.

Running the ENROLL.EXE Program

Visual C++ includes a set of four related programs that demonstrate a different version of a student registration database. The directory \MSVC20\MFC\SAMPLES\ENROLL contains the database file STDREG.MDB. The subdirectories STEP1 through STEP4 contain the four versions of project ENROLL. In this chapter, I focus on the project in directory \MSVC20\MFC\SAMPLES\ENROLL\STEP4.

Open the ENROLL project in directory \MSVC20\MFC\SAMPLES\ENROLL\STEP4; then compile and run the project. When the program starts running, it displays the Select Database dialog box (which is very similar to an Open dialog box) so that you can select the STDREG.MDB database file in directory \MSVC20\MFC\SAMPLES\ENROLL. After you select the database file, the application displays the frame window. Figure B4.1 shows the initial client area after maximizing the main frame window. The program supports two forms: the sections and course forms. The sections form (which is the initially selected form) contains edit box controls for the instructor, room, schedule, capacity, and section. In addition, the form has a drop-down combo box for the course ID. The program has a toolbar and a status bar. The toolbar has four buttons, which allow you to select the first, previous, next, and last records. In addition, there are the bitmaps with the symbols +, \, and - to add a record, cancel entering a record, and delete the current record. The **Record** menu selection duplicates these toolbar options.

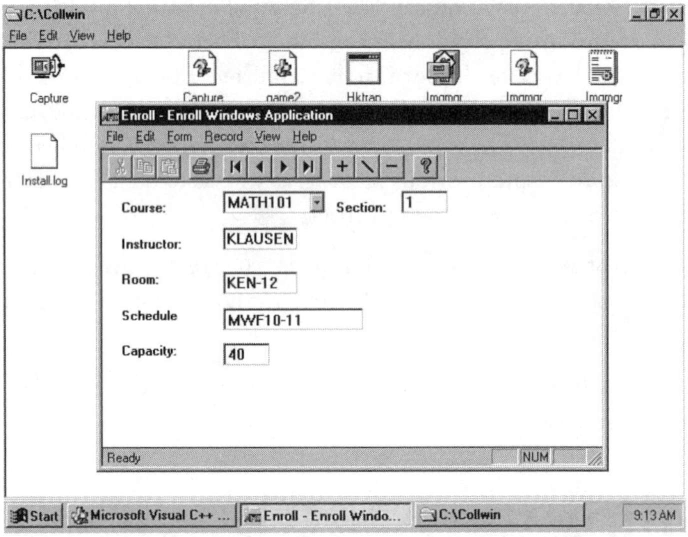

Figure B4.1. *The initial client area after maximizing the main frame window.*

To select the course form, choose **Course** from the **Form** menu. Figure B4.2 shows the course form that contains edit box controls for the course ID, title, and hours.

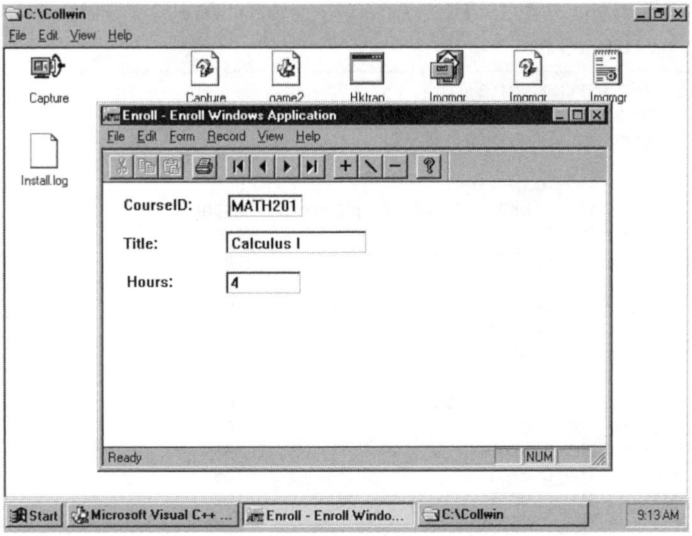

Figure B4.2. *The course form that contains edit box controls for the course ID, title, and hours.*

Experiment with selecting the two forms, and with navigating through the records—there are only a few. You can add new records and delete them later. When you are finished working with the program, choose **Exit** from the **File** menu.

The Source Code for Program ENROLL.EXE

The ENROLL.EXE program represents an interesting example of a simple database built using the MFC database classes. In this section, I present the relevant source code files and focus mainly on the code that supports the database side of the application.

The interesting aspect about program ENROLL.EXE is that it owns two related view forms: the course form and the sections form. These views have in common the course ID data. You update the courses using the course form to add, delete, or edit course recordsets. The sections form uses the course ID in a special manner—each record allows you to view the list of course IDs using the **Course** drop-down combo box. Thus, the program needs to update the combo box in the sections form when you change course records in the course form. The program uses a hint object to perform this kind of update.

Listing B4.1. The source code for the RESOURCE.H header file.

```
//{{NO_DEPENDENCIES}}
// Microsoft Visual C++ generated include file.
// Used by enroll.rc
//
#define IDR_MAINFRAME                   2
#define IDS_CANNOT_DELETE_COURSE_WITH_SECTION 3
#define IDD_ABOUTBOX                    100
#define IDD_DIALOG_FORM                 101
#define IDC_COURSE                      101
#define IDD_ENROLL_FORM                 101
#define IDC_SECTION                     102
#define IDD_COURSE_FORM                 102
#define IDC_INSTRUCTOR                  103
#define IDP_FAILED_OPEN_DATABASE        103
#define IDC_ROOM                        104
#define IDC_SCHEDULE                    105
#define IDC_CAPACITY                    106
#define IDD_COURSE                      107
#define IDC_COURSELIST                  108
#define IDC_COURSEID                    109
#define IDC_TITLE                       110
#define IDC_HOURS                       111
#define ID_RECORD_ADD                   32771
#define ID_RECORD_REFRESH               32772
#define ID_RECORD_DELETE                32773
#define ID_FORM_COURSE                  32774
#define ID_FORM_SECTIONS                32775
#define ID_FORM_COURSES                 32776
#define ID_RECORD_SAVE                  32777

// Next default values for new objects
//
#ifdef APSTUDIO_INVOKED
#ifndef APSTUDIO_READONLY_SYMBOLS
#define _APS_NEXT_RESOURCE_VALUE        103
#define _APS_NEXT_COMMAND_VALUE         32778
#define _APS_NEXT_CONTROL_VALUE         112
#define _APS_NEXT_SYMED_VALUE           101
#endif
#endif
```

Listing B4.1 shows the source code for the RESOURCE.H header file. This file declares the identifiers for the menu resource, the menu options, the About dialog, the database forms, and the controls of these forms.

Listing B4.2. The partial script for the ENROLL.RC resource file.

```
//Microsoft Visual C++ generated resource script.
//
#include "resource.h"

#define APSTUDIO_READONLY_SYMBOLS
.
.
.
/////////////////////////////////////////////////////////////////////////////
//
// Menu
//

IDR_MAINFRAME MENU PRELOAD DISCARDABLE
BEGIN
    POPUP "&File"
    BEGIN
        MENUITEM "&Print...\tCtrl+P",           ID_FILE_PRINT
        MENUITEM "Print Pre&view",              ID_FILE_PRINT_PREVIEW
        MENUITEM "P&rint Setup...",             ID_FILE_PRINT_SETUP
        MENUITEM SEPARATOR
        MENUITEM "E&xit",                       ID_APP_EXIT
    END
    POPUP "&Edit"
    BEGIN
        MENUITEM "&Undo\tCtrl+Z",               ID_EDIT_UNDO
        MENUITEM SEPARATOR
        MENUITEM "Cu&t\tCtrl+X",                ID_EDIT_CUT
        MENUITEM "&Copy\tCtrl+C",               ID_EDIT_COPY
        MENUITEM "&Paste\tCtrl+V",              ID_EDIT_PASTE
    END
    POPUP "&Form"
    BEGIN
        MENUITEM "&Course",                     ID_FORM_COURSES
        MENUITEM "&Sections",                   ID_FORM_SECTIONS
    END
    POPUP "&Record"
    BEGIN
        MENUITEM "&Add",                        ID_RECORD_ADD
        MENUITEM "&Refresh\tEsc",               ID_RECORD_REFRESH
        MENUITEM "&Delete",                     ID_RECORD_DELETE
        MENUITEM SEPARATOR
        MENUITEM "&First Record",               ID_RECORD_FIRST
        MENUITEM "&Previous Record",            ID_RECORD_PREV
        MENUITEM "&Next Record",                ID_RECORD_NEXT
        MENUITEM "&Last Record",                ID_RECORD_LAST
    END
    POPUP "&View"
    BEGIN
        MENUITEM "&Toolbar",                    ID_VIEW_TOOLBAR
        MENUITEM "&Status Bar",                 ID_VIEW_STATUS_BAR
    END
```

continues

Listing B4.2. continued

```
    POPUP "&Help"
    BEGIN
        MENUITEM "&About Enroll...",            ID_APP_ABOUT
    END
END

.
.
.
/////////////////////////////////////////////////////////////////////////////
//
// Dialog
//

IDD_ABOUTBOX DIALOG DISCARDABLE  34, 22, 217, 55
STYLE DS_MODALFRAME | WS_POPUP | WS_CAPTION | WS_SYSMENU
CAPTION "About Enroll"
FONT 8, "MS Sans Serif"
BEGIN
    ICON            IDR_MAINFRAME,IDC_STATIC,11,17,20,20
    LTEXT           "Enroll Application Version 1.0",IDC_STATIC,40,10,119,8
    LTEXT           "Copyright \251 1993",IDC_STATIC,40,25,119,8
    DEFPUSHBUTTON   "OK",IDOK,176,6,32,14,WS_GROUP
END

IDD_ENROLL_FORM DIALOG DISCARDABLE  0, 0, 196, 110
STYLE WS_CHILD | WS_BORDER
FONT 8, "MS Sans Serif"
BEGIN
    LTEXT           "Course:",IDC_STATIC,10,10,30,8
    LTEXT           "Section:",IDC_STATIC,125,10,30,8
    EDITTEXT        IDC_SECTION,160,5,25,13,ES_AUTOHSCROLL | ES_READONLY
    LTEXT           "Instructor:",IDC_STATIC,10,30,35,8
    EDITTEXT        IDC_INSTRUCTOR,65,25,40,13,ES_AUTOHSCROLL
    LTEXT           "Room:",IDC_STATIC,10,50,30,8
    EDITTEXT        IDC_ROOM,65,50,40,13,ES_AUTOHSCROLL
    LTEXT           "Schedule:",IDC_STATIC,10,70,30,8
    EDITTEXT        IDC_SCHEDULE,65,70,75,13,ES_AUTOHSCROLL
    LTEXT           "Capacity:",IDC_STATIC,10,90,30,8
    EDITTEXT        IDC_CAPACITY,65,90,25,13,ES_AUTOHSCROLL
    COMBOBOX        IDC_COURSELIST,65,5,55,65,CBS_DROPDOWNLIST | CBS_SORT |
                    WS_VSCROLL | WS_TABSTOP
END

IDD_COURSE_FORM DIALOG DISCARDABLE  0, 0, 185, 65
STYLE WS_CHILD | WS_BORDER
FONT 8, "MS Sans Serif"
BEGIN
    LTEXT           "CourseID:",IDC_STATIC,10,15,34,8
    LTEXT           "Title:",IDC_STATIC,10,30,30,8
    LTEXT           "Hours:",IDC_STATIC,10,45,30,8
    EDITTEXT        IDC_COURSEID,50,10,40,13,ES_AUTOHSCROLL | ES_READONLY
```

```
    EDITTEXT        IDC_TITLE,50,25,125,13,ES_AUTOHSCROLL
    EDITTEXT        IDC_HOURS,50,40,40,13,ES_AUTOHSCROLL
END

.
.
.
/////////////////////////////////////////////////////////////////////////////
#endif    // not APSTUDIO_INVOKED
```

Listing B4.2 shows the partial script for the ENROLL.RC resource file. The listing shows the resources for the menu, the course form, and the sections form. The resource file declares the two student registration forms as dialog resources. These form resources contain statements that define their controls—mostly static text and edit text controls.

Listing B4.3. The source code for the MAINFRM.H header file.

```
// mainfrm.h : interface of the CMainFrame class
//
/////////////////////////////////////////////////////////////////////////////

#define IDW_COURSE_FORM 1
#define IDW_SECTION_FORM 2

class CMainFrame : public CFrameWnd
{
protected: // create from serialization only
    CMainFrame();
    DECLARE_DYNCREATE(CMainFrame)

// Attributes
public:

// Operations
public:

// Overrides
    // ClassWizard generated virtual function overrides
    //{{AFX_VIRTUAL(CMainFrame)
    //}}AFX_VIRTUAL

// Implementation
public:
    virtual ~CMainFrame();
#ifdef _DEBUG
    virtual void AssertValid() const;
    virtual void Dump(CDumpContext& dc) const;
#endif


```

continues

Listing B4.3. continued

```
protected:  // control bar embedded members
     CStatusBar  m_wndStatusBar;
     CToolBar    m_wndToolBar;

     void SwitchToForm(int nForm);

// Generated message map functions
protected:
     //{{AFX_MSG(CMainFrame)
     afx_msg int OnCreate(LPCREATESTRUCT lpCreateStruct);
     afx_msg void OnFormCourses();
     afx_msg void OnUpdateFormCourses(CCmdUI* pCmdUI);
     afx_msg void OnFormSections();
     afx_msg void OnUpdateFormSections(CCmdUI* pCmdUI);
     //}}AFX_MSG
     DECLARE_MESSAGE_MAP()
};

/////////////////////////////////////////////////////////////////////
```

Listing B4.3 shows the source code for the MAINFRM.H header file. The file declares the main frame class, `CMainFrame`, as a descendant of class `CFrameWnd`. This means that the ENROLL.EXE program has an SDI view. The class declares a constructor; a destructor; and the member functions `AssertValid`, `Dump`, `SwitchToForm`, `OnCreate`, `OnFormCourses`, `OnUpdateFormCourses`, `OnFormSections`, and `OnUpdateFormSections`. The set of `OnXXXX` functions handles invoking and updating the two forms. The class also declares the data members `m_wndStatusBar` and `m_wndToolBar` to manage the status bar and the toolbar, respectively.

Listing B4.4. The source code for the ENROLL.H header file.

```
// enroll.h : main header file for the ENROLL application
//

#ifndef __AFXWIN_H__
 #error include 'stdafx.h' before including this file for PCH
#endif

#include "resource.h"       // main symbols

/////////////////////////////////////////////////////////////////////////////
// CEnrollApp:
// See enroll.cpp for the implementation of this class
//

class CEnrollApp : public CWinApp
```

```
{
public:
    CEnrollApp();

// Overrides
    // ClassWizard generated virtual function overrides
    //{{AFX_VIRTUAL(CEnrollApp)
    public:
    virtual BOOL InitInstance();
    //}}AFX_VIRTUAL

// Implementation

    //{{AFX_MSG(CEnrollApp)
    afx_msg void OnAppAbout();
// NOTE - the ClassWizard will add and remove member functions here.
//    DO NOT EDIT what you see in these blocks of generated code !
    //}}AFX_MSG
    DECLARE_MESSAGE_MAP()
};


/////////////////////////////////////////////////////////////////////////////
```


Listing B4.4 holds the source code for the ENROLL.H header file. This file declares the application class `CEnrollApp` as a descendant of class `CWinApp`. The class also declares the constructor and the member functions `InitInstance` and `OnAppAbout`.

Type

Listing B4.5. The source code for the ENROLDOC.H header file.

```
// enroldoc.h : interface of the CEnrollDoc class
//
/////////////////////////////////////////////////////////////////////////////

#define HINT_ADD_COURSE 1
#define HINT_DELETE_COURSE 2

class CUpdateHint : public CObject
{
    DECLARE_DYNAMIC(CUpdateHint);
    CUpdateHint();
    CString m_strCourse;
};
class CEnrollDoc : public CDocument
{
protected: // create from serialization only
    CEnrollDoc();
    DECLARE_DYNCREATE(CEnrollDoc)

// Attributes
protected:
```

continues

Listing B4.5. continued

```
22:      CDatabase m_database;
23:  public:
24:      CSectionSet m_sectionSet;
25:      CCourseSet m_courseSet; // for combobox in CSectionForm
26:      CCourseSet m_courseSetForForm; // for CCourseForm
27:
28:  // Operations
29:  public:
30:
31:  // Overrides
32:      // ClassWizard generated virtual function overrides
33:      //{{AFX_VIRTUAL(CEnrollDoc)
34:      public:
35:      virtual BOOL OnNewDocument();
36:      //}}AFX_VIRTUAL
37:
38:      CDatabase* GetDatabase();
39:
40:  // Implementation
41:  public:
42:      virtual ~CEnrollDoc();
43:  #ifdef _DEBUG
44:      virtual void AssertValid() const;
45:      virtual void Dump(CDumpContext& dc) const;
46:  #endif
47:
48:  protected:
49:
50:  // Generated message map functions
51:  protected:
52:      //{{AFX_MSG(CEnrollDoc)
53:         // NOTE - the ClassWizard will add and remove member functions here.
54:           //    DO NOT EDIT what you see in these blocks of generated code !
55:     //}}AFX_MSG
56:      DECLARE_MESSAGE_MAP()
57:  };
58:
59:  /////////////////////////////////////////////////////////////////////////////
```

Listing B4.5 shows the source code for the ENROLDOC.H header file. This file declares the classes `CUpdateHint` and `CEnrollDoc`. The document class `CEnrollDoc`, a descendant of class `CDocument`, declares the constructor; the destructor; and the member functions `GetDatabase`, `AssertValid`, `Dump`, and `OnNewDocument`. In addition, the class declares the following data members:

- The protected member `m_database` (line 22) is the instance of class `CDatabase`, which provides the connection with the data source.
- The member `m_sectionSet` (line 24) is the instance of class `CSectionSet`, which accesses the sections recordset.

- The member m_courseSet (line 25) is the instance of class CCourseSet, which provides the combo box with the list of courses.
- The member m_courseSetForForm (line 26) is the instance of class CCourseSet, which accesses the course recordset.

Listing B4.6 shows the source code for the COURSSET.H header file. This file contains the declaration of class CCourseSet, a descendant of class CRecordSet, to support the course recordset. The class declares the constructor and the member functions GetDefaultSQL, DoFieldExchange, AssertValid, and Dump. The class also declares the data members m_CourseID, m_CourseTitle, and m_Hours to correspond to the database fields in the course form.

Listing B4.6. The source code for the COURSSET.H header file.

```
// coursset.h : header file
//

/////////////////////////////////////////////////////////////////////////////
// CCourseSet recordset

class CCourseSet : public CRecordset
{
public:
     CCourseSet(CDatabase* pDatabase = NULL);
     DECLARE_DYNAMIC(CCourseSet)

// Field/Param Data
     //{{AFX_FIELD(CCourseSet, CRecordset)
     CString m_CourseID;
     CString m_CourseTitle;
     int     m_Hours;
     //}}AFX_FIELD


// Overrides
     // ClassWizard generated virtual function overrides
     //{{AFX_VIRTUAL(CCourseSet)
     public:
     virtual CString GetDefaultSQL();    // Default SQL for Recordset
     virtual void DoFieldExchange(CFieldExchange* pFX);  // RFX support
     //}}AFX_VIRTUAL

// Implementation
#ifdef _DEBUG
     virtual void AssertValid() const;
     virtual void Dump(CDumpContext& dc) const;
#endif
};
```

Listing B4.7. The source code for the SECTSET.H header file.

```
// sectset.h : interface of the CSectionSet class
//
////////////////////////////////////////////////////////////////////////////

class CSectionSet : public CRecordset
{
public:
     CSectionSet(CDatabase* pDatabase = NULL);
     DECLARE_DYNAMIC(CSectionSet)

// Field/Param Data
     //{{AFX_FIELD(CSectionSet, CRecordset)
     CString m_CourseID;
     CString m_SectionNo;
     CString m_InstructorID;
     CString m_RoomNo;
     CString m_Schedule;
     int m_Capacity;
     //}}AFX_FIELD
     CString m_strCourseIDParam;

// Overrides
     // ClassWizard generated virtual function overrides
     //{{AFX_VIRTUAL(CSectionSet)
     public:
     virtual CString GetDefaultSQL();      // default SQL for Recordset
     virtual void DoFieldExchange(CFieldExchange* pFX);      // RFX support
     //}}AFX_VIRTUAL

// Implementation
#ifdef _DEBUG
     virtual void AssertValid() const;
     virtual void Dump(CDumpContext& dc) const;
#endif

};
```

Listing B4.7 contains the source code for the SECTSET.H header file. This file contains the declaration of class `CSectionSet`, a descendant of class `CRecordSet`, to support the sections recordset. The class declares the constructor and the member functions `GetDefaultSQL`, `DoFieldExchange`, `AssertValid`, and `Dump`. The class also declares the data members `m_CourseID`, `m_SectionNo`, `m_InstructorID`, `m_RoomNo`, `m_Schedule`, `m_Capacity`, and `m_strCourseIDParam` to correspond to the database fields in the sections form.

Listing B4.8. The source code for the ADDFORM.H header file.

```
// addform.h : interface of the CAddForm class
//
/////////////////////////////////////////////////////////////////////////////

class CAddForm : public CRecordView
{
protected:
     CAddForm(UINT nIDTemplate);
     DECLARE_DYNAMIC(CAddForm)

protected:
     BOOL m_bAddMode;

// Operations
public:
     virtual BOOL OnMove(UINT nIDMoveCommand);
     virtual BOOL RecordAdd();
     virtual BOOL RecordRefresh();
     virtual BOOL RecordDelete();

// Implementation
public:
     virtual ~CAddForm();
// Generated message map functions
protected:
     afx_msg void OnRecordAdd();
     afx_msg void OnRecordRefresh();
     afx_msg void OnRecordDelete();
     afx_msg void OnUpdateRecordFirst(CCmdUI* pCmdUI);
     DECLARE_MESSAGE_MAP()
};
```

Listing B4.8 holds the source code for the ADDFORM.H header file. The listing declares the class `CAddForm` as a descendant of class `CRecordView`. The class `CAddForm` is also the parent of the classes modeling the course and sections forms (which I introduce in the next listings). The class declares a constructor; a destructor; and the member functions `OnMove`, `RecordAdd`, `RecordRefresh`, and `RecordDelete`. These member functions play an important role in traversing, adding, refreshing, and deleting the records. In addition, the class declares the message-handling functions `OnRecordAdd`, `OnRecordRefresh`, `OnRecordDelete`, and `OnUpdateRecordFirst`. The class `CAddForm` also declares the Boolean member `m_bAddMode`.

Listing B4.9. The source code for the CRSFORM.H header file.

```
// crsform.h : header file
//

/////////////////////////////////////////////////////////////////////////////
// CCourseForm record view

class CCourseForm : public CAddForm
{
	DECLARE_DYNCREATE(CCourseForm)
public:
	CCourseForm();           // protected constructor used by dynamic creation

// Form Data
public:
	//{{AFX_DATA(CCourseForm)
	enum { IDD = IDD_COURSE_FORM };
	CEdit	m_ctlCourseID;
	CCourseSet* m_pSet;
	//}}AFX_DATA

// Attributes
public:

// Operations
public:

// Overrides
	// ClassWizard generate virtual function overrides
	//{{AFX_VIRTUAL(CSectionForm)
	public:
	virtual CRecordset* OnGetRecordset();
	protected:
	virtual void DoDataExchange(CDataExchange* pDX);    // DDX/DDV support
	virtual void OnInitialUpdate(); // called first time after construct
	virtual BOOL OnMove(UINT nIDMoveCommand);
	//}}AFX_VIRTUAL

// Implementation
protected:
 virtual ~CCourseForm();

	// Generated message map functions
	//{{AFX_MSG(CCourseForm)
	afx_msg void OnRecordAdd();
	afx_msg void OnRecordDelete();
	afx_msg void OnRecordRefresh();
	//}}AFX_MSG
	DECLARE_MESSAGE_MAP()
};

/////////////////////////////////////////////////////////////////////////////
```

Listing B4.9 shows the source code for the CRSFORM.H header file. This file declares the class `CCourseForm` as a descendant of class `CAddForm`. The class declares a constructor; a destructor; and the member functions `OnGetRecordSet`, `OnMove`, `DoDataExchange`, `OnInitialUpdate`, `OnRecordAdd`, `OnRecordDelete`, and `OnRecordRefresh`. Some of these functions override the inherited functions to refine the actions of the inherited functions. The class also declares the data members `m_ctlCourseID` (an instance of class `CEdit`) and `m_pSet` (a pointer to class `CCourseSet`).

Type

Listing B4.10. The source code for the SECTFORM.H header file.

```
// sectform.h : interface of the CSectionForm class
//
//////////////////////////////////////////////////////////////////////////

class CSectionSet;

class CSectionForm : public CAddForm
{
public:
     CSectionForm();
     DECLARE_DYNCREATE(CSectionForm)

public:
     //{{AFX_DATA(CSectionForm)
     enum{ IDD = IDD_ENROLL_FORM };
     CEdit   m_ctlSection;
     CComboBox   m_ctlCourseList;
     CSectionSet* m_pSet;
     //}}AFX_DATA
// Attributes
public:
     CEnrollDoc* GetDocument();

// Operations
public:

// Overrides
     // ClassWizard generated virtual function overrides
     //{{AFX_VIRTUAL(CSectionForm)
     public:
     virtual CRecordset* OnGetRecordset();
     virtual BOOL OnMove(UINT nIDMoveCommand);
     protected:
     virtual void DoDataExchange(CDataExchange* pDX);     // DDX/DDV support
     virtual void OnInitialUpdate(); // called first time after construct
     virtual BOOL OnPreparePrinting(CPrintInfo* pInfo);
     virtual void OnBeginPrinting(CDC* pDC, CPrintInfo* pInfo);
     virtual void OnEndPrinting(CDC* pDC, CPrintInfo* pInfo);
     virtual void OnUpdate(CView* pSender, LPARAM lHint, CObject* pHint);
     //}}AFX_VIRTUAL

```

continues

Listing B4.10. continued

```
// Implementation
public:
     virtual ~CSectionForm();
#ifdef _DEBUG
     virtual void AssertValid() const;
     virtual void Dump(CDumpContext& dc) const;
#endif

protected:

// Generated message map functions
protected:
     //{{AFX_MSG(CSectionForm)
     afx_msg void OnSelendokCourselist();
     afx_msg void OnRecordAdd();
     afx_msg void OnRecordRefresh();
     //}}AFX_MSG
     DECLARE_MESSAGE_MAP()
};

#ifndef _DEBUG  // debug version in sectform.cpp
inline CEnrollDoc* CSectionForm::GetDocument()
   { return (CEnrollDoc*)m_pDocument; }
#endif



/////////////////////////////////////////////////////////////////////////////
```

Listing B4.10 shows the source code for the SECTFORM.H header file. The file declares the class `CSectionForm` as a descendant of class `CAddForm`. The class declares a constructor; a destructor; and the member functions `GetDocument`, `OnGetRecordset`, `OnMove`, `AssertValid`, `Dump`, `DoDataExchange`, `OnInitialUpdate`, `OnUpdate`, `OnPreparePrinting`, `OnBeginPrinting`, `OnEndPrinting`, `OnRecordAdd`, `OnRecordRefresh`, and `OnSelendokCourselist`. The class `CSectionForm` supports more operations, including printing, than class `CCourseForm`. In addition, the class declares the members `m_ctlSection` (an instance of class `CEdit`), `m_ctlCourseList` (an instance of class `CComboBox`), and `m_pSet` (a pointer to class `CSectionSet`).

Type Listing B4.11. The source code for the MAINFRM.CPP implementation file.

```
// mainfrm.cpp : implementation of the CMainFrame class
//

#include "stdafx.h"
#include "enroll.h"
```

```
#include "mainfrm.h"
#include "sectset.h"
#include "coursset.h"
#include "addform.h"
#include "crsform.h"
#include "enroldoc.h"
#include "sectform.h"

#ifdef _DEBUG
#undef THIS_FILE
static char BASED_CODE THIS_FILE[] = __FILE__;
#endif

/////////////////////////////////////////////////////////////////////////////
// CMainFrame

IMPLEMENT_DYNCREATE(CMainFrame, CFrameWnd)

BEGIN_MESSAGE_MAP(CMainFrame, CFrameWnd)
    //{{AFX_MSG_MAP(CMainFrame)
    ON_WM_CREATE()
    ON_WM_CREATE()
    ON_COMMAND(ID_FORM_COURSES, OnFormCourses)
    ON_UPDATE_COMMAND_UI(ID_FORM_COURSES, OnUpdateFormCourses)
    ON_COMMAND(ID_FORM_SECTIONS, OnFormSections)
    ON_UPDATE_COMMAND_UI(ID_FORM_SECTIONS, OnUpdateFormSections)
    //}}AFX_MSG_MAP
END_MESSAGE_MAP()

/////////////////////////////////////////////////////////////////////////////
// arrays of IDs used to initialize control bars

// toolbar buttons - IDs are command buttons
static UINT BASED_CODE buttons[] =
{
    // same order as in the bitmap 'toolbar.bmp'
    ID_EDIT_CUT,
    ID_EDIT_COPY,
    ID_EDIT_PASTE,
          ID_SEPARATOR,
    ID_FILE_PRINT,
         ID_SEPARATOR,
    ID_RECORD_FIRST,
    ID_RECORD_PREV,
    ID_RECORD_NEXT,
    ID_RECORD_LAST,
         ID_SEPARATOR,
    ID_RECORD_ADD,
    ID_RECORD_REFRESH,
    ID_RECORD_DELETE,
         ID_SEPARATOR,
    ID_APP_ABOUT,
};

static UINT BASED_CODE indicators[] =
{
```

continues

Listing B4.11. continued

```
    ID_SEPARATOR,           // status line indicator
    ID_INDICATOR_CAPS,
    ID_INDICATOR_NUM,
    ID_INDICATOR_SCRL,
};

/////////////////////////////////////////////////////////////////////////////
// CMainFrame construction/destruction

CMainFrame::CMainFrame()
{
    // TODO: add member initialization code here
}

CMainFrame::~CMainFrame()
{
}

int CMainFrame::OnCreate(LPCREATESTRUCT lpCreateStruct)
{
    if (CFrameWnd::OnCreate(lpCreateStruct) == -1)
         return -1;

    if (!m_wndToolBar.Create(this) ¦¦
         !m_wndToolBar.LoadBitmap(IDR_MAINFRAME) ¦¦
         !m_wndToolBar.SetButtons(buttons,
           sizeof(buttons)/sizeof(UINT)))
    {
         TRACE0("Failed to create toolbar\n");
         return -1;      // fail to create
    }

    if (!m_wndStatusBar.Create(this) ¦¦
         !m_wndStatusBar.SetIndicators(indicators,
           sizeof(indicators)/sizeof(UINT)))
    {
         TRACE0("Failed to create status bar\n");
         return -1;      // fail to create
    }

    // TODO: Delete these three lines if you don't want the toolbar to
    //  be dockable
    m_wndToolBar.EnableDocking(CBRS_ALIGN_ANY);
    EnableDocking(CBRS_ALIGN_ANY);
    DockControlBar(&m_wndToolBar);

    // TODO: Remove this if you don't want tool tips
    m_wndToolBar.SetBarStyle(m_wndToolBar.GetBarStyle() ¦
          CBRS_TOOLTIPS ¦ CBRS_FLYBY);

    return 0;
}


```

```
void CMainFrame::SwitchToForm(int nForm)
{
    CView* pOldActiveView = GetActiveView();
    CView* pNewActiveView = (CView*)GetDlgItem(nForm);
    if (pNewActiveView == NULL)
    {
         if (nForm == IDW_COURSE_FORM)
              pNewActiveView = (CView*)new CCourseForm;
         else
              pNewActiveView = (CView*)new CSectionForm;


         CCreateContext context;
         Context.m_pCurrentDoc = pOldActiveView->GetDocument();
         pNewActiveView->Create(NULL, NULL, 0L, CFrameWnd::rectDefault,
              this, nForm, &context);
         pNewActiveView->OnInitialUpdate();
    }

    SetActiveView(pNewActiveView);
    pNewActiveView->ShowWindow(SW_SHOW);
    pOldActiveView->ShowWindow(SW_HIDE);
    pOldActiveView->SetDlgCtrlID(
         pOldActiveView->GetRuntimeClass() == RUNTIME_CLASS(CCourseForm) ?
         IDW_COURSE_FORM : IDW_SECTION_FORM);
    pNewActiveView->SetDlgCtrlID(AFX_IDW_PANE_FIRST);
    RecalcLayout();
}


/////////////////////////////////////////////////////////////////////////////
// CMainFrame diagnostics

#ifdef _DEBUG
void CMainFrame::AssertValid() const
{
    CFrameWnd::AssertValid();
}

void CMainFrame::Dump(CDumpContext& dc) const
{
    CFrameWnd::Dump(dc);
}

#endif //_DEBUG

/////////////////////////////////////////////////////////////////////////////
// CMainFrame message handlers

void CMainFrame::OnFormCourses()
{
    if (GetActiveView()->IsKindOf(RUNTIME_CLASS(CCourseForm)))
         return; // already active
    SwitchToForm(IDW_COURSE_FORM);
}

```


continues

Listing B4.11. continued

```
172: void CMainFrame::OnUpdateFormCourses(CCmdUI* pCmdUI)
173: {
174:     pCmdUI->SetCheck(
             GetActiveView()->IsKindOf(RUNTIME_CLASS(CCourseForm)));
175: }
176:
177: void CMainFrame::OnFormSections()
178: {
179:     if (GetActiveView()->IsKindOf(RUNTIME_CLASS(CSectionForm)))
180:         return; // already active
181:     SwitchToForm(IDW_SECTION_FORM);
182: }
183:
184: void CMainFrame::OnUpdateFormSections(CCmdUI* pCmdUI)
185: {
186:     pCmdUI->SetCheck(
             GetActiveView()->IsKindOf(RUNTIME_CLASS(CSectionForm)));
187: }
```

Listing B4.11 shows the source code for the MAINFRM.CPP implementation file. The listing defines the message map macros by using entries that deal with invoking and updating the two database forms. The listing declares the following database-related member functions:

1. The member function `SwitchToForm` (lines 116 to 143) switches between the two database forms. The code for the function takes into account that initially neither form is present. The function creates the course and section forms as needed. The function also hides one form to show the other one.

2. The member function `OnFormCourses` (lines 163 to 170) handles selecting the course form. If that form is already selected, the function simply exits. Otherwise, the function `OnFormCourses` invokes the function `SwitchToForm` and supplies that function with the argument `IDW_COURSE_FORM`.

3. The member function `OnFormSections` (lines 177 to 182) handles selecting the sections form. If that form is already selected, the function simply exits. Otherwise, the function `OnFormSections` invokes the function `SwitchToForm` and supplies that function with the argument `IDW_SECTION_FORM`.

Listing B4.12. The source code for the ENROLL.CPP implementation file.

```
// enroll.cpp : Defines the class behaviors for the application.
//

```

```
#include "stdafx.h"
#include "enroll.h"

#include "mainfrm.h"
#include "sectset.h"
#include "coursset.h"
#include "enroldoc.h"
#include "addform.h"
#include "sectform.h"

#ifdef _DEBUG
#undef THIS_FILE
static char BASED_CODE THIS_FILE[] = __FILE__;
#endif

/////////////////////////////////////////////////////////////////////////////
// CEnrollApp

BEGIN_MESSAGE_MAP(CEnrollApp, CWinApp)
    //{{AFX_MSG_MAP(CEnrollApp)
    ON_COMMAND(ID_APP_ABOUT, OnAppAbout)
    // NOTE - the ClassWizard will add and remove mapping macros here.
    //    DO NOT EDIT what you see in these blocks of generated code!
    //}}AFX_MSG_MAP
    // Standard print setup command
    ON_COMMAND(ID_FILE_PRINT_SETUP, CWinApp::OnFilePrintSetup)
END_MESSAGE_MAP()

/////////////////////////////////////////////////////////////////////////////
// CEnrollApp construction

CEnrollApp::CEnrollApp()
{
    // TODO: add construction code here,
    // Place all significant initialization in InitInstance
}

/////////////////////////////////////////////////////////////////////////////
// The one and only CEnrollApp object

CEnrollApp theApp;

/////////////////////////////////////////////////////////////////////////////
// CEnrollApp initialization

BOOL CEnrollApp::InitInstance()
{
    // Standard initialization
    // If you are not using these features and wish to reduce the size
    //  of your final executable, you should remove from the following
    //  the specific initialization routines you do not need.

    Enable3dControls();

    LoadStdProfileSettings();  // Load standard INI file options (including MRU)

```

continues

Listing B4.12. continued

```
    // Register the application's document templates.  Document templates
    //  serve as the connection between documents, frame windows and views.

    CSingleDocTemplate* pDocTemplate;
    pDocTemplate = new CSingleDocTemplate(
         IDR_MAINFRAME,
         RUNTIME_CLASS(CEnrollDoc),
         RUNTIME_CLASS(CMainFrame),     // main SDI frame window
         RUNTIME_CLASS(CSectionForm));
    AddDocTemplate(pDocTemplate);


    // create a new (empty) document
    OnFileNew();

    if (m_lpCmdLine[0] != '\0')
    {
         // TODO: add command line processing here
    }


    return TRUE;
}

/////////////////////////////////////////////////////////////////////////////
// CAboutDlg dialog used for App About

class CAboutDlg : public CDialog
{
public:
    CAboutDlg();

// Dialog Data
    //{{AFX_DATA(CAboutDlg)
    enum { IDD = IDD_ABOUTBOX };
    //}}AFX_DATA

// Implementation
protected:
    virtual void DoDataExchange(CDataExchange* pDX);    // DDX/DDV support
    //{{AFX_MSG(CAboutDlg)
          // No message handlers
    //}}AFX_MSG
    DECLARE_MESSAGE_MAP()
};

CAboutDlg::CAboutDlg() : CDialog(CAboutDlg::IDD)
{
    //{{AFX_DATA_INIT(CAboutDlg)
    //}}AFX_DATA_INIT
}

void CAboutDlg::DoDataExchange(CDataExchange* pDX)
{
```

```
    CDialog::DoDataExchange(pDX);
    //{{AFX_DATA_MAP(CAboutDlg)
    //}}AFX_DATA_MAP
}

BEGIN_MESSAGE_MAP(CAboutDlg, CDialog)
    //{{AFX_MSG_MAP(CAboutDlg)
         // No message handlers
    //}}AFX_MSG_MAP
END_MESSAGE_MAP()

// App command to run the dialog
void CEnrollApp::OnAppAbout()
{
    CAboutDlg aboutDlg;
    aboutDlg.DoModal();
}

/////////////////////////////////////////////////////////////////////////////
// CEnrollApp commands
```

Listing B4.12 contains the source code for the ENROLL.CPP implementation file. The member function contains an empty-shell definition of the constructor, as well as the definition of member function `InitInstance`. The code for this function reveals that it performs straightforward initialization of an SDI-compliant application. This includes setting the dialog box color to gray, loading the standard .INI file options, registering the document template, and opening a new file. The listing also contains the definitions of the member functions of class `CAboutDlg`.

Listing B4.13. The source code for the ENROLDOC.CPP implementation file.

```
// enroldoc.cpp : implementation of the CEnrollDoc class
//

#include "stdafx.h"
#include "enroll.h"
#include "sectset.h"
#include "coursset.h"
#include "enroldoc.h"

#ifdef _DEBUG
#undef THIS_FILE
static char BASED_CODE THIS_FILE[] = __FILE__;
#endif

/////////////////////////////////////////////////////////////////////////////
// CUpdateHint

IMPLEMENT_DYNAMIC(CUpdateHint, CObject)
```

continues

Listing B4.13. continued

```

CUpdateHint::CUpdateHint()
{
}

/////////////////////////////////////////////////////////////////////////////
// CEnrollDoc

IMPLEMENT_DYNCREATE(CEnrollDoc, CDocument)

BEGIN_MESSAGE_MAP(CEnrollDoc, CDocument)
     //{{AFX_MSG_MAP(CEnrollDoc)
   // NOTE - the ClassWizard will add and remove mapping macros here.
   //    DO NOT EDIT what you see in these blocks of generated code!
     //}}AFX_MSG_MAP
END_MESSAGE_MAP()

/////////////////////////////////////////////////////////////////////////////
// CEnrollDoc construction/destruction

CEnrollDoc::CEnrollDoc()
{
     // TODO: add one-time construction code here
}

CEnrollDoc::~CEnrollDoc()
{
}

BOOL CEnrollDoc::OnNewDocument()
{
     if (!CDocument::OnNewDocument())
          return FALSE;

     // TODO: add reinitialization code here
     // (SDI documents will reuse this document)

     return TRUE;
}

/////////////////////////////////////////////////////////////////////////////
// CEnrollDoc database support

CDatabase* CEnrollDoc::GetDatabase()
{
     TRY
     {
          if (!m_database.IsOpen())
               m_database.Open("Student Registration;");
     }
     CATCH(CDBException, e)
     {
          AfxMessageBox(e->m_strError);
     }
```

```
        END_CATCH
        return &m_database;
}

////////////////////////////////////////////////////////////////////////////
// CEnrollDoc diagnostics

#ifdef _DEBUG
void CEnrollDoc::AssertValid() const
{
        CDocument::AssertValid();
}

void CEnrollDoc::Dump(CDumpContext& dc) const
{
        CDocument::Dump(dc);
}
#endif //_DEBUG

////////////////////////////////////////////////////////////////////////////
// CEnrollDoc commands
```


Listing B4.13 shows the source code for the ENROLDOC.CPP implementation file. The listing contains the empty-shell definitions of the constructor and destructor of class `CEnrollDoc`. The relevant member function is `GetDatabase`, which returns a pointer to the database. This function sends the C++ message `IsOpen` to the member `m_database`. If this message returns 0, the function sends the C++ message `Open` to the member `m_database`. The argument for this message is the literal string `"Student Registration"`. This latter message opens the database; without this step, the program has no access to a data source. The function returns the member `m_database`. The code uses a `TRY-CATCH` block to handle runtime errors of the type `CDBException`.

Type Listing B4.14. The source code for the COURSSET.CPP implementation file.

```
// coursset.cpp : implementation file
//

#include "stdafx.h"
#include "enroll.h"
#include "coursset.h"

#ifdef _DEBUG
#undef THIS_FILE
static char BASED_CODE THIS_FILE[] = __FILE__;
#endif

////////////////////////////////////////////////////////////////////////////
// CCourseSet
```

continues

Listing B4.14. continued

```

IMPLEMENT_DYNAMIC(CCourseSet, CRecordset)

CCourseSet::CCourseSet(CDatabase* pdb)
    : CRecordset(pdb)
{
        //{{AFX_FIELD_INIT(CCourseSet)
        m_CourseID = _T("");
        m_CourseTitle = _T("");
        m_Hours = 0;
        m_nFields = 3;
        //}}AFX_FIELD_INIT
}

CString CCourseSet::GetDefaultSQL()
{
        return _T("COURSE");
}

void CCourseSet::DoFieldExchange(CFieldExchange* pFX)
{
        //{{AFX_FIELD_MAP(CCourseSet)
        pFX->SetFieldType(CFieldExchange::outputColumn);
        RFX_Text(pFX, "CourseID", m_CourseID);
        RFX_Text(pFX, "CourseTitle", m_CourseTitle);
        RFX_Int(pFX, "Hours", m_Hours);
        //}}AFX_FIELD_MAP
}

/////////////////////////////////////////////////////////////////////////////
// CCourseSet diagnostics

#ifdef _DEBUG
void CCourseSet::AssertValid() const
{
        CRecordset::AssertValid();
}

void CCourseSet::Dump(CDumpContext& dc) const
{
        CRecordset::Dump(dc);
}
#endif //_DEBUG
```

Listing B4.14 contains the source code for the COURSSET.CPP implementation file. The listing contains the definitions for the following members:

1. The constructor that initializes the members `m_CourseID`, `m_CourseTitle`, `m_Hours`, and `m_nFields` by assigning them an empty string, an empty string, `0`, and `3`, respectively.

2. The member function `GetDefaultSQL` returns the default SQL string `"COURSE"`.
3. The member function `DoFieldExchange` supports exchanging data with the course recordset. The function sends the C++ message `SetFieldType` to the parameter `pFX`. The function then invokes the functions `RFX_Text` (twice) and `RFX_Int` to swap data between the members `m_CourseID`, `m_CourseTitle`, and `m_Hours` and their corresponding database fields.

Type

Listing B4.15. The source code for the SECTSET.CPP implementation file.

```
// sectset.cpp : implementation of the CSectionSet class
//

#include "stdafx.h"
#include "enroll.h"
#include "sectset.h"

/////////////////////////////////////////////////////////////////////////////
// CSectionSet implementation

IMPLEMENT_DYNAMIC(CSectionSet, CRecordset)

CSectionSet::CSectionSet(CDatabase* pdb)
     : CRecordset(pdb)
{
     //{{AFX_FIELD_INIT(CSectionSet)
     m_CourseID = "";
     m_SectionNo = "";
     m_InstructorID = "";
     m_RoomNo = "";
     m_Schedule = "";
     m_Capacity = 0;
     m_nFields = 6;
     //}}AFX_FIELD_INIT
     m_nParams = 1;
     m_strCourseIDParam = "";
}

CString CSectionSet::GetDefaultSQL()
{
     return _T("SECTION");
}

void CSectionSet::DoFieldExchange(CFieldExchange* pFX)
{
     //{{AFX_FIELD_MAP(CSectionSet)
     pFX->SetFieldType(CFieldExchange::outputColumn);
     RFX_Text(pFX, "CourseID", m_CourseID);
     RFX_Text(pFX, "SectionNo", m_SectionNo);
     RFX_Text(pFX, "InstructorID", m_InstructorID);
     RFX_Text(pFX, "RoomNo", m_RoomNo);
```


continues

Listing B4.15. continued

```
     RFX_Text(pFX, "Schedule", m_Schedule);
     RFX_Int(pFX, "Capacity", m_Capacity);
     //}}AFX_FIELD_MAP
     pFX->SetFieldType(CFieldExchange::param);
     RFX_Text(pFX, "CourseIDParam", m_strCourseIDParam);
}

/////////////////////////////////////////////////////////////////////////////
// CSectionSet diagnostics

#ifdef _DEBUG
void CSectionSet::AssertValid() const
{
     CRecordset::AssertValid();
}

void CSectionSet::Dump(CDumpContext& dc) const
{
     CRecordset::Dump(dc);
}
#endif //_DEBUG
```

Listing B4.15 shows the source code for the SECTSET.CPP implementation file. The listing defines the following member functions:

1. The constructor initializes the data members `m_CourseID`, `m_SectionNo`, `m_InstructorID`, `m_RoomNo`, `m_Schedule`, and `m_strCourseIDParams` with empty strings. The constructor also assigns `0`, `6`, and `1` to members `m_Capacity`, `m_nFields`, and `m_nParams`, respectively.

2. The member function `GetDefaultSQL` returns the default SQL string `"SECTION"`.

3. The member function `DoFieldExchange` supports exchanging data with the sections recordset. The function sends the C++ message `SetFieldType` to the parameter `pFX`. The function then invokes the functions `RFX_Text` (six times) and `RFX_Int` to swap data between the various data members and their corresponding database fields.

Type Listing B4.16. The source code for the ADDFORM.CPP implementation file.

```
// addform.cpp : implementation of the CAddForm class
//

#include "stdafx.h"
```

```
#include "enroll.h"
#include "addform.h"

#ifdef _DEBUG
#undef THIS_FILE
static char BASED_CODE THIS_FILE[] = __FILE__;
#endif

IMPLEMENT_DYNAMIC(CAddForm, CRecordView)

BEGIN_MESSAGE_MAP(CAddForm, CRecordView)
    ON_COMMAND(ID_RECORD_REFRESH, OnRecordRefresh)
    ON_COMMAND(ID_RECORD_ADD, OnRecordAdd)
    ON_COMMAND(ID_RECORD_DELETE, OnRecordDelete)
END_MESSAGE_MAP()

CAddForm::CAddForm(UINT nIDTemplate)
    : CRecordView(nIDTemplate)
{
     m_bAddMode = FALSE;
}

CAddForm::~CAddForm()
{
}

BOOL CAddForm::OnMove(UINT nIDMoveCommand)
{
    CRecordset* pRecordset = OnGetRecordset();
    if (m_bAddMode)
    {
        if (!UpdateData())
            return FALSE;
        TRY
        {
            pRecordset->Update();
        }
        CATCH(CDBException, e)
        {
            AfxMessageBox(e->m_strError);
            return FALSE;
        }
        END_CATCH

        pRecordset->Requery();
        UpdateData(FALSE);
        m_bAddMode = FALSE;
        return TRUE;
    }
    else
    {
        return CRecordView::OnMove(nIDMoveCommand);
    }
}

BOOL CAddForm::RecordAdd()
```

continues

Listing B4.16. continued

```
{
    // If already in add mode, then complete previous new record
    if (m_bAddMode)
          OnMove(ID_RECORD_FIRST);
    OnGetRecordset()->AddNew();
    m_bAddMode = TRUE;
    UpdateData(FALSE);
    return TRUE;
}

BOOL CAddForm::RecordDelete()
{
    CRecordset* pRecordset = OnGetRecordset();
    TRY
    {
          pRecordset->Delete();
    }
    CATCH(CDBException, e)
    {
         AfxMessageBox(e->m_strError);
         return FALSE;
     }
     END_CATCH

    // Move to the next record after the one just deleted
           pRecordset->MoveNext();

    // If we moved off the end of file, then move back to last record
    if (pRecordset->IsEOF())
         pRecordset->MoveLast();

    // If the recordset is now empty, then clear the fields
    // left over from the deleted record
    if (pRecordset->IsBOF())
         pRecordset->SetFieldNull(NULL);
    UpdateData(FALSE);
    return TRUE;
}


BOOL CAddForm::RecordRefresh()
{

    if (m_bAddMode == TRUE)
    {
         OnGetRecordset()->Move(AFX_MOVE_REFRESH);
         m_bAddMode = FALSE;
    }
    // Copy fields from recordset to form, thus
    // overwriting any changes user may have made
    // on the form
    UpdateData(FALSE);

    return TRUE;
```

```
115:  }
116:
117:  void CAddForm::OnRecordAdd()
118:  {
119:      RecordAdd();
120:  }
121:
122:  void CAddForm::OnUpdateRecordFirst(CCmdUI* pCmdUI)
123:  {
124:      if (m_bAddMode)
125:           pCmdUI->Enable(TRUE);
126:      else
127:           CRecordView::OnUpdateRecordFirst(pCmdUI);
128:  }
129:
130:  void CAddForm::OnRecordRefresh()
131:  {
132:      RecordRefresh();
133:  }
134:
135:  void CAddForm::OnRecordDelete()
136:  {
137:      RecordDelete();
138:  }
```

Listing B4.16 contains the source code for the ADDFORM.CPP implementation file. The listing defines the message map macros that handle the menu options to add, refresh, and delete records. The listing also contains the definitions of the following database-related member functions:

1. The constructor (lines 21 to 25) that invokes the constructor of the parent class, and then assigns `FALSE` to the data member `m_bAddMode`.
2. The member function `OnMove` (lines 31 to 58), which overrides the inherited function. The function performs the following tasks:
   - Assigns the address of the targeted recordset to the local pointer `pRecordSet`.
   - Returns the result of function `CRecordView::OnMove` if the data member `m_bAddMode` is `FALSE`. Otherwise, the function performs the remaining tasks.
   - Returns `FALSE` if a call to function `UpdateData` yields `FALSE`.
   - Updates—that is, completes editing or adding a new record—the recordset by sending the C++ message `Update` to the targeted recordset. The function uses a `TRY-CATCH` error-handling block for this task.

- ☐ Reruns the recordset's query by sending the C++ message `Requery` to the targeted recordset.
- ☐ Copies the fields from the recordset to the form by invoking the function `UpdateData` and supplying it the argument `FALSE`.
- ☐ Assigns `FALSE` to data member `m_bAddMode`.
- ☐ Returns `TRUE`.

3. The member function `RecordAdd` (lines 60 to 69) adds a new record by performing the following tasks:
   - ☐ Completes adding the previous record if already in record-add mode. This task examines the data member `m_bAddMode` and invokes the function `OnMove` if that member stores `TRUE`.
   - ☐ Sends the C++ message `AddNew` to the targeted recordset.
   - ☐ Assigns `TRUE` to the member `m_bAddMode`.
   - ☐ Copies the fields from the recordset to the form by invoking the function `UpdateData`.
   - ☐ Returns `TRUE`.
4. The member function `RecordDelete` (lines 71 to 98) deletes a record by performing the following tasks:
   - ☐ Assigns the address of the targeted recordset to the local pointer `pRecordSet`.
   - ☐ Deletes the current record by sending the C++ message `Delete` to the targeted recordset.
   - ☐ Moves to the next record by sending the C++ message `MoveNext` to the targeted recordset.
   - ☐ Moves back one record if the last task caused the record index to move past the end of the file. To test this condition, the function sends the C++ message `IsEOF` to the targeted recordset. The task of moving back one record involves sending the C++ message `MoveLast` to the targeted recordset.
   - ☐ Clears the fields if the recordset becomes empty. The function sends the C++ message `IsBOF` to determine whether the recordset is empty. If this

condition is true, the function sends the C++ message `SetFieldNull` to that targeted recordset.

- Copies the fields from the recordset to the form by invoking the function `UpdateData`.
- Returns `TRUE`.

5. The member function `RecordRefresh` (lines 101 to 115) refreshes the fields in the form by performing the following tasks:
   - Restores the record that was in view before the user started adding a new record. This task sends the C++ message `Move` (with the argument 0) to the targeted recordset, and then assigns `FALSE` to member `m_bAddMode`.
   - Copies the fields from the recordset to the form by invoking the function `UpdateData`.
   - Returns `TRUE`.
6. The member function `OnRecordAdd` merely invokes the function `RecordAdd`.
7. The member function `OnRecordRefresh` simply invokes the function `RecordRefresh`.
8. The member function `OnRecordDelete` just calls the function `RecordDelete`.

Type

Listing B4.17. The source code for the CRSFORM.CPP implementation file.

```
 1: // crsform.cpp : implementation file
 2: //
 3:
 4: #include "stdafx.h"
 5: #include "enroll.h"
 6: #include "coursset.h"
 7: #include "addform.h"
 8: #include "crsform.h"
 9: #include "sectset.h"
10: #include "enroldoc.h"
11: #include "mainfrm.h"
12: #include "resource.h"
13:
14: #ifdef _DEBUG
15: #undef THIS_FILE
16: static char BASED_CODE THIS_FILE[] = __FILE__;
17: #endif
18:
19: /////////////////////////////////////////////////////////////////////////////
20: // CCourseForm
```

continues

Listing B4.17. continued

```

IMPLEMENT_DYNCREATE(CCourseForm, CAddForm)

CCourseForm::CCourseForm()
    : CAddForm(CCourseForm::IDD)
{
    //{{AFX_DATA_INIT(CCourseForm)
    m_pSet = NULL;
    //}}AFX_DATA_INIT
}

CCourseForm::~CCourseForm()
{
}

void CCourseForm::DoDataExchange(CDataExchange* pDX)
{
    CRecordView::DoDataExchange(pDX);
    //{{AFX_DATA_MAP(CCourseForm)
    DDX_Control(pDX, IDC_COURSEID, m_ctlCourseID);
    DDX_FieldText(pDX, IDC_COURSEID, m_pSet->m_CourseID, m_pSet);
    DDX_FieldText(pDX, IDC_HOURS, m_pSet->m_Hours, m_pSet);
    DDX_FieldText(pDX, IDC_TITLE, m_pSet->m_CourseTitle, m_pSet);
    //}}AFX_DATA_MAP
}

BOOL CCourseForm::OnMove(UINT nIDMoveCommand)
{
    BOOL bWasAddMode = FALSE;
    CString strCourseID;
    if (m_bAddMode == TRUE)
    {
         m_ctlCourseID.GetWindowText(strCourseID);
         bWasAddMode = TRUE;
    }
    if (CAddForm::OnMove(nIDMoveCommand))
    {
         m_ctlCourseID.SetReadOnly(TRUE);
         if (bWasAddMode == TRUE)
         {
             CUpdateHint hint;
             hint.m_strCourse = strCourseID;
             GetDocument()->UpdateAllViews(this, HINT_ADD_COURSE, &hint);
         }
         return TRUE;
    }
    return FALSE;
}


BEGIN_MESSAGE_MAP(CCourseForm, CAddForm)
    //{{AFX_MSG_MAP(CCourseForm)
    ON_COMMAND(ID_RECORD_ADD, OnRecordAdd)
    ON_COMMAND(ID_RECORD_DELETE, OnRecordDelete)
```

```
    ON_COMMAND(ID_RECORD_REFRESH, OnRecordRefresh)
    //}}AFX_MSG_MAP
END_MESSAGE_MAP()

/////////////////////////////////////////////////////////////////////////////
// CCourseForm message handlers

CRecordset* CCourseForm::OnGetRecordset()
{
     return m_pSet;
}

void CCourseForm::OnInitialUpdate()
{
    CEnrollDoc* pDoc = (CEnrollDoc*)GetDocument();
    CDatabase* pDatabase = pDoc->GetDatabase();
    if (!pDatabase->IsOpen())
         return;
    m_pSet = &pDoc->m_courseSetForForm;
    m_pSet->m_strSort = "CourseID";
    m_pSet->m_pDatabase = pDatabase;
    CRecordView::OnInitialUpdate();
}


void CCourseForm::OnRecordAdd()
{
    CAddForm::RecordAdd();
    m_ctlCourseID.SetReadOnly(FALSE);
}


void CCourseForm::OnRecordDelete()
{
    // The STDREG.MDB Student Registration database in Access Format
    // does not require a programmatic validation to
    // assure that a course is not deleted if any sections exist.
    // That is because the STDREG.MDB database has been pre-built with
    // such an referential integrity rule.  If the user tries to
    // delete a course that has a section, a CDBException will be
    // thrown, and ENROLL will display the SQL error message
    // informing the user that the course cannot be deleted.
    //
    // A Student Registration database initialized by the STDREG
    // tool will not have any such built-in referential integrity
    // rules.  For such databases, the following code assumes the
    // burden of assuring that the course is not deleted if a section
    // exists.  The reason that STDREG does not add referential
    // integrity checks to the Student Registration database is that
    // some databases such as SQL Server do not offer SQL, via ODBC,
    // for creating referential integrity rules such as "FOREIGN KEY".
    //
    // The deletion of a course is not the only place ENROLL
    // needs a programmatic referential integrity check.  Another example
    // is a check that a duplicate course or seciton is not added.
    // For simplicity, ENROLL does not make these other checks.
```


continues

Listing B4.17. continued

```
131:
132:
133:      CEnrollDoc* pDoc = (CEnrollDoc*)GetDocument();
134:      CSectionSet sectionSet;
135:      sectionSet.m_pDatabase = pDoc->GetDatabase();
136:      sectionSet.m_strFilter = "CourseID = ?";
137:      sectionSet.m_strCourseIDParam = m_pSet->m_CourseID;
138:      BOOL b = sectionSet.Open();
139:      if (!sectionSet.IsEOF())
140:      {
141:          AfxMessageBox(IDS_CANNOT_DELETE_COURSE_WITH_SECTION);
142:          return;
143:      }
144:
145:      CUpdateHint hint;
146:      hint.m_strCourse = m_pSet->m_CourseID;
147:      if (CAddForm::RecordDelete())
148:           GetDocument()->UpdateAllViews(this, HINT_DELETE_COURSE, &hint);
149:  }
150:
151:  void CCourseForm::OnRecordRefresh()
152:  {
153:      if (m_bAddMode == TRUE)
154:          m_ctlCourseID.SetReadOnly(TRUE);
155:      CAddForm::RecordRefresh();
156:  }
```

Listing B4.17 contains the message map macros for responding to commands that add and delete records. The listing also contains the definitions of the following relevant members:

1. The constructor (line 24 to 30) of class `CCourseForm` invokes the constructor of the parent class (`CAddForm`), and then assigns `NULL` to the recordset pointer member `m_pSet`.
2. The member function `DoDataExchange` (lines 36 to 45) invokes the parent's function `DoDataExchange`, and then calls the functions `DDX_Control` and `DDX_FieldText` to swap data with the various controls in the course form.
3. The member function `OnMove` (lines 47 to 68) overrides the inherited function and performs the following tasks:
   - ☐ Declares the local Boolean variable `bWasAddMode` and assigns `FALSE` to this variable.
   - ☐ Declares the `CString` object `strCourseID`.

- If the member m_bAddMode contains TRUE, the function obtains the text in the Course control and stores that text in variable strCourseID. Then the function assigns TRUE to variable bWasAddMode.
- Invokes the parent's function OnMove and returns FALSE if the parent's function yields FALSE. Otherwise, the function OnMove performs the remaining tasks.
- If the local variable bWasAddMode contains TRUE, the function performs the following subtasks:
    - Creates the object hint as an instance of class CUpdateHint.
    - Stores the string of variable strCourseID in the member strCourse of class CUpdateHint.
    - Updates all the views by sending the C++ message UpdateAllViews to the document. Among the arguments of this message is the object hint. This message allows the sections form to be updated.
    - Returns TRUE.

4. The member function OnGetRecordset (lines 82 to 85) merely returns the recordset pointer, data member m_pSet.
5. The member function OnInitialUpdate (lines 87 to 97) initializes the form by carrying out the following tasks:
    - Assigns the address of the document to the local pointer pDoc.
    - Assigns the address of the database to the local pointer pDatabase.
    - Exits if the database is not opened.
    - Assigns the address of the course recordset to the member m_pSet.
    - Assigns the name of the sort field to the member m_strSort of the targeted recordset object (which is the course recordset).
    - Assigns the address of the database to the member m_pDatabase of the targeted recordset object.
    - Invokes the function OnInitialUpdate, of class CRecordView, to perform the rest of the initialization.
6. The member function OnRecordAdd (lines 100 to 104) invokes the function RecordAdd of the parent class CAddForm, and then sets the Course ID edit box (accessed by member m_ctlCourseID) to read-only state.

7. The member function `OnRecordDelete` (lines 107 to 149) deletes the current record by performing the following tasks:
   - ☐ Assigns the address of the document to the local document pointer `pDoc`.
   - ☐ Assigns the address of the database to the member `sectionSet.m_pDatabase`.
   - ☐ Assigns the literal string `"CourseID = ?"` to the member `sectionSet.m_strFilter`.
   - ☐ Copies the string of member `m_pSet->m_CourseID` into member `sectionSet.m_strCourseIDParam`.
   - ☐ Opens the section form by sending the C++ message `Open` to the form. The function assigns the result of this message to the local Boolean variable `b`.
   - ☐ Determines if the form is empty by sending the C++ message `IsEOF` to the form. If this message returns 0, the function displays an error message and then exits.
   - ☐ Creates the object `hint` as an instance of class `CUpdateHint`.
   - ☐ Assigns the member `m_CourseID` of the targeted recordset to the member `m_strCourse` of object `hint`.
   - ☐ Invokes the parent's Boolean function `RecordDelete`. If this function returns a non-zero value, the function `OnRecordDelete` sends the C++ message `UpdateAllViews` to update the forms. The message involves the object hint that passes the key field.
8. The member function `OnRecordRefresh` (lines 151 to 156) updates the current record. The function sets the Course ID edit box to a read-only state if the member `m_bAddMode` is `TRUE`. The function then invokes the inherited function `CAddForm::RecordRefresh`.

Listing B4.18. The source code for the SECTFORM.CPP implementation file.

```
1:  // sectform.cpp : implementation of the CSectionForm class
2:  //
3:
4:  #include "stdafx.h"
5:  #include "enroll.h"
6:  #include "sectset.h"
7:  #include "coursset.h"
```

```
#include "enroldoc.h"
#include "addform.h"
#include "sectform.h"
#include "mainfrm.h"

#ifdef _DEBUG
#undef THIS_FILE
static char BASED_CODE THIS_FILE[] = __FILE__;
#endif

/////////////////////////////////////////////////////////////////////////////
// CSectionForm

IMPLEMENT_DYNCREATE(CSectionForm, CAddForm)

BEGIN_MESSAGE_MAP(CSectionForm, CAddForm)
    //{{AFX_MSG_MAP(CSectionForm)
    ON_CBN_SELENDOK(IDC_COURSELIST, OnSelendokCourselist)
    ON_COMMAND(ID_RECORD_ADD, OnRecordAdd)
    ON_COMMAND(ID_RECORD_REFRESH, OnRecordRefresh)
    //}}AFX_MSG_MAP
    // Standard printing commands
    ON_COMMAND(ID_FILE_PRINT, CRecordView::OnFilePrint)
    ON_COMMAND(ID_FILE_PRINT_PREVIEW, CRecordView::OnFilePrintPreview)
END_MESSAGE_MAP()

/////////////////////////////////////////////////////////////////////////////
// CSectionForm construction/destruction

CSectionForm::CSectionForm()
      : CAddForm(CSectionForm::IDD)
{
    //{{AFX_DATA_INIT(CSectionForm)
    m_pSet = NULL;
    //}}AFX_DATA_INIT
}

CSectionForm::~CSectionForm()
{
}

void CSectionForm::DoDataExchange(CDataExchange* pDX)
{
    CRecordView::DoDataExchange(pDX);
    //{{AFX_DATA_MAP(CSectionForm)
    DDX_Control(pDX, IDC_COURSELIST, m_ctlCourseList);
    DDX_FieldText(pDX, IDC_SECTION, m_pSet->m_SectionNo, m_pSet);
    DDX_Control(pDX, IDC_SECTION, m_ctlSection);
    DDX_FieldText(pDX, IDC_INSTRUCTOR, m_pSet->m_InstructorID, m_pSet);
    DDX_FieldText(pDX, IDC_ROOM, m_pSet->m_RoomNo, m_pSet);
    DDX_FieldText(pDX, IDC_SCHEDULE, m_pSet->m_Schedule, m_pSet);
    DDX_FieldText(pDX, IDC_CAPACITY, m_pSet->m_Capacity, m_pSet);
    DDX_FieldCBString(pDX, IDC_COURSELIST, m_pSet->m_CourseID, m_pSet);
    //}}AFX_DATA_MAP
}

```


continues

Listing B4.18. continued

```

void CSectionForm::OnInitialUpdate()
{
    CEnrollDoc* pDoc = GetDocument();
    m_pSet = &pDoc->m_sectionSet;
    m_pSet->m_pDatabase = pDoc->GetDatabase();
    if (!m_pSet->m_pDatabase->IsOpen())
         return;

    // Fill the combo box with all of the courses

    pDoc->m_courseSet.m_strSort = "CourseID";
    if (pDoc->m_courseSet.m_pDatabase == NULL)
          pDoc->m_courseSet.m_pDatabase = pDoc->GetDatabase();
    if (!pDoc->m_courseSet.Open())
         return;

    // Filter, parameterize and sort the course recordset
    m_pSet->m_strFilter = "CourseID = ?";
    m_pSet->m_strCourseIDParam = pDoc->m_courseSet.m_CourseID;
    m_pSet->m_strSort = "SectionNo";

    CRecordView::OnInitialUpdate();

    m_ctlCourseList.ResetContent();
    if (pDoc->m_courseSet.IsOpen())
    {
        while (pDoc->m_courseSet.IsEOF() != TRUE)
        {
             m_ctlCourseList.AddString(
                   pDoc->m_courseSet.m_CourseID);
             pDoc->m_courseSet.MoveNext();
        }
    }
    m_ctlCourseList.SetCurSel(0);

}

void CSectionForm::OnUpdate(CView* pSender, LPARAM lHint, CObject* pHint)
{
    BOOL bReselectCombo = FALSE;
    int nIndex;
    CUpdateHint* pUpdateHint;
    if (lHint != 0)
    {
         pUpdateHint = (CUpdateHint*)pHint;
         ASSERT(pUpdateHint->IsKindOf(RUNTIME_CLASS(CUpdateHint)));
         switch (lHint)
         {
              case HINT_ADD_COURSE:
                   m_ctlCourseList.AddString(pUpdateHint->m_strCourse);
                   bReselectCombo = TRUE;
                   break;
              case HINT_DELETE_COURSE:
```

```
                    nIndex = m_ctlCourseList.FindStringExact(0,
                         pUpdateHint->m_strCourse);
                    ASSERT(nIndex != CB_ERR);
                    m_ctlCourseList.DeleteString(nIndex);
                    bReselectCombo = TRUE;
                    break;
          }
    }
    if (bReselectCombo)
    {
         nIndex = m_ctlCourseList.FindStringExact(0,
              m_pSet->m_strCourseIDParam);
         if (nIndex == CB_ERR)
             return;
         m_ctlCourseList.SetCurSel(nIndex);
    }
    CRecordView::OnUpdate(pSender, lHint, pHint);
}

/////////////////////////////////////////////////////////////////////////////
// CSectionForm printing

BOOL CSectionForm::OnPreparePrinting(CPrintInfo* pInfo)
{
    // default preparation
    return DoPreparePrinting(pInfo);
}

void CSectionForm::OnBeginPrinting(CDC* /*pDC*/, CPrintInfo* /*pInfo*/)
{
    // TODO: add extra initialization before printing
}

void CSectionForm::OnEndPrinting(CDC* /*pDC*/, CPrintInfo* /*pInfo*/)
{
    // TODO: add cleanup after printing
}

/////////////////////////////////////////////////////////////////////////////
// CSectionForm diagnostics

#ifdef _DEBUG
void CSectionForm::AssertValid() const
{
     CRecordView::AssertValid();
}

void CSectionForm::Dump(CDumpContext& dc) const
{
    CRecordView::Dump(dc);
}

CEnrollDoc* CSectionForm::GetDocument() // non-debug version is inline
{
    ASSERT(m_pDocument->IsKindOf(RUNTIME_CLASS(CEnrollDoc)));
    return (CEnrollDoc*)m_pDocument;
```

continues

Listing B4.18. continued

```
}
#endif //_DEBUG

/////////////////////////////////////////////////////////////////////////////
// CSectionForm database support

CRecordset* CSectionForm::OnGetRecordset()
{
    return m_pSet;
}

/////////////////////////////////////////////////////////////////////////////
// CSectionForm message handlers


void CSectionForm::OnSelendokCourselist()
{
    if (!m_pSet->IsOpen())
        return;
    m_ctlCourseList.GetLBText(m_ctlCourseList.GetCurSel(),
        m_pSet->m_strCourseIDParam);
    if (!m_bAddMode)
    {
        m_pSet->Requery();
        if (m_pSet->IsEOF())
        {
            m_pSet->SetFieldNull(&(m_pSet->m_CourseID), FALSE);
            m_pSet->m_CourseID = m_pSet->m_strCourseIDParam;
        }
        UpdateData(FALSE);
     }
}

void CSectionForm::OnRecordAdd()
{
    // If already in add mode, then complete previous new record
    if (m_bAddMode)
        OnMove(ID_RECORD_FIRST);

    CString strCurrentCourse = m_pSet->m_CourseID;
    m_pSet->AddNew();
    m_pSet->SetFieldNull(&(m_pSet->m_CourseID), FALSE);
    m_pSet->m_CourseID = strCurrentCourse;
    m_bAddMode = TRUE;
    m_ctlSection.SetReadOnly(FALSE);
    UpdateData(FALSE);
}


void CSectionForm::OnRecordRefresh()
{
    if (m_bAddMode == TRUE)
         m_ctlSection.SetReadOnly(TRUE);
```

```
    CAddForm::RecordRefresh();

}
BOOL CSectionForm::OnMove(UINT nIDMoveCommand)
{
    if (CAddForm::OnMove(nIDMoveCommand))
          m_ctlSection.SetReadOnly(TRUE);
     return TRUE;
}
```

Listing B4.18 contains the source code for the SECTFORM.CPP implementation file. The listing contains the message map macros to support adding, refreshing, and updating records, as well as printing and print previewing. The listing also contains the definitions for the following database-related member functions:

1. The constructor (lines 37 to 43) invokes the constructor of the parent class and assigns `NULL` to the data member `m_pSet`.
2. The member function `DoDataExchange` (lines 49 to 62) invokes the parent's function `DoDataExchange`, and then calls the functions `DDX_Control`, `DDXFieldCBString`, and `DDX_FieldText` to swap data with the various controls in the sections form.
3. The member function `OnInitialUpdate` (lines 65 to 100) initializes the sections form by performing the following tasks:
   - Assigns the address of the document to the local pointer `pDoc`.
   - Assigns the address of the sections recordset to the member `m_pSet`.
   - Assigns the address of the document's database to the local pointer `pDatabase`.
   - Exits if the database is not open.
   - Inserts the names of the courses in the combo box control.
   - Sets the parameter for the course recordset, and then sorts that recordset.
   - Invokes the `OnInitialUpdate` function of class `CRecordView`.
   - Clears the contents of the combo box by sending the C++ message `ResetContent` to member `m_ctlCourseList`.
   - Inserts the names of the courses in the combo box. This task uses a `while` loop, which adds the name of the courses to the combo box control. The loop contains two statements. The first sends the C++ message `AddString`

to the combo box control. The argument for this message is the member `m_CourseID` of the course recordset. The second loop statement visits the next record by sending the C++ message `MoveNext` to the source recordset.

- Selects the first item in the combo box by sending the C++ message `SetCurSel` to that control.

4. The member function `OnUpdate` (lines 102 to 135) updates the forms by adding a new course name or deleting a course name from the course ID combo box. The function uses `CUpdateHint` objects to determine how to update the course ID combo box.
5. The member function `OnGetRecordset` (lines 180 to 183) simply returns the member `m_pSet`.
6. The member function `OnMove` (lines 230 to 235) handles traversing the records on the sections form. The function invokes the parent's function `OnMove`. If that function returns `TRUE`, the function `OnMove` sets up the read-only state of the Section edit control. The function `OnMove` always returns `TRUE`.
7. The member function `OnRecordAdd` (lines 207 to 220) responds to the record add command by carrying out the following tasks:
   - Completes the previous record addition if the member `m_bAddMode` is `TRUE`. This task invokes the function `OnMove` with the argument `ID_RECORD_FIRST`.
   - Assigns a string of the recordset's member `m_CourseID` to the local `CString` instance `strCurrentCourse`.
   - Adds a new record by sending the C++ message `AddNew` to the targeted recordset.
   - Fills the fields with null values by sending the C++ message `SetFieldNull` to the targeted recordset.
   - Assigns the string of the local variable `strCurrentCourse` to the recordset's member `m_CourseID`.
   - Assigns `TRUE` to the member `m_bAddMode` to ensure that the record addition mode is true.
   - Turns on the read-only state of the Section edit control.
   - Copies the fields from the recordset to the form by invoking the function `UpdateData`.

8. The member function `OnRecordRefresh` (lines 223 to 229) responds to the record refresh command by performing the following tasks:
   - Turns on the read-only state of the Section edit control if the member `m_bAddMode` is `TRUE`.
   - Invokes the parent's function `RecordRefresh`.

Summary

This chapter introduces you to the MFC classes that support ODBC drivers and the new database features of Visual C++. The chapter covers the following topics:

- The MFC database classes, which include `CDatabase`, `CRecordset`, `CFieldExchange`, `CRecordView`, `CLongBinary`, and `CDBException`. These classes support databases, recordsets, data exchange with database fields, recordset views, storage of large binary objects, and database-related runtime errors, respectively.
- The ENROLL.EXE example, which shows an application with a small database and two recordset views.
- The source code listing that implements the ENROLL.EXE. In addition, the chapter discusses the various header and implementation files.

Q&A

Q Does AppWizard support ODBC applications?

A Yes. AppWizard offers a dialog box that allows you to select Microsoft Access, dBASE, Paradox, and FoxPro files.

Q Does AppWizard generate a working ODBC application?

A Yes. However, the application contains a form with a single static text control. In other words, you can't do much with the ODBC program generated by AppWizard.

Q Can I change the type of database at runtime?

A No. The selection you make while creating the database program locks you into the database file format(s).

Q Does the ENROLL.EXE program use a popular database format?

A No. The program uses its own format.

Exercise

To further study the source code files of project ENROLL, insert several breakpoints in different files and run the program. Select variables to watch and observe their values at the breakpoint. Perhaps the best way to conduct this debug-based study is in several sessions. In each session, focus on member functions in the same implementation file. This approach permits you to have relatively few variables to watch.

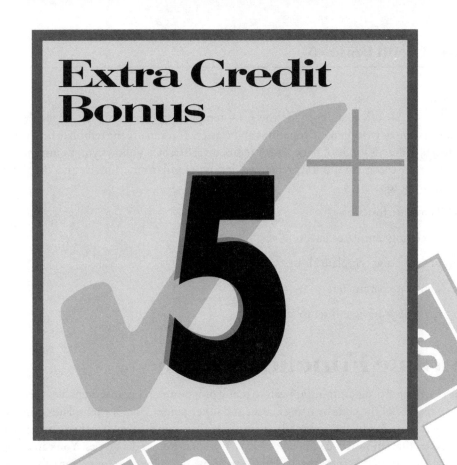

Extra Credit Bonus

5+

Working with C++ Templates

Visual C++ 2.0 offers support for the C++ template feature. This language feature empowers you to write generic functions and classes. You can use the template functions to process different kinds of data. As for template classes, C++ allows you to instantiate them to create classes for specific predefined data types and classes. This chapter discusses the following topics:

- Template functions
- Declaring template classes
- Instantiating template classes
- Template parameters
- Class derivation and templates

Template Functions

Object-oriented programming appeals to many programmers because it enables them to reduce the size of the code by using classes and inheritance. The C++ templates provide another aspect of reducing your code. Templates allow you to develop generic functions and classes that support the same operations, but for different data types. You can write template functions that sort, search, and swap various data types. Likewise, you can create template classes that model generic data structures, like arrays, matrices, hash tables, lists, trees, and graphs. This book contains template classes that model most of these data structures.

The most common types of functions used by programmers are ones that swap, search, and sort data. Let's look at different versions of functions that swap data for different types. Such functions are typical (and short) examples. Here are three versions of the function swap:

```
void swap(int &i, int &j)
{
  int temp = i;
  i = j;
  j = temp;
}

void swap(char &i, char &j)
{
  char temp = i;
  i = j;
  j = temp;
}
```

```
void swap(double &i, double &j)
{
  double temp = i;
  i = j;
  j = temp;
}
```

The preceding functions can coexist in a C++ program since the compiler regards them as overloaded functions. You can add more overloaded versions of the `swap` functions to cover the other predefined data types as well as the ones you create. The end result is a long list of very similar code. The C++ template feature enables you to substitute the code for all of these overloaded functions with a single template function, shown here:

```
template<class T>
void swap(T& i, T& j)
{
  T temp = i;

  i = j;
  j = temp;
}
```

Notice that the declaration of a `template` function begins with the keyword `template` followed by a list of template class names. In this case, the list includes the `class T` (which I call the template class.) The term `class T` is a dummy class that is not yet defined but can still be used by the `template` function. Notice that the swapped data type of the previous versions of the function is replaced with the template `class T`. When the compiler sees a `template` function and a template class, it stores the template code for future reference. The template code itself is not compiled because the template classes are not yet defined. To employ the `template` function, you need to associate it with a data type or a class. The compiler then instantiates a copy of the `template` function for the data type you specify. This process may bring out any compile-time error for the instantiated `template` function.

DO	DON'T

DO develop a `template` function by deriving it from a non-`template` function that has been tested.

DON'T assume that just because a source code containing `template` functions compiles fine, there are no errors.

The C libraries include generic (C-style) functions for searching and sorting. The ANSI C supports the following functions to support generic sorting of arrays and to perform binary searching in arrays:

```
/* the generic QuickSort function */
void qsort(void *base, // the pointer to the array
           size_t nelem, // number of array items
           size_t width, // size of each element
           // the element-comparison function
           int (*fcmp)(const void *, const void *));

/* the binary search function */
void *bsearch(const void *key, // search key
              const void *base, // pointer to the array
              size_t nelem, // number of elements
              size_t width, // size of each element
              // the element-comparison function
              int (*fcmp)(const void*, const void*));
```

The following shows a `template` function that sorts a generic array using the Combsort method:

```
template<class T>
void combSort(T array[], unsigned num)
{
  unsigned i, j, n, offset;
  long k;
  Boolean isSorted;

  offset = num; // get the initial offset
  // start loop to sort the array elements in the
  // range [first..last]
  do {
    // update the offset, making sure that it
    // does not become less than 1
    k = (offset * 8L) / 11;
    offset = (k == 0) ? 1 : (unsigned)k;
    isSorted = true;
    // start comparing array elements that are
    // offset members apart
    for (i = 0; i < (num - offset); i++) {
      j = i + offset;
      // need to swap elements i and j?
      if (array[i] > array[j]) {
        // swap the elements i and j
        isSorted = false;
        swap(array[i], array[j]);
      }
    }
  } while (!(isSorted && offset == 1));
}
```

Here is a `template` function that supports generic search in arrays:

```
template<class T>
unsigned binarySearch(T& searchData, T array[], unsigned num)
{
  T median;
  unsigned m = (num - 1) / 2;
```

```
  do {
    m = (first + last) / 2;
    if (searchData < array[m])
      last = m - 1;
    else
      first = m + 1;
  } while (!(searchData == array[m] ¦¦ first > last));

  // found a match
  return (searchData == array[m]) ? m : 0xffff;
}
```

Compare the parameter lists of the `qsort` and `combSort` functions and of the `bsearch` and `binarySearch` functions. Notice that the C++ template functions require fewer parameters. There is no need for the size of each element and the comparison functions. These items are provided by the template class. You can readily instantiate a template function with a predefined data type. In the case of a user-defined class, that class must already be defined before you can use it to instantiate a template function or a template class. This means defining a class that has the relational operators <, <=, >, >=, ==, and `!=` to cover all possible ways of comparing elements of the template class.

Template Classes

Visual C++ also supports template classes. These classes model generic objects that provide similar operations for different data types. The best example for using template classes is data structures. Using a template class, you can create a generic stack, for example, that can be instantiated for various predefined and user-defined data types. Likewise, you can have template classes for queues, arrays, matrices, lists, trees, hash tables, graphs, and any other general-purpose data structure.

Declaring Template Classes

Declaring template classes is similar, but more evolved, than declaring a `template` function. Here is an example of a simple template class which supports dynamic arrays. You can access, sort, and search the elements of these arrays. Listing B5.1 shows the source code for the TEMPAR1.H header file.

Type

Listing B5.1. The source code for the TEMPAR1.H header file.

```
#ifndef _TEMPAR1_H_
#define _TEMPAR1_H_
```

continues

Listing B5.1. continued

```
 3:
 4:  template<class T> class DynArray
 5:  {
 6:   public:
 7:     enum Boolean { false, true };
 8:
 9:     DynArray(int nMaxSize = 10);
10:     ~DynArray();
11:
12:     int GetWorkSize()
13:       { return m_nWorkSize; };
14:     T& operator [](int nIndex);
15:     void Sort();
16:     int LinearSearch(T& searchData);
17:     int BinarySearch(T& searchData);
18:
19:   protected:
20:     T* m_pData;
21:     int m_nWorkSize;
22:     int m_nMaxSize;
23:     Boolean m_bInOrder;
24:  };
25:
26:  #endif
```

The keyword `template` informs the compiler that you are about to declare a template class or function. The template keyword is then followed by a template parameter list that is enclosed in angle brackets. Typically, the list contains a single class item. The type `T` is the popular choice for the template class. The template parameter list may include additional template classes and/or other data types (predefined or user-defined structures). The template class declares the following protected data members:

- The member `m_pData` (in line 20) is the pointer to the template class type `T`. This member accesses the dynamically allocated array.
- The member `m_nWorkSize` (in line 21) stores the working size of the array (that is, the number of array elements, starting with the one at index 0, which contain meaningful data).
- The member `m_nMaxSize` (in line 22) stores the number of elements allocated to the dynamic array.
- The Boolean member `m_bInOrder` (in line 23) stores the sorted state for the array.

The template class declares the nested enumerated type Boolean in line 7. The class also declares a constructor, a destructor, and the member functions `GetWorkSize`, operator `[]`,

Sort, LinearSearch, and BinarySearch. These member functions provide a minimal set of operations which include accessing array elements, sorting, and searching. The array supports both linear search (mainly for unsorted array elements) and binary search (for sorted array elements).

> **Note:** Any reference to the class itself inside its declaration requires appending the template class type (enclosed in angle brackets). In the case of class DynArray, you need to use DynArray<T>. In addition, notice the use of the template class T with member functions LinearSearch and BinarySearch, which manipulate the basic to-be-yet-defined data type.

What about the definition of the member functions? Does it require any special syntax? The answer is a firm yes! Examine the source code for the TEMPAR1.CPP library file, shown in Listing B5.2. Notice that the definition of every member function begins with template<class T>. In addition, the class name qualifier is DynArray<T> and not just DynArray. A good example is the member function Sort:

```
template<class T>
void  DynArray<T>::Sort()
```


> **Note:** The template class declaration and definition of its member functions require the use of the class name and parameter identifiers when making a reference to the template class.

Listing B5.2 shows the source code for the TEMPAR1.CPP implementation file. Examine the code in Listing B5.2.

Type

Listing B5.2. The source code for the TEMPAR1.CPP implementation file.

```
// implementation file for class DynArray

#include "tempar1.h"

template<class T>
DynArray<T>::DynArray(int nMaxSize)
{
```

continues

Listing B5.2. continued

```
  m_nMaxSize = (nMaxSize < 0) ? 10 : nMaxSize;
  m_pData = new T[m_nMaxSize];
  m_nWorkSize = 0;
  m_bInOrder = false;
}

template<class T>
DynArray<T>::~DynArray()
{
  delete [] m_pData;
}

template<class T>
T& DynArray<T>::operator [](int nIndex)
{
  m_bInOrder = false; // clear order flag
  // is index valid?
  if (nIndex > -1 && nIndex < m_nMaxSize) {
    // update the work size
    if (nIndex >= m_nWorkSize && m_nWorkSize < m_nMaxSize)
      m_nWorkSize++;
    return m_pData[nIndex];
  }
  else
    return m_pData[0];
}

template<class T>
void DynArray<T>::Sort()
{
  int offset, i, j;
  int n = m_nWorkSize;
  long k;
  T temp;

  // exit if array is small or array is already sorted
  if (m_nWorkSize < 2 || m_bInOrder == true)
    return;

  offset = n; // get the initial offser
  do {
    // update the offset, making sure that
    // it does not become less than 1
    k = (offset * 8L) / 11;
    offset = (k == 0) ? 1 : (int)k;
    m_bInOrder = true;
    // start comparing elements
    for (i = 0, j = i + offset; i < (n - offset); i++, j++)
      if (m_pData[i] > m_pData[j]) {
        m_bInOrder = false;
        temp = m_pData[i];
        m_pData[i] = m_pData[j];
        m_pData[j] = temp;
      }
```

```
62:
63:     } while (!(m_bInOrder == true && offset == 1));
64:  }
65:
66:  template<class T>
67:  int DynArray<T>::LinearSearch(T& searchData)
68:  {
69:    Boolean notFound = true;
70:    int i = 0;
71:
72:    while (i < m_nWorkSize && notFound == true)
73:      if (searchData != m_pData[i])
74:        i++;
75:      else
76:        notFound = false;
77:
78:    // return search index
79:    return (notFound == false) ? i : -1;
80:  }
81:
82:  template<class T>
83:  int DynArray<T>::BinarySearch(T& searchData)
84:  {
85:    T medianElem;
86:    int lo = 0;
87:    int hi = m_nWorkSize - 1;
88:    int median;
89:
90:    if (m_bInOrder == false)
91:      return LinearSearch(searchData);
92:
93:    do {
94:      median = (lo + hi) / 2;
95:      medianElem = m_pData[median];
96:      if (searchData < medianElem)
97:        hi = median - 1;
98:      else
99:        lo = median + 1;
100:   } while (!(searchData == medianElem || lo > hi));
101:
102:   return (searchData == medianElem) ? median : -1;
103: }
```

Listing B5.2 defines the following member functions for the template class `DynArray`:

- The constructor (defined in lines 5 to 12) creates the class instances by initializing the data members and allocating the dynamic space for the instantiated array. The array maintains the same size during its life cycle.
- The destructor (defined in lines 14 to 18) removes the elements of the dynamic array associated with the instance of the template class.

- The operator `[]` (defined in lines 20 to 33) returns the reference to the array element accessed by the index `nIndex`. Thus, the operator supports storing and recalling data in the array. The operator systematically assigns `false` to the member `m_bInOrder`, since storing data in the array will most likely corrupt any array order. The operator validates the argument of parameter `nIndex`. The operator also updates the value in member `m_nWorkSize` when the routine accesses elements at higher indices. If the argument for parameter `nIndex` is not valid, the operator returns the reference to the element at index 0.
- The function `Sort` (defined in lines 35 to 64) sorts the first `m_nWorkSize` elements of the dynamic array using the Combsort method. When the function finishes sorting the array elements, the data member `m_bInOrder` ends up with the value `true`.
- The function `LinearSearch` (defined in lines 66 to 80) searches in the array for an element that matches the argument of parameter `searchData`. The function returns the index of the first matching array element, or yields -1 if no match is found. The function uses a linear search method which works with both unsorted and sorted array elements.
- The function `BinarySearch` (defined in lines 82 to 103) searches in the array for an element that matches the argument of parameter `searchData`. The function returns the index of the first matching array element, or yields -1 if no match is found. The function uses a binary search method which works with sorted array elements.

Instantiating Template Classes

Instantiating template classes requires that you observe a few rules:

1. The first rule deals with how to include the source code template classes. The C++ compiler does NOT compile template classes. Instead it reads them and stores them pending their use. Therefore, you need to include the code for both declaring the template class and defining its member functions. You can either put these two code segments in one file or use a header file and a .CPP file. I choose to apply the latter approach, simply to be more consistent with non-template classes. Using this approach, you need to include the .CPP in your client programs. Of course, the .CPP needs to include the related header file.

2. The template class is instantiated by specifying predefined data types or a user-defined class. The general syntax for instantiating a simple template class is:

```
templateClass<type> instance(constructorArguments);
```

To illustrate the instantiation of class `DynArray`, I present Listing B5.3 which shows the source code for the TSARR1.CPP program file. The program tests the template class `DynArray` by creating instances that have the basic types `int`, `char`, and `double`. Each array has 15 elements. The program tests the various arrays in a similar way. Here are the operations that the program performs on each array:

1. Assigns values to the array elements.
2. Displays the elements of the unsorted array elements.
3. Searches for the data in the unsorted array elements. The program displays the indices of the matching array elements.
4. Sorts the array elements.
5. Displays the elements of the sorted array elements.
6. Searches for the data in the sorted array elements. The program displays the indices of the matching array elements.

Listing B5.3. The source code for the TSARR1.CPP program file.

```
// C++ program to test class DynArray

#include <iostream.h>
// include template .CPP file!!
#include "tempar1.cpp"

void pressEnter();

main()
{
  const ARR_SIZE = 15;
  DynArray<int> intArr(ARR_SIZE);
  DynArray<char> charArr(ARR_SIZE);
  DynArray<double> dblArr(ARR_SIZE);
  int i, j, n;
  char c;
  double x;

  cout << "Testing array of integers\n\n";
  for (i = 0; i < ARR_SIZE; i++)
    intArr[i] = 999 - i;
```

continues

Listing B5.3. continued

```
  // display array
  cout << "Unsorted array is:\n";
  for (i = 0; i < ARR_SIZE; i++)
    cout << intArr[i] << "\n";
  pressEnter();
  for (i = 0; i < ARR_SIZE; i++) {
    n = 999 - i;
    cout << "Searching for " << n << " : ";
    j = intArr.LinearSearch(n);
    if (j > -1)
      cout << "found at index " << j << "\n";
    else
      cout << "no match found\n";
  }
  pressEnter();

  // sort the array
  intArr.Sort();
  cout << "Sorted array is:\n";
  for (i = 0; i < ARR_SIZE; i++)
    cout << intArr[i] << "\n";
  pressEnter();
  for (i = 0; i < ARR_SIZE; i++) {
    n = 999 - i;
    cout << "Searching for " << n << " : ";
    j = intArr.BinarySearch(n);
    if (j > -1)
      cout << "found at index " << j << "\n";
    else
      cout << "no match found\n";
  }
  pressEnter();

  cout << "Testing array of characters\n\n";
  for (i = 0; i < ARR_SIZE; i++)
    charArr[i] = char(int('z') - i);
  // display array
  cout << "Unsorted array is:\n";
  for (i = 0; i < ARR_SIZE; i++)
    cout << charArr[i] << "\n";
  pressEnter();
  for (i = 0; i < ARR_SIZE; i++) {
    c = char(int('z') - i);
    cout << "Searching for " << c << " : ";
    j = charArr.LinearSearch(c);
    if (j > -1)
      cout << "found at index " << j << "\n";
    else
      cout << "no match found\n";
  }
  pressEnter();

  // sort the array
  charArr.Sort();
  cout << "Sorted array is:\n";
```

```
  for (i = 0; i < ARR_SIZE; i++)
    cout << charArr[i] << "\n";
  pressEnter();
  for (i = 0; i < ARR_SIZE; i++) {
    c = char(int('z') - i);
    cout << "Searching for " << c << " : ";
    j = charArr.BinarySearch(c);
    if (j > -1)
      cout << "found at index " << j << "\n";
    else
      cout << "no match found\n";
  }
  pressEnter();

  cout << "Testing array of doubles\n\n";
  for (i = 0; i < ARR_SIZE; i++)
    dblArr[i] = 200.0 - i;
  // display array
  cout << "Unsorted array is:\n";
  for (i = 0; i < ARR_SIZE; i++)
    cout << dblArr[i] << "\n";
  pressEnter();
  for (i = 0; i < ARR_SIZE; i++) {
    x = 200.0 - i;
    cout << "Searching for " << x << " : ";
    j = dblArr.LinearSearch(x);
    if (j > -1)
      cout << "found at index " << j << "\n";
    else
      cout << "no match found\n";
  }
  pressEnter();

  // sort the array
  dblArr.Sort();
  cout << "Sorted array is:\n";
  for (i = 0; i < ARR_SIZE; i++)
    cout << dblArr[i] << "\n";
  pressEnter();
  for (i = 0; i < ARR_SIZE; i++) {
    x = 200.0 - i;
    cout << "Searching for " << x << " : ";
    j = dblArr.BinarySearch(x);
    if (j > -1)
      cout << "found at index " << j << "\n";
    else
      cout << "no match found\n";
  }
  pressEnter();

  return 0;
}

void pressEnter()
```

continues

Listing B5.3. continued

```
{
  char c[3];
  cout << "press Enter to continue...";
  cin.getline(c, 2);
}
```

Here is a portion of the output in a session with the test program. The output fragment shows how the program tests the array of integers:

```
Testing array of integers

Unsorted array is:
999
998
997
996
995
994
993
992
991
990
989
987
986
press Enter to continue...
Searching for 999 : found at index 0
Searching for 998 : found at index 1
Searching for 997 : found at index 2
Searching for 996 : found at index 3
Searching for 995 : found at index 4
Searching for 994 : found at index 5
Searching for 993 : found at index 6
Searching for 992 : found at index 7
Searching for 991 : found at index 8
Searching for 990 : found at index 9
Searching for 989 : found at index 10
Searching for 988 : found at index 11
Searching for 987 : found at index 12
Searching for 986 : found at index 13
Searching for 999 : found at index 14
press Enter to continue...
Sorted array is:
986
987
989
990
991
992
993
994
995
```

```
996
997
998
999
press Enter to continue...
Searching for 999 : found at index 14
Searching for 998 : found at index 13
Searching for 997 : found at index 12
Searching for 996 : found at index 11
Searching for 995 : found at index 10
Searching for 994 : found at index 9
Searching for 993 : found at index 8
Searching for 992 : found at index 7
Searching for 991 : found at index 6
Searching for 990 : found at index 5
Searching for 989 : found at index 4
Searching for 988 : found at index 3
Searching for 987 : found at index 2
Searching for 986 : found at index 1
Searching for 999 : found at index 0
press Enter to continue...
```

Analysis Notice that line 5 in Listing B5.3 includes the TEMPAR1.CPP file and not TEMPAR1.H. The program needs to include the header and implementation files for the template classes. This inclusion permits the compiler to read the declarations for the template classes.

The function `main` declares the following dynamic arrays:

- The array `intArr` (in line 12), which instantiates the template class `DynArray` using the predefined type `int`. The constant `ARR_SIZE` sets the number of elements in this array.
- The array `charArr` (in line 13), which instantiates the template class `DynArray` using the predefined type char. The constant `ARR_SIZE` sets the number of elements in this array.
- The array `dblArr` (in line 14), which instantiates the template class `DynArray` using the predefined type `double`. The constant `ARR_SIZE` sets the number of elements in this array.

Lines 19 to 53 test the array of integers, `intArr`, in the manner that I described earlier. The `for` loop in lines 20 and 21 initializes the array elements. The statements in lines 23 to 25 display the elements of the unsorted array. Lines 27 to 35 search for the values in the unsorted array. The statement in line 30 sends the C++ message `LinearSearch` to the object `intArr` to search for data. Line 39 sorts the array `intArr` by sending it the C++ message `Sort`. The statements in lines 40 to 42 display the elements of the sorted array. Lines 44 to 52 search for the values in the sorted array. The statement in line 47 sends the C++ message `BinarySearch` to the object `intArr` to search for data.

B5

The statements in lines 55 to 89 test the array of characters, `charArr`. These statements are similar to the ones which test the array `intArr`. The statements in lines 91 to 125 test the array of doubles, `dblArr`. These statements are also similar to the ones which test the array `intArr`.

Template Parameters

The template parameter list enables you to specify multiple classes and/or additional data types. Most template classes that model generic data structure have only one template class. A few employ more than one template class. Let me present a new version of the template class `DynArray` that uses an additional template parameter to specify the number of array elements. Listing B5.4 shows the source code for TEMPAR2.H header file.

Type

Listing B5.4. The source code for the TEMPAR2.H header file.

```
 1: #ifndef _TEMPAR2_H_
 2: #define _TEMPAR2_H_
 3:
 4: template<class T, int nCount> class DynArray
 5: {
 6:  public:
 7:    enum Boolean { false, true };
 8:
 9:    DynArray();
10:
11:    int GetWorkSize()
12:      { return m_nWorkSize; };
13:    T& operator [](int nIndex);
14:    void Sort();
15:    int LinearSearch(T& searchData);
16:    int BinarySearch(T& searchData);
17:
18:  protected:
19:    T m_Data[nCount];
20:    int m_nWorkSize;
21:    int m_nMaxSize;
22:    Boolean m_bInOrder;
23: };
24:
25: #endif
```

Notice that line 4 declares the new version of the template class `DynArray` with two parameters: class `T` and int `nCount`. The new template parameter specifies the number of array elements. The new class version has the following changes:

- The constructor has no parameter to specify the number of elements, since template parameter `nCount` now performs this task.
- The class uses the member `m_Data` as an array of the type `T` and not a pointer to `T`. Thus the new class version uses a static array (its size is determined during the instantiation of the template class).
- There is no destructor to remove the dynamic array since the class does not use a dynamic array.

Listing B5.5 shows the source code for the TEMPAR2.CPP implementation file.

Type

Listing B5.5. The source code for the TEMPAR2.CPP implementation file.

```
// implementation file for class DynArray

#include "tempar2.h"

template<class T, int nCount>
DynArray<T,nCount>::DynArray()
{
  m_nMaxSize = nCount;
  m_nWorkSize = 0;
  m_bInOrder = false;
}

template<class T, int nCount>
T& DynArray<T,nCount>::operator [](int nIndex)
{
  m_bInOrder = false; // clear order flag
  // is index valid?
  if (nIndex > -1 && nIndex < m_nMaxSize) {
    // update the work size
    if (nIndex >= m_nWorkSize && m_nWorkSize < m_nMaxSize)
      m_nWorkSize++;
    return m_Data[nIndex];
  }
  else
    return m_Data[0];
}

template<class T, int nCount>
void DynArray<T,nCount>::Sort()
{
  int offset, i, j;
  int n = m_nWorkSize;
  long k;
  T temp;

```

continues

Listing B5.5. continued

```
  // exit if array is small or array is already sorted
  if (m_nWorkSize < 2 || m_bInOrder == true)
    return;

  offset = n; // get the initial offser
  do {
    // update the offset, making sure that
    // it does not become less than 1
    k = (offset * 8L) / 11;
    offset = (k == 0) ? 1 : (int)k;
    m_bInOrder = true;
    // start comparing elements
    for (i = 0, j = i + offset; i < (n - offset); i++, j++)
      if (m_Data[i] > m_Data[j]) {
        m_bInOrder = false;
        temp = m_Data[i];
        m_Data[i] = m_Data[j];
        m_Data[j] = temp;
      }

  } while (!(m_bInOrder == true && offset == 1));
}

template<class T, int nCount>
int DynArray<T,nCount>::LinearSearch(T& searchData)
{
  Boolean notFound = true;
  int i = 0;

  while (i < m_nWorkSize && notFound == true)
    if (searchData != m_Data[i])
      i++;
    else
      notFound = false;

  // return search index
  return (notFound == false) ? i : -1;
}

template<class T, int nCount>
int DynArray<T,nCount>::BinarySearch(T& searchData)
{
  T medianElem;
  int lo = 0;
  int hi = m_nWorkSize - 1;
  int median;

  if (m_bInOrder == false)
    return LinearSearch(searchData);

  do {
    median = (lo + hi) / 2;
    medianElem = m_Data[median];
    if (searchData < medianElem)
```

```
      hi = median - 1;
    else
      lo = median + 1;
  } while (!(searchData == medianElem ¦¦ lo > hi));

  return (searchData == medianElem) ? median : -1;
}
```

Listing B5.5 is very similar to Listing B5.2. The main differences are:

- The various member functions access the array elements using the member `m_Data`.
- The template-related syntax now includes the template parameters `T` and `nCount`.
- The constructor does not allocate dynamic memory. It simply initializes the members `m_nMaxSize`, `m_nWorkSize`, and `m_bInOrder`.

Let's look at the test program for the new version of the template class `DynArray`. Listing B5.6 shows the source code for the TSARR2.CPP program file. The test program is very similar to program TSARR1.CPP (in Listing B5.3) and performs the similar tasks.

Listing B5.6. The source code for the TSARR2.CPP program file.

```
// C++ program to test class DynArray

#include <iostream.h>
// include template .CPP file!!
#include "tempar2.cpp"

void pressEnter();

main()
{
  const int ARR_SIZE = 15;
  DynArray<int, ARR_SIZE> intArr;
  DynArray<char, ARR_SIZE> charArr;
  DynArray<double, ARR_SIZE> dblArr;
  int i, j, n;
  char c;
  double x;

  cout << "Testing array of integers\n\n";
  for (i = 0; i < ARR_SIZE; i++)
    intArr[i] = 999 - i;
  // display array
```

continues

Listing B5.6. continued

```
  cout << "Unsorted array is:\n";
  for (i = 0; i < ARR_SIZE; i++)
    cout << intArr[i] << "\n";
  pressEnter();
  for (i = 0; i < ARR_SIZE; i++) {
    n = 999 - i;
    cout << "Searching for " << n << " : ";
    j = intArr.LinearSearch(n);
    if (j > -1)
      cout << "found at index " << j << "\n";
    else
      cout << "no match found\n";
  }
  pressEnter();

  // sort the array
  intArr.Sort();
  cout << "Sorted array is:\n";
  for (i = 0; i < ARR_SIZE; i++)
    cout << intArr[i] << "\n";
  pressEnter();
  for (i = 0; i < ARR_SIZE; i++) {
    n = 999 - i;
    cout << "Searching for " << n << " : ";
    j = intArr.BinarySearch(n);
    if (j > -1)
      cout << "found at index " << j << "\n";
    else
      cout << "no match found\n";
  }
  pressEnter();

  cout << "Testing array of characters\n\n";
  for (i = 0; i < ARR_SIZE; i++)
    charArr[i] = char(int('z') - i);
  // display array
  cout << "Unsorted array is:\n";
  for (i = 0; i < ARR_SIZE; i++)
    cout << charArr[i] << "\n";
  pressEnter();
  for (i = 0; i < ARR_SIZE; i++) {
    c = char(int('z') - i);
    cout << "Searching for " << c << " : ";
    j = charArr.LinearSearch(c);
    if (j > -1)
      cout << "found at index " << j << "\n";
    else
      cout << "no match found\n";
  }
  pressEnter();

  // sort the array
  charArr.Sort();
  cout << "Sorted array is:\n";
```

```
  for (i = 0; i < ARR_SIZE; i++)
    cout << charArr[i] << "\n";
  pressEnter();
  for (i = 0; i < ARR_SIZE; i++) {
    c = char(int('z') - i);
    cout << "Searching for " << c << " : ";
    j = charArr.BinarySearch(c);
    if (j > -1)
      cout << "found at index " << j << "\n";
    else
      cout << "no match found\n";
  }
  pressEnter();

  cout << "Testing array of doubles\n\n";
  for (i = 0; i < ARR_SIZE; i++)
    dblArr[i] = 200.0 - i;
  // display array
  cout << "Unsorted array is:\n";
  for (i = 0; i < ARR_SIZE; i++)
    cout << dblArr[i] << "\n";
  pressEnter();
  for (i = 0; i < ARR_SIZE; i++) {
    x = 200.0 - i;
    cout << "Searching for " << x << " : ";
    j = dblArr.LinearSearch(x);
    if (j > -1)
      cout << "found at index " << j << "\n";
    else
      cout << "no match found\n";
  }
  pressEnter();

  // sort the array
  dblArr.Sort();
  cout << "Sorted array is:\n";
  for (i = 0; i < ARR_SIZE; i++)
    cout << dblArr[i] << "\n";
  pressEnter();
  for (i = 0; i < ARR_SIZE; i++) {
    x = 200.0 - i;
    cout << "Searching for " << x << " : ";
    j = dblArr.BinarySearch(x);
    if (j > -1)
      cout << "found at index " << j << "\n";
    else
      cout << "no match found\n";
  }
  pressEnter();

  return 0;
}

void pressEnter()
```

continues

Listing B5.6. continued

```
131: {
132:    char c[3];
133:    cout << "press Enter to continue...";
134:    cin.getline(c, 2);
135: }
```

The output of the program in Listing B5.6 is the same as that of Listing B5.3. The two programs differ mainly in how they instantiate the template class `DynArray`. Notice lines 12 to 14 in Listing B5.6. These lines contain the statements that declare the array objects `intArr`, `charArr`, and `dblArr`. Notice that the instantiation of the template class `DynArray` involves two arguments: the basic type of the array element and the constant `ARR_SIZE`. The rest of the statements in Listing B5.6 are identical to those in Listing B5.3.

Class Derivation and Templates

Class derivation in template classes obey the general rules for class derivation, as well as the syntax rules for template classes. Let's look at an example that uses the first version of the template class `DynArray`. Listing B5.7 shows the source code for the TEMPAR3.H header file that declares the template classes `DynArray` and `XDynArray`. The class `XDynArray` is a descendant of class `DynArray`. This descendant class supports the capability to expand the number of array elements during runtime.

Type

Listing B5.7. The source code for the TEMPAR3.H header file.

```
#ifndef _TEMPAR3_H_
#define _TEMPAR3_H_

template<class T> class DynArray
{
 public:
   enum Boolean { false, true };

   DynArray(int nMaxSize = 10);
   ~DynArray();

   int GetWorkSize()
     { return m_nWorkSize; };
   T& operator [](int nIndex);
   void Sort();
   int LinearSearch(T& searchData);
   int BinarySearch(T& searchData);

 protected:
```

```
    T* m_pData;
    int m_nWorkSize;
    int m_nMaxSize;
    Boolean m_bInOrder;
};

template<class T>
class XDynArray : public DynArray<T>
{
 public:
  XDynArray(int nMaxSize = 10)
    : DynArray<T>(nMaxSize) {}

  int Expand(int nNewSize);
};

#endif
```

Listing B5.7 declares the class `DynArray` just like in Listing B5.1. The listing declares the descendant class `XDynArray` along with its constructor and member function `Expand`. Listing B5.8 shows the source code for the TEMPAR3.CPP implementation file.

Listing B5.8. The source code for the TEMPAR3.CPP implementation file.

```
// implementation file for class DynArray

#include "tempar3.h"

template<class T>
DynArray<T>::DynArray(int nMaxSize)
{
  m_nMaxSize = (nMaxSize < 0) ? 10 : nMaxSize;
  m_pData = new T[m_nMaxSize];
  m_nWorkSize = 0;
  m_bInOrder = false;
}

template<class T>
DynArray<T>::~DynArray()
{
  delete [] m_pData;
}

template<class T>
T& DynArray<T>::operator [](int nIndex)
{
  m_bInOrder = false; // clear order flag
  // is index valid?
  if (nIndex > -1 && nIndex < m_nMaxSize) {
```

continues

Listing B5.8. continued

```
    // update the work size
    if (nIndex >= m_nWorkSize && m_nWorkSize < m_nMaxSize)
      m_nWorkSize++;
    return m_pData[nIndex];
  }
  else
    return m_pData[0];
}

template<class T>
void DynArray<T>::Sort()
{
  int offset, i, j;
  int n = m_nWorkSize;
  long k;
  T temp;

  // exit if array is small or array is already sorted
  if (m_nWorkSize < 2 || m_bInOrder == true)
    return;

  offset = n; // get the initial offser
  do {
    // update the offset, making sure that
    // it does not become less than 1
    k = (offset * 8L) / 11;
    offset = (k == 0) ? 1 : (int)k;
    m_bInOrder = true;
    // start comparing elements
    for (i = 0, j = i + offset; i < (n - offset); i++, j++)
      if (m_pData[i] > m_pData[j]) {
        m_bInOrder = false;
        temp = m_pData[i];
        m_pData[i] = m_pData[j];
        m_pData[j] = temp;
      }

  } while (!(m_bInOrder == true && offset == 1));
}

template<class T>
int DynArray<T>::LinearSearch(T& searchData)
{
  Boolean notFound = true;
  int i = 0;

  while (i < m_nWorkSize && notFound == true)
    if (searchData != m_pData[i])
      i++;
    else
      notFound = false;

  // return search index
  return (notFound == false) ? i : -1;
```

```
}

template<class T>
int DynArray<T>::BinarySearch(T& searchData)
{
  T medianElem;
  int lo = 0;
  int hi = m_nWorkSize - 1;
  int median;

  if (m_bInOrder == false)
    return LinearSearch(searchData);

  do {
    median = (lo + hi) / 2;
    medianElem = m_pData[median];
    if (searchData < medianElem)
      hi = median - 1;
    else
      lo = median + 1;
  } while (!(searchData == medianElem || lo > hi));

  return (searchData == medianElem) ? median : -1;
}

template<class T>
int XDynArray<T>::Expand(int nNewSize)
{
  T* pData;

  if (nNewSize < m_nMaxSize)
    return 0; // 0 is no-expansion code
  // create new dynamic array
  pData = new T[nNewSize];
  // allocation failed?
  if (pData == NULL)
    return -1; // negative value is allocation error code
  // copy data
  for (int i = 0; i < m_nMaxSize; i++)
    pData[i] = m_pData[i];
  // delete old array
  delete [] m_pData;
  // access new array with member m_pData
  m_pData = pData;
  // update maximum size
  m_nMaxSize = nNewSize;
  return 1;
}
```

Listing B5.8 is a superset of Listing B5.2. The preceding listing adds the definition of member function `Expand`. This function creates a new dynamic array, copies the data from the old array to the new array, deletes the old dynamic array, and updates the data members `m_pData` and `m_nMaxSize`.

Let's look at a simple test program for class `XDynArray`. Listing B5.9 shows the source code for the TSARR3.CPP program file. The test program instantiates the template class `XDynArray` using the predefined `int` type. The program creates the array of integers with an initial size, manipulates the array, expands the array, and then manipulates the expanded array. The program manipulates each of the original and expanded arrays as follows:

1. Assigns values to the array elements.
2. Displays the elements of the unsorted array elements.
3. Searches for the data in the unsorted array elements. The program displays the indices of the matching array elements.
4. Sorts the array elements.
5. Displays the elements of the sorted array elements.
6. Searches for the data in the sorted array element. The program displays the indices of the matching array elements.

Type

Listing B5.9. The source code for the TSARR3.CPP program file.

```
// C++ program to test class XDynArray

#include <iostream.h>
// include template .CPP file!!
#include "tempar3.cpp"

void pressEnter();

main()
{
  const SMALL_ARR_SIZE = 7;
  const LARGE_ARR_SIZE = 10;
  XDynArray<int> intArr(SMALL_ARR_SIZE);
  int i, j, n;

  cout << "Testing array of integers\n\n";
  for (i = 0; i < SMALL_ARR_SIZE; i++)
    intArr[i] = 999 - i;
  // display array
  cout << "Unsorted array is:\n";
  for (i = 0; i < SMALL_ARR_SIZE; i++)
    cout << intArr[i] << "\n";
  pressEnter();
  for (i = 0; i < SMALL_ARR_SIZE; i++) {
    n = 999 - i;
    cout << "Searching for " << n << " : ";
    j = intArr.LinearSearch(n);
```

```
      if (j > -1)
        cout << "found at index " << j << "\n";
      else
        cout << "no match found\n";
    }
    pressEnter();

    // sort the array
    intArr.Sort();
    cout << "Sorted array is:\n";
    for (i = 0; i < SMALL_ARR_SIZE; i++)
      cout << intArr[i] << "\n";
    pressEnter();
    for (i = 0; i < SMALL_ARR_SIZE; i++) {
      n = 999 - i;
      cout << "Searching for " << n << " : ";
      j = intArr.BinarySearch(n);
      if (j > -1)
        cout << "found at index " << j << "\n";
      else
        cout << "no match found\n";
    }
    pressEnter();

    // expand the array
    if (intArr.Expand(LARGE_ARR_SIZE) < 1) {
      cout << "Error in expanding the array!\n\n";
      return 0;
    }

    cout << "Testing the expanded array of integers\n\n";
    for (i = SMALL_ARR_SIZE; i < LARGE_ARR_SIZE; i++)
      intArr[i] = 999 - i;
    // display array
    cout << "Unsorted array is:\n";
    for (i = 0; i < LARGE_ARR_SIZE; i++)
      cout << intArr[i] << "\n";
    pressEnter();
    for (i = 0; i < LARGE_ARR_SIZE; i++) {
      n = 999 - i;
      cout << "Searching for " << n << " : ";
      j = intArr.LinearSearch(n);
      if (j > -1)
        cout << "found at index " << j << "\n";
      else
        cout << "no match found\n";
    }
    pressEnter();

    // sort the array
    intArr.Sort();
    cout << "Sorted array is:\n";
    for (i = 0; i < LARGE_ARR_SIZE; i++)
      cout << intArr[i] << "\n";
```

continues

Listing B5.9. continued

```
    pressEnter();
    for (i = 0; i < LARGE_ARR_SIZE; i++) {
      n = 999 - i;
      cout << "Searching for " << n << " : ";
      j = intArr.BinarySearch(n);
      if (j > -1)
        cout << "found at index " << j << "\n";
      else
        cout << "no match found\n";
    }
    pressEnter();

    return 0;
  }

  void pressEnter()
  {
    char c[3];
    cout << "press Enter to continue...";
    cin.getline(c, 2);
  }
```

Here is the output for the program in Listing B5.9:

```
Testing array of integers

Unsorted array is:
999
998
997
996
995
994
993
press Enter to continue...
Searching for 999 : found at index 0
Searching for 998 : found at index 1
Searching for 997 : found at index 2
Searching for 996 : found at index 3
Searching for 995 : found at index 4
Searching for 994 : found at index 5
Searching for 993 : found at index 6
press Enter to continue...
Sorted array is:
993
994
995
996
997
998
999
press Enter to continue...
Searching for 999 : found at index 6
```

```
Searching for 998 : found at index 5
Searching for 997 : found at index 4
Searching for 996 : found at index 3
Searching for 995 : found at index 2
Searching for 994 : found at index 1
Searching for 993 : found at index 0
press Enter to continue...
Testing the expanded array of integers
993
994
995
996
997
998
999
992
991
990
press Enter to continue...
Searching for 999 : found at index 6
Searching for 998 : found at index 5
Searching for 997 : found at index 4
Searching for 996 : found at index 3
Searching for 995 : found at index 2
Searching for 994 : found at index 1
Searching for 993 : found at index 0
Searching for 992 : found at index 7
Searching for 991 : found at index 8
Searching for 990 : found at index 9
press Enter to continue...
990
991
992
993
994
995
996
997
998
999
press Enter to continue...
Searching for 999 : found at index 9
Searching for 998 : found at index 8
Searching for 997 : found at index 7
Searching for 996 : found at index 6
Searching for 995 : found at index 5
Searching for 994 : found at index 4
Searching for 993 : found at index 3
Searching for 992 : found at index 2
Searching for 991 : found at index 1
Searching for 990 : found at index 0
press Enter to continue...
```

Analysis

The program in Listing B5.9 declares the constants `SMALL_ARR_SIZE` and `LARGE_ARR_SIZE` in lines 11 and 12. Line 13 instantiates the class `XDynArray` using the predefined type `int` to create the array of integers `intArr`. The program

B5

manipulates the array intArr in a manner similar to the programs in Listing B53 and B5.6. Line 53 expands the array intArr by sending it the C++ message Expand. This message appears in an if statement that determines the success or failure of the message. Lines 59 contains a for loop that assigns values to the new elements of array intArr. The rest of the statements in the program manipulate the expanded array in a manner similar to manipulating the original array.

Summary

This chapter presented the C++ feature which supports template functions and template classes. You learned about the following:

- Template functions that empower you to develop generic routines to handle a wide variety of data types. Template functions enable you to consolidate your code and make it easier to maintain.
- Declaring template classes. This step states that a class is generic using the general syntax:

  ```
  template<parameterList>
  class className
  {
       // declarations of members
  };
  ```

  The *parameterList* is a list of one or more template classes. The list may also include predefined data types and user-defined structures. The class declaration requires the use of fully qualified class names.

  The definition of the various member functions must employ a special syntax. The general syntax for template functions is shown below:

  ```
  template<parameterList>
  type className<paramNamesList>::memberFunction(
                     functionParameterList)
  ```

  The *paramNamesList* is the list of parameter names and does not include the associated classes and data types.

- Instantiating template classes. This is a process that creates an instance from the template class by specifying the instantiating data type. The general syntax for the instantiation of a template class is:

```
className<instantiatingType>
     classInstance(constructurArguments);.
```

- Template parameters include one or more classes as well as any other valid data type. The chapter illustrated how dynamic arrays are modeled using a C++ class with two template parameters.
- Class derivation and templates. C++ supports the normal rules of deriving classes and inheritance for template classes. C++ allows you to create class hierarchies that are either solely made up of template classes or both template and non-template classes.

Q&A

Q Can I derive a non-template class from a template class?

A Yes. The non-template descendant class would offer specific operations based on the inherited general operations of the parent template class.

Q How do I instantiate a template class with a non-template class?

A You need to make sure that the instantiating class defines all of the operators (such as `=`, `==`, `!=`, and so on) used in the template class. Otherwise you get a compiler error, since it cannot complete the instantiation process.

Q Can I create an abstract template class?

A Yes, indeed. Abstract template classes are commonly used in implementing template classes which support popular data structures such as arrays, lists, and trees.

Q Does the template class save in code space?

A No. Each instantiation of a template class adds to the code space.

Exercise

Modify the second version of template class `DynArray` to use a dynamic array. Moreover, add the member function `Expand` to your class version to support runtime array expansion.

A

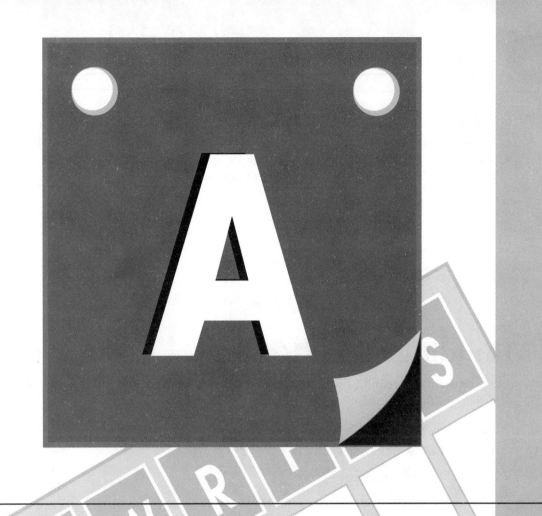

Controls Resource Script

This appendix presents the syntax for the menu resource and the controls resource scripts. The resource script itself was defined by Microsoft long before it created the MFC class hierarchy. However, as you see in Day 19, dialog box instances are created using resources. In this appendix, you learn about the following resources:

- The menu resources
- The dialog box resource
- The `DIALOG` option statements
- The general control resource
- The resources for the default controls

Building Menu Resources

The menu resource file (which is usually stored in an .RC file extension) may contain the following statements:

- The `MENU` statement
- The `MENUITEM` statement
- The `POPUP` statement
- The `MENUITEM SEPARATOR` statement
- The `ACCELERATORS` statement

The `MENU` statement defines the contents of a menu resource. The general syntax for the `MENU` statement is

```
menuID MENU [load options] [mem options]
BEGIN
  item definitions
END
```

The *`menuID`* is the unique name or integer ID of the menu resource. The keywords associated with resource files appear in uppercase. This is optional—they are not case-sensitive. I maintain the uppercase letters to make it easier to distinguish between resource keywords and non-keywords. The following are the load options:

- `PRELOAD` loads the resource immediately.
- `LOADONCALL` loads the resource as needed (the default option).

The following are the memory options:

- FIXED keeps the resource in a fixed memory location.
- MOVABLE moves the resource when needed for the sake of memory compaction (the default option).
- DISCARDABLE discards the resource when no longer needed (this option is also selected by default).

The MENUITEM statement defines the name and attributes of an actual menu item. The general syntax for the MENUITEM statement is

```
MENUITEM text, result [, option list]
```

The text field accepts a string literal (enclosed in double quotes) that designates the name of the menu item. To define a hot key for a menu item, place the ampersand character (&) before the letter you want to make the hot key (the selection is case-insensitive). To display the ampersand as part of the menu name, use a sequence of two ampersand characters (that is, &&). You can also include the \t sequence to insert a tab in the menu item name. The \a sequence can be inserted to align all text that follows, by flushing it to the right.

The result field contains an integer, usually a CM_XXXX constant, that represents the command emitted by the menu item.

The option list may contain the following items:

- CHECKED displays a check mark next to the menu item.
- GRAYED displays the menu item in a gray color to indicate the menu item is not active.
- HELP puts a vertical separator bar to the left of the menu item.
- INACTIVE displays the menu item but prevents its selection. This option is usually combined with the GRAYED option to give a better visual indication that the menu item is inactive.
- MENUBARBREAK places the menu item on a new line for static menu bar items. In the case of pop-up menu items (presented next), it separates the new and old columns with a vertical line.
- MENUBREAK places the menu item on a new line for static menu bar items. In the case of pop-up menus, it places the menu item in a new column, without any dividing line between the columns.

The POPUP statement defines the beginning of a pop-up menu. The general syntax for the POPUP statement is

```
POPUP text [,option list]
BEGIN
  item definitions
END
```

The *text* and option list fields are similar to their counterparts in the MENUITEM statement. The item definitions are made up of MENUITEM and/or other POPUP statements. The latter statements enable you to create nested menus.

The MENUITEM SEPARATOR statement is a special form of the MENUITEM statement that creates an inactive menu item and displays a dividing bar between two active menu items.

The ACCELERATORS statement defines one or more accelerators for your MFC application.

NEW TERM An *accelerator* is a keystroke defined to give the application user a quick way to select a menu item and carry out a specific task.

The general syntax for the ACCELERATORS statement is

```
accTableName ACCELERATORS
BEGIN
  event, idValue, [type] [NOINVERT] [ALT] [SHIFT] [CONTROL]
END
```

The *accTableName* field defines a unique name or integer ID that distinguishes an accelerator resource from any other type of resources. The event field specifies the keystroke used as an accelerator and can be one of the following:

- A single ASCII character is enclosed in double quotes. You can place a caret symbol before the character to signal that it is a control character. In this case, the *type* field is not required.
- An integer value designates an ASCII code of a character. In this case, the *type* field must be the keyword ASCII.
- An integer value represents a virtual key. In this case, the *type* field must be the keyword VIRTKEY.

The *idValue* field is an integer that identifies the accelerator. The *type* field is required only when the event field is an ASCII character code or a virtual key.

The NOINVERT option prevents a top-level menu item from being highlighted when the accelerator is used. The ALT, SHIFT, and CONTROL options activate the accelerator when the Alt, Shift, and Control keys are pressed down, respectively. The following is an example of an accelerator resource:

```
"EditKeys" ACCELERATORS
BEGIN
     "h",        IDDHEADING                              ; the H key
     "H",        IDDHOLD                                 ; the Shift-H keys
     "^B",       IDDBOLD                                 ; the Control-B keys
     64,         IDDADD                                  ; The Shift-A keys
     97,         IDDAPPEND                               ; The A key
     "s",        IDDSEARCH, ALT                          ;  The Alt-S keys
     VK_F7,      IDDSAVE, VIRTKEY                        ; The F7 function key
     VK_F2,      IDDLOAD, SHIFT, VIRTKEY                 ; The Shift-F2 keys
     VK_F3,      IDDSAVEAS, CONTROL, VIRTKEY             ; The Control-F3 keys
     VK_F1,      IDDNEW, ALT, SHIFT, VIRTKEY             ; The Alt-Shift-F1
; keys
END
```

Dialog Box Resource

The `DIALOG` statement defines the resource that can be utilized in a Windows program to build dialog boxes. The general syntax for the `DIALOG` statement is

```
nameID DIALOG [load-option][mem-option] x, y, width, height
 [option-statements]
BEGIN
  control-statements
END
```

The *nameID* is the unique name or integer ID of the dialog box resource. The keywords associated with resource files appear in uppercase. This is optional—they are not case-sensitive. I maintain the uppercase letters to make it easier to distinguish between resource keywords and non-keywords. The following are the load options:

- `PRELOAD` loads the resource immediately.
- `LOADONCALL` loads the resource as needed (the default option).

The following are the memory options:

- `FIXED` keeps the resource in a fixed memory location.
- `MOVABLE` moves the resource when needed for the sake of memory compaction (the default option).
- `DISCARDABLE` discards the resource when no longer needed (this option is also selected by default).

The `x` and `y` parameters specify the location of the upper left corner of the dialog box. The `width` and `height` parameters define the dimensions of the dialog box.

An example of a dialog box resource definition is shown next. The example is taken from the DIALOG1.RC file:

```
#include <windows.h>
#include <afxres.h>

NEW DIALOG DISCARDABLE LOADONCALL PURE MOVEABLE 30, 50, 200, 100
STYLE WS_POPUP ¦ DS_MODALFRAME
CAPTION "Message"
BEGIN
  CTEXT "Exit the application?", 1, 10, 10, 170, 15
  CONTROL "OK", IDOK, "BUTTON", WS_CHILD ¦ WS_VISIBLE ¦
        WS_TABSTOP ¦ BS_DEFPUSHBUTTON, 20, 50, 70, 15
  CONTROL "Cancel", IDCANCEL, "BUTTON", WS_CHILD ¦ WS_VISIBLE ¦
        WS_TABSTOP ¦ BS_PUSHBUTTON, 110, 50, 70, 15
END
```

DIALOG Option Statements

The DIALOG option statements designate the special attributes of the dialog box, such as style, caption, and menu. These statements are optional. If you do not incorporate any option statements in your dialog box resource definition, you end up with a dialog box that has default attributes. The DIALOG option statements include the following items:

- STYLE
- CAPTION
- MENU
- CLASS
- FONT

In the following subsections, I explain each of these dialog box attributes.

The *STYLE* Statement

The STYLE statement specifies the window style of the dialog box. This attribute indicates whether the dialog box is a child window or a pop-up window. The default style for the dialog box has the WS_POPUP, WS_BORDER, and WS_SYSMENU styles. The general syntax for the STYLE statement is

```
STYLE style
```

The *style* parameter takes an integer value made up of bitwise OR style attributes. The following is an example of the STYLE option statement:

```
STYLE WS_POPUP ¦ DS_MODALFRAME
```

The *CAPTION* Statement

The `CAPTION` statement defines the title for the dialog box. This title appears in the caption bar of the dialog box, if the box has that bar. By default, the title is an empty string. The general syntax for the `CAPTION` statement is

```
CAPTION title
```

The *title* parameter is a string literal. The following is an example of the `CAPTION` statement:

```
CAPTION "Replace Text"
```

The *MENU* Statement

The `MENU` statement specifies the menu attached to the dialog box. By default, the dialog box has no menu. The general syntax for the `MENU` statement is

```
MENU menuName
```

The *menuName* parameter is the name or number of the menu resource. The following is an example of the `MENU` statement:

```
#include <windows.h>
#include <afxres.h>

YesNo MENU LOADONCALL MOVEABLE PURE DISCARDABLE
BEGIN
  MENUITEM "&Ok", IDOK
  MENUITEM "&Cancel", IDCANCEL
END

NEW DIALOG DISCARDABLE LOADONCALL PURE MOVEABLE 30, 50, 200, 100
STYLE WS_POPUP ¦ DS_MODALFRAME
CAPTION "Message"
MENU YesNo
BEGIN
  CTEXT "Exit the application?", 1, 10, 10, 170, 15
  CONTROL "OK", IDOK, "BUTTON", WS_CHILD ¦ WS_VISIBLE ¦
          WS_TABSTOP ¦ BS_DEFPUSHBUTTON, 20, 50, 70, 15
  CONTROL "Cancel", IDCANCEL, "BUTTON", WS_CHILD ¦ WS_VISIBLE ¦
          WS_TABSTOP ¦ BS_PUSHBUTTON, 110, 50, 70, 15
END
```

The *CLASS* Statement

The `CLASS` statement specifies the Windows registration class (and not the MFC library class) of the dialog box. The general syntax for the `CLASS` statement is

```
CLASS className
```

The `className` parameter defines the integer or string name of the registration class. The following is an example of the `CLASS` statement:

```
CLASS "ChitChat"
```

The *FONT* Statement

The `FONT` statement specifies the font used by Windows to draw text in the dialog box. The specified font must already be loaded, either from WIN.INI or by invoking the `LoadFont` API function. The general syntax for the `FONT` statement is

```
FONT pointSize, typeface
```

The *`pointSize`* parameter is an integer that specifies the size of the font in points. The *`typeface`* parameter is a string that indicates the name of the font. The following is an example of the `FONT` statement:

```
FONT 10, "Helv"
```

Dialog Box Control Resources

The resource script supports two types of control resources. The first one is the `CONTROL` statement, which provides a general way for declaring the resource of a control. The other type of resource controls are the modifiable default control resources. These resources use statements with keywords that are descriptive of the control they define. For example, the `RADIOBUTTON` statement defines the resource for a radio button. In the next section, I present the `CONTROL` statement. In the sections after the next one, I present the statements that define the resources for specific controls.

The General Control Resource

The `CONTROL` statement allows you to define the resource for any standard or user-defined control that is owned by a dialog box. The general syntax for the `CONTROL` statement is

```
CONTROL text, id, class, style, x, y, width, height
```

The *`text`* parameter specifies a string literal for the text that appears in the control.

The *`id`* parameter declares the control's unique ID.

> **Note:** The *class* parameter is a string that indicates the name of the Windows registration class for the control. Table A.1 shows the Windows registration class names for the various standard controls. Notice that the pushbutton, check box, radio button, and group box all share the same registration class name! How are they distinguished from each other? The answer lies with the *style* parameter.

> **Note:** The *style* parameter, which is usually a bitwise `OR` expression, sets all the styles associated with the control. There are *no default style values!*

The *x*, *y*, *width*, and *height* parameters specify the location and dimensions of the control. These parameters are typically integer constants. You can also use the addition operator to build simple expressions.

Table A.1. Windows registration class names for the various standard controls.

Control	Registration Class Name
Check box	`BUTTON`
Combo box	`COMBOBOX`
Edit box	`EDIT`
Group box	`BUTTON`
List box	`LISTBOX`
Pushbutton	`BUTTON`
Radio button	`BUTTON`
Scroll bar	`SCROLLBAR`
Static text	`STATIC`

Examples of using the `CONTROL` statement to create dialog box controls are shown next. These examples are taken from the DIALOG6.RC resource file:

```
ID_DIALOG DIALOG DISCARDABLE LOADONCALL PURE MOVEABLE 10, 10, 200, 150
STYLE WS_POPUP | WS_CLIPSIBLINGS | WS_CAPTION | WS_SYSMENU | DS_MODALFRAME
CAPTION "Controls Demo"
BEGIN
  CONTROL "Find", ID_FIND_TXT, "STATIC", WS_CHILD | WS_VISIBLE |
          SS_LEFT, 20, 10, 100, 15

  CONTROL "", ID_FIND_CMB, "COMBOBOX", WS_CHILD | WS_VISIBLE |
          WS_BORDER | WS_TABSTOP | CBS_DROPDOWN, 20, 25, 100, 50

  CONTROL "Replace", ID_REPLACE_TXT, "STATIC", WS_CHILD | WS_VISIBLE |
          SS_LEFT, 20, 45, 100, 15

  CONTROL "", ID_REPLACE_CMB, "COMBOBOX", WS_CHILD | WS_VISIBLE |
          WS_BORDER | WS_TABSTOP | CBS_DROPDOWN, 20, 60, 100, 50

  CONTROL " Scope ", ID_SCOPE_GRP, "BUTTON", WS_CHILD | WS_VISIBLE
          | WS_GROUP | BS_GROUPBOX, 20, 80, 90, 50

  CONTROL "Global", ID_GLOBAL_RBT, "BUTTON", WS_CHILD | WS_VISIBLE
          | WS_TABSTOP | BS_AUTORADIOBUTTON, 30, 90, 50, 15

  CONTROL "Selected Text", ID_SELTEXT_RBT, "BUTTON", WS_CHILD |
         WS_VISIBLE | WS_TABSTOP | BS_AUTORADIOBUTTON, 30, 105, 60, 15

  CONTROL "Case Sensitive", ID_CASE_CHK, "BUTTON", WS_CHILD |
         WS_VISIBLE | WS_TABSTOP | BS_AUTOCHECKBOX, 20, 130, 80, 15

  CONTROL "Whole Word", ID_WHOLEWORD_CHK, "BUTTON", WS_CHILD |
          WS_VISIBLE | WS_TABSTOP | BS_AUTOCHECKBOX, 100, 130, 80, 15

  CONTROL "&OK", IDOK, "BUTTON", WS_CHILD | WS_VISIBLE | WS_TABSTOP
           | BS_DEFPUSHBUTTON, 120, 90, 30, 20

  CONTROL "&Cancel", IDCANCEL, "BUTTON", WS_CHILD | WS_VISIBLE |
          WS_TABSTOP, 160, 90, 30, 20
END
```

The *LTEXT* Statement

The LTEXT statement defines the resource of a static text control whose text is flush left. The general syntax for the LTEXT statement is

```
LTEXT text, id, x, y, width, height [, style]
```

The *text* parameter specifies the static control text. This text may include an & character to underline a hot-key character. The *id* parameter defines the ID of the static control. The *x*, *y*, *width*, and *height* parameters specify the location and dimensions of the control. The optional *style* parameter specifies the additional styles for the resource. The default style is SS_LEFT and WS_GROUP. The *style* parameter can be the WS_TABSTOP style, the WS_GROUP style, or both.

The characters of the *text* parameter are displayed left-justified. If the entire text does not fit in the specified width, the additional characters are wrapped to the beginning of the next line.

The following are examples of the LTEXT statement:

```
LTEXT "Current Drive:", ID_DRIVE_TXT, 10, 10, 50, 10

LTEXT "Current Dir:", ID_DIR_TXT, 10, 50, 50, 10, WS_TABSTOP
      | WS_GROUP
```

The *RTEXT* Statement

The RTEXT statement defines the resource of a static text control whose text is flush right. The general syntax for the RTEXT statement is

```
RTEXT text, id, x, y, width, height [, style]
```

The *text* parameter specifies the static control text. This text may include an & character to underline a hot-key character. The *id* parameter defines the ID of the static control. The *x*, *y*, *width*, and *height* parameters specify the location and dimensions of the control. The optional *style* parameter specifies the additional styles for the resource. The default style is SS_RIGHT and WS_GROUP. The *style* parameter can be the WS_TABSTOP style, the WS_GROUP style, or both.

The characters of the text parameter are displayed right-justified. If the entire text does not fit in the specified width, the additional characters are wrapped to the next line and also appear right-justified.

The following is an example of the RTEXT statement:

```
RTEXT "Current Drive:", ID_DRIVE_TXT, 70, 10, 50, 10
```

The *CTEXT* Statement

The CTEXT statement defines the resource of a static text control whose text is centered. The general syntax for the CTEXT statement is

```
CTEXT text, id, x, y, width, height [, style]
```

The *text* parameter specifies the static control text. This text may include an & character to underline a hot-key character. The *id* parameter defines the ID of the static control. The *x*, *y*, *width*, and *height* parameters specify the location and dimensions of the control. The optional *style* parameter specifies the additional styles for the resource. The default style is SS_CENTER and WS_GROUP. The *style* parameter can be the WS_TABSTOP style, or the WS_GROUP style, or both.

The characters of the *text* parameter are displayed as centered. If the entire text does not fit in the specified width, the additional characters are wrapped to the next line and also appear as centered.

The following is an example of the CTEXT statement:

```
CTEXT "Current Drive:", ID_DRIVE_TXT, 10, 10, 50, 10
```

The *CHECKBOX* Statement

The CHECKBOX statement defines a check box control resource that has the BUTTON registration class. The general syntax for the CHECKBOX statement is

```
CHECKBOX text, id, x, y, width, height [, style]
```

The *text* parameter specifies the caption of the control. This text may include an & character to underline a hot-key character. The *id* parameter defines the ID of the check box control. The *x*, *y*, *width*, and *height* parameters specify the location and dimensions of the control. The optional *style* parameter specifies the additional styles for the resource. The default style is BS_CHECKBOX and WS_TABSTOP. The *style* parameter can be the WS_DISABLED style, the WS_TABSTOP style, or both.

The following is an example of the CHECKBOX statement:

```
CHECKBOX "Case-Sensitive", ID_CASE_CHK, 10, 10, 100, 10
```

The *PUSHBUTTON* Statement

The PUSHBUTTON statement defines a push button control resource that has the BUTTON registration class. The general syntax for the PUSHBUTTON statement is

```
PUSHBUTTON text, id, x, y, width, height [, style]
```

The *text* parameter specifies the caption of the control. This text may include an & character to underline a hot-key character. The *id* parameter defines the ID of the pushbutton control. The *x*, *y*, *width*, and *height* parameters specify the location and dimensions of the control. The optional *style* parameter specifies the additional styles for the resource. The default style is BS_PUSHBUTTON and WS_TABSTOP. The *style* parameter can be the WS_TABSTOP style, the WS_DISABLED style, or the WS_GROUP style, or any bitwise OR combination of these styles.

The following is an example of the PUSHBUTTON statement:

```
PUSHBUTTON "Calculate", ID_CALC_BTN, 10, 10, 100, 10, WS_DISABLED
```

The *DEFPUSHBUTTON* Statement

The DEFPUSHBUTTON statement defines a default pushbutton control resource that has the BUTTON registration class. The general syntax for the DEFPUSHBUTTON statement is

```
DEFPUSHBUTTON text, id, x, y, width, height [, style]
```

The *text* parameter specifies the caption of the control. This text may include an & character to underline a hot-key character. The *id* parameter defines the ID of the default pushbutton control. The *x*, *y*, *width*, and *height* parameters specify the location and dimensions of the control. The optional *style* parameter specifies the additional styles for the resource. The default style is BS_DEFPUSHBUTTON and WS_TABSTOP. The *style* parameter can be the WS_TABSTOP style, the WS_DISABLED style, the WS_GROUP style, or any bitwise OR combination of these styles.

The following is an example of the DEFPUSHBUTTON statement:

```
DEFPUSHBUTTON "Calculate", ID_CALC_BTN, 10, 10, 100, 10
```

The *LISTBOX* Statement

The LISTBOX statement defines a list box control resource that has the LISTBOX registration class. The general syntax for the LISTBOX statement is

```
LISTBOX id, x, y, width, height [, style]
```

The *id* parameter defines the ID of the list box control. The *x*, *y*, *width*, and *height* parameters specify the location and dimensions of the control. The optional *style* parameter specifies the additional styles for the resource. The default style is LBS_NOTIFY, WS_VSCROLL, and WS_BORDER. The *style* parameter can be the WS_BORDER style, the WS_VSCROLL style, or both.

The following is an example of the LISTBOX statement:

```
LISTBOX ID_OPERAND_LST, 10, 10, 100, 100
```

The *GROUPBOX* Statement

The GROUPBOX statement defines a group box control resource that has the BUTTON registration class. The general syntax for the GROUPBOX statement is

```
GROUPBOX text, id, x, y, width, height [, style]
```

The *text* parameter specifies the caption of the control. This text may include an & character to underline a hot-key character. The *id* parameter defines the ID of the group box control. The *x*, *y*, *width*, and *height* parameters specify the location and dimensions of the control. The optional *style* parameter specifies the additional styles for the resource. The default style is BS_GROUPBOX and WS_TABSTOP. The *style* parameter can be the WS_TABSTOP style, the WS_DISABLED style, or both.

The following is an example of the GROUPBOX statement:

```
GROUPBOX "Angle", ID_ANGLE_GRP, 10, 10, 200, 200
```

The *RADIOBUTTON* Statement

The RADIOBUTTON statement defines a radio button control resource that has the BUTTON registration class. The general syntax for the RADIOBUTTON statement is

```
RADIOBUTTON text, id, x, y, width, height [, style]
```

The *text* parameter specifies the caption of the control. This text may include an & character to underline a hot-key character. The *id* parameter defines the ID of the radio button control. The *x*, *y*, *width*, and *height* parameters specify the location and dimensions of the control. The optional *style* parameter specifies the additional styles for the resource. The default style is BS_RADIOBUTTON and WS_TABSTOP. The *style* parameter can be the WS_TABSTOP style, the WS_GROUP style, the WS_DISABLED style, or any bitwise OR combination of these styles.

The following is an example of the RADIOBUTTON statement:

```
RADIOBUTTON "Degrees", ID_DEGREES_RBT, 10, 10, 100, 10
```

The *EDITTEXT* Statement

The EDITTEXT statement defines an edit box control resource that has the EDIT registration class. The general syntax for the EDITTEXT statement is

```
EDITTEXT id, x, y, width, height [, style]
```

The *id* parameter defines the ID of the edit box control. The *x*, *y*, *width*, and *height* parameters specify the location and dimensions of the control. The optional *style* parameter specifies the additional styles for the resource. The default style is WS_TABSTOP, ES_EDIT, and WS_BORDER. The *style* parameter can be the WS_TABSTOP, the WS_GROUP, the WS_VSCROLL, the WS_HSCROLL, or the WS_DISABLED styles, or any bitwise OR combination of these styles.

The following is an example of the EDITTEXT statement:

```
EDITTEXT ID_INPUT_BOX, 10, 10, 200, 200
```

The *COMBOBOX* Statement

The COMBOBOX statement defines a combo box control resource that has the COMBOBOX registration class. The general syntax for the COMBOBOX statement is

```
COMBOBOX id, x, y, width, height [, style]
```

The *id* parameter defines the ID of the combo box control. The *x*, *y*, *width*, and *height* parameters specify the location and dimensions of the control. The optional *style* parameter specifies the additional styles for the resource. The default style is WS_TABSTOP and CBS_SIMPLE. The *style* parameter can be the WS_TABSTOP, the WS_GROUP, the WS_VSCROLL, or the WS_DISABLED styles, or any bitwise OR combination of these styles.

The following is an example of the COMBOBOX statement:

```
COMBOBOX ID_INPUT_BOX, 10, 10, 200, 200
```

The *SCROLLBAR* Statement

The SCROLLBAR statement defines a scroll bar control resource that has the SCROLLBAR registration class. The general syntax for the SCROLLBAR statement is

```
SCROLLBAR id, x, y, width, height [, style]
```

The *id* parameter defines the ID of the scroll bar control. The *x*, *y*, *width*, and *height* parameters specify the location and dimensions of the control. The optional *style* parameter specifies the additional styles for the resource. The default style is SBS_HORZ. The *style* parameter can be the WS_TABSTOP, the WS_GROUP, the WS_DISABLED styles, or any bitwise OR combination of these styles.

The following is an example of the SCROLLBAR statement:

```
SCROLLBAR ID_INDEX_SCR, 10, 10, 20, 200
```

Summary

This appendix briefly introduces you to the resource statements used to create the dialog box and its controls. You learn about the following topics:

- The `DIALOG` statement defines a dialog box resource.
- The `DIALOG` option statements include the `STYLE`, `CAPTION`, `MENU`, `CLASS`, and `FONT` statements.
- The `CONTROL` statement defines the resources for both standard and user-defined controls.
- The `LTEXT` statement defines the resource for a left-justified static text control.
- The `RTEXT` statement defines the resource for a right-justified static text control.
- The `CTEXT` statement defines the resource for a centered-text static text control.
- The `CHECKBOX` statement defines the resource for a check box control.
- The `PUSHBUTTON` statement defines the resource for a pushbutton control.
- The `DEFPUSHBUTTON` statement defines the resource for a default pushbutton control.
- The `LISTBOX` statement defines the resource for a list box control.
- The `GROUPBOX` statement defines the resource for a group box control.
- The `RADIOBUTTON` statement defines the resource for a radio button control.
- The `EDITTEXT` statement defines the resource for an edit box control.
- The `COMBOBOX` statement defines the resource for a combo box control.
- The `SCROLLBAR` statement defines the resource for a scroll bar control.

B

Answers

Note: Due to space limitations, not every Exercise is answered.

Answers to Day 1, "Getting Started"

Quiz

1. The program generates the string `C++ in 21 Days?`.
2. The program generates no output because the `cout` statement appears inside a comment! The function `main` simply returns 0.
3. The `cout` statement is missing the semicolon.

Exercise

```
// Exercise program

#include <iostream.h>

main()
{
  cout << "I am a C++ Programmer";
  return 0;
}
```

Answers to Day 2, "C++ Program Components"

Quiz

1. The following table indicates which identifiers are valid and which are not (and why):

Identifiers	Valid?	Reason (if Invalid)
`numFiles`	Yes	
`n0Distance_02_Line`	Yes	
`0Weight`	No	Starts with a digit

Identifiers	Valid?	Reason (if Invalid)
`Bin Number`	No	Contains a space
`static`	No	Reserved keyword
`Static`	Yes	

2. The output of the program is

   `a = 10` and `b = 3`

   The function `swap` fails to swap the arguments `a` and `b` because it only swaps a copy of their values.

3. The output of the program is

   `a = 3` and `b = 10`

   The function `swap` succeeds in swapping the arguments `a` and `b` because it uses reference parameters. Consequently, the changes in the values of parameters `i` and `j` go beyond the scope of the function itself.

4. The second version of function `inc` has a default argument, which, when used, hinders the compiler from determining which version of `inc` to call. The compiler flags a compile-time error for such functions.

5. Because the second parameter has a default argument, the third one must also have a default argument. Here is one version of the correct definition of function `volume`:

```
double volume(double length, double width = 1, double height = 1)
{
  return length * width * height
}
```

6. The parameter `i` is a lowercase letter. However, the function uses the uppercase `I` in the assignment statement. The compiler complains that the identifier `I` is not defined.

7. The function `main` requires a prototype of function `sqr`. The correct version of the program is

```
#include <iostream.h>
// declare prototype of function sqr
double sqr(double);
main()
{
```

```
    double x = 5.2;
    cout << x << "^2 = " << sqr(x);
    return 0;
  }
  double sqr(double x)
  { return x * x ; }
```

Exercise

Here is my version of program OVERLOD2.CPP:

```
// C++ program illustrates function overloading
// and default arguments

#include <iostream.h>

// inc version for int types
void inc(int& i, int diff = 1)
{
  i = i + diff;
}

// inc version for double types
void inc(double& x, double diff = 1)
{
  x = x + diff;
}

// inc version for char types
void inc(char& c, int diff = 1)
{
  c = c + diff;
}

main()
{
  char c = 'A';
  int i = 10;
  double x = 10.2;

  // display initial values
  cout << "c = " << c << "\n"
       << "i = " << i << "\n"
       << "x = " << x << "\n";
  // invoke the inc functions using default arguments
  inc(c);
  inc(i);
  inc(x);
  // display updated values
  cout << "After using the overloaded inc function\n";
  cout << "c = " << c << "\n"
       << "i = " << i << "\n"
```

```
        << "x = " << x << "\n";
  return 0;
}
```

Answers to Day 3, "Operators and Expressions"

Quiz

1. The output is

```
12
8
2
3.64851
150.5
```

2. The output is

```
12
8
2
```

3. The output is

```
12
27
```

4. The output is

```
TRUE
TRUE
TRUE
FALSE
```

Exercises

1. Here is my version of the function `max`:

```
int max(int i, int j)
{
  return (i > j) ? i : j;
}
```

2. Here is my version of the function `min`:

```
int min(int i, int j)
{
  return (i < j) ? i : j;
}
```

3. Here is my version of the function `abs`:

```
int abs(int i)
{
  return (i > 0) ? i : -i;
}
```

4. Here is my version of the function `isOdd`:

```
int isOdd(int i)
{
  return (i % 2 != 0) ? 1 : 0;
}
```

Answers to Day 4, "Managing I/O"

Quiz

1. The output statement cannot contain the inserter operator >>. The statement can be corrected as follows:

```
count << "Enter a number ";
cin >> x;
```

2. Because the variable `x` appears in the first and last items, the last number overwrites the first number.

Exercises

1. Here is my version of program OUT3.CPP:

```
// C++ program uses the printf function for formatted output
 #include <stdio.h>
 #include <math.h>
 main()
 {
```

```
  double x;
  // display table heading
  printf("      X          Sqrt(X)\n");
  printf("-----------------------\n");
  x = 2;
  printf("    %3.0lf          %3.4lf\n", x, sqrt(x));
  x++;
  printf("    %3.0lf          %3.4lf\n", x, sqrt(x));
  x++;
  printf("    %3.0lf          %3.4lf\n", x, sqrt(x));
  x++;
  printf("    %3.0lf          %3.4lf\n", x, sqrt(x));
  x++;
  printf("    %3.0lf          %3.4lf\n", x, sqrt(x));
  x++;
  printf("    %3.0lf          %3.4lf\n", x, sqrt(x));
  x++;
  printf("    %3.0lf          %3.4lf\n", x, sqrt(x));
  x++;
  printf("    %3.0lf          %3.4lf\n", x, sqrt(x));
  x++;
  printf("    %3.0lf          %3.4lf\n", x, sqrt(x));
  return 0;
}
```

2. Here is my version of program OUT4.CPP:

```
// C++ program which displays octal and hexadecimal integers
#include <iostream.h>
#include <stdio.h>
main()
{
  long i;
  cout << "Enter an integer : ";
  cin >> i;
  printf("%ld = %lX (hex) = %lo (octal)\n", i, i, i);
  return 0;
}
```

Answers to Day 5, "The Decision-Making Constructs"

Quiz

1. The simpler version is

```
if (i > 0 && i < 10)
  cout << "i = " << i << "\n";
```

2. The simpler version is

```
if (i > 0) {
  j = i * i;
  cout << "j = " << j << "\n";
}
else if (i < 0) {
  j = 4 * i;
  cout << "j = " << j << "\n";
}
else {
  j = 10 + i;
  cout << "j = " << j << "\n";
}
```

3. False. When the variable `i` stores values between -10 and -1, the statements in the clauses of the two `if` statements execute. In this case, all the assignment statements are executed. By contrast, it is impossible to execute the statements in both the `if` and `else` clauses of the supposedly equivalent `if-else` statement.

4. The simplified version is

```
if (i > 0 && i < 100)
     j = i * i;
else if (i >= 100)
     j = i;
else
     j = 1;
```

   Notice that I eliminate the original first `else if` clause because the tested condition is a subset of the first tested condition. Consequently, the condition in the first `else if` never gets examined and the associated assign statement never gets executed. This is an example of what is called *dead code.*

5. The tested condition is always false. Consequently, the statements in the clause are never executed. This is another example of dead code.

Exercises

1. Here is my version of program IF5.CPP:

```
// C++ program to solve quadratic equation
#include <iostream.h>
#include <math.h>
main()
{
  double A, B, C, discrim, root1, root2, twoA;
  cout << "Enter coefficients for equation A*X^2 + B*X + C\n";
  cout << "Enter A: ";
  cin >> A;
  cout << "Enter B: ";
  cin >> B;
  cout << "Enter C: ";
  cin >> C;
  if (A != 0) {
     twoA = 2 * A;
     discrim = B * B - 4 * A * C;
     if (discrim > 0) {
       root1 = (-B + sqrt(discrim)) / twoA;
       root2 = (-B - sqrt(discrim)) / twoA;
       cout << "root1 = " << root1 << "\n";
       cout << "root2 = " << root2 << "\n";
     }
     else if (discrim < 0) {
       discrim = -discrim;
       cout << "root1 = (" << -B/twoA
            << ") + i (" << sqrt(discrim) / twoA <<")\n";
       cout << "root2 = (" << -B/twoA
            << ") - i (" << sqrt(discrim) / twoA << ")\n";
     }
     else {
       root1 = -B / 2 / A;
       root2 = root1;
       cout << "root1 = " << root1 << "\n";
```

```
      cout << "root2 = " << root2 << "\n";
    }
  }
  else
    cout << "root = " << (-C / B) << "\n";
  return 0;
}
```

2. Here is my version of program SWITCH2.CPP:

```
// C++ program which uses the switch statement to implement
// a simple four-function calculator program
#include <iostream.h>
const int TRUE = 1;
const int FALSE = 0;
main()
{
  double x, y, z;
  char op;
  int error = FALSE;
  cout << "Enter the first operand: ";
  cin >> x;
  cout << "Enter the operator: ";
  cin >> op;
  cout << "Enter the second operand: ";
  cin >> y;
  switch (op) {
    case '+':
      z = x + y;
      break;
    case '-':
      z = x - y;
      break;
    case '*':
      z = x * y;
      break;
    case '/':
      if (y != 0)
        z = x / y;
      else
```

```
            error = TRUE;
          break;
        default:
          error = TRUE;
      }
      if (!error)
        cout << x << " " << op << " " << y << " = " << z << "\n";
      else
        cout << "Bad operator or division-by-zero error\n";
      return 0;
    }
```

Answers to Day 6, "Loops"

Quiz

1. The statements inside the loop fail to alter the value of `I`. Consequently, the tested condition is always true and the loop iterates endlessly.
2. The output of the program consists of the numbers 3, 5, and 7.
3. The output of the program is an endless sequence of lines that display the value of 3. The reason for the indefinite looping is that the loop control variable is not incremented.
4. The nested `for` loops use the same loop control variable. This program will not run.
5. Both `for` loops declare the variable `i` as their loop control variable. The compiler generates an error for this duplication.
6. The condition of the `while` loop is always true. Therefore, the loop iterates endlessly.
7. The program lacks a statement which explicitly initializes the variable factorial to 1. Without this statement, the program automatically initializes the variable `factorial` to 0—the wrong value. Consequently, the `for` loop ends up assigning 0 to the variable `factorial` in every iteration. Here is the correct version of the code:

```
int n;
double factorial = 1;
cout << "Enter positive integer : ";
```

```
cin >> n;
for (int i = 1; i <= n; i++)
  factorial *= i;
cout << n << "!= " << factorial;
```

Exercises

1. Here is my version of program FOR5.CPP:

```
// Program calculates a sum of odd integers in
// the range of 11 to 121
#include <iostream.h>
const int FIRST = 11;
const int LAST = 121;
main()
{
    double sum = 0;
    for (int i = FIRST; i <= LAST; i += 2)
      sum += (double)i;
    cout << "Sum of odd integers from "
         << FIRST << " to " << LAST << " = "
         << sum << "\n";
    return 0;
}
```

2. Here is my version of program WHILE2.CPP:

```
// Program calculates a sum of squared odd integers in
// the range of 11 to 121
#include <iostream.h>
const int FIRST = 11;
const int LAST = 121;
main()
{
    double sum = 0;
    int i = FIRST;
    while (i <= LAST) {
      sum += double(i * i++);
    }
    cout << "Sum of squared odd integers from "
```

```
        << FIRST << " to " << LAST << " = "
        << sum << "\n";
    return 0;
}
```

3. Here is my version of program DOWHILE2.CPP:

```
// Program calculates a sum of squared odd integers in
// the range of 11 to 121
#include <iostream.h>
const int FIRST = 11;
const int LAST = 121;
main()
{
    double sum = 0;
    int i = FIRST;
    do {
      sum += double(i * i++);
    } while (i <= LAST);
    cout << "Sum of squared odd integers from "
         << FIRST << " to " << LAST << " = "
         << sum << "\n";
    return 0;
}
```

Answers to Day 7, "Arrays"

Quiz

1. The program displays the factorials for the numbers 0 to 4:

```
x[0] = 1
x[1] = 1
x[2] = 2
x[3] = 6
x[4] = 24
```

2. The program displays the square roots for the numbers 0 to 4:

```
x[0] = 0
x[1] = 1
x[2] = 1.41421
```

```
x[3] = 1.73205
x[4] = 2
```

3. The first `for` loop should iterate between 1 and `MAX-1` and not between 0 and `MAX-1`. The first loop iteration uses an out-of-range index.

Exercise

Here is my version of program ARRAY7.CPP:

```
// C++ program that sorts arrays using the Comb sort method
#include <iostream.h>

const int MAX = 10;
const int TRUE = 1;
const int FALSE = 0;

int obtainNumData()
{
  int m;
  do { // obtain number of data points
    cout << "Enter number of data points [2 to "
         << MAX << "] : ";
    cin >> m;
    cout << "\n";
  } while (m < 2 || m > MAX);
  return m;
}

void inputArray(int intArr[], int n)
{
  // prompt user for data
  for (int i = 0; i < n; i++) {
    cout << "arr[" << i << "] : ";
    cin >> intArr[i];
  }
}

void showArray(int intArr[], int n)
{
  for (int i = 0; i < n; i++) {
    cout.width(5);
    cout << intArr[i] << " ";
  }
  cout << "\n";
}

void sortArray(int intArr[], int n)
{
  int offset, temp, inOrder;

  offset = n;
  while (offset > 1) {
    offset /= 2;
```

```
    do {
      inOrder = TRUE;
      for (int i = 0, j = offset; i < (n - offset); i++, ++) {
        if (intArr[i] > intArr[j]) {
          inOrder = FALSE;
          temp = intArr[i];
          intArr[i] = intArr[j];
          intArr[j] = temp;
        }
      }
    } while (!inOrder);
  }
}

main()
{
  int arr[MAX];
  int n;

  n = obtainNumData();
  inputArray(arr, n);
  cout << "Unordered array is:\n";
  showArray(arr, n);
  sortArray(arr, n);
  cout << "\nSorted array is:\n";
  showArray(arr, n);
  return 0;
}
```

Answers to Day 8, "User-Defined Types and Pointers"

Quiz

1. The enumerated values on and off appear in two different enumerated types. Here is a correct version of these statements:

```
enum Boolean { false, true };
enum State { state_on, state_off };
enum YesNo { yes, no };
enum DiskDriveStatus { drive_on , drive_off };
```

2. False. The enumerated type YesNo is correctly declared.
3. The program lacks a delete statement before the return statement. Here is the correct version:

```
#include <iostream.h>
main()
```

```
{
  int *p = new int;
  cout << "Enter a number : ";
  cin >> *p;
  cout << "The square of " << *p << " = " << (*p * *p);
  delete p;
  return 0;
}
```

Exercises

1. Here is my version of PTR6.CPP:

```
/* C++ program that demonstrates pointers to structured types */
#include <iostream.h>
#include <stdio.h>
#include <math.h>
const MAX_RECT = 4;
const TRUE = 1;
const FALSE = -1;
struct point {
  double x;
  double y;
};
struct rect {
  point ulc; // upper left corner
  point lrc; // lower right corner
  double area;
  int id;
};
typedef rect rectArr[MAX_RECT];
main()
{
  rectArr r;
  rect temp;
  rect* pr = r;
  rect* pr2;
  double length, width;
  int offset;
```

```
  int inOrder;
  for (int i = 0; i < MAX_RECT; i++, pr++) {
    cout << "Enter (X,Y) coord. for ULC of rect. # "
         << i << " : ";
    cin >> pr->ulc.x >> pr->ulc.y;
    cout << "Enter (X,Y) coord. for LRC of rect. # "
         << i << " : ";
    cin >> pr->lrc.x >> pr->lrc.y;
    pr->id = i;
    length = fabs(pr->ulc.x - pr->lrc.x);
    width = fabs(pr->ulc.y - pr->lrc.y);
    pr->area = length * width;
  }
  // sort the rectangles by areas
  offset = MAX_RECT;
  do {
    offset = (8 * offset) / 11;
    offset = (offset == 0) ? 1 : offset;
    inOrder = TRUE;
    pr = r;
    pr2 = r + offset;
    for (int i = 0;
         i < MAX_RECT - offset;
         i++, pr++, pr2++)
      if (pr->area > pr2->area) {
        inOrder = FALSE;
        temp = *pr;
        *pr = *pr2;
        *pr2 = temp;
      }
  } while (!(offset == 1 && inOrder));
  pr = r; // reset pointer
  // display rectangles sorted by area
  for (i = 0; i < MAX_RECT; i++, pr++)
    printf("Rect # %d has area %5.4lf\n", pr->id, pr->area);
  return 0;
}
```

2. Here is my version of structure intArrStruct:

```
struct intArrStruct {
  int* dataPtr;
  unsigned size;
};
```

3. Here is my version of structure matStruct:

```
struct matStruct {
  double* dataPtr;
  unsigned rows;
  unsigned columns;
};
```

Answers to Day 9, "Strings"

Quiz

1. The string s1 is smaller than string s2. Consequently, the call to function strcpy causes a program bug.

2. Using the function strncpy to include the constant MAX as the third argument ensures that string s1 receives MAX characters (excluding the null terminator) from string s1:

```
#include <iostream.h>
#include <string.h>
const in MAX = 10;
main()
{
  char s1[MAX+1];
  char s2[] = "1234567890123456789012345678 90";
  strncpy(s1, s2, MAX);
  cout << "String 1 is " << s1
       << "\nString 2 is " << s2;
  return 0;
}
```

3. Because the string in variable s1 is greater than that in variable s2, the statement assigns a positive number (1 to be exact) in variable i.

4. The call to function strcmp compares the substrings "C++" with "Basic" because the arguments include an offset value. Because "C++" is greater than "Basic", the statement assigns a positive number (1 to be exact) in variable i.

5. False! Although the basic idea for the function is sound, dimensioning the local variable requires a constant. One solution is to use the same constant, call it MAX_STRING_SIZE, to size up the arguments of parameter s:

```
int hasNoLowerCase(const char* s)
{
  char s2[MAX_STRING_SIZE+1];
  strcpy(s2, s);
  strupr(s2);
  return (strcmp(s1, s2) == 0) ? 1 : 0);
}
```

   The other solution uses dynamic allocation to create a dynamic local string which stores a copy of the argument of parameter s. This solution works with all arguments of parameter s:

```
int hasNoLowerCase(const char* s)
{
  char *s2 = new char[strlen(s)+1];
  int i;
  strcpy(s2, s);
  strupr(s2);
  // store result in variable i
  i = (strcmp(s1, s2) == 0) ? 1 : 0);
  delete [] s2; // first delete local dynamic string
  return i; // then return the result of the function
}
```

Exercises

1. Here is my version of function strlen:

```
int strlen(const char* s)
{
  int i = 0;
  while (s[i] != '\0')
    i++;
  return i;
}
```

2. Here is the other version of function `strlen`:

```
int strlen(const char* s)
{
  char *p = s;
  while (p++ != '\0')
    /* do nothing */;
  return p - s;
}
```

3. Here is my version of program STRING5.CPP:

```
#include <stdio.h>
#include <string.h>
main()
{
   char str[] = "2*(X+Y)/(X+Z) - (X+10)/(Y-5)";
   char strCopy[41];
   char* tkn[3] = { "+-*/ ()", "( )", "+-*/ " };
   char* ptr;
   strcpy(strCopy, str); // copy str into strCopy
   printf("%s\n", str);
   printf("Using token string %s\n", tkn[0]);
   // the first call
   ptr = strtok(str, tkn[0]);
   printf("String is broken into: %s",ptr);
   while (ptr) {
     printf("  ,%s", ptr);
     // must make first argument a NULL character
     ptr = strtok(NULL, tkn[0]);
   }
   strcpy(str, strCopy); // restore str
   printf("\nUsing token string %s\n", tkn[1]);
   // the first call
   ptr = strtok(str, tkn[1]);
   printf("String is broken into: %s",ptr);
   while (ptr) {
     printf("  ,%s", ptr);
     // must make first argument a NULL character
     ptr = strtok(NULL, tkn[1]);
   }
```

```
    strcpy(str, strCopy); // restore str
    printf("\nUsing token string %s\n", tkn[2]);
    // the first call
    ptr = strtok(str, tkn[2]);
    printf("String is broken into: %s",ptr);
    while (ptr) {
      printf("  ,%s", ptr);
      // must make first argument a NULL character
      ptr = strtok(NULL, tkn[2]);
    }
    printf("\n\n");
    return 0;
}
```

B

Answers to Day 10, "Advanced Functions Parameters"

Quiz

1. The function is

```
double factorial(int i)
{ return (i > 1) ? double(i) * factorial(i-1) : 1; }
```

2. At first glance, the function may seem correct, though somewhat unusual. The `case` labels offer quick results for arguments of 0 to 4. However, the catch-all `default` clause traps arguments that are greater than 4 *and* are negative values! The latter kind of arguments causes the recursion to overflow the memory resources. Here is a corrected version which returns a very large negative number when the argument is a negative number:

```
double factorial(int i)
{
  if (i > -1)
    switch (i) {
        case 0:
        case 1:
            return 1;
             break;
```

```
            case 2:
                 return 2;
                 break;
            case 3:
                 return 6;
                 break;
            case 4:
                 return 24;
                 break;
            default:
                 return double(i) * factorial(i-1);
       }
  else
    return -1.0e+30; // numeric code for a bad argument
}
```

3. The nonrecursive version of function `Fibonacci` is

```
double Fibonacci(int n)
{
  double Fib0 = 0;
  double Fib1 = 1;
  double Fib2;
  if (n == 0)
    return 0;
  else if (n == 1 || n == 2)
    return 1;
  else
    for (int i = 0; i <= n; i++) {
      Fib2 = Fib0 + Fib1;
      Fib0 = Fib1;
      Fib1 = Fib2;
    }
    return Fib2;
}
```

4. True. The first function uses a formal reference parameter, whereas the second parameter uses a pointer parameter.

Exercise

Here is my version of program ADVFUN9.CPP:

```
/*
C++ program that uses pointers to functions to implement a
a linear regression program that supports temporary
mathematical transformations.
*/

#include <iostream.h>
#include <math.h>

const unsigned MAX_SIZE = 100;

typedef double vector[MAX_SIZE];

struct regression {
  double Rsqr;
  double slope;
  double intercept;
};

// declare array of function pointers
double (*f[2])(double);

// declare function prototypes
void initArray(double*, double*, unsigned);
double linear(double);
double sqr(double);
double reciprocal(double);
void calcRegression(double*, double*, unsigned, regression&,
double (*f[2])(double));
int select_transf(const char*);

main()
{
  char ans;
  unsigned count;
  vector x, y;
  regression stat;
  int trnsfx, trnsfy;

  do {
    cout << "Enter array size [2.."
         << MAX_SIZE << "] : ";
    cin >> count;
  } while (count <= 1 || count > MAX_SIZE);

  // initialize array
  initArray(x, y, count);
  // transform data
  do {
    // set the transformation functions
    trnsfx = select_transf("X");
```

```
    trnsfy = select_transf("Y");
    // set function pointer f[0]
    switch (trnsfx) {
      case 0 :
        f[0] = linear;
        break;
      case 1 :
        f[0] = log;
        break;
      case 2 :
        f[0] = sqrt;
        break;
      case 3 :
        f[0] = sqr;
        break;
      case 4 :
        f[0] = reciprocal;
        break;
      default :
        f[0] = linear;
        break;
    }
    // set function pointer f[1]
    switch (trnsfy) {
      case 0 :
        f[1] = linear;
        break;
      case 1 :
        f[1] = log;
        break;
      case 2 :
        f[1] = sqrt;
        break;
      case 3 :
        f[1] = sqr;
        break;
      case 4 :
        f[1] = reciprocal;
        break;
      default :
        f[1] = linear;
        break;
    }

    calcRegression(x, y, count, stat, f);

    cout << "\n\n\n\n"
         << "R-square = " << stat.Rsqr << "\n"
         << "Slope = " << stat.slope << "\n"
         << "Intercept = " << stat.intercept << "\n\n\n";
    cout << "Want to use other transformations? (Y/N) ";
    cin >> ans;
  } while (ans == 'Y' || ans == 'y');
  return 0;
}
```

```
void initArray(double* x, double* y, unsigned count)
// read data for array from the keyboard
{
  for (unsigned i = 0; i < count; i++, x++, y++) {
    cout << "X[" << i << "] : ";
    cin >> *x;
    cout << "Y[" << i << "] : ";
    cin >> *y;
  }
}

int select_transf(const char* var_name)
// select choice of transformation
{

  int choice = -1;
  cout << "\n\n\n";
  cout << "select transformation for variable " << var_name
       << "\n\n\n"
       << "0) No transformation\n"
       << "1) Logarithmic transformation\n"
       << "2) Square root transformation\n"
       << "3) Square  transformation\n"
       << "4) Reciprocal transformation\n";
  while (choice < 0 || choice > 4) {
    cout << "\nSelect choice by number : ";
    cin >> choice;
  }
  return choice;
}

double linear(double x)
{ return x; }

double sqr(double x)
{ return x * x; }

double reciprocal(double x)
{ return 1.0 / x; }

void calcRegression(double* x,
                    double* y,
                    unsigned count,
                    regression &stat,
                    double (*f[2])(double))

{
  double meanx, meany, sdevx, sdevy;
  double sum = (double) count, sumx = 0, sumy = 0;
  double sumxx = 0, sumyy = 0, sumxy = 0;
  double xdata, ydata;

  for (unsigned i = 0; i < count; i++) {
    xdata = (*f[0])(*(x+i));
    ydata = (*f[1])(*(y+i));
    sumx += xdata;
```

```
    sumy += ydata;
    sumxx += sqr(xdata);
    sumyy += sqr(ydata);
    sumxy += xdata * ydata;
  }

  meanx = sumx / sum;
  meany = sumy / sum;
  sdevx = sqrt((sumxx - sqr(sumx) / sum)/(sum-1.0));
  sdevy = sqrt((sumyy - sqr(sumy) / sum)/(sum-1.0));
  stat.slope = (sumxy - meanx * meany * sum) /
  sqr(sdevx)/(sum-1);
  stat.intercept = meany - stat.slope * meanx;
  stat.Rsqr = sqr(sdevx / sdevy * stat.slope);
}
```

Answers to Day 11, "Object-Oriented Programming and C++ Classes"

Quiz

1. By default, the members of a class are protected. Therefore, the class declaration has no public member and cannot be used to create instances.
2. The third constructor has a default argument, which makes it redundant with the fourth constructor. The C++ compiler detects such an error.
3. True. `String("Hello Visual C++")` creates a temporary instance of class `String` and then assigns it to the instance `s`.
4. Yes. The new statements are valid.

Exercise

Here is the implementation of function `main` in my version of program CLASS7.CPP:

```
main()
{

  Complex c[5];
  c[1].assign(3, 5);
  c[2].assign(7, 5);
  c[4].assign(2, 3);
```

```
  c[3] = c[1] + c[2];
  cout << c[1] << " + " << c[2] << " = " << c[3] << "\n";
  cout << c[3] << " + " << c[4] << " = ";
  c[3] += c[4];
  cout << c[3] << "\n";
  return 0;
}
```

Answers to Day 12, "Basic Stream File I/O"

Quiz

1. False. The `read` and `write` functions cannot store and recall the dynamic data, which is accessed by a pointer member of a structure or a class.
2. True.
3. True.
4. False.

Exercise

Here is the code for member function `binSearch` and the updated function `main` in program IO4.CPP (the output also shows the new global constant `NOT_FOUND` and the updated class declaration):

```
const unsigned NOT_FOUND = 0xffff;

class VmArray
{
 protected:
  fstream f;
  unsigned size;
  double badIndex;

 public:
  VmArray(unsigned Size, const char* filename);
  ~VmArray()
     { f.close(); }
  unsigned getSize() const
     { return size; }
  boolean writeElem(const char* str, unsigned index);
  boolean readElem(char* str, unsigned index);
  void Combsort();
  unsigned binSearch(const char* search);
};
```

```
unsigned VmArray::binSearch(const char* search)
{
  unsigned low = 0;
  unsigned high = size - 1;
  unsigned median;
  char str[STR_SIZE+1];
  int result;

  do {
    median = (low + high) / 2;
    readElem(str, median);
    result = strcmp(search, str);
    if (result > 0)
      low = median + 1;
    else
      high = median - 1;
  } while (result != 0 && low <= high);
  return (result == 0) ? median : NOT_FOUND;
}

main()
{
  const unsigned NUM_ELEMS = 10;
  char* data[] = { "Michigan", "California", "Virginia", "Main",
                   "New York", "Florida", "Nevada", "Alaska",
                   "Ohio", "Maryland" };
  VmArray arr(NUM_ELEMS, "arr.dat");
  char str[STR_SIZE+1];
  char c;
  unsigned index;

  // assign values to array arr
  for (unsigned i = 0; i < arr.getSize(); i++) {
    strcpy(str, data[i]);
    arr.writeElem(str, i);
  }
  // display unordered array
  cout << "Unsorted arrays is:\n";
  for (i = 0; i < arr.getSize(); i++) {
    arr.readElem(str, i);
    cout << str << "\n";
  }
  // pause
  cout << "\nPress any key and then Return to sort the array...";
  cin >> c;
  // sort the array
  arr.Combsort();
  // display sorted array
  cout << "Sorted arrays is:\n";
  for (i = 0; i < arr.getSize(); i++) {
    arr.readElem(str, i);
    cout << str << "\n"
  }
  // pause
```

```
    cout << "\nPress any key and then Return to search the array...";
    cin >> c;
    // search for array elements using the pointer data
    for (i = 0; i < NUM_ELEMS; i++) {
      index = arr.binSearch(data[i]);
      if (index != NOT_FOUND)
        cout << "Found " << data[i]
             << " at index " << index << "\n";
      else
        cout << "No match for " << data[i] << "\n";
    }
    return 0;
  }
```

Answers to Day 13, "Programming Windows Using the MFC Library"

Quiz

1. The message box needs the following MB_xxxx expression:

   ```
   MB_YESNOCANCEL ¦ MB_ICONQUESTION
   ```

2. The message box needs the following MB_xxxx expression:

   ```
   MB_OK ¦ MB_ICONEXCLAMATION
   ```

3. The MessageBox function returns IDYES.
4. The MessageBox function returns IDCANCEL.

Answers to Day 14, "Creating Basic MFC Applications"

Quiz

1. True.
2. False. The associated function is OnActivate and not Onactivate.
3. True.
4. True.

Answers to Day 15, "Basic Windows"

Quiz

1. False. The function `OnPaint` also initially draws the window. Windows are drawn and redrawn when the application receives the Windows message `WM_PAINT`.
2. False. The inherited scrolling function offers no scrolling features.
3. False. The member function `OnSize` is only required when the window class scrolls its contents. In this case, the run-time system supplies the `OnSize` with the updated window dimensions.
4. False. The absence of function `OnKeyDown` only disables using the cursor control keys, such as PageUp and PageDown.

Answers to Day 16, "MFC Controls"

Quiz

1. False. Only the text for static controls with the `SS_SIMPLE` style are unchangeable.
2. True.
3. False. The pointer is needed at least to delete the dynamic instance of the static control.
4. True.
5. True, because every control is a window.
6. False. The Windows messages emitted by a pushbutton must be mapped using the `ON_BTN_CLICKED` map.

Answers to Day 17, "Grouped Controls"

Quiz

1. False. The check box can replace the two radio buttons only if these buttons offer opposite alternatives.
2. True.
3. True. Each check box can be independently toggled.
4. False. Radio buttons in a group control are mutually exclusive.

Answers to Day 18, "List Boxes"

Quiz

1. True.
2. True.
3. False. The list box notification message LBN_CHANGE indicates that a new item is selected.
4. False. The list box notification message LBN_DBLCLK indicates that a list item is selected with a double mouse click.
5. False. The LBS_STANDARD style does include the LBS_SORT style and therefore creates ordered list boxes.

Answers to Day 19, "Scroll Bars and Combo Boxes"

Quiz

1. True.
2. False. The correct notification message is CBN_EDITUPDATE.

3. False. The items in the list box components are sorted, but not unique. You can insert multiple copies of the same string.
4. True, otherwise the items inserted in the list box components are not in chronological order. Instead, they are in sorted order.
5. False.
6. True. The program illustrates this concept: when you alter the value of either control, the other control changes accordingly.
7. False. The program CTLSCRL1.CPP demonstrates that you can alter the range of values for a scroll bar at run-time.

Answers to Day 20, "Dialog Boxes"

Quiz

1. False. You may compile the .RC files after you compile your .CPP files.
2. False. The OK and Cancel buttons are mandatory.
3. True. However, these buttons must be treated in the program as the OK and Cancel buttons. In other words, you can alter the caption of standard OK and Cancel buttons.
4. False. The best examples of nested dialog boxes are those related to setting up the printer.
5. False. Dialog boxes can be stand-alone windows.

Answers to Day 21, "MDI Windows"

Quiz

1. False.
2. False.
3. False.
4. True! Congratulations on completing the book.

Glossary

address: The location of each memory byte in the computer's memory. The lowest memory address is 0. The highest memory address depends on the amount of memory in a computer.

ancestor class: A class that is one or more levels higher in the class hierarchy than a referenced class.

argument: The value that is passed to a parameter of a function or a procedure.

array: A collection of variables which share the same name and use one or more indices to access an individual member.

ASCII: Acronym for *American Standard Code for Information Interchange.*

ASCII file: A file which contains readable text. ASCII files are also called *text files.*

AUTOEXEC.BAT: A special batch file which the computer automatically executes if it finds it in the root directory of the boot disk.

backup file: A duplicate copy of a file which protects your work in case you damage the text or data in the main file.

.BAK: The common file extension for backup files.

base class: The root of a class hierarchy. A base class has no parent class.

batch file: An executable file which contains MS-DOS commands and other special commands. Batch files assist in automating various tasks.

binary: A numbering system which includes 0 and 1.

bit: The short name for *binary digit.* Bits are the smallest units of data storage. Programs commonly use groups of 8, 16, 32, and 64 bits to represent different kinds of data.

Boolean: Synonomous with logical (true or false). The word Boolean comes from the name of the English mathematician George Bool who studied logical values and created the truth table.

bubblesort: The slowest and simplest method for ordering the elements of an array in ascending or descending order.

buffer: A memory location where transient data flows in and out.

bug: A common name for a logical program error.

byte: A unit of data storage which contains 8 bits.

.C: The extension of a C file.

CGA: Acronym for *Color Graphics Adapter*. CGA screens have a resolution of 640 by 200 pixels.

class: A category of objects.

clipboard: A special memory area in the Windows environment which holds text that you copied or deleted.

clock tick: The duration based on the CPU's internal clock. One second contains 18.2 clock ticks.

Comb sort: A new and efficient method for sorting the elements of an array. This method is based on improving the bubblesort method.

compiler: A tool which converts the source code of a program file into a binary object code (.OBJ) file. The object code must be linked with other object files and library files to generate an executable .EXE file.

concatenation: The process of joining two or more strings by chaining their characters.

conditional loop: A loop which iterates until or while a tested condition is true.

CONFIG.SYS: The name of the system configuration file. When a machine boots, it reads the CONFIG.SYS file in the root directory of the boot disk.

constant: Information that remains fixed during the execution of a program.

.CPP: The extension of a C++ source file.

CPU: Acronym for *Central Processing Unit*, the computer's brain.

crash: The state in which a computer seems to freeze and does not respond to the keyboard, mouse, or any other input device.

cursor: The blinking underline or block which appears on the screen to indicate where the next character insertion will occur.

data member: The fields in a class which store data.

data processing: The manipulating and/or managing of information.

data record: A collection of data items which convey meaningful information. Your mailing address, for example, is a data record.

debug: To detect and remove logical errors in the program.

debugger: A tool which assists you in debugging the program. The environment contains a powerful debugger.

.DEF: The extension of a Windows program definition file.

default: A preselected action or value that is used when no other action or value is offered.

descendant class: Any child class derived from a parent class.

dialog box: A special pop-up screen which prompts you for input.

directory: A section or compartment of a hard, floppy, or electronic disk which contains files.

disk: The magnetic medium which stores data.

disk drive: The device which reads and loads data and programs in a disk.

diskette: A removable thin disk. Also called *floppy disk.*

display: The screen, console, or monitor in a computer.

display adapter: The board inside a computer which assists in displaying text and graphics.

DOS: Acronym for *Disk Operating System.*

drag: The act of holding a mouse button down while moving the mouse. This action moves a window from one location in the screen to another.

EGA: Acronym for *Enhanced Graphics Adapter.* The resolution of an EGA display is 640 by 350 pixels.

element (of an array): The member of an array, which is accessed by specifying one or more indices.

file: The name of a location in a disk which contains a program, text, or other data.

file extension: The three letters used by DOS files to identify the type of a file. Programs have file extensions of .COM or .EXE.

file I/O: File input and/or output.

filename: The name of a DOS file.

floppy disk: *See* **diskette**.

format: The image or map used to output data.

function: A subprogram that executes one or more statements and returns a single value.

function key: The keys labeled F1 to F10 on a keyboard. Some keyboards also have keys labeled F11 and F12.

global variable: A variable that is accessible to all functions and procedures in a program.

graphics monitor: A monitor that is able to display high-resolution graphics.

.H: The extension of a header file.

header file: A file that contains the declarations of constants, data types, function prototypes, and class declarations.

hertz: The unit of measuring frequency. One hertz is one cycle per second. Abbreviated Hz.

HGA: Acronym for *Hercules Graphics Adapter.*

inheritance: The ability of a class to reuse data members and member functions in a parent class.

input: The data which a program obtains from the keyboard, disk drive, communication port, or any other input device.

I/O: Acronym for *Input/Output.*

kilobyte (K): A unit of measuring memory. 1K is 1,024 bytes.

least significant bit: The rightmost bit in a byte, word, or any other unit of memory.

linker: A tool that combines the various .OBJ files generated by the compiler with the various library files to create the executable .EXE file.

local variable: A variable which is declared inside a function or procedure.

loop: A set of statements which are repeatedly executed.

main module: The program section containing the function `main`.

.MAK: The extension of a project make file.

make file: A special file which invokes the compiler and linker as needed to compile and link the source and/or object files.

math operator: A symbol which performs a mathematical operation, such as addition, subtraction, multiplication, division, and raising to powers.

matrix: A two-dimensional array. The elements of a matrix are accessed by specifying the row and column indices.

MCGA: Acronym for *Multi-Color Graphics Adapter.*

MDA: Acronym for *Monochrome Display Adapter.*

megabyte (M): The unit of memory. 1M is approximately one million bytes.

member function: A function that is a member in a class.

memory: The part of the computer that retains programs and data while the computer is on.

menu: A display which offers a set of options to select from.

menu-driven: A program which depends on one or more menus to perform its tasks, as guided by the user.

message: What an object-oriented program does to an object.

method: How an object-oriented program manipulates an object.

modulus: The integer remainder of a division.

monitor: The screen, console, or display.

monochrome: Single color. Monochrome monitors can display neither colors nor high-resolution graphics.

most significant bit: The leftmost bit in a byte, word, or other unit of memory.

MS-DOS: Acronym for *Microsoft Disk Operator System.*

multidimensional arrays: Arrays which have multiple subscripts.

nested loop: A loop inside another loop.

null string: An empty string.

numeric functions: A function which returns a numerical value.

object: An instance of a class.

object file: The output of the compiler. The linker combines various object and library files to create the executable .EXE file.

object-oriented programming (OOP): Programming techniques which focus on modeling objects and their operations.

open loop: A loop which in principle iterates indefinitely. In practice, most open loops use an exit mechanism located in a statement inside the loop.

order of operators: The priority of executing operations in an expression.

output device: A device which receives output. Common output devices are the screen, the printer, the disk drive, and the communication port. Some output devices also support input, such as the communication port and the disk drive.

palette: A set of possible colors.

parameter: A special variable which appears after the declaration of a function or procedure, and which fine-tunes the operations of the function or procedure.

passing by reference: The task of passing an argument to a function or procedure by providing its reference. Consequently, the parameter receiving the reference becomes an alias to the argument. Any changes made to the parameter inside the function or procedure also affect the argument.

passing by value: The task of passing an argument to a function or procedure by providing a copy of its value. Consequently, any changes made to the parameter inside the function or procedure do not affect the argument.

pixel: The short name for *picture element.*

pointer: A special variable which stores the address of another variable or system information.

polymorphism: The feature of object-oriented programming that supports abstract functionality.

precedence of operators: *See* **order of operators**.

program: A collection of executable statements or instructions.

programming language: The high-level human interface for communicating with a machine.

pseudocode: A text outline which describes in English the tasks of a program.

RAM: *See* **random access memory (RAM)**.

random access file: A file which permits you to access its fixed-length records for input and output by specifying the record number. Random access files are suitable for databases.

random access memory (RAM): Memory that can be accessed by specifying an address.

.RC: The extension of a resource script file.

read only memory (ROM): A class of memory which contains fixed data.

record: A unit of storing information in a data file. Typically, text files have variable-length records. Random access files contain fixed-length records.

relational operators: Symbols which compare two compatible data items and return a logical value.

.RES: The extension of a compiled resource file.

resolution: The sharpness of an image which appears on a screen.

resource file: A file which defines resources to be used by one or more Windows applications. Resource files can be shared by applications written in different programming languages. Resources include strings, keyboard, menu, controls, and dialog box resources.

ROM: *See* **read only memory (ROM)**.

scientific notation: A special form for representing numbers by specifying the mantissa and the exponent. In a number such as 1.23E+44, the 1.23 is the mantissa and +44 is the exponent (the power of ten). Therefore 1.23E+44 is a more convenient way to write 1.23 x 10+44.

sequential file: A file which stores readable text using variable-length records.

single-dimensional arrays: An array which requires a single subscript to access its elements.

sorting: The task of arranging the elements of an array in either ascending or descending order. The array is ordered using part or all of the value in each element.

static variable: A variable with a fixed memory location. Usually, static variables are declared in functions and are able to retain their values between function calls.

string constant: A constant associated with a string literal.

string literal: A set of characters enclosed in a pair of double quotes.

string variable: A variable which stores a string of characters.

structure: A user-defined data type. C++ allows you to define a structure using the `TYPE` statement.

structured array: An array that contains elements that have a user-defined data type.

structured variable: A variable whose type is a user-defined data type.

subdirectory: A directory which is connected to a parent directory.

subscript: The index of an array.

SVGA: Acronym for *Super Vector Graphics Array. See also* **VGA**.

syntax error: An error in writing a statement.

system hang: *See* **crash**.

text file: *See* **ASCII file**.

unary operator: Symbols that require only one operand.

user-defined data type: *See* **structure**.

user-defined functions: A function defined by a programmer to conceptually extend the C++ language and serve the host program.

variable: A tagged memory location which stores data.

variable-length record: A record with a varying number of bytes or characters.

variable-length string variables: A string variable which can accommodate a varying number of characters.

variable scope: The visibility of a variable in the different components of a program.

VGA: Acronym for *Vector Graphics Array*. The resolution of VGA is 640 by 480 pixels.

virtual function: A function which, when overridden by a descendant class, must have the same purpose and parameter list as the one in an ancestor class.

Windows message: A message sent by one Windows component to another.

word: A unit of data storage which contains 2 bytes or 16 bits.

Index

Symbols

A

B

C

F

I–J

K–L

M

P

Q–R

menus, 373-385, 818-821
modal dialog boxes (DIALOG2.RC), 589-590
modeless dialog boxes (DIALOG3.RC), 597
multiple selection list boxes (CTLLST2.RC), 525
.RC, 871
.RES, 872

Resource menu, 23

responding
menus (Windows), 378-385
messages
combo boxes controls, 561-562
list boxes, 511
scroll bars, 544
Windows, 359-360

reversing strings, 237-240

ROM (Read Only Memory), 871

roots (binary trees), 268-271

RTEXT statement, 827

rules in virtual functions, 307-308

Run-Time Object Model Support subhierarchy, 352

S

cSquare classes, 306-307

Save All command (File menu), 10

Save As command (File menu), 9

Save As dialog box, 9

Save command (File menu), 9

sayError function, 194-195

scientific notation, 872

screens
CGA (Color Graphics Adapter), 867
display, 868
EGA (Enhanced Graphics Adapter), 868
MCGA (Multi-Color Graphics Adapter), 869
MDA (Monochrome Display Adapter), 869
SVGA (Super Vector Graphics Array), 872
VGA (Vector Graphics Array), 873

scroll bars, 540
count-down timer application, 544-553
messages, responding, 544

SCROLLBAR statement, 831

scrolling windows, 409-429

ScrollWindow function, 411-412

Search command (Edit menu), 13

searching arrays, 159-169

searchInUnorderedArray function, 169

sections in classes, 289-292

seekg functions (I/O), 336-337

segmented memory pointers, 216

Select All command (Edit menu), 12

select_transf function, 279-280

SelectString function
CComboBox class, 560
CListBox class, 508

SellItemRange function, 508-509

semicolon (;), 29

SendDlgItemMessage function (API), 360-361

sending messages (Windows), 360-365

SendMessage function (API), 360-361

sequential binary file stream I/O, 329-336

sequential files, 872

sequential text stream I/O, 324-329

Serialize function, 715

SetButtonStyle function, 446-468

SetCharHeight function, 427

SetCheck function, 472

SetCurSel function
CComboBox class, 556
CListBox class, 509

setHeight function, 302

SetLineSize function, 428

SetPageSize function, 428

SetScrollPos function, 411, 543

SetScrollRange function, 410-411, 543

SetSel function
CListBox class, 509
edit control, 443-444

Settings command (Project menu), 19

SetTopIndex function, 509-510

SetVScrollMax function, 428

SetWindowText function, 435-468

showArray function, 162

showColumnAverage function, 178

ShowDropDown function, 557

showTree function, 271

T

U

V

W–Z

Disk Offer

The programs in *Teach Yourself Visual C++ 2 in 21 Days* are available on disk from the author. Fill out this form and enclose a check for only $10.00 to receive a copy. Outside the U.S., please enclose a check for $14.00 in U.S. currency, drawn on a U.S. bank. Please make the check payable to **Namir C. Shammas**. Sorry, no credit card orders. Mail this form to

Namir C. Shammas
3928 Margate Drive
Richmond, VA 23235

Name ______________________________

Company (for company address) ______________

Street ______________________________

City ________________________________

State/Province ______________

ZIP or Postal Code ______________

Country (outside USA) ______________

Disk format (check one):

5.25 inch ______________ 3.5 inch ______________